THE GREAT GALLERY OF SCULPTURE

Acknowledgments

The author would like thank the three establishments which originated the present volume, beginning with their respective heads:
Henri Loyrette, president-director of the Musée du Louvre
Serge Lemoine, president of the Musée d'Orsay
Bruno Racine, president of the Centre Pompidou;

Alfred Pacquement, director of the Musée National d'Art Moderne-Centre de Création Industrielle;
the curators:
Geneviève Bresc-Bautier, Jean-René Gaborit, Marc Bormand;
Catherine Chevillot;
Isabelle Monod-Fontaine, Brigitte Léal.

The editorial staff
at the Centre Pompidou: Annie Pérez, Philippe Bidaine, and Françoise Bertaux, who oversaw the publication of the volume with talent and passion,
Evelyne Pomey, Martial Lhuillery;
at the Louvre Museum: Violaine Bouvet-Lanselle;
at the Musée d'Orsay: Annie Dufour.

This book owes a great deal to conversations and exchanges with the author's sculptor friends and he pays particular tribute to the late Erik Dietman and Piotr Kowalski.
The text has gained much from the thoughts and works of Jean-Christophe Bailly, Klaus Bussmann, Bruno Corà, Eric Darragon, François Fossier, Claude and Françoise Frontisi, Daniela Gallo, Dario Gamboni, Itzhak Goldberg, Antje von Graevenitz, Michel Hochmann, Pontus Hulten, Christian Klemm, Antoinette Le Normand-Romain, Christa Lichtenstern, Jean-Marc Poinsot, Paul-Louis Rinuy, Philippe Sénéchal, Marina Vanci, José Vovelle and Karen Wilkin.

French Edition
ISBN: 2-35031-045-0 Musée du Louvre
ISBN: 2-905724-27-7 Musée d'Orsay
ISBN: 2-84426-264-3 Centre Pompidou
Publication number: 1264
Legal deposition: october 2005

English Edition
ISBN: 2-35031-046-9 Musée du Louvre
ISBN: 2-905724-37-4 Musée d'Orsay
ISBN: 2-84426-272-4 Centre Pompidou
Publication number: 1265
Legal deposition: october 2005

Author

Former student at the Ecole Normale with an *agrégation* in history, Thierry Dufrêne is professor of history of contemporary art at Université Paris X-Nanterre, where he is director of the Centre de Recherches en Histoire de l'Art et Histoire des Représentations. Author of studies on Surrealism, public art, and the writings of 20th-century artists, he has already produced several works and exhibition catalogues on sculpture, including *Giacometti. Les dimensions de la réalité* (Geneva: Skira, 1994), prepared the publication of the acts of the colloquium *De la sculpture au XXe siècle* (in collaboration with P.-L. Rinuy, Grenoble: P.U.G., 2001), and more recently contributed the main essay to the catalogue *Carpeaux/Shapiro* for the Musée d'Orsay (2005). Scientific secretary to the Comité International d'Histoire de l'Art (CIHA) and member of the Association Internationale des Critiques d'Art (AICA), he is presently preparing a volume on Jean Tinguely's *Cyclop* (to be published by Gallimard in the collection "Art et artistes").

Musée du Louvre

Henri Loyrette, **President-Director**
Didier Selles, **Chief Executive Director**
Aline Sylla, **Deputy Executive Director**

Musée d'Orsay

Serge Lemoine, **President**
Thierry Gausseron, **Chief Executive Director**

Centre national d'art et de culture Georges Pompidou

Bruno Racine, **President**
Bruno Maquart, **Managing Director**
Alfred Pacquement, **Director of the Musée national d'art moderne-Centre de création industrielle**

Editions du Centre Pompidou

Director
Annie Pérez
Sales Manager
Benoît Collier
Rights and Contracts Managers
Mathias Battestini, Claudine Guillon
Publications Administrator
Nicole Parmentier

Musée du Louvre

Head of Publications
Violaine Bouvet-Lanselle

Musée d'Orsay

Head of Publications
Annie Dufour

Cover Illustrations

Antonio Canova,
Psyche Revived by the Kiss of Love,
1787-1801 (detail)

Auguste Rodin,
Man with a Broken Nose,
1864/1878 (detail)

Alberto Giacometti,
Suspended Ball,
1930-31 (detail)

Publication

Editor
Françoise Bertaux
Translator
David Radzinowicz
Graphic Designer
Robaglia design:
Antoine Robaglia
Assisted by Nathalie Bigard
Copy Editors
Geneviève Munier (**French**)
Natasha Edwards (**English**)
Documentation
Catherine Dupont, Carole Nicolas (**Louvre**)
Virginie Berri, Alice Ertaud (**Orsay**)
Evelyne Pomey (**Centre Pompidou**)
Production
Martial Lhuillery

Musée du Louvre, Musée d'Orsay, Centre Pompidou/Musée national d'art moderne
PERSPECTIVES ON THREE COLLECTIONS

THE GREAT GALLERY OF SCULPTURE

Thierry Dufrêne

Translated by
David Radzinowicz

© Éditions du Centre Pompidou/Musée du Louvre Éditions/Musée d'Orsay, Paris, 2005

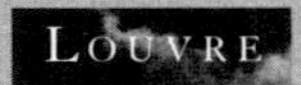
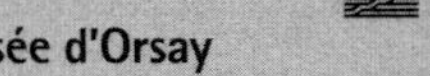

Foreword

'Sculpture? That's what you trip over when you step back to look at a picture.' So runs one celebrated definition, often ascribed to the American painter Barnett Newman. It's true we live in a world of images and that the modernity cherished by Charles Baudelaire has tended to give greater prominence to painting. Nonetheless, due to its sensual qualities, its manner of apprehending space, in a word, its *embodiment*, sculpture has found new ways of imposing itself visually in our increasingly technological society.

The public comes in droves to revel in the spatial experiences proposed by sculptures and installations, something one can witness for oneself in the halls of French sculpture in the Musée du Louvre, looking down over the sculpture gallery in the Musée d'Orsay, or following visitors round Dubuffet's *Jardin d'hiver* or Beuys' *Plight* in the Musée National d'Art Moderne at the Centre Pompidou.

Following on from *The Big Picture, Paintings in Paris*, the object of the present volume is to unite a reflection on sculpture with the joy of discovering — or rediscovering — in our museums members of an artistic family that is both more ancient and more varied than painting. In 1954, André Malraux wrote in his introduction to the *Imaginary Museum of World Sculpture*: 'No art is more highly charged with the languages of artists whose faith and race we have long forgotten and with the presence of the most enigmatic qualities of Art.'

What is the common factor between a three-thousand-year-old Egyptian figurine and a Brancusi? It is the extraordinary stylistic freedom with which the artist treated the object.

In fact, sculptures from very different epochs resemble each more by the striking manner in which they go beyond outward appearances than by any imitation of a natural, or more specifically human, form.

The Great Gallery of Sculpture confirms the publishing principles embraced by the museums concerned in presenting a three-fold itinerary around the French national collections that is neither a conventional guide nor a mere anthology of reproductions. The work of an academic, Thierry Dufrêne, professor of history of art and a specialist in the history of sculpture, it is above all the fruit of individual choice. Nevertheless, thanks to active assistance on behalf of the departments of sculpture in the museums concerned and suggestions by their staff, it is also the outcome of the collaboration between the museums and the university. This has been a positive move and one we would dearly hope to pursue.

Like Georges Perec, for instance, the author, rather than slavishly adhering to a set of rules, has chosen the self-imposed constraint of a 'triptych' that combines *at least one* sculpture from *each* institution. Occasionally, he has allowed himself the luxury of selecting more than one piece: no complaint there — variety is the spice of any system. The resulting juxtapositions seldom rely on one-to-one equivalences, on quotations from work to work — although the practice has been resorted to by sculptors at least as much as by painters — and echoes between museums and periods abound. Rather than formal resemblance or assonance, though the results can be exceedingly revealing when these do occur (as in the 'Geometry' sequence, which places side by side Pierre Julien's *Dying Gladiator,* Maillol's *Mediterranean* and a *Spatial Sculpture* by Katarzyna Kobro), the author highlights

the transpositions, the diverse approaches to problems or themes espoused by each artist and each period.
Few other arts are as deeply rooted in the anthropological context as sculpture. This is brought out
particularly in the first part, '(Hi)stories of sculptures' (whose title is a homage to Jean-Luc Godard),
through sequences treating the idol or the mask and the fundamental techniques of sculptural image-
making — the imprint, touch, modelling, and so on.
A shell, a tree trunk goes a long way to explaining the origins of the *sculpter*. Encounters between
works cast light on the rifts beneath the apparent continuity: witness, in the 'Assemblage' sequence
the astonishing Roman ready-made opposite Duchamp's *Bicycle Wheel*, or the Etruscan canopic jar
side by side with Picasso's *Absinthe Glass*.
The second part, 'Embodiment, allusion' throws up evidence of the dual alchemy performed
by sculptors, who not only create bodies in every conceivable state but also endow ideas with
a material form. The confrontation between Pradier's *Satyr and Bacchante* and Giacometti's
Suspended Ball, both pieces where the chaos of passion and cruelty is reined in within the rigours
of form, encapsulates this perfectly.
Elsewhere, González's *Montserrat*'s cry vibrates alongside that of Puget's *Milon of Crotona,* while
Pigalle's gripping self-portrait joins forces with the imprint of Penone's face in *Soffio*.
From the outset, the third part chimes in with contemporary sensibilities, as it is sculpture's capacity
'to recreate space, to give form to time' that gives this rhythmical, interactive art such appeal.
Whereas the philosopher Lessing strove to draw a distinction between the arts of time, such as poetry,
and the arts of space, such as sculpture, developments in the latter have belied this convention.
One sequence in particular exemplifies how sculptors can question time better than anyone:
'The Ages of Man' links a child carved by Houdon, a man in the prime of life by Camille Claudel
and a modern *vanitas* in the shape of Anselmo's lettuce, whose wilting form would undermine
the entire construction were it not replaced by the curator.
With Tinguely, sculpture comes to life: the era of the sculpture-machine is upon us, going beyond
the freeze-frame of the 'decisive moment' which, like photographers (yet well before the invention
of that technique), sculptors had always sought.
 Since we have just mentioned photography, this is perhaps the place to congratulate the work of the
photographers and of the graphic designer, who, in spite of the notorious difficulties of reproducing
sculpture, have succeeded in recreating the spatial environment in which it operates within the pages
of a book.
No doubt the present volume, a product of experience and of personal preference, will prove of
singular assistance to readers when, through an analysis of the emotions encountered on confronting
sculpture, they go on to unearth its interrelationships and evolutionary trends, and engage with visual
and intellectual experiences of their own. At that point, to quote Stendhal, beauty truly will appear
as 'a promise of happiness'.

Henri Loyrette, president-director of the Musée du Louvre
Serge Lemoine, president of the public establishment of the Musée d'Orsay
Bruno Racine, president of the Centre d'art et de culture Georges Pompidou

Contents

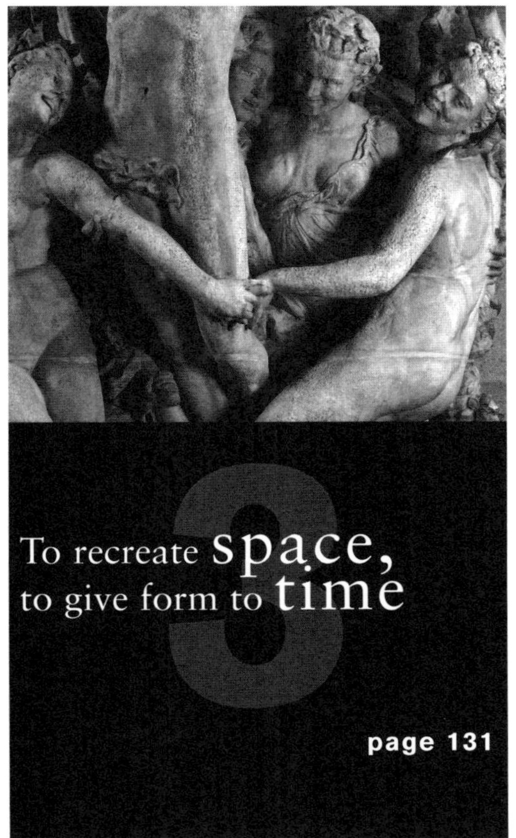

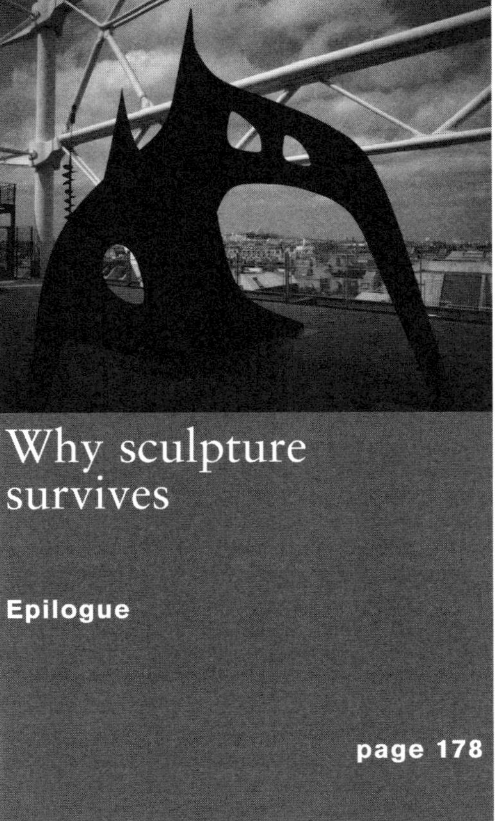

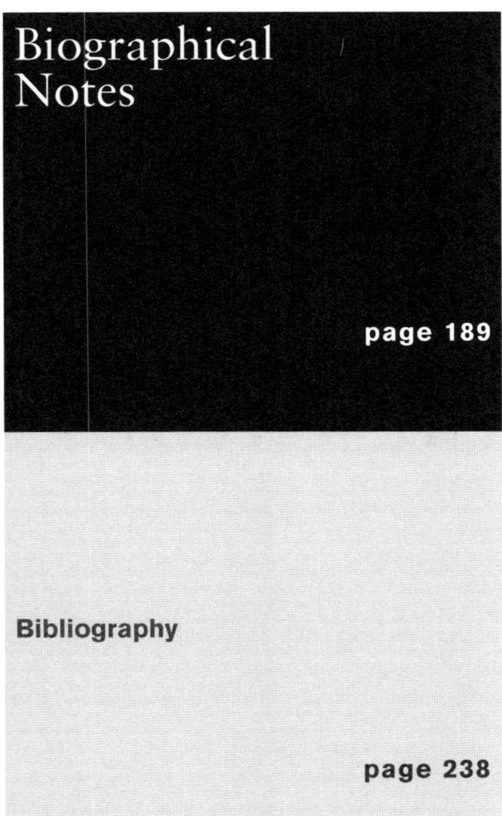

Walking through
the Great Gallery of Sculpture

1. Origins

'The origin of sculpture is lost in the mists of time,' wrote Baudelaire in his *Salon de 1846*. Its foundations lay in the sacred, in magic, in ritual. People of agro-pastoral civilisations believed that man had been created by a demiurge out of mud deposited by the rising rivers. They worshipped the remains of meteors that fell from the sky, however. If there are no painting deities, there are on the other hand plenty of sculptor gods: the God of the Bible models man out of silt in his image, just as the gods of Mesopotamia had done before Him. Every civilisation composes at least one chapter of its mythology in sculptural form. In Hawaii, Pele, the goddess of the volcano who burns the forests, jealous of the beauty of Hopo'e, elder daughter of Nature, transforms her into a vibrating, singing stone. Since then, there grew up on the island the habit of striking lava stones against one another as an accompaniment to the rain dance. In Greece, Prometheus steals the gods' fire and brings it to Man, paving the way for the invention of metalwork. Mythical blacksmiths are dubbed Hephaistos in Greece, Thor in Scandinavia or Gu — the blacksmith god of the Yoruba — in Africa.

Thus, when the contemporary sculptor Giuseppe Penone embraces a mass of clay leaving an imprint of his whole body, when Charles Simmonds films himself clambering out of a heap of soil under which he is buried, or when James Turrell alters the landscape of a volcano in the middle of the American desert, all three are but taking part in a history of sculpture many thousands of years old, a history directly related to the creation of the world.

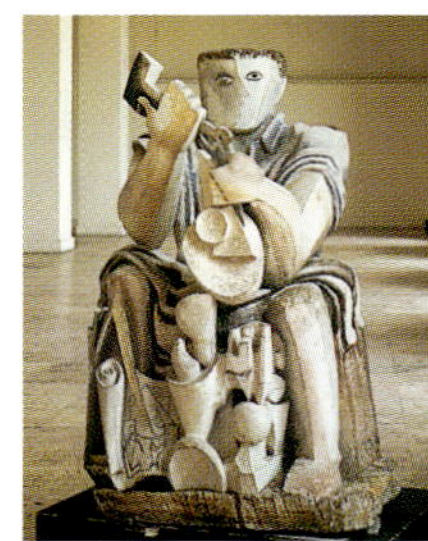

Ossip Zadkine
The Sculptor, 1939
Painted wood. 195 x 129 x 100 cm - CP

Since the most distant times, sculpture has embodied and rendered present whatever is not by nature visible (a divinity, a spirit), whatever cannot be seen everywhere at the same time (the sovereign on an equestrian statue) or what is no longer visible (an ancestor or the deceased by way of a totem). Sculpture thereby possesses three functions: a sacred and religious one; a political one intended to display power; and, finally, one of commemoration, establishing a bond with the past. It goes without saying that these three are closely link-ed: funerary ritual, for instance, presupposes that the effigy of the defunct serves in the ancestor worship from which its power emanates.

Because it makes material the image it forms, sculpture is always the earliest victim of iconoclasm. Thus Napoleon, who had seen statues of kings of France trampled under foot during the French Revolution, had great mis-givings before finally accepting any in his image. And more recently how many *Lenins* and *Stalins* and other politicians in bronze or granite have we seen toppled?

There is a distinction between monumental sculpture, always linked to archi-tecture and as such not the subject of the present volume, and independent sculpture, be it in the form of carved group, stand-alone statue or relief. If free-standing sculpture, around which one can turn and admire from every point of view, is surely the most attractive for true-blue lovers of the form, those with a nostalgia for pictorial effects might prefer the relief, which pre-supposes a ground, and which can be appreciated from only one viewpoint. Throughout history, there has been an ongoing discussion (known as the

paragone) of the respective merits of painting and sculpture, sometimes in an attempt to establish the superiority of one art over the other. The argument of multi-faciality — the multiplicity of angles of vision — was often advan-ced in favour of sculpture. An advocate of the superiority of painting, Leonardo da Vinci denied it, alleging that the sculptor in fact works from only two sides: front and back. Benvenuto Cellini, on the other hand, affir-med in his *Treatise on Sculpture and the Art of Goldsmithery* (1568) that 'painting fixes but one of the eight principal points of view sculpture demands.' Still, if for Mannerist sculptors in the 16th century, such as Giambologna and his epigone Adriaen de Vries, multi-faceted viewpoints were paramount, they were less so for the Baroque sculptor Bernini, who preferred his dynamic works to be viewed from a single station point. Thus multi-faciality is not necessarily perceived as an intrinsic quality of sculpture. In his *Salon de 1846*, Baudelaire complained that sculpture 'shows too many faces at the same time', apparently making it 'imprecise and ungraspable'. At the end of the century, the sculptor and theorist Adolf von Hildebrand went further than Baudelaire in *Das Problem der Form in der bildenden Kunst* (*The Problem of Form in the Visual Arts*), published in 1893, when he defi-ned relief as the most authentic form of sculpture, in opposition to Rodin. In the 20th century, 'modern' sculpture totally rehabilitated the third dimension. The discovery by the Expressionists and, even more so, by the Cubists of Black African statuary (called by Carl Einstein 'total form') reasserted the legitimacy of volume. In the wake of Brancusi, it was soon the relationship to space that, beyond the object sculpted, became the principal subject of the sculptor, whether in the sense that the piece is presented in the form of a draw-ing in space (González, Picasso), maintains a dialectical relation with depth (Giacometti), measures space logically (Judd), or regards it as a setting in which it is deployed (Cragg, Hesse). Environments, such as those by Dubuffet and Beuys presented in this book, and installations even allow visitors to enter a sculpture that has become, even if temporarily, architecture. Lastly, with the kinetic art of a Calder or a Tinguely, inherent motion is added to the viewer's circular path.

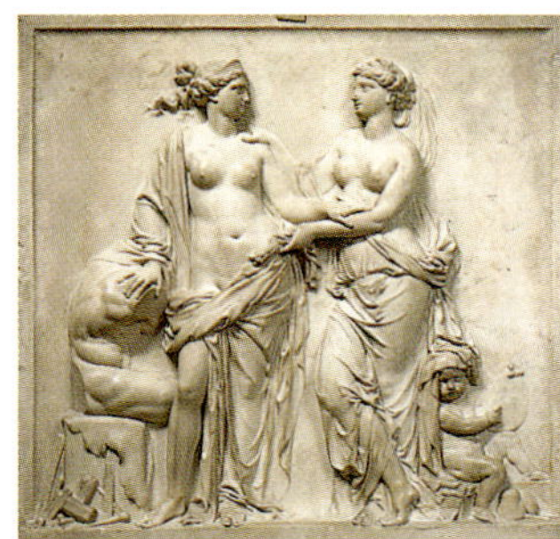

Jacques Buirette
The Marriage of Painting and Sculpture, 1663
Marble bas-relief. 78 x 76 x 8 cm - ML

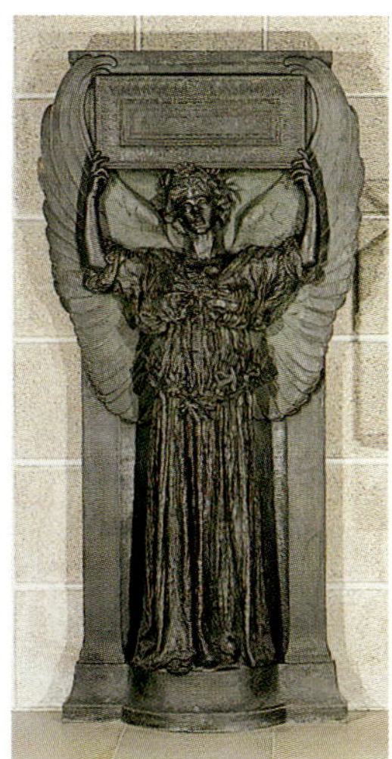

Augustus Saint-Gaudens

Amor Caritas, before 1899

Bronze - MO

2. History

Homer defined sculpture as 'numerous beautiful bodies in beautiful postures'. But the origins of Greek statuary lie in the *xoana*, pieces of wood
or stones (*betyles*) considered as symbols of a divine presence and often
hidden from the eyes of mere mortals under a cloth or in a casket. For the
art historian David Freedberg, the power of such ancient images derived
precisely from the absence of any anthropomorphic character owed to the
fact that they were *acheiropoietes*, 'not made by the hand of the man', an
exceptional quality that facilitated the transition between the realm of the
living and the kingdom of the dead. It is only on the cusp of the 4th century BC that the theory of *mimesis* (imitation), outlined by Xenophon and
elaborated by Plato, led in Greece to increasingly realistic figuration.
Antiquity thereafter sought to arrive at perfect proportions — square and
solid for Polycletes as against tall and slender for Lysippus. The 'beautiful
postures' about which Homer speaks thus constitute a repertory of gestures, attitudes and actions bequeathed to posterity by sculpture, in addition to its experience of the ingenious machine called the body.

The Middle Ages saw the appearance of ymaigiers, image-makers, an integral part of the great cathedral building sites, corporations of them active
in carving stone tombs or funerary effigies, statues representing saints or
decorated capitals. The artist began to become an entity independent from
the stonemason, one of the first to sign his work being Gislebertus at the
cathedral of St-Lazare at Autun in Burgundy. 'This will kill that': in his
historical novel *Notre-Dame de Paris* (1831), Victor Hugo opposes the
paper book of the printed word ('this') to the stone book of statuary
('that'). Yet the book did not kill statuary because, from the Renaissance
on, the latter began increasingly to serve in the cause of another great narrative form — mythology. Only later would sculpture open up to the reality of the outside world.

3. Antiquity or nature

For as long as sculpture was coupled with narrative, the fledgling artist had to be able to master a basic vocabulary of human types and gestures (Gombrich). It is not possible to understand Puget's *Milon of Crotona* without reference to the ancient Hellenistic group of the Laocoon that supplied the *exemplum doloris*.

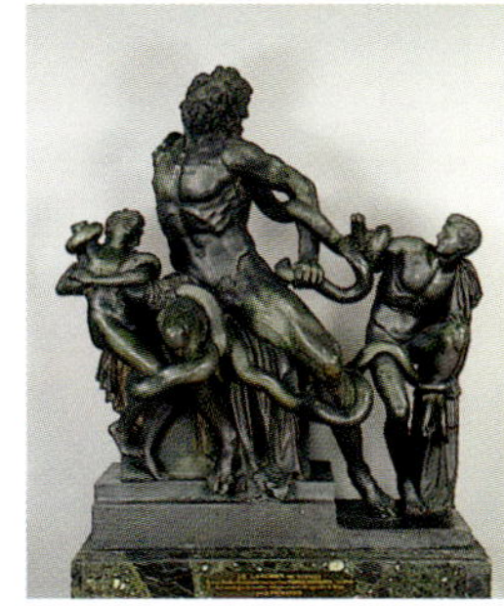

Primaticcio
Laocoon (Vatican), 1543
Bronze - Château de Fontainebleau

The male nude straining in effort or expiring refers back, in the work of Jean-Jacques Pradier or Pierre Julien for instance, to the *Borghese Gladiator* or *The Dying Gladiator*. It was all the more common to borrow a repertory of forms from Antique sculpture since, unlike painting ancient examples of which have practically disappeared, sculpture offered permanence, and even renewal. Roman copies made after Greek originals were returned to both in the Renaissance and in the Baroque age. Antique sculpture always aroused interest, being completed on occasion precisely *because* it was admired. Thus, the Antique *Hermaphrodite* reposes on a mattress carved by Bernini in the 17th century. As for the red porphyry and white marble *Galatian,* a Roman work of the 2nd century, its head is not original, while the tunic was reworked by Lorenzo Nizza in 1610 and the arms are wholly modern.

It was only in the 1770s that the painter Anton Raffael Mengs voiced what only a few had dared even to think: sculptures considered Greek cannot all be original, and in fact only a handful are. It is from this revelation that the dogma

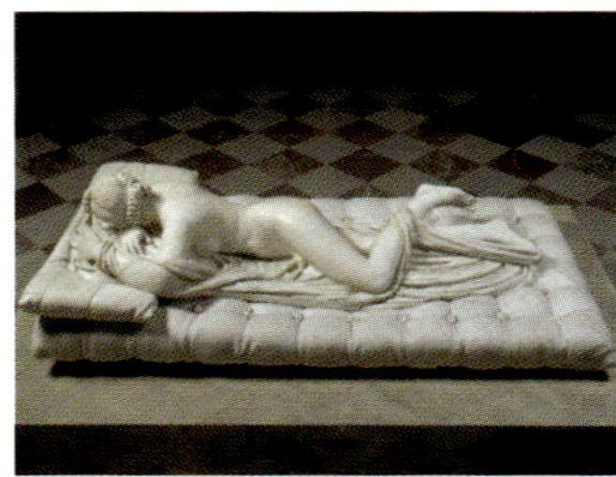

Sleeping Hermaphrodite,
Roman copy, second half of the 2nd century BC
Marble. 169 x 89 cm - ML

of originality sprang, one that modern sculpture has pursued to extremes. Academic teaching, the subjects tabled for the Prix de Rome, the conventions of the Salons and official commissions ended up by substituting the observation of Nature for the Greco-Roman repertory of forms. Nonetheless, the 18th century possessed a far richer, less mechanistic conception of the body than previous centuries, one increasingly marked by physiology, the study of the temperaments and of the organism in general. Nature as corrected by the Antique would henceforth be the goal of sculptors such as Houdon and Caffieri, or Pigalle in his naked *Voltaire*. If in the 17th century the Baroque took into account solely violent passions, the following century, as Aline Magnien reminds us, had a predisposition for depicting 'softer' passions: melancholy, affliction, sleep, repose.

In the name of 'character' or to convey some explosive action, even deformation of proportion was permitted. In his *Chevaux de Marly,* Guillaume Coustou the Elder showed no hesitation in shortening the left leg of the man reining in the horse so as to render his exertion. In the same period, Bouchardon and Falconet were far from alone in striving to attain a synthesis between the beautiful Antique and Nature studied from life. Philippe Sénéchal has shown that at the beginning of the 19th century, Jean-Galbert Salvage sought to achieve a 'reciprocal validation of nature and the antique' in the same vein by analysing the anatomy of certain ancient statues, such as the *Borghese Gladiator,* in *écorché*, as sectional figures. A little later, Stendhal wrote that, because she is alive, a simple countrywoman is more beautiful than an Antique Venus, even though she does not inspire the love of people of taste. Sculpture thus calls for more than the imitation of the Antique, and more too than a slavish copy of Nature.

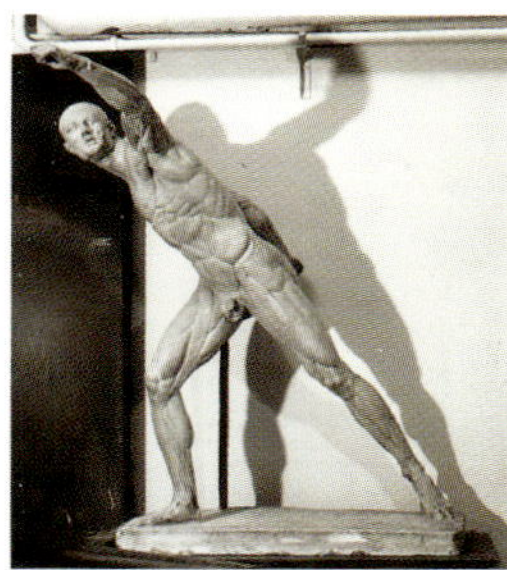

Jean-Galbert Salvage
The Borghese Gladiator in écorché, 1804
Plaster. H : 157 cm, L : 199 cm.
Paris, Ecole nationale des beaux-arts

The 19th century continued to depict the subject thinking and feeling through the physical envelope. The academic nude began to lose ground. Whereas in 1804, in the *Journal des arts*, Vivant Denon had defended a nude statue of Napoleon commissioned from Chaudet, by 1828 Stendhal was writing in the *Revue trimestrielle*: 'Sculpture has less and less to do with our world, because it cannot achieve anything without the nude, and that we no longer like.' He appealed for a 'revolution' in 'sculpture, able to interest us deeply and to move us', a sensual sculpture, an emotion 'clothed' which would equal a Canova. The 'expressive head' met with great success in the Romantic era. By the time of Carpeaux and Rodin, psychology and feeling

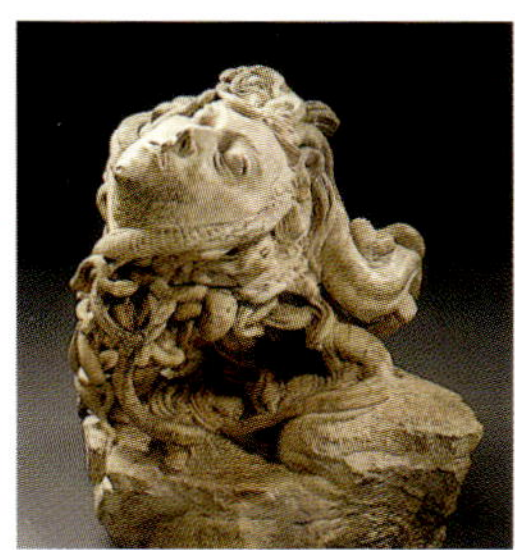

Paul Dardé
Eternal Grief, Head with Serpents, 1913
Gypsum - MO

have ousted physiology. Even the way the work of a sculptor was appreciated had altered: the artist's autograph work, the clay model was now being more highly rated than the finished product in marble carved by technicians.

4. Modern and contemporary sculpture

The history of 20th-century art has altered the concept of sculpture considerably. In less than a century, one has witnessed the promotion of the Object by Marcel Duchamp, Pop artists and Nouveaux Réalistes; the adoption of 'poor' non-noble materials (soil, textiles, industrial waste), as much by Dadaists and the proponents of junk art, such as Chamberlain, as in Arte Povera; the opening on to real space initiated by the environments and installations of the 1970s; and, finally, the deployment of the real body in performance art.

Since Brancusi and Duchamp, the renewal of themes and materials has been accompanied by a constant questioning of the very definition of sculpture. One might almost speak of a de-construction of everything that the essence

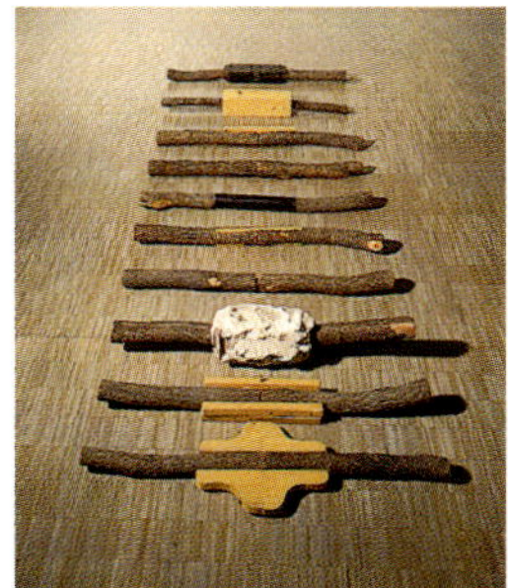

Bernard Pagès
Ten Assemblages End to End, 1974
Wood, diverse materials. 40 x 110 cm - CP

of sculpture seemed to stand for, leading away from direct carving, durable stone and the perennial verticality of statuary and onto the informal, the 'soft' (Robert Morris, Claes Oldenburg), the transformable, the perishable (Giovanni Anselmo), the horizontal (Carl Andre). No longer just an object observed from every angle, moving sculpture (Tinguely), 'environments' which one enters, such as Beuys' *Plight*. Not so much forms hewn by the sculptor, but found, recycled or machined objects. Not modelled volume, but a hollow imprint, as in Penone's *Soffio*.

The industrial age has also placed at the disposal of sculptors new materials (glass, resin, polystyrene), mechanisms, technologies (kinetic art, electronics), and processes (such as mass production), all of which can be marshalled to the cause of art.

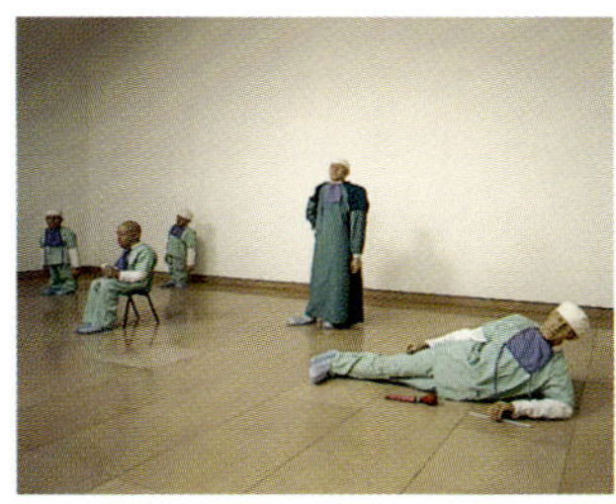

Gilles Barbier

Polyfocus, 1999

Five mannequins, wax heads and diverse materials - CP

If the ready-made demonstrated that skill is not the only way to make art, ephemerality and performance in particular have shaken the foundations of sculpture more than any other forms. How should one consider the record of an action like Richard Serra's in his film *Hand Catching Lead*? Are the three-dimensional forms in a hologram or a video installation, like *Moon is the Oldest TV* by Nam June Paik, sculpture? The question then arises of the limits of an art which, since Lessing's text *Laocoon* (1766), has been confined exclusively to the third dimension. Frank Popper showed that in our electronic age (and with kinetic art) temporality too is part and parcel of sculpture. The autonomy of the contemporary artist makes him or her free to create independently from the time-consuming, constricting process of the commission, even if they remain sensitive to the social demands and the spirit of the age. The acceptance of abstraction has released the artist from the need to refer to reality: in 'built art', to borrow Serge Lemoine's evocative expression, an artist can invent whatever they want.

5. Overture

This book has been conceived as a walk through an imaginary museum. Thanks to photography, here one can place side by side sculptures located today in three different museums.

The shortcomings of this type of enterprise, such as loss of scale and historical context, are obvious, yet, in reality, one always visits a museum accompanied by the baggage of all the artworks one has seen and thanks to which one is able to experience an aesthetic emotion when presented with a sensory experience. The reader can amble through the itinerary suggested in the *Great Gallery of Sculpture* just as they would among works in a real museum. And whenever they next visit the museum, the image of a sculpture compared to another in this book might come to mind, forming a kind of counterpoint. Just as in Jean-Luc Godard's *Histoire(s) de cinéma*, we propose '*(hi)stories* of sculpture': beginnings of stories — shots, snippets, sequences —, visual comparisons that all feed into the sculptural imagination. Words surface: 'embody', because sculpture renders things present; 'suggest', because it is more elliptic than painting — 'recreate space and give form to time.' As Richard Serra writes: 'I think that sculpture, if it has any potential at all, has the potential to create its own place and space.'

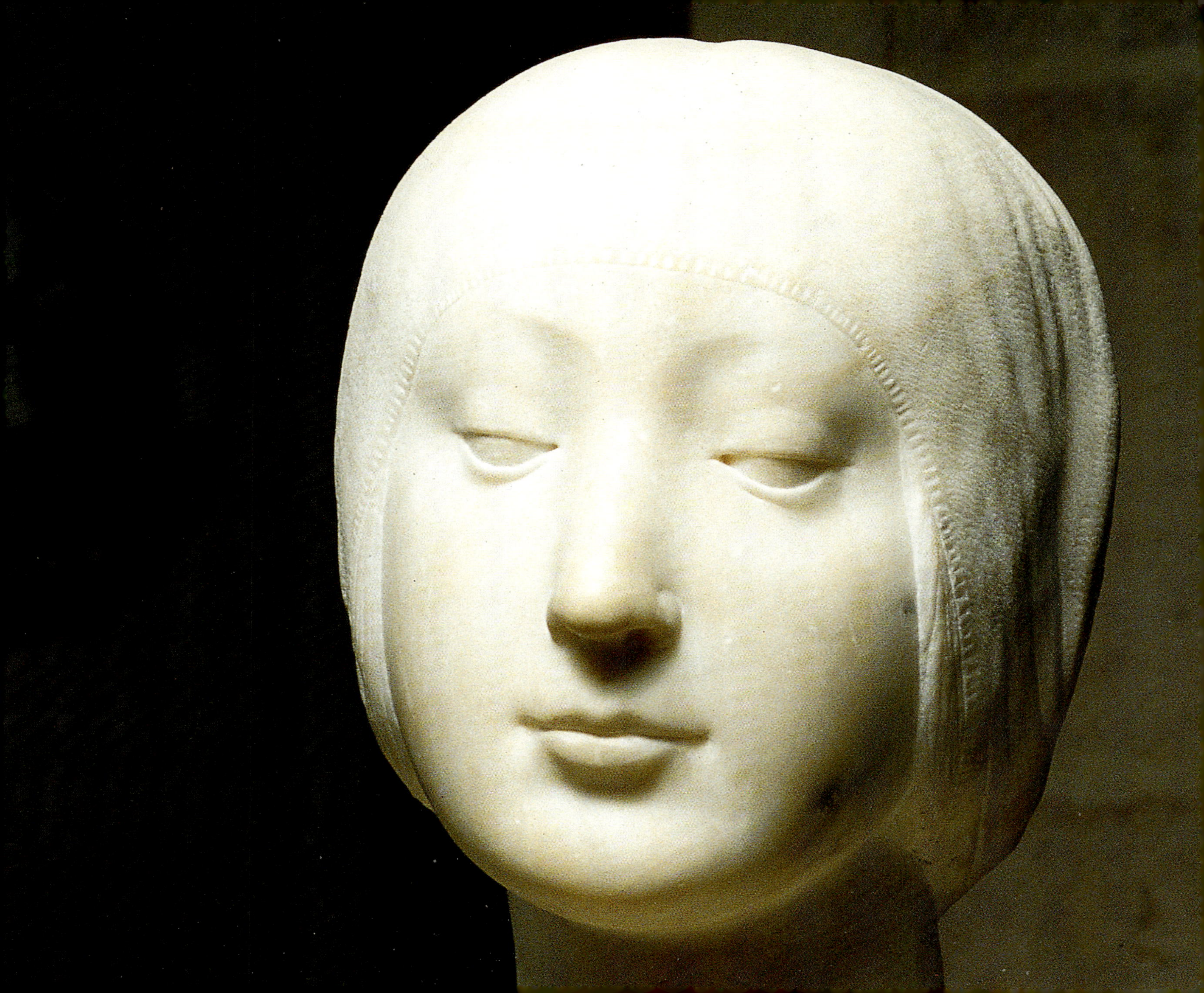

1

(Hi)stories
of Sculptures

Marble is well suited to the pure and luminous forms of woman.
For goddesses, white marble; for great men and for heroes, bronze
that brings out male, violent beauty with greater vigor. Marble is ideal for flesh,
simulating its appearance and imperceptible roughness.

Théophile Thoré, *Salon de 1847*, Paris: Librairie internationale, chez Lacroix et Verboeckhoven, 1868

The Idol

The idol was the first form of sculpture. It is present in prehistoric art as ample-bodied goddesses of fecundity, as well as in Ancient Greece where 'bell-idols' from late 8th-century BC Boeotia were paraded in funeral processions (*ekphorai*). The articulated legs striking the bell symbolise the voyage of the dead to the Beyond. 'Terrifically grotesque' was the initial verdict on their accession to the Louvre in 1894.

Modern art often recalls the schematic forms of the idol, as in this *Figure* by the Cubist sculptor Jacques Lipchitz. Although according to the artist himself comparisons should be made to African art if 'only in a very general sense', it is more reminiscent of the rock formations the artist examined on the Brittany coast in the company of his friend, Le Corbusier. Nevertheless, its hieratic quality and marked sexual overtones make it a totemic sculpture (it is also known as *Totem*), whereas the transparency of its structure shows links to experiments by those 20th-century artists who tried to integrate the void into sculpture.

Paul Gauguin himself wished his last major ceramic sculpture, *Oviri*, to be set up on his tomb at Atuona in the Marquesas Islands; and a long time after, in 1973, a bronze version was indeed erected there. He called it *La Tueuse* 'the killer' (in the feminine) and, in a letter to his friend the poet Mallarmé, qualified it as a 'strange figure, cruel enigma'. In Tahitian, *oviri* means 'wild, savage' and symbolises retreat into the self. Syncretic, the *Tueuse* refers back to female figures of fecundity at Borobudur and to mummified craniums of Maori chieftains, while the dilated eyes are reminiscent of Easter Island statuary. To the artist's mind, *Oviri* is perhaps the 'savage' who dispatches the Old World, the Europe the artist had fled from and which would in that case be represented by the wolf drowning in its gore. Or maybe this stands instead for the 'the savage in-spite-of-myself', a figure of melancholy that invariably made Gauguin — like his art — alien to others.

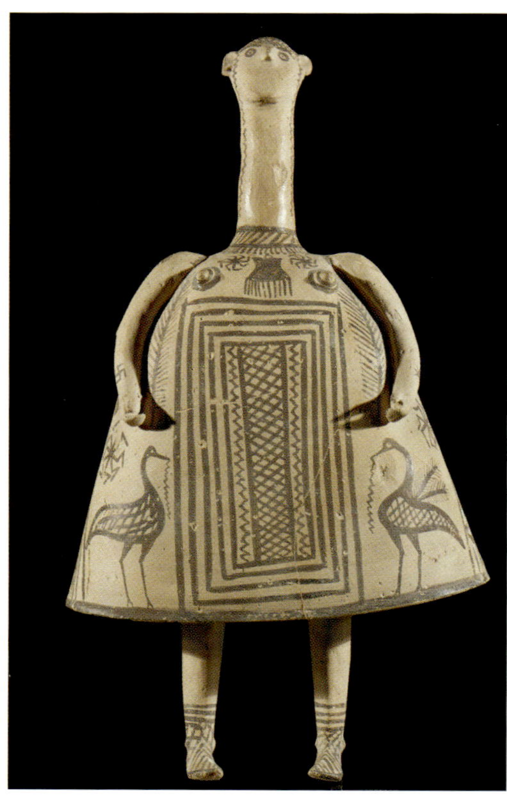

Bell-Idol, Thebes, Archaic period, c. 700 BC.
Terracotta.
H: 39.5 cm - ML

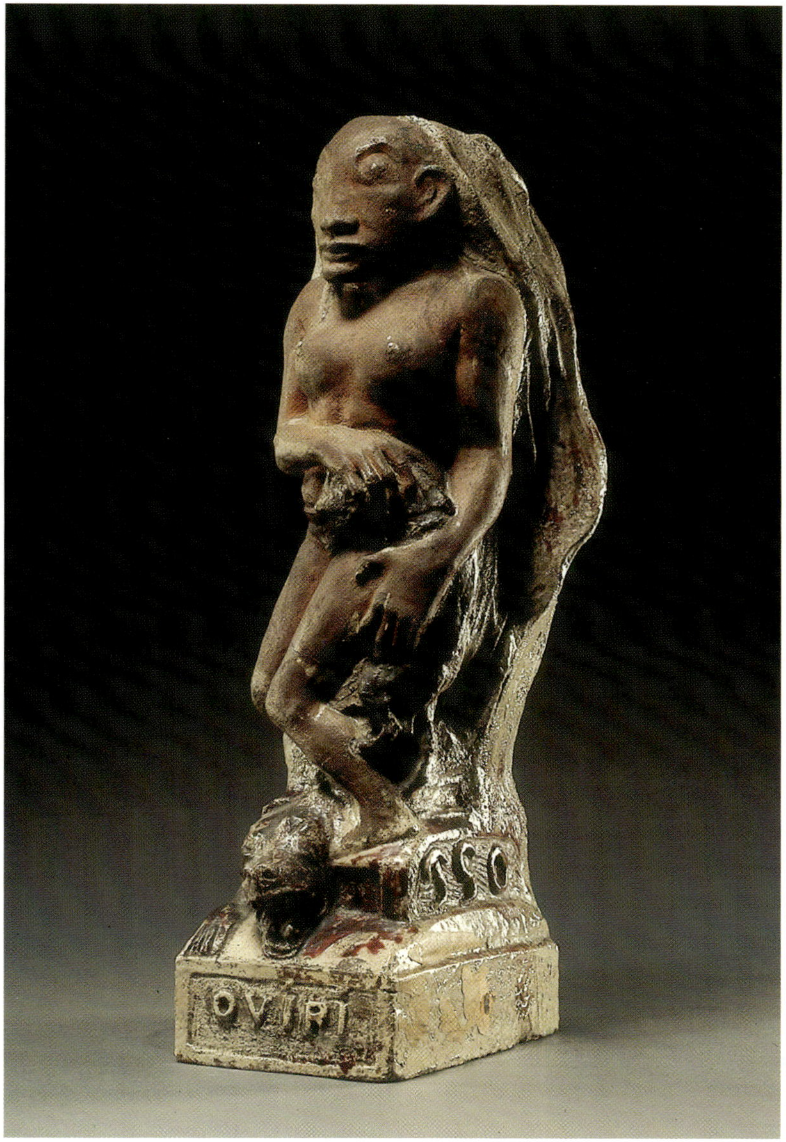

Paul Gauguin

Oviri, 1894

Partially enamelled vitrified sandstone. 75 x 19 x 27 cm - MO

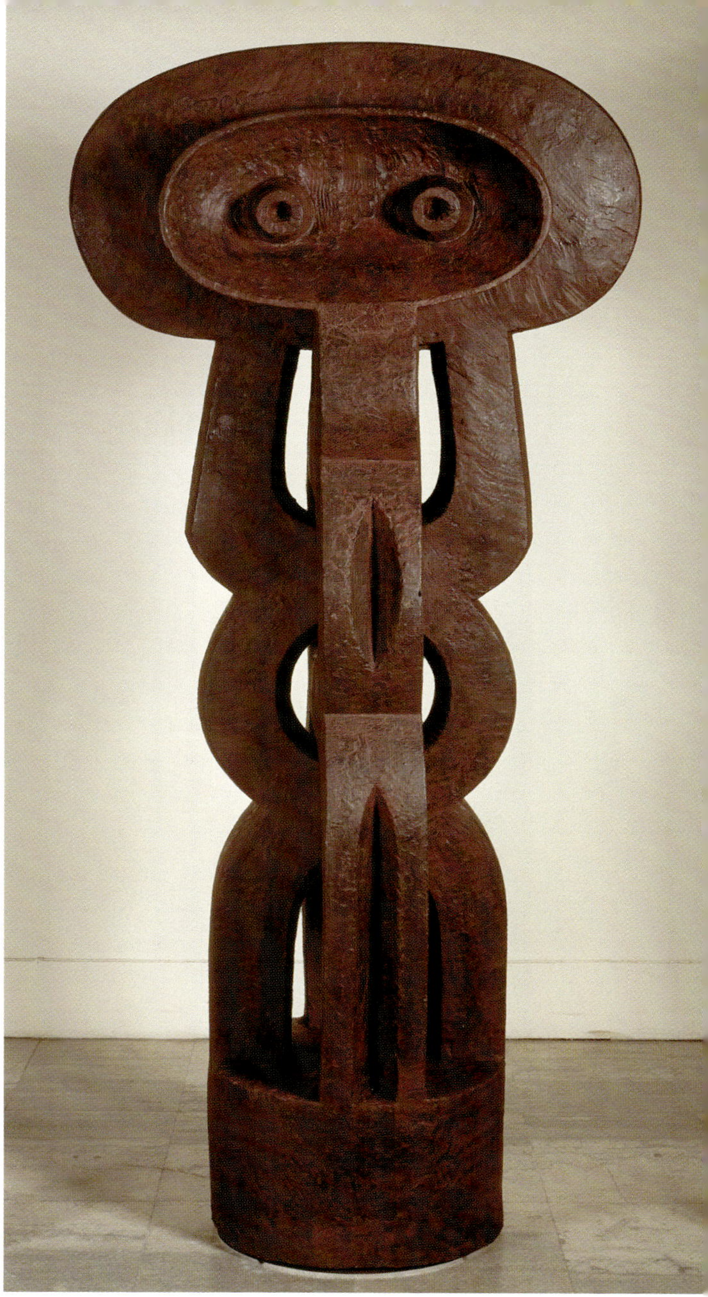

Jacques Lipchitz

Figure, 1926-30

Painted plaster. 220 x 95 x 75 cm - CP

Mask

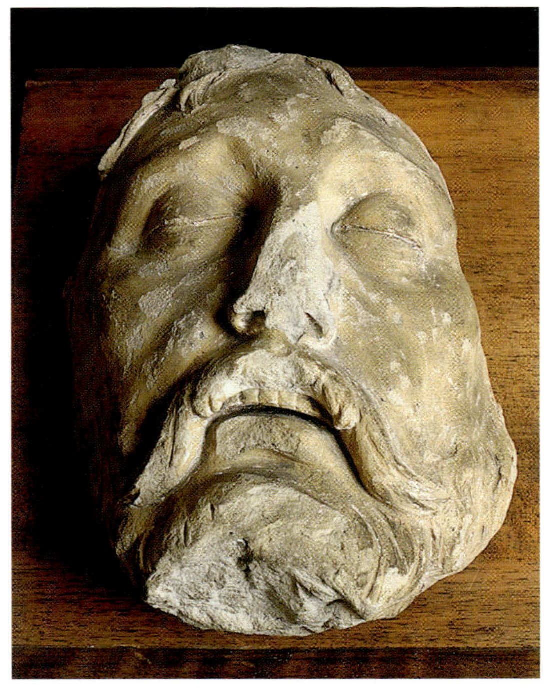

Germain Pilon (attributed to)
Mask of Henri II, second half of the 16th century
Terracotta. 21 x 16 x 11 cm - ML

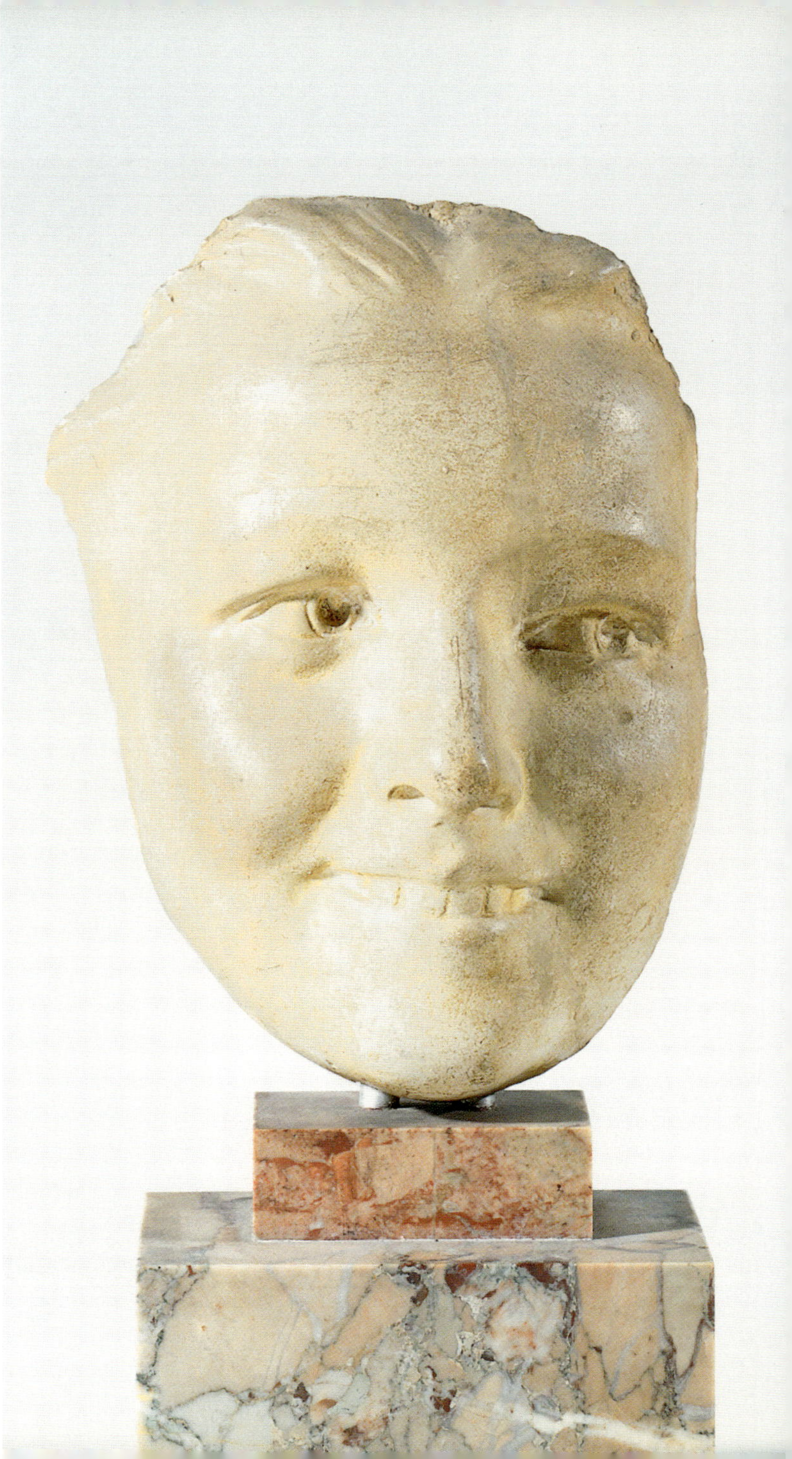

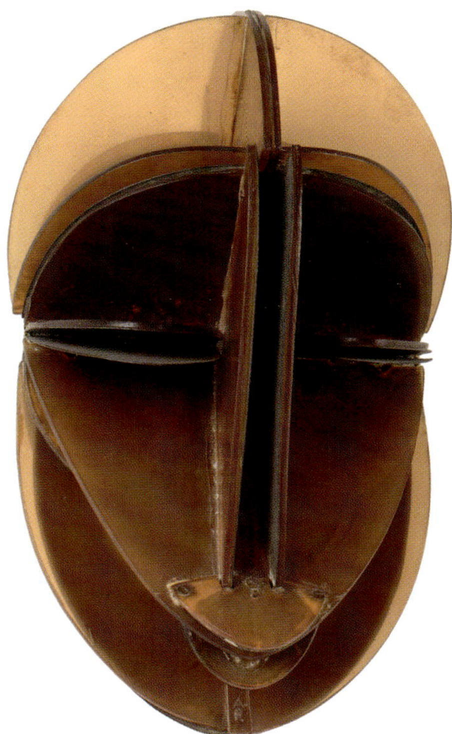

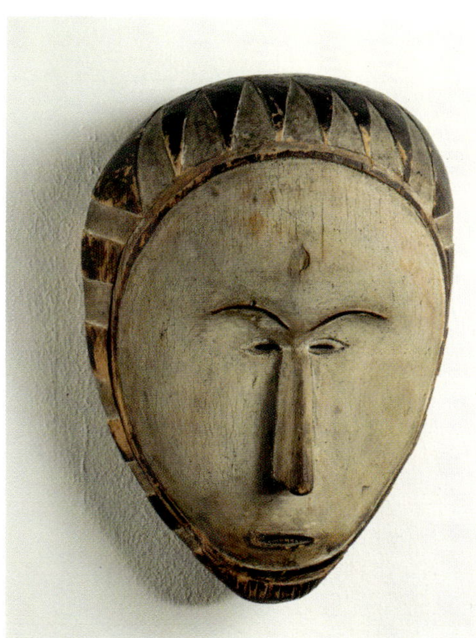

For a carved mask, one can either aim at a likeness, or, on the contrary, eschew it completely.

The mask of Henri II returns us to the practice of the posthumous mask. Its discoverer Louis Courajoud wrongly identified it as the one taken directly from the king's corpse that served as the model for the wax funerary mask executed in 1559 by the painter François Clouet. In point of fact, it is a model made after the mortuary mask for the gisant (the prone statue on a sculpted tomb) of the monarch taken in 1565 by Germain Pilon for the tomb of Henri II and Catherine de' Medici intended for the Valois Rotunde at the abbey of Saint-Denis; the work was transferred to the basilica after its demolition at the beginning of the 18th century.

Jean-Baptiste Carpeaux's objective in making the mask of Anna Foucart, the daughter of a friend from Valenciennes, and a relatively rare preserved example of a moulding from a head, was to compose a study that would capture the most lifelike expression possible. From this fugitive, instantaneous reaction, the sculptor manages to create an image of eternal freshness. He also turned to this sprightly girl's smile in other works, such as the *Laughing Girl with Vine Branches*.

On the other hand, the common trait between the Fang mask and Antoine Pevsner's *Mask* is their complete freedom from imitation. The first belonged to the painter André Derain, who, along with the poet Guillaume Apollinaire, was one of the first to initiate modern practitioners to the arts of Black Africa. The Constructivist sculptor's piece may be redolent of an African mask, but it was built out of modern materials: metal and Plexiglas. The work dates from the high-water mark of the cult of the machine and alludes to the gas masks worn in the war of 1914-18 as well as prefiguring the face of the robot Eve in Fritz Lang's film *Metropolis* (1927).

Jean-Baptiste Carpeaux

Anna Foucart, 1860

Patinated plaster mask. 19 x 13 x 7 cm - MO

Antoine Pevsner

Mask, 1923

Celluloid, zinc. 33 x 20 x 20 cm - CP

Fang Mask, **Gabon, late 19th century (?)**

Dried gourd with pokerwork design

42 x 28.5 x 14.7 cm - CP

Ritual

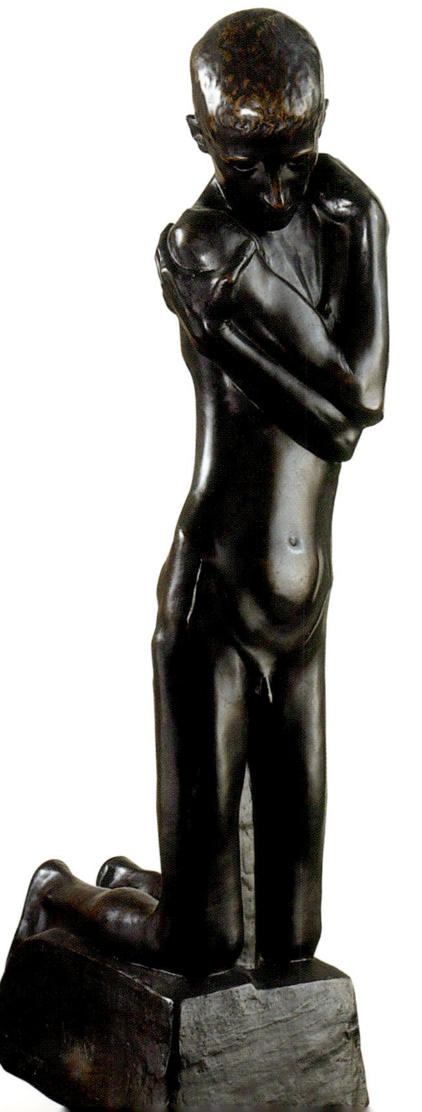

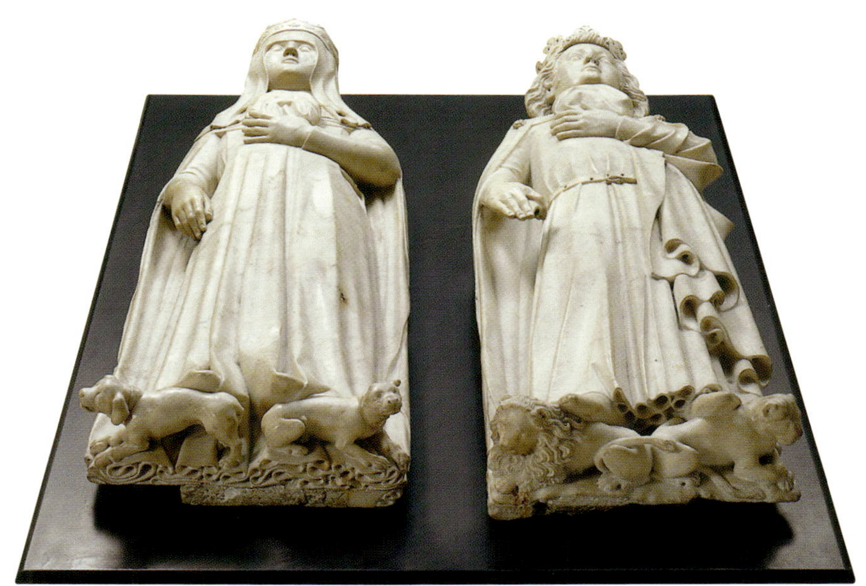

Georges Minne
Kneeling Youth at the Fountain, 1898
Bronze. 78 x 19 x 43 cm - MO

Jean de Liège
*Tomb for the Entrails of Charles the Fair
and Jeanne d'Evreux*, second half of the 14th century
Marble. 135 x 36 x 160 cm - ML

Wolfgang Laib
Milk-Stone, 1977
Marble and milk. 143.5 x 139.5 x 2 cm - CP

Ernst Gombrich noted that the earliest objects of artistic representation were ritualised acts: gestures of prayer, lamentation, thanksgiving, instruction and triumph. André Chastel called them 'primordial signs'. From the outset, ritual and sculpture went hand in hand.

Wolfgang Laib thus forms part of a long history when he kneels before the *Milk-Stone* that he has beforehand polished and slightly hollowed out — as was done formerly with cupule stones, in which cavities collected the blood of sacrificial victims. By pouring milk over the slab, Laib performs an act of purifying libation in the heart of the museum, which emphasises how 'white marble possesses a purity and density that harmonise with the purity of milk.'

In this, the German artist recalls the sublime, slender adolescent silhouette of the *Kneeling Youth at the Fountain* by George Minne. In keeping with the device that consists in multiplying the same figure seen from various viewing angles initiated by Auguste Rodin with the *Three Shades* for the *Gates of Hell*, the Belgian sculptor placed five bronzes of this kneeling figure around fountains in Brussels and Ghent, thus the kneelers endow the act of cleansing with a ritual character.

The marble table of the *Milk-Stone* also evokes stone tombs, such as the *Tomb for the Entrails of Charles le Bel and Jeanne d'Evreux*, carved by Jean de Liège. In his will and testament in 1324, the king had stipulated that his body be interred at the abbey of Saint-Denis, his heart at the monastery of the Predicant Friars in Paris, and his entrails in the monastery at Maubuisson, in accordance with the medieval tradition of multiple burial places. In this tomb, executed under his widow Jeanne d'Evreux, the sovereigns, figured by smaller than life-size 'alabaster images', each bear 'a round object': a bag containing the entrails.

Magic

This Egyptian possession figurine was intended literally to *prick* love in the person to whom it was directed. Formerly, a herb would have been placed under a statue to instil passion into passers-by. The magic object can be a box containing secrets, like that by the Symbolist sculptor Fix-Masseau, carried by a modern Pandora copied exactly from a casket in the medieval collections of the Musée National du Moyen-Age (Cluny) in Paris.

At the instigation of André Breton and Salvador Dalí, and following Alberto Giacometti's *Suspended Ball* (1930), the Surrealists created 'symbolically functioning objects' intended to plug directly into the Unconscious. These might be mechanical in the case of Marcel Duchamp and Man Ray; or else 'natural,' as in Joan Miró's *Objet du couchant.* The latter artist looked to the rural magical practices of his Catalan village of Montroig, from where this red rootstock of carob originally came. It is cut into the shape of a foot: for Miró, strength and fertility could spring only from the earth. The strange atmosphere of a setting sun haloes this erotic object, in which stand side by side a bird and a female sex, figuratively reunited with Nature in the guise of a slit in the bark and an outline of a spider. The metal spring suggests a bed and the cords, some hair. This erotic reading should not, however, detract from broader concerns. The Spanish artist was faced with the drama that was drenching western Europe, the land of the 'setting sun', in blood: the Spanish Civil War. In this case, the *Objet du couchant* might well be performing a kind of counter-spell.

Possession Figurine with Needles, **Roman Egypt**
3rd-4th centuries AD
Terracotta. 9.6 x 4.2 x 7.2 cm - ML

Fix-Masseau
The Secret, 1894
Mahogany, ivory casket. 76 x 17 x 18 cm - MO

Joan Miró
L'Objet du couchant, 1935-36
Assemblage: painted carob-tree trunk, bedspring, gas jet, gas burner, chain, shackle, string. 68 x 44 x 26 cm - CP

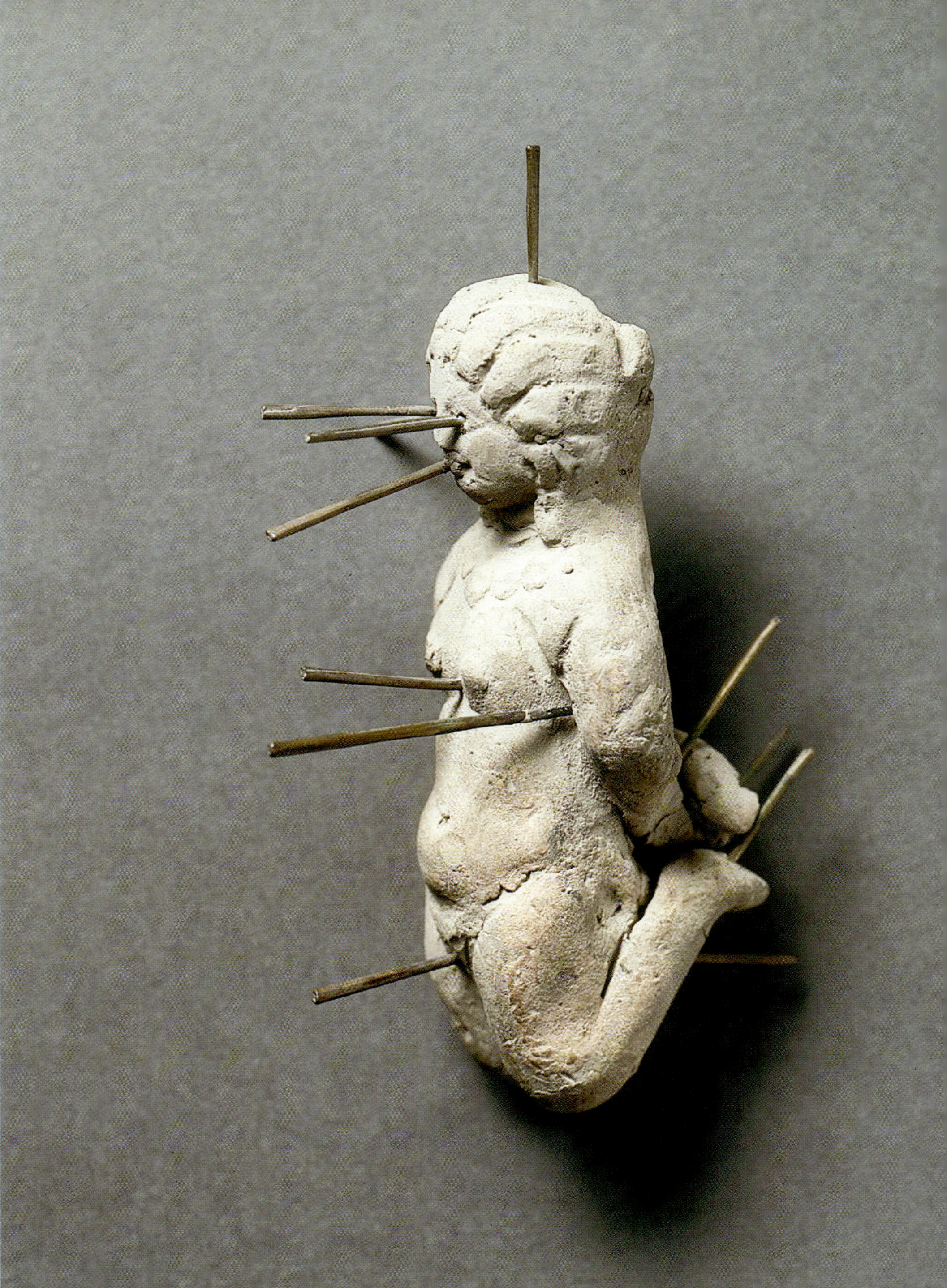

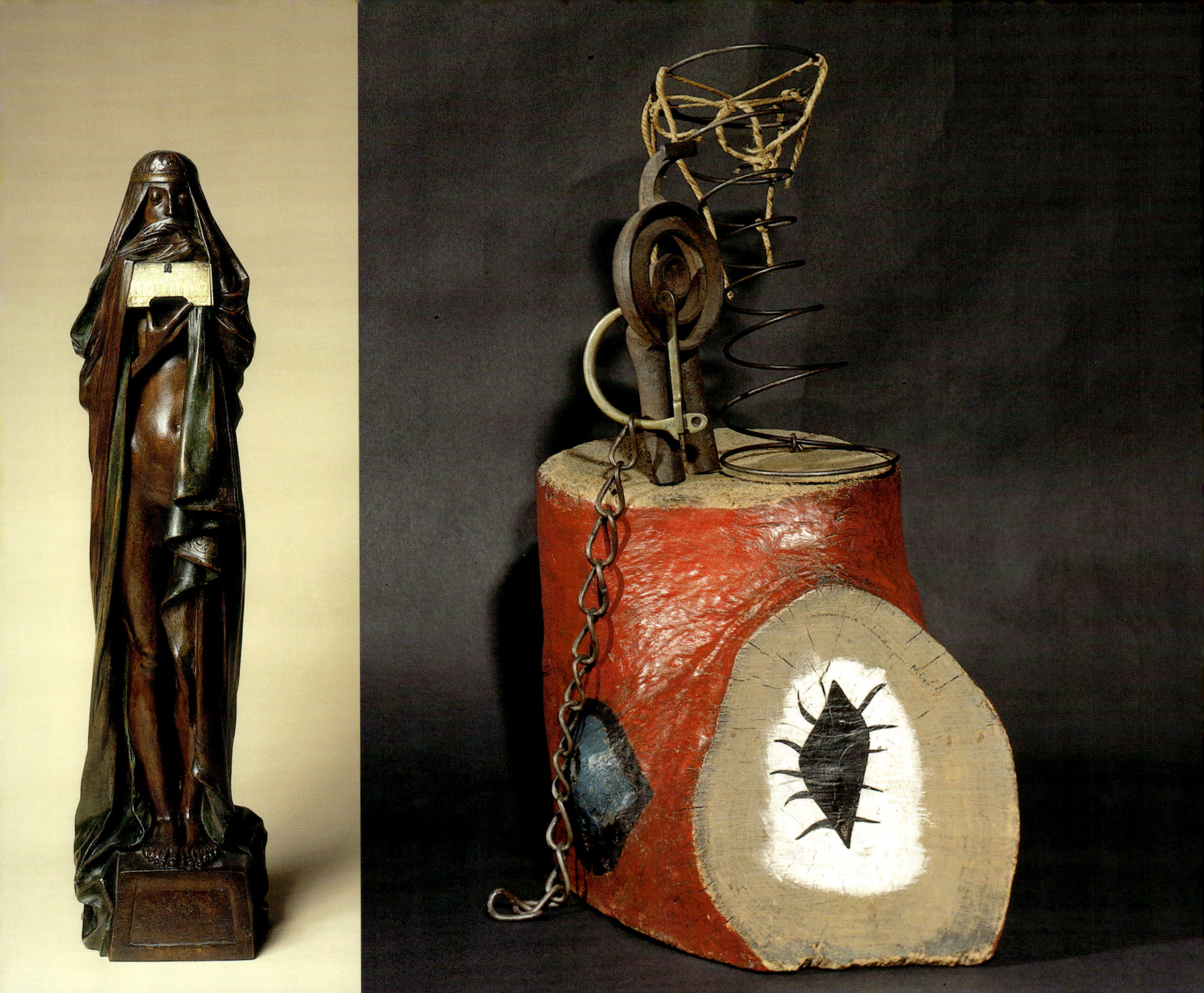

Shell

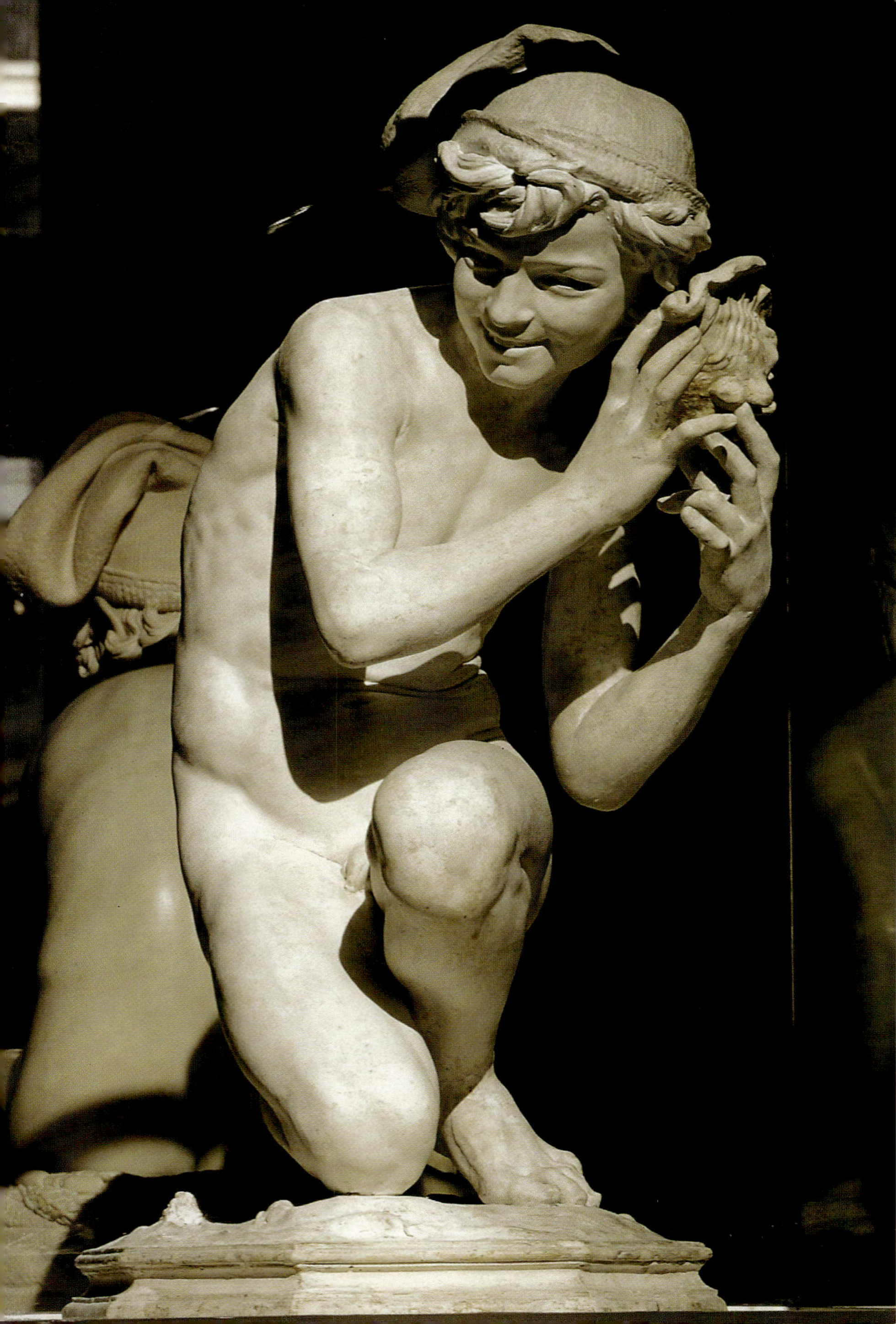

Jean-Baptiste Carpeaux
Young Fisherman with a Shell or *The Fisherboy*, **1858 Salon**
Original plaster model. 91 x 47 x 54 cm - ML

Why, we wonder, do sculptors adore shells? Long ago, poets and painters turned the creature into a floating cradle for the birth of Venus. In sculpture, moreover, the shell is a metaphor for Nature that carves. The scroll of its pearly concretions entrap the universe in hidden, 'turned' forms. Have not shells, fossils and even a stone carved in the shape of shell been found in the caves at Lascaux? In an effort to outdo his master François Rude, the creator of the *Neapolitan Fisherman Playing with a Tortoise* (p. 110), Jean-Baptiste Carpeaux by exchanging carapace for shell realises the astonishing *Young Fisherman with a Shell*. Observed from life, the subject is absorbed, attentive and fascinated by a single thing, one of a family of carved figures that harbour or transmit a secret. To listen to sculpture is to harken to Nature herself. In *Idol with Shell*, Gauguin places the sculptor on the same level as Nature: like her, he combines elements from the sea and exotic woods in a Gallé-like treasure-trove, a kind of tropical art nouveau.

The image of Aphrodite Anadyomene ('she who leaves the water') is deliberately present in the work of Vito Acconci, who cultivates, to the limits of kitsch, the mannerism of paradox and of changes in dimension: here, a miniature shell is gigantically upscaled. Through a metonymic sleight of hand, it becomes the bed of seduction: a huge starlet's bra that reminds one, in the thunderous roll pouring from one 'shell' to another, at the same time of the sea, of Aurora*'s rocaille* chariot and of that period furniture style that lifts its forms from the world of the shell and from the Rococo.

Paul Gauguin
Idol with Shell, 1892
Ironwood (*tua*), mother-of-pearl, pharyngeal tooth from a parrot-fish
34 x 12 x 11 cm - MO

Vito Acconci
Convertible Clam Shelter, 1990
Sound installation: fibreglass, steel, rope, shells, lighting
Each shell: 150 x 240 x 280 cm - CP

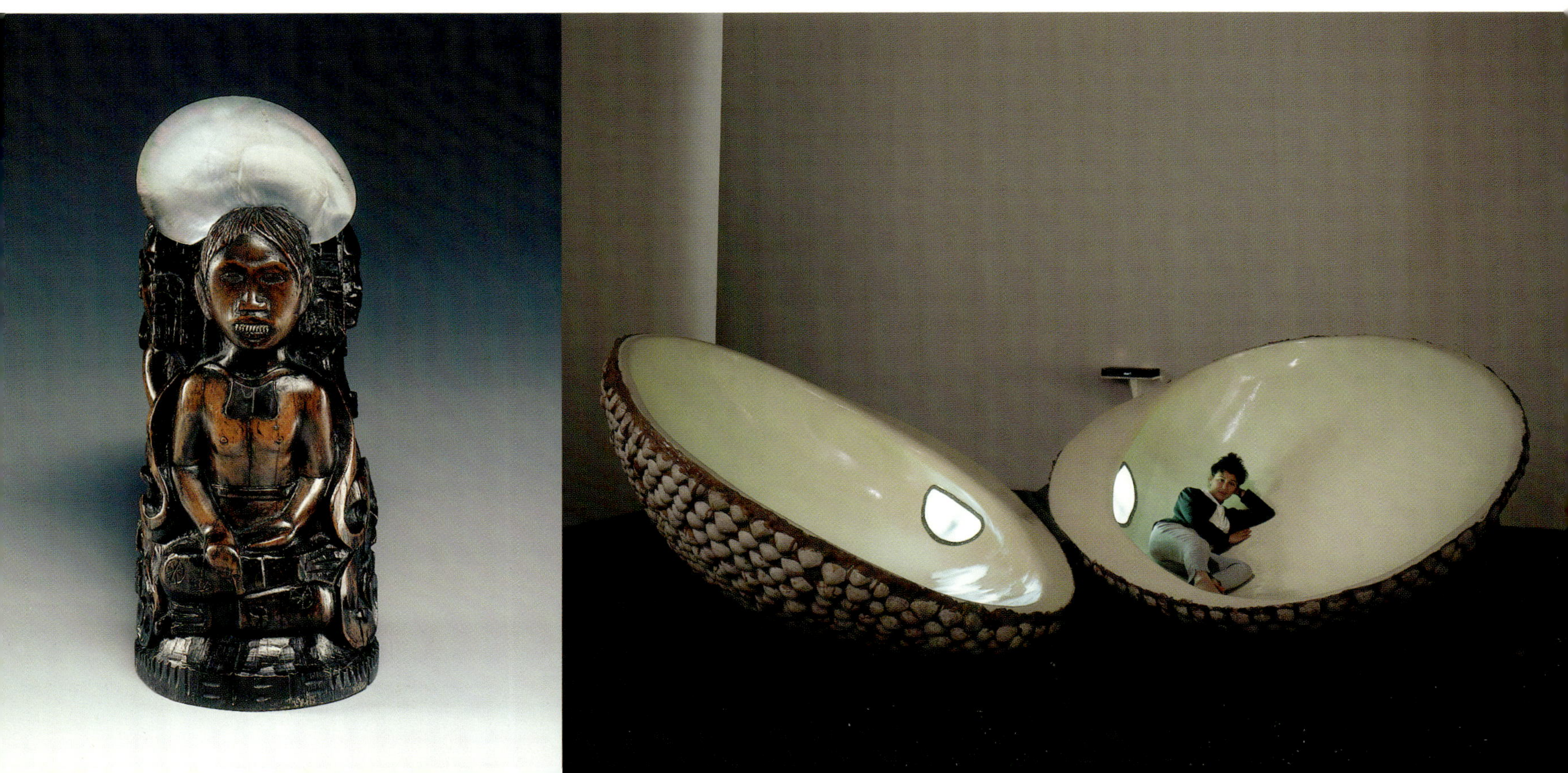

Dream of stone or pale phantom

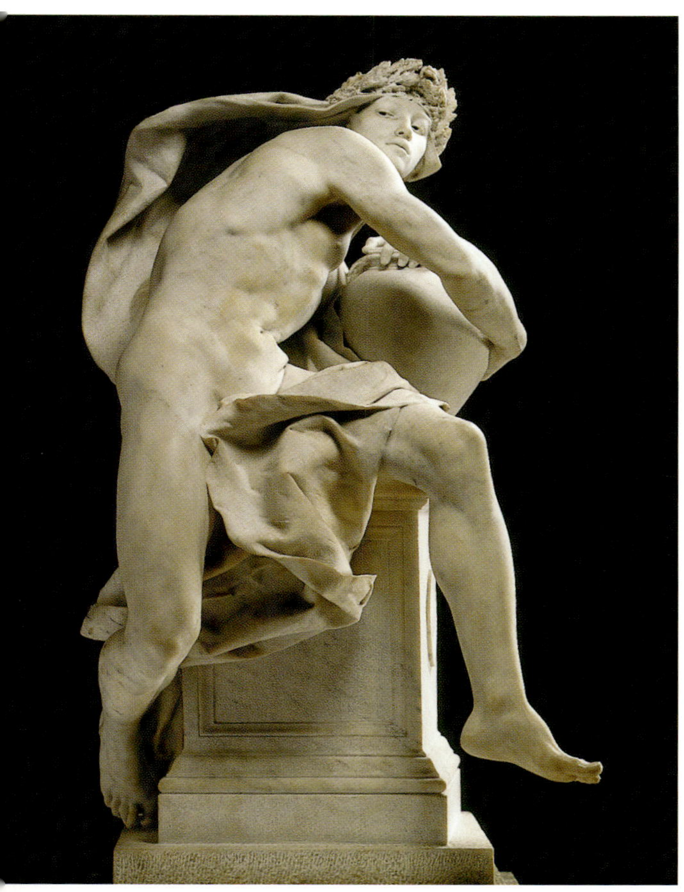

Who haunts the white stone? 'I am beautiful, Oh mortals, like a dream of stone,' wrote Charles Baudelaire. To whom did this face carved by Francesco Laurana, with its pure volumes, the individual features melding into the fullness of the form, belong? One might think it a retrospective portrait but the Neapolitan's models were in fact perhaps alive. The essence of the face crystallises to compose an 'accomplished beauty' (Daniela Gallo).

Who are these creatures, gliding through the air to encircle tombs and keep them inviolate? One of these funerary geniuses, the *Genius Keeping the Secret of the Tomb* by René de Saint-Marceaux, translates one of Michelangelo's decorative figures from the Sistine Chapel into marble, though its gestures also evoke that of a Sibyl closing the Book. As it gyrates upward, the figure, pure energy, seems stripped of all bodily weight.

The whiteness of marble or that of a ghost? What does Claes Oldenburg's *Soft Sculpture* most resemble? When contours grow blurred, when volumes collapse, when structure looks the worse for wear, only the phantom of a sculpture remains: a ghost. But a

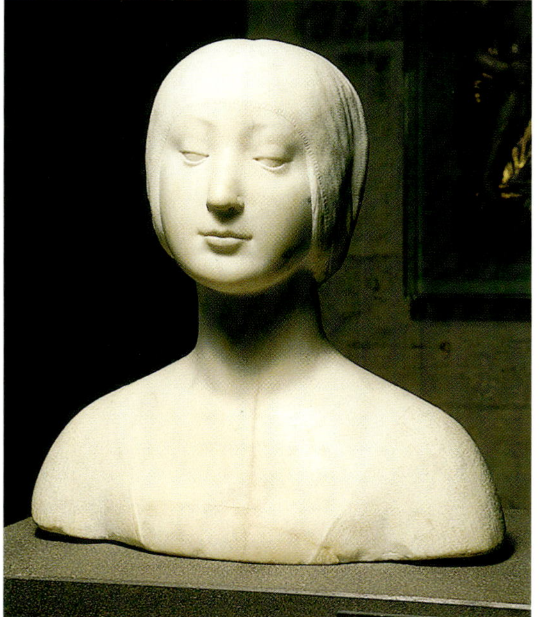

phantom is also called a 'spirit': so the spirit of sculpture endures. What is it made of, if not of that projection of our own body onto the world of objects which allows us to inhabit them, to invade them from the inside, and to fill them with our sullenness and negligence, our plumpness, and our tenderness too? 'Tell me who you haunt, and I'll tell you who you are,' runs the saying as rewritten by André Breton at the beginning of his novel, *Nadja* (1928). It is Oldenburg who haunts these objects of soft sculpture, ghosts of himself. By the same token, he haunts the Unconscious of sculp-

ture that ordered it to stand to attention, stiff, straight-backed, to constrain and build up its forms. Oldenburg, on the contrary, lets everything hang slack, unlacing, loosening the pitiable, shapeless materials he employs. His humour smacks of Rabelais' roly-poly giants, or else of those joyous and satirical displays of everyday objects in which Pop artists indulged so enthusiastically.

René de Saint-Marceaux
Genius Keeping the Secret of the Tomb, 1879
Marble. 168 x 95 x 119 cm - MO

Francesco Laurana
Unknown Princess, second half of the 15th century
Marble. 44 x 44 x 24 cm - ML

Claes Oldenburg
Ghost Drum Set, 1972
Ten elements in sewn and painted cloth filled with polystyrene balls
80 (with plinth) x 183 x 183 cm - CP

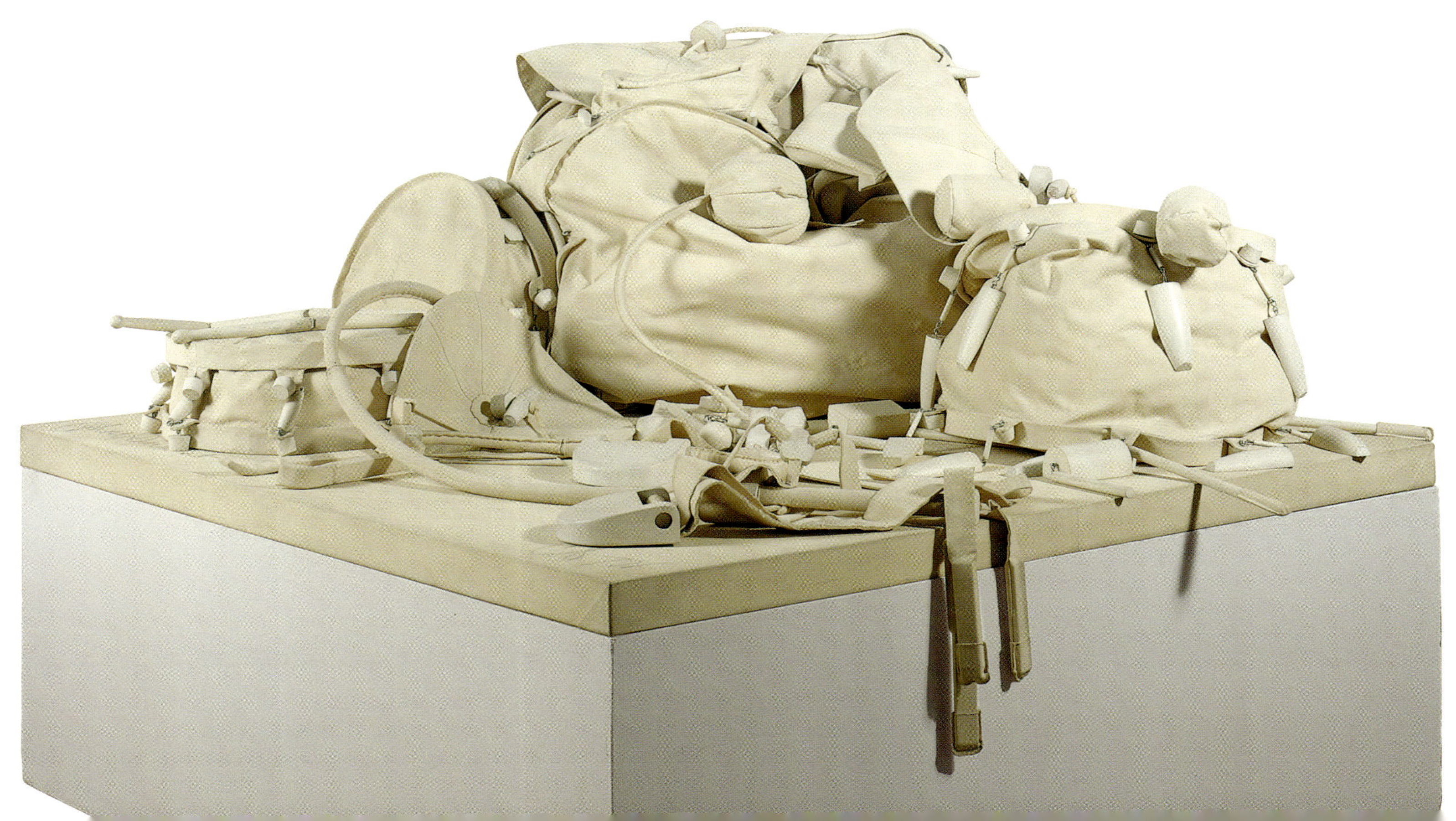

Making signs

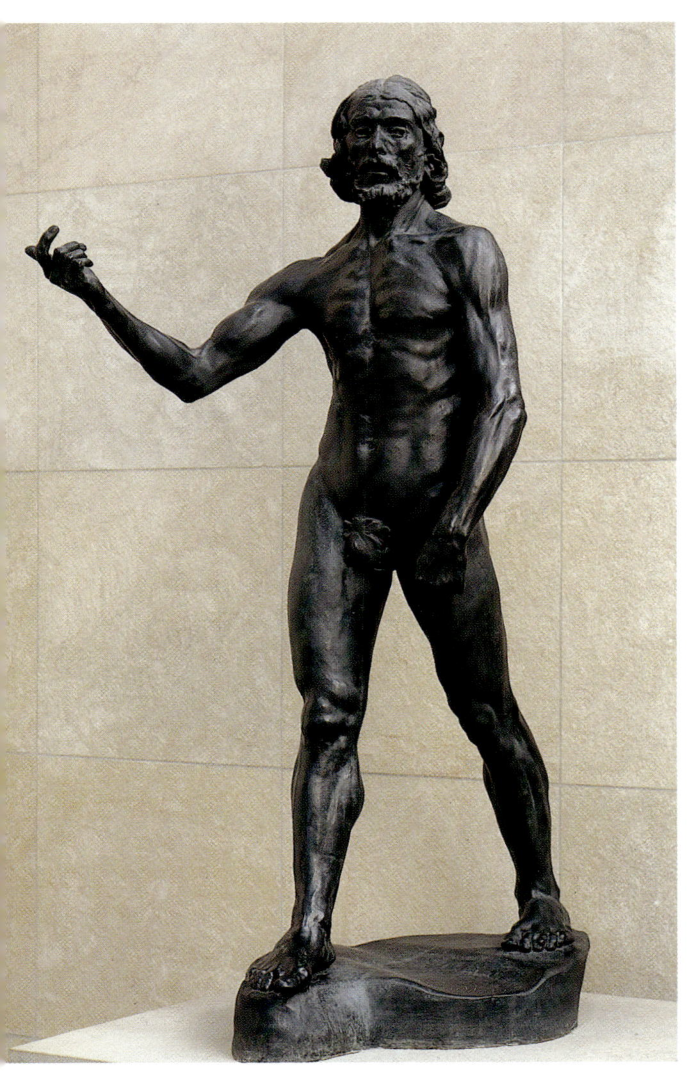

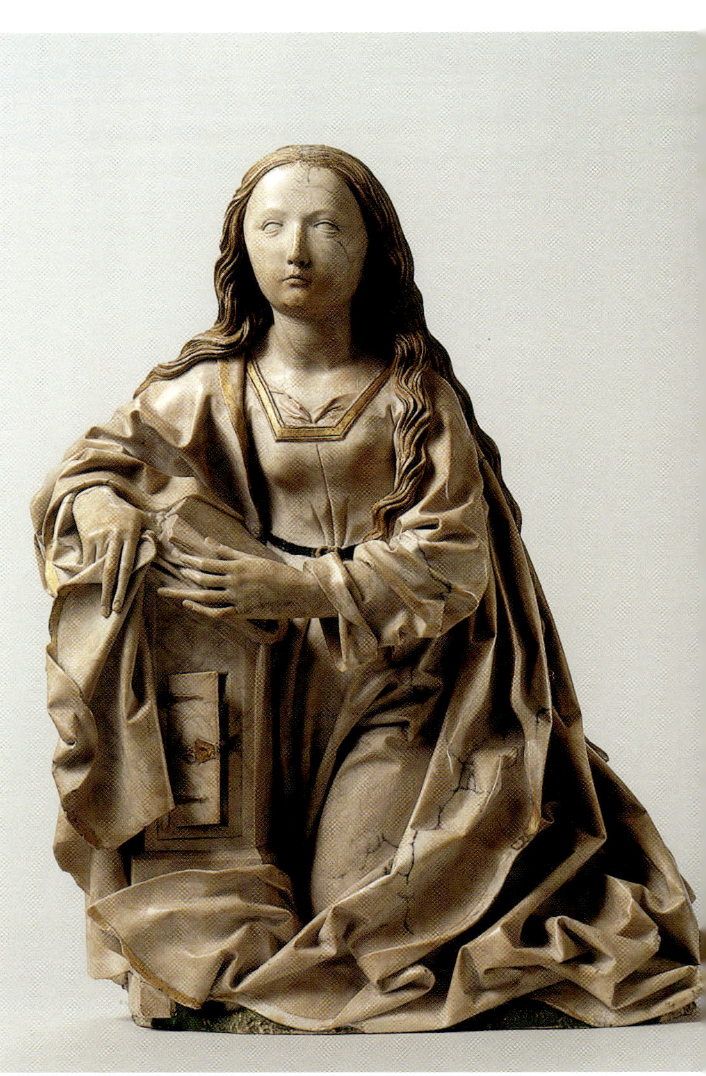

Auguste Rodin
St John the Baptist, 1879-81
Bronze. 204 x 63 x 113 cm - MO

Tilman Riemenschneider
Virgin of the Annunciation, c. 1495
Alabaster, polychrome highlights. 53 x 40 x 19 cm - ML

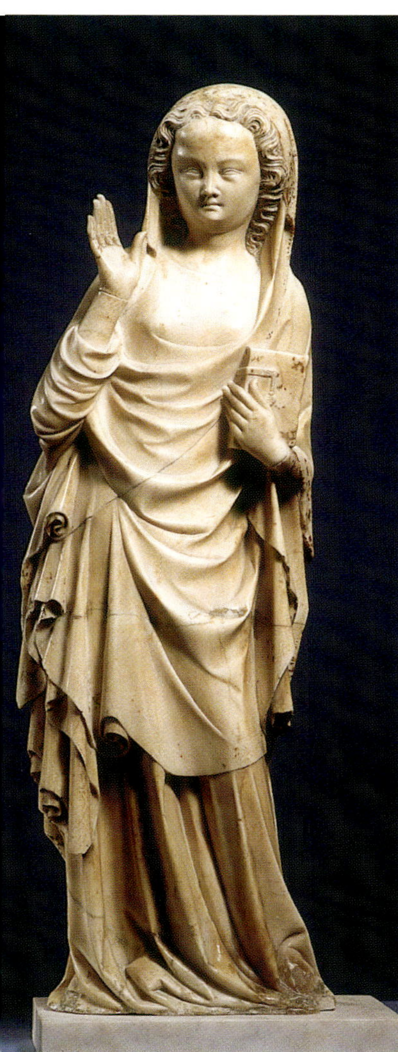

Virgin of the Annunciation, Ile-de-France
second third of the 14th century
Alabaster, flecks of gilding. 69 x 20 x 12 cm - ML

Hermes at the crossroads, columns, herms, obelisks — the function of sculpture here is to give a sign that establishes a reciprocal relationship with the passer-by: one makes the sign of the Cross in front of the Cross.

The codified gestures of a Quattrocento Virgin of the Annunciation mirror her state of mind: it can thus be seen whether she is astonished, acquiescent or grateful. But we no longer look with the eye of the Quattrocento and these gestures have lost, to our way of seeing, much of their content. The *Virgin* from Javernant in Champagne, holding a book and without the crown worn by Virgins of the Annunciation, responds to the angel (today in the museum at Cleveland) who unrolls a phylactery emblazoned with the address, *Ave Maria gratiae plena*, by raising her hand in a sign of acceptance.

The Virgin carved by Tilman Riemenschneider from Franconia in about 1495 is a masterpiece of Late Gothic art (*Spätgotik*). The attitude is realistic, the face attentive, the unmoving hands resting on the book. She harkens to the angel (today no longer extant) who would have stood to her right. The drapery with its broken folds is all the more lyrical for that. Whereas the Annunciation is conceived like a stage scene, like a mystery, Auguste Rodin needs only the body and the pose of his *St John the Baptist* to make a sign. In fact, the entire, outstretched body is a kind of semaphore. The sculptor could even remove the cross he had initially placed in St John's hand as his index finger alone is sufficiently eloquent.

The modern world has given over the production of signs to technical devices that transmit and receive and has abandoned it to the industrial world and its advertising billboards. In 1926, in *Paris Peasant*, Louis Aragon affirmed that, in the modern era, filling stations are the new 'statues at the crossroads'. The American sculptor David Smith made his postwar *Tanktotem* out of industrial surplus: here they are, the sculptures that produce signs for today! Using electronic signals in both light and sound, Takis goes even further. The American sociologist Marshall MacLuhan coined the famous formula, 'the medium is the message'. In *Large Signal*, the medium — the transmitting sculpture — becomes the message: energy put to use. Indeed, the spindly, Giacometti-like silhouettes don't so much speak through their forms as through the signals they emit to the viewer from a distance.

Takis

Le Grand Signal, 1964
Metal and light signal. 499 x 50 x 34 cm - CP

31

Nature

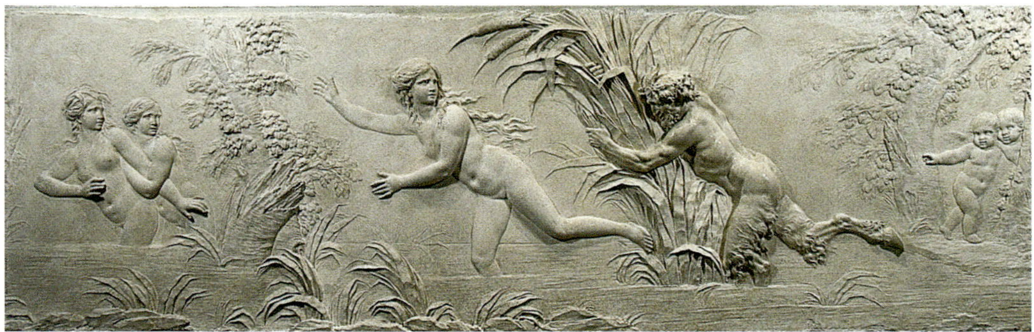

Pan pursues the nymph Syrinx, but she is transformed into a clump of reeds into which the satyr stumbles. Under Clodion's Attic chisel, the unrestrained rhythm of the pursuit is subjected to the parallelism of line and the symmetry of number. The vegetal universe of Alexander Calder, composed of just a few leaves, a swaying black stem and the movement occasioned by a fleeting draught, is also surprisingly mobile. Calder called this type of form, in which certain parts move on others that remain fixed, a 'mobile-stabile'. Red, blue, yellow — primary colours spinning in space: Calder stated that he wanted to set in motion Mondrian's studio, a painter whose work achieves a subtle equilibrium of coloured planes. As opposed to this energetic suppleness, works by Georges Lacombe and Germaine Richier evince instead the brute force of Nature at its most powerful and awesome. In 1895, the Nabi artist Lacombe produced an image of Nature with the features of Isis in painted mahogany. The goddess presses a nourishing liquid out of her breasts. A splendid, barbaric image, it recalls many miracles ascribed in the Middle Ages to statues of the Virgin Mary. The fluid runs in channels and waters burgeoning flowers, whereas, in the upper part of the relief, trees take root in the figure's hair. The ever-changing natural cycle, the solidity of great trees and, above all, a homage to Woman. The reverse of the relief bears the inscription: 'This piece of wood belongs to my Lady Gabrielle Wenger.' Germaine Richier's *Storm* is a powerful silhouette in which gesture and attitude are almost animalised. It is impossible to tell if it is Nature taking on human shape, or if it is a man who reverts to the world of the animal and of telluric forces. To some, the work may bring to mind the petrified bodies of Pompeii.

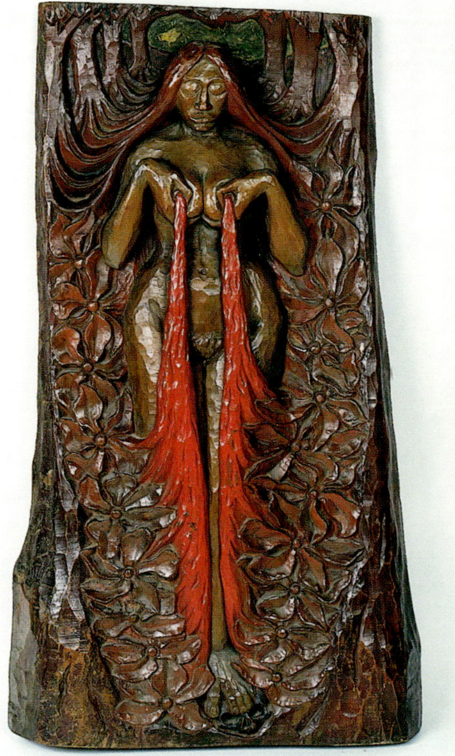

Clodion

Pan and Syrinx, 1782.

Tonnerre stone. 104 x 323 x 23 cm - ML

Georges Lacombe

Isis, 1895

Partially polychrome mahogany. 111 x 62 x 10 cm - MO

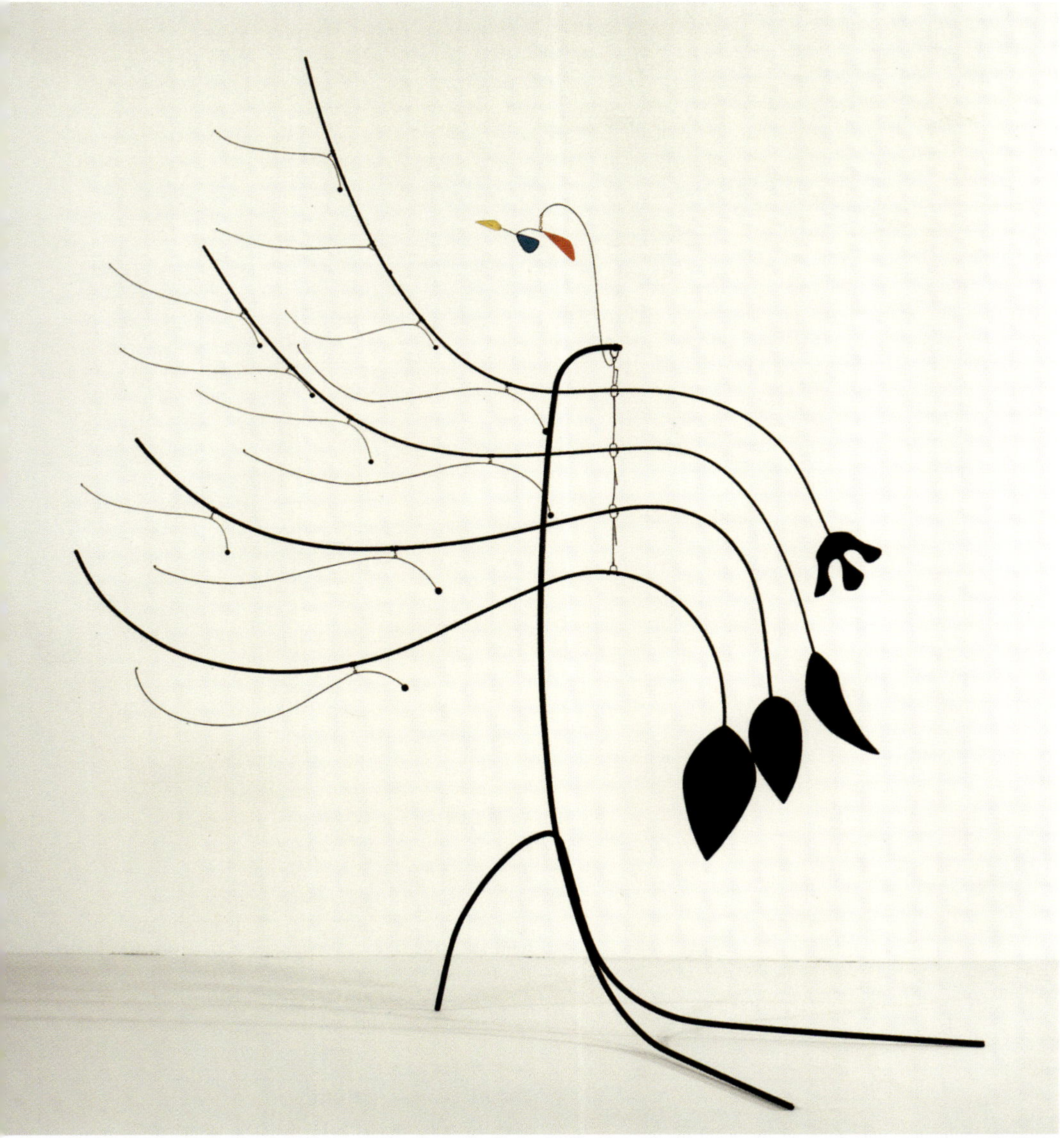

Alexander Calder

Four Leaves and Three Petals, 1939
Mobile on foot: sheet-steel, painted metal struts and wire. 205 x 174 x 135 cm - CP

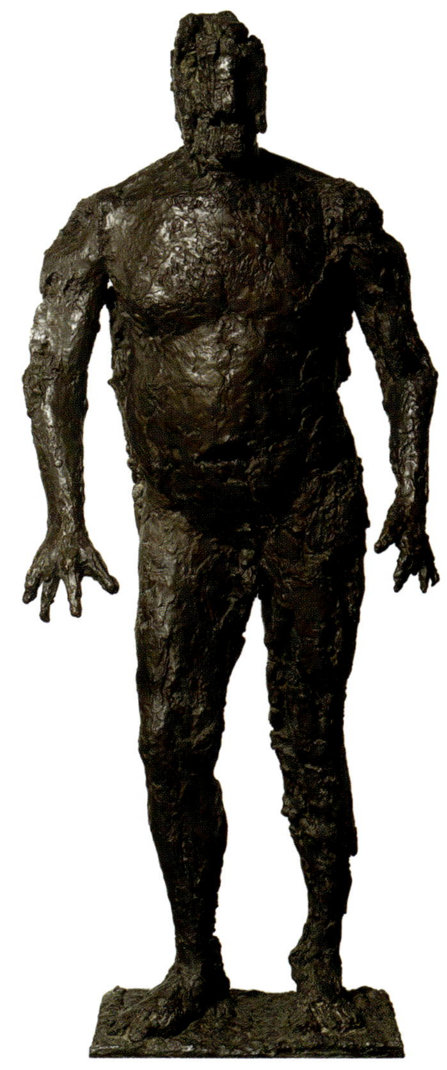

Germaine Richier

The Storm, 1947-48
Bronze. 200 x 80 x 52 cm - CP

33

Animal sculpture

Antoine-Louis Barye made the subject of a fight between animals a speciality of Romantic sculpture. Théophile Gautier wrote: 'At the sight of this terrible and superb animal with its bristling mane [...] all the poor marble lions stuffed their tails between their legs!' Bourdelle, who much admired Barye, affirmed: 'Having analysed tigers and wolves, he fled from Man.' A fair number of these combats display heroic and moral connotations. More especially it was the imposing spectacle of a Nature untainted by human presence that attracted the sculptor. For the first time the animal is dominant. The popularity of *animalier* sculpture, which developed just as landscape painting was taking off in earnest, proved considerable. The edition of small bronzes, which was the artist's main livelihood, soon ensured his work appeared on many mantelpieces. François Pompom's *Polar Bear* and Xavier Veilhan's red *Rhinoceros* have a number of features in common: convincing sculptures in the round, their masses are stylised and they impose themselves powerfully in space. Along with a handful of others, such as Rembrandt Bugatti, it was Pompom, earning his living as a stoneworker cutting marble for designs by masters such as Rodin, who really put the animal world into sculpture. The repertoire grew ever richer thanks to the accounts and sketches brought back by explorers and the practice of visiting Paris's Natural History Museum and Zoological Gardens. As for the contemporary artist Xavier Veilhan, he seems to be in dialogue with another great of 19th-century animal sculpture, Alfred Jacquemart, whose own *Rhinoceros* was made in 1878 for the Trocadéro Palace at the Paris World Fair and whose strange colossus stands today on the esplanade in front of the Musée d'Orsay. Veilhan's is painted with red automobile lacquer, endowing the animal with a hyper-Pop character. Fulfilling an order from a *grand couturier*, the artist is here deliberately poking fun at that advertising commonplace that assimilates a marque of car to a swift-footed animal — horse for Ferrari, lion for Peugeot, the Jaguar, and so on.

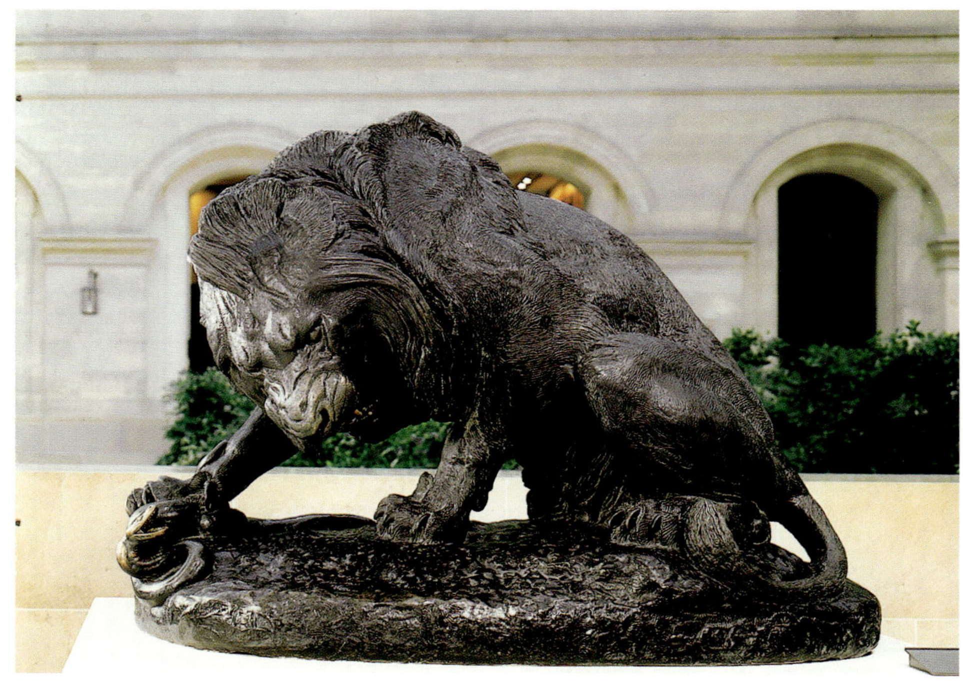

Antoine-Louis Barye
Lion with Snake, 1835 Salon
Bronze.
135 x 178 x 96 cm - ML

François Pompon
Polar Bear, 1922/1929
Lens stone. 163 x 251 x 90 cm - MO

Xavier Veilhan
The Rhinoceros, 1999-2000
Resin, polyester paint, varnish. 110 x 415 x 140 cm - CP

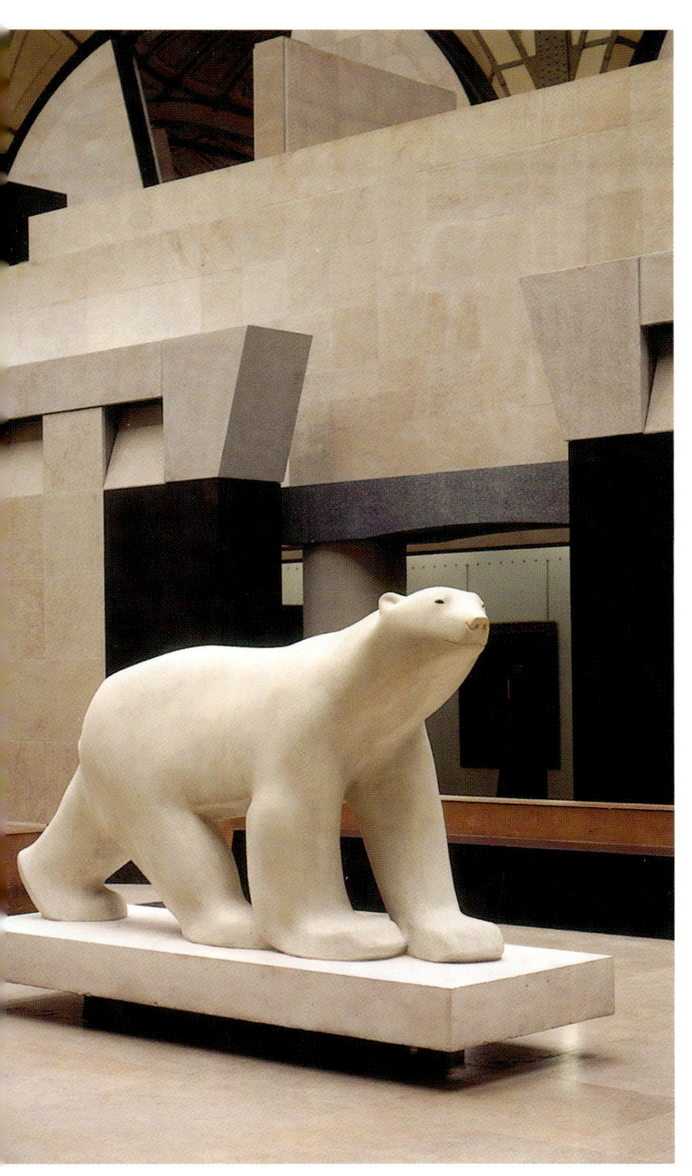

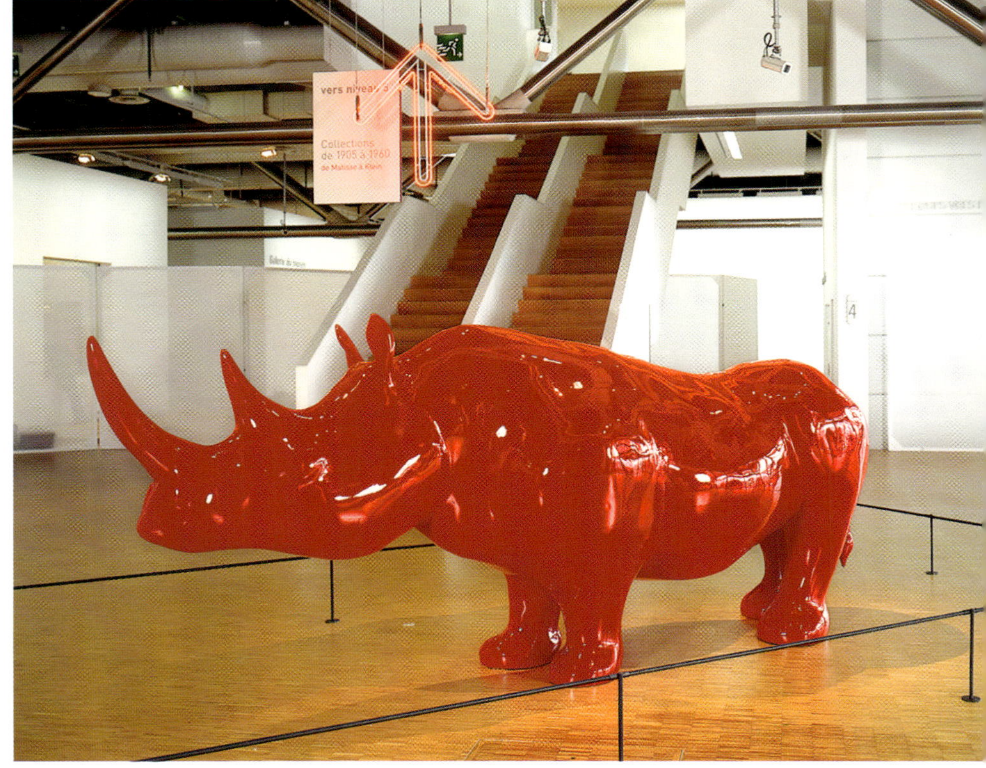

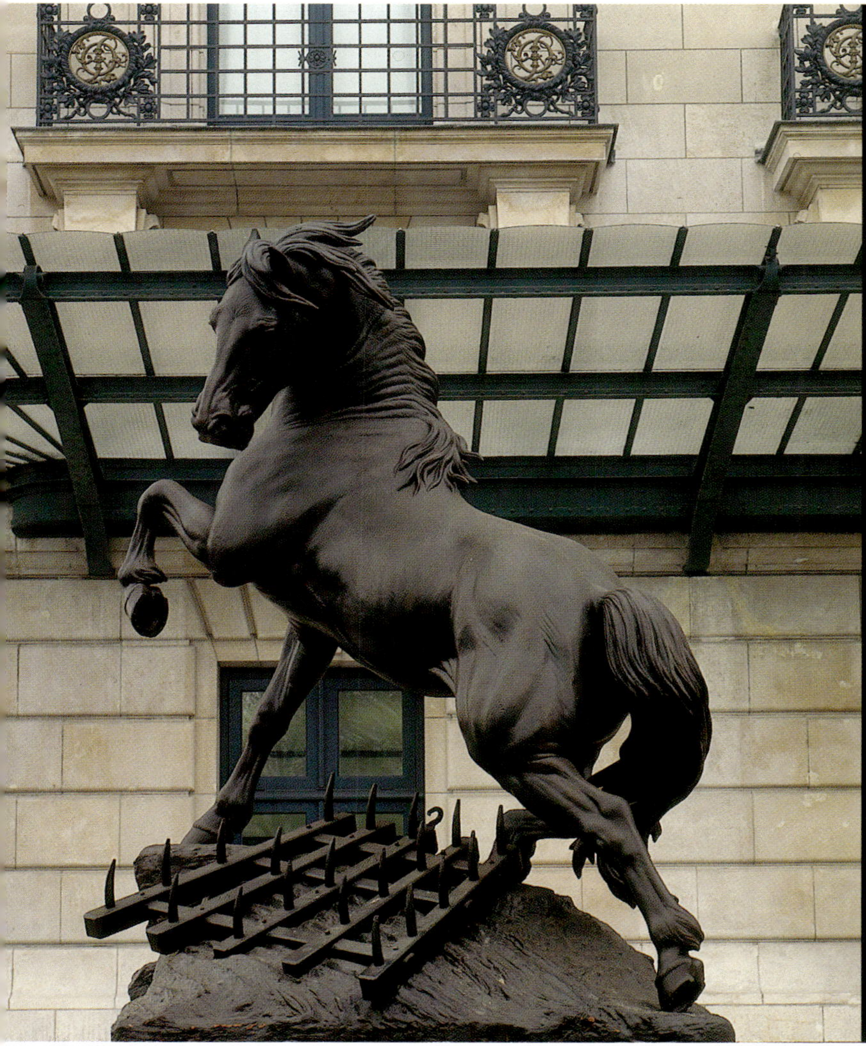

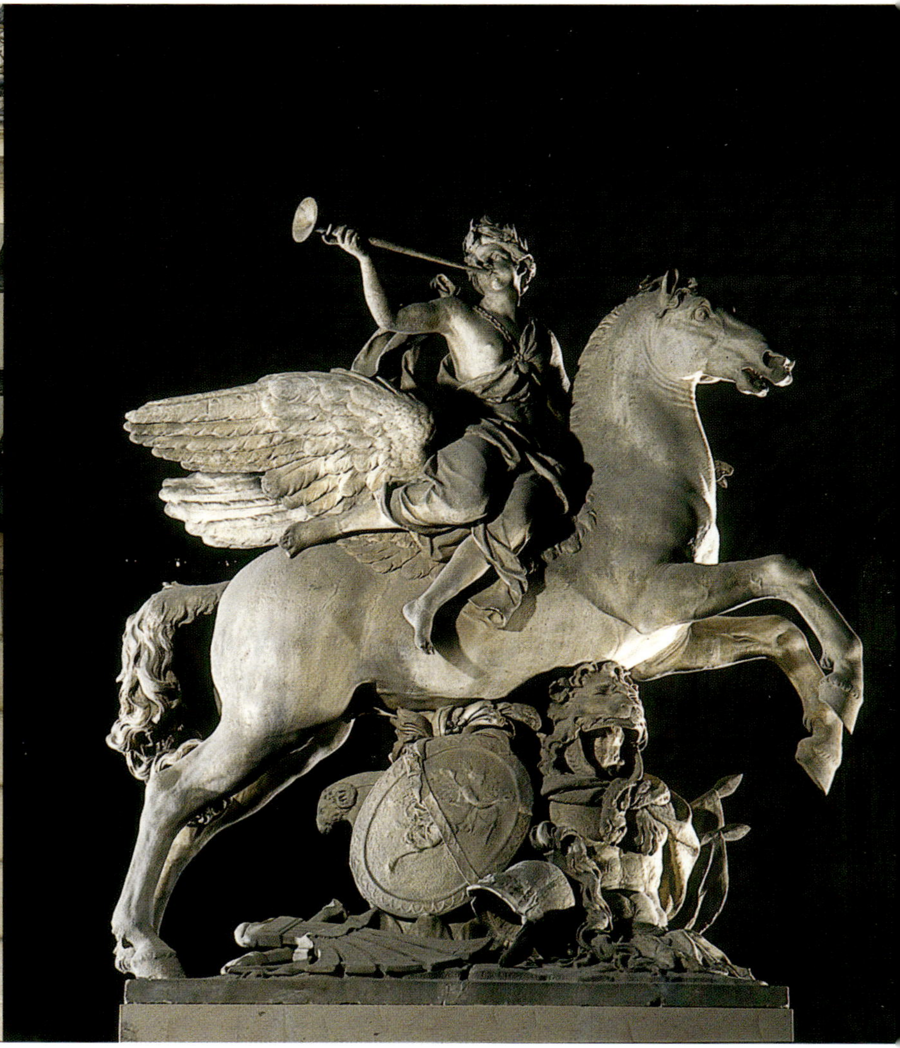

Pierre-Louis Rouillard

Horse with a Harrow, 1878

Cast iron. 350 x 223 x 220 cm - MO

Antoine Coysevox

Fame Mounted on Pegasus, 1699-1702

Carrara marble. 315 x 291 x 128 cm - ML

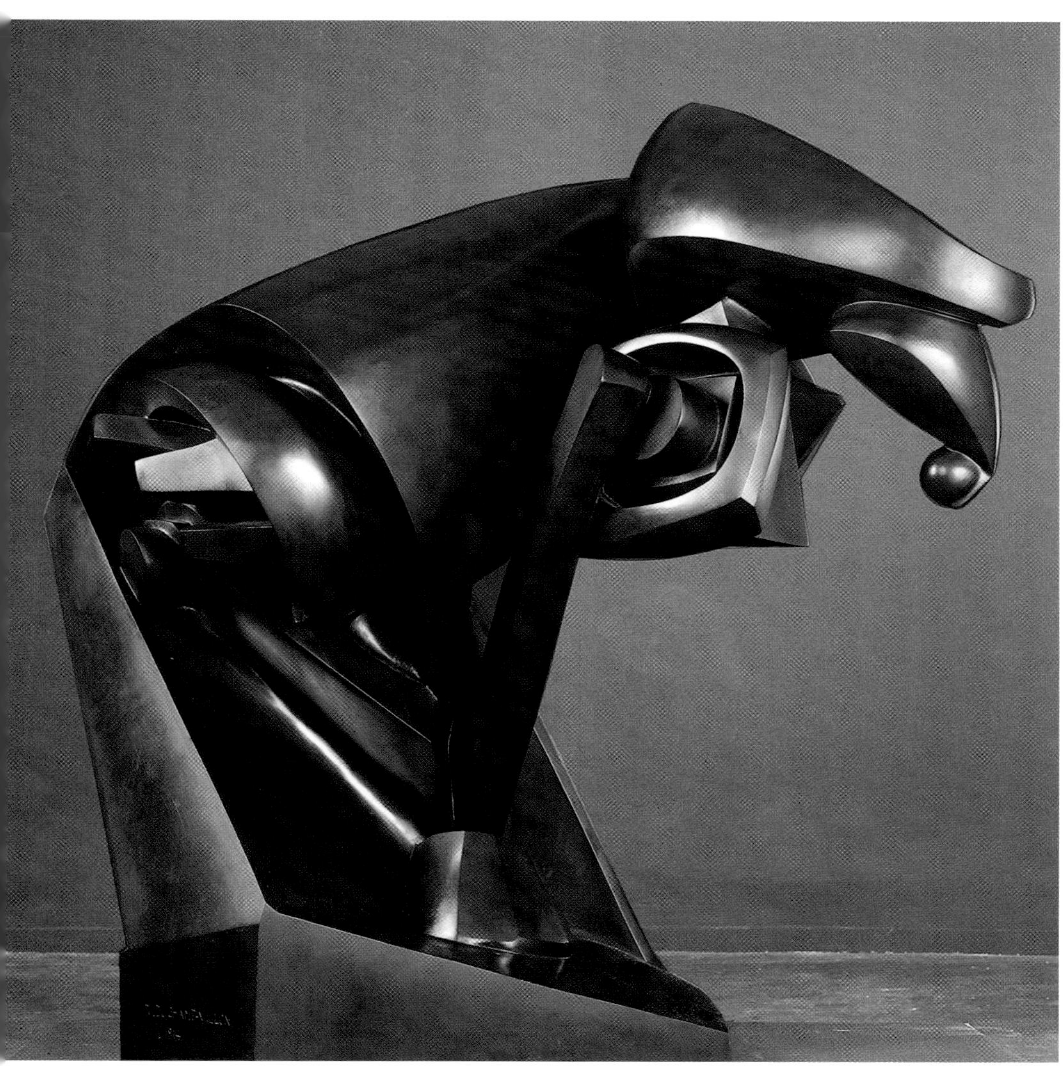

Raymond Duchamp-Villon
Le Cheval majeur, 1914/1976
Bronze with black patina. 150 x 97 x 153 cm - CP

The horse has always been the sculptor's most noble conquest. While working on his unfinished *Cavallo*, Leonardo pondered the Marcus Aurelius on the piazza of the Capitol in Rome, one of Antiquity's last great metal casts. The admirable *Horseman* of Bamberg on its pillar, Donatello's *Gattamelata* on its elevated base in Padua, Verrocchio's *Colleoni* in Venice, or Falconet's *Peter the Great* in St Petersburg climbering up a rock as his horse rears, are legends of the art.

And it is yet another legendary horse, Pegasus, the flying steed, that Antoine Coysevox readied as the mount for his *Fame of Louis XIV*. Plenty of others come to mind, too, from ancient majesties in the saddle — Girardon's *Charlemagne*, *Louis XIV* or the *Napoleon*s by Barye and by Fremiet, not forgetting Bernini's controversial *Louis XIV*, a version of which now stands next to the Pyramid of the Louvre — to the more modern *Miracoli* by Marino Marini, and even the centaur in César's *Homage to Picasso*.

It is hardly surprising that, after the slaughter of inappropriately mounted horses during the French Revolution, the Republic preferred to be represented on foot. It is to be recalled too that, in iconographic tradition, the horse symbolises lust, absence of control, even madness, as the theme of Mazeppa testifies. Rouillard's splendid stallion, carried out, like Jacquemart's *Rhinoceros*, for the 1878 World Fair in Paris, has the excuse of being decorative, medieval in spirit, while the harrow curbs its frantic dash, making it rear up.

Le Cheval majeur by Marcel Duchamp's brother, Raymond Duchamp-Villon, who died in World War I, evokes, just before the outbreak of the conflict, a new-found power: that of the machine, of 'horsepower' or, in Zola's phrase, 'the human beast'. The sculpture, for which the original plaster is in the museum at Grenoble, was to have been cast in steel (as recently carried out for the museum at Nancy) in a forthright statement of the innovative industrial treatment of an equestrian theme. This horse-cum-locomotive, this mechanical creature, was created at the same time as the British sculptor Jacob Epstein stuck his *Rock Drill* in the earth to power sculpture into action. The sculptor Emile Gilioli affirmed that, even though the base clearly remained at rest, Duchamp-Villon's piece would vibrate when you placed your hand on it.

Battles with monsters

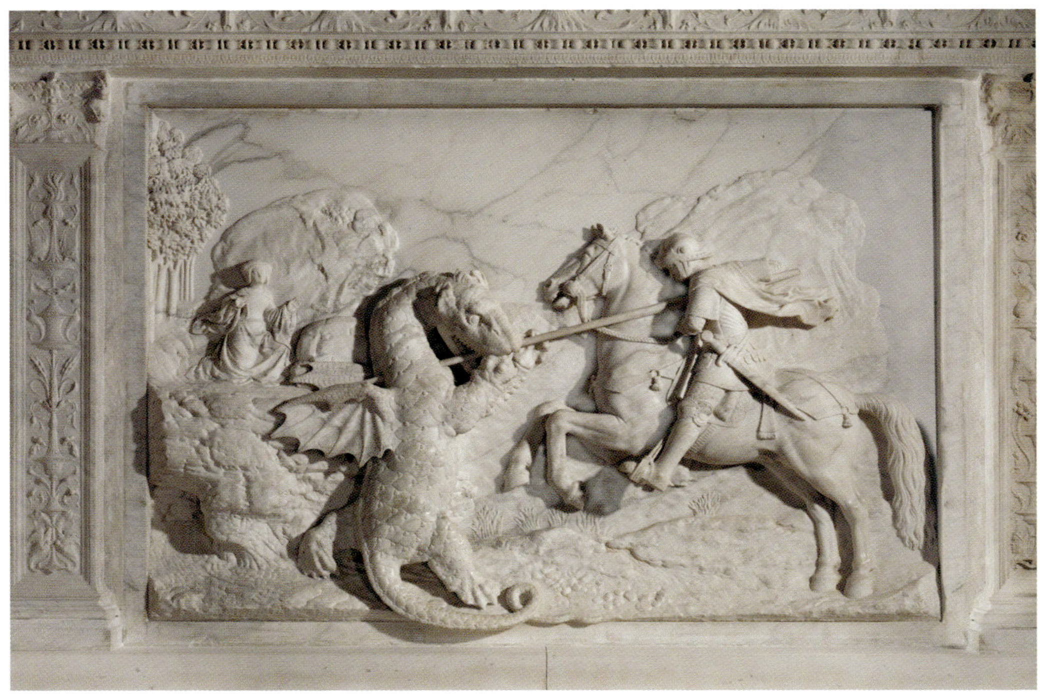

Michel Colombe
St George Slaying the Dragon, 1509-10
Marble. 128 x 182 x 17 cm - ML

Jean Dampt
Fireplace in the Salle du Chevalier, 1900-06
Comblanchien marble
196 x 224 x 14 cm - MO

Niki de Saint Phalle
The Monster of Soisy, c. 1962-63
Paint and diverse objects on metal framework
253 x 161 x 63.3 cm - CP

Early on in her career, Niki de Saint Phalle placed the figure of the 'monster', and in particular that of the dragon, at the centre of her artistic universe. By 1962, the beast had turned into King Kong, and it is on him the artist fires her rifle, the bullets bursting plastic bags containing paint, which, as its spurts out, makes it seem less ghostly, more human. *The Monster of Soisy*, named after a village in the forest of Fontainebleau where Jean Tinguely and Niki de Saint Phalle set up a studio, is covered with plastic figurines symbolising various traumatic targets: war, suffering, alienation. In this manner, the artist reinvents the iconographical tradition of the monster-slaying saint. As one can judge for instance from the chimney-piece for the Hôtel de Béarn, by the beginning of the 20th century this theme had become purely decorative, even if the bird's-eye view of the cityscape above which the sculptor Jean Dampt depicts the figure of the dragon remains intriguing.
Niki de Saint Phalle found inspiration in Uccello, Donatello and Michel Colombe, who had represented St George dispatching the dragon. In Colombe's relief for the chapel in the Château de Gaillon, the horseman, seen in profile like at a tournament, transfixes the fantastic animal who embodies his malevolent double. The monster has raised up its bristling wing to the same level as the knight, so mirroring the fluttering cape of the warrior, while its tail, resting against the frame, echoes that of the saint's horse.

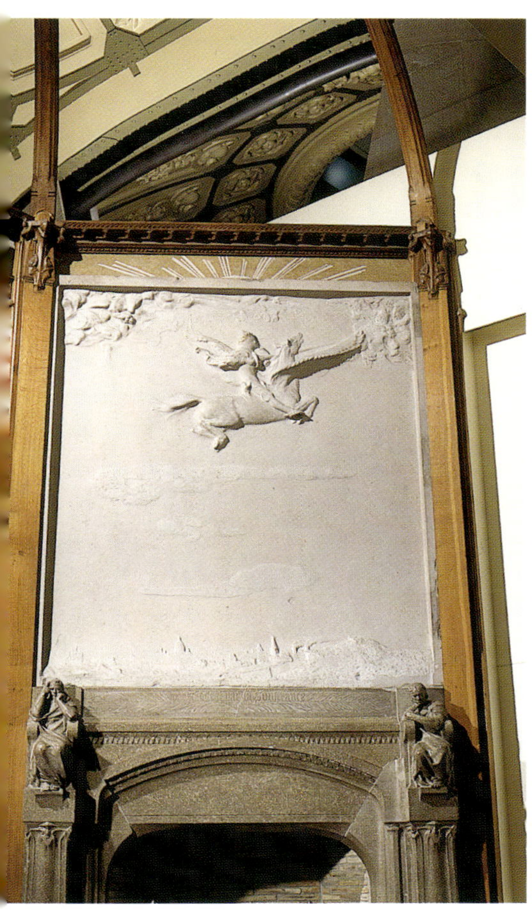

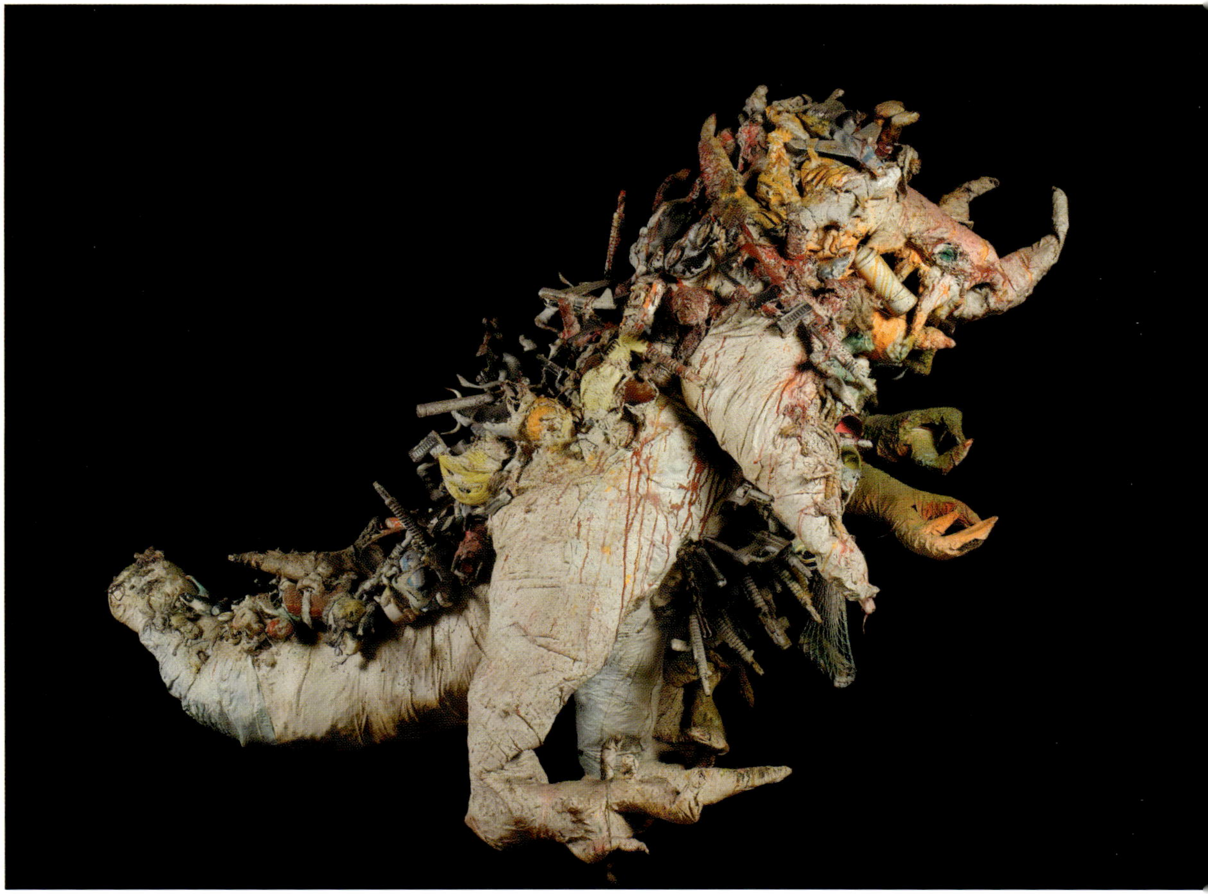

Sculptor's drawings

Does a drawing specific to sculpture exist? Not, if one recalls that academic teaching preached that drawing was the foundation of all the visual arts.

It is from his father, the celebrated sculptor Pierre Puget, that François Puget learned his mastery of linear space, the acute sense of volume and even of weight, which are so startling in this drawing of his father's *Milon de Crotona*.

'Statuary does not possess the resources of the painter', Falconet admitted, adding: 'The sculptor has no palette.' But the sculptor can rely on drawing, closer to the touch than all the colour. It is truth to line, to the profile, to contours and, one might add, to weight, which — as Jacqueline Lichtenstein has it —from the second half of the 17th century on, places the sculptor on the side of the philosopher, whereas the painter remains in thrall to illusion. Thus the opposition between painter-artist and sculptor-philosopher grew up. In his text *Plastik*, Johann Gottfried Herder affirmed: 'In vision lies the dream; in touch, truth.'

In Edgar Degas' studies of dancers one finds the same liberty and spontaneity as in his pieces in clay and wax: the essence of the movement is caught in a few lines and as if modelled in charcoal. When Eduardo Chillida creates drawings that evolve in space, dense and enigmatic like some Pre-Socratic poem, he entitled them significantly, *Gravitation*. As for Richard Serra, his powerful forms succeed in the optical suggestion of weight.

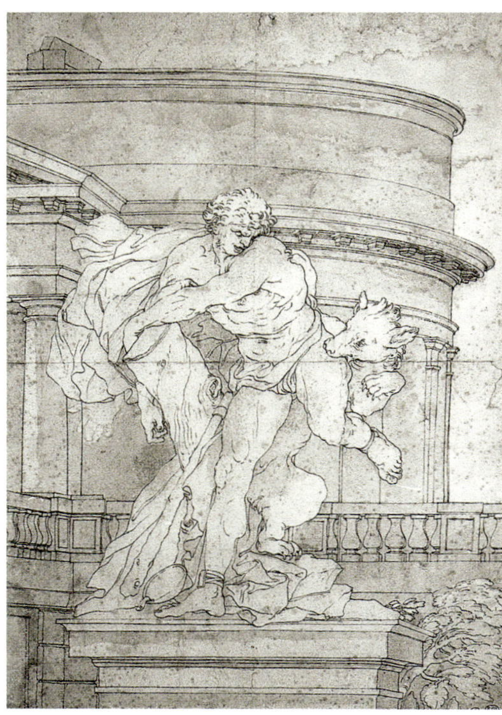

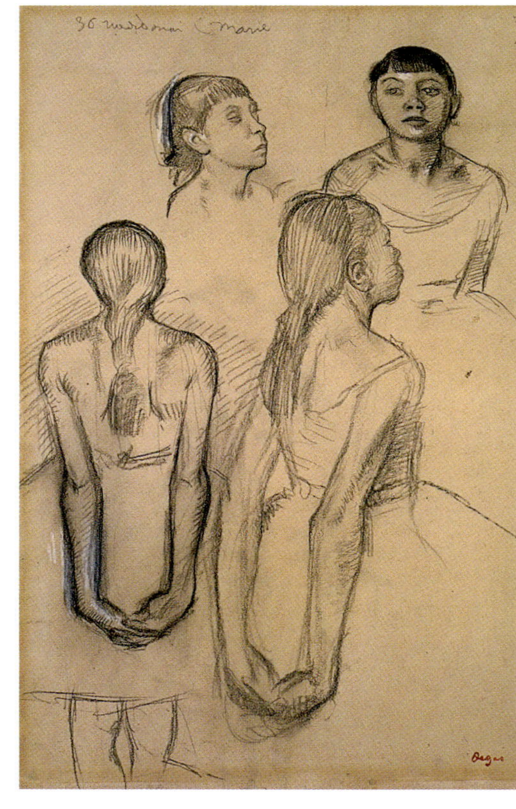

François Puget

Milon of Crotona, his Hands Trapped in the Trunk of an Oak-Tree, **second half of the 17th century**

Pen and brown ink, pencil, grey wash. 45 x 31 cm - ML

Edgar Degas

Four Studies of a Dancer, **1878-79**

Charcoal, white highlights on vellum. 49 x 32.1 cm - ML

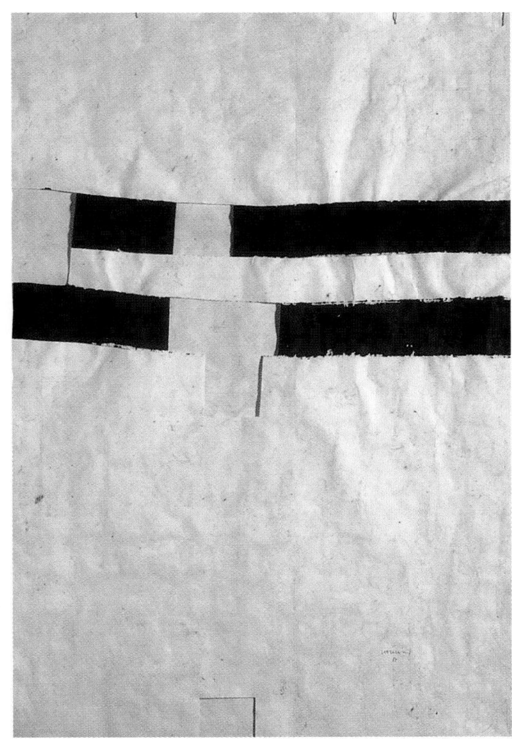

Eduardo Chillida
Gravitation, 1989
Cut-outs and Indian ink on handmade amate paper glue-mounted
on paper. 122 x 80.5 cm - CP

Richard Serra
Père Lachaise, 1990
Lithograph on vellum with paintstick highlights
119 x 190 cm - CP

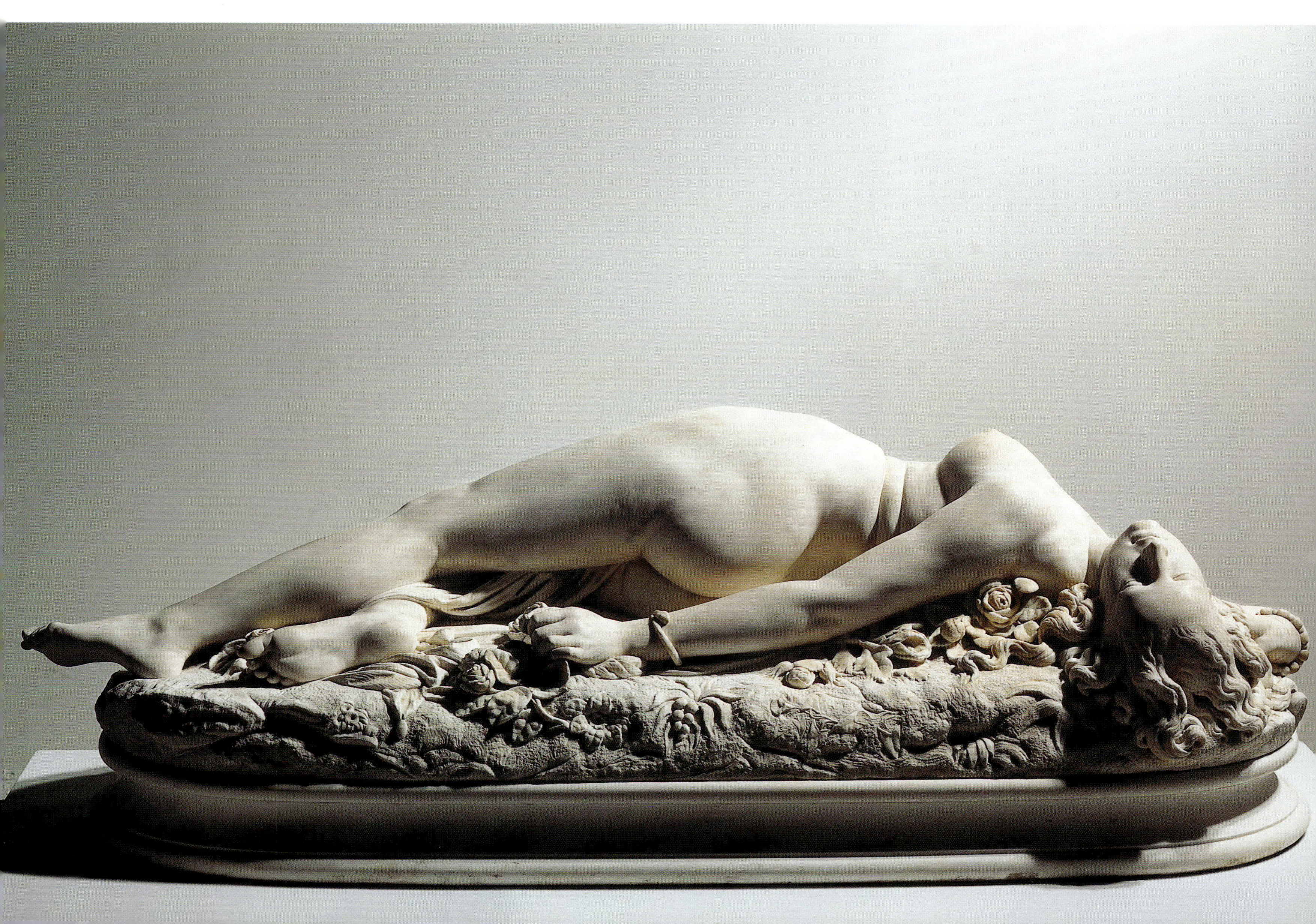

Auguste Clésinger

Woman Bitten by a Snake, 1847

Marble. 56 x 180 x 70 cm - MO

George Segal

Movie House, 1966-67

Light installation: plaster, wood, Plexiglas, electric lamps

259 x 376 x 370 cm - CP

Statue in Human Form, Jordan, 7th millennium BC

Gypsum plaster, bitumen (eyelids and pupils)

105 x 33 x 13 cm - ML

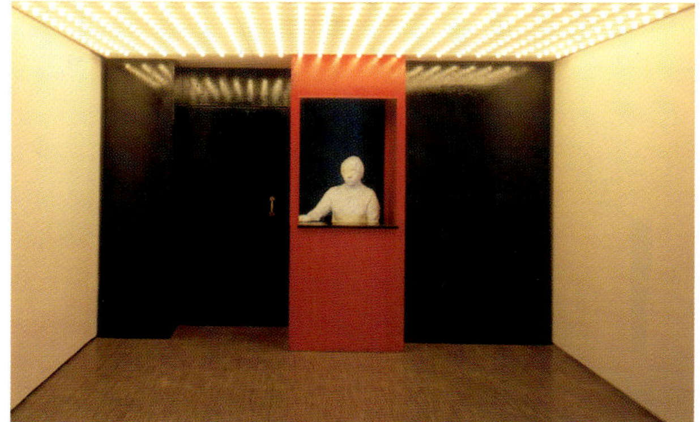

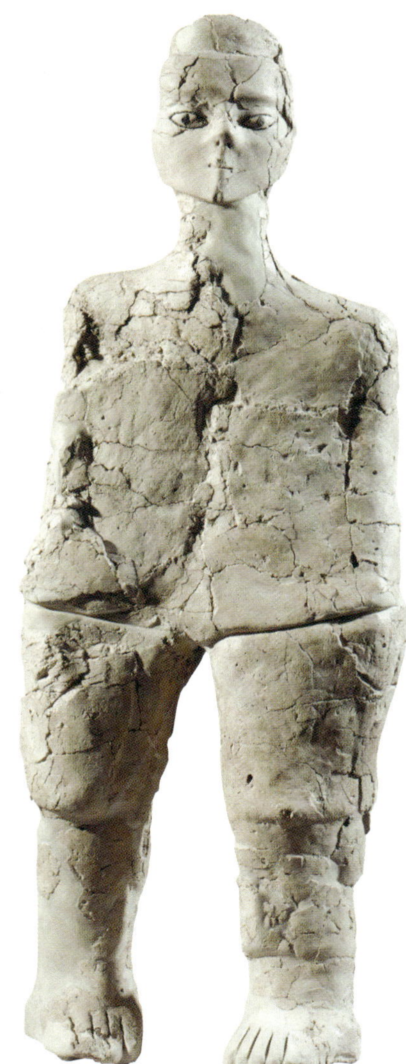

Many sacred texts present a god who models human beings out of the silt of a river and breathes life into them. Kneading a human effigy and placing it over an armature of whipped rope, the sculptor of the 7th millennium BC seems to be repeating this primeval gesture.

For *Woman Bitten by a Snake*, presented at the Salon of 1847, Auguste Clésinger lifted the cast directly from the body of Madame Sabatier, known as the 'Présidente', a literary muse much-vaunted by Théophile Gautier and Charles Baudelaire. He is even meant to have incorporated a little of the lady's puppy-fat! The marble statue stirred up a furore. To justify female convulsions, which Paul Mantz for one — like the Président de Brosses commenting in an earlier century on Bernini's *St Teresa* — placed at the door of an 'extreme pleasure' ('You can be sure that she is loved, that she quivers beneath some invisible kiss, and that she is happy'), the sculptor simply appended a serpent to his wrist, thereby turning the voluptuous figure into a *Cleopatra* or *Eurydice*.

But the argument raged less over the young woman herself than over the method. Gustave Planche wrote: 'The process employed by Mr Clésinger is to statuary what daguerreotype is to painting.' This assimilation of moulding to the photographic imprint, by associating sculpture and photography, is further evidence of the debate at the time as to the artistic value of the latter: in the eyes of its detractors, recording reality with a camera could only be mechanical and never artistic.

Interestingly, when American Hyperrealism confronted photography once more in the 1970s, sculptors like George Segal and Edward Kienholz employed moulds in their 'environments', composite sculptures in which figures are arranged in reconstituted locales. Segal's cinema cashier is of course a far cry from Clésinger's Madame Sabatier bitten by her snake: condemned to the anonymity of vapid plaster, lost in the overwhelming indifference of the urban crowd, she seems to merge with her function. The artist, however, exposes her to the gaze of the onlooker.

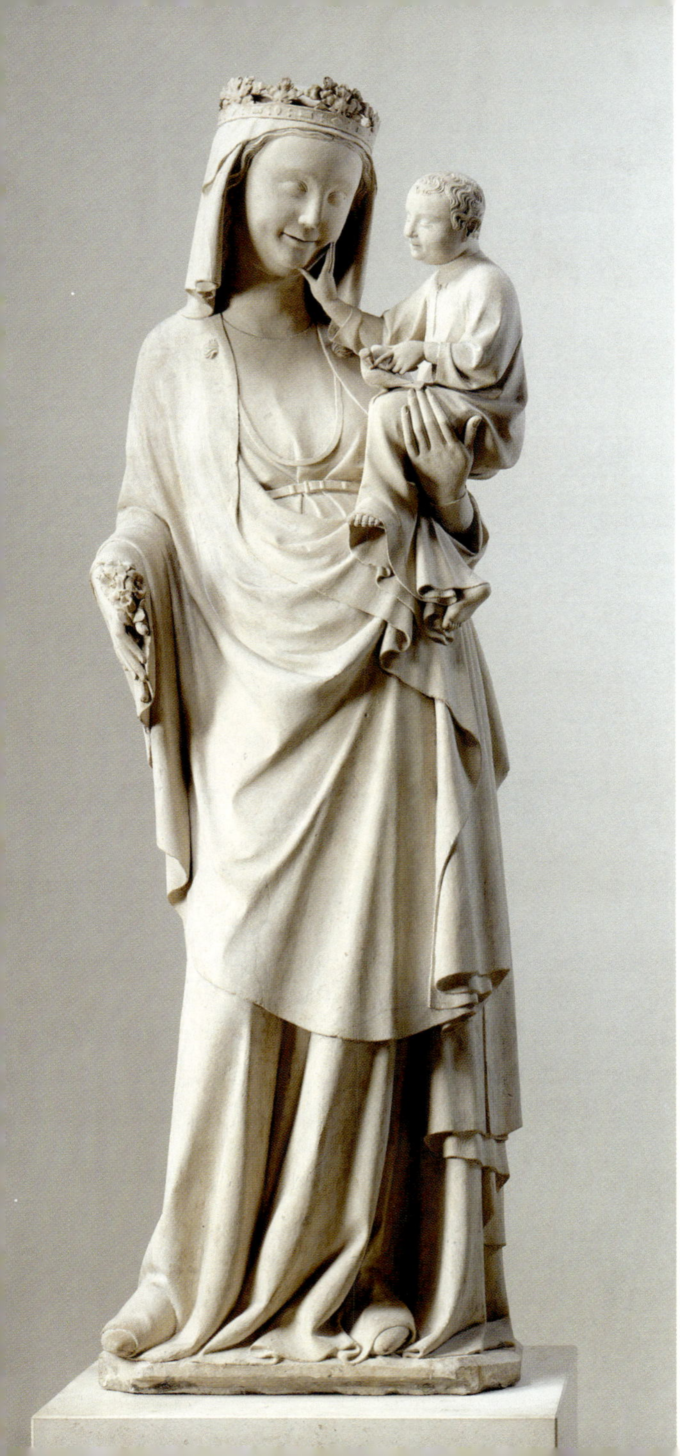

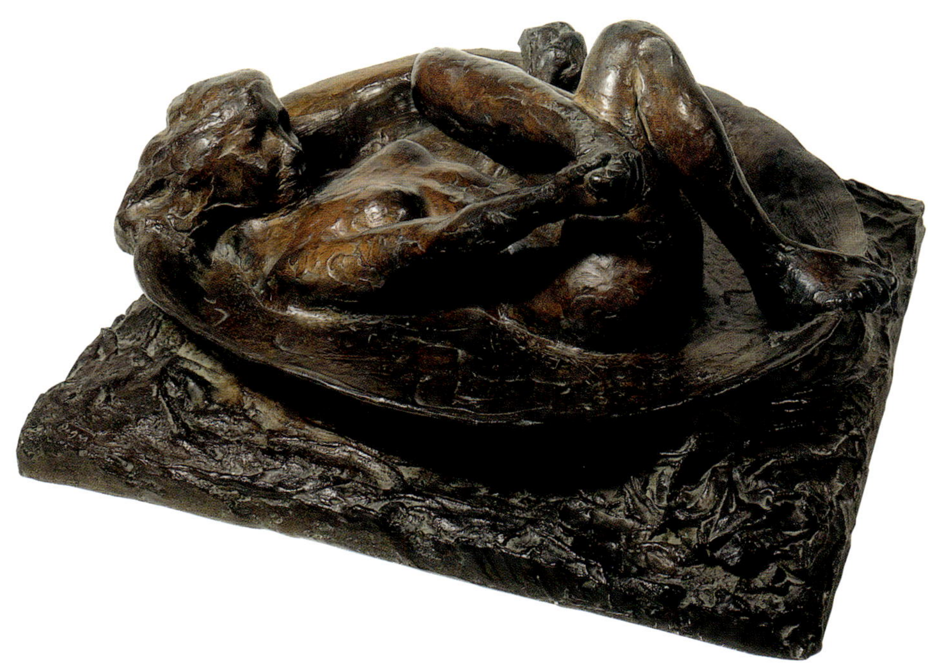

Virgin and Child
Normandy, first third of the 14th century.
Stone. 175 x 57 x 34 cm - ML

Edgar Degas
The Bathtub, **1889**
Bronze. 22 x 43 x 45 cm - MO

Richard Serra
Hand Catching Lead, **1968**
16mm black and white silent film stock
Length: 3 min - CP

The tactile art par excellence, in which the hand plays the primary role, sculpture is forever striving to convey the feel of materials, to express the effects of touch. In Edgar Degas' *The Bathtub*, the impact of this insistence on contact with flesh is highly sensual. He captures his bather in an act of intimate acrobatics in the splashing water. In the circular pool of unruffled water, the study reveals a complex geometry and sensual forms that recall those of another of the artist's recurrent themes, ballerinas at the barre.

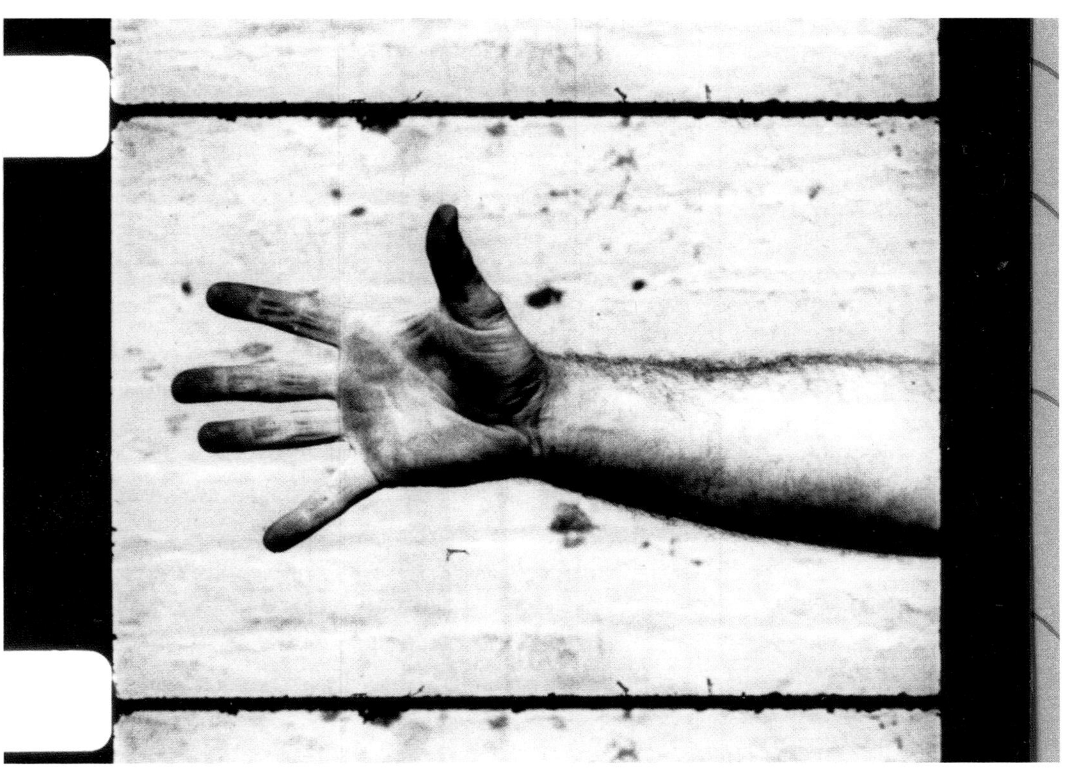

Worth a thousand words of dogma, the gesture of the Christ Child brushing the cheek of his mother in the 14th-century *Virgin with Child* (incidentally, the first medieval work to be purchased by the Louvre) is treated in accordance with the type of the *Virgin Eleousa* (Virgin of tenderness) adopted by Byzantine and Coptic sculptors and ivory-carvers. The sculpture expresses the humanity of Christ in one simple act. In his other hand Jesus holds a bird, which pecks at his finger. Could this be an allusion to the Passion? I prefer to think of the legend of the Christ Child fashioning sparrows out of clay and giving them life, as found in Pseudo-Matthew (Ch. 27) and in the Koran (III, 43): this, then, would be Christ as sculptor.

The American Richard Serra made several films along the lines of *Hand Catching Lead* at the end of 1960s, in which he shows a close-up of his palm stopping pieces of lead fired at him. At a time when Minimalist artists were delegating the task of sculpture-making to industry, the performance amounted to an appeal to return to materials. The sculptor is not for all that a doubting Thomas who has to touch to create; but in this way he is better able to gauge the resistance of his materials, their consistency, their autonomous life, as well as the energy required to put them to use.

Direct carving

Michelangelo established a distinction between sculpture *per via di porre*, by the addition of matter, as the modeller does, and sculpture *per forza di levare*, by subtraction, by carving into a block of marble, the practice he considered superior. The art historian Rudolf Wittkower viewed the areas the master left unfinished, the famous *non finitò*, as a typical manifestation of Neo-Platonic dissatisfaction, born from the discrepancy between initial design — the Ideal — and its material manifestation.

What do Michelangelo and Giuseppe Penone have in common? The first said he could see a work inside a block of stone, that he only had to release it, patiently exposing it, like ore from the gangue. Similarly Penone rolls back time, intuiting how it once was, by use of a wooden purloin from which he peels off ring after ring of the sapwood, stopping halfway at the one corresponding to year twenty, his own age at the time, and going on to expose the heart of the tree. This tree, then, becomes a kind of self-portrait

Even if Brancusi rightly stated: 'Direct or indirect carving: it means nothing — only the thing made counts,' to carve straight into a material does forge a strong and instantly apparent bond between the work and its maker. A sculptor who works his materials himself produces a unique piece that bears his stamp, far more than one in bronze, which is obtained only with the aid of many intermediaries. Thus, in 1908, when Joseph Bernard carved this stone head, which he significantly entitled *Effort Towards Nature,* he was reverting to the technique of Michelangelo: beyond the physical effort, Bernard's quest was for an authentic gesture and respect for materials.

Joseph Bernard
Effort towards Nature, 1905-06
Lens stone. 32 x 29 x 31 cm - MO

Giuseppe Penone
Albero, 1973
Wood. 550 x 19.5 x 7.5 cm - CP

Michelangelo
The Captive or *The Rebel Slave*, 1513-15
Marble. 209 x 49 x 75.5 cm - ML

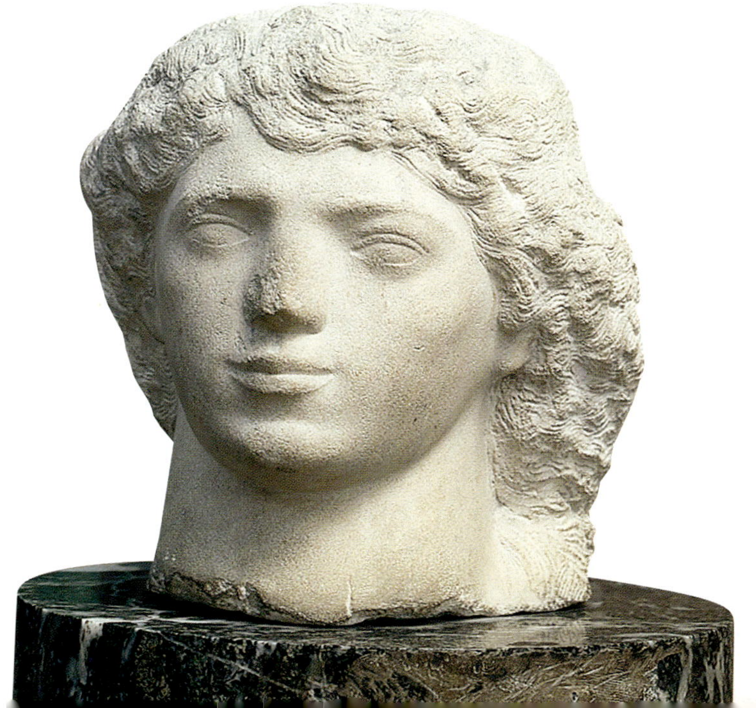

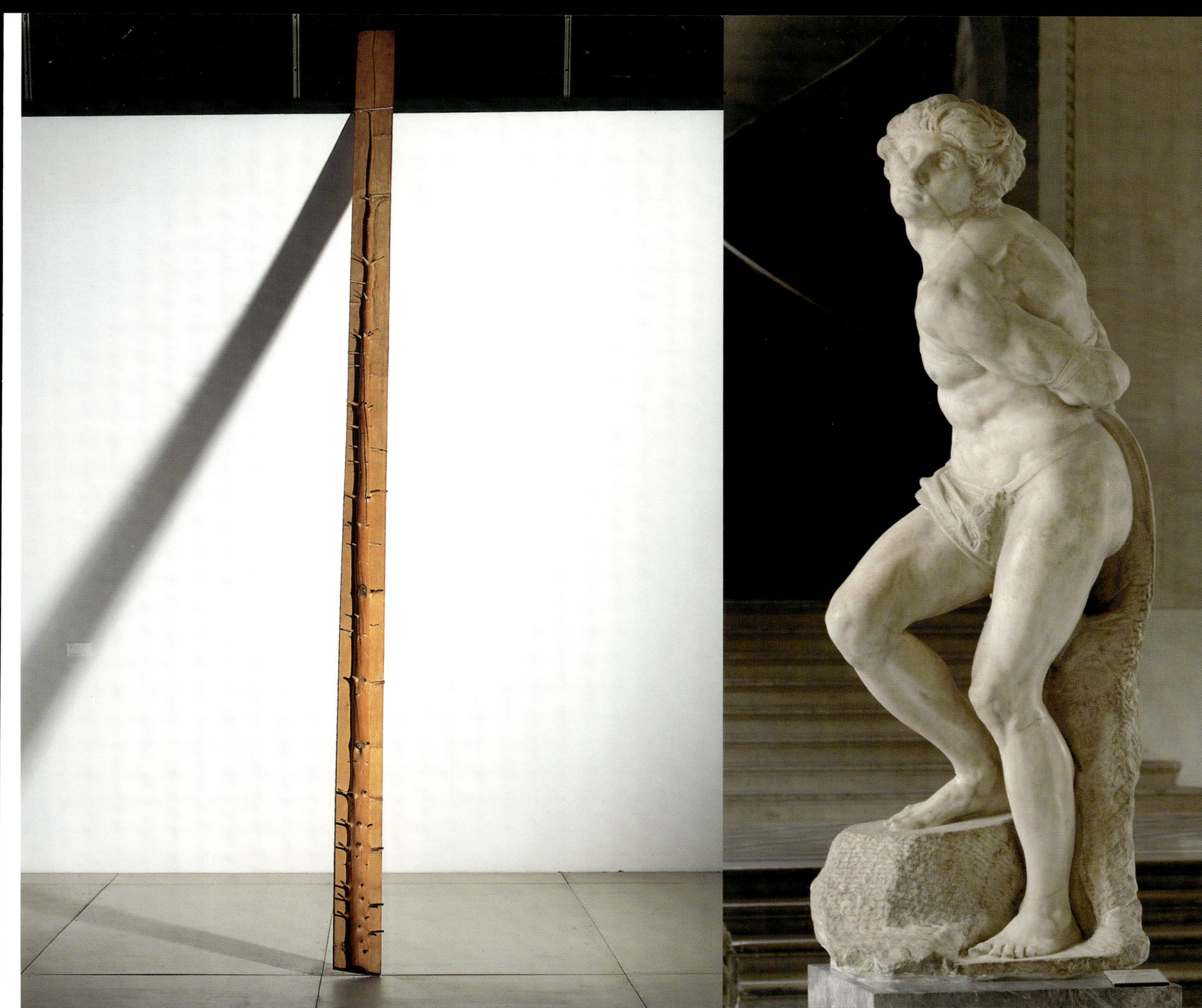

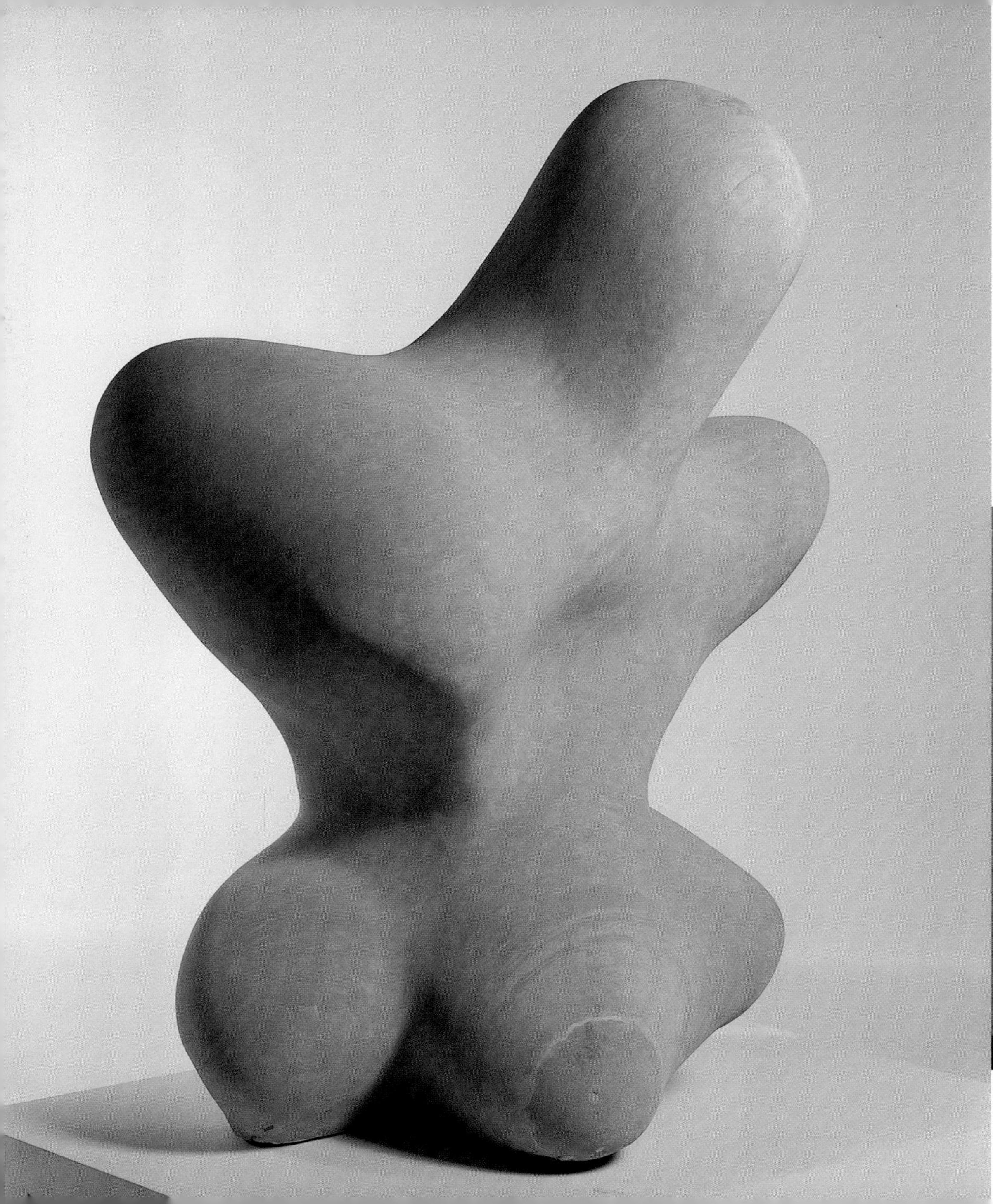

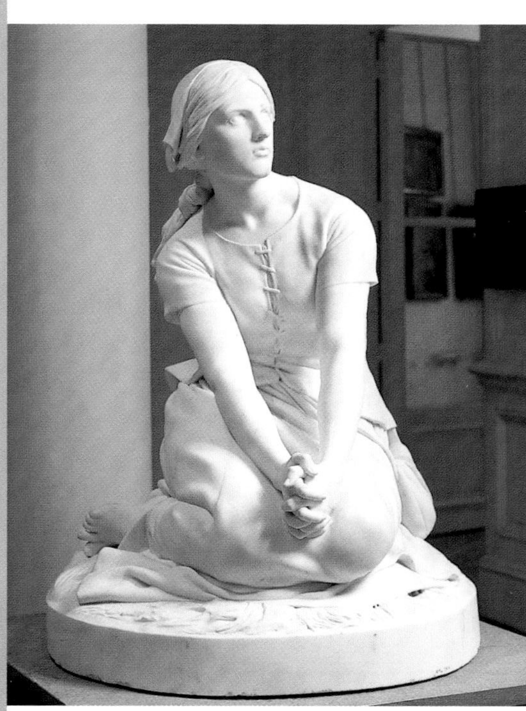

Sculpture in the round

Sculpture in the round is three-dimensional form, the body-sculpture free-standing in space, released from the wall to which bas-relief is confined. However, Augustin Pajou's *Psyche Abandoned*, an admirable 18th-century nude in which the flesh is riven by torment, fully conveys its elegiac tone only when looked at from the front, a viewpoint stipulated by the sculptor.

Joan of Arc at Domrémy by Henri Chapu, presented at the Salon of 1872, is very different. Full of allusions to the still fresh memory of the provinces lost by France in the Franco-Prussian war of 1870 and to a long-awaited national revival, the figure has been studied so that, as Joan's body reacts to the voices she hears, she turns, with singular naturalness, on a foot exposed as her dress rides up, and lifts her face to the heavens. Chapu took the theme of the countrywoman of Lorraine as an expression of rural France from his master François Rude's *Joan Listening to her Voices* (1852), but the sculptor has here created an image of perfect simplicity and the eye never tires of following the inspired figure round as she slowly twists on her axis.

Sculpture in the round did not disappear with abstract art, as the work of Jean Arp clearly demonstrates. After a Dada phase, he moved on to a biomorphic abstraction that he dubbed 'Concrete art'. He better than anyone knew how to exploit the analogy between the forms of femininity and maternity on the one hand and the concretions and shapes of the natural world on the other. These first 'human concretions', which heralded his return to sculpture in the round, were scooped out of plaster then filed down, although later Arp turned to stone, as is the case here. We sense the same vitality of form here as in the Chapu.

Jean Arp
Giant Pip, 1937
Stone. 162 x 125 x 77 cm - CP

Henri Chapu
Joan of Arc at Domrémy, 1870/1871
Marble. 117 x 92 x 83 cm - MO

Augustin Pajou
Psyche Abandoned, 1785/1790
Marble. 177 x 86 x 86 cm - ML

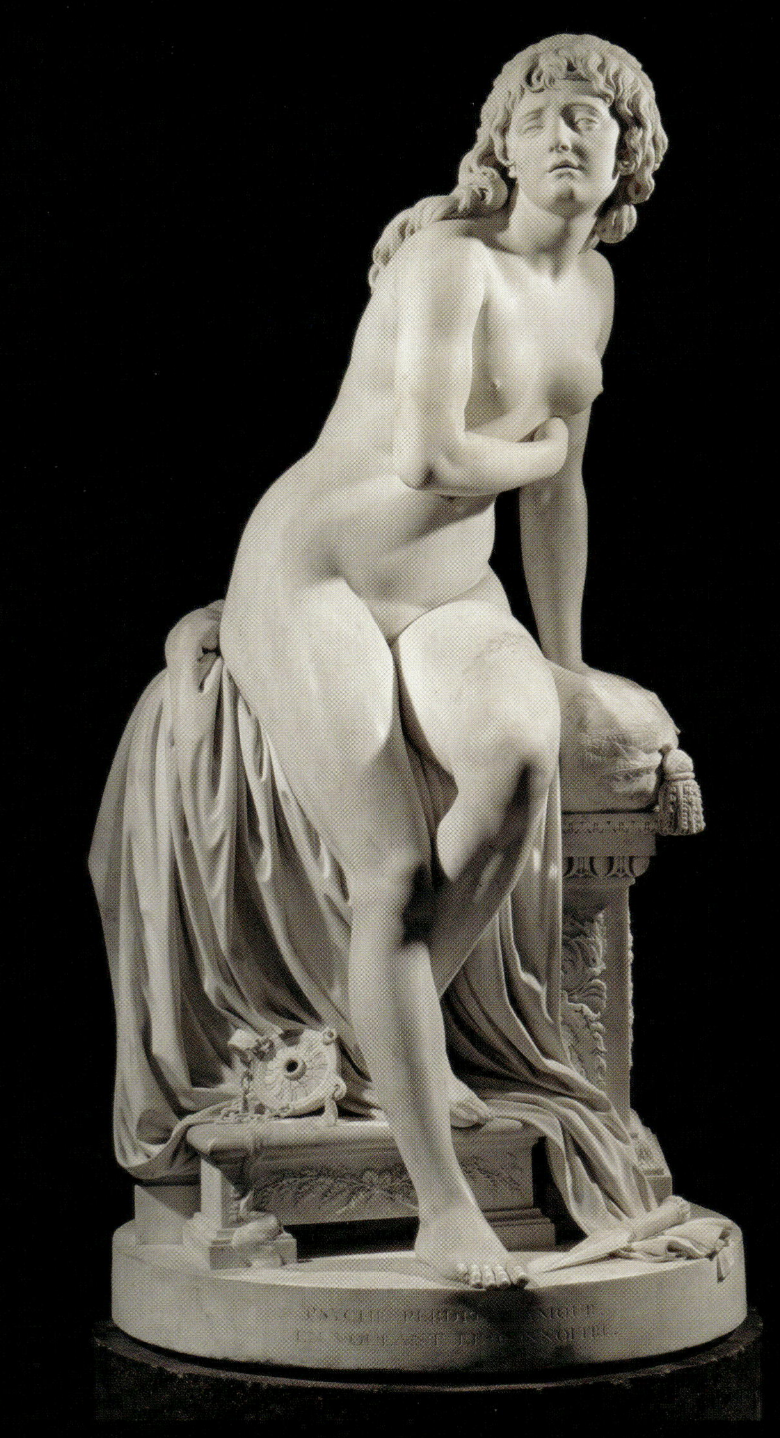

Medallion

'Homage to an Antique poet', one reads beneath the study for this work by Gino Pascali, an Arte Povera artist who died prematurely. The work is a homage to the Greek fabulist Aesop, whose apologias in which animals play the roles of men were used as a model by the French 17th-century poet La Fontaine. He could hardly receive a better celebration than this *tondo*, perfectly apt for a man who wielded the quill. Moreover, these hundred cockerel feathers stand for arrows that Pascali fires into a particular target: the vanity of Man, whose violence he had roundly condemned in other pieces incorporating real weapons. The shuddering, rustling feathers also evoke the act of drawing. Once again, Pascali harks back to the art of the past the better to transform it, since carved medals, oval or round in shape (*tondi*), placed drawing at the heart of sculpture. Made as an admission piece to the Académie Royale in 1657, François Girardon's *Mater Dolorosa* presents the Virgin face-on, her hands crossed over her breast, her body draped in ample folds against which the long, finely drawn fingers stand out. Viewed in three-quarters as if in motion, her head, turning and leaning towards the right shoulder, imparts a singular impression of space. Like Pascali, the Romantic sculptor Auguste Préault returned time and again to the genre of famous literary celebrities: the noble profile of his *Virgil*, prince of poets, head girt with laurel, stands out in high relief. Dear to the heart of the Romantics for having guided Aeneas to the Underworld from which the hero emerged victorious, Virgil also appears in Delacroix's painting *The Barque of Dante* (1822), the boat that twice crossed the Acheron, the river of Death. Perhaps a medallion is a kind of viaticum for posterity that the sculptor bestows on the man of letters…

Auguste Préault
Virgil, 1853
Bronze. 95 x 85 x 23 cm - MO

Pino Pascali
Aesop's Feathers, 1968
Bird feathers, braided steel wool mounted on a wooden plank
Diam: 150 cm; depth: 35 cm - CP

François Girardon
Virgin of Sorrows, 1657
Marble. 85 x 65 x 10 cm - ML

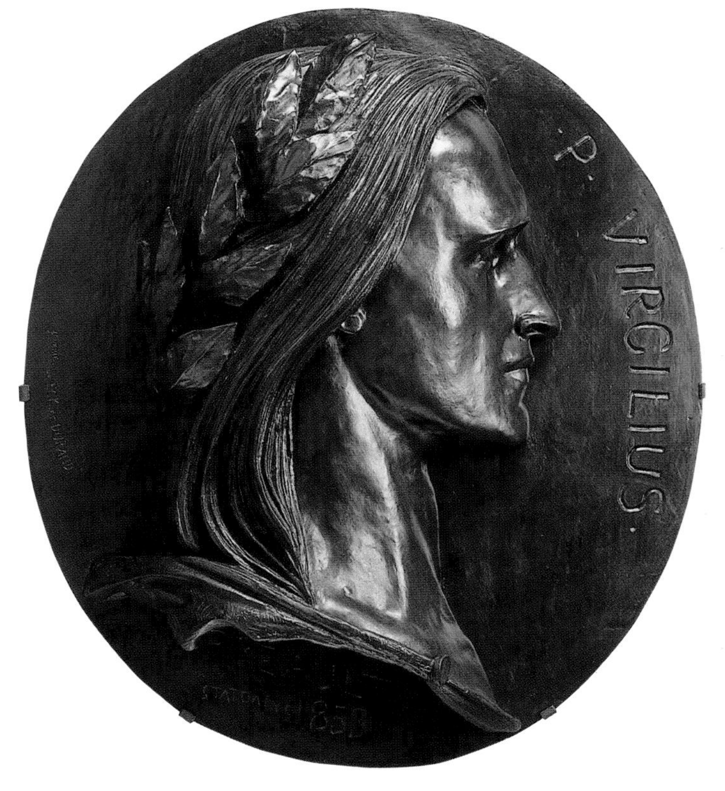

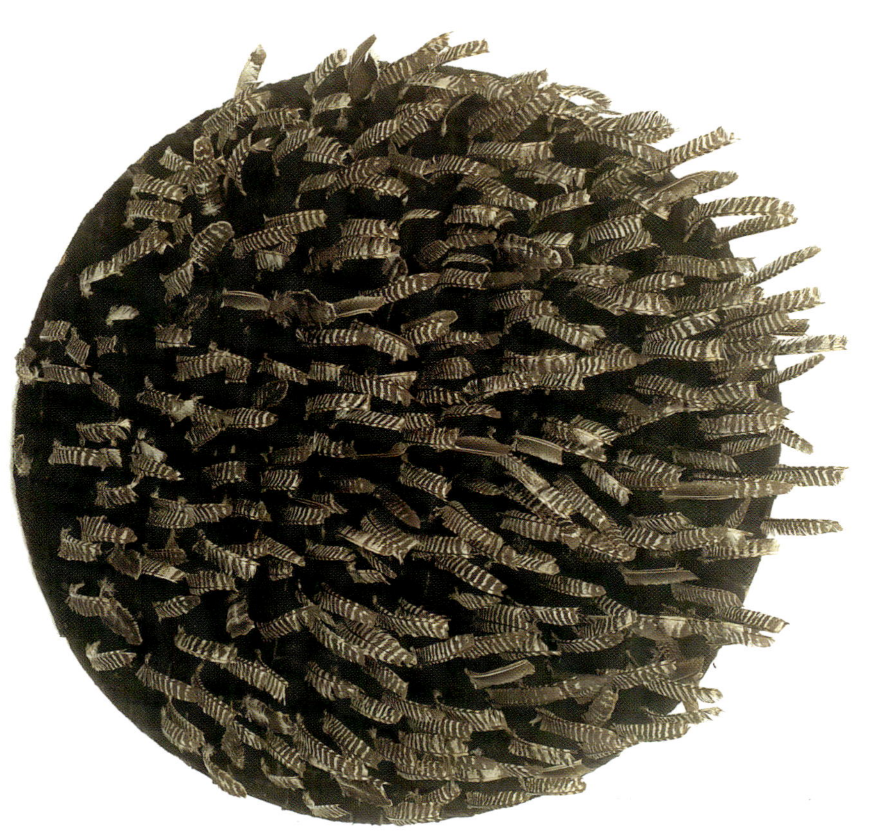

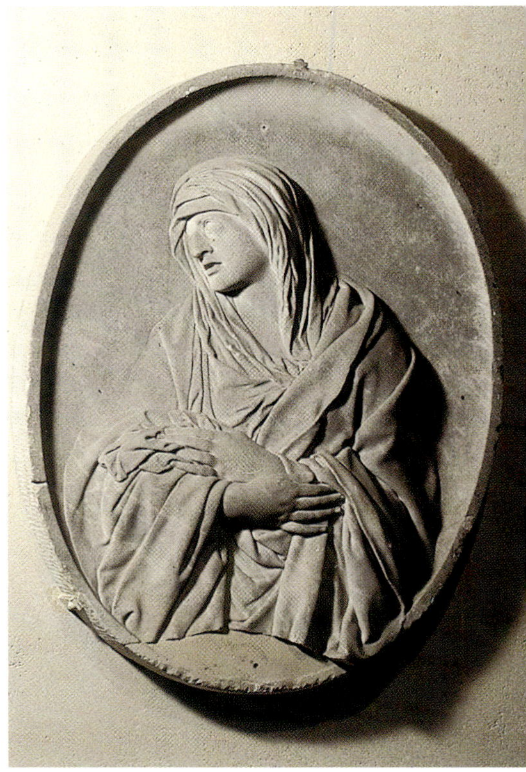

Assemblage

Etruscan Canope Vase, Vulci
Second half of the 6th century BC
Terracotta. H: 50 cm - ML

Pablo Picasso
The Absinthe Glass, 1914
Painted and sand-coated bronze, absinthe spoon. 21.5 x 16.5 x 6.5 cm - CP

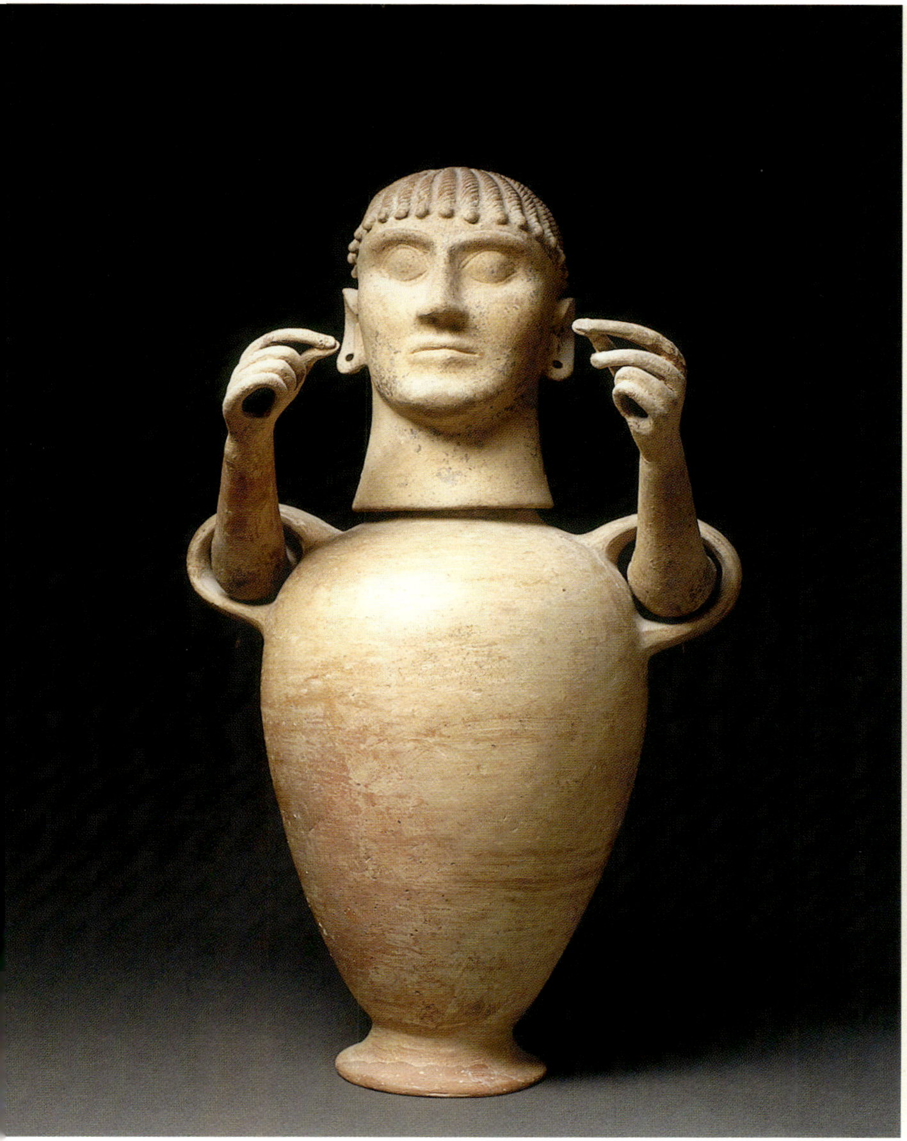

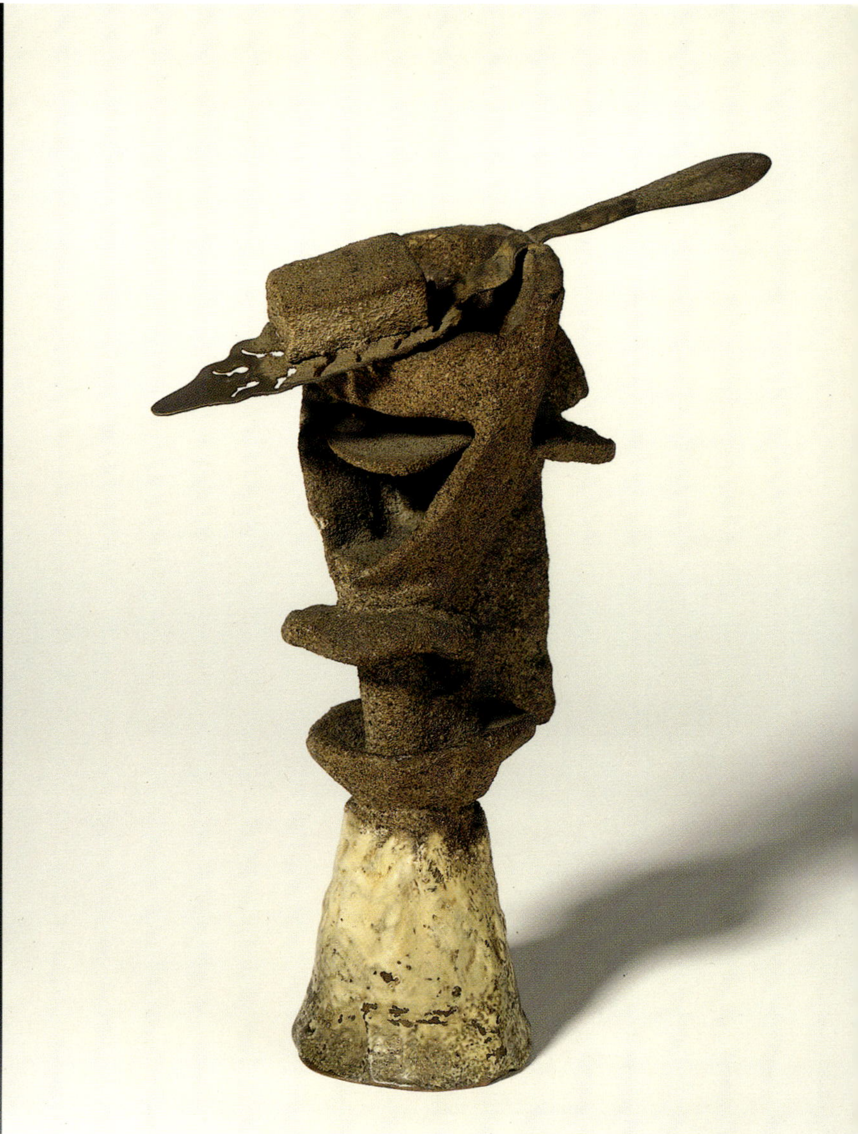

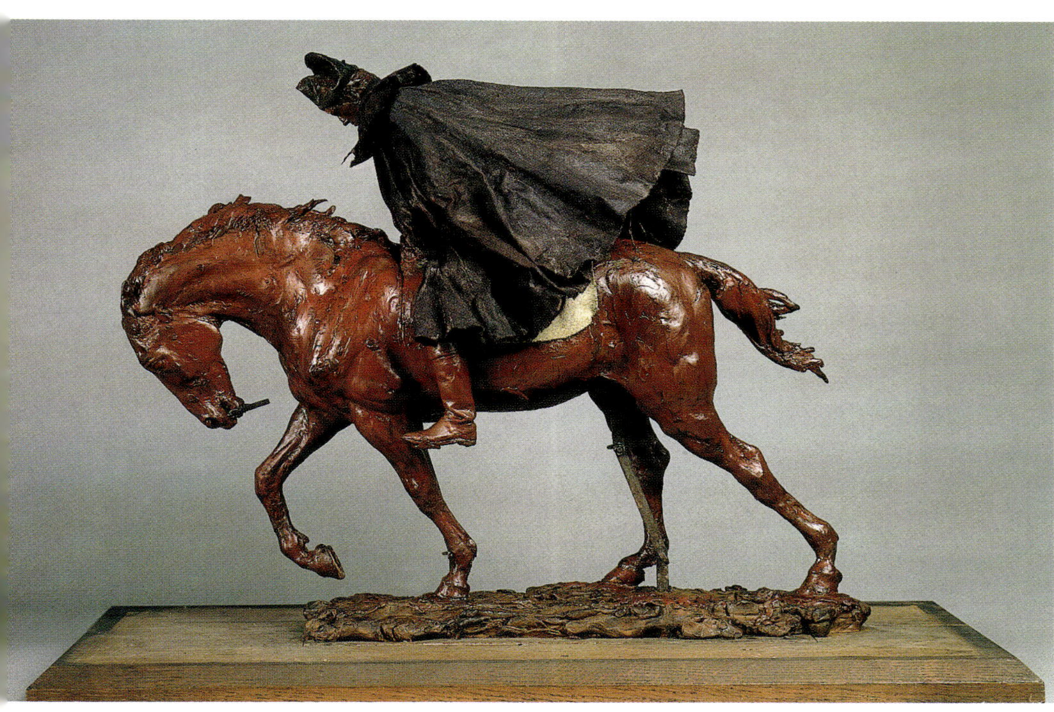

A pair of arms is enough to turn the bulge of an Etruscan canope into a belly belonging to one of those effigies of funerary art. Cobbling together is, as Claude Lévi-Strauss suggested in *The Savage Mind*, characteristic of the artistic act. When the painter Ernest Meissonier, whom Dalí hailed as a genius, needed a study of a rider for one of his celebrated battle scenes, he assembled this small working sculpture from a wooden model horse, a scrap of cloth and some leather for a bridle.

In the same way, Gustave Moreau fashioned little figurines for studies of the movement in his *Salome*. Poussin and, closer to our time, Giorgio Morandi staged miniature theatrics. To make sculptures for a painting is thus no irrelevant detour. Meissonier, whose assemblage is not far removed from Degas dressing up his *Little*

Fourteen-Year-Old Dancer (p. 72), placed his rider in an enduringly tangible space: it is easy to picture him struggling against the wind over the great plains of Germany or Poland during one of the most dramatic episodes of the Napoleonic saga, the retreat from Russia. Picasso's *Absinthe Glass* (1914) proved a revolution in the field of 20th-century sculpture. The work at the Centre Pompidou belongs to a series of six sculptures, of which each one is an 'original', since they are all painted differently. The trick of the piece, as it were, lies in the real perforated absinthe spoon integrated into the ana-lytical representation of the glass and the mimetic treatment of the lump of sugar. Oddly, the object plays the role of itself — a test then for the work of art: 'The relationship between real spoon and model glass interests me,' said Picasso. In 1912, and for similar

reasons, he had already introduced a piece of oilcloth into his *Still Life with Cane Chair*. The use of a real object, one that had not been specially made, like the tutu in Degas' *Dancer*, opened a vast field of possibilities to contemporary sculpture — indeed, quite as many as the conundrums arising from Duchamp's ready-mades. Picasso uses some everyday article, something from the world of objects, rather like a slang term coming to the aid of the elevated language of art.

Ernest Meissonier

Traveller in the Wind, **1878**

Grey and red wax, cloth and leather on wooden plinth. 47 x 60 x 39 cm - MO

Lifting, carrying

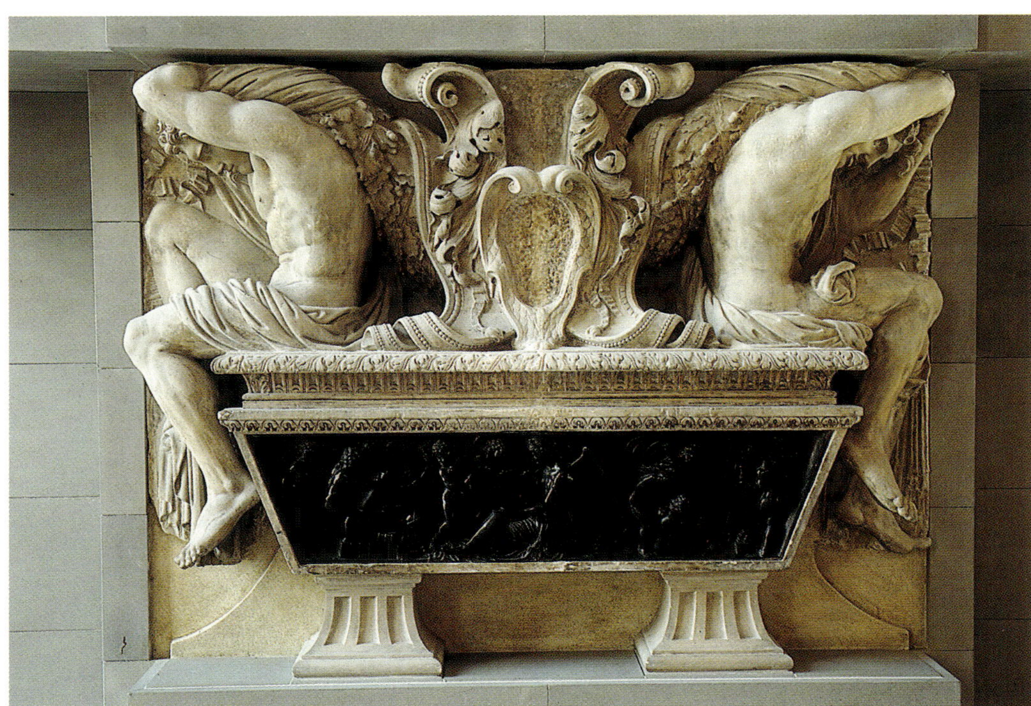

Atlantes, caryatids, *moscophores* (water-carriers), bearers of offerings, but also telamons, Atlas with the world on his shoulders, Hercules relieving the same of his burden, Aeneas saving his father Anchises, the Virgin and Child, St Christopher carrying Jesus as a child, Christ bearing the Cross, the Pietà, the Entombment, divinities ravishing mortals and gods *psychopompe*, mounted horses, and every stripe of amoretti and putti making off with all manner of objects: there is a whole tribe of porters and weightlifters, right up to Picasso's *Man with Sheep*.

François Anguier's mighty atlantes belong to this selfsame race: they support the praying figure of the Magistrat de Thou, who was chief librarian to the king and one of the negotiators of the Edict of Nantes. Constantin Brancusi's *Newborn* possesses a deeper meaning. The ovoid form standing for the infant is borne on a number of bases. One of them is open at the centre, seemingly the belly or matrix that carried the embryo. Inspecting the polished surface of the bronze egg, one sees that it reflects the entire surrounding space. By way of a striking effect of inversion, the most concentrated and simplest form contains within it the entire world. The round-dance in the *Four Quarters of the World Bearing the Celestial Sphere* by Jean-Baptiste Carpeaux endows the fountain in the Jardins de l'Observatoire in Paris with a truly baroque energy enhanced by Emmanuel Fremiet's four sculptures of horses. Campagna had already made a spectacular high altar with the *Heavenly Father on the Globe Borne by the Evangelists* (1591-93) in the church of San Giorgio Maggiore in Venice. Carpeaux sets in motion the allegorical figures representing the four known continents holding a vast armillary sphere: in an alliance between astronomy, geography and sculpture, a round-dance of naked female figures embodies the rotation of the Earth.

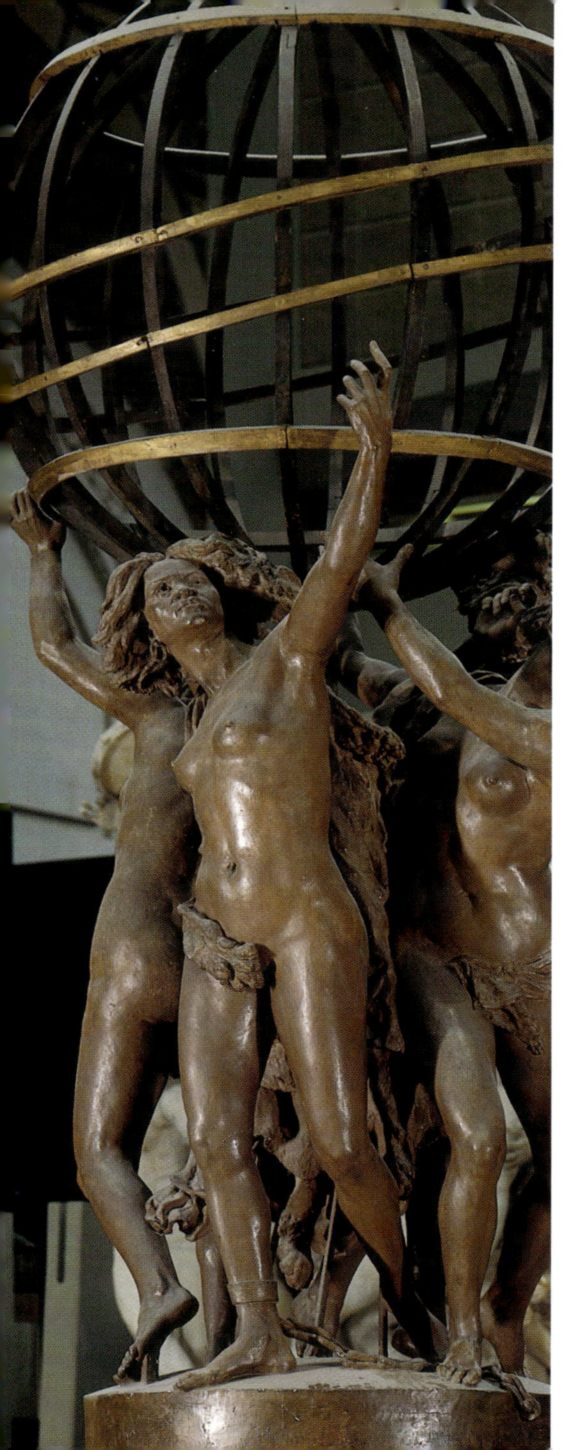

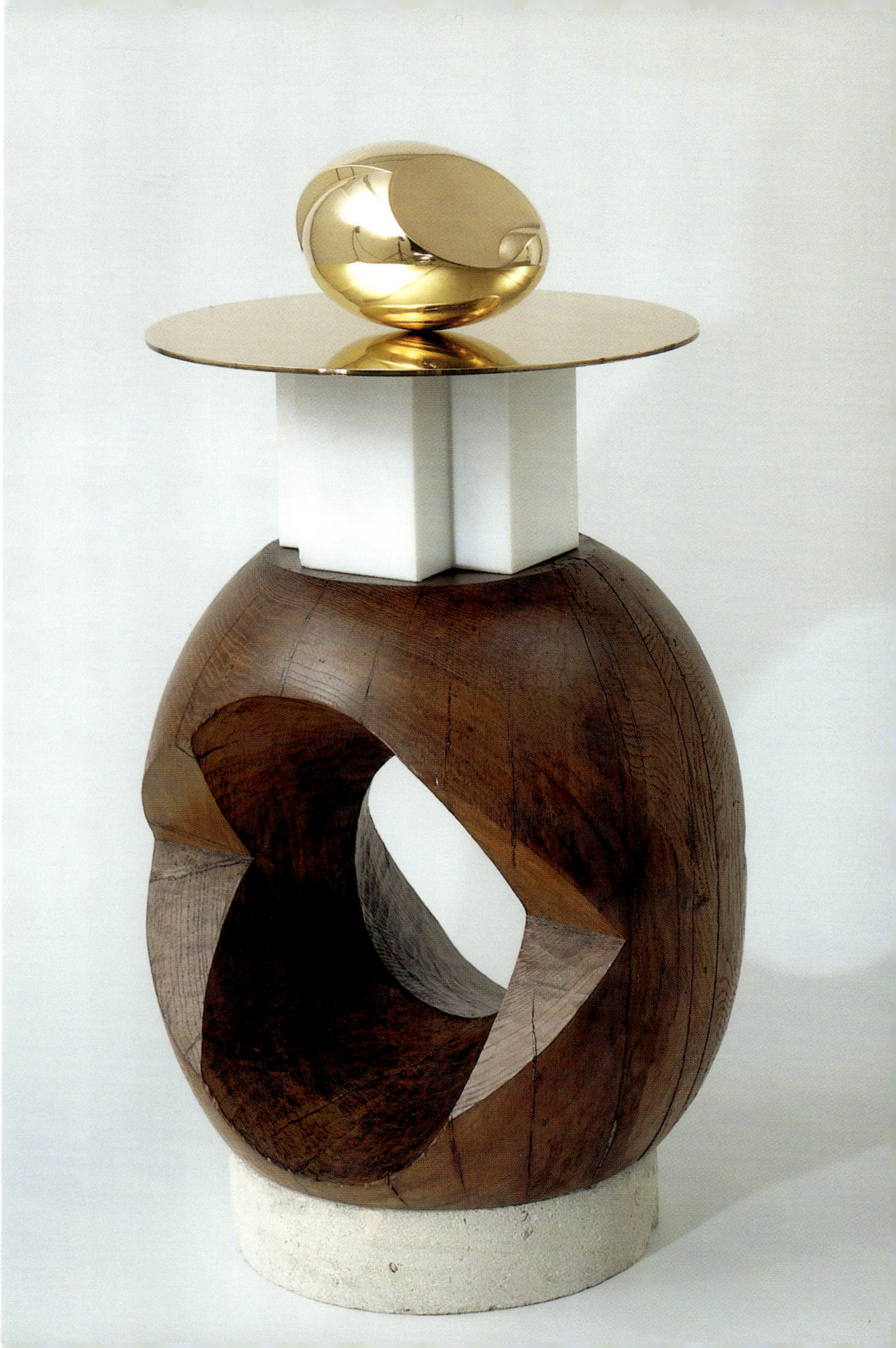

Plinths

The plinth sets the stage for a theatre of ascension. Like those clouds which in paintings of Baroque 'Glories' serve as engines of saintly propulsion, here the plinth, footboard to the celestial world, elevates the founder of the Oratory, Cardinal de Bérulle, as sculpted by Jacques Sarazin in an attitude of prayer, high above our mortal condition and into full-blown Counter-Reformation rapture. The sides of the base open the picture book of St Filippo Neri and Moses. It is the plinth then that turns the sculpture into a monument.

It can, however, play a more active role in the composition. In the replica of the finial for the abbey of the Mont-Saint-Michel by Emmanuel Fremiet, this is the case for the pillar that raises up the archangel: it is an allusion to the battle for heaven, as well as a reminder of the divers monsters trampled underfoot that adorned capitals in the medieval iconographical tradition.

Can one say that Constantin Brancusi abolished the plinth? Rather, he integrated it into the sculpture and reinterpreted it in accordance with a new idea of verticality, of the sculptural pile. Far from remaining an inert base, a mere podium, the plinth enters into dialogue with the other elements, conjointly through its volume and the outline of its contours. By permutation, it can even end up in the median position. The whole sculpture maintains a dynamic relationship with the ground. It is the energy of a formal relation within a vertical ascent that gives *The Cockerel* such power: however unwilling these fowl may be in nature to get airborne, this one is certainly ready to take off.

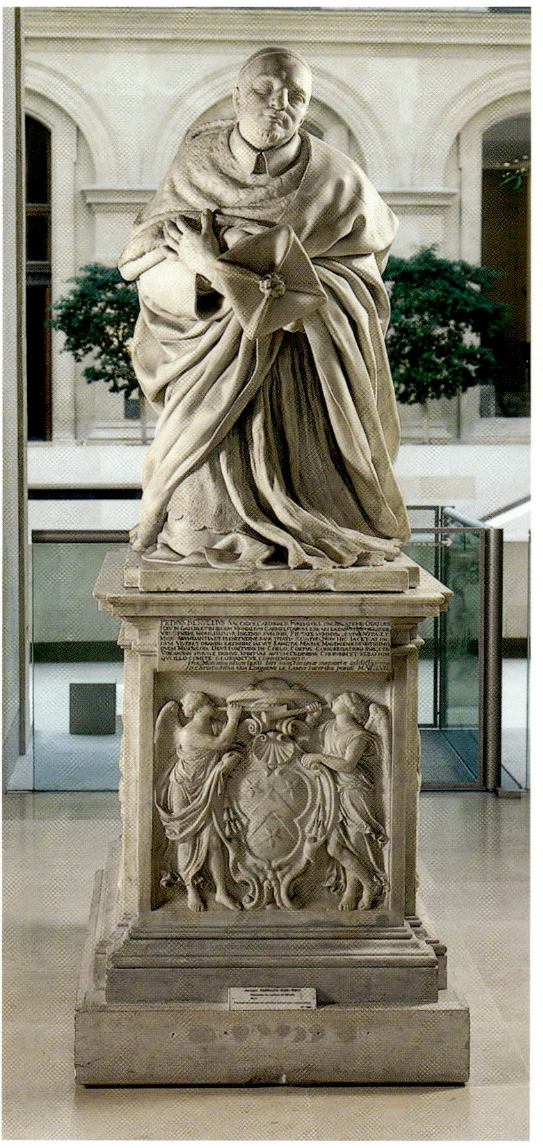

Jacques Sarazin
Monument for the Heart of Cardinal Pierre de Bérulle
1653-57
Marble. 216.5 (including plinth) x 80 x 135 cm - ML

Emmanuel Fremiet
St Michael Slaying the Dragon, 1897
Hammered copper. 617 x 260 x 120 cm - MO

Constantin Brancusi
The Cockerel, 1935
Polished bronze. 103.4 x 12.1 x 29.5 cm
plinth in four parts: limestone, oak. H: 150 cm - CP

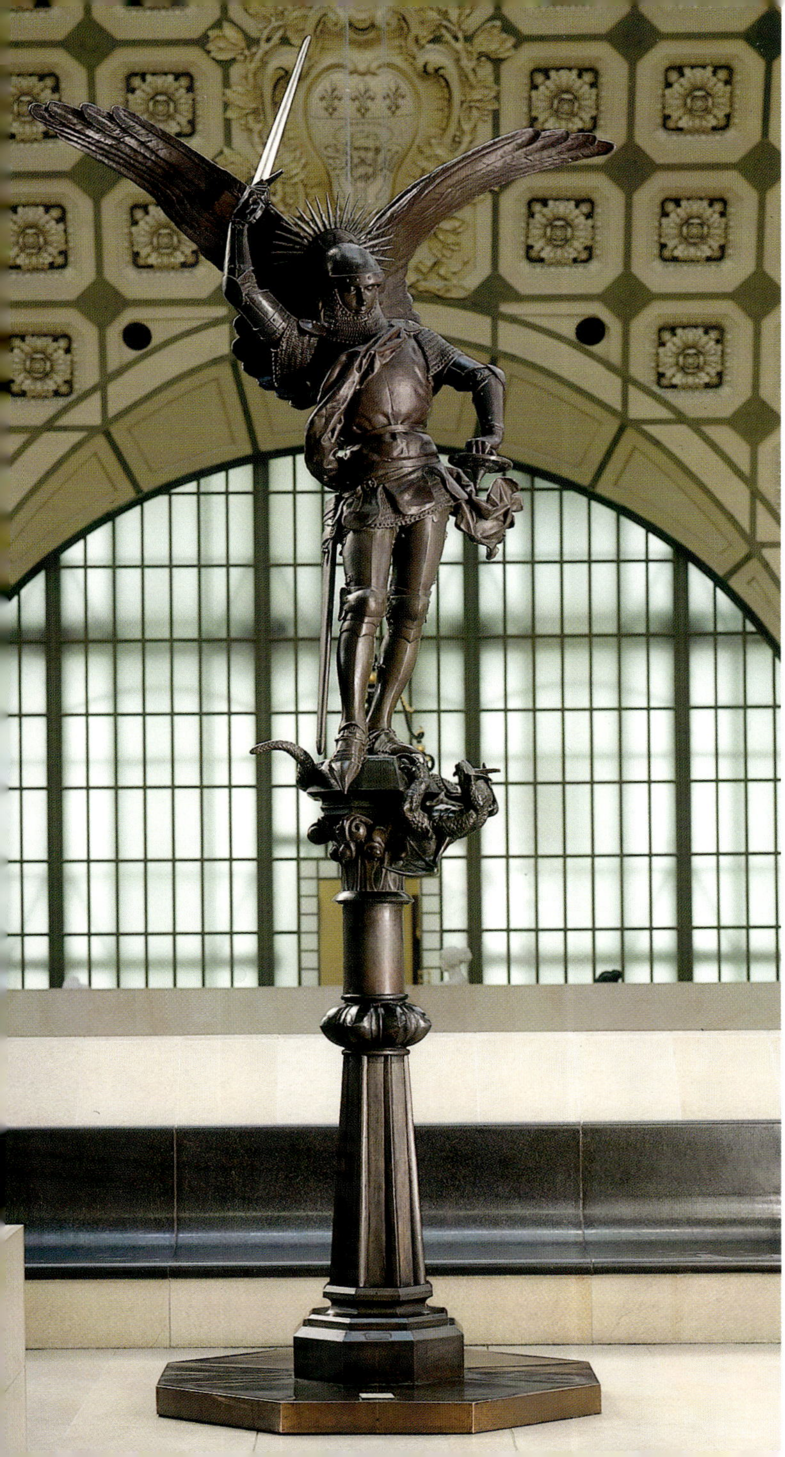

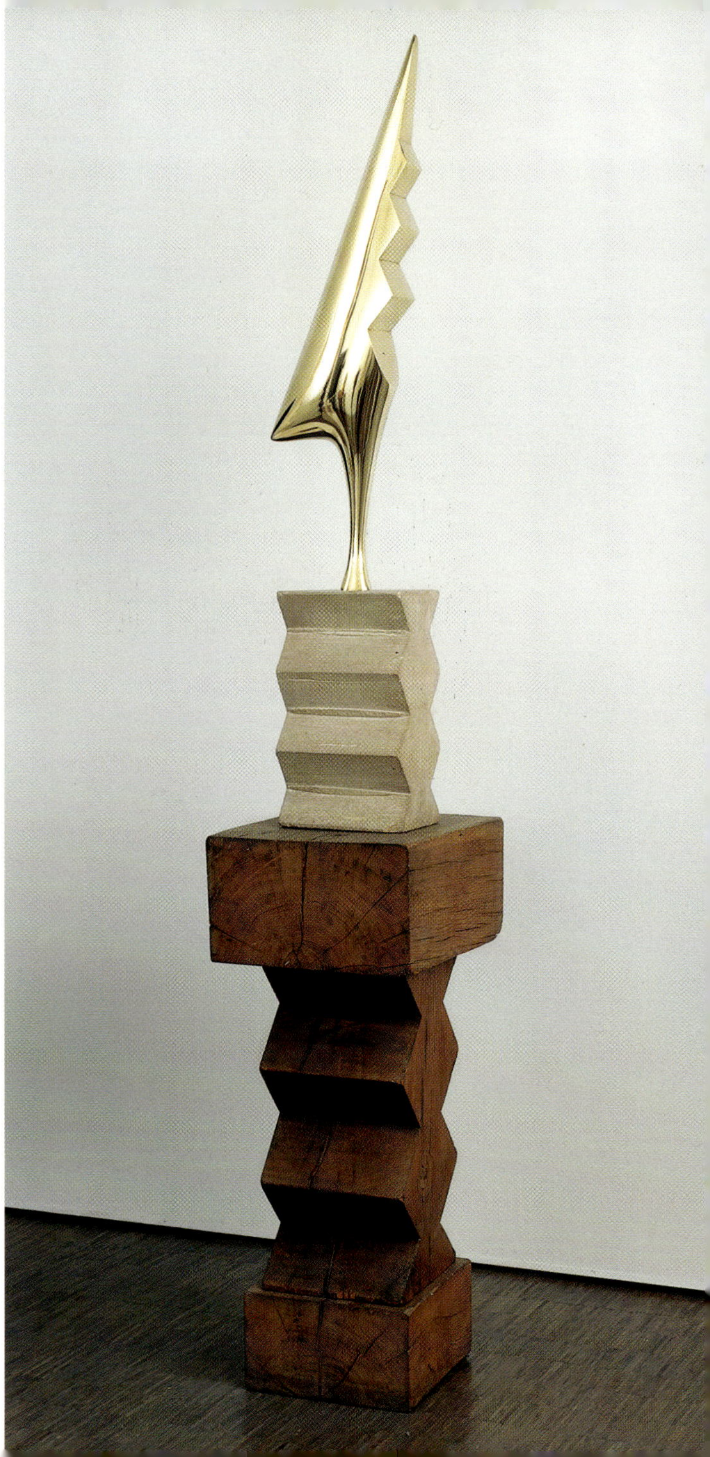

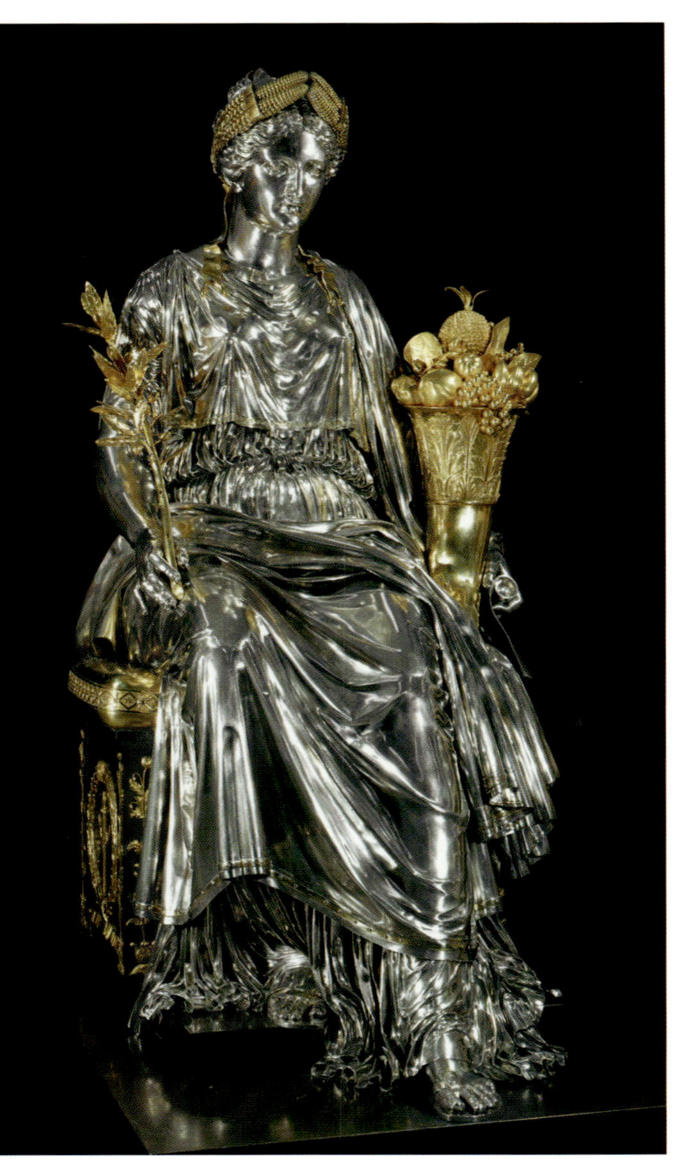

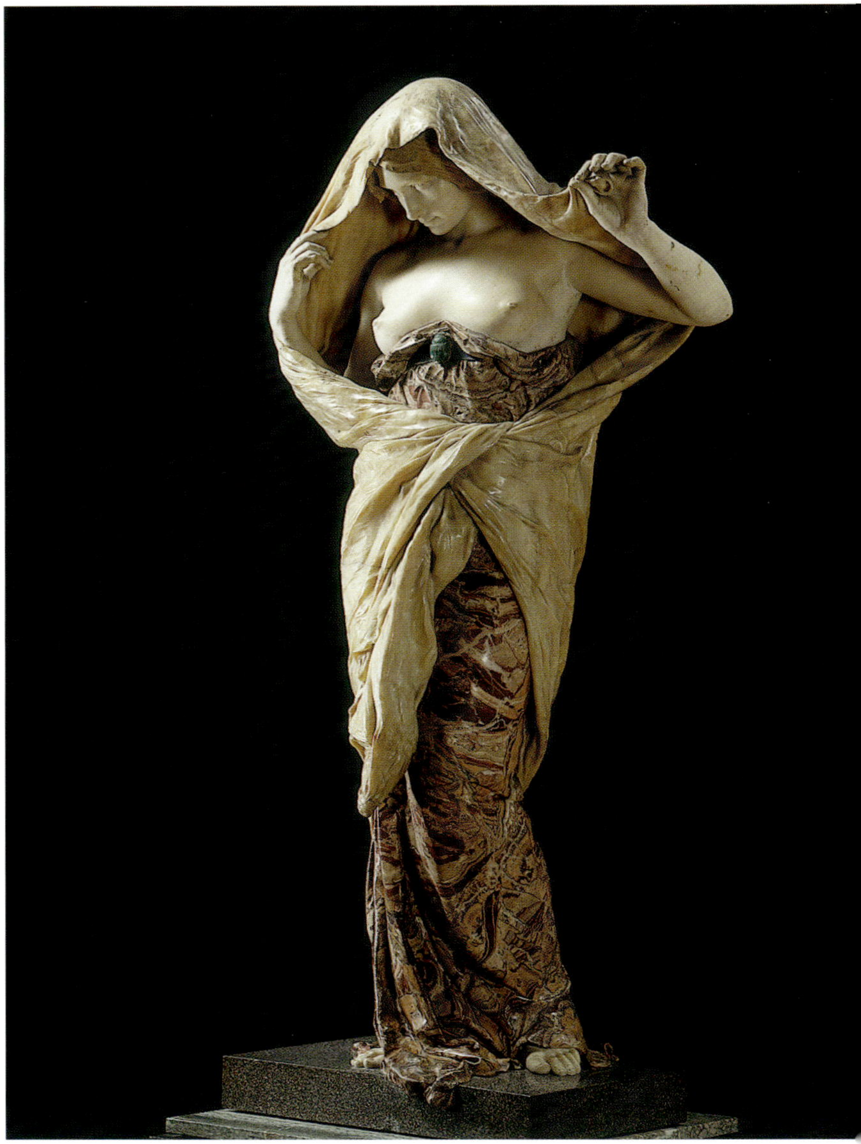

Antoine-Denis Chaudet

Peace, 1806

Silver, silver gilt, bronze and gilded bronze. 167 x 108 x 84 cm - ML

Louis-Ernest Barrias

Nature Revealing Herself to Science, 1899

Diverse materials. 200 x 85 x 55 cm - MO

Allegory

To embody an abstract idea, to show it by way of human figures is the principle of allegory. So *Peace*, commissioned from Antoine-Denis Chaudet by Vivant Denon for the First Consul, was to have celebrated the Peace of Amiens signed with England in 1802. The resumption of hostilities, however, delayed its realisation until 1806-07. The image of Ceres, goddess of the harvest, sporting an olive branch and a horn of plenty, was perfectly suited to official iconography. A consummate masterpiece of multi-material sculpture, *Peace* was cast in bronze and silver by Chéret, and then gilded.

Nature Revealing Herself to Science, also known as *Woman with a Scarab* because of the jewel motif adorning the breast of the allegorical figure, was deliberately designed by Louis-Ernest Barrias as a rich display of materials so as to convey the bounty of Nature. Nature herself is presented in more conventional fashion, in the guise of a woman revealing her secrets to the scientist.

Allegory can be deployed to work negatively too. As an illustration of the spirit of modern times, the Berlin Dadaist Raoul Hausmann hijacked a real hairdresser's dummy: 'For a long time,' he wrote, 'I had noticed that people have no character and that their faces are mere pictures composed by their hairdresser [...]. I wanted to unmask the spirit of our era, the spirit of each of us in his rudimentary state.' As well as labels, Hausmann's head is covered with all kinds of oddments, such as an scrap from a wallet, a bit of radio receiver, and a tinplate goblet in an allusion to brainwashing.

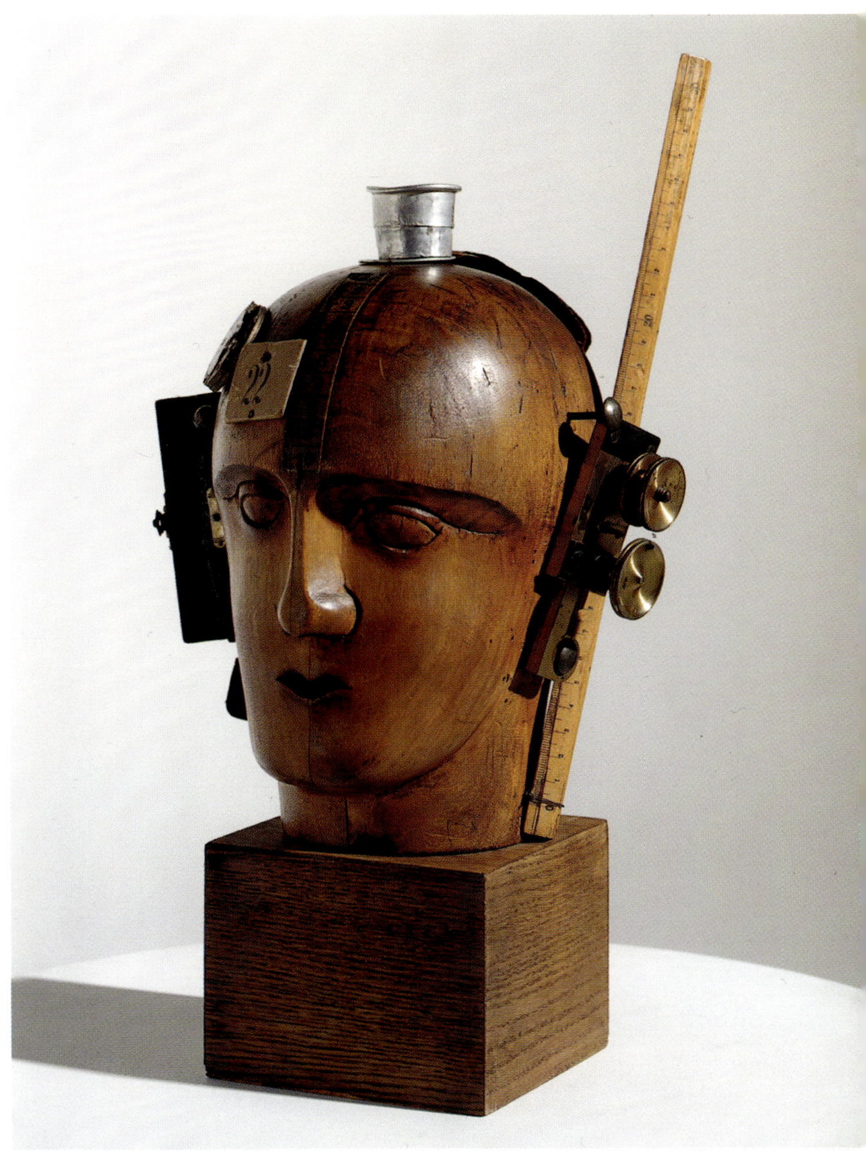

Raoul Hausmann
The Spirit of Our Time or *Mechanical Head*, 1919
Wooden dummy head with diverse materials. 32.5 x 21 x 20 cm - CP

Ready-made

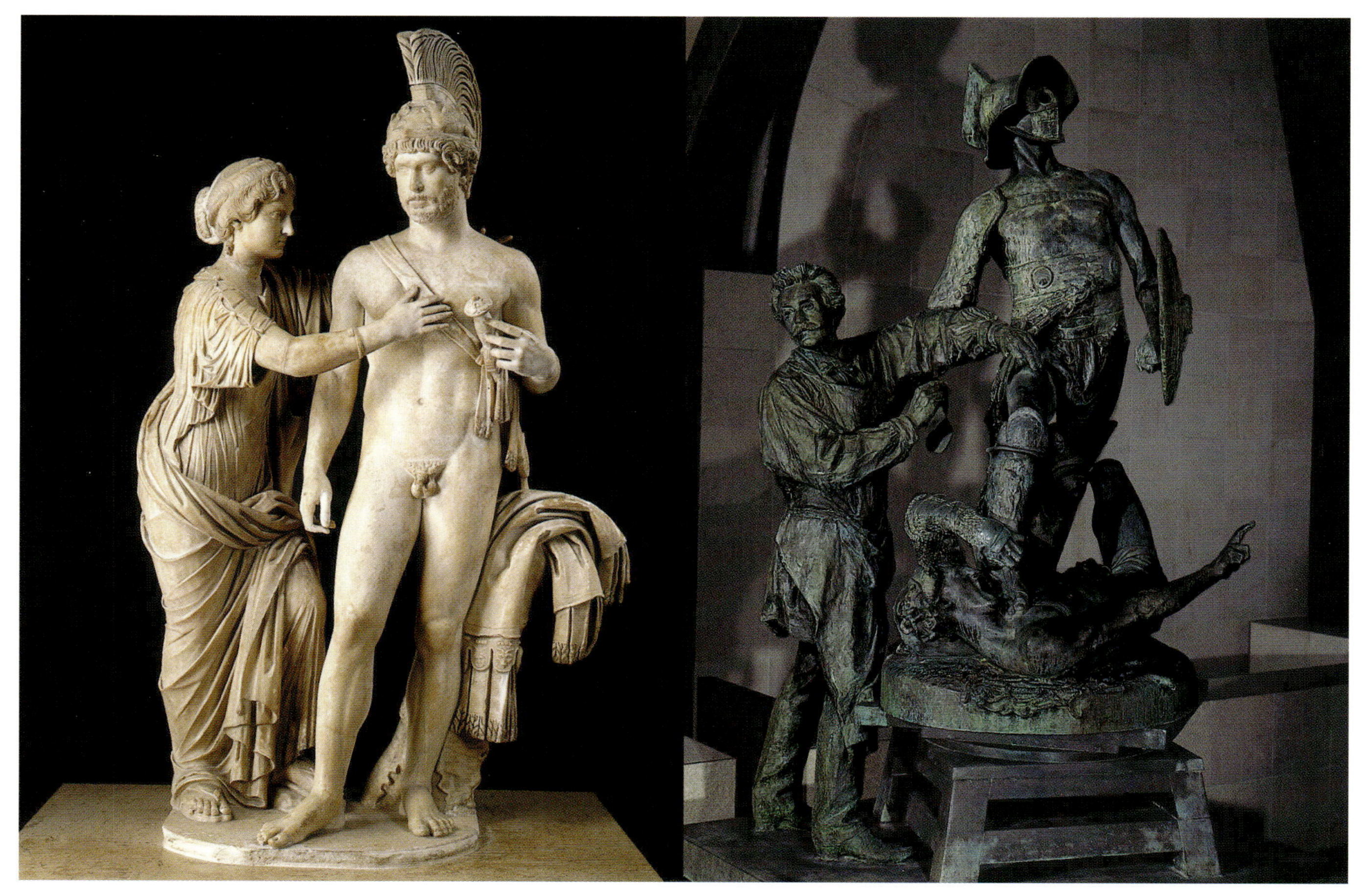

Imperial Group as Mars and Venus
Roman, c. 120-140; reworked c. 170-175
Marble. H: 173 cm - ML

Jean-Léon Gérôme and Aimé Morot
The Gladiators, 1878. Monument to Gérôme, 1909
Bronze. 360 x 182 x 170 cm - MO

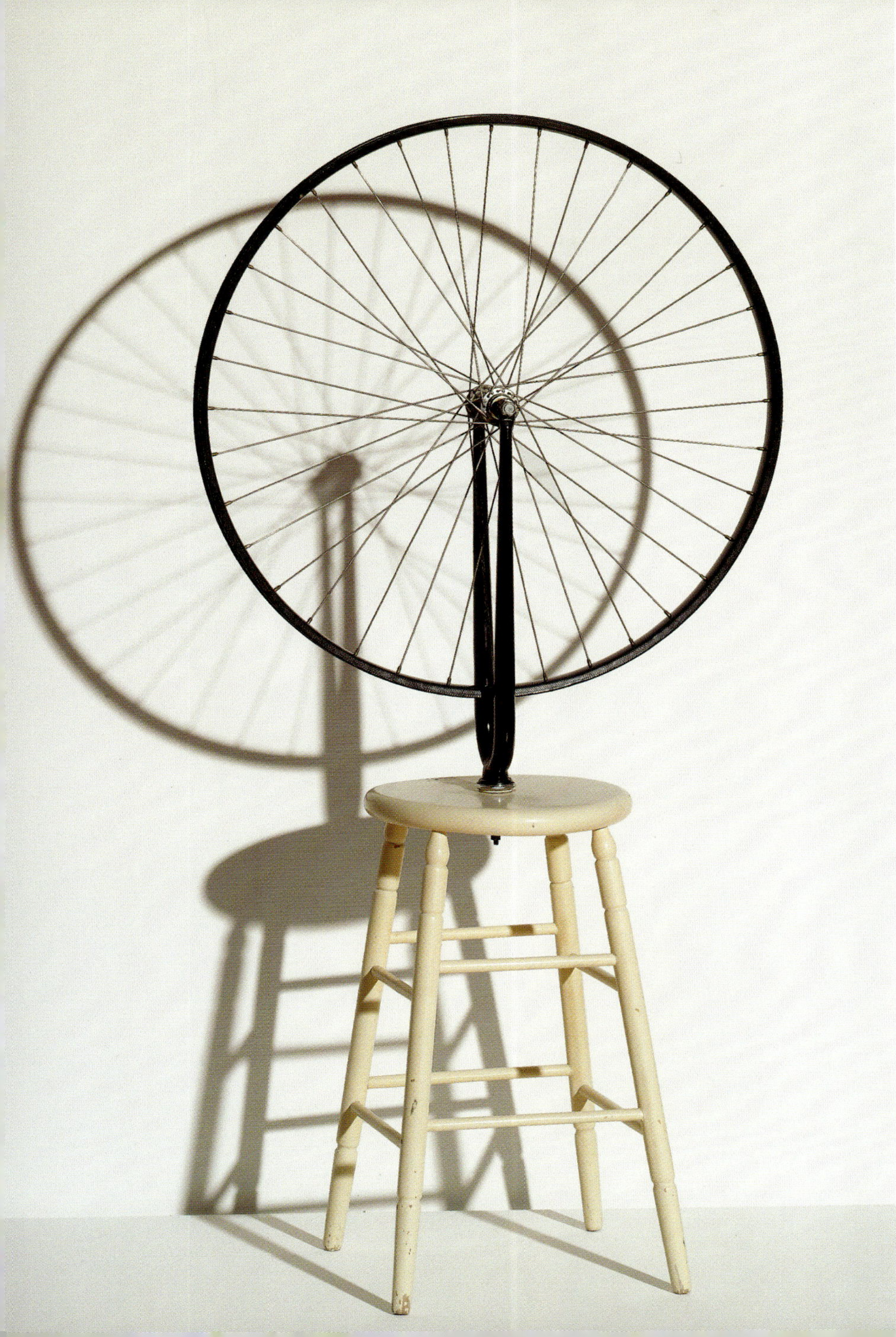

A living couple lends their features to Mars and Venus in this fashionable mythological remake that anticipates those funfair photographs of the 19th century, where holiday-makers pop their head through a hole in a piece of painted cloth. Adhering to the standard repertory of mythological types, the patron chose what was a well-trodden path, simply updating it with his own features and those of his wife.

The original bronze of Jean-Léon Gérôme's *Gladiators* was long looked for in vain, to the point that it was thought lost. It was then realised, by examining the dates of the cast, that Gérôme's son-in-law Aimé Morot had brazenly co-opted it into his own homage to the artist entitled *Gérôme Carving the Gladiators*, in which he camped his father-in-law at work before the sculptor's banker on which stands the famous bronze: a ready-made before the letter!

Marcel Duchamp's decisive move was to sidestep the games of quotation and borrowing on which the art world had always relied. His *Bicycle Wheel* of 1913 kicked off the well-known series of manufactured objects converted into art *objets* known as ready-mades. On a chair that functions as a plinth, he presents an idea of movement, a concept on everybody's lips since the *Futurist Manifesto* of 1909. The wheel is indeed mobile, at least virtually, unlike pictures and traditional sculptures that are condemned to represent movement without ever actually effecting it. In this manner, the accent falls on 'the free choice of the artist' and on the pertinence of his demonstration, rather than on the fabrication of an object belonging to any accepted family of artworks. Should the sculptor so wish, the world of everyday objects, of technology, industry and ideas can henceforth find a place in the workshop. Unlike the *Bull's Head* made by Picasso out of bicycle saddle and a pair of handlebars, the *Bicycle Wheel* whisks us away from the spirit of metamorphosis and the retinal and places our perception of art on a more intellectual plane.

Marcel Duchamp
Bicycle Wheel, 1913 (original), 1964 (current edition)
Ready-made: metal, painted wood. 126.5 x 31.5 x 63.5 cm - CP

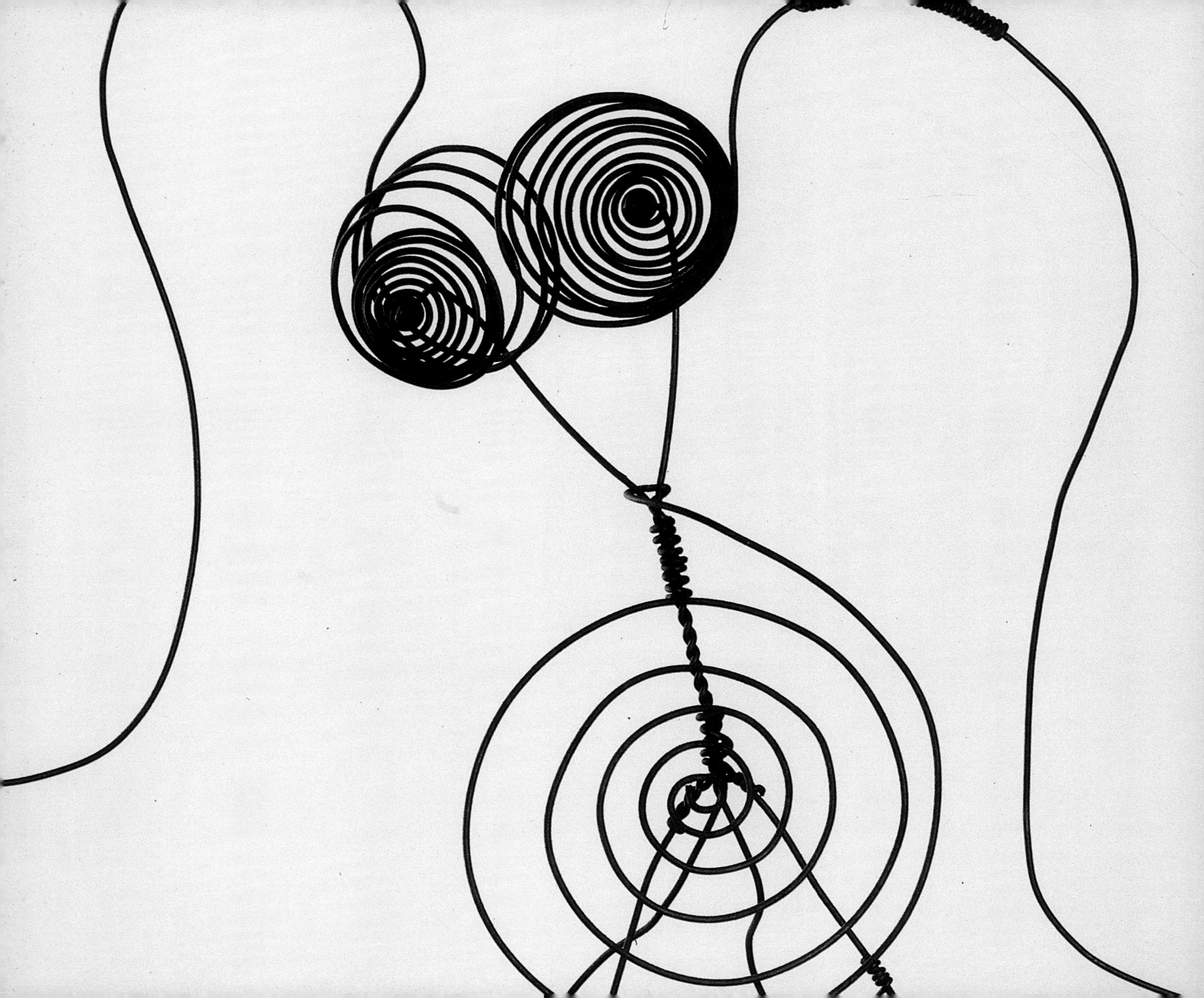

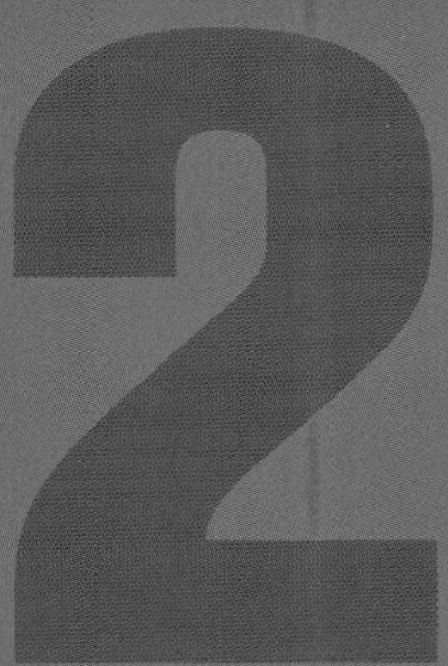

2

Embodiment, allusion

It's not just marble and colour,

–there's also the imaginative power of those who make sculptures and paintings.

(Aretino, Letter to Sansovino, December 1553)

Lettres de l'Arétin (trans. André Chastel), Paris: Scala, 1988

Stare

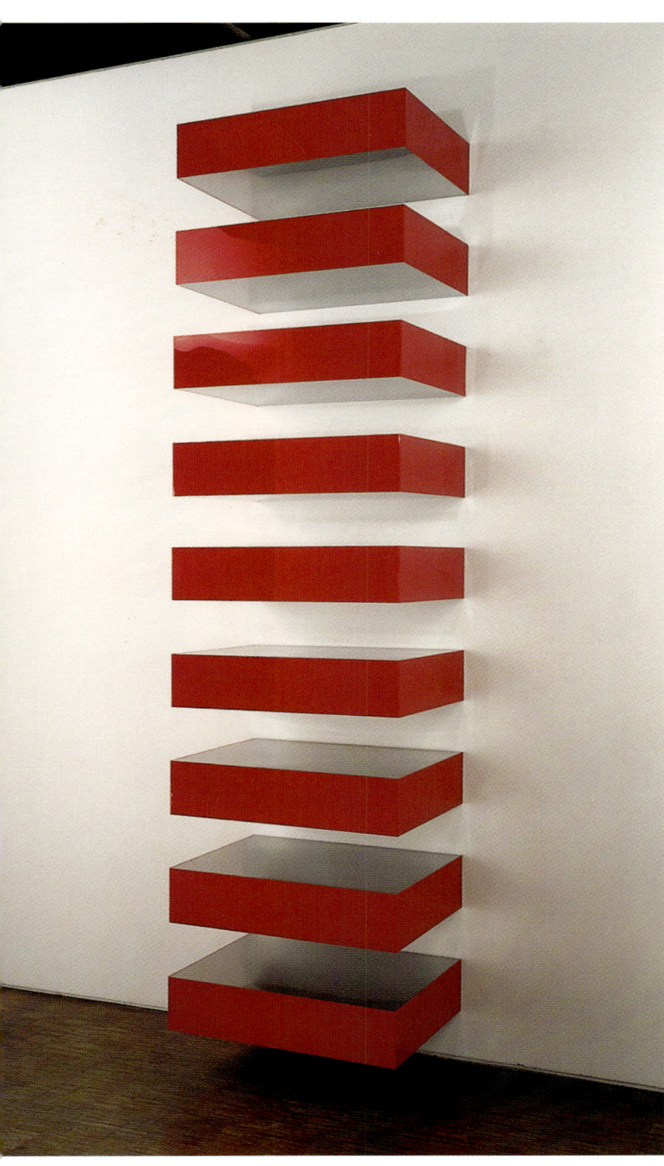

Donald Judd
Stack, 1972
Stainless steel, red Plexiglas. 470 x 102.5 x 79.2 cm - CP

Kore, Samos, c. 570-560 BC
Marble. H: 192 cm - ML

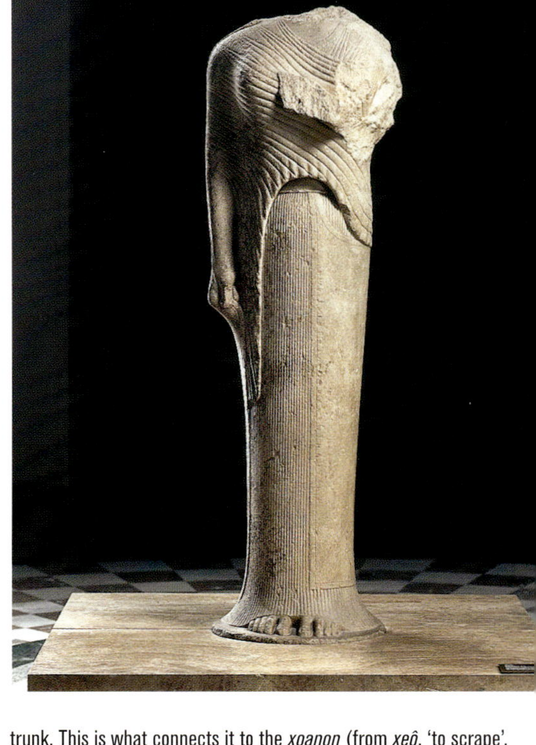

Stare. In Latin: to stand, to draw oneself up, like a tree or a stone being raised. An essential component of sculpture lies in asserting its presence by erection, projection and verticality. This is what Donald Judd's *Stack* makes apparent. A Jacob's ladder of sculpture, it alternates a series of enigmatic metal boxes and empty space of like dimensions. The work is more an object of thought, a principle of organisation, a measure of architectural space, than a material thing. The eye is borne aloft on a vertical structure seemingly constructed in collaboration with the void itself.

Antique *kore* too seem to stand firm, like trees. The cylindrical sheath into which the legs are inserted indeed resembles a tree trunk. This is what connects it to the *xoanon* (from *xeô*, 'to scrape', a word pertaining to the vocabulary of woodworking), the barely hewn beam that constituted the earliest form of Greek sculpture. Yet, beneath the fabric of the mantel, the sculptor has modelled the arm in a very adroit, realistic manner, prefiguring later, large-scale cult statues.

The monument to Balzac commissioned from Auguste Rodin by the Société des Gens de Lettres on Emile Zola's initiative makes one think instead of a menhir. Unveiled at the Salon of 1898, the star of an exhibit of works by Rodin at the Pavillon de l'Alma in 1900, the statue was rejected: the Société failed to see Balzac in it at all.

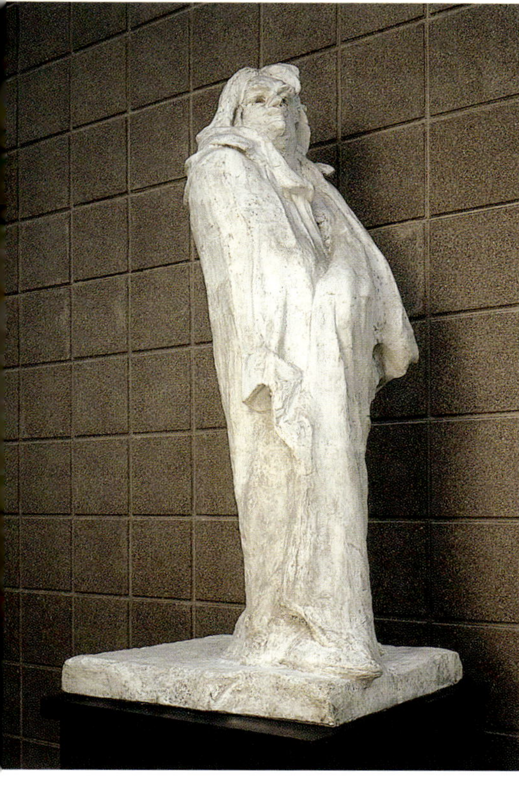

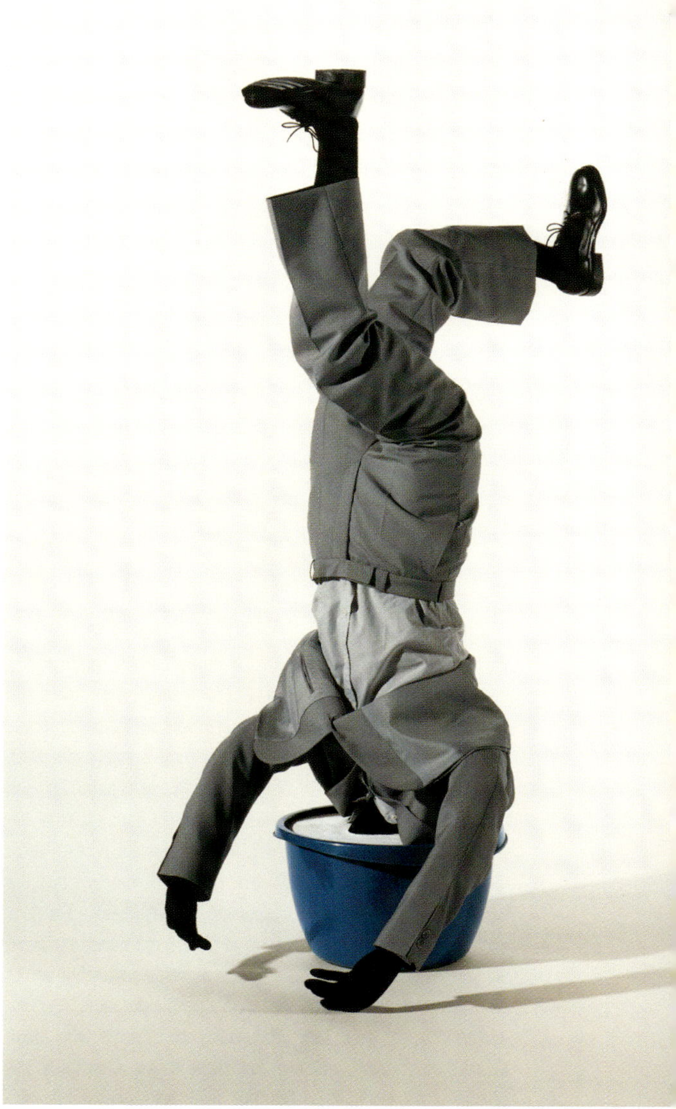

The sculptor, however, had researched his rendering meticulously, going as far as to travel to the Touraine where he found the dressing-gown the writer liked to don when writing — a kind of literary man's equivalent of the sculptor's apron. And this was the crucial thing: Rodin had broken with the conventional representation of the writer seated at his desk inspired by his muse or crowned by fame and instead depicted Balzac as artists often had been, casually, collar unbuttoned. The heroic nonchalance of the gown, physically incorporated into the plaster model, endows the figure with an imposing stature. His face? A mask. His garment? The coat of *The Human Comedy* replaces the Virgin's mantel that sheltered all humanity. The bronze was finally erected at the junction of rue Vavin and boulevard Raspail in Paris in 1939.

The inverted figure of Alain Séchas' *The Dummy* well translates the crisis of vertical sculpture in contemporary art. This switch, which brings to mind certain paintings by Baselitz where the figures are shown upside-down, reveals an artist who uses humour and who is not afraid of plunging his head into his art or, indeed, into the plaster!

Women standing

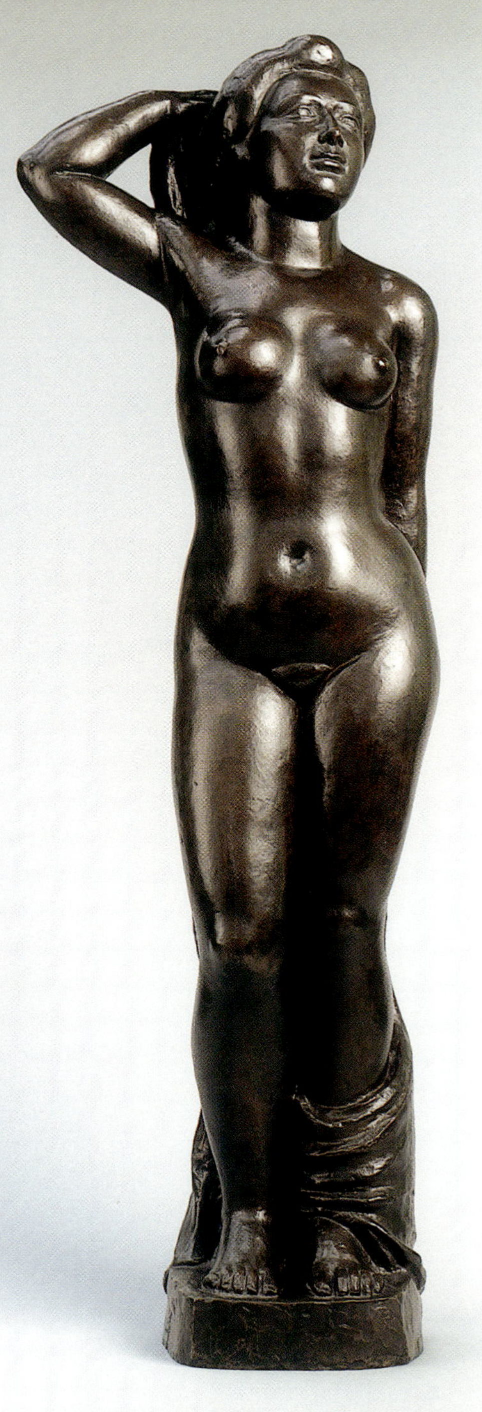

Only the knees and breasts jut out from the flat slab representing the body of *Nemi Aphrodite* draped in a long chiton. If certain details are brought out, such as the hair and the upturned shoes, the simplified overall form recalls that of some primitive idol. Such vertical stretching is surely explained by this *ex-voto* quality with magical overtones. The comparison that might be made with one of Alberto Giacometti's *Women of Venice* unveiled at the Venice Biennale is not, however, sufficient reason to conclude that the sculptor was influenced by Etruscan art. This lengthening and thinning, which became a key feature of his art, are better explained by Giacometti's desire to make figures of 'women standing' and of 'men walking' that could be seen from a certain distance. Their disproportionately large feet ('fabulously club-footed' was Jean Genet's description), which makes them appear even taller and slenderer, act as a built-in plinth that keeps the viewer at a respec-

ful distance. Thus, beholders feel the sculptures as a living presence, whereas were they to approach any closer, they would notice little more than the artist's fingerprints and the marks of the modelling knife.

By contrast, a *Bather* by Aristide Maillol, here based on the archetype of the Venus Genitrix, affirms the plenitude of a linear volume intended to take possession of the space. The sculptor declared that he always began with a figure engaged in a column, or in any case from a geometrical form, 'since these are the figures that best hold their own in a space.'

Giacometti's filiform figures, however, express a crisis in thought and representation. They seem to be losing ground before the advancing void. They resist, nevertheless, as if energised by the ordeal, like humanity struggling to its feet after the wars and upheavals of the 20th century.

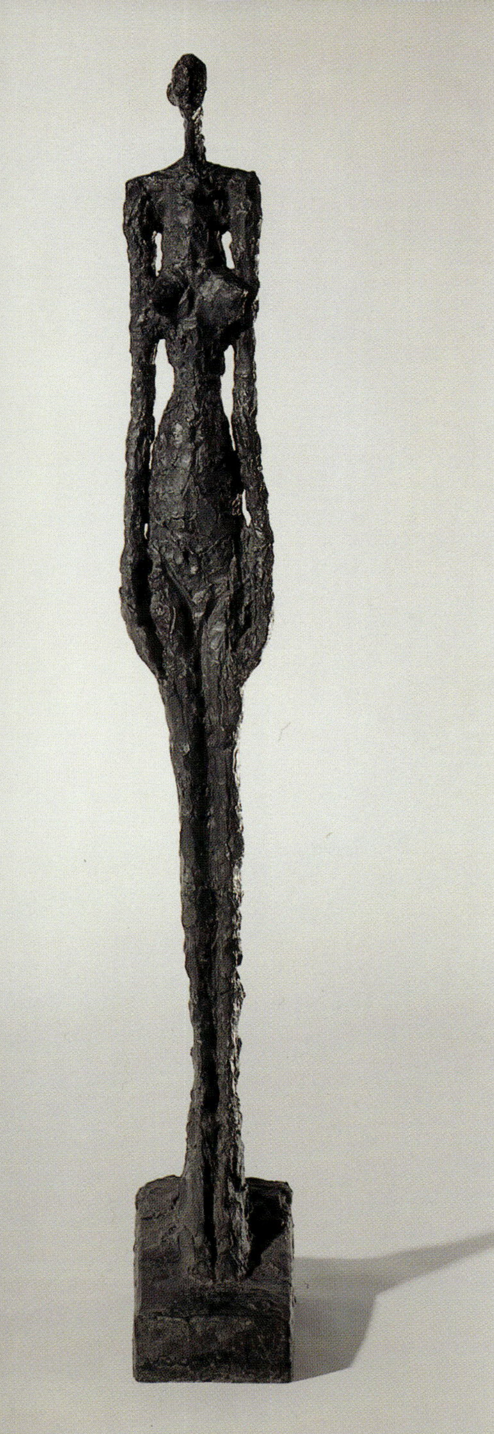

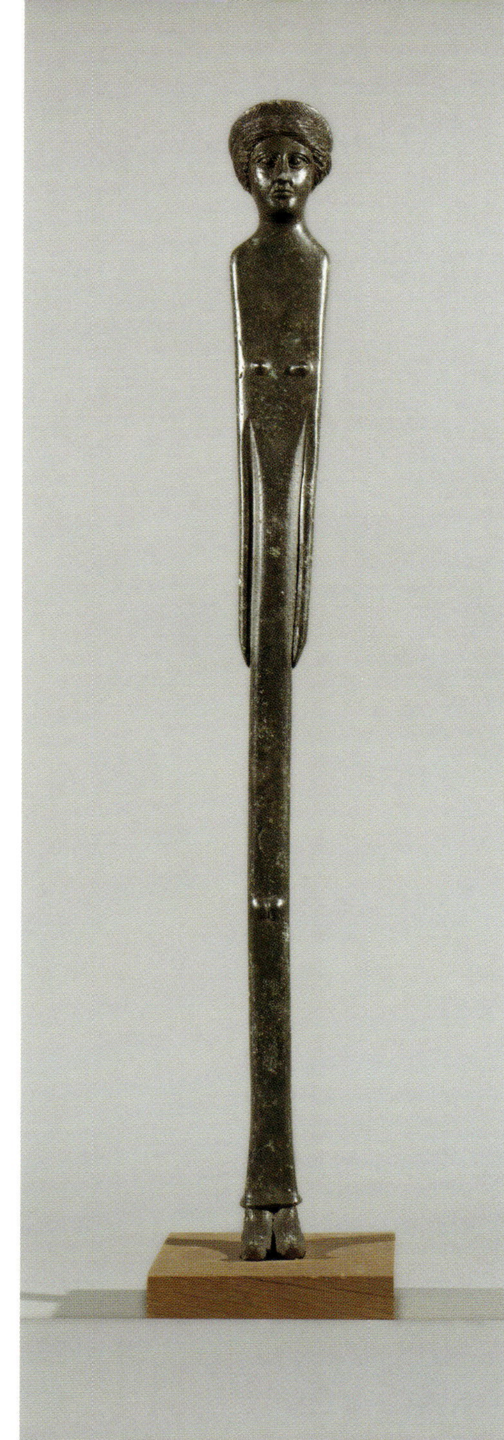

Aristide Maillol
Standing Bather, 1898-1900
Bronze. 78 x 25 x 15 cm - MO

Alberto Giacometti
Woman of Venice V, 1956
Bronze. 110.5 x 31.3 x 14 cm - CP

Nemi Aphrodite, Etruscan and Italiot art
4th century BC
Bronze. H: 50.5 cm - ML

The nude

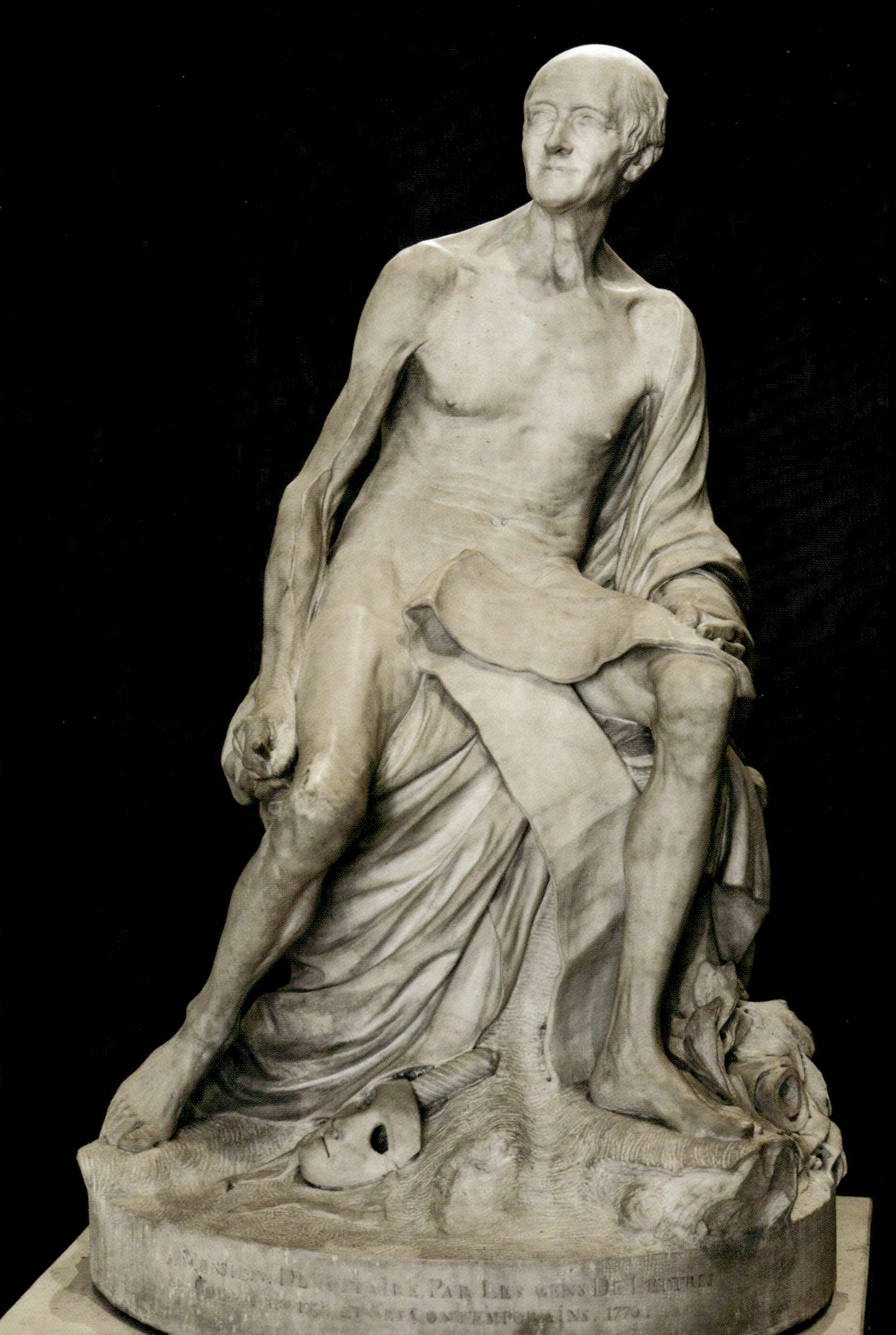

Jean-Baptiste Pigalle
Voltaire Nude, 1770-76
Marble. 150 x 89 x 77 cm - ML

Paul Gauguin
Nude Woman and Tree with Red Fruit, 1901
Right door jamb from the Maison du Jouir.
Polychrome giant sequoia wood. 159 x 40 x 2 cm - MO

André Derain
Standing Nude, 1907
Stone. 95 x 33 x 17 cm - CP

Whenever one refers to the nude in sculpture, one thinks naturally enough of beautiful young bodies, of which this book contains many examples. Carved by Paul Gauguin, this *vahine* by a tree bearing red fruit departs from such canons of beauty. The exposed body becomes a pretext for formal study and expressive distortion, as it would also in its treatment by the Fauves and Cubists.

When he came to carve his *Standing Nude*, a work that plainly heralds Cubism in its geometrical simplification of the volumes, and one that Isabelle Monod-Fontaine has rightly hailed as an 'essential historical milestone', André Derain harked back as much to Gauguin as to Cézanne.

But there was another nude, that of the elderly figure, which was to inspire many 19th-century sculptors, such as Jules Desbois, Camille Claudel and Rodin, who made it the subject of a number of *vanitas*. A century earlier, Jean-Baptiste Pigalle had confronted the public with his *Voltaire Nude*. As the great Enlightenment philosopher had written in his *Philosophical Dictionary*: 'It would be a fine thing to see one's soul.' Pigalle seems to have taken Voltaire at his word and laid it bare for all to see. It proved the most controversial sculpture of the 18th century, both because it depicted an old man unclothed and because, for the first time, a statue showed a living writer: Voltaire was 73 at the time. The latter didn't know what to make of it either, comforting himself with the wry observation: 'At least I will no longer inspire ladies with any indecorous thoughts.' Diderot, who was behind the original commission, had cherished the idea of an heroic nude in the manner of the *Dying Seneca* in the Borghese collection: 'What do you think a sculptor is to make of your jackets, your breeches, and your rows of buttons?' he thundered. There remains a handful of conventional attributes: Thalia's dagger (symbolising tragedy), Melpomene's mask (comedy), the lyre, and the poet's crown. But this aged body, posed for by a veteran of the Seven Years War, the face jotted down by the artist at Ferney as the philosopher refused to keep still, ought to be seen as an allegory of naked truth: exactly the one so passionately espoused by the writer, who defended Jean Calas, wrongfully condemned to death for the murder of his son.

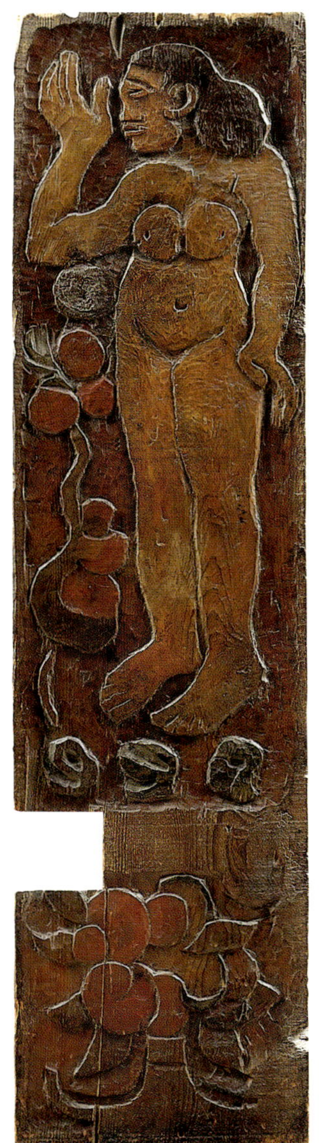

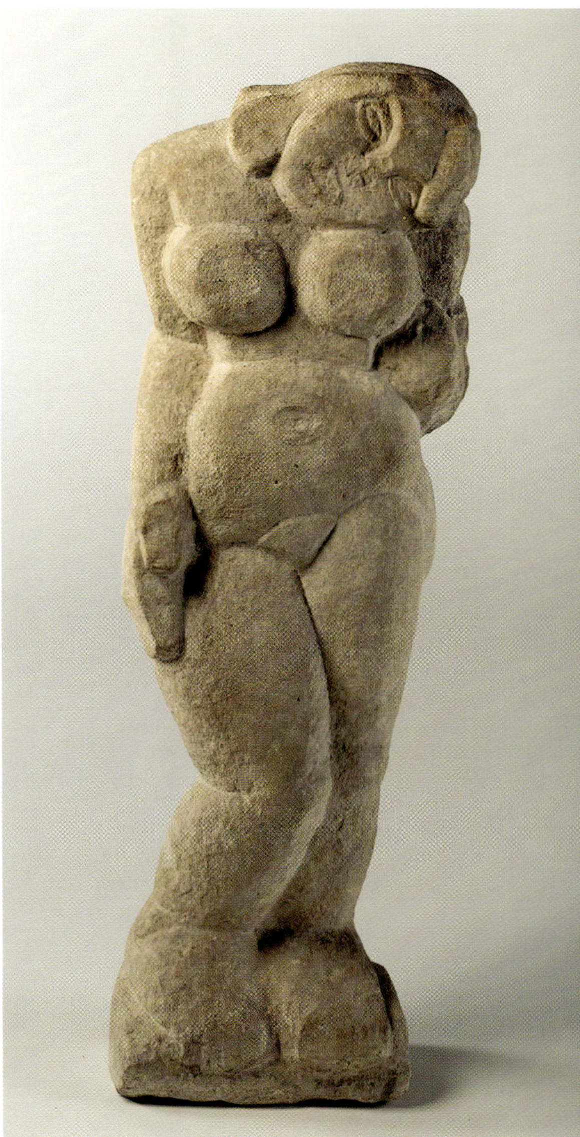

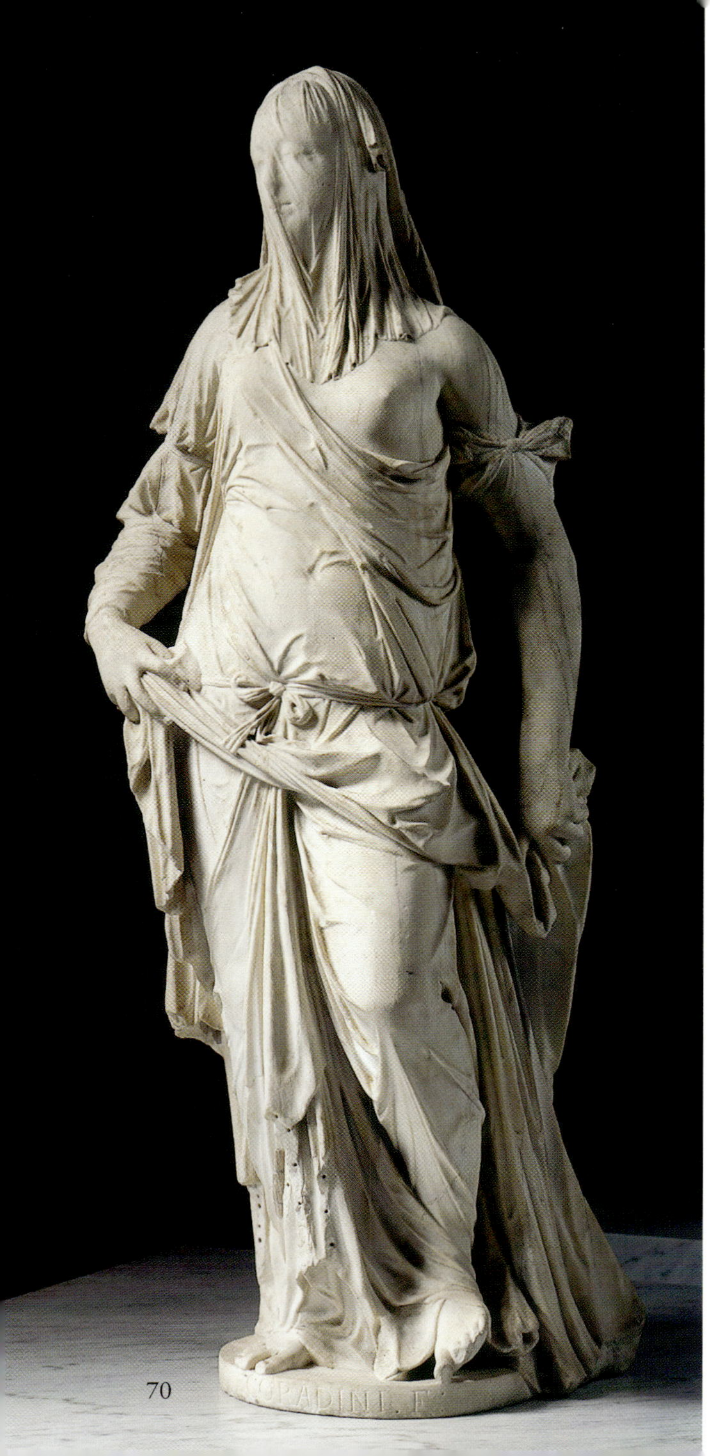

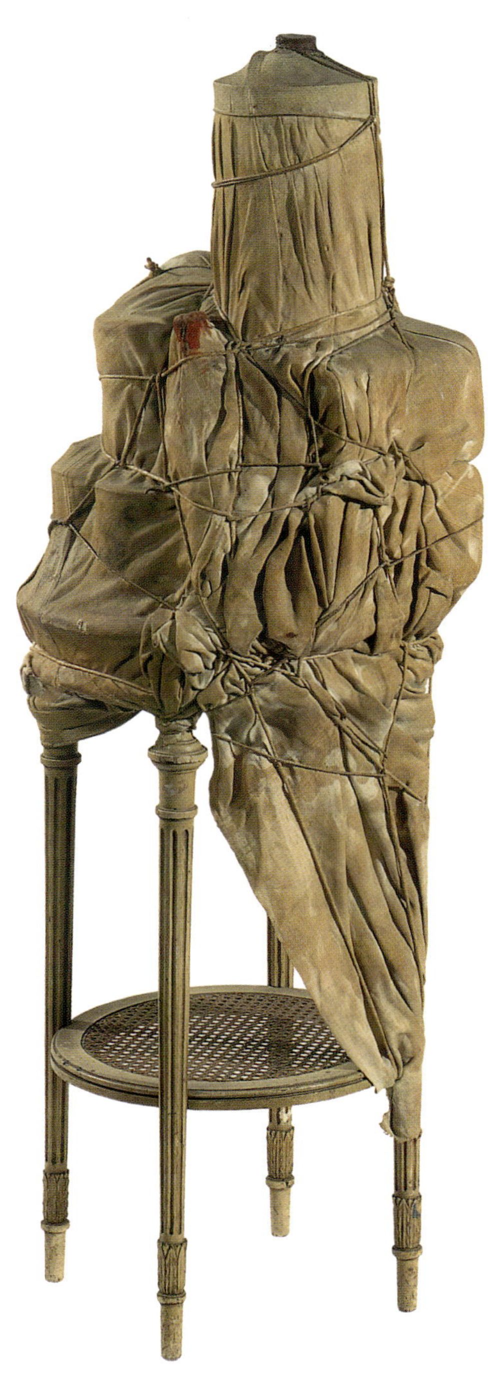

Veils

The veil as the skin of sculpture. Applied to the body or other objects, it at once dissimulates and reveals. Why does the Italian sculptor Antonio Corradini enwrap Faith in a veil? Like the Greek statue of Aidos, the incarnation of decency or propriety, which was, for that very reason, covered with a veil, Faith is chaste. One can divine the body beneath the veil, however, because Faith, like Truth, is naked. Similarly, in Titian's picture *Profane Love and Sacred Love*, it is the profane variety that sports the fashionable, worldly attire. Sacred love, the love that endures, is unclad. Nudity is thus a sign of truth and authenticity. It has to be conceded though that this is also a typically Baroque method of seduction. Corradini had besides made a speciality of these veils that expose more than they hide, starting with the figure of *Modesty* (after 1749), which stands next to the *Christ with the Shroud* by Sanmartino in the Sansevero chapel in Naples.

This process of veiling and unveiling reappears in the child sculpted by Medardo Rosso and in the table wrapped by the artist Christo. It was the unusual shape made by a child hiding in a curtain that inspired the bust Rosso entitled *Ecce Puer*: 'Behold the Child', in the same way as one says, *Ecce Homo*, 'Behold the Man.' It is like an apparition in which light plays over a cloth plastered over the face, blurring angles and contours alike.

In the same vein, the shapes of the objects wrapped by Christo evaporate, and other structures emerge from the crisscrossed ropes tied over the cloth, creating new volumes. For a time, one forgets the function of the objects: here they are, beautiful, useless — objects then of belief and emotion. To wrap a whole monument, as the artists Christo and Jeanne-Claude, did Paris's Pont-Neuf and the Reichstag in Berlin, brings out its basic lines, its essential volumes. It is difficult to know whether this is revelation or transfiguration; probably a little of both. Afterwards the transitory spectacle lets the building return to its humdrum existence, but its architecture is no longer the same for the passer-by, as if it has moulted and grown a fresh skin.

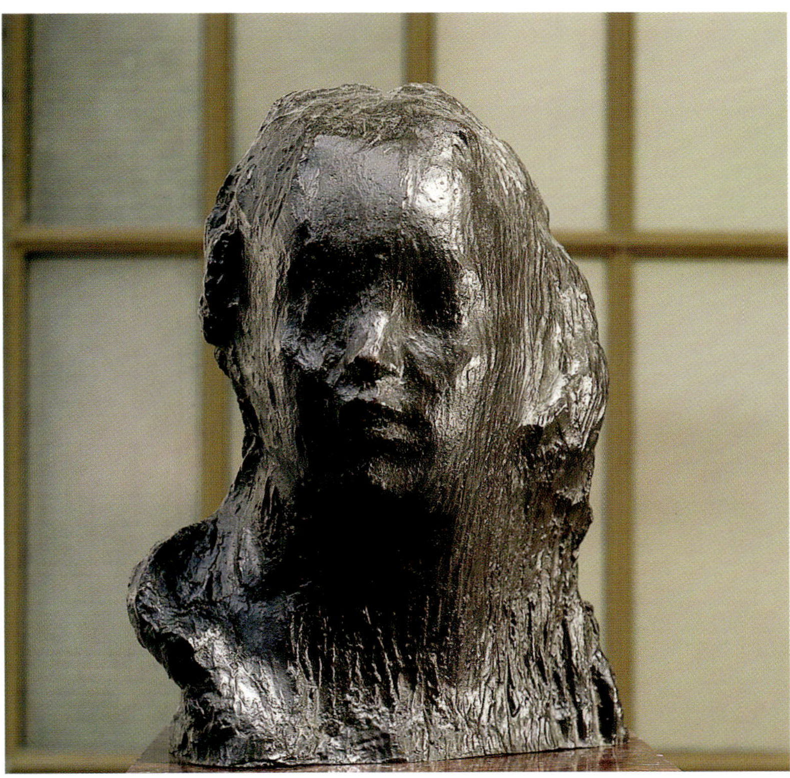

Antonio Corradini

Veiled Woman (Faith), **first half of the 18th century**

Marble. 138 x 48 x 36 cm - ML

Christo

Package on a Table, **1961**

Wood, various objects, velvet, canvas, string. 134.5 x 43.5 x 44.5 cm - CP

Medardo Rosso

Ecce Puer or *Behold the Child*, **1906**

Bronze. 44 x 37 x 27 cm - MO

Period dress

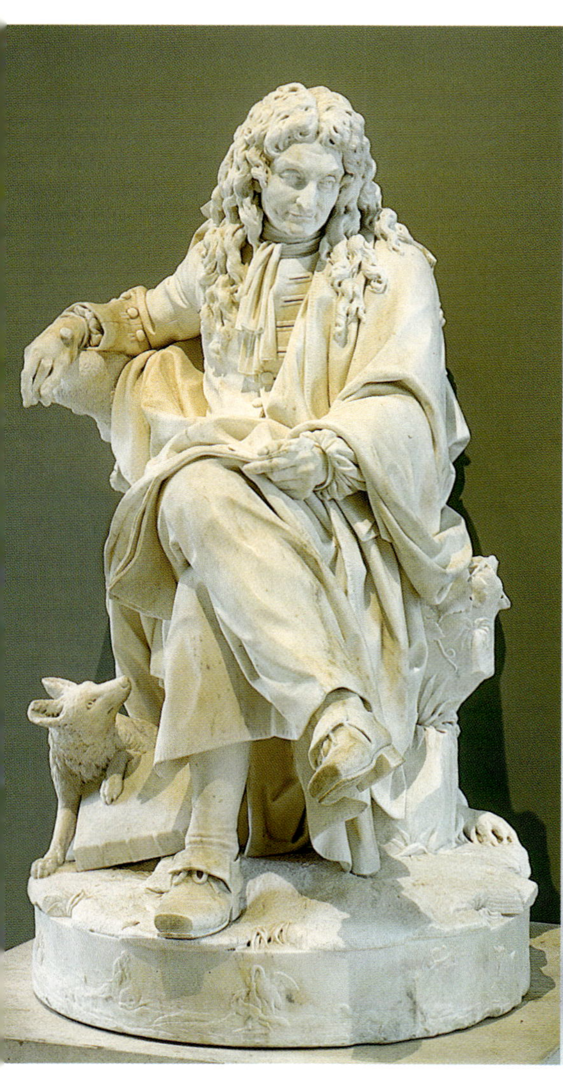

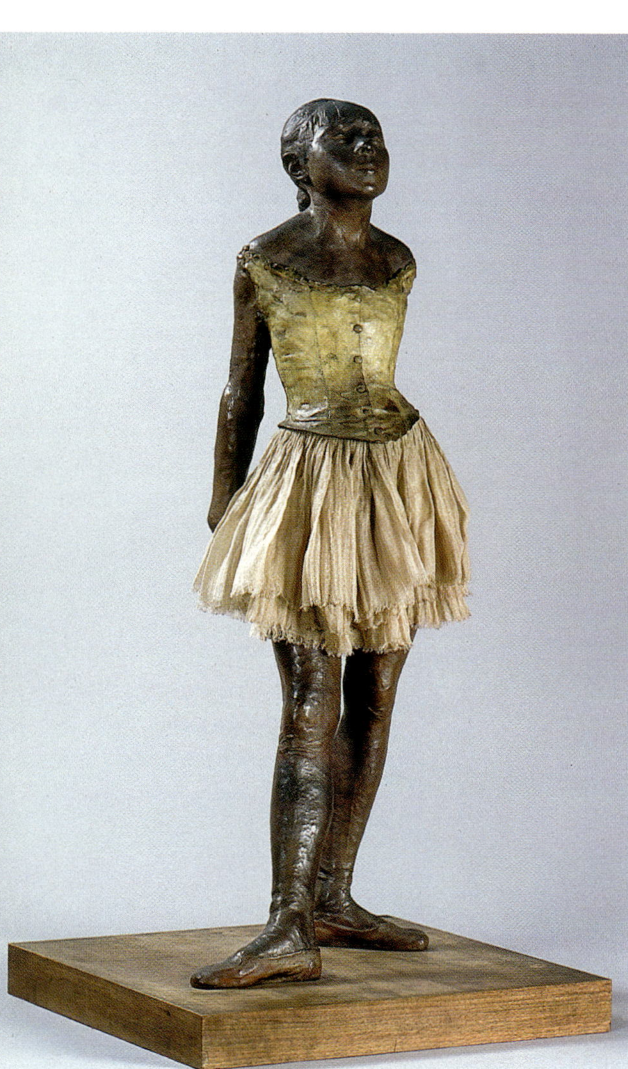

Pierre Julien

Jean de La Fontaine (1621-1695), **1785 Salon**
Marble. 173 x 110 x 129 cm - ML

Edgar Degas

Little Fourteen-Year-Old Dancer or *Large Dressed Dancer*, **1881**
Bronze patinated in various tints, tulle, satin ribbon. 90 x 35 x 24 cm - MO

Etienne-Martin

Coat (Dwelling 5), **1962**
Fabric, trimmings, rope, leather, metal, tarpaulin
250 x 230 x 75 cm - CP

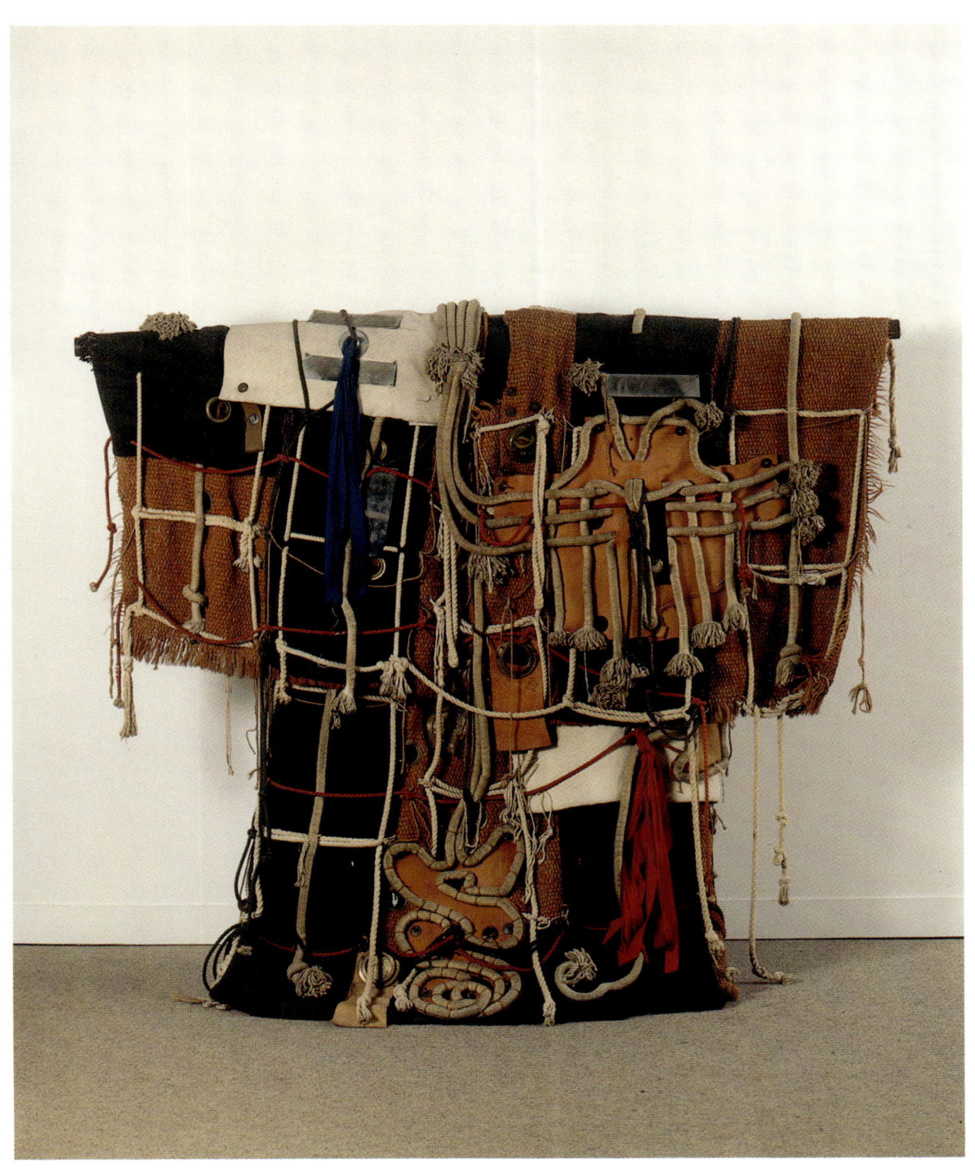

To dress *The Little Fourteen-Year-Old Dancer* in a real tutu, to tie a pink ribbon in her hair, might seem rather fetishistic of Edgar Degas. But before him, Spanish masters had dressed their statues. Anne Pingeot underlines the ground-breaking character of the work: 'It could find a place in various chapters entitled, for instance, "assemblage", "the polychrome" or "realism". It is a benchmark, heralding the introduction of the object into sculpture.' But to consider it in this manner should not obscure the impact of the figure's pose: the dancer hails the public arrayed before her like a toreador launches a challenge to the bull. Her one-night bullfighter's costume and her shop-new cape might one day become the trappings of a streetwalker, since at that period many showgirls, lowborn in general, descended the slippery slope into prostitution.

The frock-coat and overcoat worn by La Fontaine smell of his time, the era of Louis XIV. They too are an element of realism. Etienne-Martin's coat is, on the contrary, quasi-mythological attire, cobbled together from string, fabric, glass and odds and ends, like a home-made wendy house, but also like a costume for an opera.

D'Angiviller, Superintendent of the King's Works, who in 1775 ordered a series of statues commemorating the 'great men of France' to which Pierre Julien's *La Fontaine* forms a part, had stipulated that they all appear in the costume of the time, and not draped 'in the antique manner'. The only exception for the series was to be Poussin, who looks as if he'd been dragged out of bed by the force of his inspiration. Julien represents the fabulist in his finery, in the act of writing a story featuring the fox, the sly-boots who also appears in the little incidents on the plinth.

Etienne-Martin's *Coat* belongs to the series of *Demeures* (residences or living spaces). These are walk-in sculptures, or at least the eye can pay them a flying visit. They refer in plan and layout to the artist's childhood home in Loriol-sur-Drôme. The *Coat* too is a place: whoever puts it on immediately provides it with an axis. Worn by the artist, it is not unlike the poncho of a mountain dweller in the Andes or the garb worn by a Caucasian peasant chief. But, for the sculptor, it is above all the protecting dress of a mother.

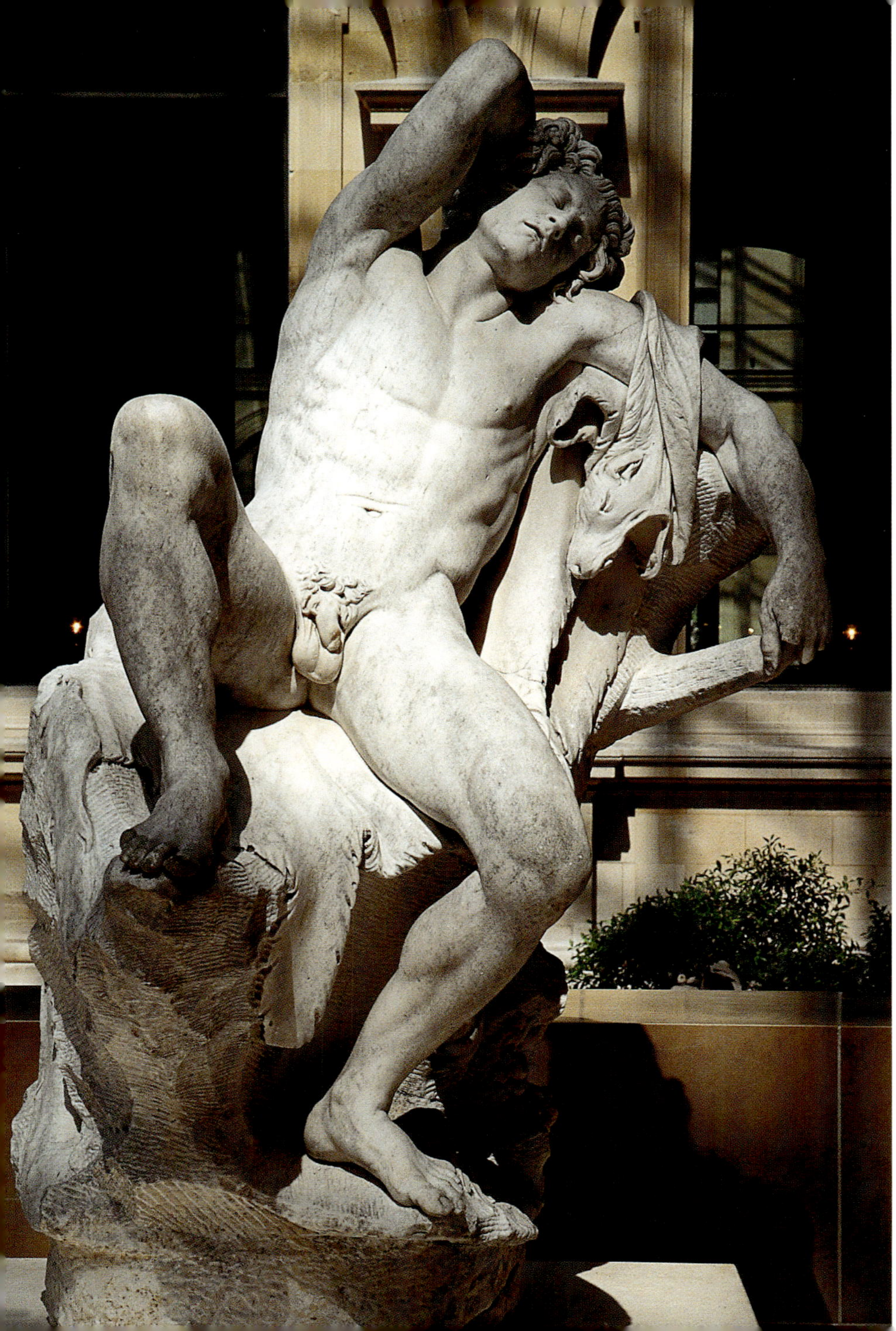

At rest

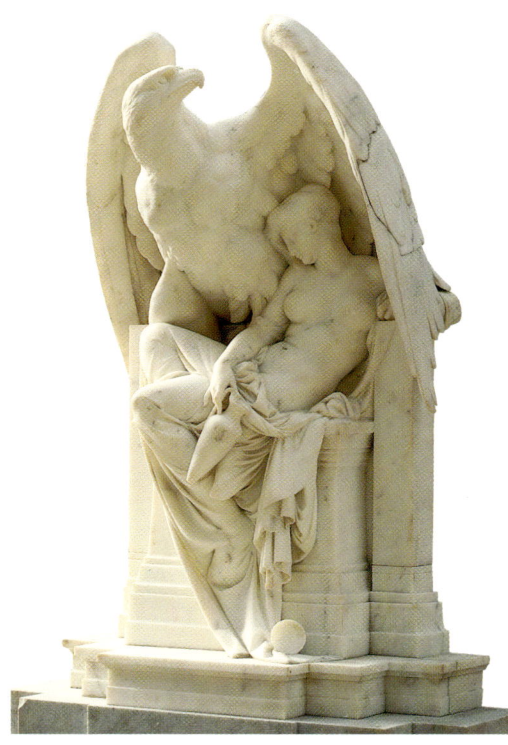

Languid, like Michelangelo's *Dying Slave* or one of Canova's funerary geniuses, Edmé Bouchardon's *Sleeping Faun* exhibits his genitals with no fig-leaf to conceal them. This was permitted by the example of the ancient model since Bouchardon's is an admirable reinterpretation of the *Barberini Faun*, today in Munich. Winckelmann described the original as follows: 'It is not ideally beautiful, but a naive image of unadorned nature left to itself.'

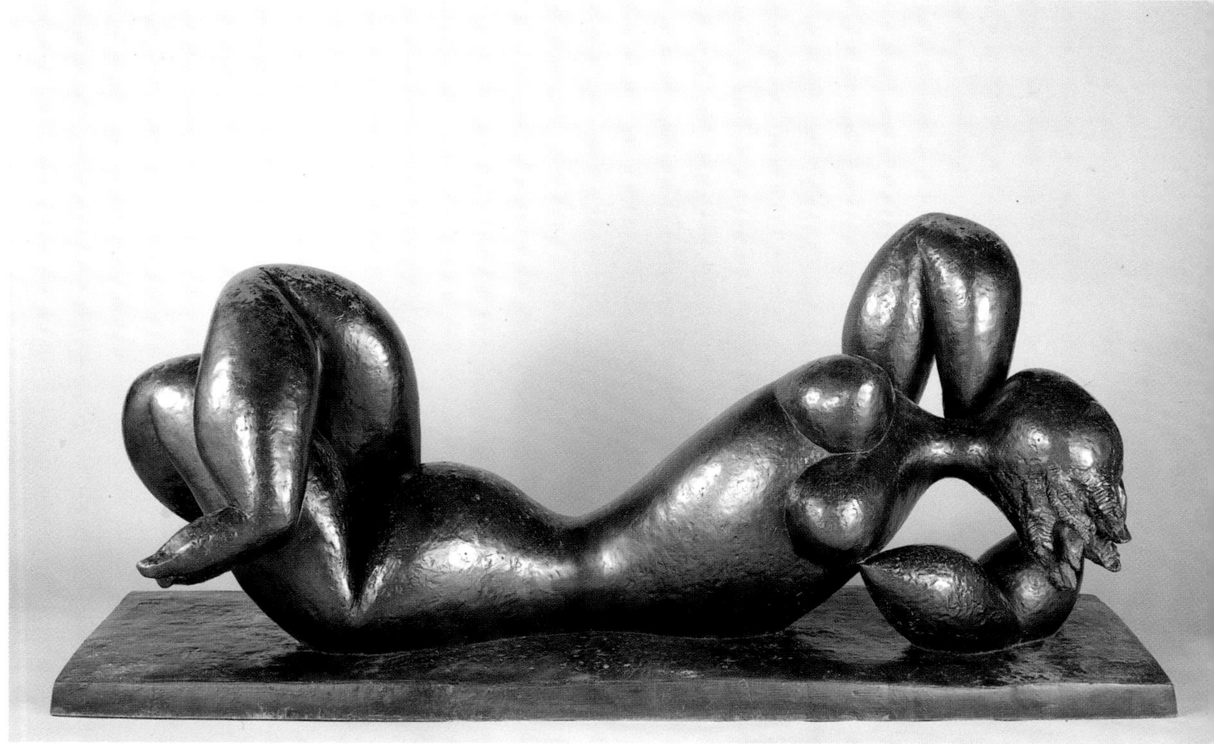

Closer to our time, Dominique Fernandez sees it as a 'virile pendant to Bernini's *St Teresa*.'
The long stretched-out pose also suits *Autumn*, the season of fruitfulness in which plant growth gradually slows down. Henri Laurens returns to the tradition of the limber nudes of the School of Fontainebleau. He gives the reclining figure a rhythmic undulating form in a virtuoso composition.

In the *Hebe* made in 1869 by Rodin's master Carrier-Belleuse, the world of the dream joins forces with an intimation of history. This woman, fast asleep beneath the wing of an immense bird of prey, stands for France slumbering under the imperial eagle. The very next year, she was to be rudely awoken with the defeat of Napoleon III by the Prussians at Sedan that brought down the Second Empire and ushered in the Commune. But quite beyond the almost incidental echoes of French history, the sculpture is stunningly erotic in itself, with its suggestive intimacy between flesh and feather, between woman and beast.

In motion

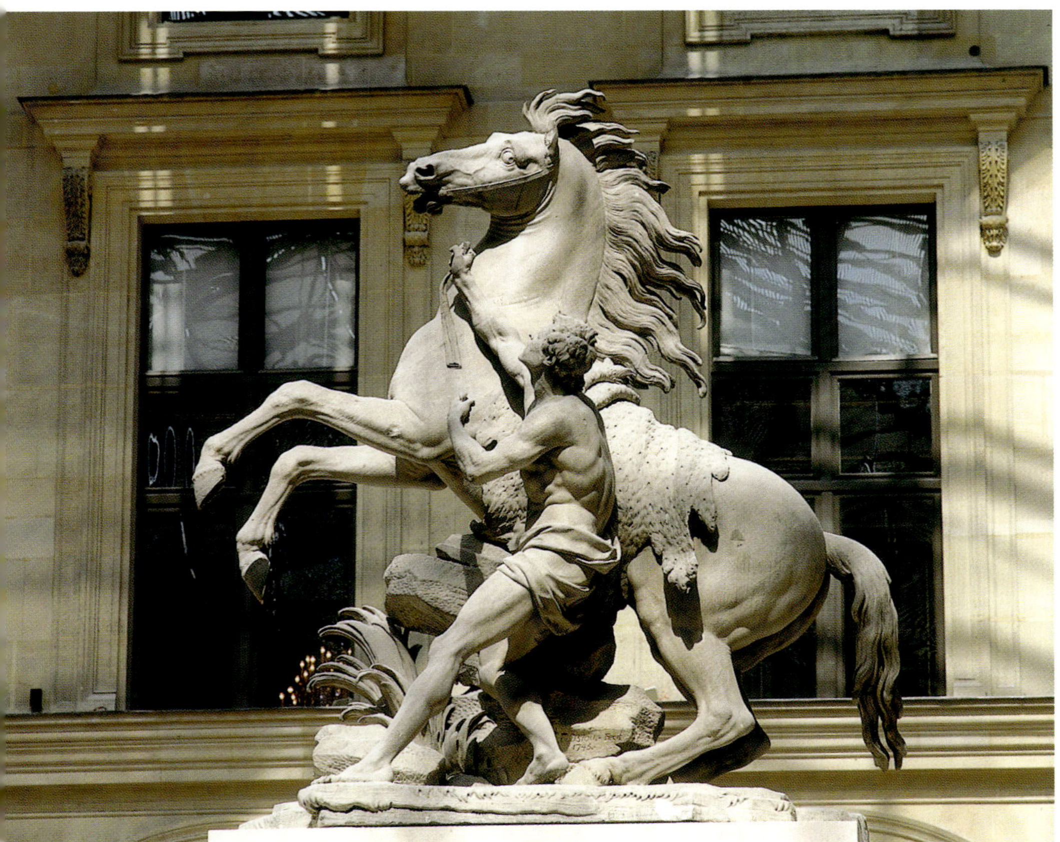

The movement that Guillaume Coustou the Elder studies in his *Horse Restrained by a Groom* is twofold: the onward dash of the horse who, pulled back, can only rear up; the more complex movement of the man, whose arms react to the traction, while his arched legs brace him against it. Two opposing lines: a convex one for the horse and a concave one for the groom. Two movements clash: one forwards and upwards, the other backwards and downwards. It is interesting to observe that, when the sculpture is viewed from the rear, the horse obscures the man completely: the sculptor seems to be toying with the beholder's point of view. Together with a companion piece, the horse was initially set up at the Château de Marly, then at the entrance to the Champs-Elysées (where there is still a copy), before finally being placed at the Louvre in the Cour Marly. The triumph of man over animal, of intelligence over instinct, does not completely mask the spectacular expression of savagery. The painter Géricault recalled these Marly horses in his famous picture of the *Wounded Cuirassier Leaving the Field of Battle* (1814).

Auguste Rodin was one of the very first to treat man as a being essentially in motion: movement does not have to bring about any particular action, as in the Coustou, except that of walking. Rodin himself compared his *Walking Man* to a temple. The legs would be the columns and the imposing chest, derived from that of Miletos (p. 82), the entablature and pediment. But it is a 'temple that walks'. This obliteration of the parts less concerned with movement, such as the head or the arms, was to resurface in Umberto Boccioni's Futurist sculpture, *Unique Forms in the Continuity of Space*.

However, it was Alberto Giacometti, whose work is in constant dialogue with Rodin, who was to situate motion in an urban space. If this woman making her way between two houses resembles a bearer of an offering in an Egyptian funerary model, if she moves as in a game, on a white square between two black ones, the direction she faces is, nevertheless, fixed. She can be seen only side-on, or conceivably from above, as if propelled along a specific trajectory.

Guillaume Coustou the Elder
Horse Restrained by a Groom, or *Cheval de Marly*, **1739-45**
Carrara marble. 340 x 284 x 127 cm - ML

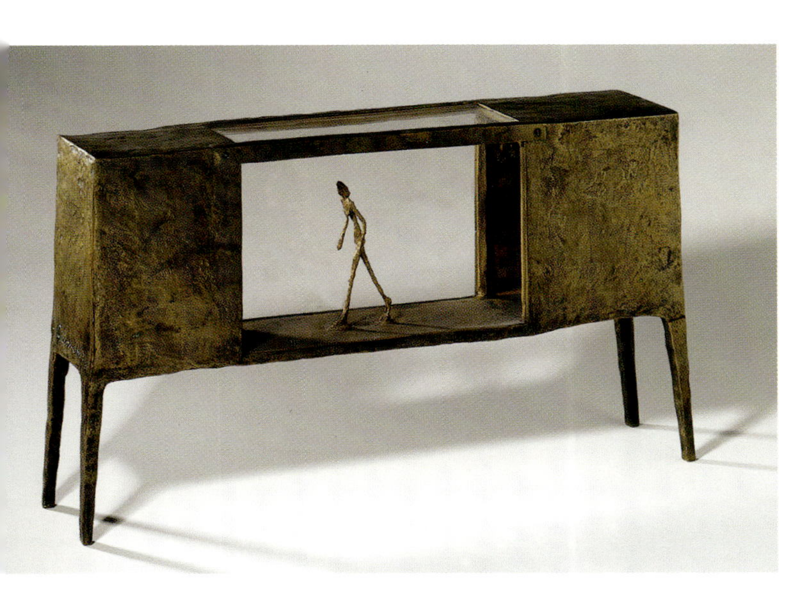

Alberto Giacometti

Figurine in a Box between Two Houses, 1950

Painted bronze. 29.5 x 53.5 x 9.4 cm - CP

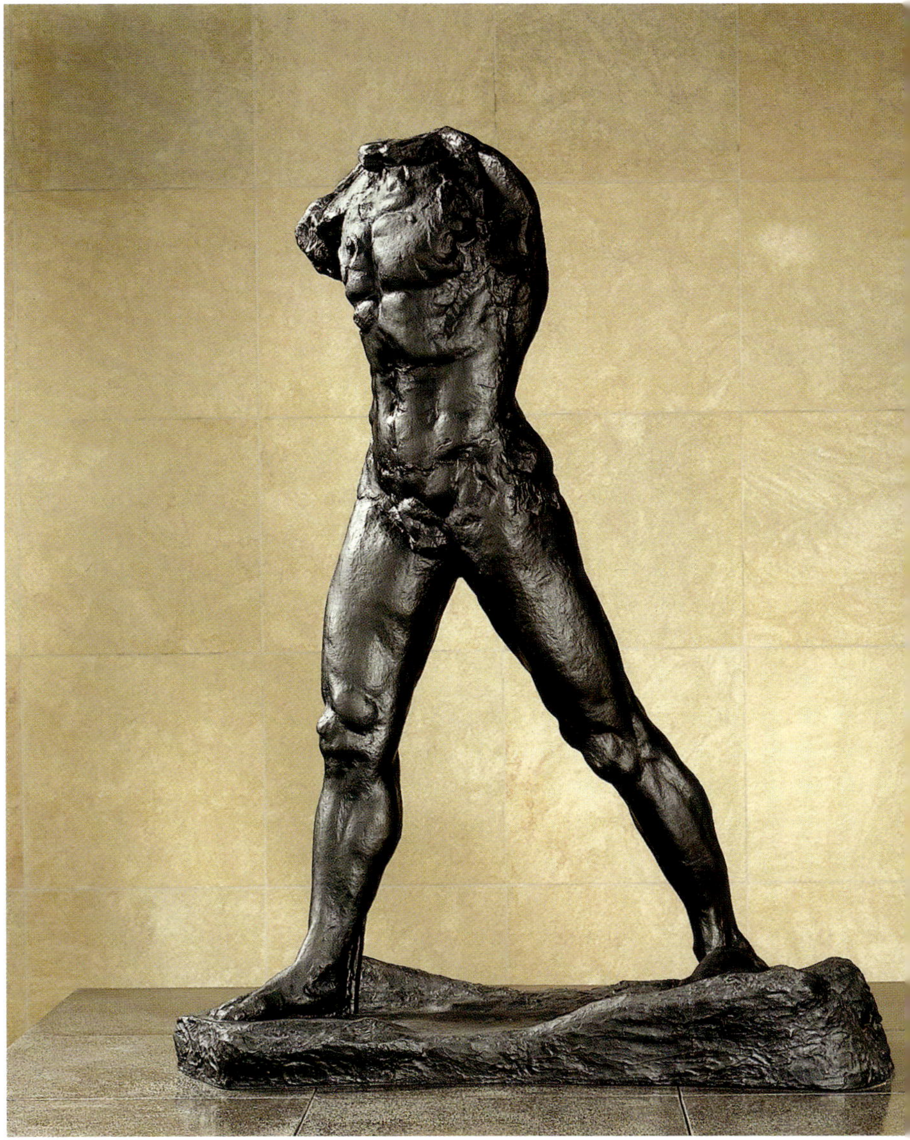

Auguste Rodin

Walking Man, 1905

Bronze. 213 x 161 x 72 cm - MO

Serpentine line

Why did photographer Man Ray regard the spiral entitled *Lampshade* as his 'contribution as a sculptor'? Agreeable to look at, the spiral, suspended like a mobile, a genuine light trap, patently had its parallels in sculpture. With her leg strongly projecting beneath the drapery, the belly drawn in as 'broad as the sea', as Rodin finely put it, and the gyration of the upper part, the *Venus de Milo* herself describes a harmonious spiral. The incomparable torsion of her body is surely explained by the fact that Venus had just been embracing Ares, god of war, with whom, before time pulled them asunder, she had formed a group. The motion the artist has impressed upon the *Venus de Milo*, and which recurs in many Greek statues (right shoulder and left leg thrust forward, left shoulder pulled back, and the body resting on the right leg), results in a slightly projecting hip. In contrapposto, the sculptors of the Italian Quattrocento, who could not have known the Venus (she was unearthed only in 1820), accentuated this opposition between upper and lower parts of the body, turning it into a principle of composition. In their wake, more precisely in that of Donatello, Antonin Mercié, who along with Paul Dubois belonged to a group of Frenchmen who so admired Florentine art that they were dubbed the 'Florentins', treats the theme of *David*, famously taken up in the Tuscan capital itself by Donatello and Michelangelo, as a youthfully muscled figure in dynamic *contrapposto*. The act of sheathing the sword situates Mercié's figure some way between François Rude's sculpture of Maréchal Ney wielding his blade and Donatello's *David*, where it is stuck in the ground, and adds still more to the impression of a serpentine line. Was Mercié perhaps thinking of the *Venus de Milo*? The advancing leg does appear to be a variation of the same movement.

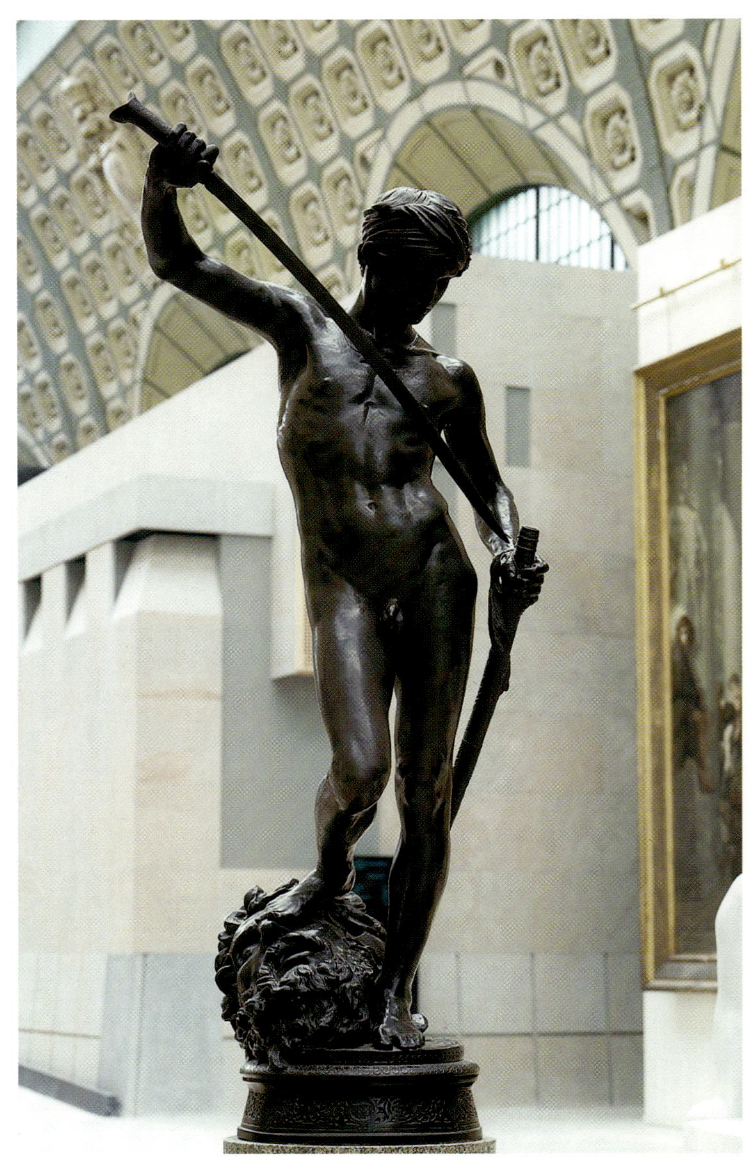

Antonin Mercié
David, 1869-70/1873
Bronze. 184 x 76 x 83 cm - MO

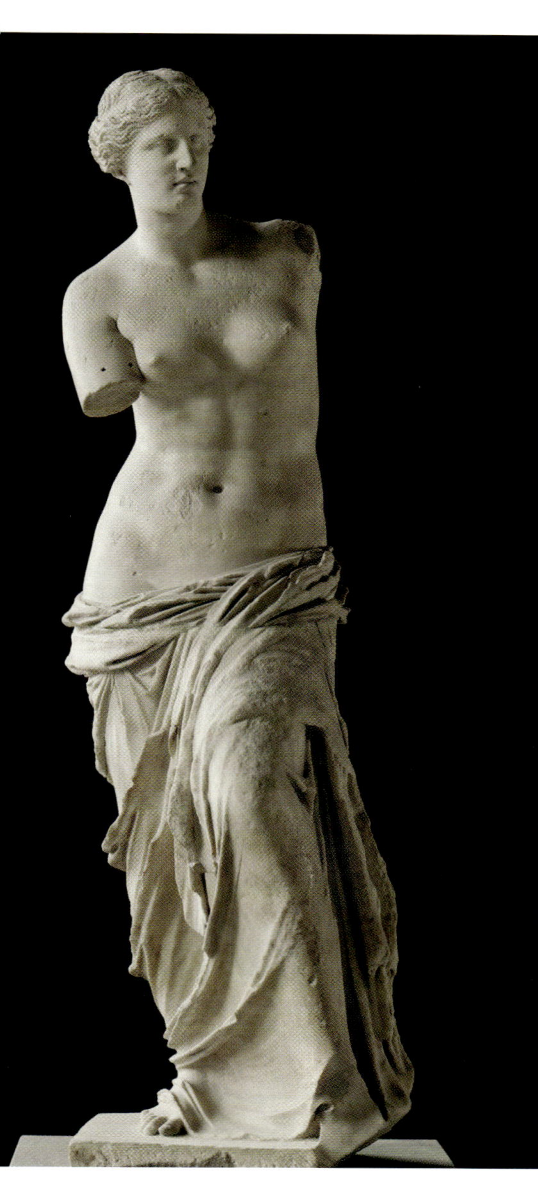

Aphrodite, known as the *Venus de Milo*
Island of Melos (Greece), c. 100 BC.
Marble. 202 x 63 x 64 cm - ML

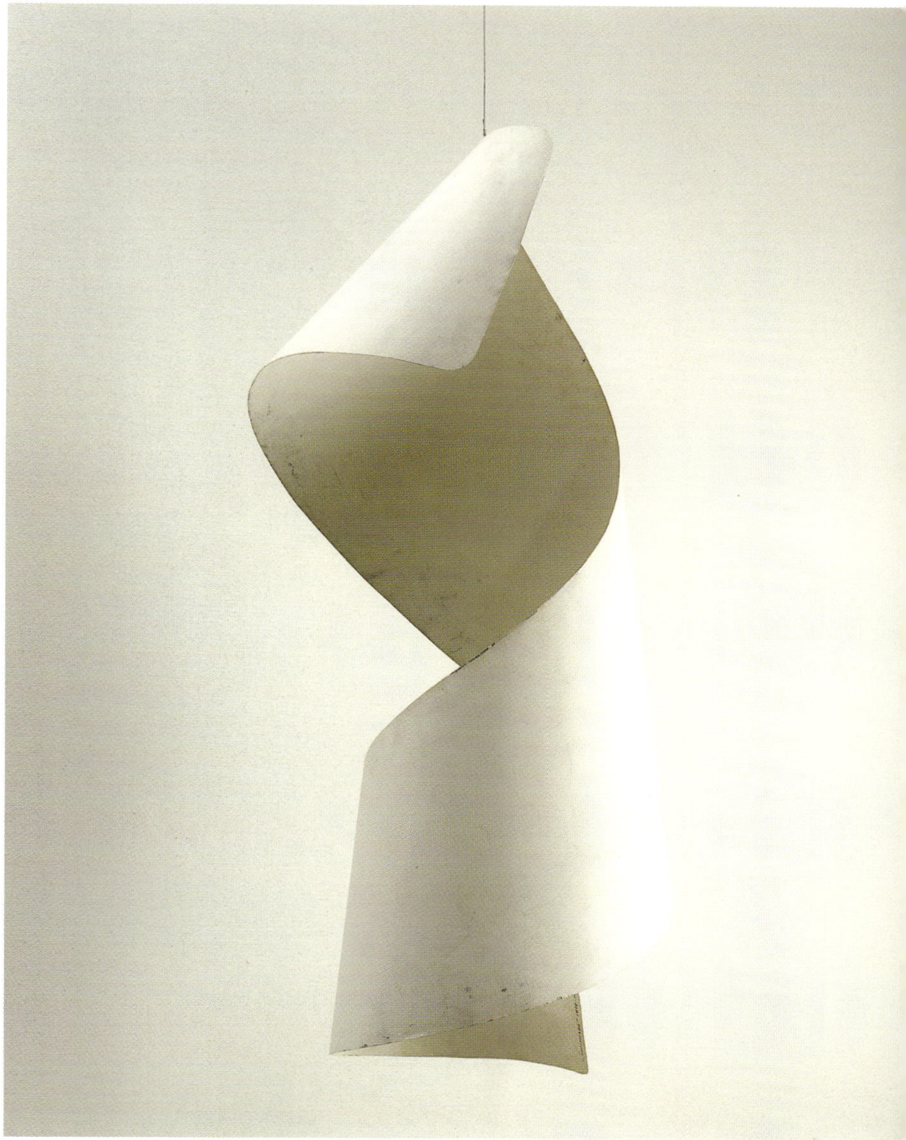

Man Ray
Lampshade, 1919 (original), 1954 (current edition)
Painted aluminium. 152.5 x 63.5 cm - CP

Gestures

First of all, comes the heroic gesture, that of combat, as in the *Borghese Gladiator* carved by Agasias of Ephesus in around 100 BC, discovered in pieces south of Rome in about 1610, and reconstituted by the Borgheses' sculptor, Nicolas Cordier, known as Il Franciosino. A main line traversed by a powerful diagonal, the arms crossing the axis perpendicularly, it was called an 'anatomical marvel' by Théophile Gautier. A model for sculptors, it was abundantly commented on and diversely interpreted, though no-one sees it any longer as a gladiator. Is it some heroic warrior confronting a horseman towering over him, perhaps an Amazon? Is this Alexander, Achilles, maybe? Many have been reminded of the spirit of the great decorations at Pergamon or of the School of Lysippus of Sicyon (4th century BC).

Then comes the gesture of work, as conjured up by the Republican sculptor Aimé-Jules Dalou, a Socialist exiled under the Empire to whom we owe *The Triumph of the Nation*. Dalou's project had been to carve a monument to work, but he only managed to carry out the figure of the *Large Peasant*. This is not a labourer engaged in his toil; he is caught instead just as he rolls up his sleeves, and gazes down at the soil he is about to till, a secular counterpart to Millet's *Angelus*. Unless of course the positions of the hands and his bowed head are meant to evoke the attitude of a prisoner, like that of the *Captive Barbarian* that Dalou could see in the Louvre, thus introducing an undercurrent of social protest.

Lastly comes the gesture of the sculptor. César's is enduringly present, petrified in an *Expansion*, like Pompeii under the volcano's dust-cloud. A cast: '*Expansions* are traditional sculpture,' the artist claimed. 'I can control the way it's poured, and, by hand or body, accentuate the folds…' And it is true that, if at the outset the *Expansion*s played as performances from which pieces were removed, the *Expansion*s became sculptures the moment the movement, the pleating, became fixed under the successive coats of vinyl covering the expanded polyurethane cast.

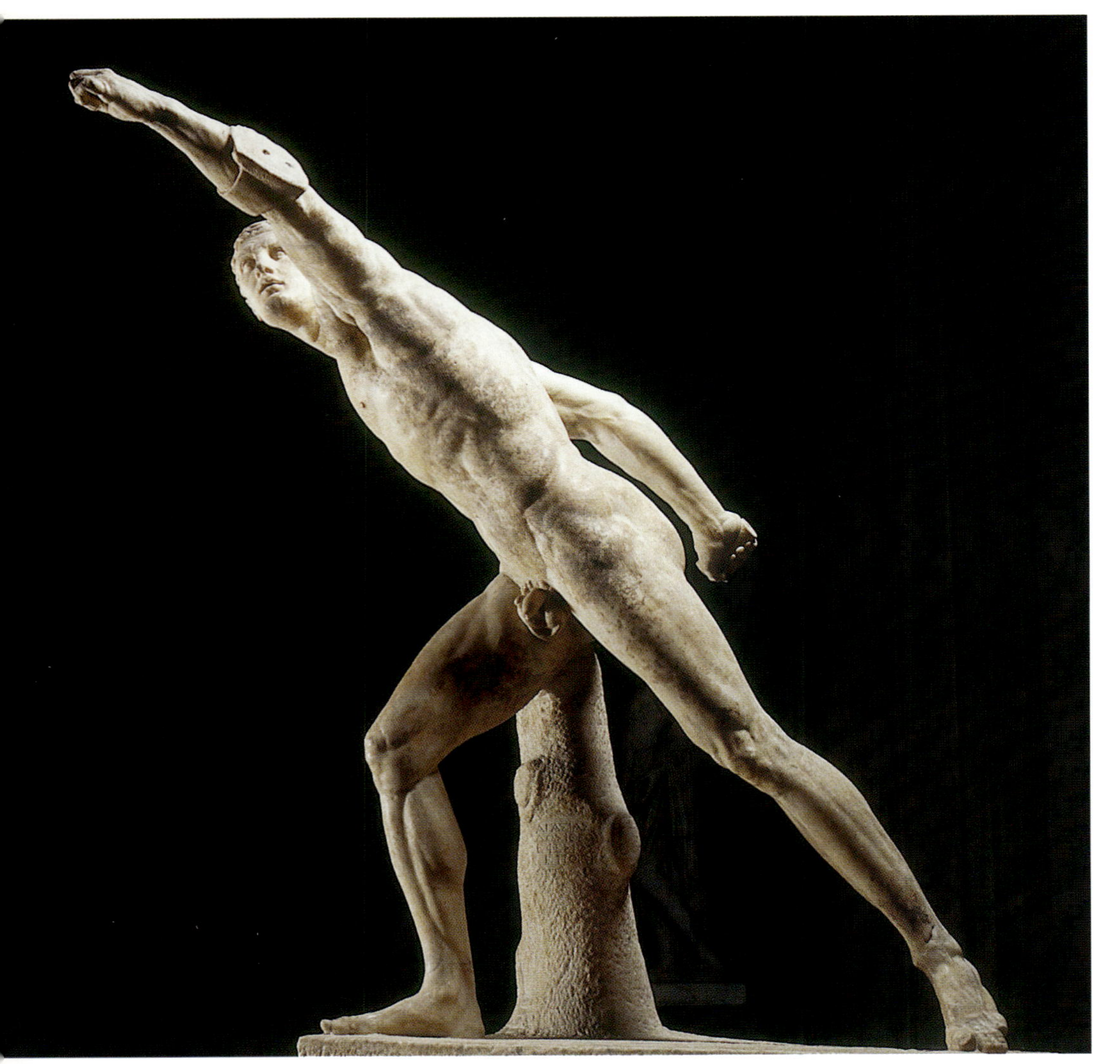

The Borghese Gladiator, Italy, c. 100 BC
Marble. H: 199 cm - ML

Aimé-Jules Dalou
Large Peasant, 1898-1902
Bronze. 197 x 70 x 68 cm - MO

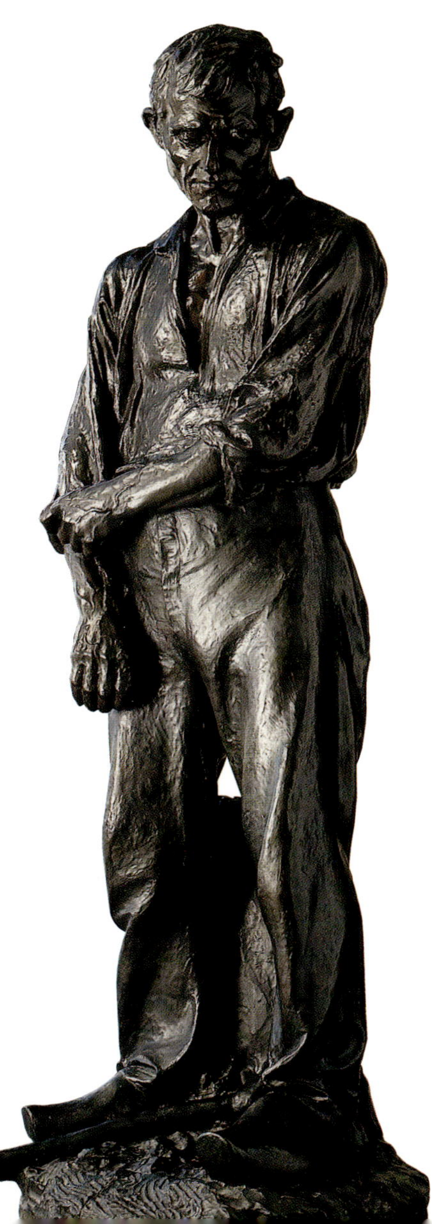

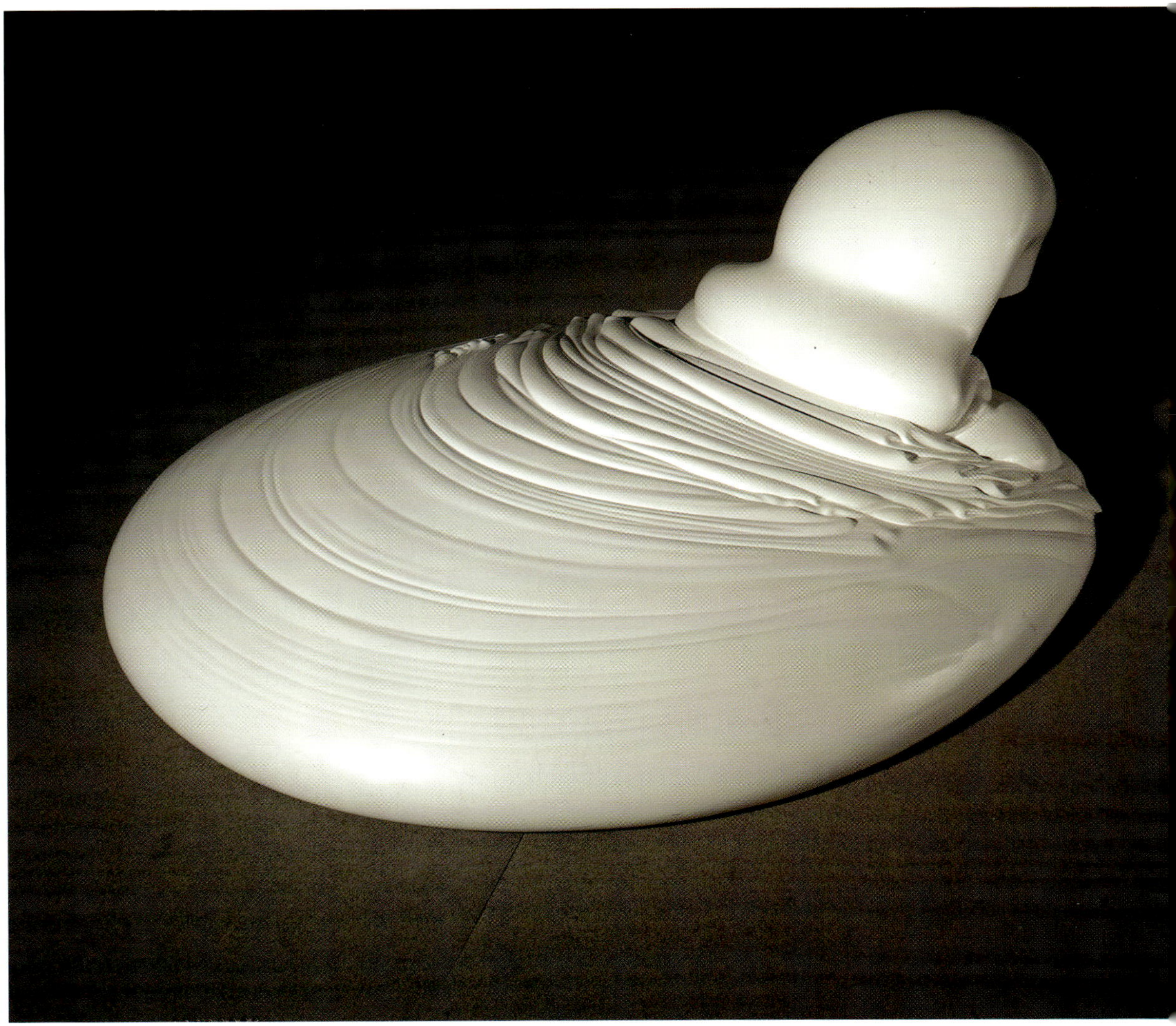

César

Expansion No. 14, 1970

Expanded polyurethane, laminated and varnished. 100 x 270 x 220 cm - CP

Torso

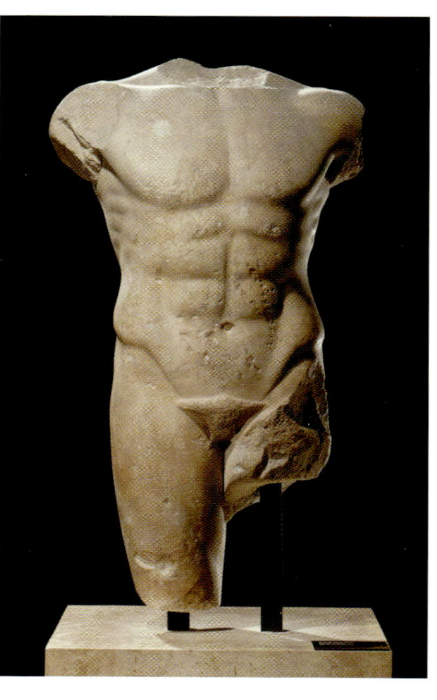

Long after their discovery, torsos, vestiges of Antique art, would often be subjected to additions. As we have seen, the limbs and heads affixed by Bernini and Cordier are such masterpieces that today it would be barbaric to 'un-restore' them. From the 19th century on, our way of seeing has changed, and the torso is regarded, in a manner of speaking, as a 'complete fragment'. Besides, at that time new torsos were being hewn that were not just studies: think of Rodin, who derived such aesthetic mileage from the fragmentation and mutilation of Antique torsos. In the sweep of the back and the rendering of the pubic area, the *Torso of Miletos* remains conventional and close to the initial block. Rilke had it that this *kouros*, by its sense of proportion and of modelling that goes well beyond mere design, 'shone out like a candelabrum' (1908).

The torso continued to attract artists in the 20th century. That of Aristide Maillol's *Youth* reflects the inspiration of Greece, which the artist had visited thanks to the good offices of his patron, Count Kessler: the lines and proportions are in keeping with one of those 'tranquil artists' (according to André Gide's expression) who reinvented classicism. A member of the Rodin stable, Eugène Dodeigne treats the torso as a *cosmos* in which form is born from a magma-like chaos of energies.

Yves Klein co-opts the accepted schema of the torso so as to transcend realism. The portrait of Arman, moulded over the artist's body, is impregnated with the famous 'Klein blue', emerging from a golden ground redolent of the gilded mosaics on Byzantine cupolas emblazoned with the Christ Pantocrator. Klein's intention was to compose a sculpture gallery of portraits of his friends, Arman, Martial Raysse and Claude Pascal, placing his own image in the centre, this time gold on a blue ground.

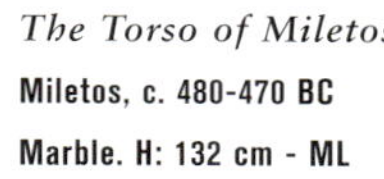

The Torso of Miletos
Miletos, c. 480-470 **BC**
Marble. H: 132 cm - ML

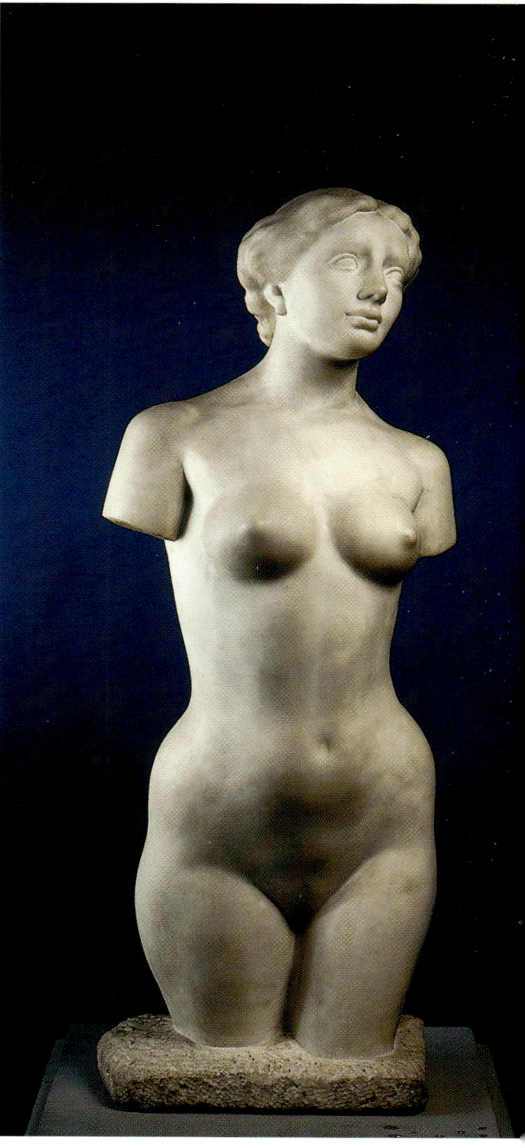

Aristide Maillol
Youth, 1910
Marble. 106 x 44 x 34 cm - MO

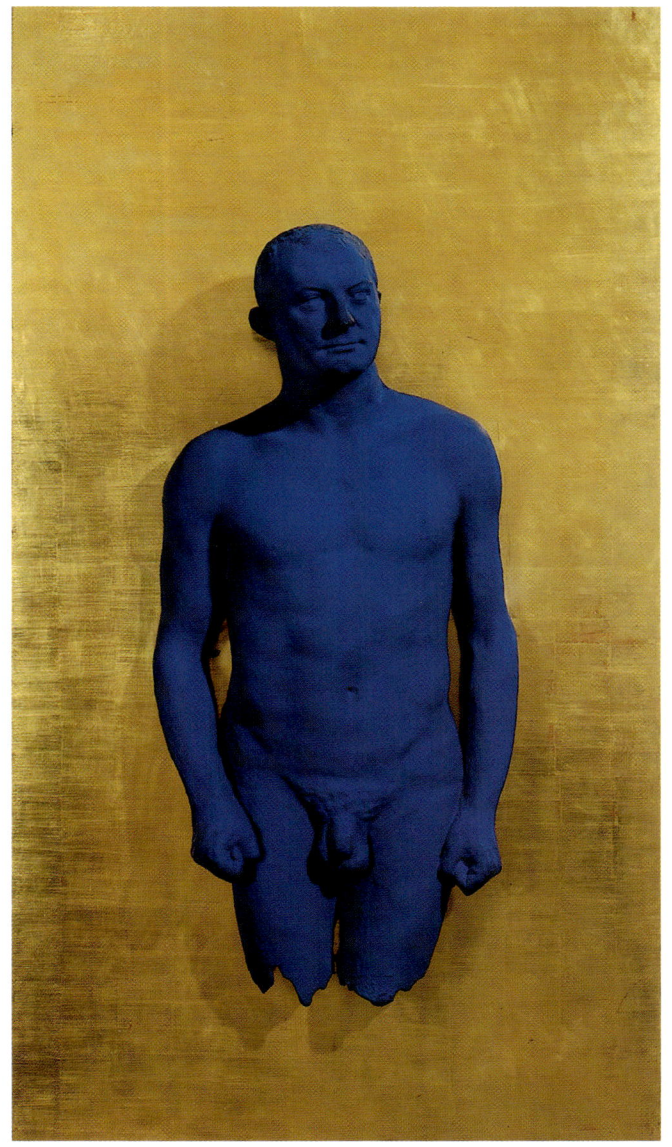

Yves Klein
Portrait-Relief Arman, 1962
Bronze, plywood, gold-leaf. 175 x 95 x 26 cm - CP

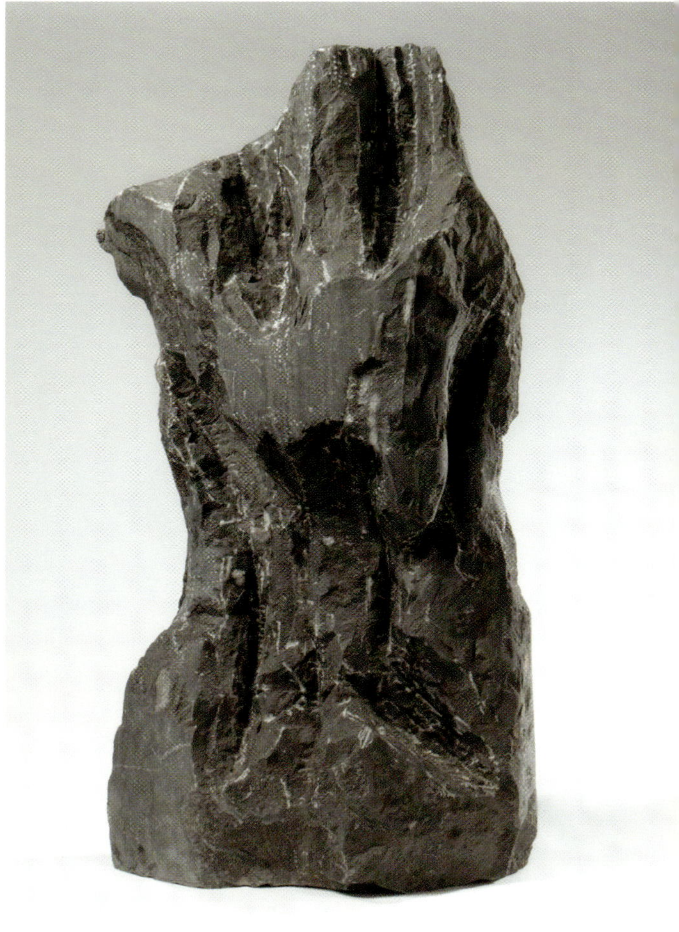

Eugène Dodeigne
Large Torso, 1960-61
Black granite. 120 x 56 x 45 cm - CP

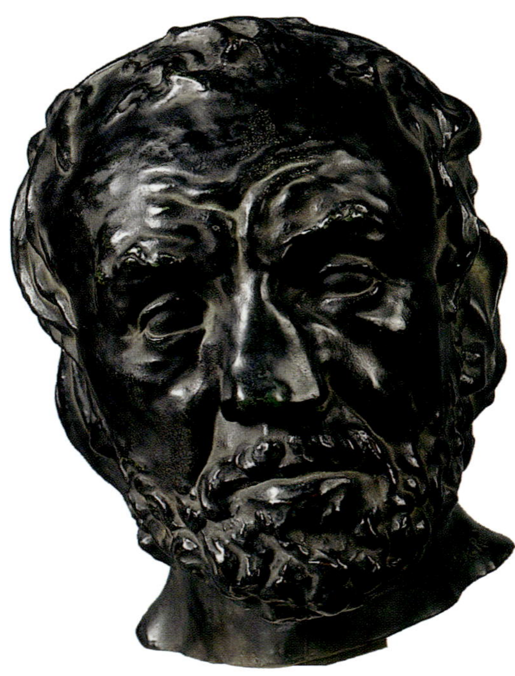

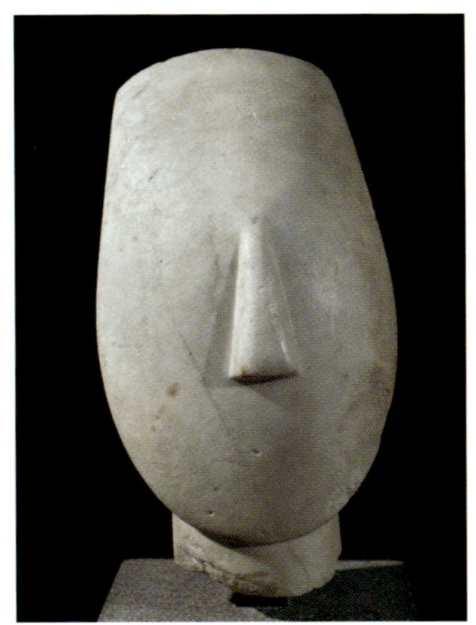

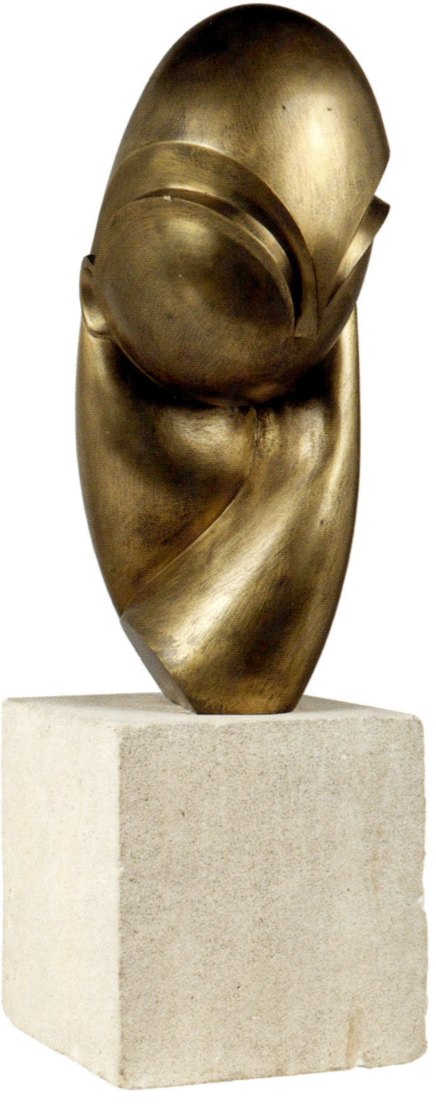

If Rodin decided to cast the *Man with a Broken Nose* (the result of an accident to the clay model) in enduring bronze, it was not only because he was always ready to make creative use of haphazard events, but also because the shape enhanced the play of light over the modelling of the face and off-kilter nose.

On the other hand, the Cycladic head and the portrait of Mademoiselle Pogany by Constantin Brancusi are perfectly geometrical. The nose — conical in one case, while in the other created from double curves that generate a triangle from the continuum skull-prominent brow-eye-nose — is all-important in that it marks the axis of symmetry in a very complicated construction.

The formal analogies between these two works should not though be over-stated: they appear more obvious today, since the red, black and blue motifs that picked out the features on the Cycladic head have long disappeared. In addition, the first *Mlle Pogany*, which whipped up a scandal at the New York Armory Show of 1913 and which the press christened 'Miss Egg', preceded the reevaluation of archaic Greek art, which dates rather from between the wars. As a whole, Brancusi's chosen task was a fascinating and unrelenting process of formal simplification, of abstraction from the live model, a search for the essence of form as encapsulated in one fundamental idea, in this case that of a primeval ovoid.

In what was a crucial two-pronged assault, Dadaism and Cubism both attacked the 'head'. What lies inside a head? This is the iconoclastic question that Cubist sculptor Henri Laurens poses in 'breaking' the head open and operating a synthesis of the resulting volumes. As for Sophie Taeuber-Arp's *Dada Head*, it can be compared to the masks worn at Dadaist soirees staged in Zurich in 1916-17 and to Hausmann's *Mechanical Head*. In what was a crucial two-pronged assault, Dadaism and Cubism both attackted the 'head'...

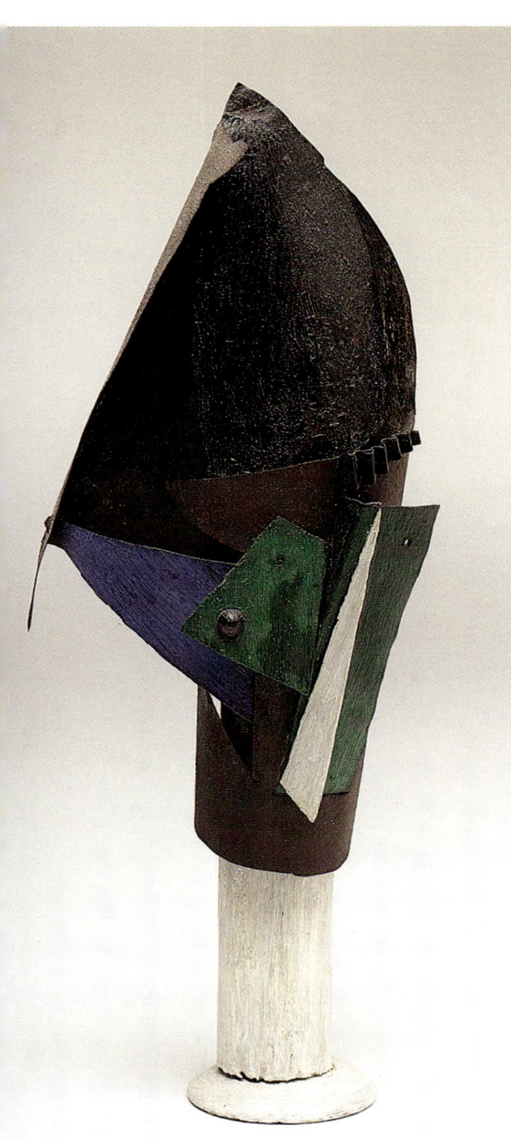

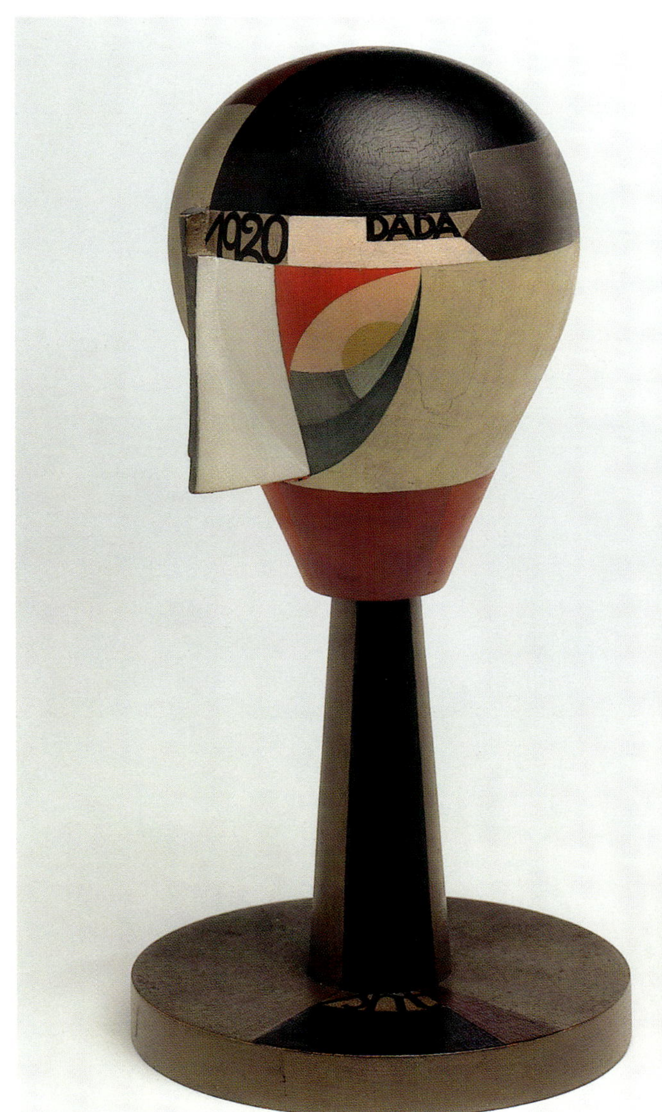

Auguste Rodin

Man with a Broken Nose, 1864/1878
Bronze. 26 x 21 x 23 cm - MO

Female Head, Early Cycladic II (2700-2300 BC)
Marble. H: 27 cm - ML

Constantin Brancusi

Mlle Pogany III, 1933
Bronze. 44.5 x 19 x 27 cm - CP

Henri Laurens

Construction, Small Head, 1915
Wood and polychrome iron sheeting. 30 x 13 x 10 cm - CP

Sophie Taeuber-Arp

Dada Head, 1920
Painted lathed wood. H: 29.43 cm - CP

The cheek

François Rude shared in the painter Jacques Louis David's exile. This last had been banished from France at the Restoration for having voted for Louis XVI's execution when he was in the Convention and for having been guilty of painting the *Coronation of Napoleon*. On the death of David, Rude produced a first bust, dated 1826, considered more than adequate by the deceased's family. A second bust, executed in 1838, also represents the painter. No longer garbed in the Antique fashion, David is treated here without idealisation: he is the 'man with a swollen cheek', whose face was deformed by a lipoma. In Medardo Rosso's *The Golden Age* (in fact his wife and son), the junction between the cheeks speaks of their intimacy, as well as providing a study of how light plays over an unbroken surface.

As for Marcel Duchamp, he harks back to one of the legends of the origin of sculpture: in Pliny the Elder's *Natural History* (1st century AD), the potter Butades is described as first having the idea of modelling a face when requested by his daughter to make an image of her beloved for her to keep. Butades set to work using a profile of the subject his daughter had made by drawing around her beloved's shadow. Thus the origins of sculpture and of drawing

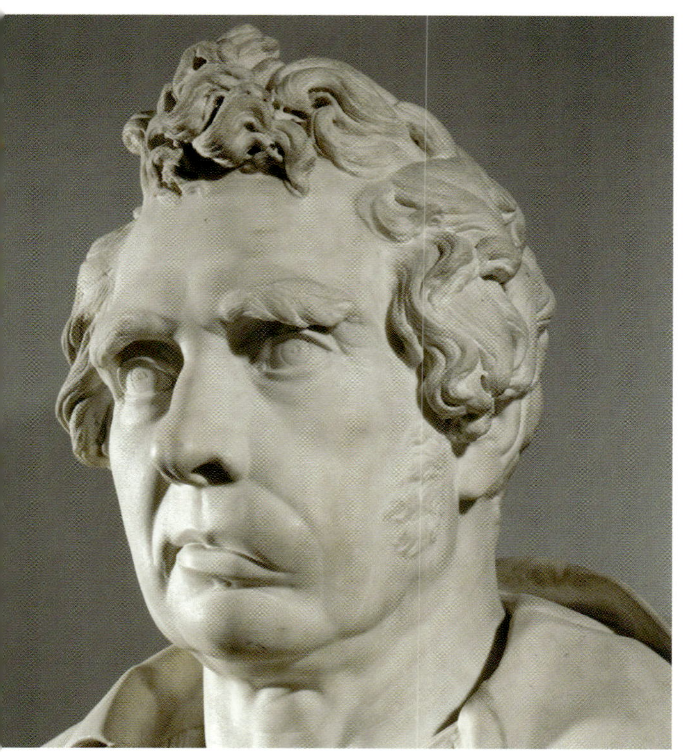

François Rude

Jacques Louis David, Painter, 1838

Marble. 86 x 75 x 50 cm (detail) - ML

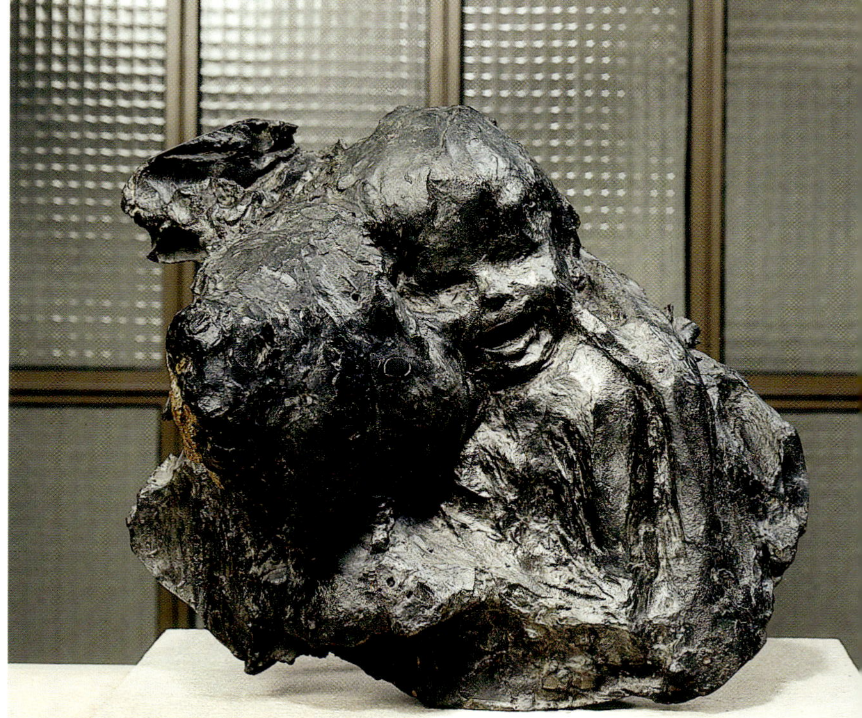

Medardo Rosso

Aetas aurea or *The Golden Age*, 1886

Bronze. 50 x 37 x 26 cm - MO

both stem from love. Did sculpture spring from the erotic? This seems to be what the inventor of the *objet trouvé* affirms, be it ironically, in tracing his self-portrait: a shift, then, from the second to the third dimension? There is a fourth to be added: that of the spirit, since the witty title, *With My Tongue in My Cheek,* possesses obvious ironic connotations.

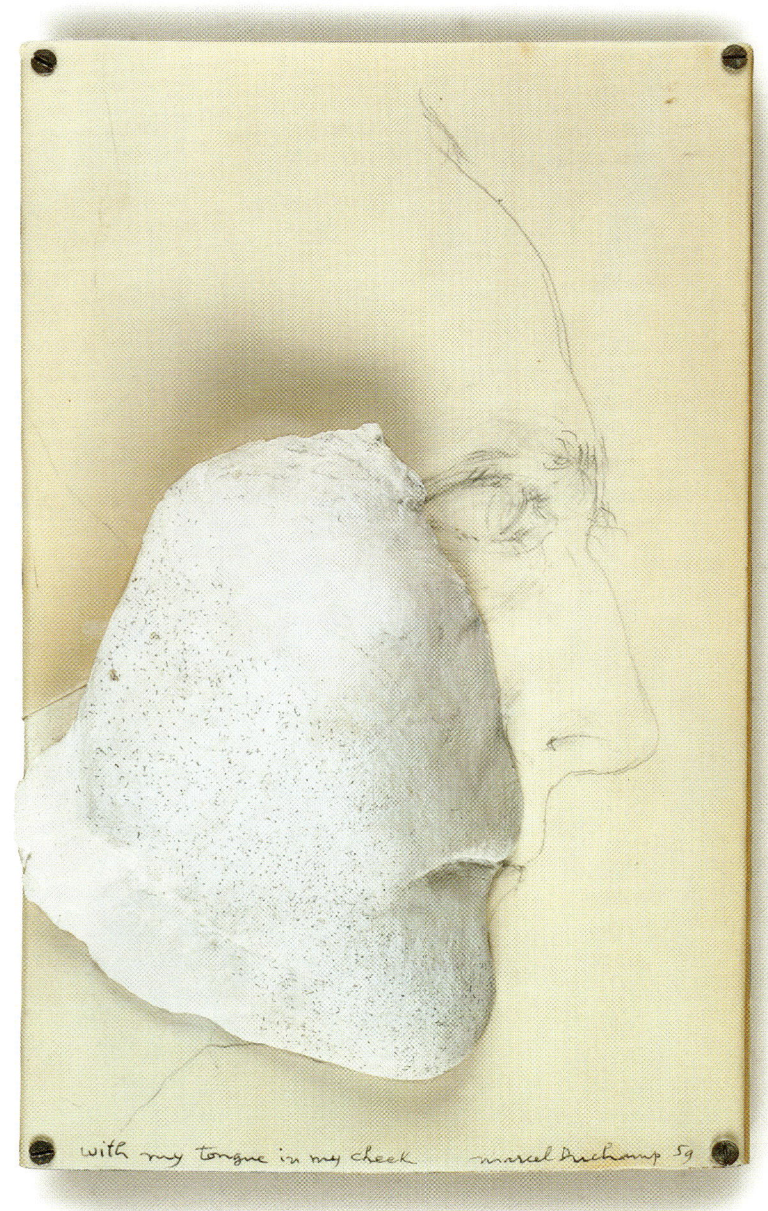

Marcel Duchamp

With My Tongue in My Cheek, 1959

Plaster, pencil on paper mounted on wood. 25 x 15 x 5.1 cm - CP

Back

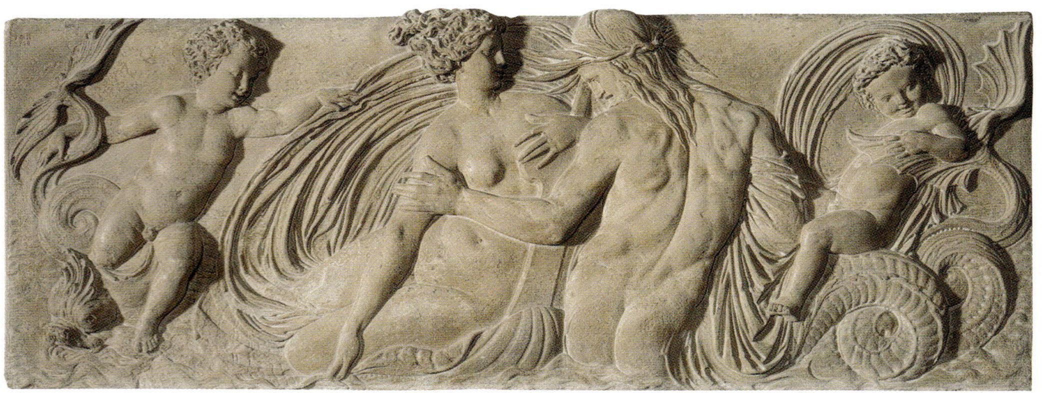

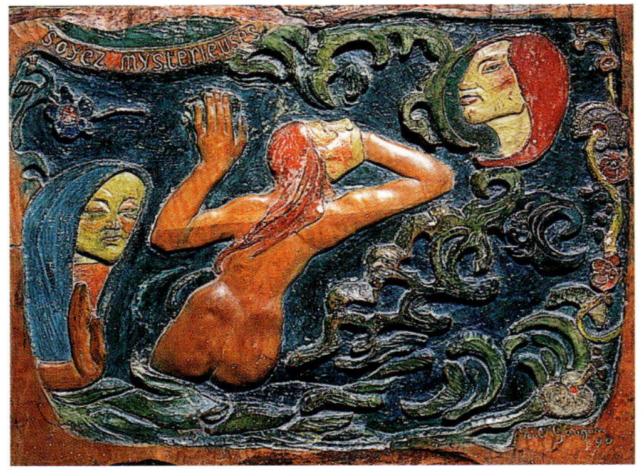

There exist two main types of figuration in bas-relief: profile and three-quarter face. Here, as is less frequently the case, the artist has chosen to emphasise the back. In this relief, carried out for the Fontaine des Innocents, an architectural dais erected in the heart of Paris for the ceremonial entry of Henri II in 1549, Jean Goujon rewrites a scene lifted from an Antique sarcophagus: with an intellectual concern to outstrip reality, the projection formed by the triton's back contrasts with the elongated lines of a nymph drawn in keeping with Mannerist aesthetics. The incredible thing about Goujon is how he manages, starting from painterly premises — his borrowings from Rosso and Parmigianino are well documented — and respecting the rule of the frame, to create a balanced imbalance, an interplay between line and sculptural expression. This beguiling talent was recalled by Georges Lacombe when he came to work on the reliefs for his cycle of life (p. 172).

This wooden bas-relief by Gauguin that belongs to a series of panels from his Maison du Jouir, which was covered with maxims encouraging love, reveals the inswept back of a woman in motion, shown fleeing from an allegorical figure of austere wisdom and throwing herself into the arms of voluptuous pleasure. The hand enjoining silence is at one with the injunction 'Soyez mystérieuses' ('Women, be mysterious') in advocating an existence outside society. The woman invites the beholder to follow her...

Yet only the imagination of a sculptor who was also a fully fledged painter like Henri Matisse could come up with a figure that turns its back completely on the viewer. Through a process of simplification and condensation of the structural schema, of which he provides other examples in the *Jeannette* and *Henriette* series, Matisse manages to morph the spinal column into a vertical divide down the middle of the panel. The artist ends up with a near-abstract, yet still dynamic form.

Jean Goujon
Nymph and Triton, mid-16th century
Stone. 73 x 195 x 12 cm - ML

Paul Gauguin
Be Mysterious, 1890
Polychrome-painted limewood. 73 x 95 x 5 cm - MO

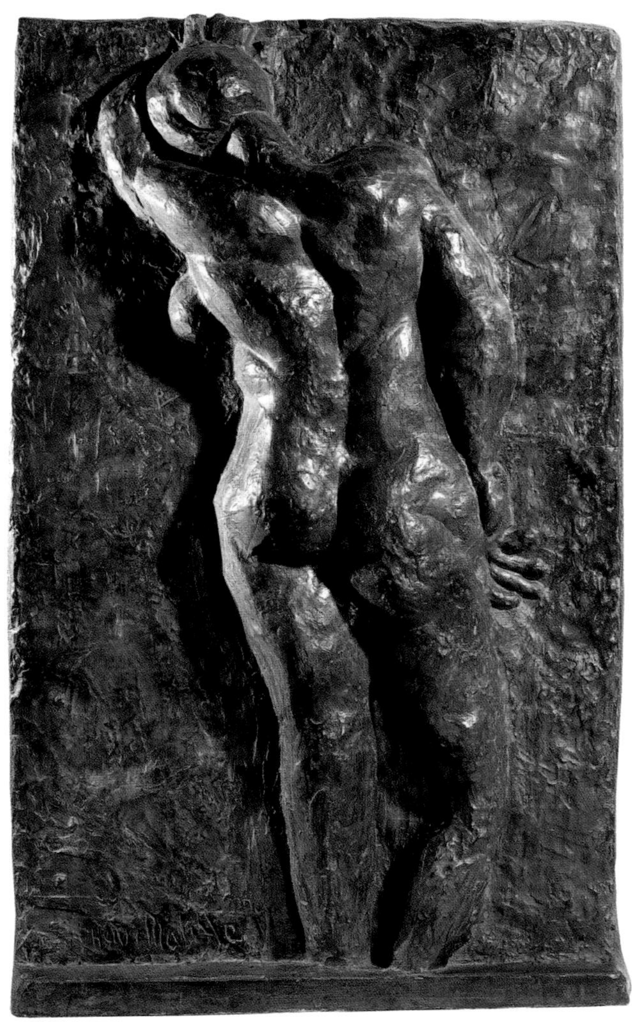

Henri Matisse

Nude from the Back - First State or *Back I*, 1950

Lost-wax process bronze. 190 x 116 x 17 cm - CP

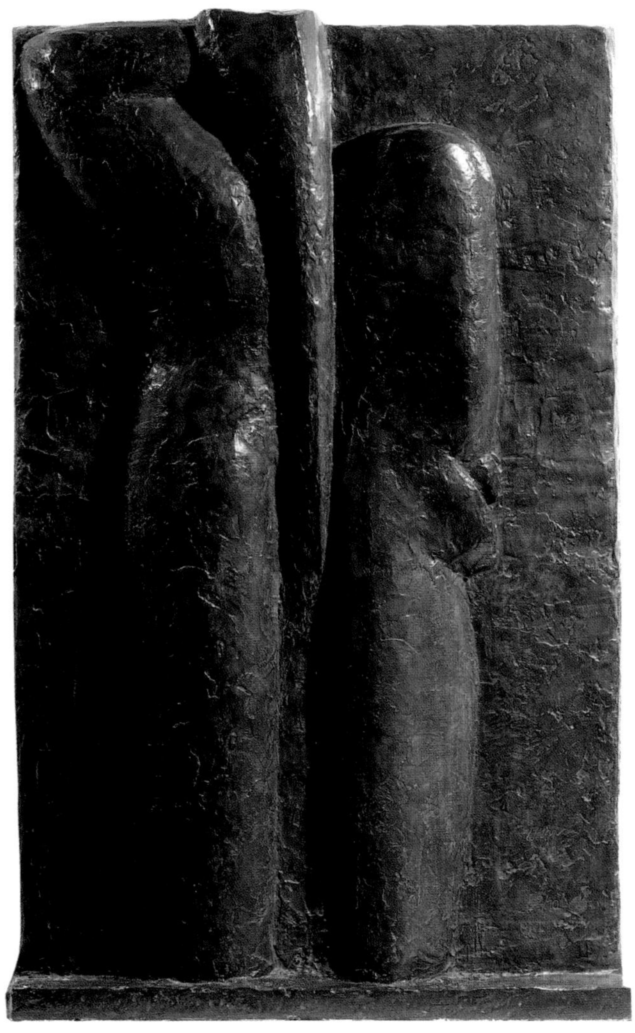

Henri Matisse

Nude from the Back - Fourth State or *Back IV*, 1960-63

Bronze, dark patina. 190 x 114 x 16 cm - CP

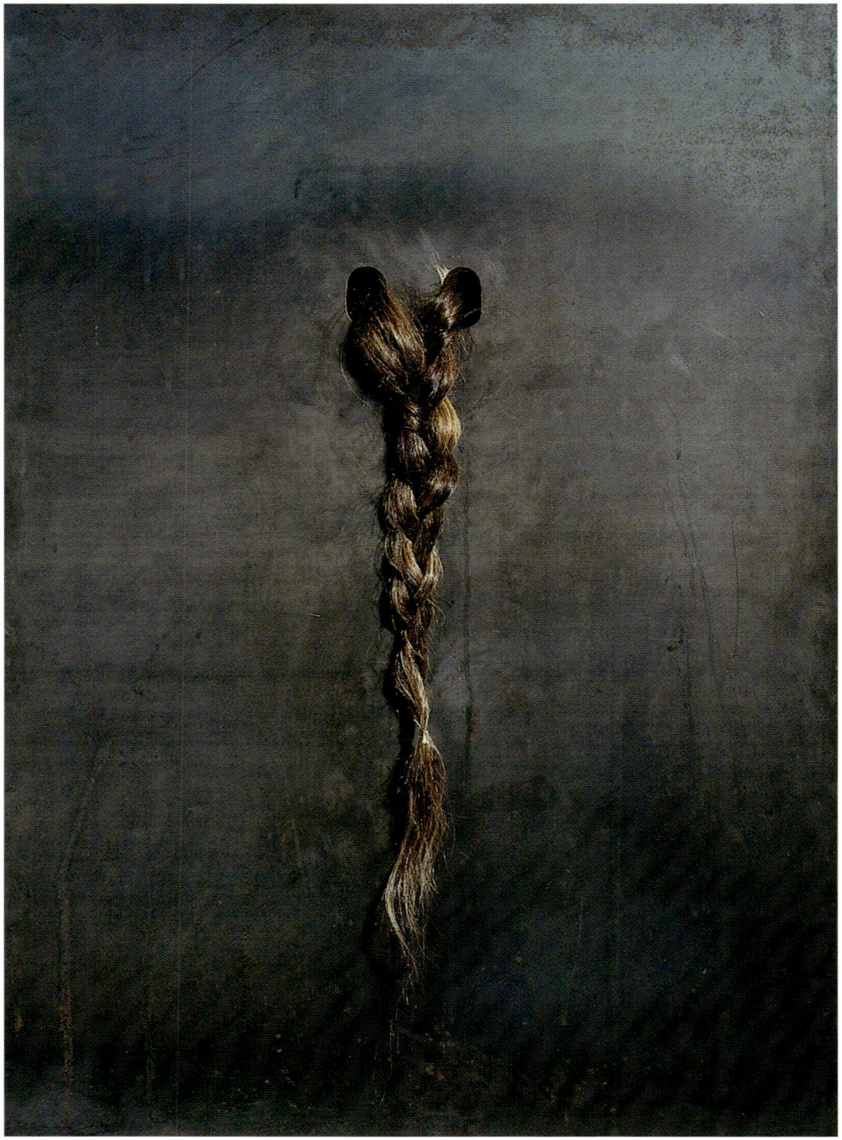

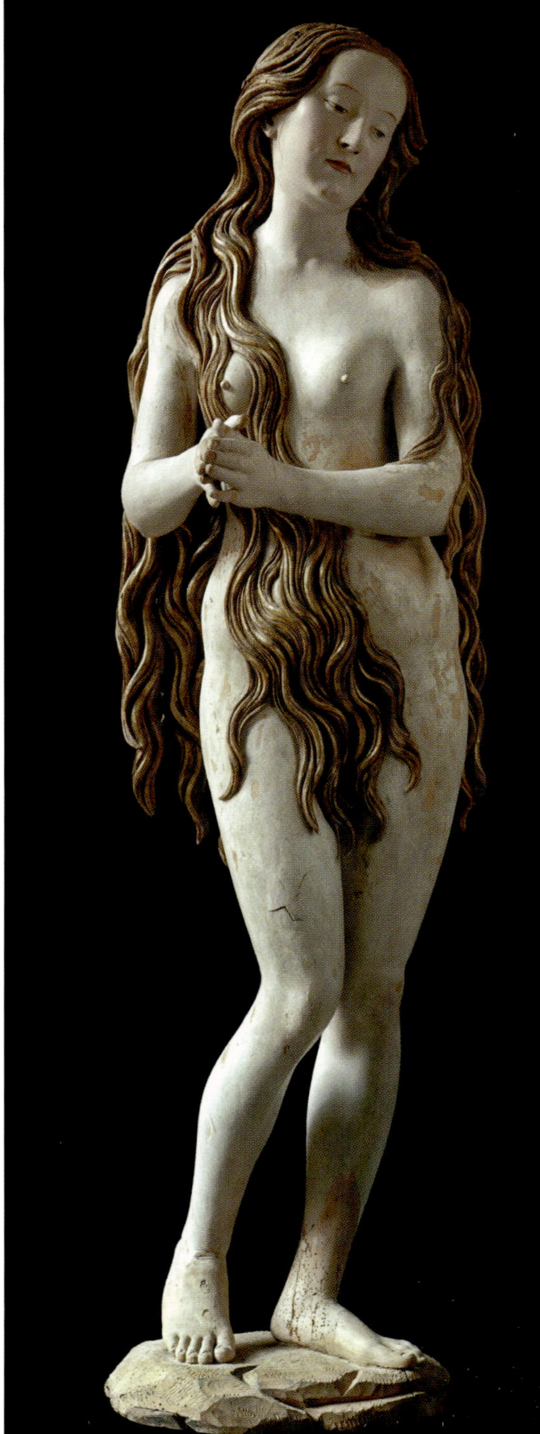

Hair

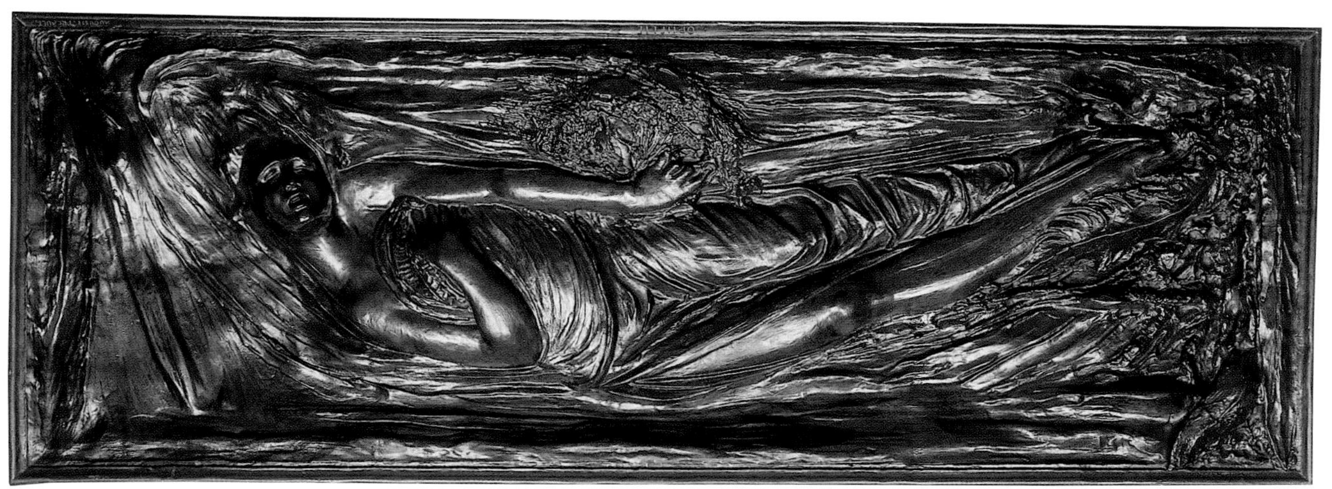

Jannis Kounellis
Untitled, 1969
Metal, hair. 100.5 x 70.5 x 5 cm - CP

Gregor Erhart
Mary Magdalene, c. 1615-20
Limewood, original polychromy. 177 x 44 x 43 cm - ML

Auguste Préault
Ophelia, 1863/1876
Bronze. 75 x 200 x 20 cm - MO

The invitation Jannis Kounellis offers the beholder is a cruel one: to pull or even to cut off a plait. Perhaps one should here evoke all the legends in which captive princesses escape from the prison tower by letting their hair grow long and using it as a rope ladder, or should one perhaps praise an economy of means that fashions materials considered a priori poor — hair on metal — into a sculpture by the age-old practice of plaiting. Still, it has been less the plait than the full head of loose hair that has received attention from artists for its sensual suggestiveness. The German sculptor Gregor Erhart treated his *Magdalene* like a Venus. It is true that the repentant Magdalene, dressed in little more than her tumbling locks, is undoubtedly one of the most erotic figures in the Christian repertory of images. This female figure, her breast jutting out through a mass of hair, is quite unlike the ravaged apparition of Donatello's *St Magdalene*, intended for the baptistery in Florence (c. 1455). Erhart's version was displayed in an elevated position, possibly alluding to a legend that had the saint borne aloft by angels above the cave where she had taken refuge in the Sainte-Baume massif in southern France.

Auguste Préault treats hair as an unruffled stretch of water floating around the body of the drowned Ophelia from which sprouts a tangle of aquatic plant life. In addition to Shakespeare, Préault took as his starting point these lines by Victor Hugo in *Les Fantômes*: 'As Ophelia by the river borne/Dies gathering flowers.' This liquid gravestone might be compared to the tomb of the Sieur de Rocquencourt, a relief of dream-like depth, as well as to paintings by the English Pre-Raphaelites.

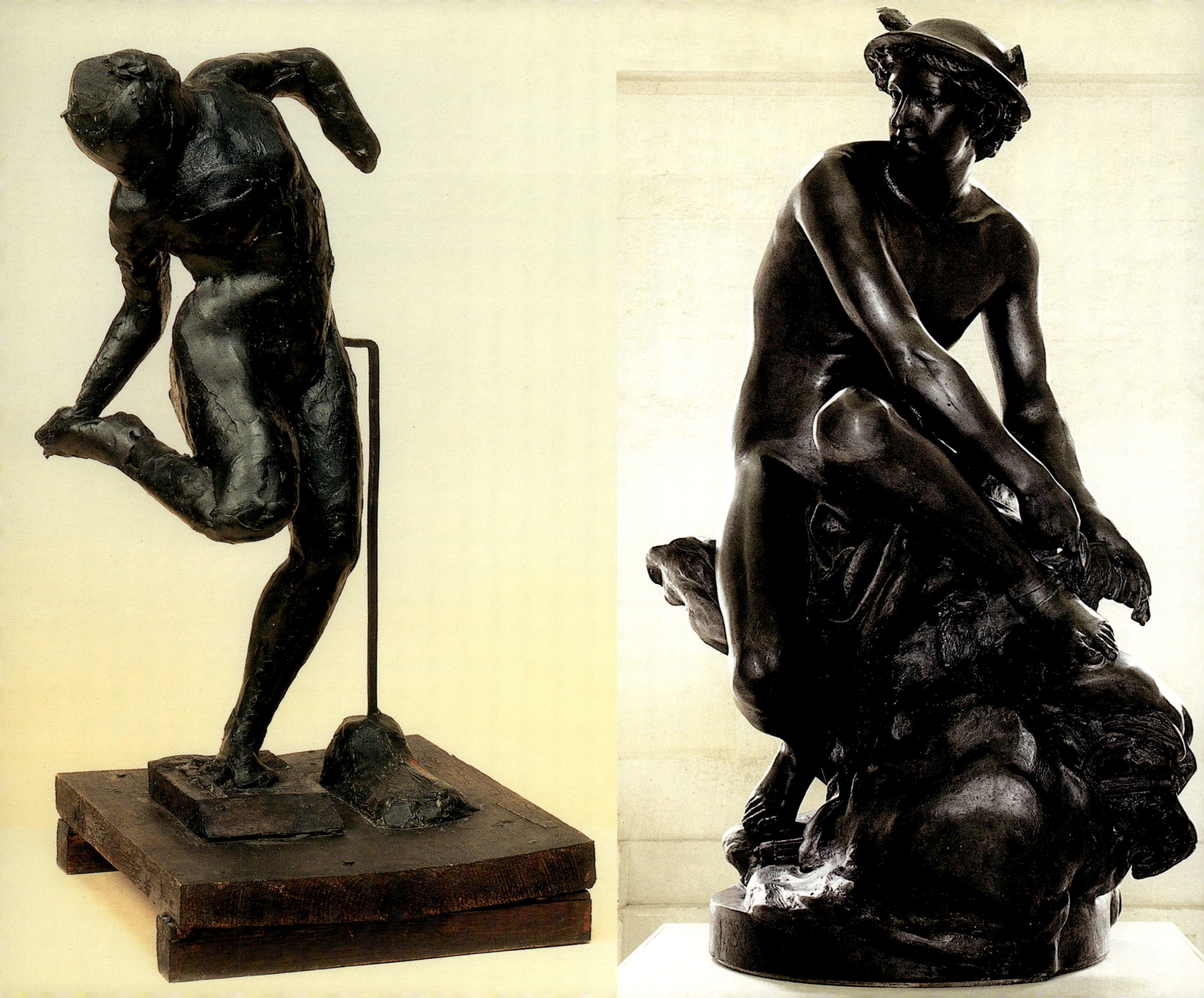

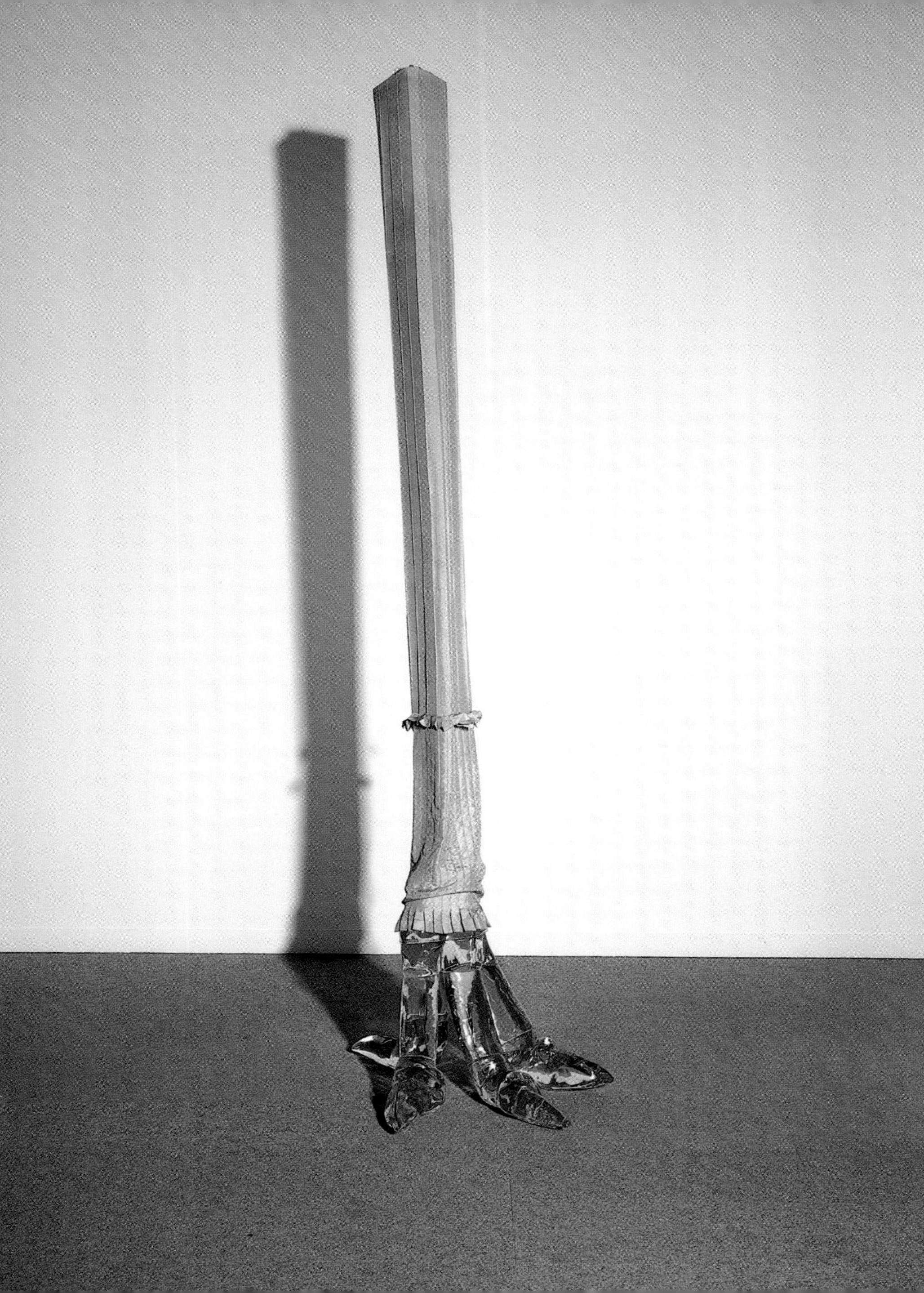

Feet

Before attempting his wax figure, how many study drawings did Edgar Degas have to undertake to map out the various stages of this dancer flexing her leg? In the gesture of a ballerina grasping her foot, reminiscent of the girl in the *Bathtub* (p. 44), the sculptor captures the essence of movement, one common to both sculpture and dance: unstable equilibrium.

The pose of Jean-Baptiste Pigalle's *Mercury* had already demonstrated this perfectly adequately: the messenger of the gods, tutelary divinity for both merchants and robbers, was originally shown carrying off a missive from his pendant, a *Venus*. Still sitting and hastily lacing up the *talaria* that endow him with the power of flight, he is already straining forwards, about to leap to his feet. The sculptor treated the base with the drill, coiling the figure up like a spring that can be released with the heel like a pedal.

In sculpture, the foot is a fundamental point of support on the ground and in the passage from the horizontal to the vertical. In his series of *Piede*, the Italian sculptor Luciano Fabro brings this out amply. Made of metal, wood or, as here, glass, his 'feet', which evoke those of a large wading-bird, give new meaning to the thematic of the plinth as treated by Brancusi and Giacometti. The choice of glass underlines the fragility of the support and creates an impression that the body of the sculpture is almost levitating. This fragile foot also suggests the *Mezzogiorno*, the south of the 'boot' of Italy.

Edgar Degas
Dancer Looking at the Sole of her Right Foot,
first preliminary study, **1895-1910**
Wax. 45 x 21 x 18 cm (without plinth)

Jean-Baptiste Pigalle
Mercury Tying his Talaria, **1753**
Lead. 187 x 108 x 106 cm - ML

Luciano Fabro
Foot, **1968-72**
Murano glass, silk shantung. 333.5 x 108 x 79 cm - CP

Venustà

As much as Etienne-Maurice Falconet's *Bather* — slightly turning and bending at the knee, as in *Love Cutting his Bow* (p. 127) — exalts the Neoclassical line in ageless and immaculate white marble, so Jean-Léon Gérôme paints his *Tangara* consistent with the lessons of archaeology in which he was profoundly interested.

It was generally agreed that this 'Parisian of Antiquity', with her 'rosy pallor' and with 'carmine smeared' over her lips, was actually Gérôme's mistress Madame Siot, depicted as the incarnation of the 'spirit of the city'. The hieratic quality of the enthroned pose, however, does nothing to detract from the life study. The polychromy, which evokes turn-of-the-century Orientalism, shows the links between painting and sculpture, arts Gérôme practised conjointly, being of the opinion that 'painting breathed sculpture into life'. *Sculpturae vitam insufflat Pictura* was indeed the title of one of the pictures he painted while engaged on *Tanagra*. In another, Gérôme reconstituted an Antique studio in which the dancer with the hoop (placed here in the woman's hand) was being made. The artist, with a wink to the viewer, even places a reduction of his own *Tanagra* on a shelf in the sculptor's shop.

What, then, is missing from this *venustà*? Duchamp replies, 'a female fig-leaf', underlining the contrast between what is considered permissible in the display of female genitalia — except in scandalously overt cases such as Courbet's *The Origin of the World* — and the concealment of the male member. Remember that disciple of Michelangelo, Daniele da Volterra, notoriously summoned by the pope to paint 'breeches' over the *ignudi* in the Sistine Chapel. Duchamp's piece, belonging, like the *Objet Dard* and *Prière de toucher*, to a family of 'selected pieces' of the human body, and which is no more moulded from nature than a fig-leaf is from a phallus, demonstrates that sexuality is a *cosa mentale*, and the representation of the genitals in sculpture nothing but a *vanitas*.

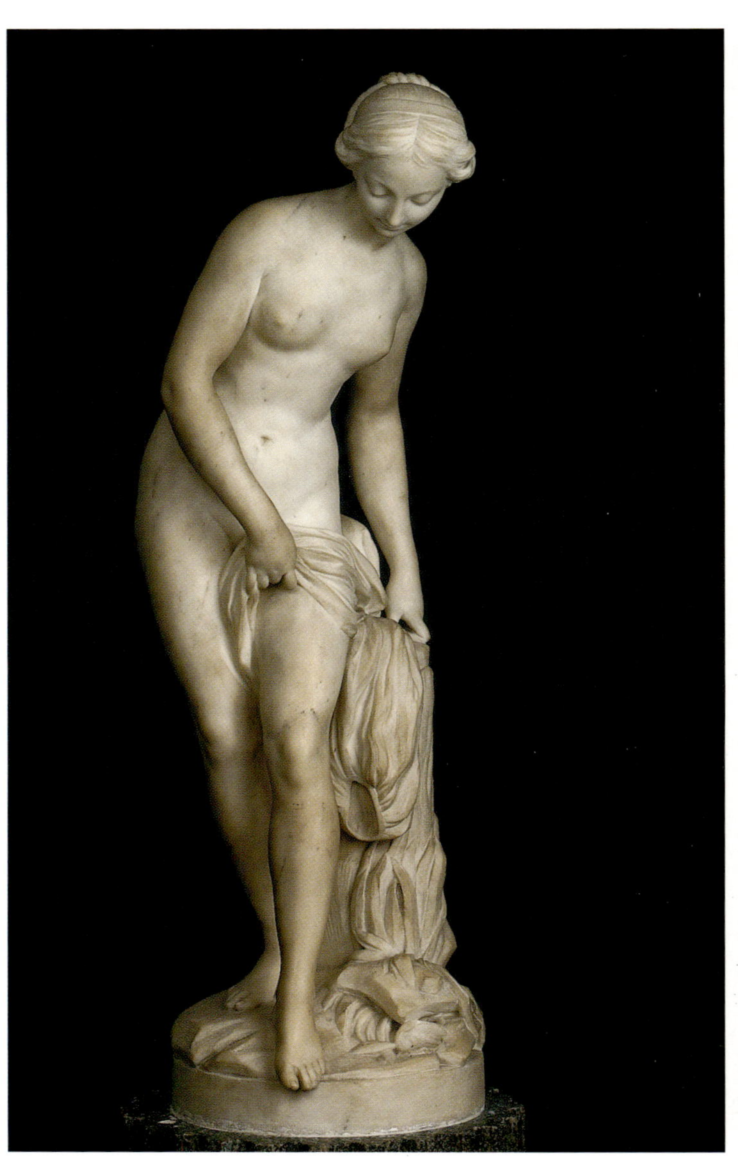

Etienne-Maurice Falconet
Bather, 1757
Marble. 80 x 25 x 29 cm - ML

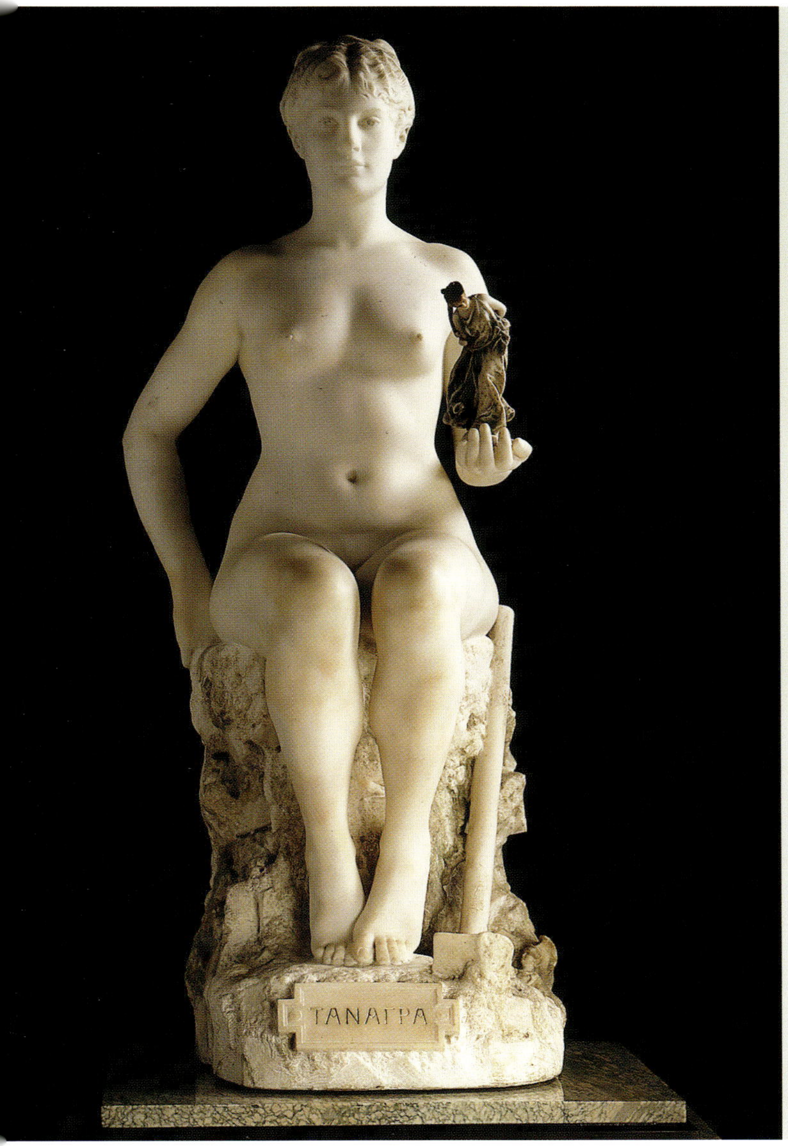

Jean-Léon Gérôme

Tanagra, 1890

Marble. 154 x 56 x 57 cm - MO

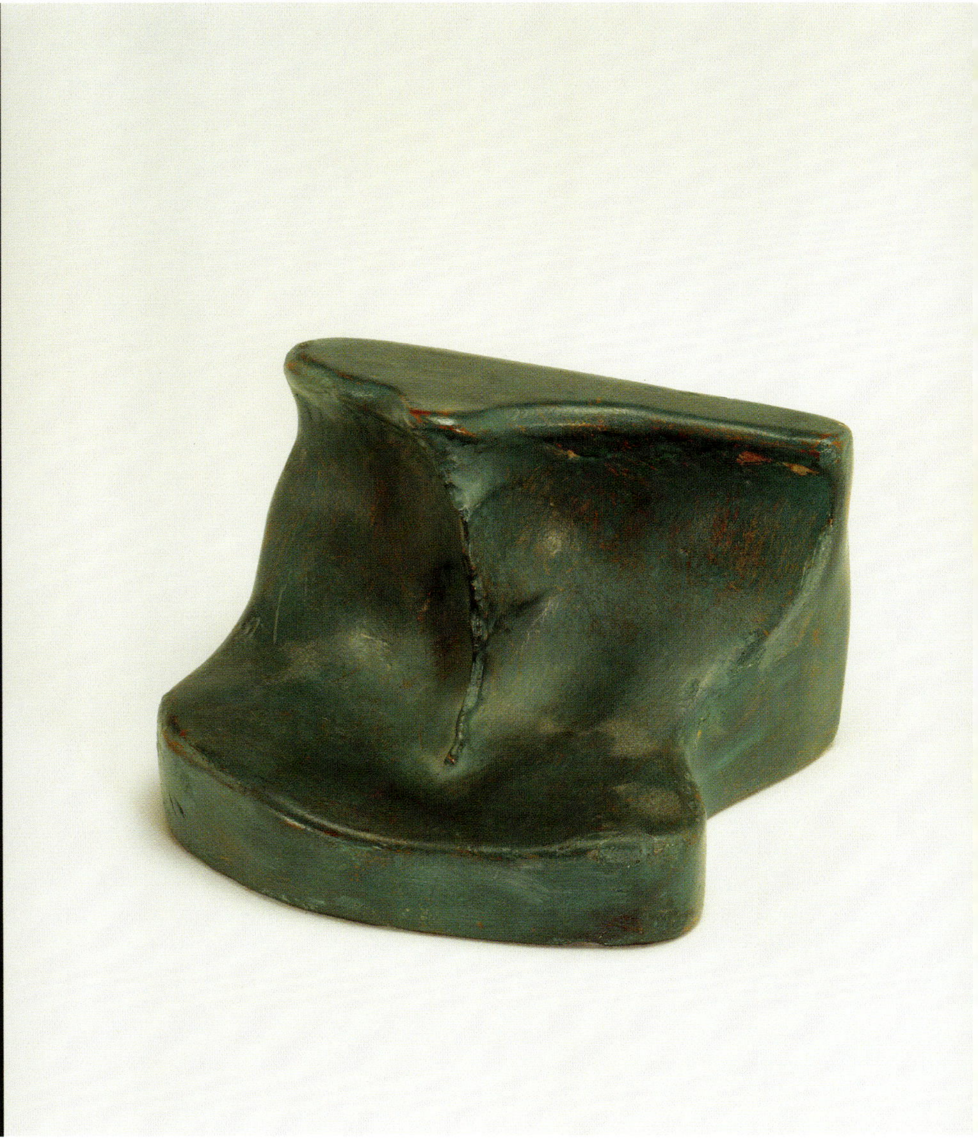

Marcel Duchamp

Female Fig-Leaf, 1950/1951

Green-painted plaster. 8.5 x 13 x 11 cm - CP

Embracing

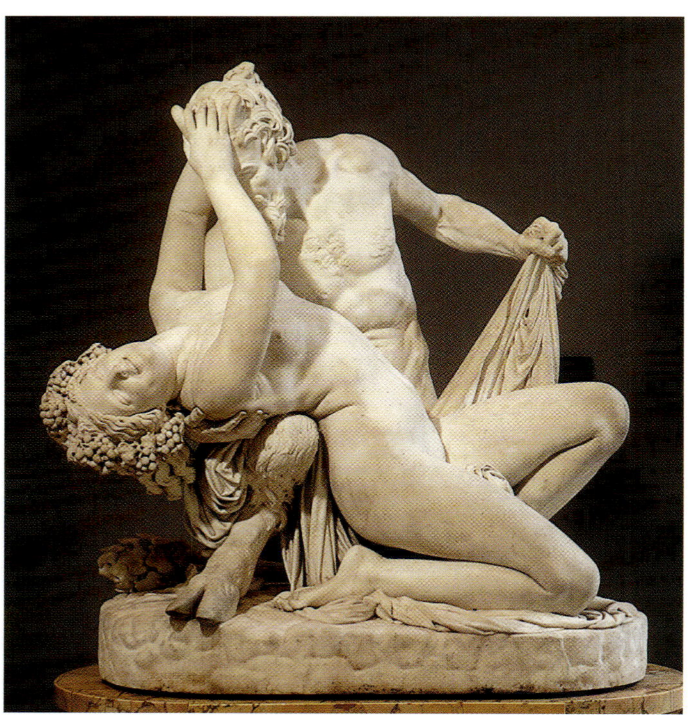

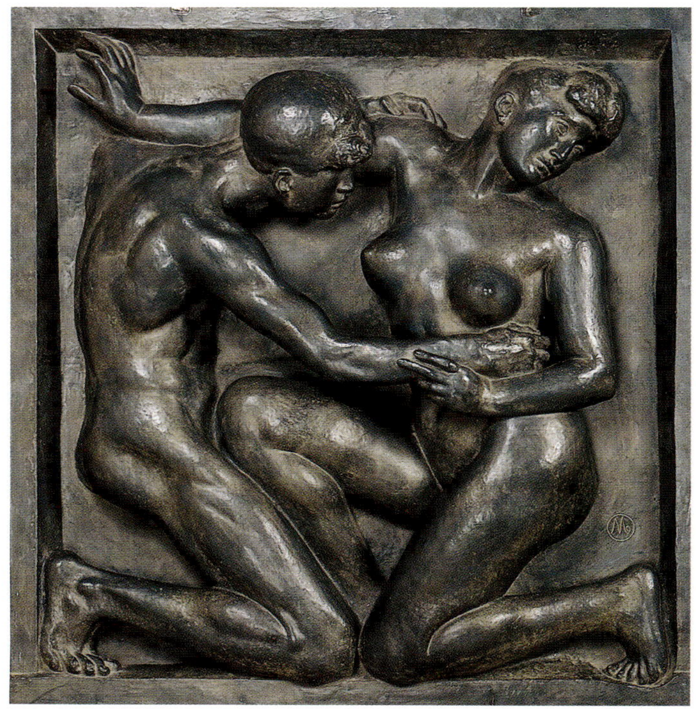

Public reaction to James Pradier's group, *Satyr and Bacchante*, was overwhelmingly hostile, the journal *Le Cabinet de lecture* lambasted the sculpture as 'ignoble, disgusting and wretched'. Louis-Philippe's government was unwilling to countenance its acquisition. The theme itself was not novel, but it had previously always been treated schematically, or in a reduced format, whereas here, the abduction is violent, life size and of unbridled sensuality. The sculptor lent his own features to the satyr, choosing his mistress, Juliette Drouet, for the bacchante. Patently, Pradier is here thinking of Rubens' picture entitled *The Abduction of the Daughters of*

Leucippus: the nymph's complexion and the motion of the bodies are in the same vein. The classical temperament of the sculptor, however, is betrayed by the perfect line running down the viewing side of the sculpture. Drawn in the way of a relief, it shows the young woman resisting just enough to make victory worth the struggle. It was said that Pradier set off 'every morning for Athens'. Known for his sharp tongue, Auguste Préault quipped that it was to spend most of his time where the whores ply their wares!

In Aristide Maillol's relief, the remarkable manner the poses intersect and the gestures answer one another, the expressive diagonal

of the legs, create a vibrant dynamism which nonetheless takes place over a underlying geometric grid. It might be described as a squared-up rendering of desire. And much the same could be said of Raymond Duchamp-Villon's relief, *The Lovers*, also at the Centre Pompidou. Maillol 'detaches' the limbs of the shaven-headed faun and the recalcitrant young woman, just as Matisse does with figures in his gouache cut-outs.

The *Suspended Ball* (1930), 'mobile and silent object' as Alberto Giacometti's own expression has it, also presents two bodies facing one another within a frame. Hanging from a wire in a cage, a

James Pradier
Satyr and Bacchante, 1834
Marble. 125 x 112 x 78 cm - ML

Aristide Maillol
Desire, 1905-07
Lead. 120 x 115 x 25 cm - MO

Alberto Giacometti
Suspended Ball, 1930-31
Wood, iron and string. 60.4 x 36.5 x 34 cm - CP

ball with a notch in its base swings over a crescent shape. No-one can look at this piece without feeling vaguely disconcerted. Salvador Dalí persuaded André Breton to buy it immediately (which is why it features in the rue Fontaine studio reconstituted at the Centre Pompidou), before coming up with a theory on 'symbolically functioning objects' in the review *Le Surréalisme au service de la Révolution* where he based the concept on the *Suspended Ball* and Miró's *Objet du couchant*. Francis Bacon, who had a fondness for Giacometti's oeuvre, painted many figures in cages.

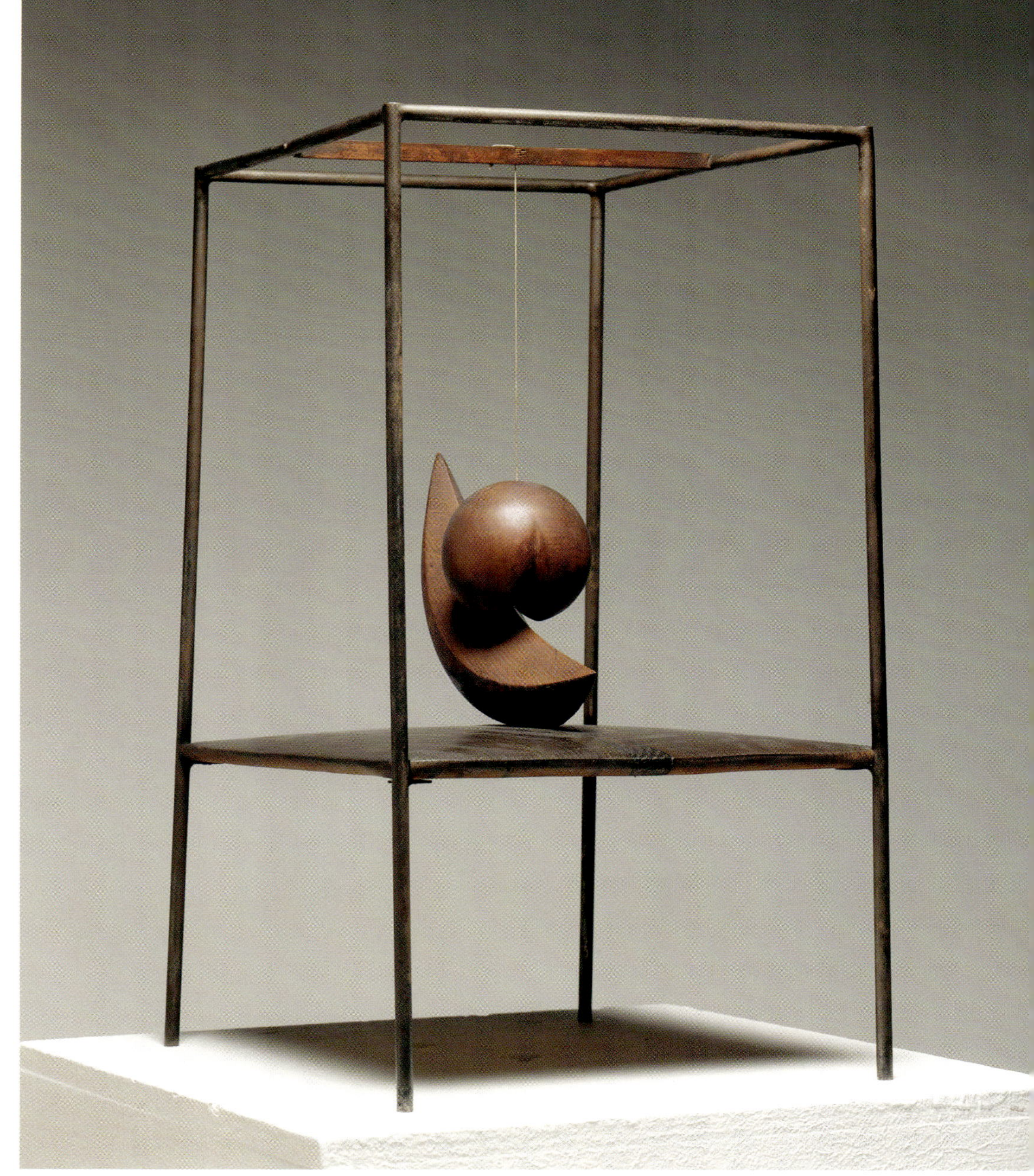

The erotic

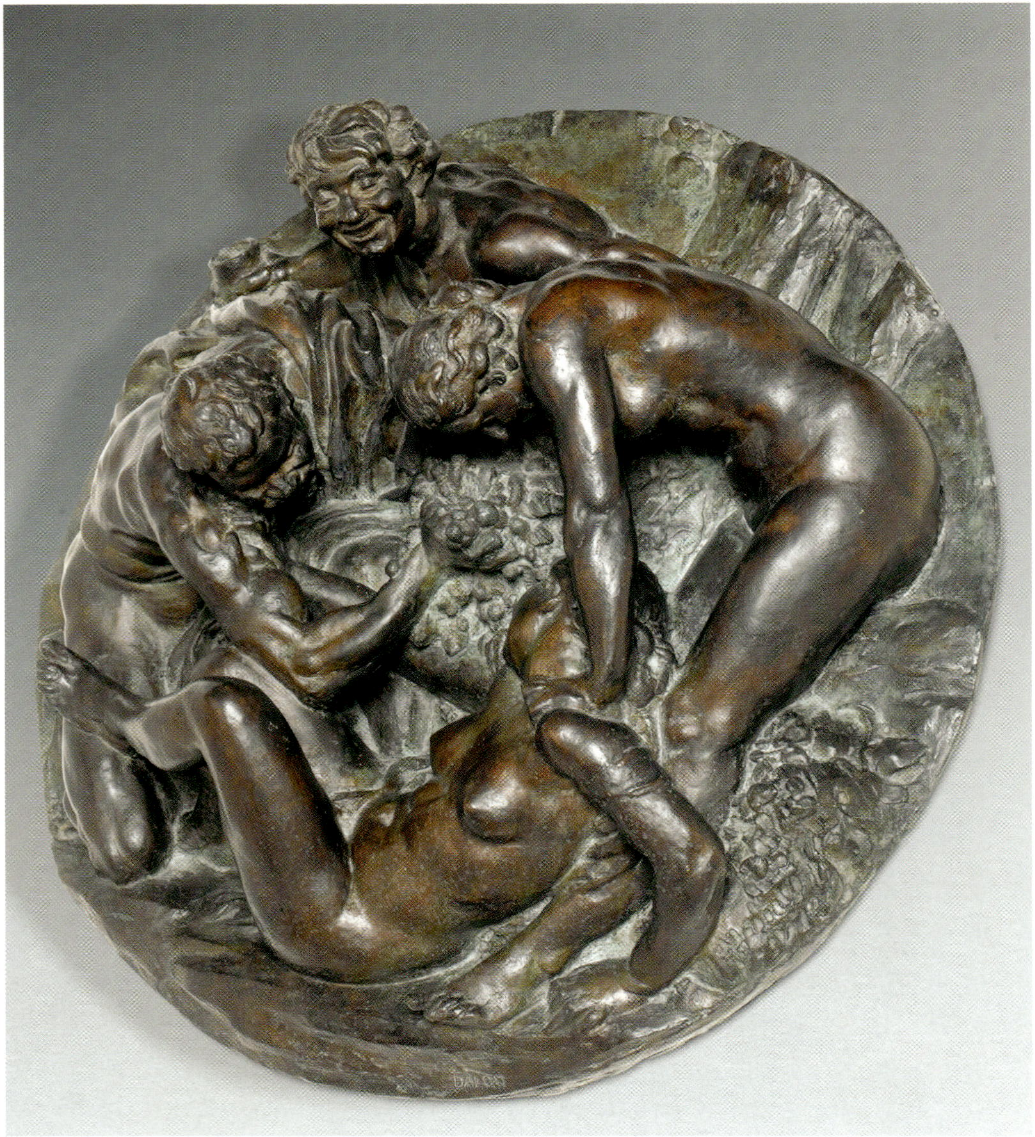

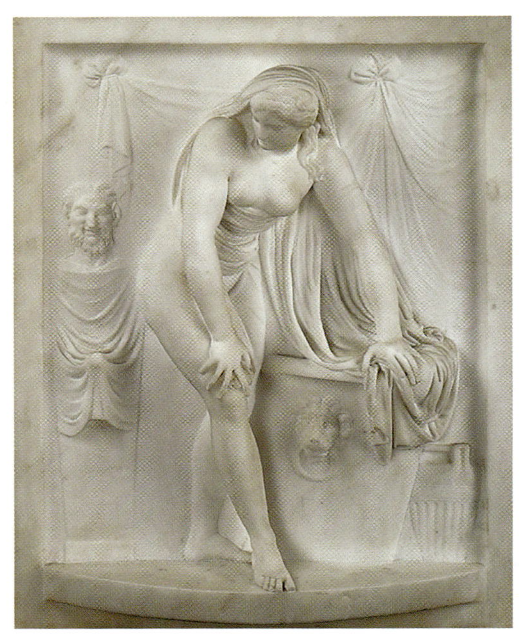

The phallus is one of sculpture's major themes, from Hermes and the oversized phalluses of Antiquity to Brancusi's *Princess X* and Jean Tinguely's *Vittoria*, erected on the Piazza del Duomo in Milan in 1970. The Swedish artist Johan Tobias Sergel, won over to Neoclassicism after encountering Canova and Thorvaldsen, takes as his starting point an ancient Bacchic sarcophagus he saw during his first sojourn in Rome.

In his tondo, Aimé-Jules Dalou captures the swirling movement of a bacchanalia, using the circular form to present a plunging view in which the background serves as the earth. Beside civic and

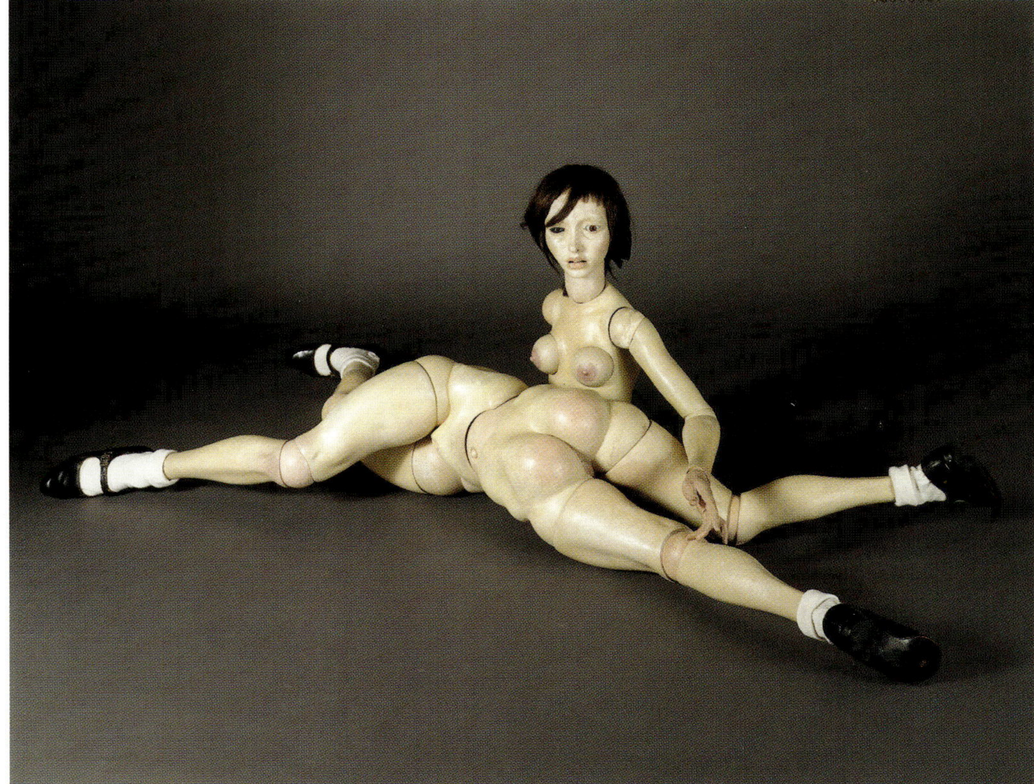

social subjects, the sculptor often drew on this bacchic vein, as in *The Drunkenness of Silenus* and the *Laughing Bacchante*, and even in the project for a monument to work which, towards the end of his life, he envisaged as a phallic structure. The seething mass of this trance-crazed orgy makes one think of one of Rubens' village fairs as amended by Carpeaux…

A plethora of very different desires is aroused by the disjointed poses of Hans Bellmer's 'articulated minor' made in 1937, a year before the artist settled in Paris. He had designed the first model of *The Doll* in 1932-34, having seen a production of one of Hoffmann's tales concerning an artificial girl called Olympia, and following conversations with Rilke and Lotte Pritzel, who herself had built a doll for Oskar Kokoschka. Responding with enthusiasm, the Surrealists published photographs of the dolls in a special number of *Cahiers d'art* devoted to the Object in 1936, as well as in their review, *Minotaure*. Beyond renewing the theme of the mannequin that the Surrealists held in such esteem, Bellmer compared the variable positions adopted by the doll's body to a language in which every word and expression can be twisted however one chooses, *ad infinitum*. It is said the idea first came to him after spotting a wooden mannequin with ball-and-socket limbs ascribed to the School of Dürer in a Berlin museum. Prior to fleeing Nazi Germany, the artist had featured his *Doll* in photographs taken in the garden of a property owned by his parents. In 1949, some of these were published by Paul Eluard in a book inspired by Bellmer's work, *Les Jeux de la poupée*. The polymorphic imagery of this bizarre female centaur testifies to its creator's freedom of thought as well as imagination and to his rejection of the dictatorship beleaguering his homeland.

Terribilità

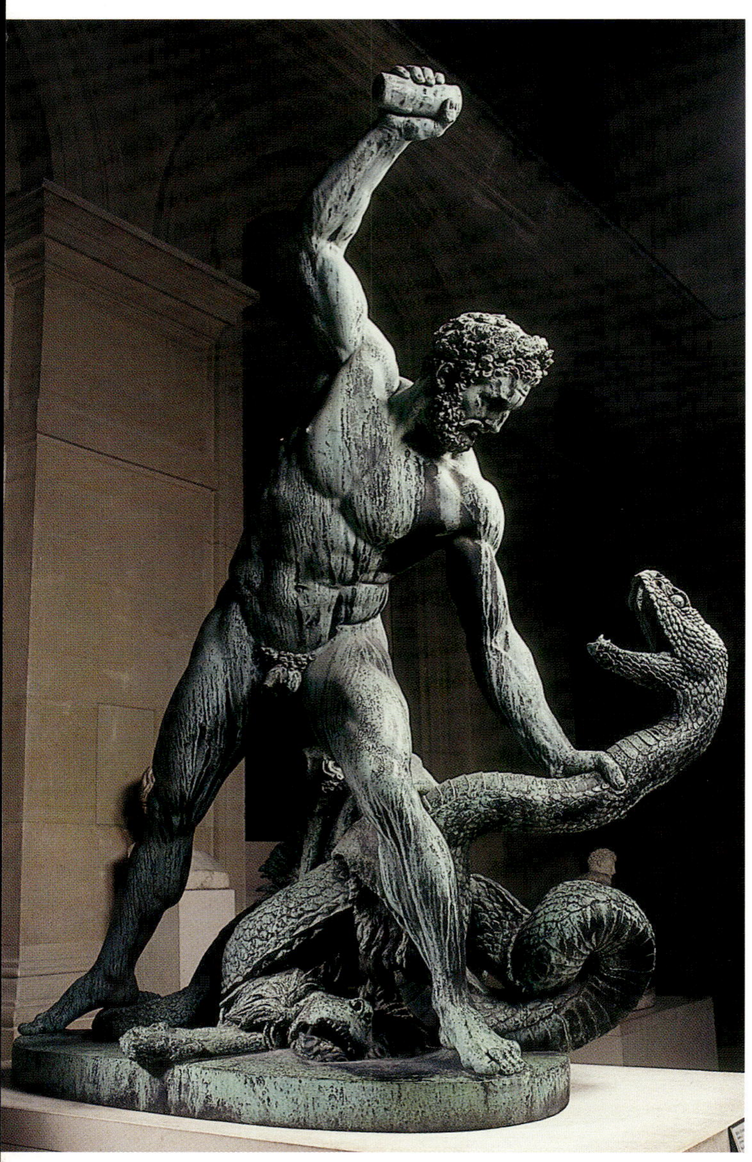

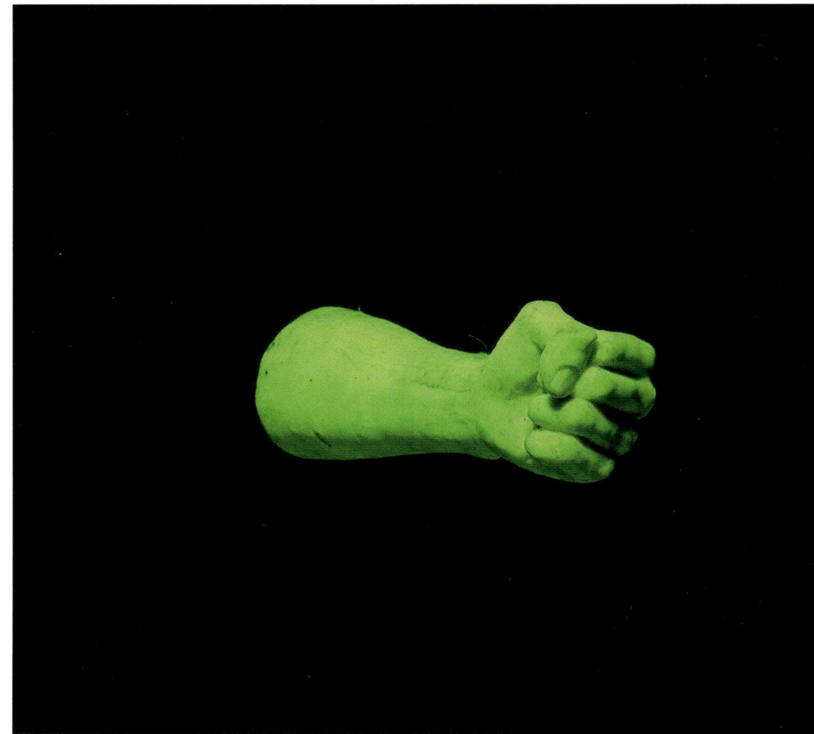

François-Joseph Bosio
Hercules Fighting with Achelous Transformed into a Snake, 1814/1824
Bronze. 260 x 210 x 95 cm - ML

Gilberto Zorio
Phosphorescent Fist, 1971
Phosphorescent wax, two Wood lamps. 170 x 180 x 50 cm - CP

Emile-Antoine Bourdelle
Herakles Killing the Stymphalian Birds, or Herakles Archer (second version), 1909
Gilt bronze. 248 x 247 x 123 cm - MO

The word was forged to characterise the power of the figurative forms that, in the wake of Michelangelo, made their way into Mannerism, such as Giulio Romano's frescoes of the *Giants* at the Palazzo del Tè in Mantua. There also exists, however, a 'black' Neoclassicism, a forerunner of the frenzies of Romanticism, that of *Hercules Fighting with Achelous Transformed into a Snake* by Baron Bosio, an echo of Antonio Canova's masterful *Hercules and Lichas*, with the same heroic profile, the same linear developments, and the same ample gestures constructed around a counterpoint between passive and active curves.

In place of Rodin's Attic rotundity, Antoine Bourdelle substitutes an architectonic sculpture that greatly emphasises the planes. In his *Herakles Archer*, the extreme tension of the leg bracing itself against a rock cut into facets in an almost Cubist manner and the arm stretching to bend the bow elongates the line of the entire body. Such an alliance of constructed power and line in a sculpture so open to the space around it had hardly been encountered before, save in Géricault's *Faun and Nymph*, today in the museum at Rouen.

'My works are themselves energy,' declared Gilberto Zorio. *Pugno fosforescente*, presented at Documenta V in Kassel (1972), acts directly on the human brain through its luminosity and its candid refusal to please. The aggressive upraised fist seems like a rewrite (in the light of the events at the 1968 Mexico Olympic Games when three black sprinters had mounted the podium raising a black-gloved fist) of Rodin's theme of the hand, those hands with which he had created *Cathedral* or *Secret*, the modelled hands of Pierre de Wissant — a sculptor's hands associated with the Hand of God. Every eight minutes, the two iodine lamps go out and the fist, modelled in wax and phosphorus, glows green in the darkness for five seconds. The *antigrazioso*, a principle in which Boccioni delighted, is here extended to light.

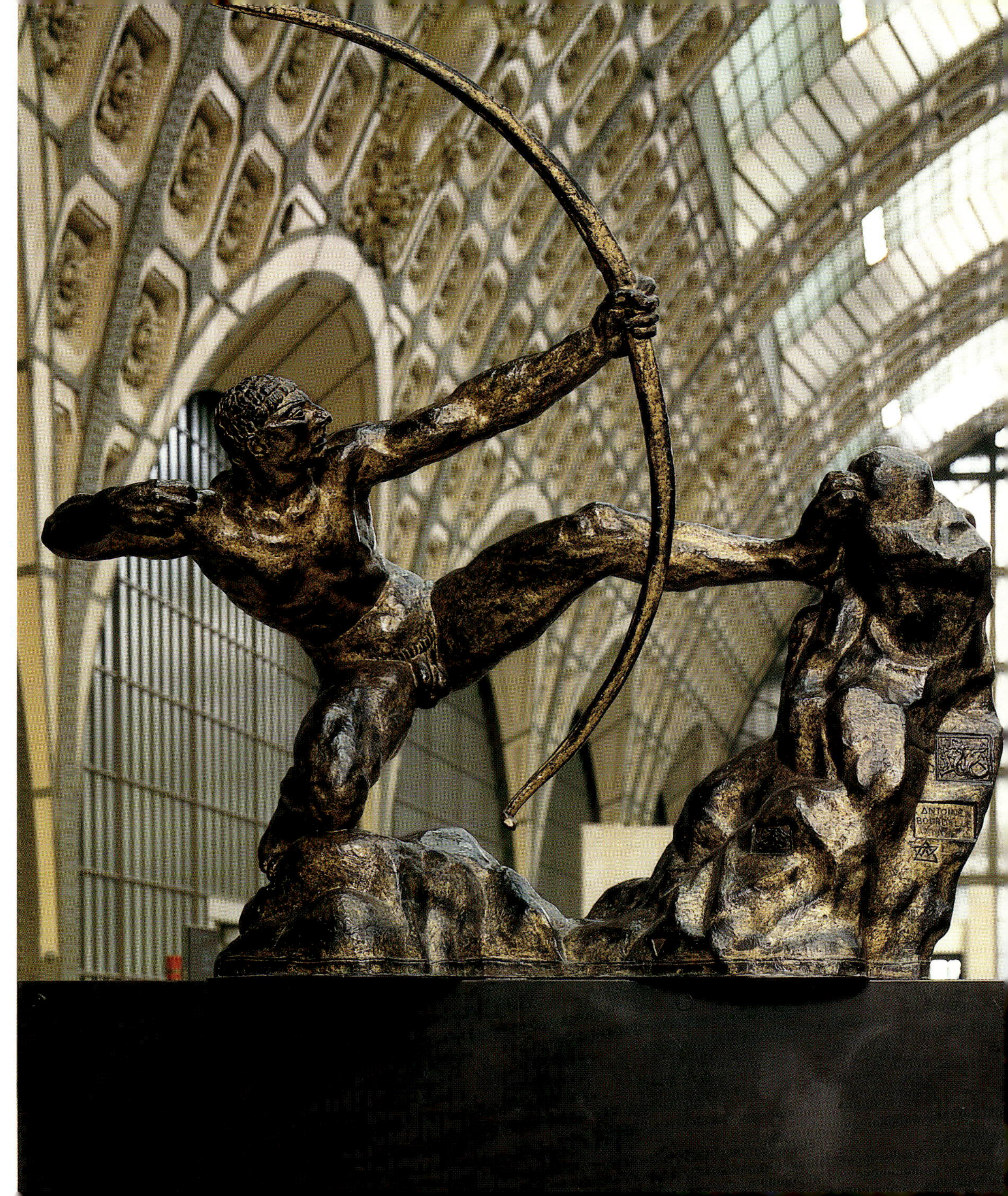

The scream

The ageing athlete, Milon of Crotona, presumptuously boasted he would rip a tree apart with his bare hands, but, the punishment fitting the crime, the trunk shut on his hand like a trap, leaving him helpless against an attack by a lion. When Maria-Teresa saw the version of his agony by the sculptor Pierre Puget, she exclaimed compassionately: 'The poor fellow!' Puget here harks back to the famous Antique group of the *Laocoon* in the collection of the Vatican, and especially to its principal figure, the Trojan priest screaming in pain. As the German philosopher Lessing pointed out, his cry does nothing to detract from the beauty of his face. In the case of *Milon de Crotona*, the historian Herding has shown that the sculptor captures the physical pain, his body is shot through by powerful intersecting diagonals that translate the extreme suffering that grips him. 'Puget the melancholic, the emperor of convicts', as Baudelaire dubbed him in his poem *Les Phares*, would often seize the opportunity to study the physiques of the stevedores slaving away in the ports and arsenals of Marseille and Genoa where he worked. Puget paved the way for the Romantic genius unafraid to put the scream at the forefront of sculpture, as in the case of François Rude, who, for the Arc de Triomphe in Paris, rallies the nation with a cry that became an anthem — *La Marseillaise*.

Let us finish with the cry of a simple countrywoman who is none other than Montserrat, daughter of the Holy Land of Spain. And her cry is *'No Pasaran'*, which Julio González intended as a 'genius' for Spanish Republicans to act as a pendant to the upraised fist that was the emblem of their struggle.

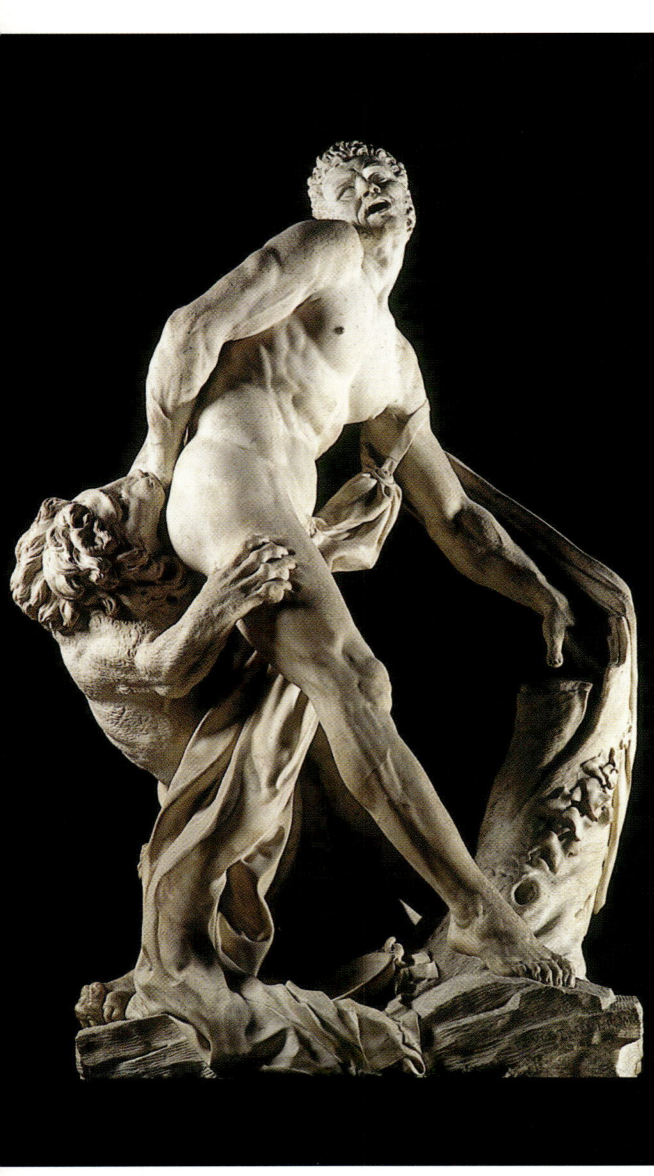

Pierre Puget

Milon of Crotona, 1670-82

Carrara marble. 270 x 140 x 80 cm - ML

Julio González

Mask of Montserrat Shouting, c. 1938-39

Welded wrought iron, patina. 22 x 15.5 x 12 cm - CP

François Rude

Génie de la Patrie, 1836/1898

Plaster. 224 x 196 x 90 cm - MO

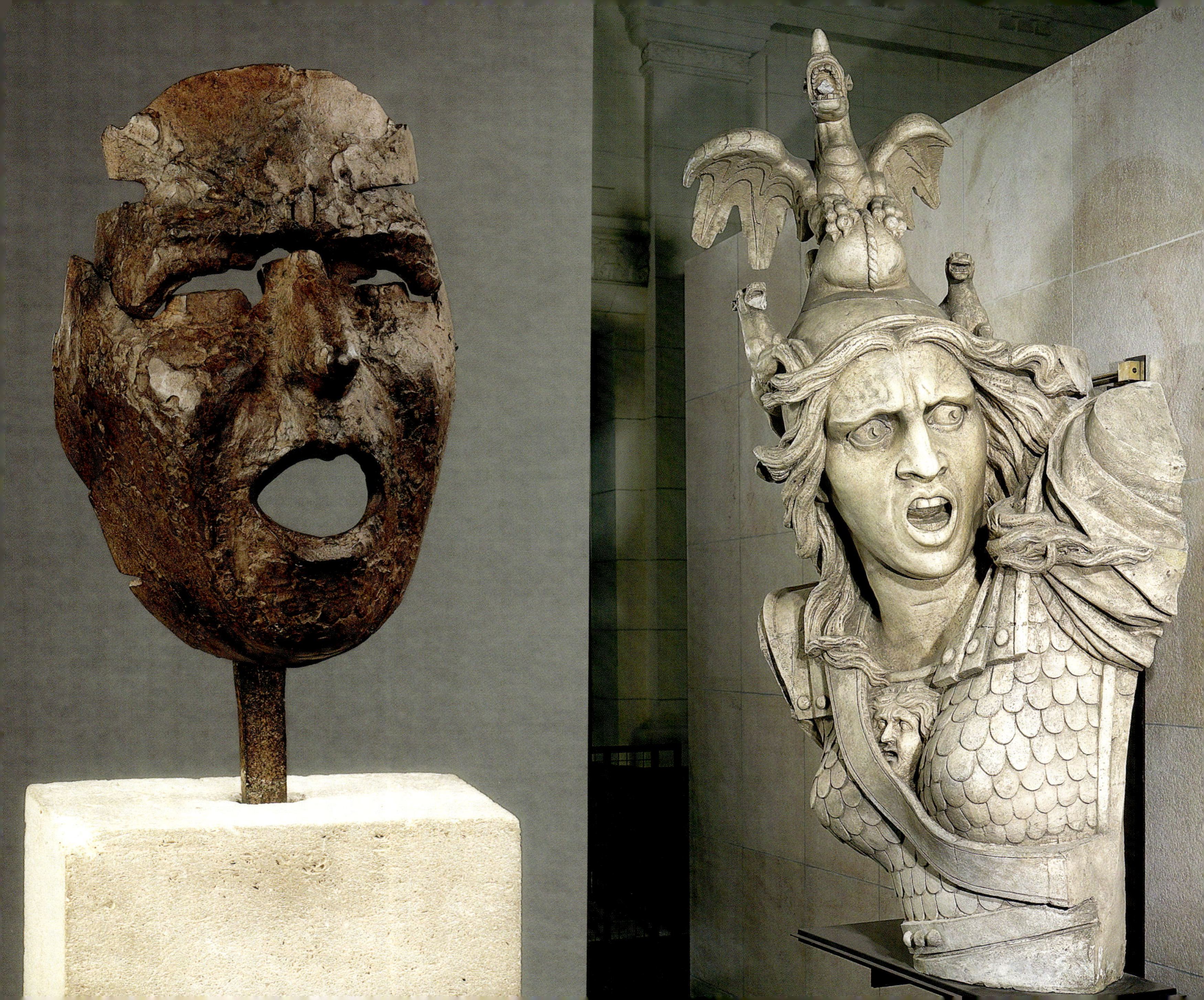

Eyes and glances

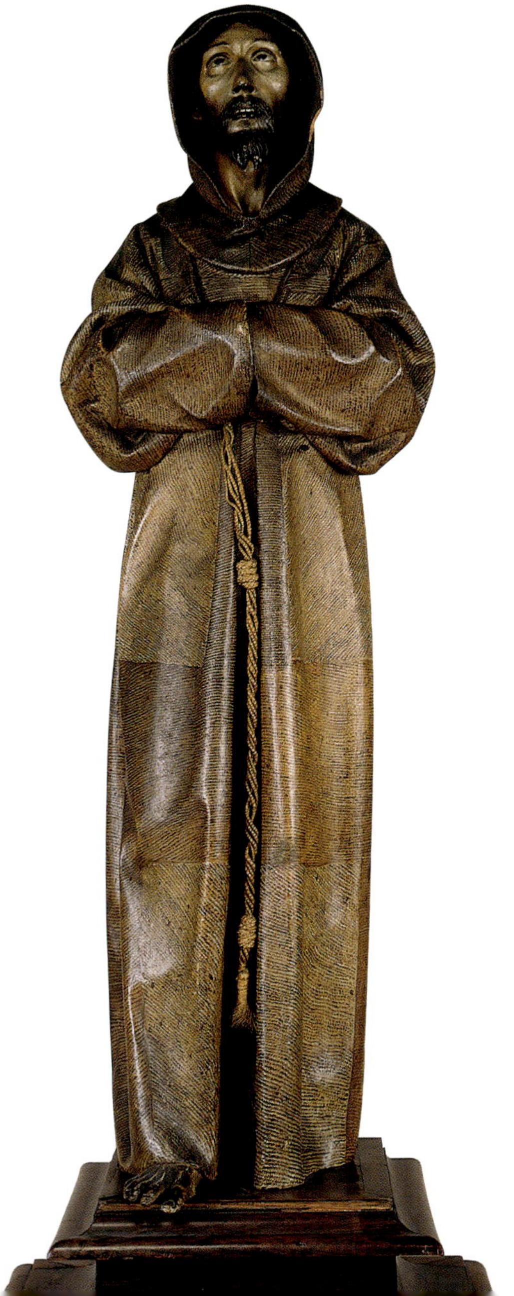

Alberto Giacometti took against the use of coloured stones by the creator of the Egyptian *Seated Scribe* to indicate the statue's eyes: 'Eyes, but unseeing!' he protested. The ecstatic glance of this Spanish School *Dead St Francis* reveals nothing vacuous or artificial, on the contrary. These are glass eyes, nonetheless, but used in the spirit of Hispanic statuary that habitually clothes its figures, revelling in a wealth of materials. Here, the teeth are made of bone, the cord is real hemp; the saint, complete with stigmata, is portrayed in an unusual pose, standing up in his tomb.

Max Klinger underscores the eyes of *Cassandra* the seer — she, who, unheeded, predicted the fall of Troy and who, brought back captive to Greece, witnessed the tragic end of Agamemnon — with cornelian incrustations. This Symbolist artist was a skilful exponent of polychrome sculpture, which was coming back into vogue in the final decades of the 19th century. His familiarity with the thought of Nietzsche, in particular *The Birth of Tragedy*, endowed the rebirth of mythology in both poetry and arts in central Europe with especial aesthetic profundity. It is hard to say whether the sheer beauty of the figure is diminished or, on the contrary, increased by its sexual ambivalence — an alliance of the masculine and female that seems to have fused Phidias' *Athena* to Praxiteles' *Hermes* — as well as by startling oscillation between the Apollinian and the Dionysian poles.

Giacometti said that he only wanted to paint the glance and that the head just came with it. His *Annette* is proof positive that he followed no inalterable recipe; this time, he took to rendering the eyes only following protracted study of a model holding the pose. For Giacometti, it was not a question of encapsulating some unspecified psychological expression, but of capturing the mysterious, living entity expressed in a glance.

Dead St Francis, Spain, mid-17th century

Walnut, glass (eyes), bone (teeth), hemp (cord), original polychromy

87 x 26 x 24 cm - ML

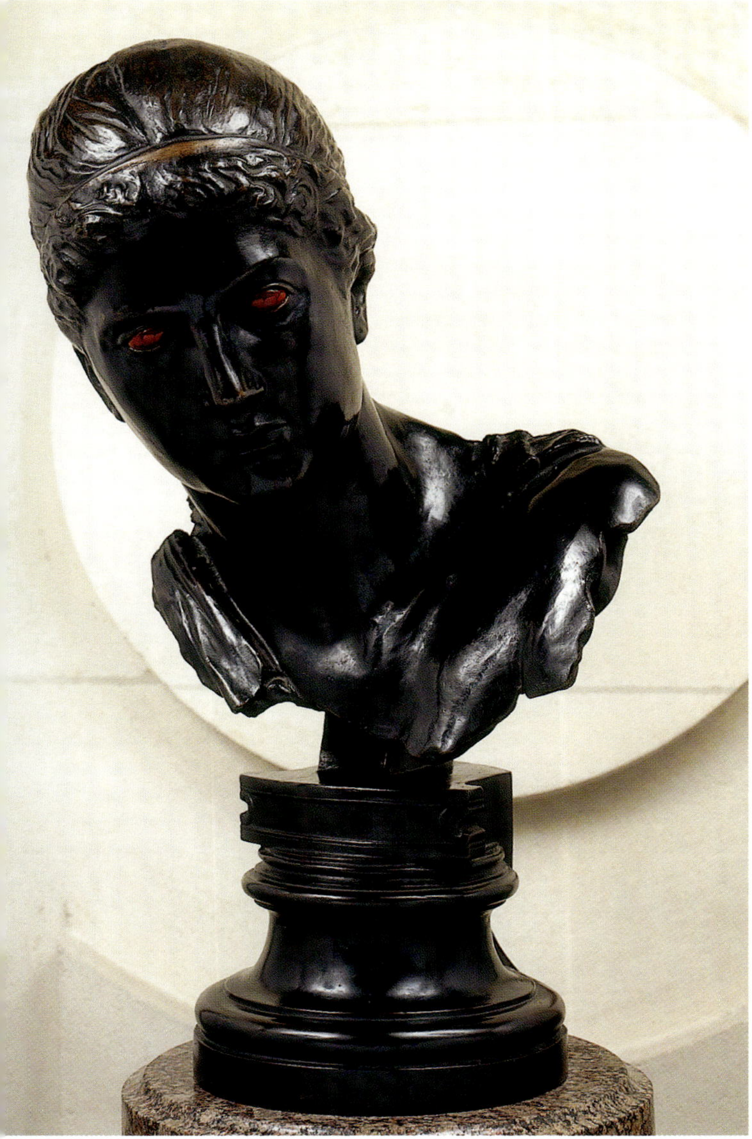

Max Klinger

Cassandra, 1886-95/1903

Bronze, cornelian, traces of gold. 59 x 32 x 35 cm - MO

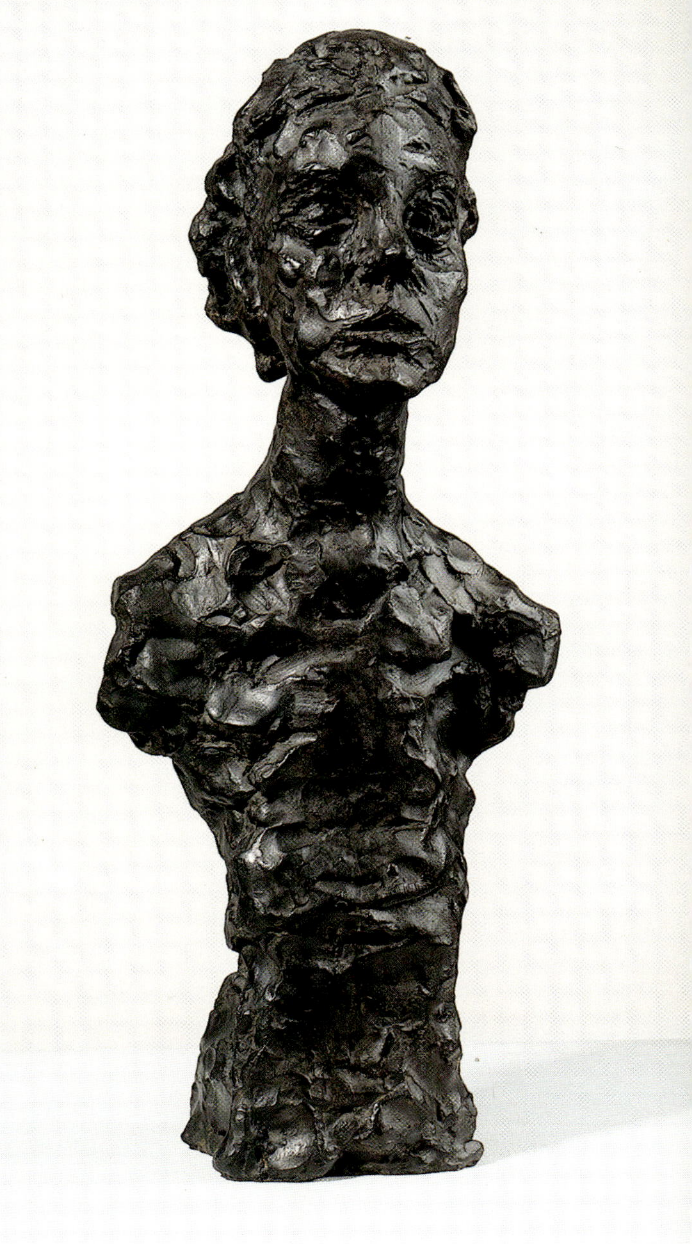

Alberto Giacometti

Annette X, 1965

Bronze. 44 x 18.5 x 13.5 cm - CP

105

Madness

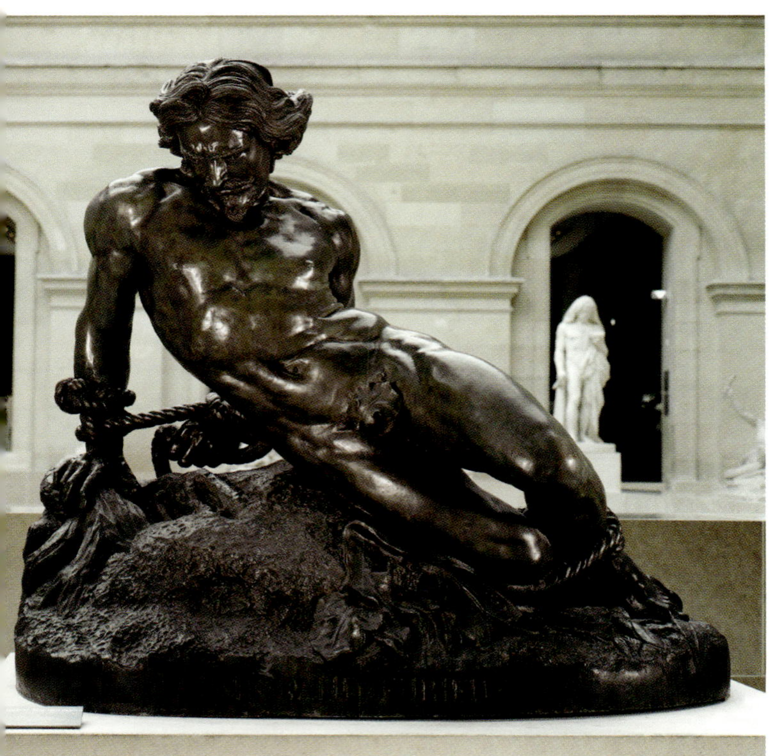

Sculpture has the propensity of unearthing its wildest figures from literature. *Roland Furious (Orlando Furioso)*, a masterpiece by a young man of twenty-three, the model for which was unveiled at the Salon of 1831, is a *Milon of Crotona* prey to overriding passion. Théophile Gautier saw him as 'Roland the Paladin, frothing at the mouth, who, beneath a furrowed brow, rolls a feral, dubious eye.' Jehan Duseigneur has perfectly conveyed Ariosto's text, which describes Orlando driven insane by his disappointed love for Angelica and tied up by his companions.

Jean-Baptiste Carpeaux's *Ugolino*, imprisoned and condemned to devour his own children so as not to die of hunger, is a figure from Dante's *Hell*. The famished father consumes his fingers, his 'own flesh and blood' — a metonymy for his offspring. As his children grasp at his knees pleading — one even offering himself as a sacrifice — they manage one final moment of contact as a prolongation of the father's body, whose race is condemned to die with him. Sculpture cannot depict actual cannibalism as Goya did in painting: the pose would be unbearable, the resulting fragmentation otiose, and colour misplaced. Nonetheless, by dint of the prominent, Michelangelo-esque image of the father, the striking pyramidal structure that places the sons at the foot of their forbear, and by positioning the damned soul plumb in front of the viewer, Carpeaux constructs one of the most expressive images in all sculpture: a figure surging forth from an accumulation of bodies.

To make his *accumulation* that ironically points up the collective folly of mass murder, Arman drew from the real: a gas-mask is morphed into a 20th-century warrior helm, worn to defend the 'home' (*Home, Sweet Home*), one's native soil. The artist, himself a collector of African masks, exploits the formal analogy to reflect back onto Western audiences an image of cruelty that it all too readily projects onto other continents, and onto Africa in particular.

Jehan Duseigneur
Orlando Furioso, 1867
Bronze. 130 x 140 x 90 cm - ML

Jean-Baptiste Carpeaux
Ugolino, 1860
Bronze. 194 x 148 x 119 cm - MO

Arman
Home, Sweet Home, 1960
Gas masks in a box under Plexiglas.
160 x 140.5 x 20.3 cm - CP

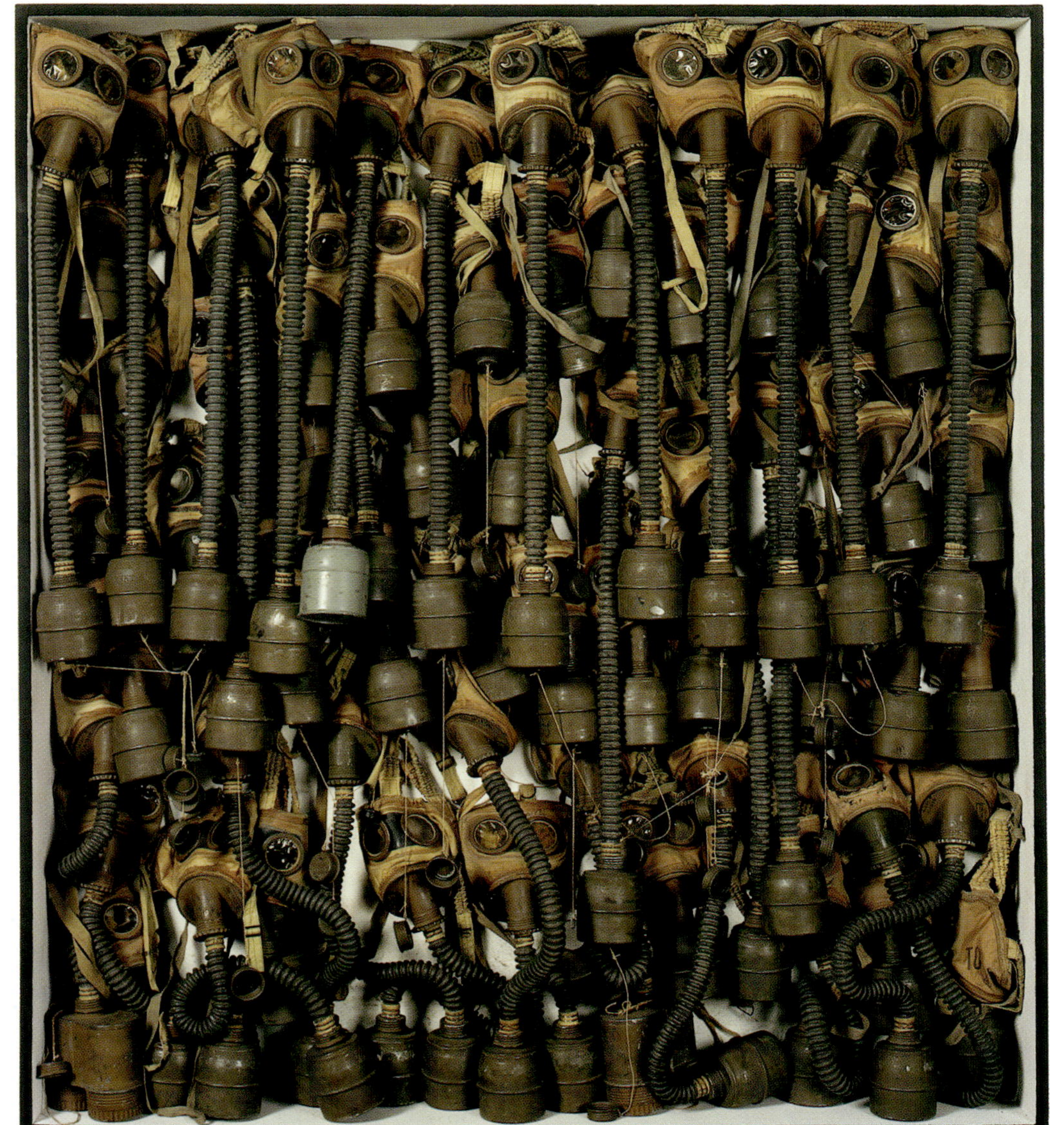

Pain

Alexandre Falguière

Tarcisius, Christian Martyr, 1868
Marble. 64 x 140 x 59 cm - MO

Gina Pane

Francis of Assisi Three Times with the Stigmata, 1985-87
Zinc-plated iron, iron, rust, frosted glass.
169.6 x 198 x 2.2 cm - CP

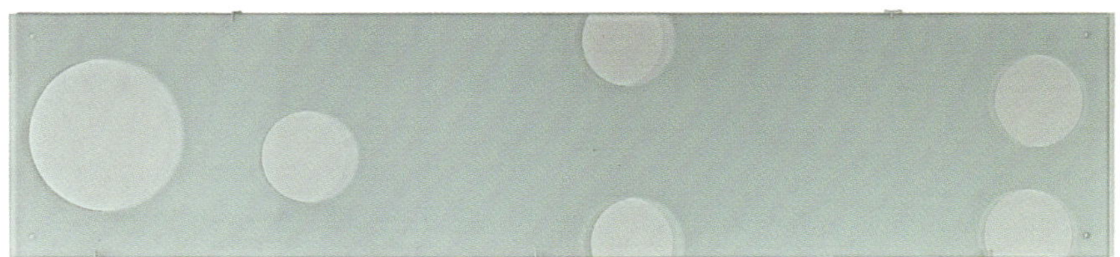

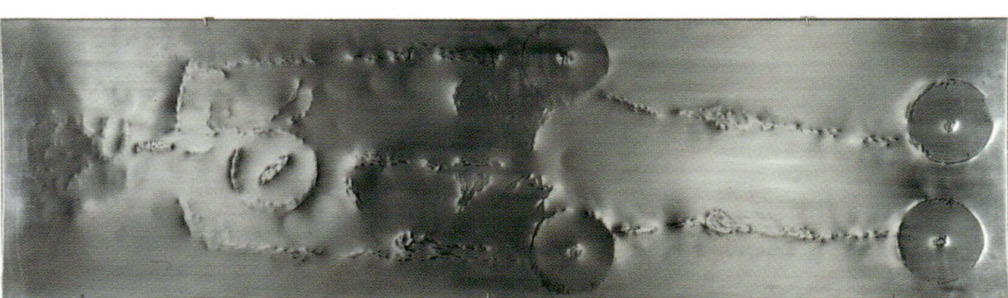

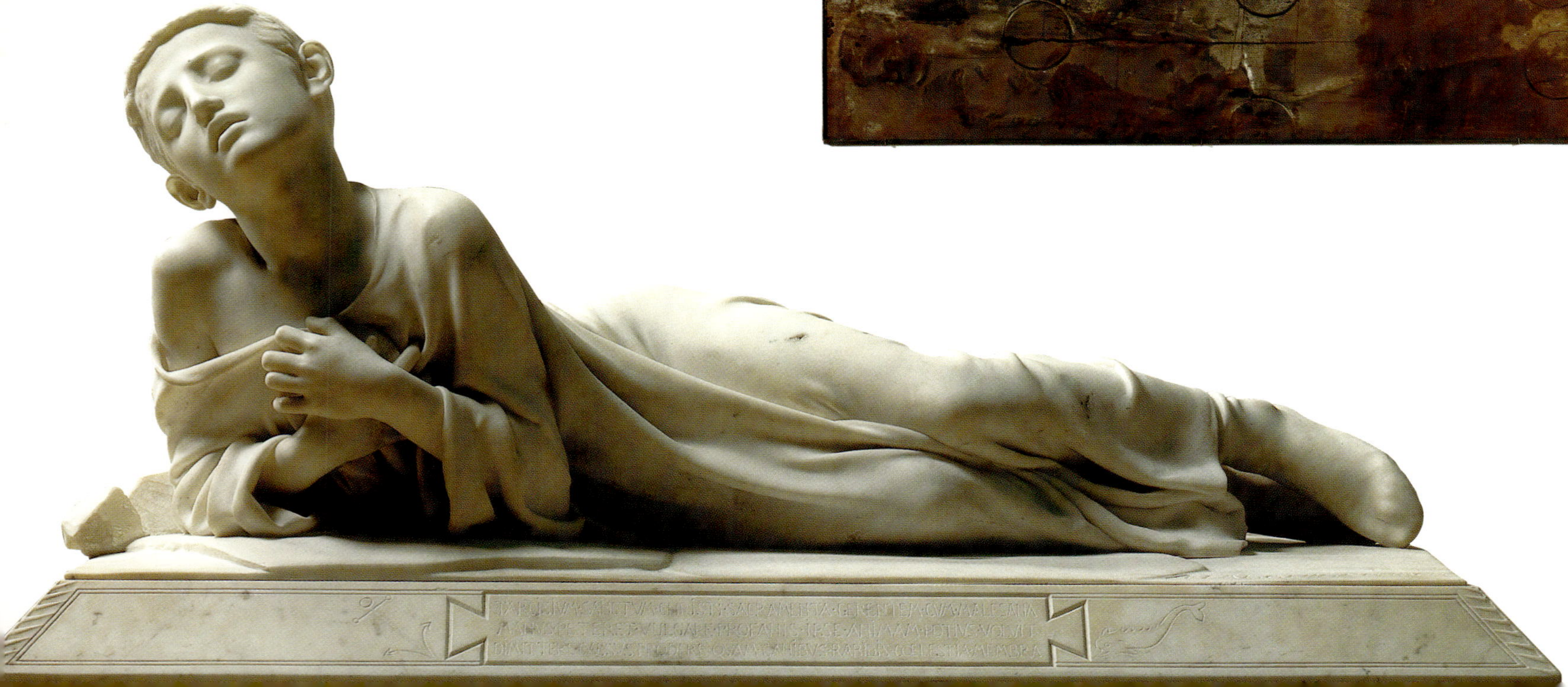

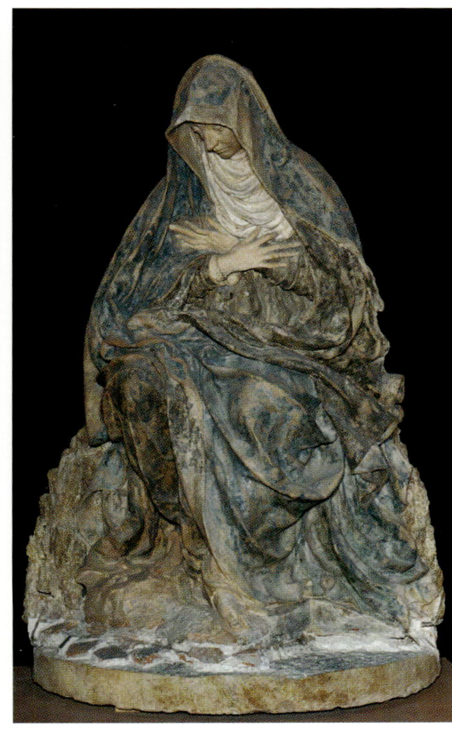

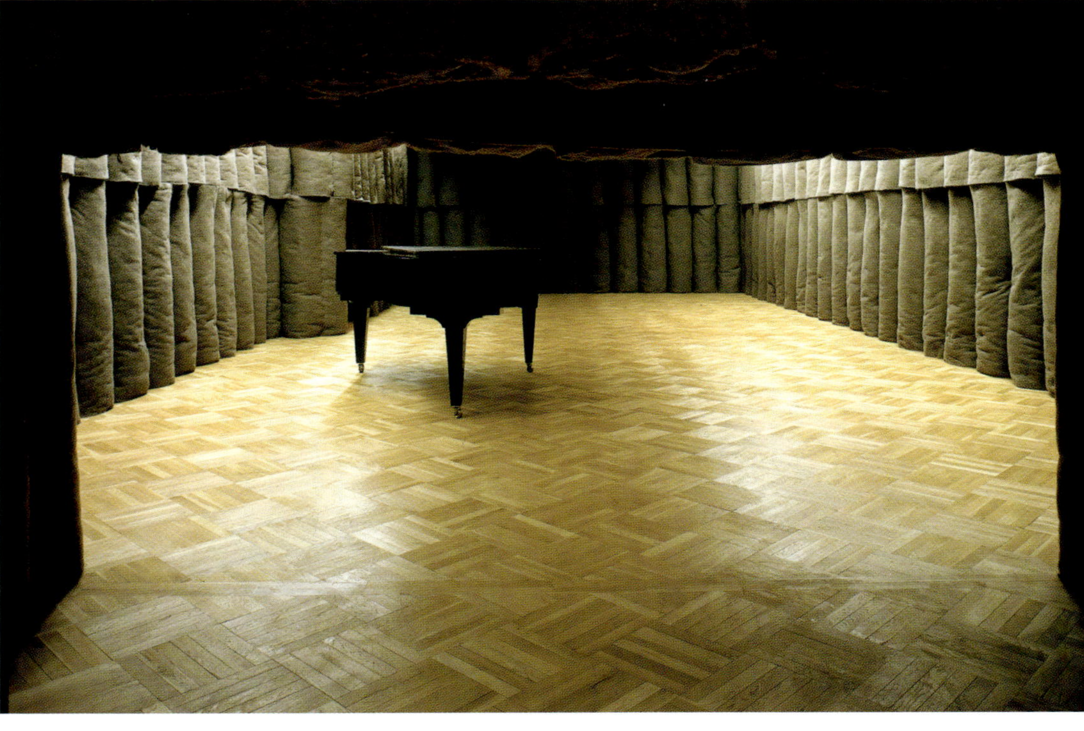

Marks of pain, evidence of divine election: slumped headlong, the young martyr Tarcisius depicted by Alexandre Falguière boasts a sublime face, transfigured, like that of the Blessed Ludovica Albertoni in the unforgettable funerary effigy carved by Bernini.

As a practitioner of body art, for many years Gina Pane gave performances during which she would mutilate her own body in what she saw as a symbolic protest against the violence perpetrated on others (by war, racism, sexism, intolerance and so on). During a visit to Sienna, she was forcibly struck by the resemblance between her own self-mutilation and certain paintings of the stigmatisation of St Francis. The work in which she preserved the memory of this encounter consists of three lengthwise panels forming a progression: 'wound of the body, decomposition, transfiguration.' Repoussé zinc-plated iron figures the stigmata, then comes untreated iron left to rust, and finally frosted glass suggesting an immaterial presence.

By the sunken folds of the *Virgin of Sorrows*' mantle, Germain Pilon expresses the suffering that grips a mother grieving for her lost child. These are neither the pleats of Gothic statuary, nor the drapery that covers the lamenting figures in funerary sculpture. These ample folds translate a new gravity, while the drooping head conveys the resigned acceptance of the sacrifice.

Josef Beuys' *Plight* also concerns redemptive suffering. The dual impression of constraint — one has to bend down to pass the threshold — and of enclosure, created by the double row of rolls of felt one on top of the other, turns finally into a sense of inner peace: the heated environment is a physical equivalent of 'warming' the soul. This viewers experience as they pass from a first room into a second in which stands a piano whose music they can only hear with their inward ear, like the memory of something pleasant or a striving for harmony: later, leaving as one came in, one is as if galvanised by a source of new life. Beuys was feeling his way to this piece in a preliminary version entitled *Ulysses* as early as 1958, a homage to two themes in James Joyce's novel of the same name: the journey and the labyrinth.

Germain Pilon

Virgin of Sorrows, 1590

Polychrome terracotta and gypsum. 159 x 119 x 81 cm - ML

Joseph Beuys

Plight, 1985

Installation: 43 elements with 5 felt rolls (each), grand piano, blackboard, thermometer. 310 x 890 x 1813 cm - CP

Happiness, happiness?

Paul Gauguin
Soyez amoureuses, vous serez heureuses, 1901
Right-hand plinth from the Maison du Jouir
Polychrome giant sequoia wood. 45 x 204 x 2 cm - MO

François Rude
Neapolitan Fisherman Playing with a Tortoise, 1833 Salon
Marble. 82 x 88 x 48 cm - ML

Louise Bourgeois
Precious Liquids, 1992
Environment: water tank in cedarwood ringed in metal, glass,
alabaster, fabric, embroidery, water, rubber balls
H: 427 cm ; diam: 442 cm - CP

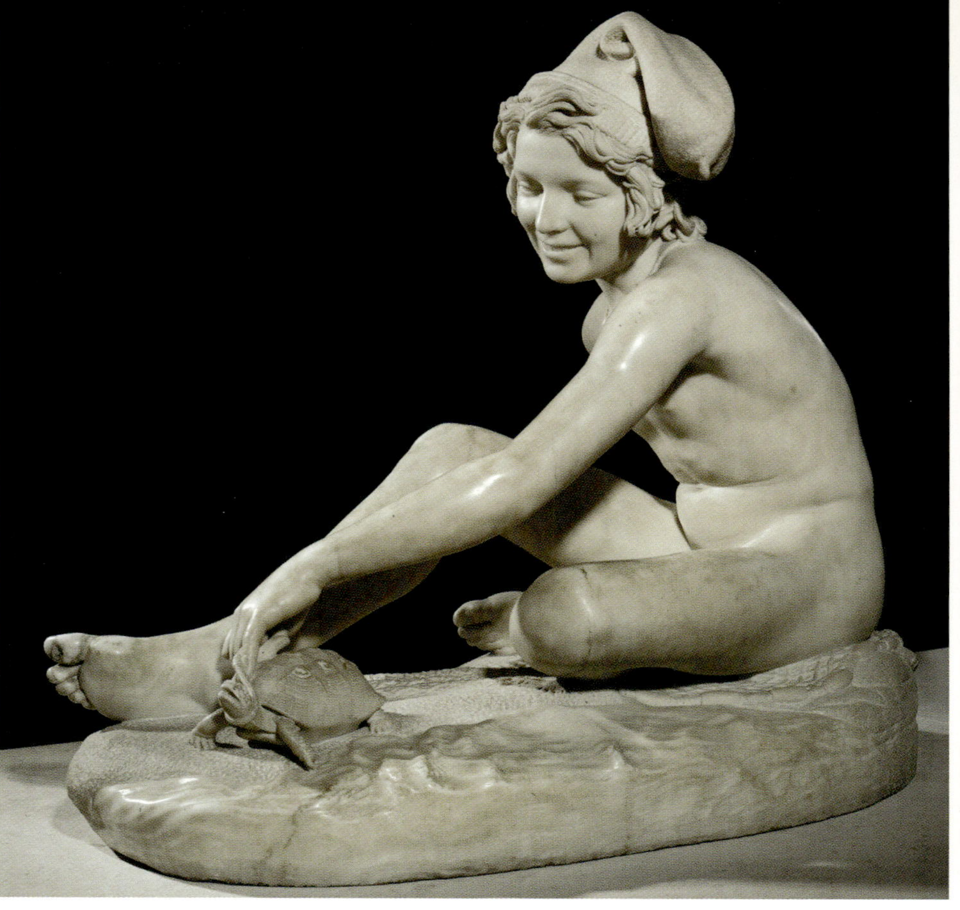

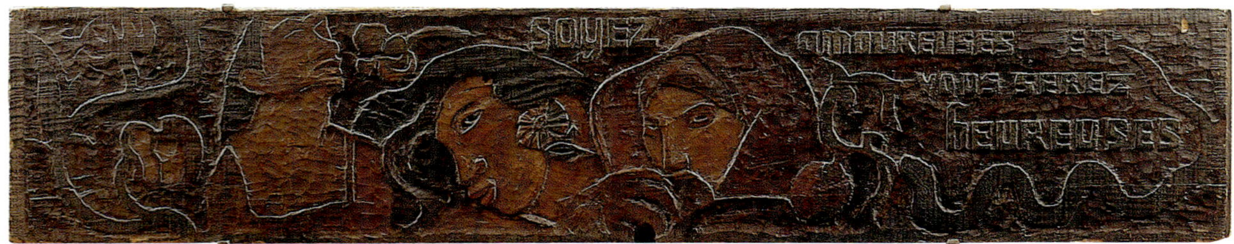

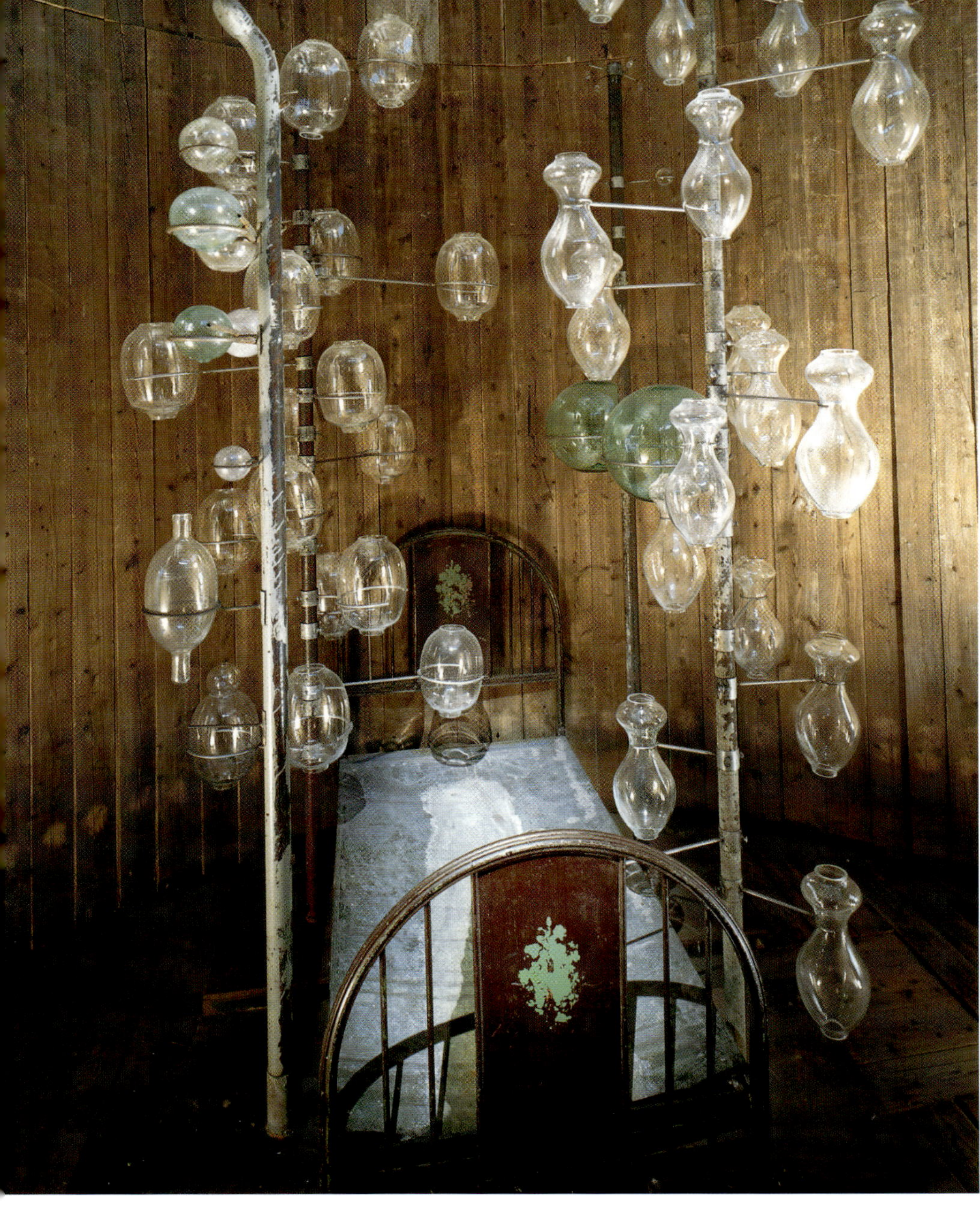

In *Neapolitan Fisherman Playing with a Tortoise*, the plaster model for which was exhibited at the 1831 Salon, François Rude returned to the Hellenistic theme of children playing. The boyish fisher with his bonnet and scapular, whose brilliant, broad smile exposes his teeth far back in his mouth (a formula Carpeaux was to remember), hails from a romanticised Italy, the Italy of Madame de Staël's novel *Corinne* and the one painted by artists such as Léopold Robert, in which the lower classes were thoroughly idealised. *Young Fisherman Dancing the Tarentella* by Francisque Duret is in much the same spirit.

Paul Gauguin and Louise Bourgeois address the question of happiness in two entirely distinct contexts. 'In primitive art you will always find nourishing milk,' wrote Gauguin in 1897. For him, the paradise of Tahiti was also that of a free, sincere love whose precepts he emblazoned on a panel in his Maison du Jouir: *Soyez amoureuses et vous serez heureuses*, 'Be in love and you'll be happy.'

Happiness is also departure: 'flee, far over there', Gauguin's friend Mallarmé had written. In *Precious Liquids*, the Franco-American artist Louise Bourgeois places the following recommendation on a wooden tank similar to those one finds on roofs in New York: 'Art is a guarantee of sanity.' In the heart of the modern metropolis, the artist proposes an answer, a woman's answer, to the mechanics of the exchange of liquids and gases in Duchamp's *Large Glass*: elements for the explanation of such a piece are to be sought in symbolism and depth psychology.

The bed, in which we spend a substantial part of our life from birth to death, stands in the centre of the wooden tank. Within the flasks takes place the transmutation of the humours and secretions occasioned by anguish, suffering, desire and anger into 'precious liquids'. Through art, human beings at last encounter passion instead of terror.

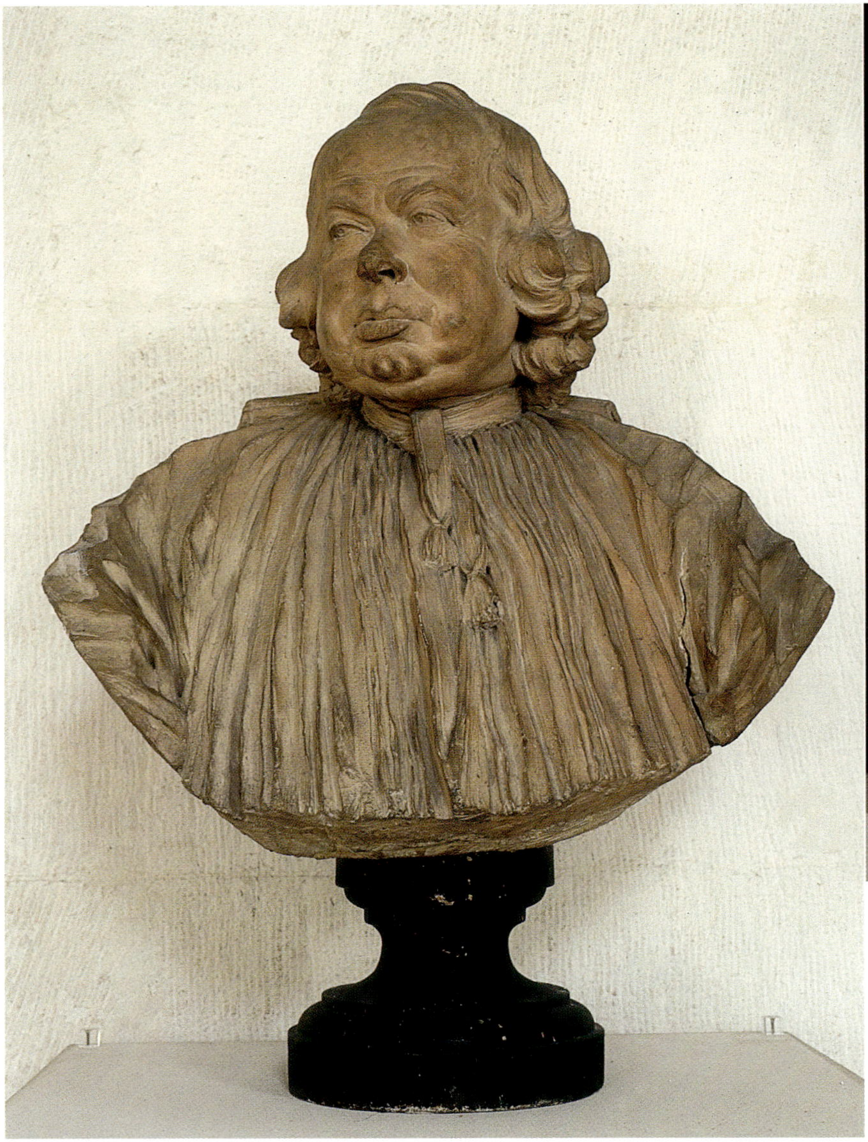

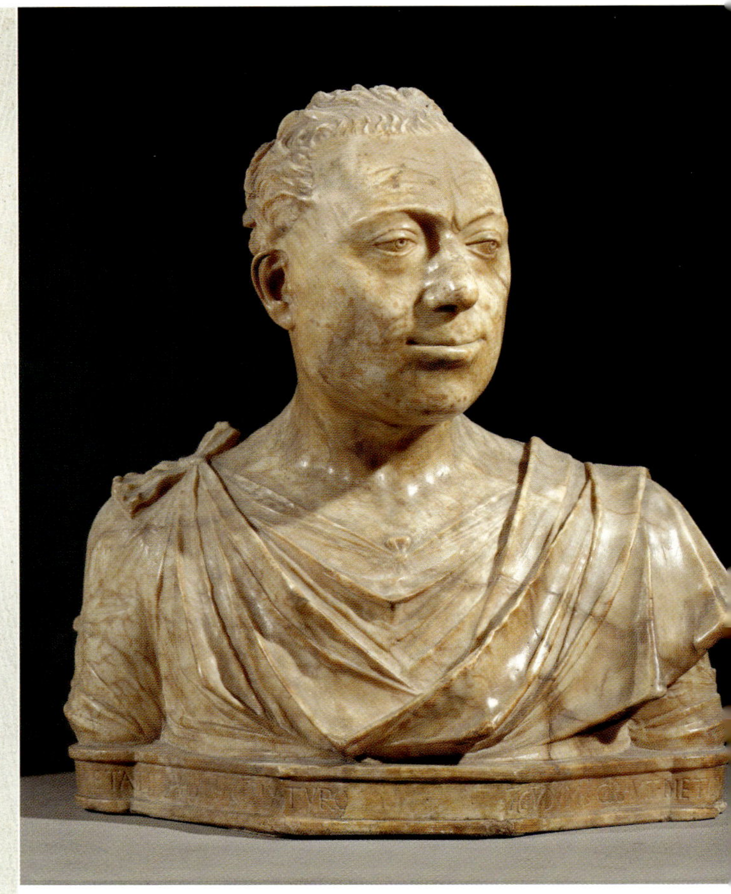

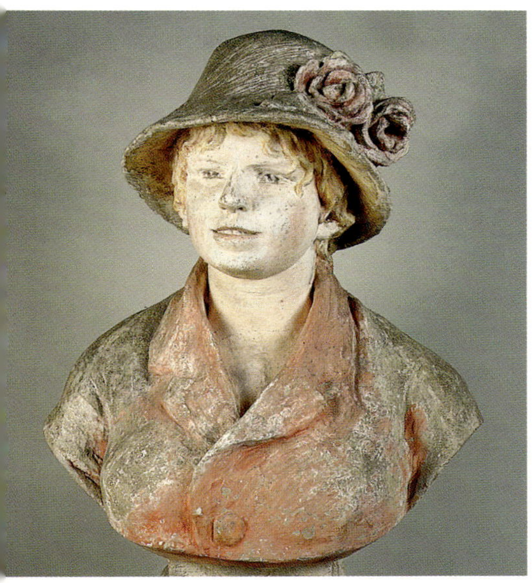

Jean-Jacques Caffieri
Canon Alexandre-Gui Pingré (1711-1796), 1788
Terracotta. 51 x 51 x 34 cm - ML

Mino da Fiesole
Dietisalvi Neroni (1406-1482), 1464
Marble. 57 cm x 50 cm - ML

Auguste Renoir and Richard Guino
Madame Renoir, 1916
Polychrome mortar. 82 x 53 x 34 cm - MO

Alberto Giacometti
Bust of Diego, 1954
Bronze. 40 x 33.7 x 19 cm - CP

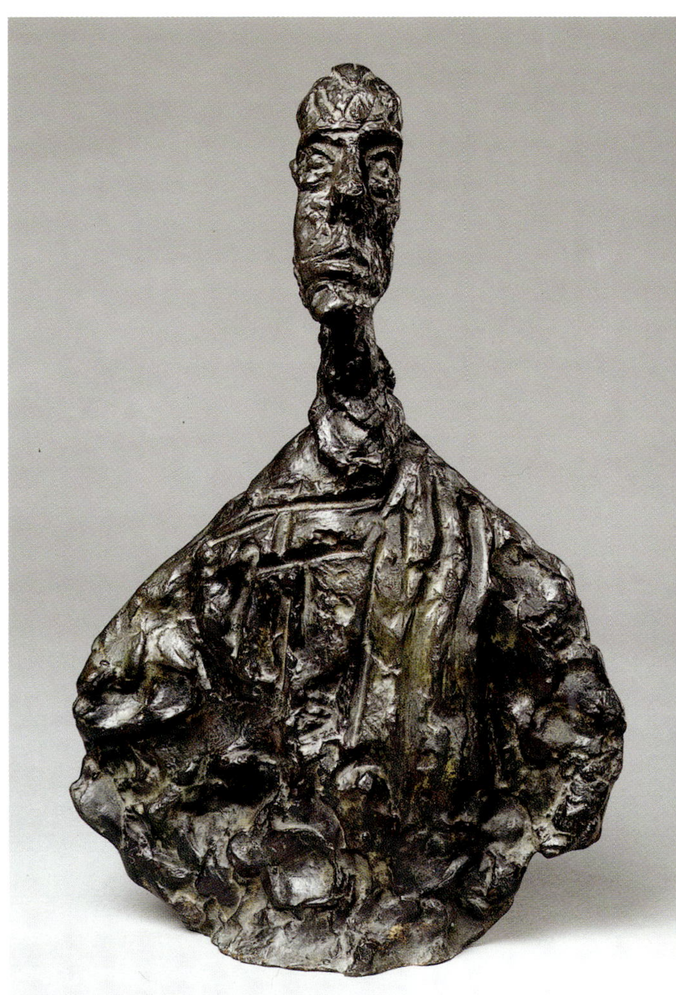

Five centuries separate the revival of carved portraiture by Mino da Fiesole and the *Bust of Diego* by Alberto Giacometti. The first portrait bust of the Quattrocento to be dated with certitude is that of Piero de Medici carved in 1453 by Mino. It was not yet a portrait in strict accordance with nature, as was to become increasingly the practice after 1460, but a true realistic portrait and not just an inflated heroic effigy devised to exalt the *fama* or *virtù* of the patron-sitter. Portrayed at around the age of sixty, this is Diotisalvi Neroni, a Florentine humanist and opponent of the Medicis who died in exile in Rome.

The portrait of the '*bonhomme Pingré*', French Astronomer Royal and a canon of Sainte-Geneviève in Paris, presented at the 1789 Salon by Jean-Jacques Caffieri, and that of *Madame Renoir*, designed and painted by Auguste Renoir, displays the same vigorous vitality. While plumpness and brightness characterise the portrait of the artist's wife, the double chin and jovial mien of the bon vivant, the epicure's mouth and the mischievous glint in the astronomer's eye seem to confirm his motto: *Uti conviva satur* ('Die like a satisfied diner').

Diego is one of the innumerable portraits of his brother that Giacometti realised after breaking with the Surrealist group and reverting to figuration in 1934-35. The sculptor's intention had been to study a head for a number of weeks with a view to executing some figure groups: the study was in fact to last his whole life. The resemblance he sought was less one fixed by physiognomy than the reality of a presence.

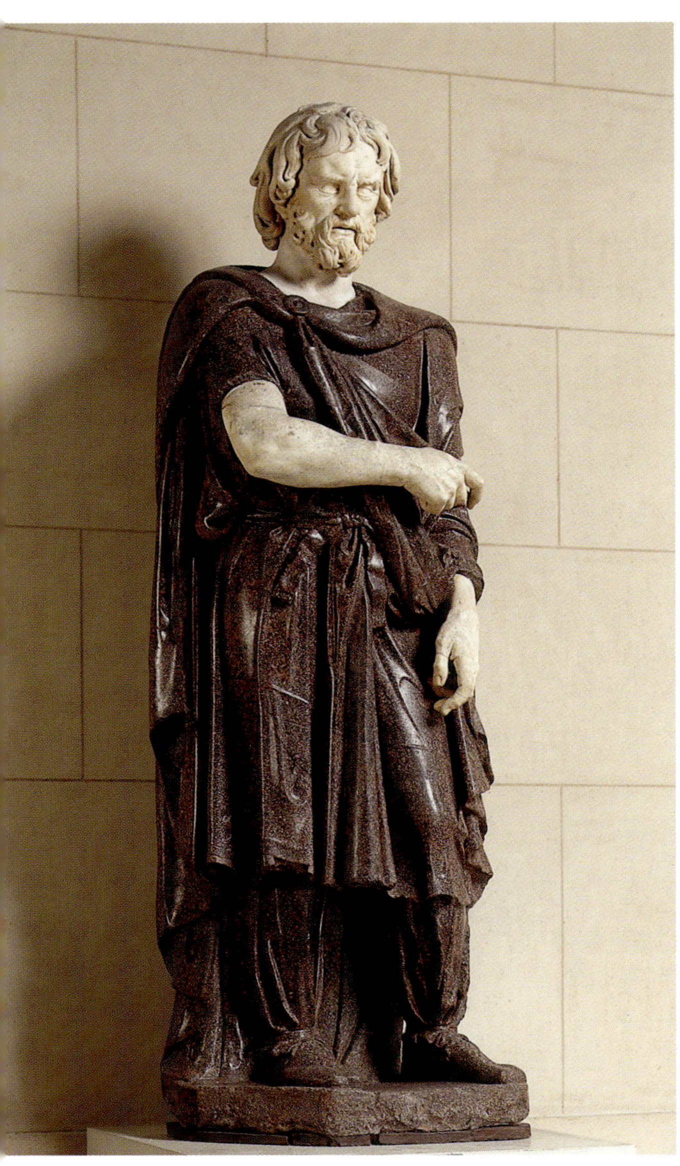

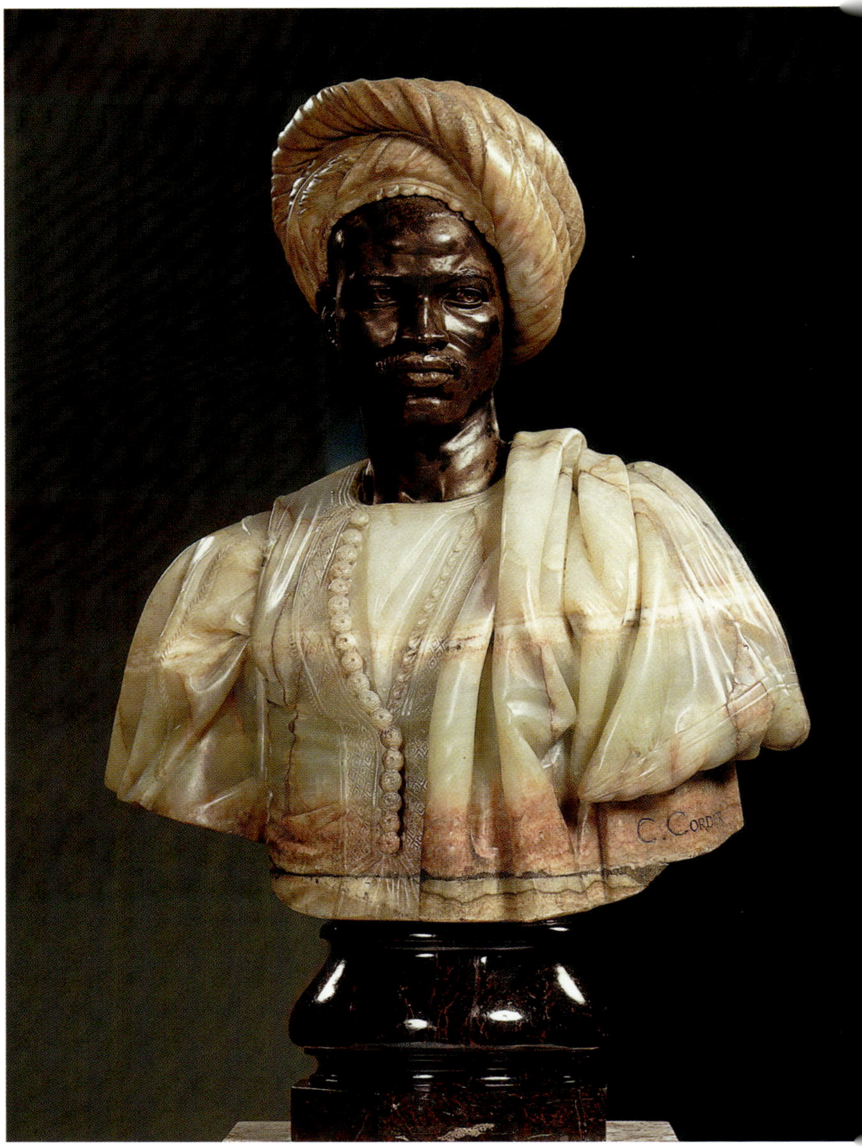

Captive Barbarian, Rome, 2nd century
Red porphyry and white marble
H: 240 cm - ML

Charles Cordier
Negro of the Sudan or *Negro in Algerian Costume,* 1856
Bronze, onyx, Vosges porphyry
96 (of which stand 20) x 66 x 36 cm - MO

Ernesto Neto
We Stopped Just Here at the Time, 2002
Cloth, clove, turmeric, cumin, pepper
400 x 506 x 506 cm - CP

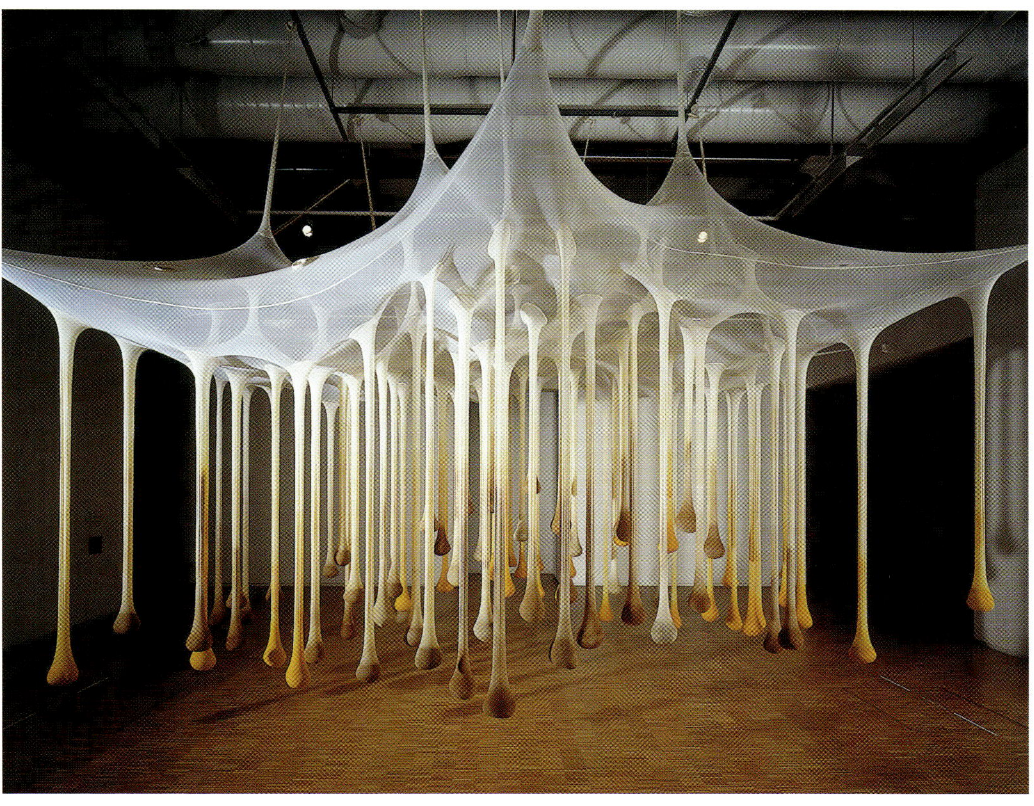

In sculpture, exoticism was at first embodied by faces and postures: those of prisoners placed at the foot of statues depicting the victors in memorials. There was, for example, a black captive among the four figures decorating the pedestal of the Pierre Franqueville's equestrian statue of Henri IV, which, until its destruction in the French Revolution, used to stand on the Pont-Neuf.

The Antique statue of Decius, the *Captive Barbarian*, and the *Negro of Sudan* by Charles Cordier further their theme by the use of a wide range of materials. The costume of the hirsute and bearded 'barbar-ian' consists of porphyry. Polychromy came at an opportune moment in the 19th century, embellishing a gallery of foreign types that colonial expeditions and the new imagery they ushered in was to make popular. In this connection, the incomparable Cordier was an opulent and delicate craftsman. His sculpture resembles a three-dimensional colour daguerreotype, with a sense of contrast where onyx cuts across bronze, the visual impact being enhanced by the porphyry pedestal. Closer to our time, the Brazilian artist Ernesto Neto tackles the sense of smell, hanging exotic spices in astonishing sheaths redo-lent of the models made by Gaudí (the architect used to hang weights from them and mount them upside-down), forming a bizarre structure through which one can walk. Is it a forest? A space buzzing with electrons? Or is Neto, in his way, offering to take us on a voyage inside the body, starting at the base of the hair, the origin of our secretions? A prime example of scientific exoticism.

Grotesques

The unbridled ugliness of the satyr's face and the repulsive task being performed in the *The Rustic Flayer* — stabbing through the beast's pelt as its entrails spurt out — belongs to the grotesque obverse of Greco-Roman statuary. *The Mask of Horror,* carved in enamelled sandstone by the astonishing Jean Carriès, also presents a reinterpretation, in the manner of a grotesque mascaron, of the genre of the expressive head.

This illustration of the alliance between the ironical and the fantastic attains its limit in the environments of the Californian Edward Kienholz, whose art is a pessimistic exploration, at once tender and scathing, of the soft underbelly of America. His environments feature characters from the present-day 'American scene' whose attitudes and clothing are recognisable but whose heads have been metamorphosed. *State Hospital* denounces the inhumanity of the psychiatric ward, while *The Art Show* mocks the 'pettiness of the art world'. The sculptor readily reworks the great scenes of Hollywood cinema, which loom so large in the popular imagination: in *The Dodge* he treats with crude realism the inevitable backseat love scene. Here, we have the story of a couple's break-up as they make love in a shabby room, each thinking of something else, as shown on miniature monitors that record their fantasies. The plum-like shape of their heads is explained in the childish ditty that plays on unaccountably in the background of this extraterrestrial yet human, all too human, world.

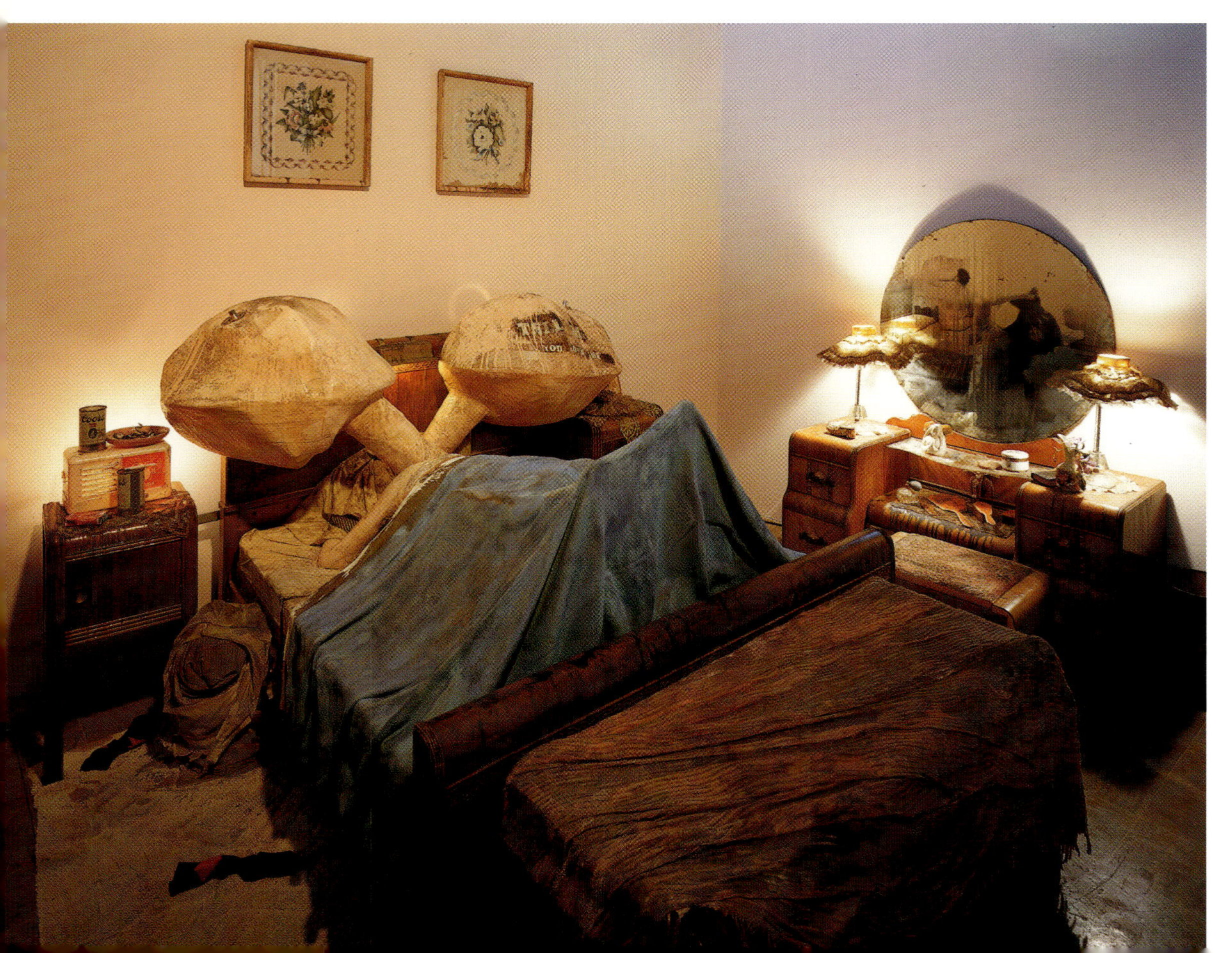

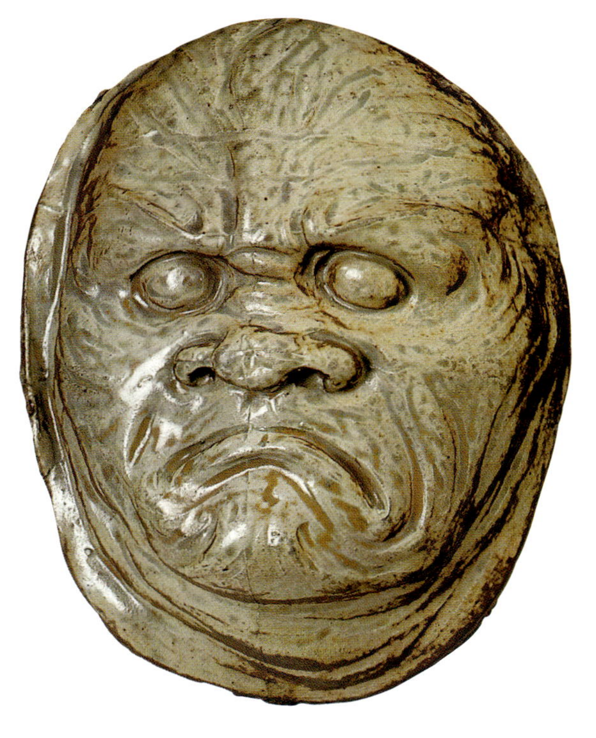

Edward Kienholz
While Visions of Sugar Plums Danced in their Heads, 1964
Sound installation: furniture, bedding, radio, framed prints, fibreglass
dummies. 180 x 360 x 270 cm - CP

Jean Carriès
Masque of Horror, 1891
Enamelled stoneware. 28 x 22 cm - MO

The Rustic Flayer, Rome, 1st-2nd century
Marble. H: 107 cm - ML

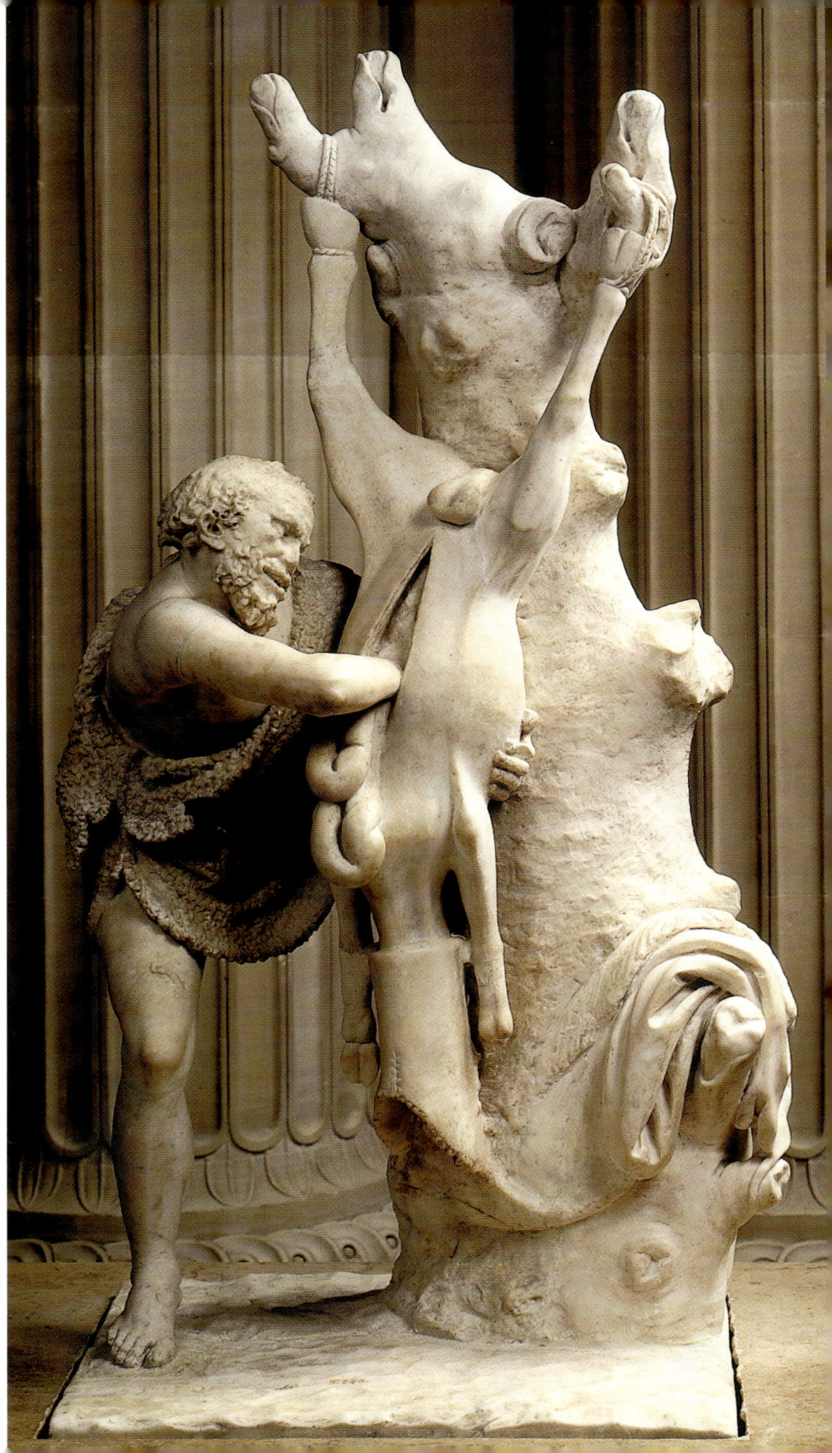

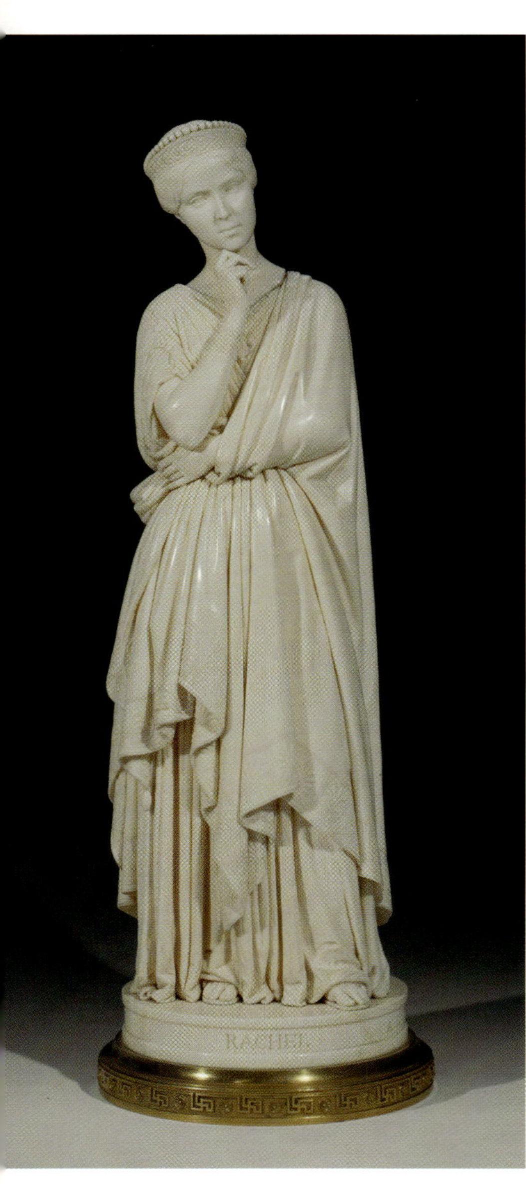

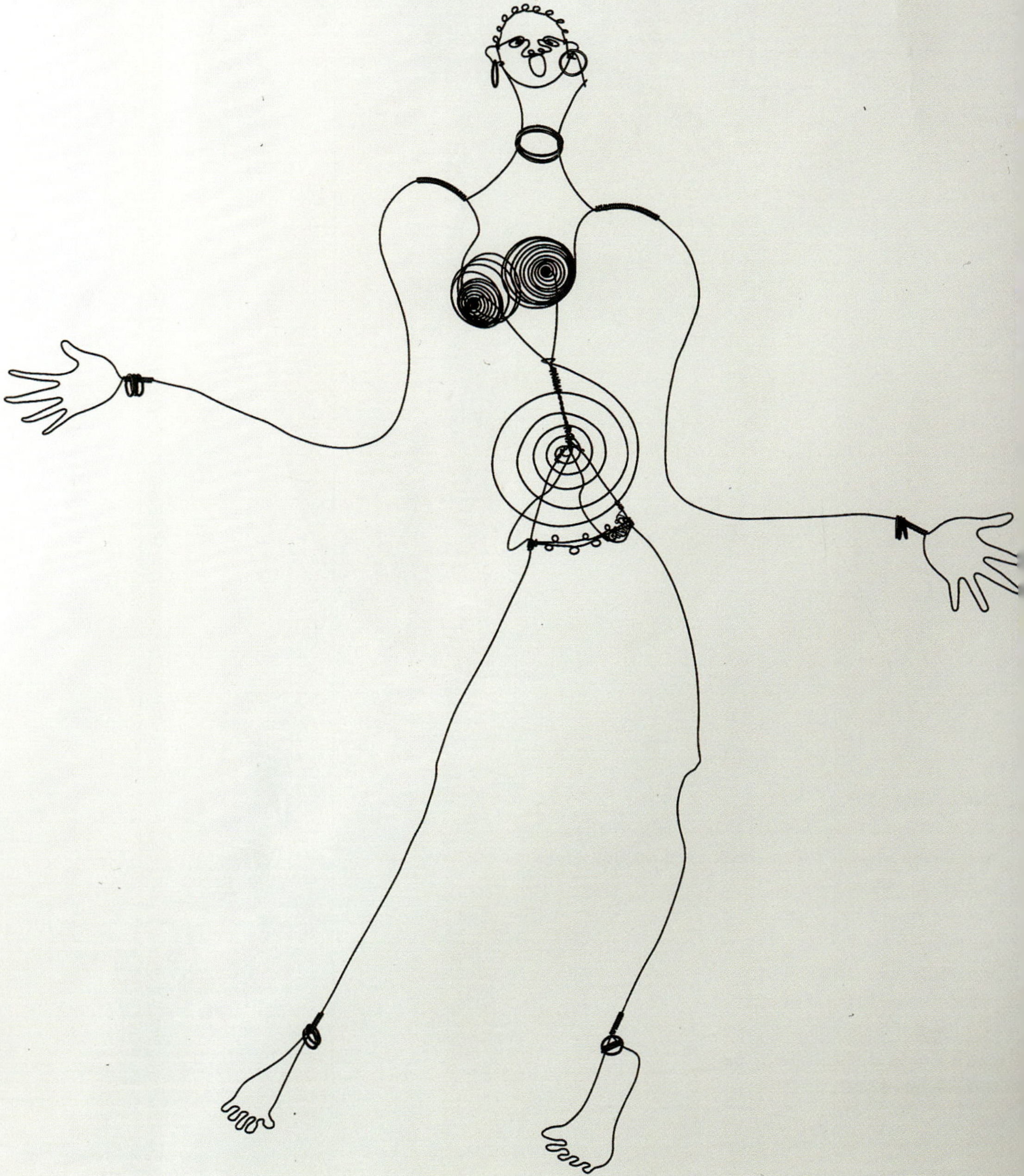

Women on the stage

'This is Tragedy!' the poet Alfred de Musset exclaimed when he saw the actress Rachel in the role of Camille. The Prince de Joinville, son of Louis-Philippe, declared she 'had a genius for costume, for drapery.' Beneath her peplum, one seemed to glimpse an Antique statue. She had moreover become an allegory in her own lifetime and was represented singing the *Marseillaise* wrapped in the French flag during the Revolution of 1848. Here, her pensive figure illustrates the vogue for Romantic statuettes. Another actress, Sarah Bernhardt, was also a great sculptor: this is why Jean-Léon Gérôme paid her the homage of this richly coloured and expressive bust, with, affixed to the base, figurines referring at once to her work as a sculptor and to her career as a tragic actress. In the same vein, Milhomme had already carved a bust of Andromaque historiated with piquant scenes, today also in the Louvre.

This silhouette of the variety artist Josephine Baker amply demonstrates the fascination she must have exerted on the young Alexander Calder, who was a devoted spectator whenever she appeared in Paris. His memory abuzz, the American artist would fashion little sculptures as lively as those in the miniature circuses for which he became renowned. At the outset, it is a drawing in space made out of wire. A twisting treble clef rolls up round the navel, whereas the bracelets and necklaces indicating the dancer's joints amount to humorous suggestions of volume.

Jean Auguste Barre
Rachel (1821-1858), **1848**
Ivory on a gilded bronze plinth. 46 x 13 x 13 cm - ML

Alexander Calder
Josephine Baker I, also called *Dance,* **1926**
Wire. 100.5 x 84 x 21 cm - CP

Jean-Léon Gérôme
Sarah Bernhardt, **1895**
Stained marble. 69 x 41 x 29 cm - MO

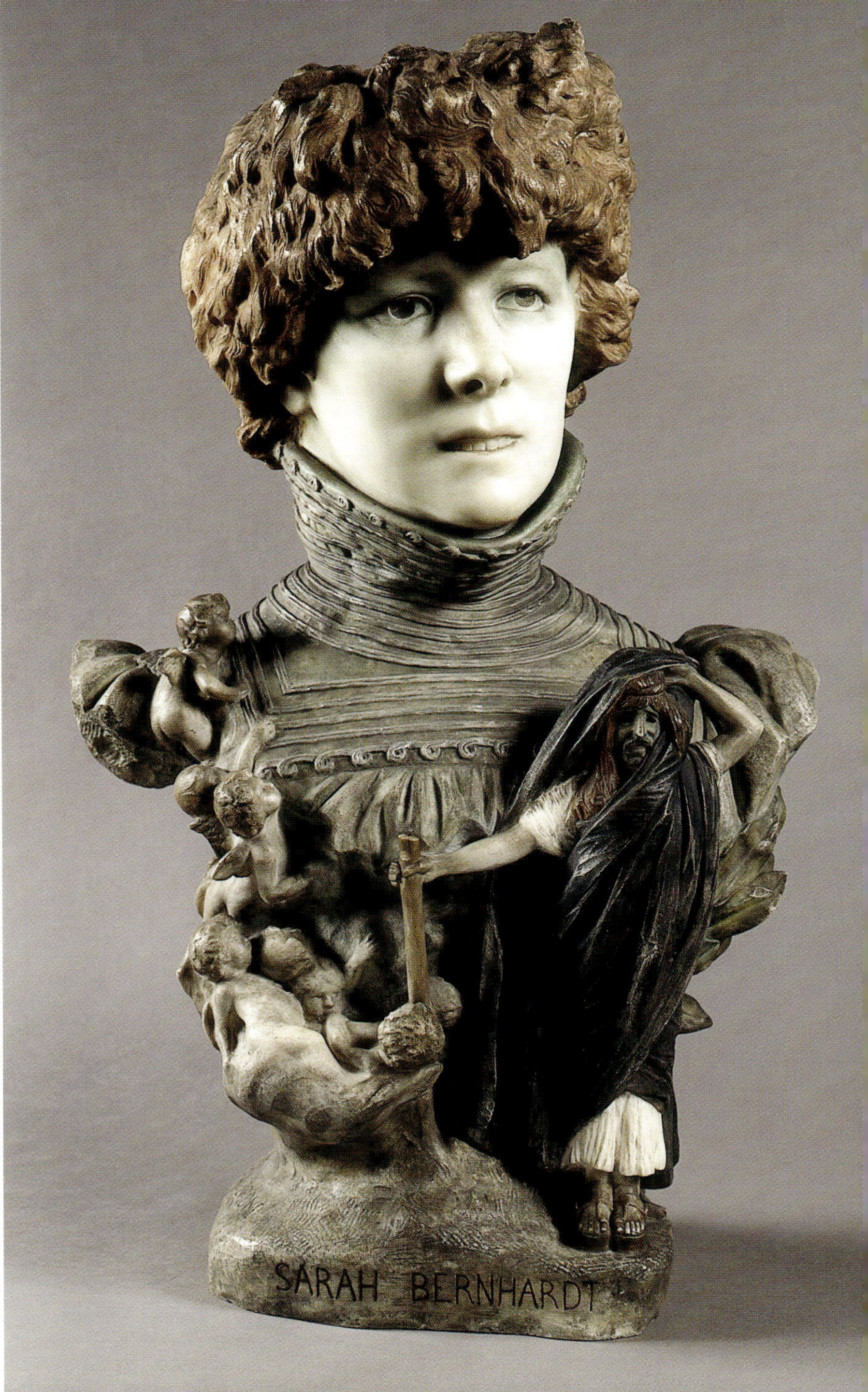

Commemoration

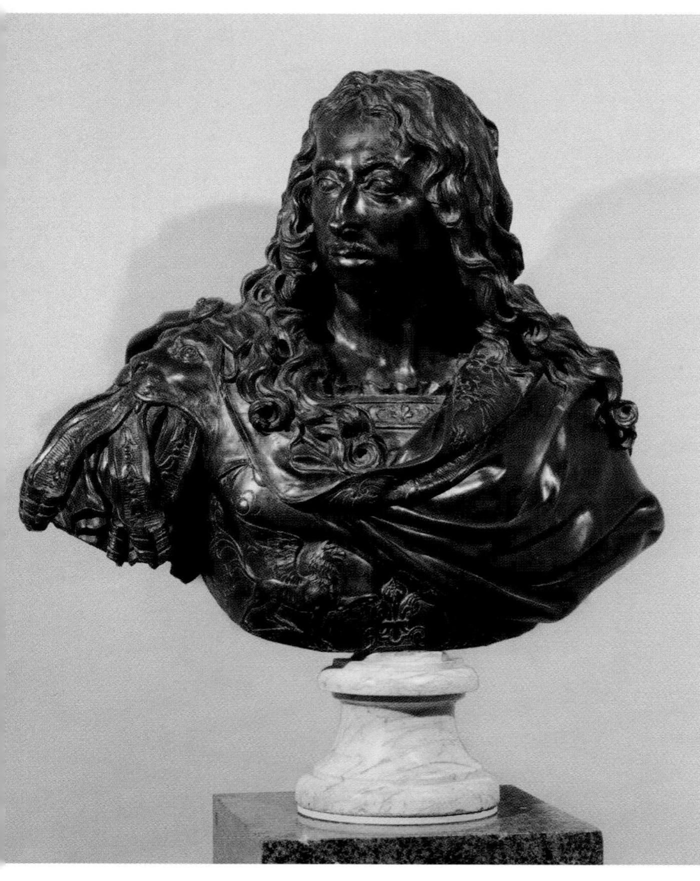

Antoine Coysevox
*Louis II of Bourbon, called Le Grand Condé
(1621-1686)*, **1688**
Bronze. 60 x 68 x 34 cm - ML

David d'Angers
Johann Wolfgang von Goethe, 1829
Plaster. 83 x 58 x 51 cm - MO

Dan Flavin
Untitled (Monument for Vladimir Tatlin), 1975
Fluorescent light tubes, metal. 304.5 x 62.5 x 12.5 cm - CP

Antoine Coysevox's *Grand Condé* is portrayed in the heat of action. The head, by turning in a different direction from the body, endows the figure with an immense impression of life. The virtuoso artist here recalls Bernini's portrait of Louis XIV: the same edginess in the attitude, the enveloping Baroque ampleness, the same unbroken sweep of wig and coat.

David d'Angers reveals his talent as much in studies of expressive heads, which he elevated to a fully fledged genre, as in the retrospective medal, of which the Louvre's collection possesses many examples. In this colossal head of Goethe, he combines both strands. The man of genius, with the broad forehead of a thinker — according to Lessing, 'the face is the seat of the expression' — topped by jagged locks of hair like a laurel wreath, is also 'Goethe the man' exemplified by some incisive features and the thin mouth.

Dan Flavin, at the forefront of those contemporary artists who use light, here pays homage to an earlier colleague he much admired: the Russian Constructivist Vladimir Tatlin, author of *The Monument to the Third International*. In deploying industrial materials, the neon structures of the *Monuments for Vladimir Tatlin* keep faith with the spirit of Constructivism. The fluorescent light tubes emit a diffuse glow, which pervades both the room and the viewers attracted to the halo.

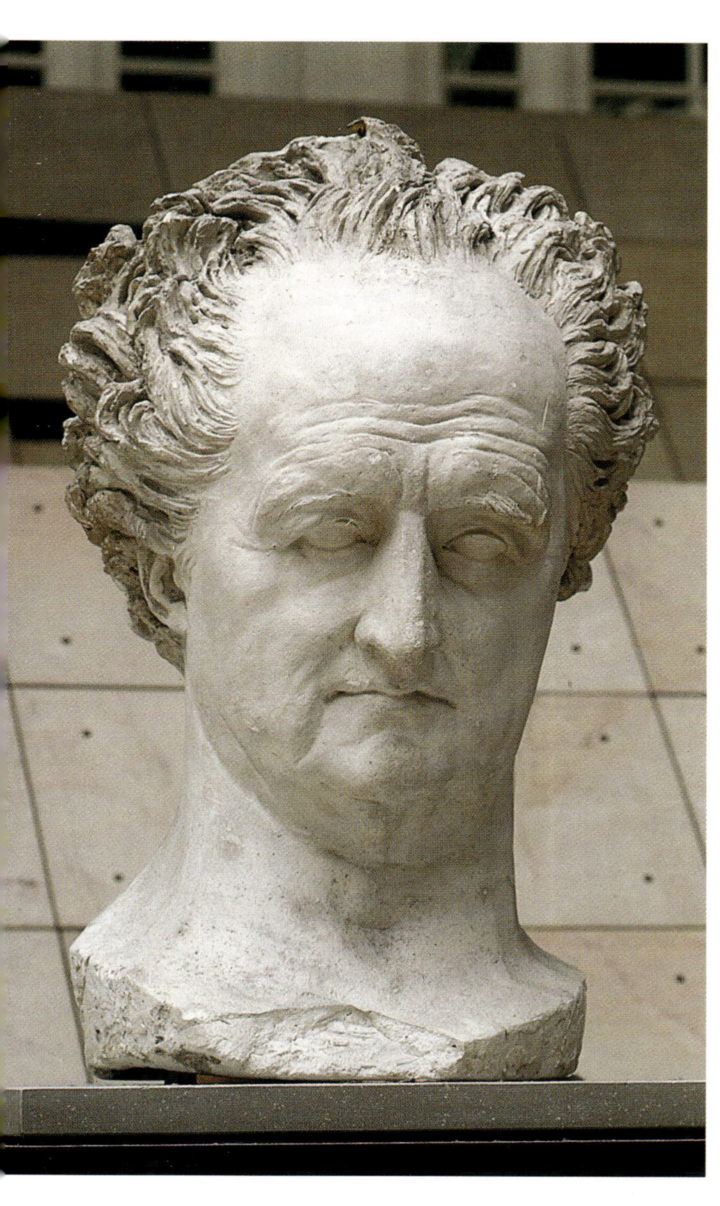

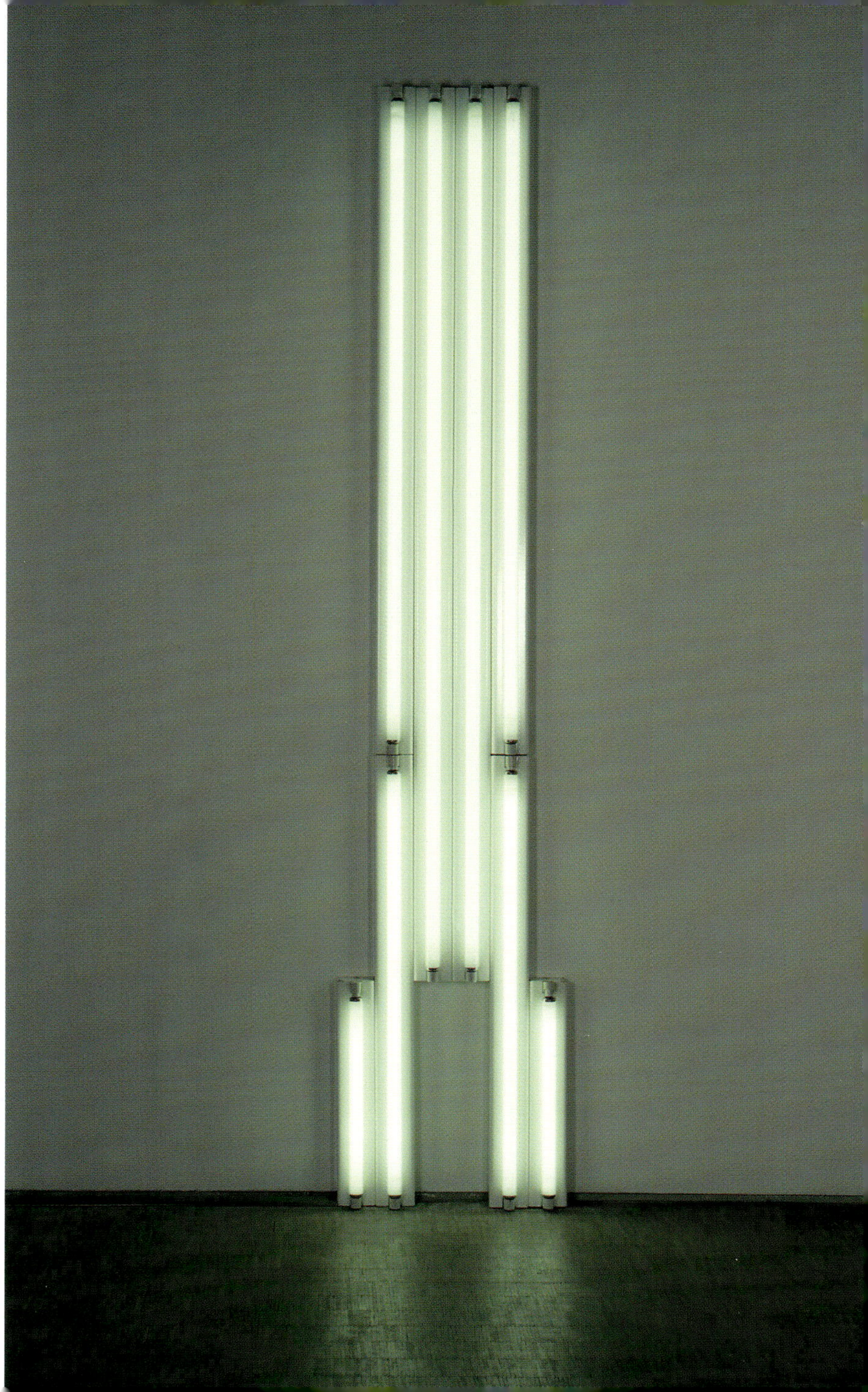

Self-portraits

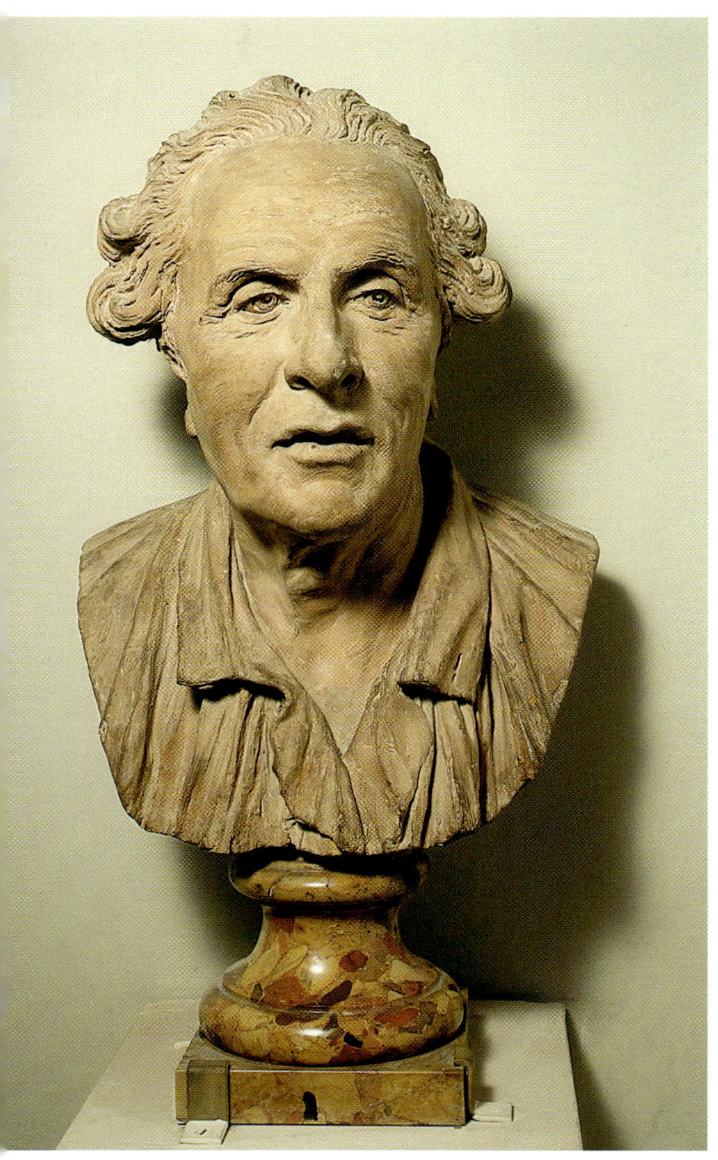

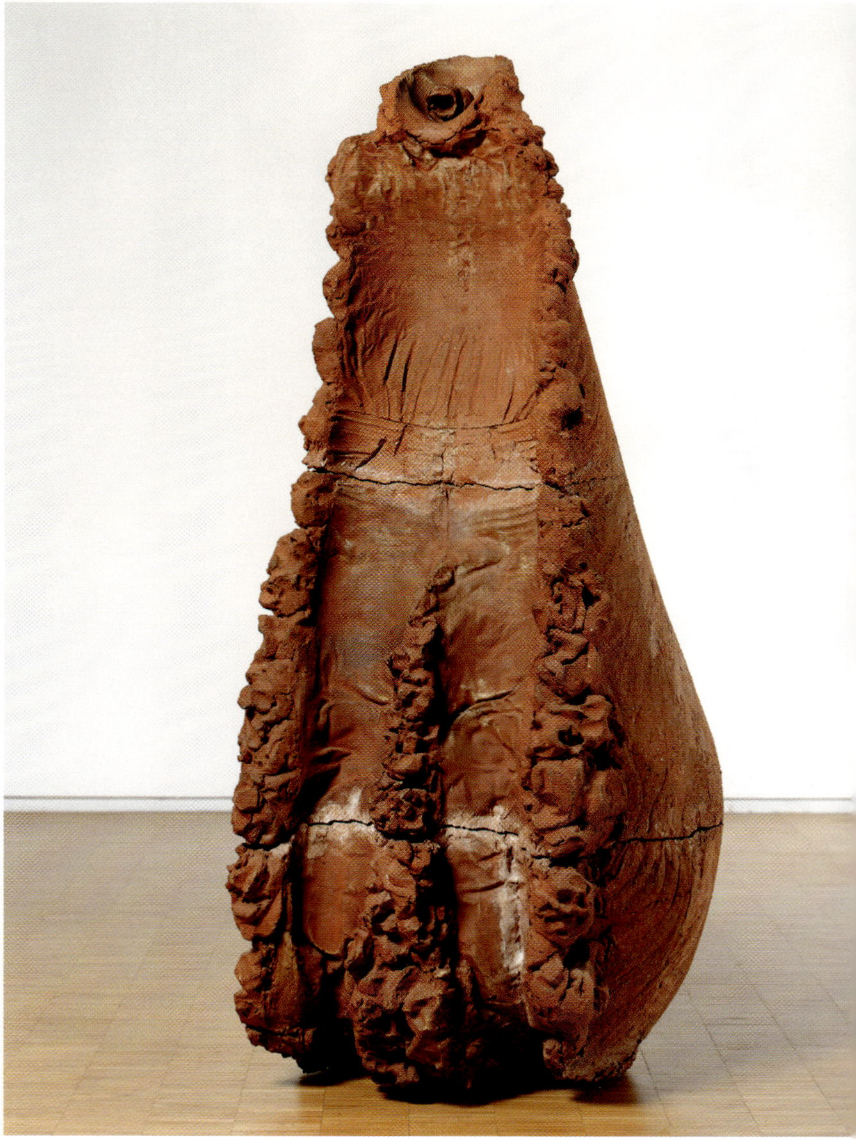

Jean-Baptiste Pigalle

Self-Portrait, c. 1777

Terracotta. 44 x 27 x 25 cm - ML

Giuseppe Penone

Soffio 6, 1978; general view and detail

Terracotta. 158 x 75 x 79 cm - CP

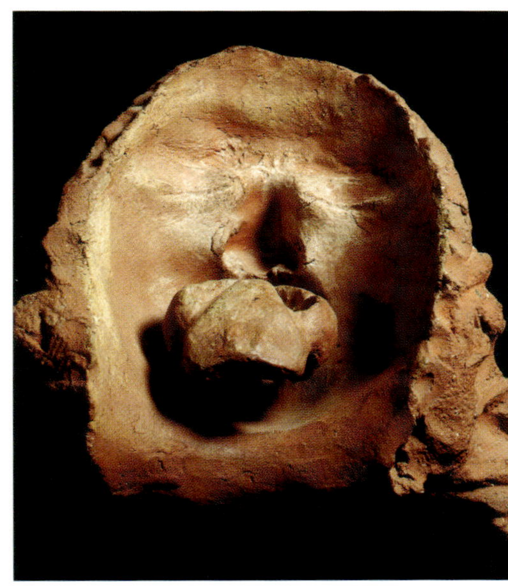

What could be more radical than the work of Giuseppe Penone? Imprinting the shape of his own body and face in clay, he directly revisits a number of myths relating both to the origin of sculpture and the creation of man. In Mesopotamian mythology, man was first modelled by the gods out of the fertile silt that accumulated as the rivers rose. Genesis names the first man Adam, from a Semitic root meaning 'made of red earth'. It should also be remembered that Paleolithic peoples exploited the natural relief of rock faces, applying pigment to suggest figures, animals for the most part, and creating what would later be termed bas-reliefs. The shape of the jar in *Soffio 6* recalls not only the legend of the potter Butades, the inventor of sculpture, but also Pandora, the first woman. This union of man and a female earth gives rise to an image evoking jointly a phallus and a pregnancy.

Jean-Baptiste Pigalle's self-portrait is equally simple and devoid of pomposity. He captures his face in the mirror, virtually in the way of those sketches in which he so excels. The trademark casualness of the sculptor's professional garb — the open-necked blouse — is accompanied by an air by infinite sadness more revealing than any Romantic confession.

Jean Carriès, meanwhile, transposed his self-portrait into the strange world of the faun, those hybrid, grotesque creatures that loomed so large in his world. The theme of the faun flute-player and pursuer of nymphs seems to characterise this artist perfectly and anticipates by more than a century an identity adopted by Picasso and Matthew Barney.

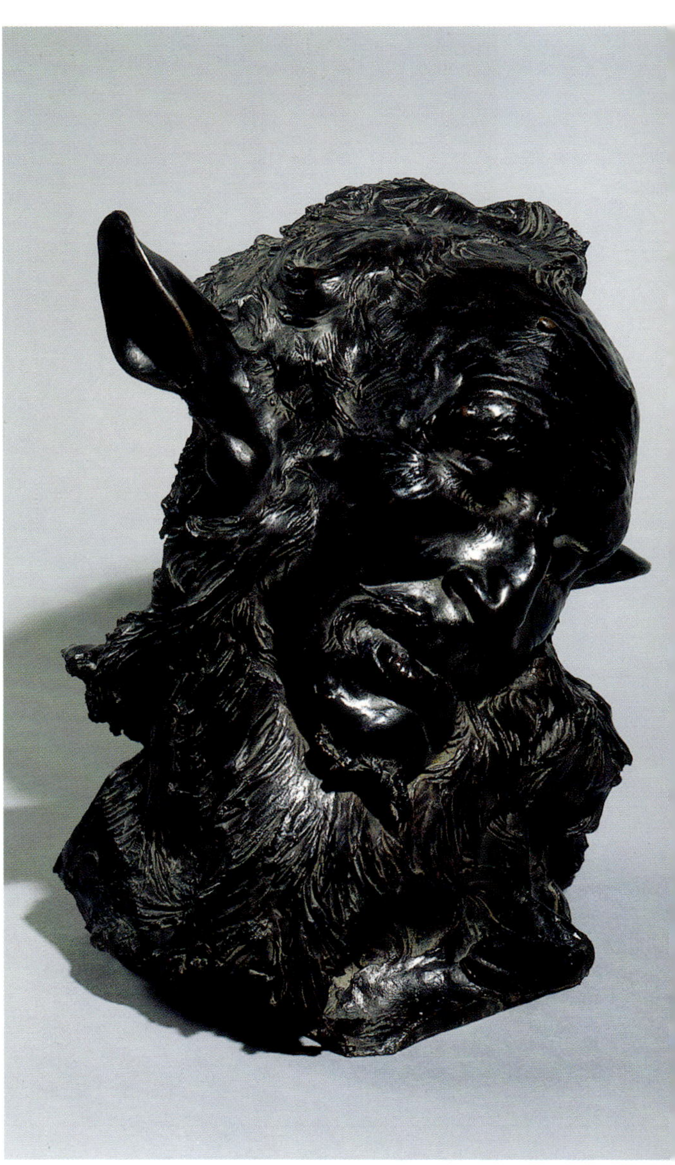

Jean Carriès
Faun, 1893
Bronze. 35.3 x 34 x 23 cm - MO

123

Work

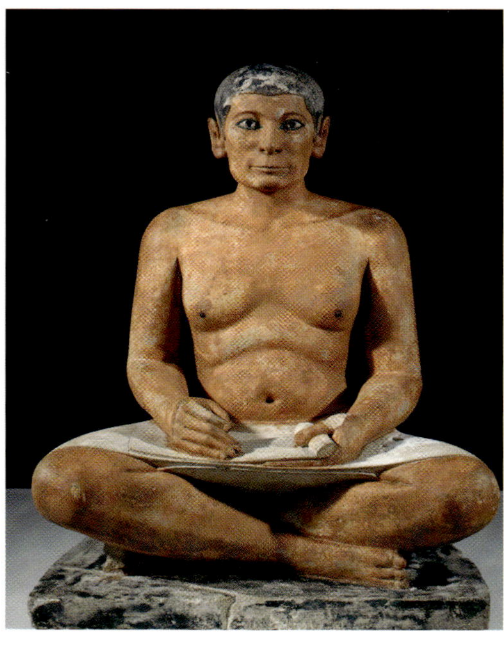

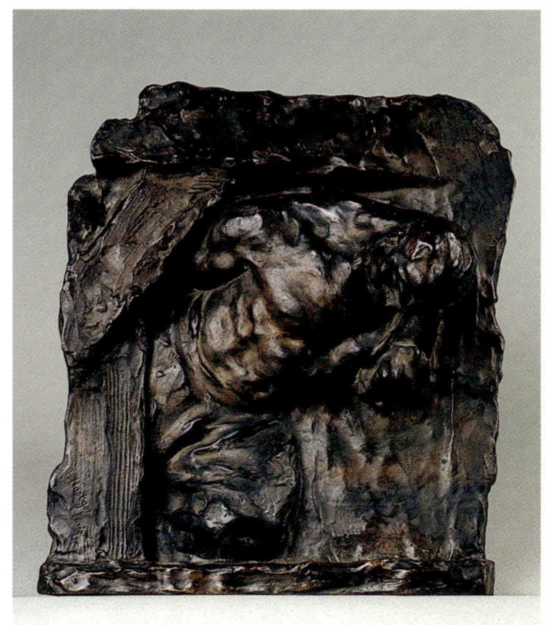

Over time, *The Seated Scribe* with the penetrating eye — probably the portrait of a steward or overseer — has become the archetype of the man writing. It was with this figure in mind that Alberto Giacometti painted the portrait of Jean Genet. Giacometti, however, had little time for the gemstones inserted in the ancient statue for eyes, considering them too inert and inexpressive to capture a human gaze. Recent X-ray studies have demonstrated the exceptional knowledge the Egyptian artist must have possessed of both the form and structure of the eye, as well as the virtuosity he showed in rendering them in appropriate materials.

In *The Human Machine*, Bernhard Hoetger evokes a very different universe of work, striking in the manner it characterises an exhausted miner literally enmeshed in the oppressive net of stays supporting the gallery. Images of atlantes, of the 'salt of the earth', and of a man condemned to labour beneath a yoke or be thrown into the stocks come together. The direct impact of this art of social protest is in some respects a forerunner of Socialist Realism. That Hoetger's work was purchased by Marcel Duchamp induces us to try to view it through the latter's eyes as a 'bachelor machine', a simile for the alienation of work and desire: the beam holds the worker down in the lower world, that of the 'bachelors' those who aspire to the 'belle', the bride or, perhaps, revolution.

With Jean Tinguely's *Requiem for a Dead Leaf*, we pass from the human machine to the machine that crushes mankind. The piece immediately reminds one of Charlie Chaplin as the worker trapped in the remorseless mechanism of the assembly line in the movie *Modern Times* (1936) that so incensed American audiences still enthralled by the marvels of Ford and Taylor. Here, however, the falling leaf is borne aloft by the cog wheels. The machine, which in passing pokes fun at the mechanist conceptions of a post-Cartesian and technologist Nature, is here commandeered for its potential as art. It becomes poetical, amalgamating in one and the same movement the autumnal decline of the natural cycle, the mindless alienation of routine work, like that of a machine that seizes up or breaks down, and the meditation of a man no longer young observing transfixed the transitory fall of the leaf. There is an inscription on the mausoleum of Hadrian in Rome (now the Castello Sant'Angelo) that records a quotation by the emperor: 'Little soul, tender, floating soul, companion of my body who was your host, you will go down to those places, pale, unyielding, unadorned, where you will have to forgo all the games of long ago.' This autumn leaf is perhaps Tinguely's own soul, a portrait of the artist at work: 'As long as it's black, my name is Jean,' he used to say.

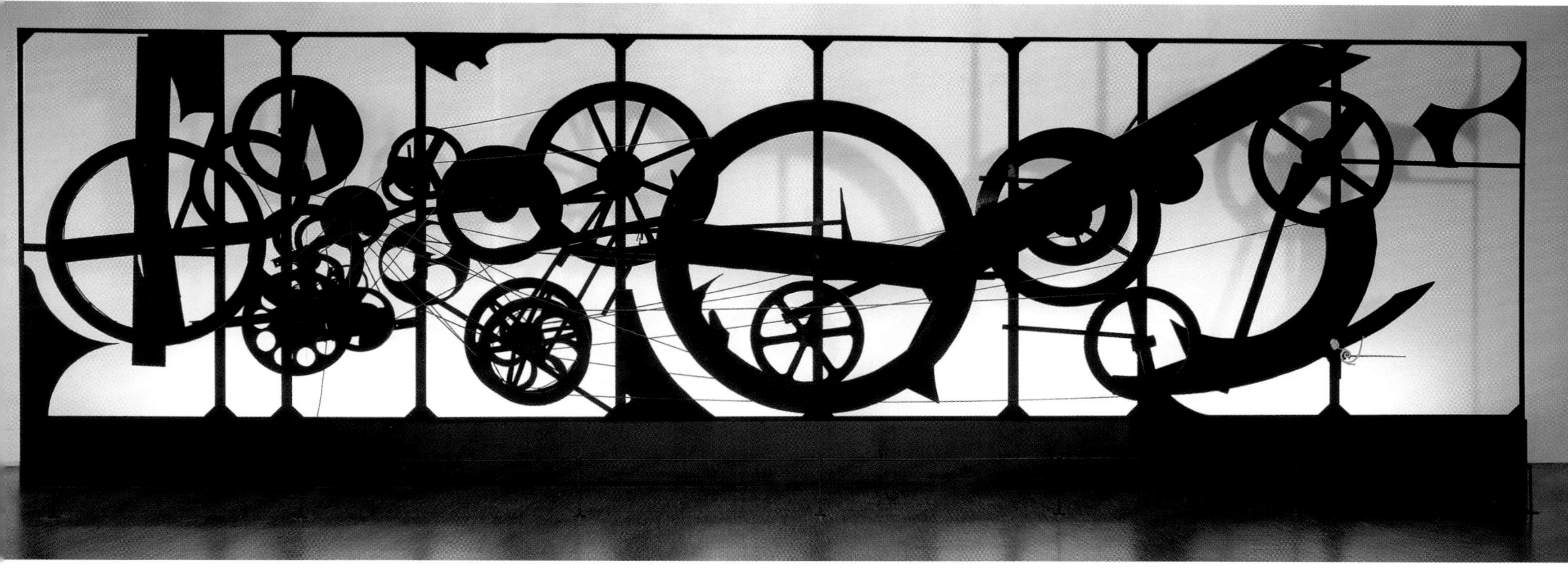

The Seated Scribe, Egypt, 4th or 5th Dynasty, 2600-2350 BC.
Painted limestone; eyes incrusted with rock crystal in copper.
53.70 x 44 x 35 cm - ML

Bernhard Hoetger
The Human Machine, 1902
Bronze. 44 x 37 x 18 cm - MO

Jean Tinguely
Requiem for Dead Leaf, 1967
General view and detail
Painted steel and wood, leather. 305 x 1105 x 80 cm - CP

125

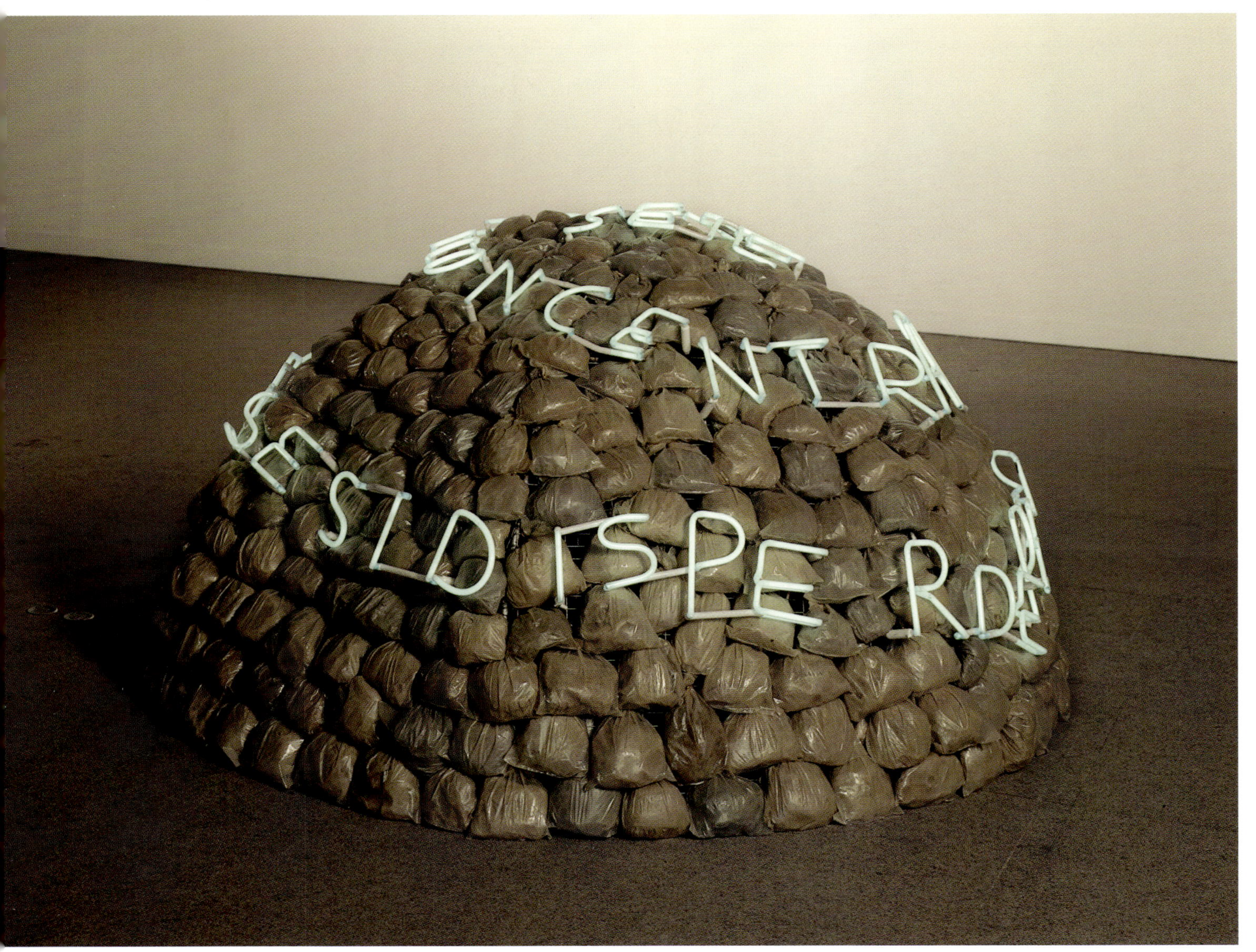

War and peace

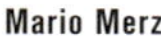

Mario Merz

Igloo di Giap, 1968

Iron armature, plastic bags filled with earth, neon tubes, batteries.

120 x 200 cm - CP

Edme Bouchardon

Love Cutting his Bow from the Club of Hercules, 1750

Marble. 173 x 75 x 75 cm - ML

Antoine-Louis Barye

Peace, 1855

Stained plaster. 105 x 91 x 70 cm - MO

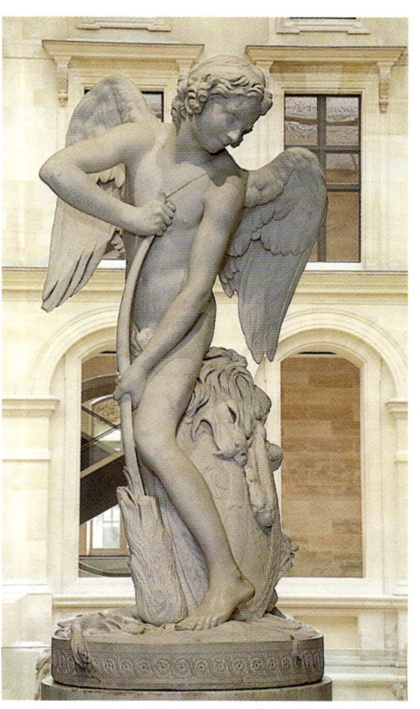

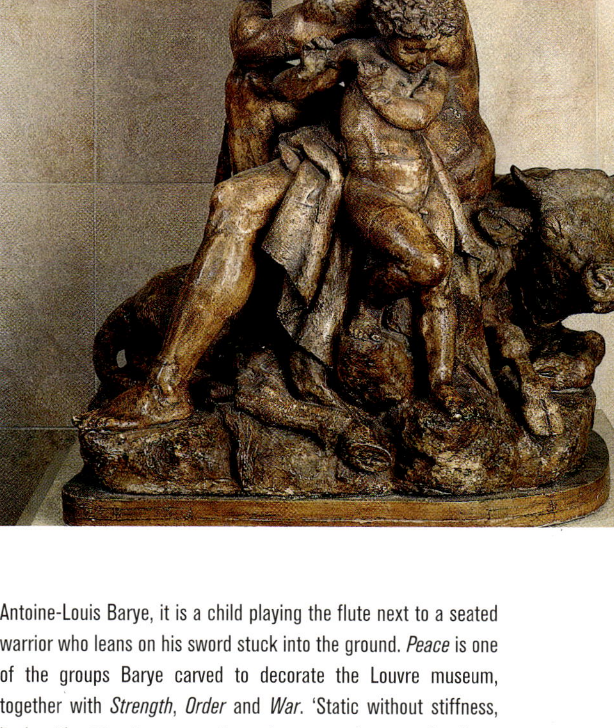

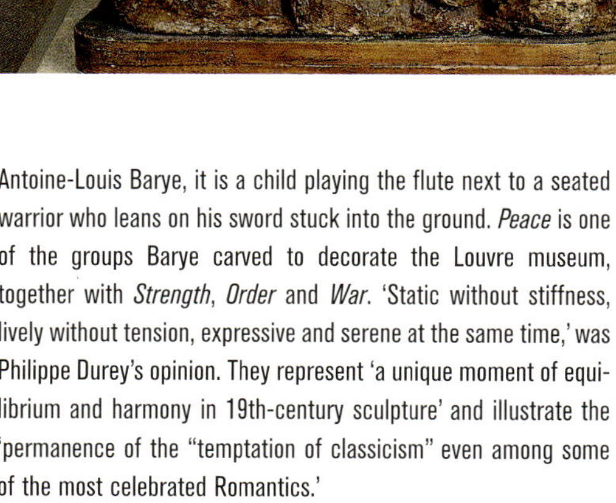

It was an 'impromptu monticule' (Didier Semin) — in fact bags of earth laid over a metal armature in the shape of an igloo — that the artist Mario Merz dedicated to General Giap in 1968, right in the middle of the Vietnam war. The form, evoking both pillbox and shelter, perfectly reflects the formula the strategist had made his own and which one reads spelled out in strip lights affixed to the igloo: 'If the Enemy Masses his Forces he Loses Ground, if he Scatters he Loses Strength. Giap.' Seldom have words and spatial composition been as demonstrably correlated in a sculpture. The piece belongs to the first generation of earthworks that the exponents of Land art were to develop further, sometimes in a more formalist manner. The artist resolutely takes the side of those who defend their native land and who turn their territory into a bastion against the aggressor, whose blinding weapons are suggested by the neon. This light of the future, neon, is finally emblazoned to the glory of Giap whose name shines out.

Compared to the sculpture of combat, to the evocation of war, the return of peace often takes the guise of a child, figure for the future. For Edme Bouchardon, this was Eros, Love, who cut his bow in Hercules' club. 'Love as sculptor!' as Voltaire neatly put it. For Antoine-Louis Barye, it is a child playing the flute next to a seated warrior who leans on his sword stuck into the ground. *Peace* is one of the groups Barye carved to decorate the Louvre museum, together with *Strength*, *Order* and *War*. 'Static without stiffness, lively without tension, expressive and serene at the same time,' was Philippe Durey's opinion. They represent 'a unique moment of equilibrium and harmony in 19th-century sculpture' and illustrate the 'permanence of the "temptation of classicism" even among some of the most celebrated Romantics.'

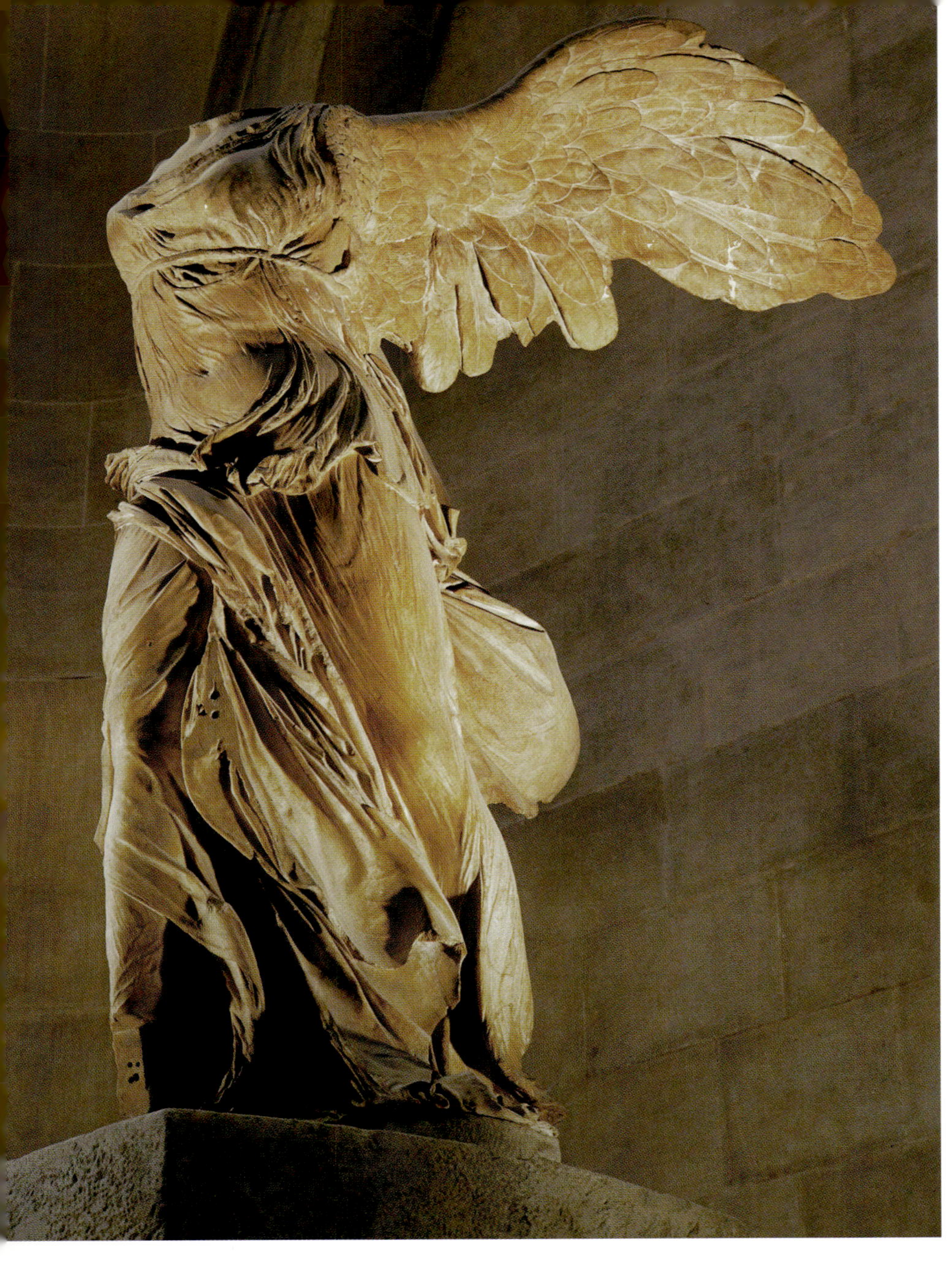

Dynamism or stability: which of the two images best translates power? The creator of the Victory unearthed at Samothrace in 1863 and transported to the Louvre in 1866 chose dynamism, though this choice was imposed by the subject, a celebration of a naval victory. The marble allegorical figure is set on a stone plinth in an allusion to the prow of a galley. Whereas the right leg provides firm support, the left is in motion, and the drapery, plastered to the body by the wind, reveals a vigorous form borne aloft by a pair of outstretched wings. The *Winged Victory of Samothrace* is very much in an image of the dynamism that Marinetti's *Futurist Manifesto*, published in 1909, challenged the car to embody.

Contrariwise, for his *Imperial France,* Carpeaux, recalling Michelangelo, opted on this occasion for a static composition designed to fit in with the voluminous decorum of the Louvre museum

Winged Victory of Samothrace, c. 190 BC
Grey Lartos marble (boat), Paros marble (statue)
H: 328 cm - ML

Political power, symbolic power

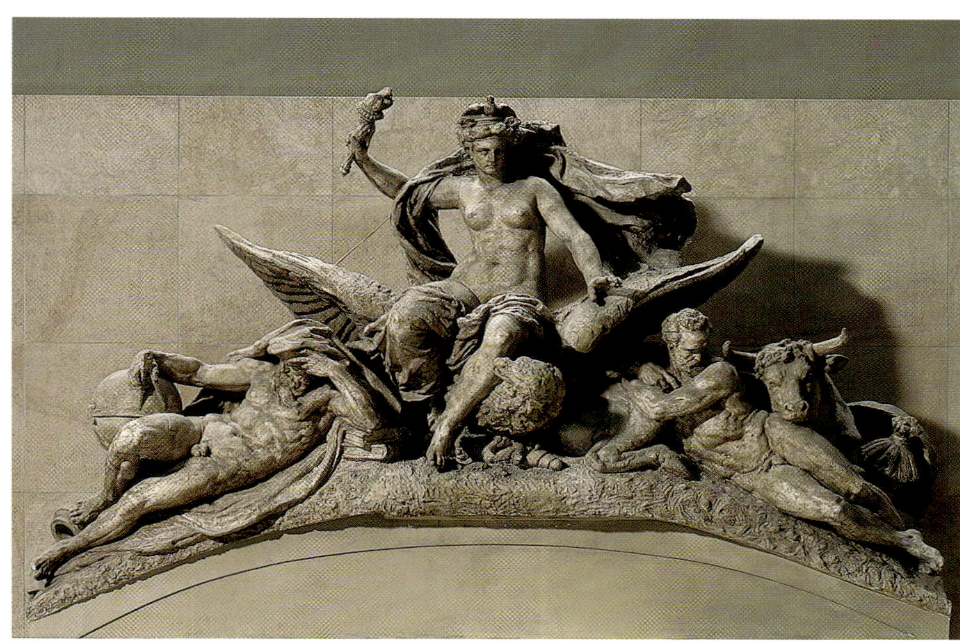

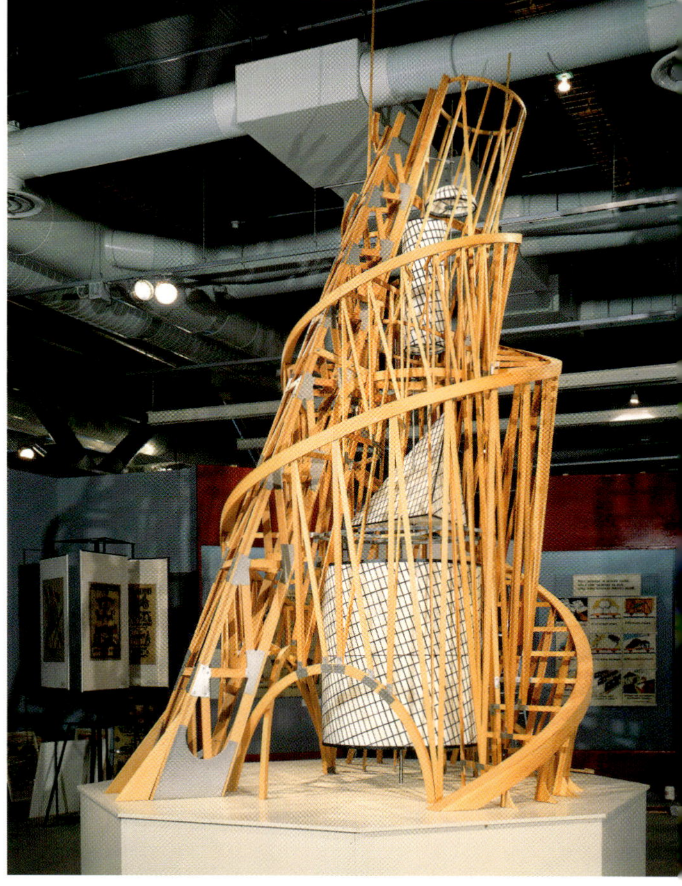

during the Second Empire. An allegory of France, accompanied by an eagle, urges on figures representing agriculture and industry.

Vladimir Tatlin's *Monument to the Third International* was to have been of a colossal height, taller than New York's Empire State Building, at the time in the course of completion, and taller too than the Eiffel Tower, which it was intended to upstage. The monument, which never got further than a model, combined both stability and dynamism: stability, in its geometric shape designed to accommodate the organs and assemblies of Soviet power, right up to the summit with its radio stations and agit-prop; dynamism, in its double helix form and in areas to designed to rotate differentially — once a day at the top and once a year at the base.

Jean-Baptiste Carpeaux

Imperial France Bringing Light to the World and Protecting Agriculture and Science, 1866
Plaster model. 268 x 427 x 162 cm - MO

Vladimir Tatlin

Model for the Monument to the Third International, 1919/reconstruction 1979
Wood, metal. H: 500 cm; diam (base): 300 cm - CP

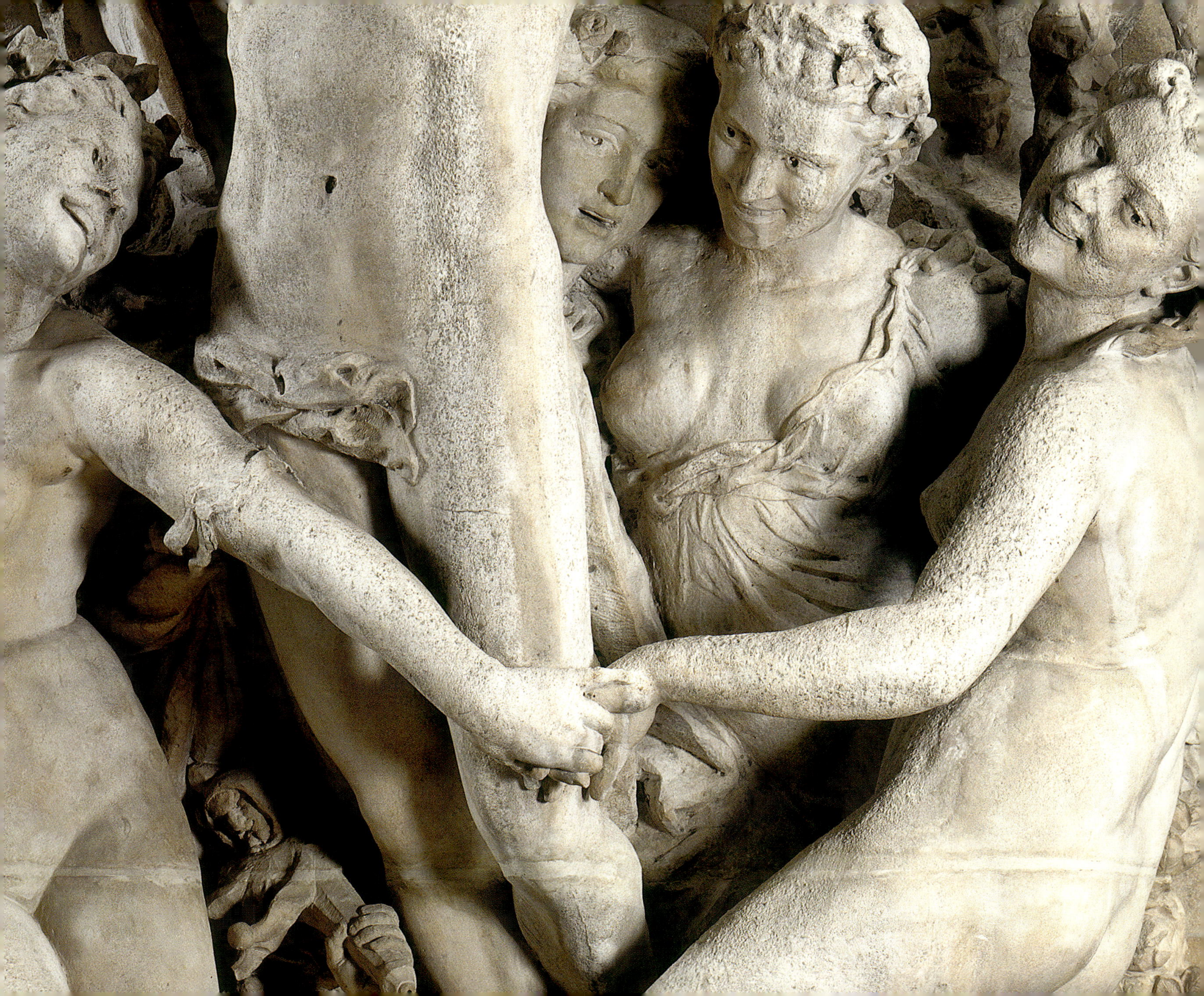

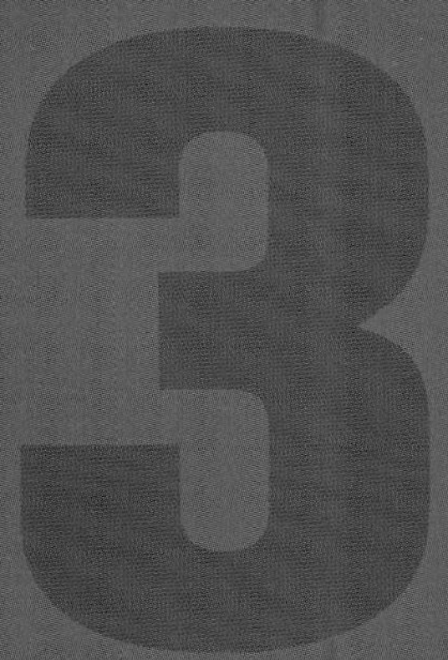

3

To recreate space, to give form to time

Everything moves continuously. Immobility does not exist. [...] Accept instability. Live in Time. Be static - with movement. For a static of the present movement. [...] You are movement and gesture.

Jean Tinguely, *For Statics*, 1959

Cosmos

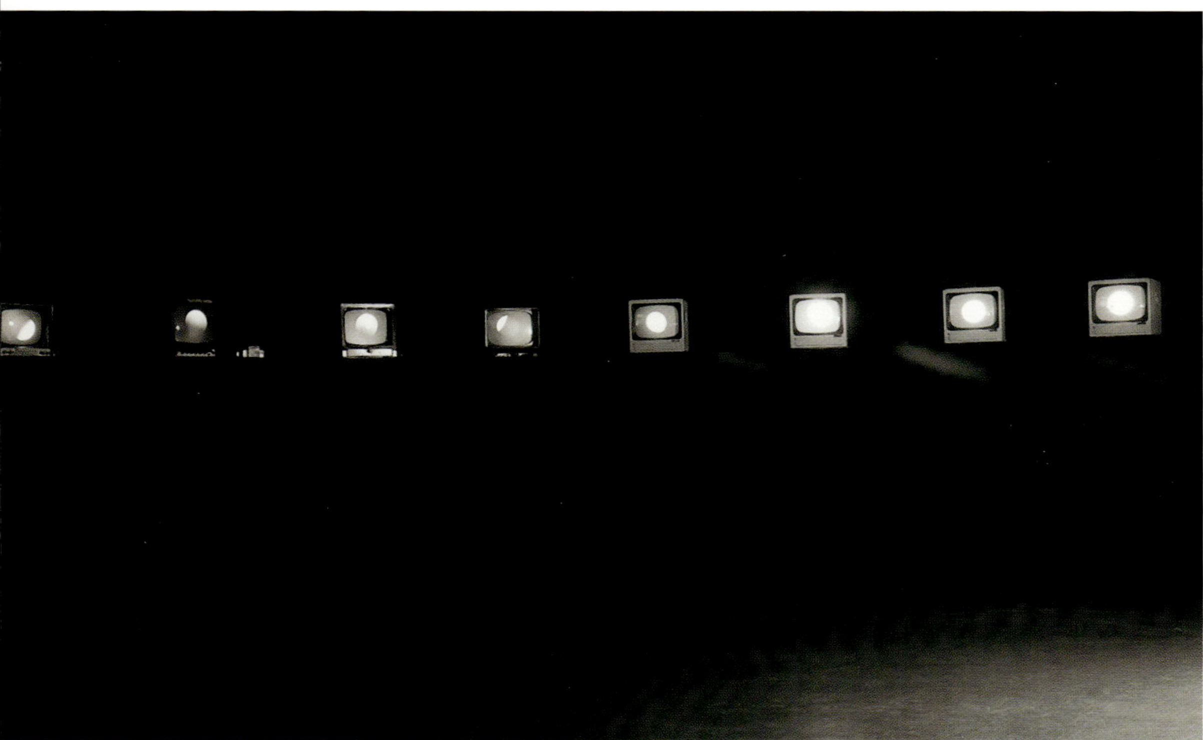

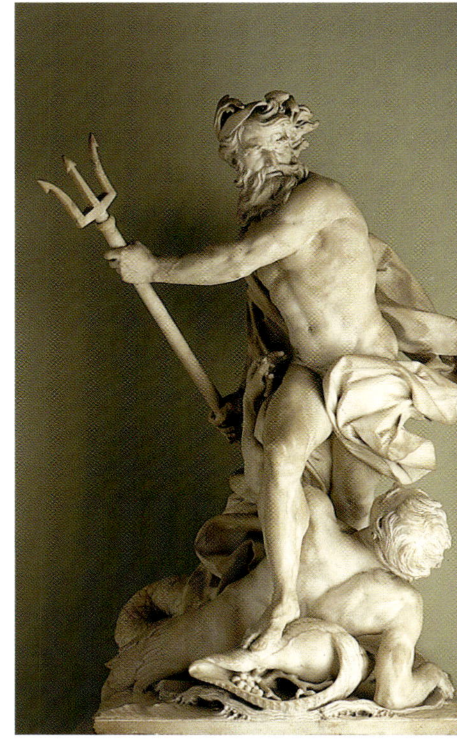

Following in the vein of Bernini's *Neptune and Triton* (1620), Lambert-Sigisbert Adam choreographs the god of the sea — he whom the Ancients called the 'ruler of the waves' — sitting astride a triton: the cosmos comes into being. This dynamic composition, imbued with a typically Baroque ardour, was the sculptor's reception piece to the French Academy in 1737. Adam was to amplify its movement still further in the group *The Triumph of Neptune and Amphitrite* (1740), set up in the middle of the Bassin de Neptune at Versailles.

For the Fontaine de l'Observatoire in Paris (the horses are by Emmanuel Fremiet), Jean-Baptiste Carpeaux positions the vault of heaven — an armillary sphere with the signs of the zodiac — atop female figures representing the four known continents. In 1878 for the Paris World Fair, six others sculptures including the two Americas and Oceania were commissioned from various artists and are presently dis-played on the terrace at the Musée d'Orsay. The roundelay performed by Carpeaux's gambolling caryatids evokes the rotation of the globe. Interestingly, only Europe, towards whom both America and Asia turn, actually touches the sphere with her head. This is the vision of an European who moreover finds fault with an America shown enslaving Africa, her foot standing on a chain attached to the latter's legs. In the heat of the American Civil War, Carpeaux is here clearly alluding to the

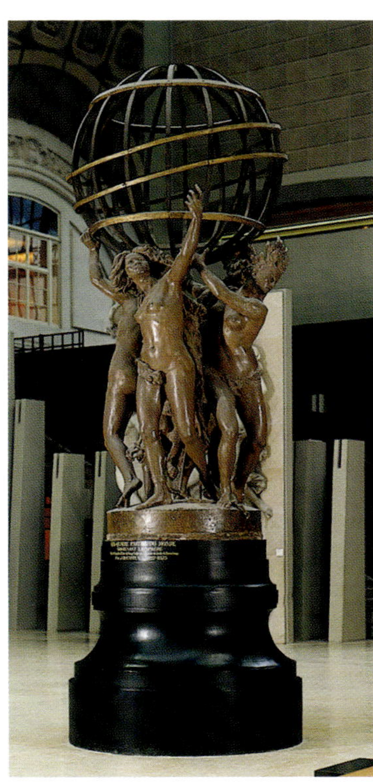

Nam June Paik

Moon is the Oldest TV, 1965

Installation: 12 to 17 black and white TV sets, 12 to 17 magnets

Dark room from 10 x 7 m - CP

Lambert-Sigisbert Adam

Neptune Calming the Waters, 1733

Marble. 85 x 59 x 48 cm - ML

Jean-Baptiste Carpeaux

The Four Parts of the World Holding up the Celestial Sphere, 1873

Patinated plaster model. 280 x 177 x 145 cm - MO

Boris Achour

Cosmos, 2001

Coloured resin, engine, soundtrack on CD

191 x 218 cm - CP

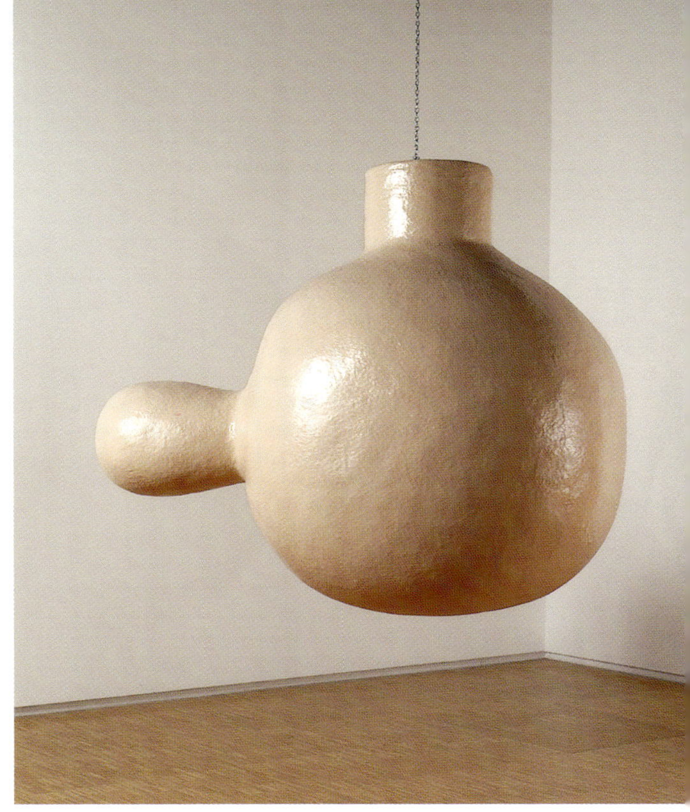

question of abolition. However, the sculptor does subscribe to the universalist spirit of the Enlightenment in suggesting that all four figures are in fact one, Humanity, seen from different points of view.

Nam June Paik's television monitors present the spectacle of the various phases of the moon displayed along a curved line that apes the satellite's trajectory. Technological tools, though, are as nothing: curiosity is all. Had not astronomers of the school of Alexandria already calculated the distance from the earth to the moon? Well before Méliès' famous film, *Le Voyage dans la Lune*, the moon was pictured as a face in early times. This 'gogglebox' in the sky was also the young artist Boris Achour's inspiration for the protuberant nose in his *Cosmos*, accompanied by a thumping *Lambada* as an ersatz music of the spheres: a fusion of sound and matter.

133

Imaginary space, real space

'You could move out of my sun!' This, according to legend, was Diogenes' answer to Alexander the Great when he said he would grant him a wish, reminding us that all men, omnipotent or puny, dwell beneath the same sun and that freedom of thought can neither be confined nor bought. This large-scale relief by Pierre Puget recalls, as Geneviève Bresc-Bautier has observed, 'together with classical language and ancient history, the great principles of Christian philosophy.' In the manner of a painter, the sculptor, turning to the topography of a Rome with which he was familiar, rebuilds the ancient city and unfolds an urban panorama of singularly evocative power.

But an imaginary space is created in sculpture not only by means of reliefs. A comparison between Joseph Bernard's *The Water-Carrier* and one of Robert Morris's *Felt Pieces* allows us to better appreciate the distinction between a space inherent in a work and the space of reality, a theme tirelessly rehearsed by contemporary art. An updated peasant-girl with her pot of milk, cousin to Ingres' *The Spring* and to many faces by Greuze, *The Water-Carrier* creates her own space, like an ingénue Gradiva, advancing towards her destiny with measured step. Viewers can thus savour the delectable spectacle of the eternal water-carrier walking past with concentrated grace, unheeding of the solid ground on which they themselves stand and whose presence is nullified by the sculpture's plinth.

The space defined by the sections of felt detached from the wall in the work by Robert Morris is eminently real. The work shares its space with the beholder who can literally walk on it. With cavities as tall as a man cut into the centre of the bolts of cloth that fall symmetrically to either side, the piece seems designed as a place *for* the viewer. However, the ambiguity between real and imaginary space subsists and the impression is of experiencing a work at once approachable yet elusive.

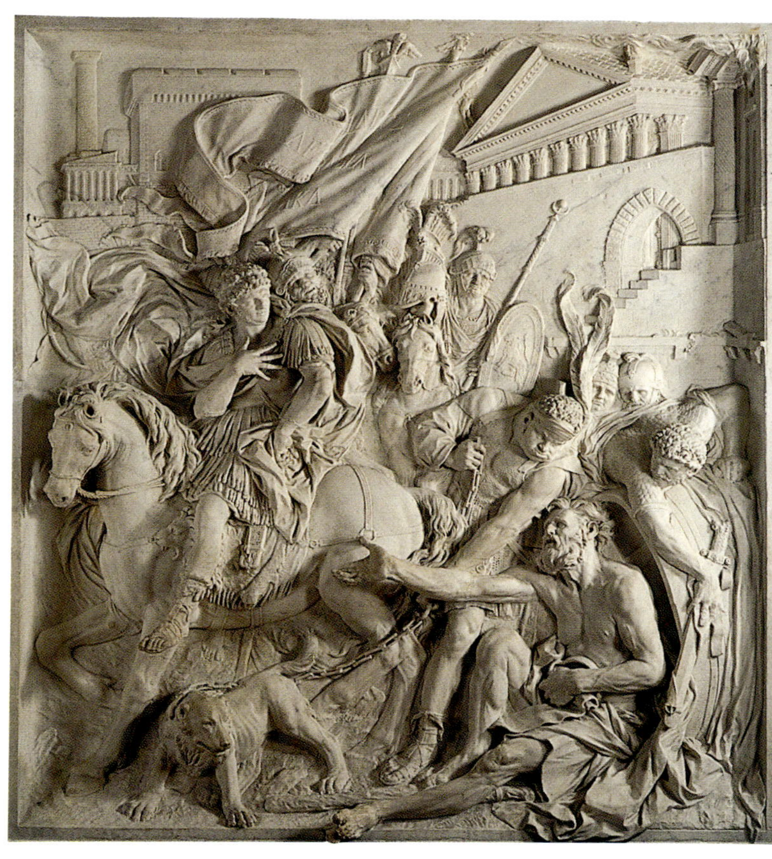

Pierre Puget
Alexander and Diogenes, 1670-89
Carrara marble. 332 x 296 x 44 cm - **ML**

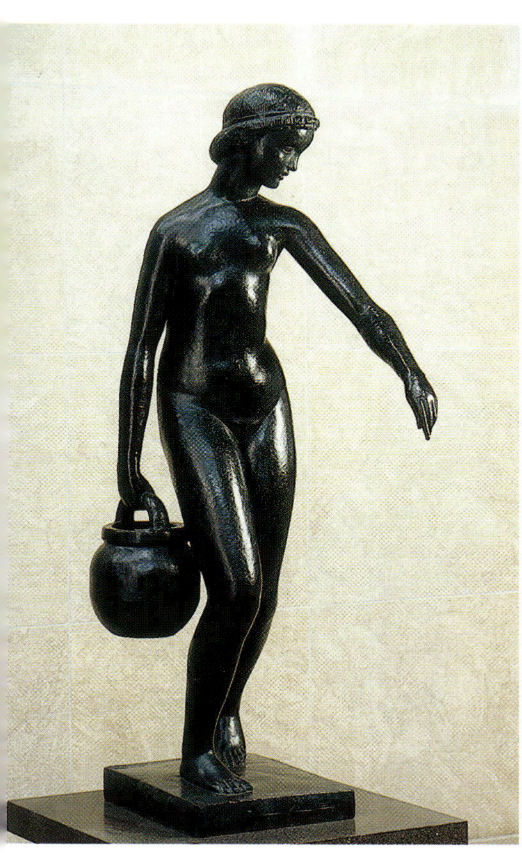

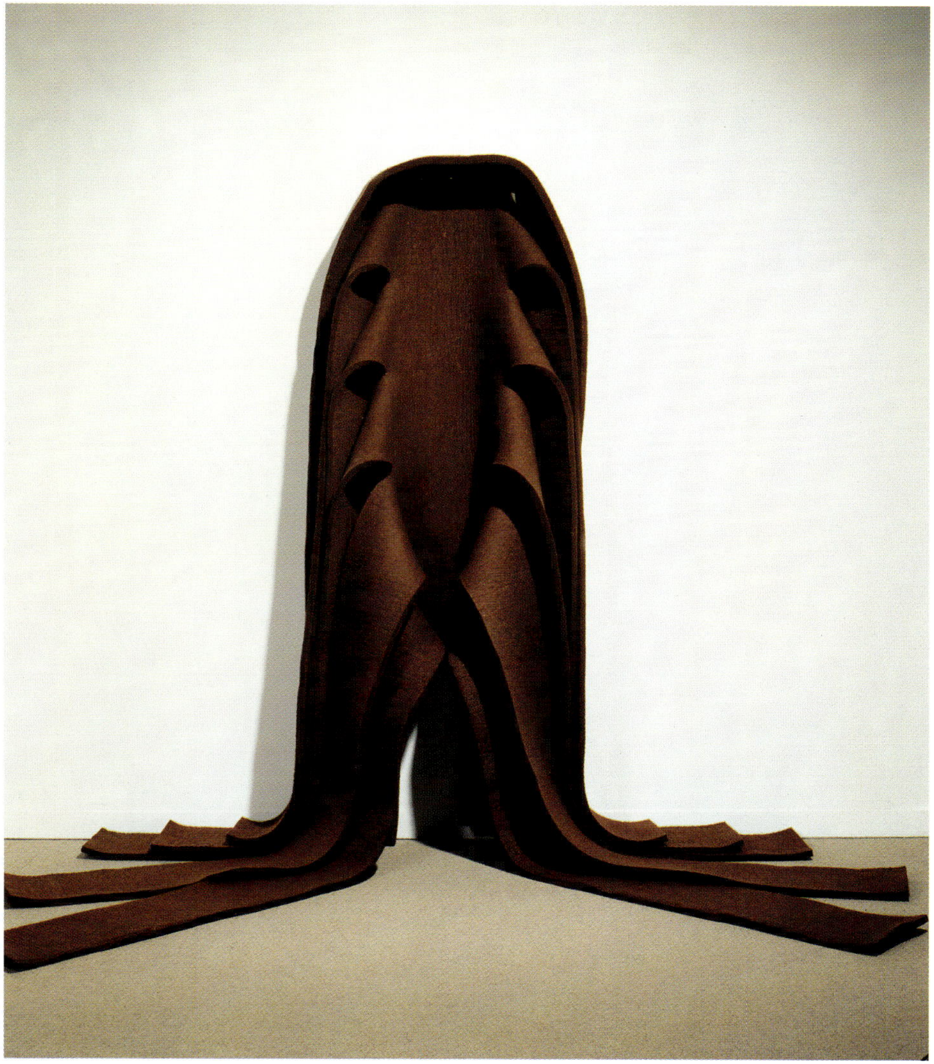

Joseph Bernard
The Water-Carrier, 1912
Bronze. 175 x 40 x 52 cm - MO

Robert Morris
Wall Hanging, 1971-73
Cut felt. 247 x 355 x 120 cm - CP

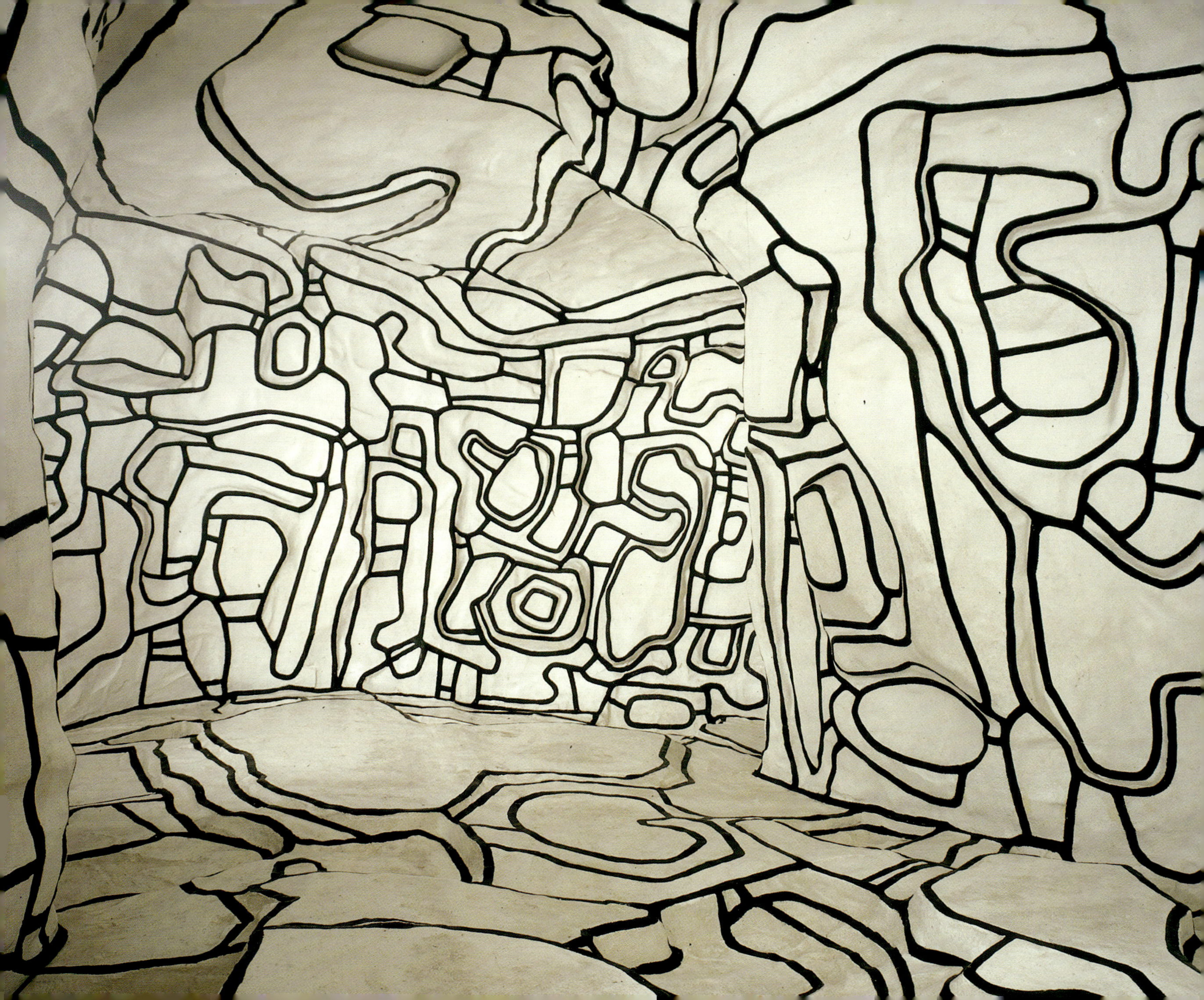

Wild nature or domesticated garden

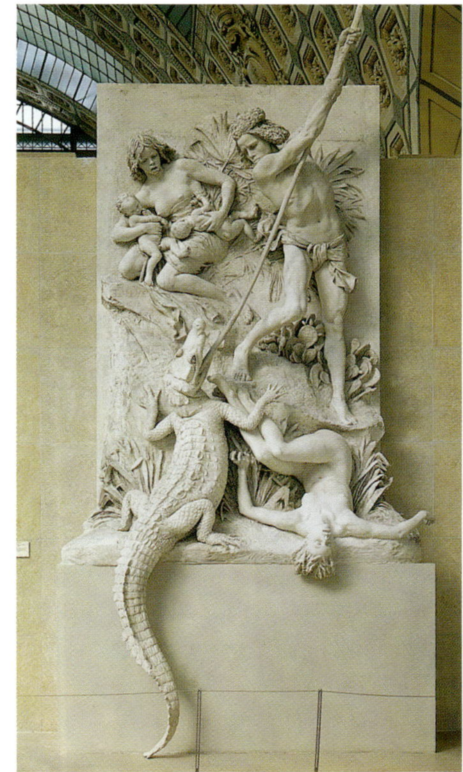

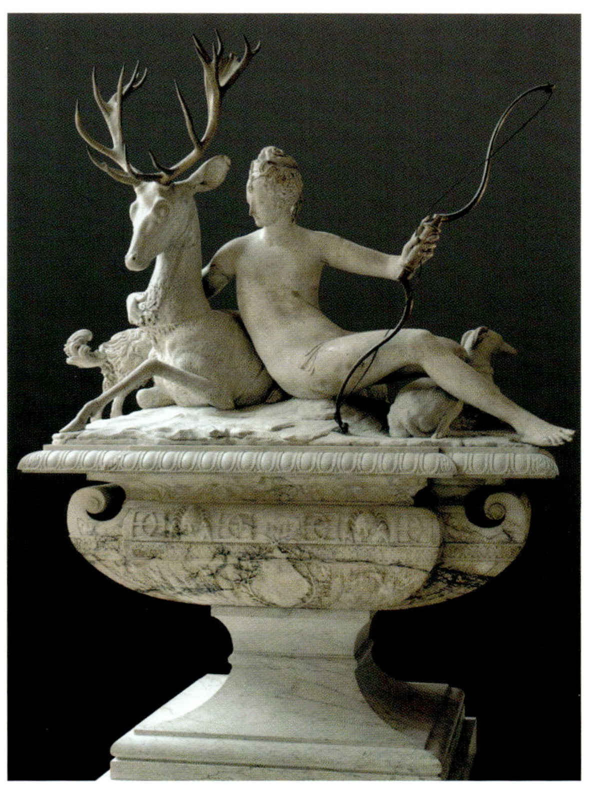

Unbridled nature and courtly refinement have seldom been more closely fused than in this *Diana the Huntress with Stag*, sometimes ascribed to Ponce Jacquiot, and in which one recognises the elegant lines of the School of Fontainebleau. Of a steady classicism, the piece stood on a basin in the park of the Château d'Anet. The subject is an allusion to the first name of Henri II's favourite, Diane de Poitiers, the owner of the château, whereas the real stag antlers inserted in the sculpture recall aristocratic pastimes and the passion for hunting.

The work by Ernest Barrias is truly spectacular, like a St George slaying an alligator! The plaster piece was in fact used for a commission to decorate the Natural History Museum in Paris. The sculptor combines the evocation of a primordial age when one had to fight to survive with the exoticism of a world whose horizons were being broadened by colonial campaigns. Barrias' neo-baroque taste treats the scene in a lively and hugely virtuoso vein redolent of great Baroque subjects, such as the fall of the rebel angels or the battle against the Amazons.

Jean Dubuffet, on the other hand, purloins the charms of natural landscape only to lock them in a cave in an artificial garden. On entering the den, the visitor discovers a twofold ideal of the external world, a modern equivalent of the nympheums and of the grotesque-adorned halls of the Renaissance: a condensation of nature. The relative lack of light, a colour scheme restricted to black lines on a white surface, and the uneven nature of the ground culminate in a disorientating experience for visitors. Only by attending more than usual to their senses can the visitor get an idea of where they are, to move about freely, and, finally, to take possession of a disquieting environment that weds sculpture and architecture.

On the ground

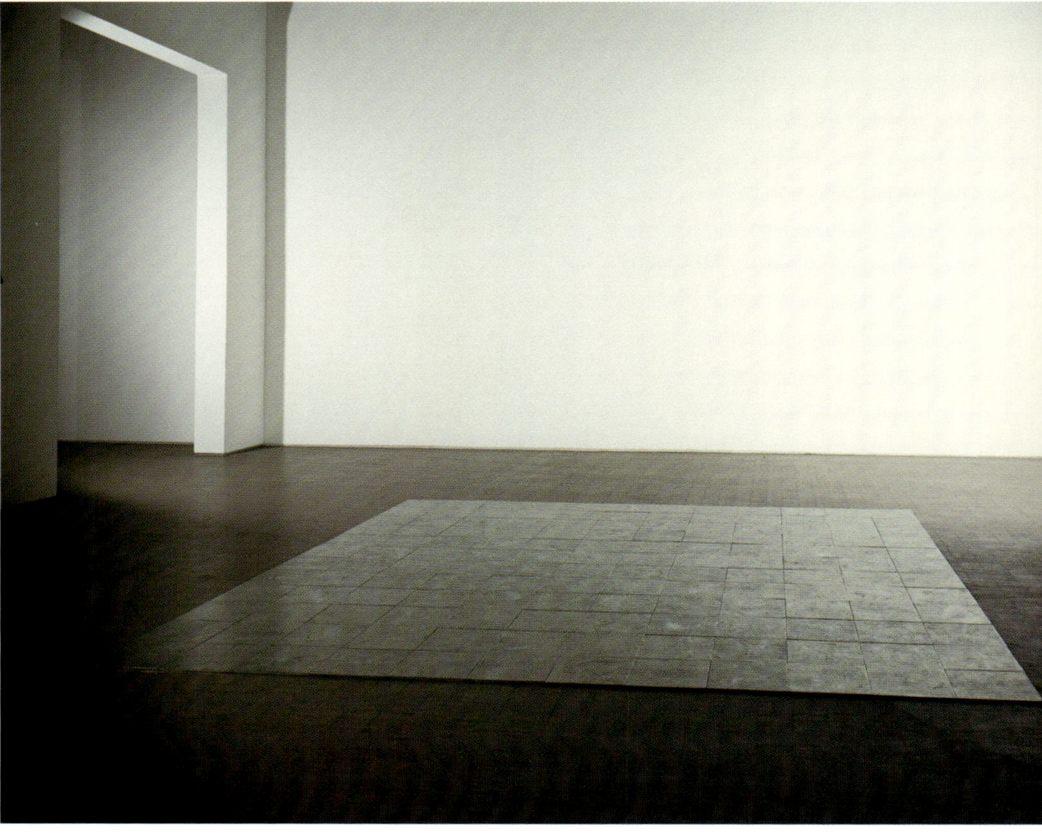

If, ordinarily, sculpture is stood up, there exist cases where it is 'brought back down to earth' and has to be viewed, unusually, from above. American sculptor Carl Andre's rejection of the phallic verticality of traditional sculpture is a deliberate choice: according to his own fulsome expression, 'Priapus has been laid on the ground!' The horizontal disposition of the metal plates invites us to walk over them. Once we do, the piece becomes less a form strictly speaking than a location. The viewer no longer skirts round an object but discovers the potential of acting in and experiencing a place transformed by a sculpture. Andre likes to say that, in the history of sculpture, interest initially focused on form, then structure, and that, lately, contemporary art has come to emphasise place. To illustrate his contention, he takes as an example the Statue of Liberty: at first, the vigorous figure was praised; then its structure (armature, footings, pedestal); and finally one came to consider the zone with which it interacts, Bedloe's Island opposite Ellis Island and Manhattan.

Comparing *144 Tin Square* with a 'horizontal' sculpture, such as that of the *Young Tarentine* by Pierre-Alexandre Schoenewerk, one can readily see what is new in a contemporary piece with respect to those forms of sculpture that were set on the ground in the past. Older works were almost always affected by a degree of pathos: the languid pose of sleep, abandonment after love, let alone the more dramatic register of the dying and of posthumous effigies.

In this regard, it is probably Ponce Jacquiot, four centuries ago, who comes closest to a vision exempt of all pathetic solemnity in his tomb for the Seigneur de Rocquencourt, a piece characterised by a tenderness devoid of lethargy. Jacquiot manages to reconcile the depiction of an heroic and strongly muscular physique with that of the sleep of death, symbolised, in accordance with ancient precepts, by the poppies. The prone corpse's eternalised features are bequeathed to posterity, flattened out like in an engraving. In their different ways, Jacquiot's and Andre's works each create a transitional place.

Carl Andre
144 Tin Square, 1975
Assemblage on the ground of 144 tin squares in rows of 12.
367 x 367 cm - CP

Pierre-Alexandre Schoenewerk
Young Tarentine, 1871
Marble. 74 x 171 x 68 cm - MO

Ponce Jacquiot (attributed to)
André Blondel de Rocquencourt,
third quarter of the 16th century
Bronze. 59 x 173 x 6 cm - ML

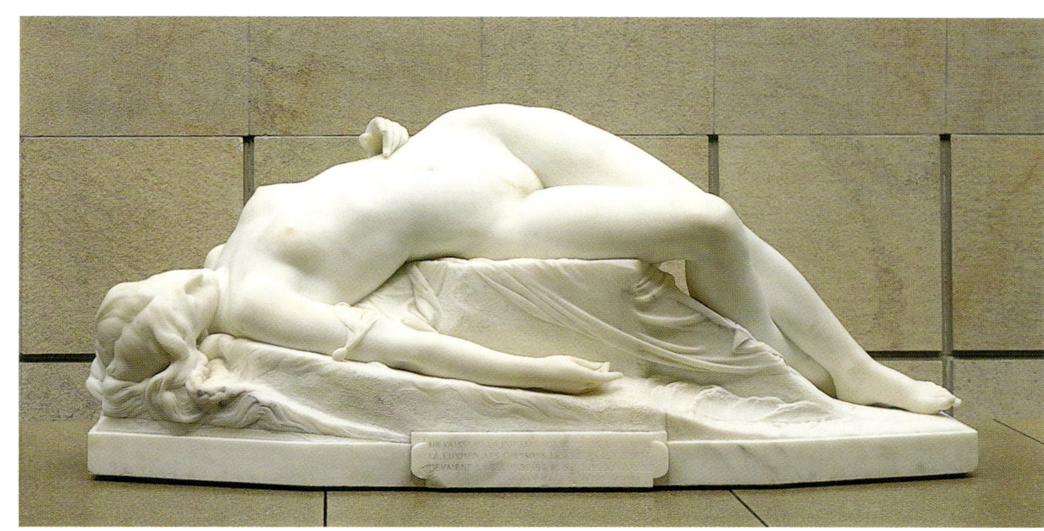

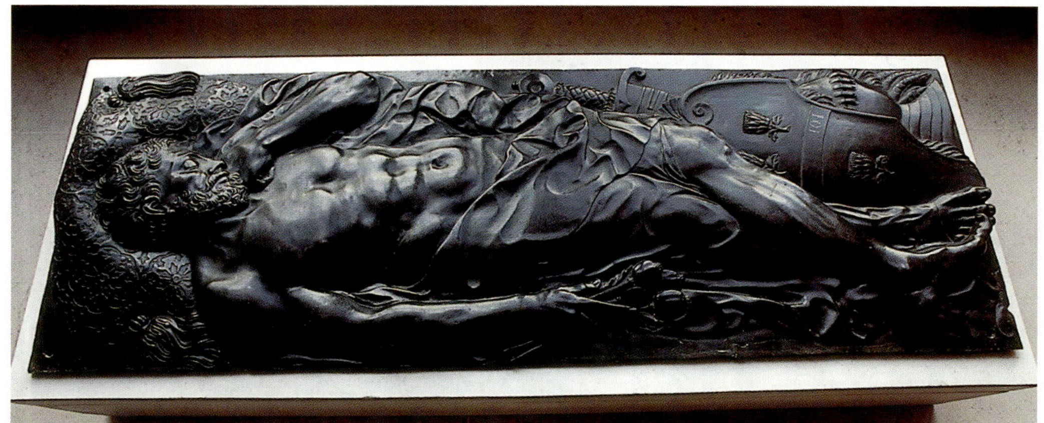

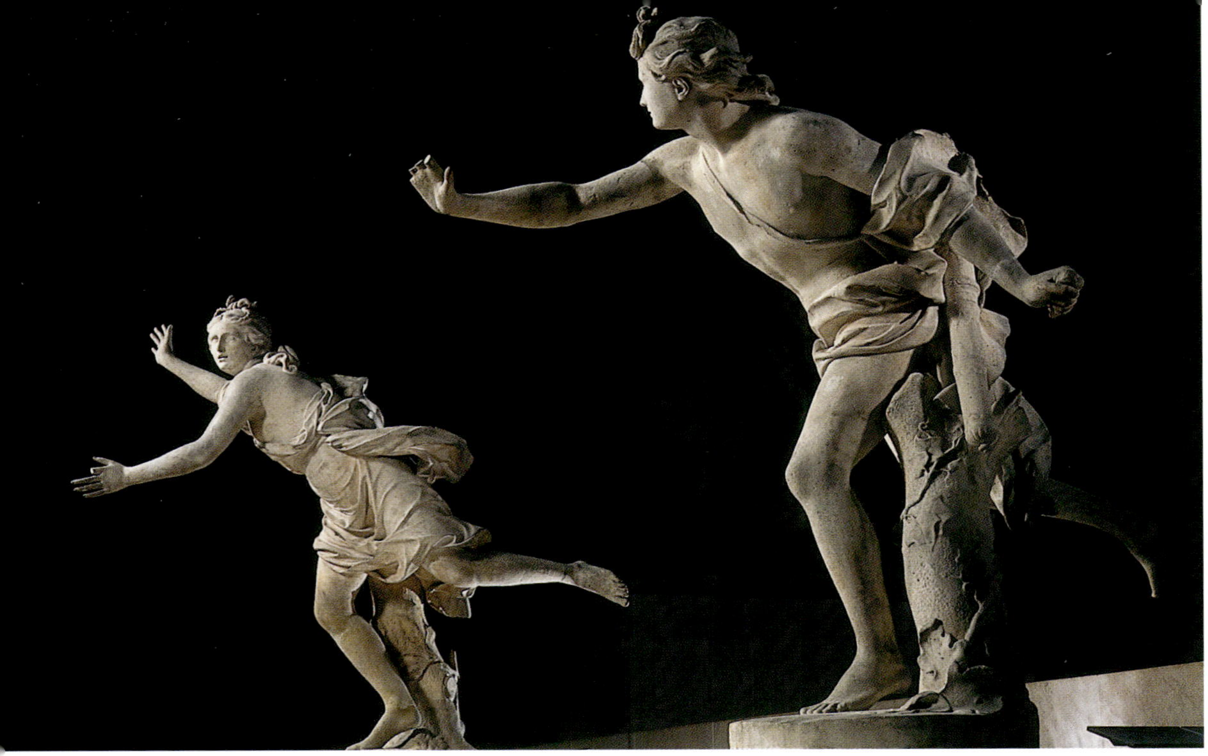

The Gracchi by Eugène Guillaume, the plaster model of which was executed by the artist in Rome in 1847-48 based on the archetype of late imperial cenotaphs, is just one in a family of heroic two-somes, such as the *tyrannoctones* Harmodios and Aristogiton, Romulus and Remus and, even, closer to our time, Vera Muhina's group, *The Worker and the Peasant Woman* (1937). The Roman-style double bust of the tribunes of the plebe, who famously intro-duced measures favourable to the populace of the ancient city, is a prime example of the current of severity that appeared in France in the late 1840s. Guillaume exploits the symmetry between the two men and, intuitively, between two eras: the Roman Republic and the impending 1848 Revolution. The fact that in 1853 the Second Empire ordered it in bronze attests to the desire of Napoleon III (author of *The Eradication of Pauperism*) to give cre-dence to the 'social Empire'. The sculptures of Apollo and Daphne,

respectively commissioned from the brothers Nicolas and Guillaume Coustou the Elder for the Château de Marly, form a pair engaged in a single action, even though they were actually placed at a certain distance apart, standing in two of the park's ponds that flanked the central pavilion. They illustrate a scene described in Ovid's *Metamorphoses*, where the god pursuing the nymph sees her escape by being transformed into a laurel tree. The sculptors were inspired by Bernini's famous group of *Apollo and Daphne* that now stands in the Galleria Borghese in Rome. The novel element, how-ever, is how the surrounding space is encompassed in the interplay and symmetry of the pair: the bodies are in parallel, their faces turning towards one another. This correlation is of course rein-forced by their reflection in the glassy waters. Marly possessed two other such 'runners' *Atalanta* and *Hippomenes*, by, respectively, Pierre Lepaultre and, once again, Guillaume Coustou the Elder.

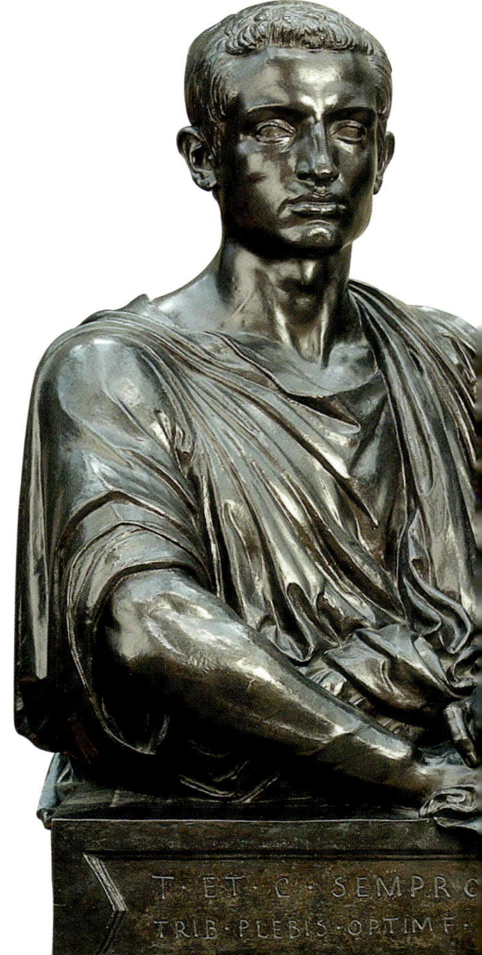

Duos

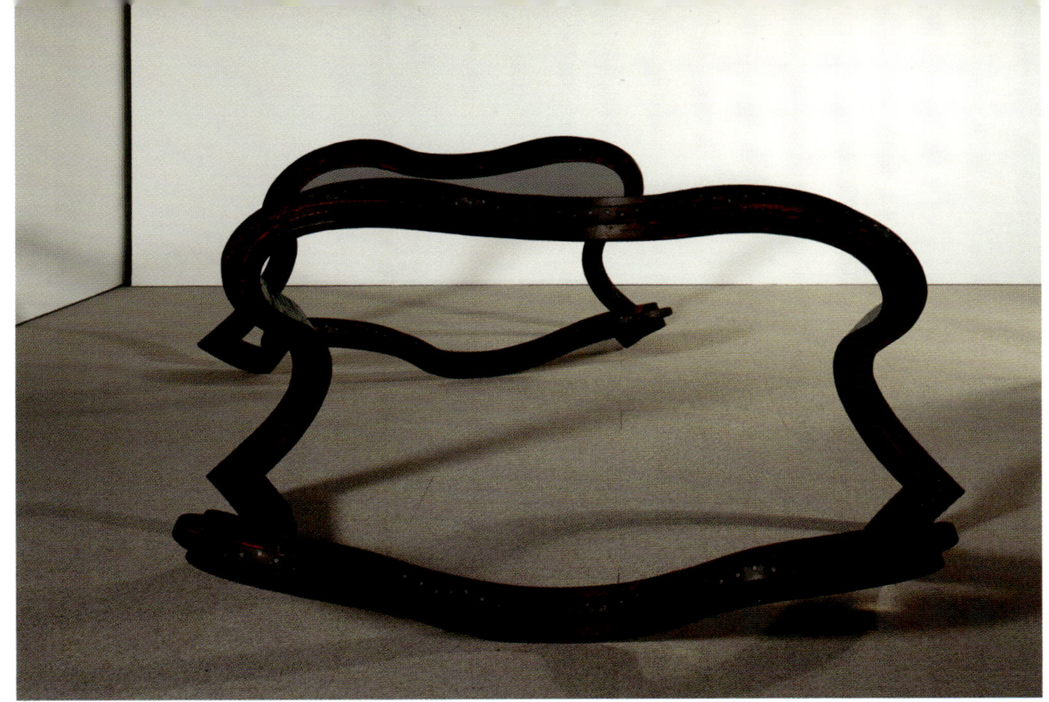

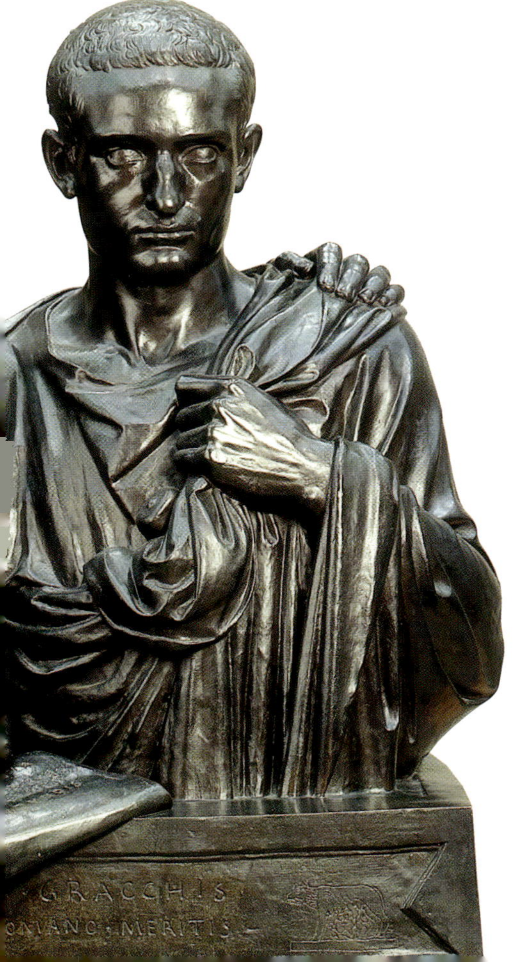

The complex contours of the two sections of *Breed* by the British sculptor Richard Deacon do not seem to refer to any precise form. At most, the viewer, as he moves round the sculpture, will make out, taking shape in the space, and depending on his angle of view and on the projections of his imagination, human body parts, something like hearts or genitals. The title chosen by Deacon does of course suggest ideas of birth and generation, themes particularly prevalent in modern British sculpture and especially in the work of its founder, Henry Moore. Procreation reappears expressed in a ternary rhythm that penetrates the piece's binary structure, since the hollowed-out shapes constituting the 'couple' are actually borne on three points of support.

Guillaume Coustou the Elder
Daphne Pursued by Apollo, 1710
Marble. 132 x 135 x 65 cm - ML

Nicolas Coustou
Apollo Pursuing Daphne, 1713
Marble. 135 x 106 x 113 - ML

Eugène Guillaume
The Gracchi, 1847/1853
Bronze. 85 x 90 x 60 cm - MO

Richard Deacon
Breed, 1989
Wood, hardboard, laminate, aluminium, pigments
138 x 285 x 150 cm and 142 x 287 x 150 cm - CP

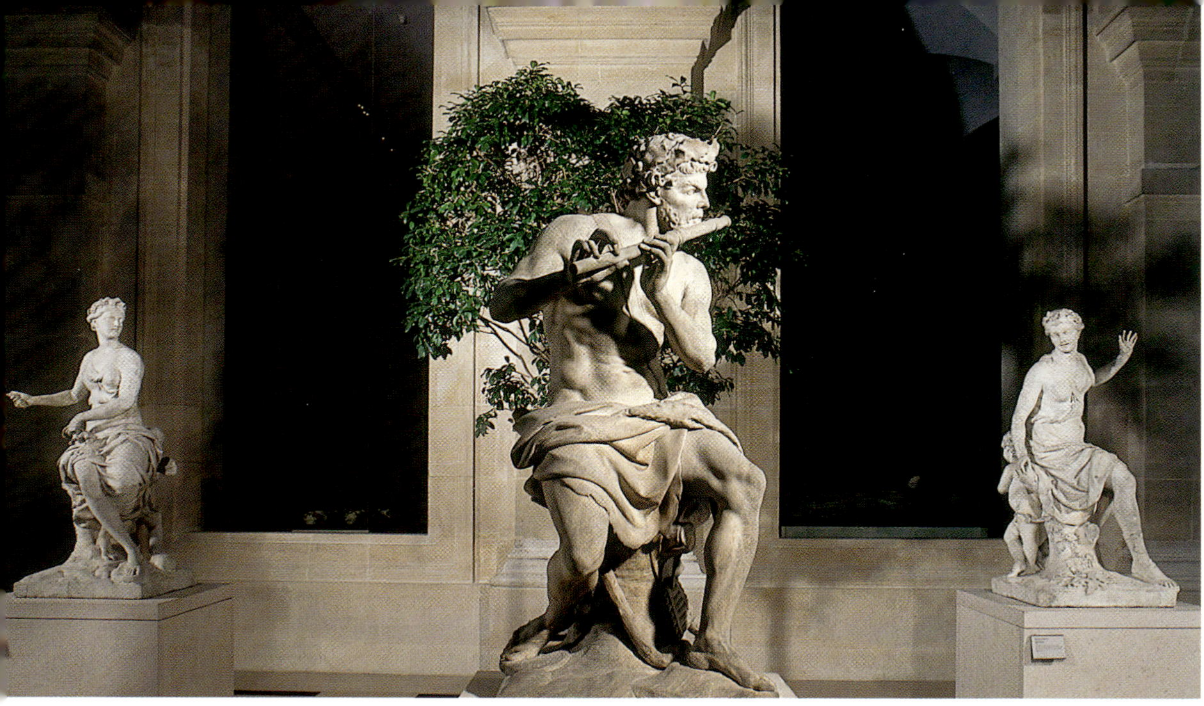

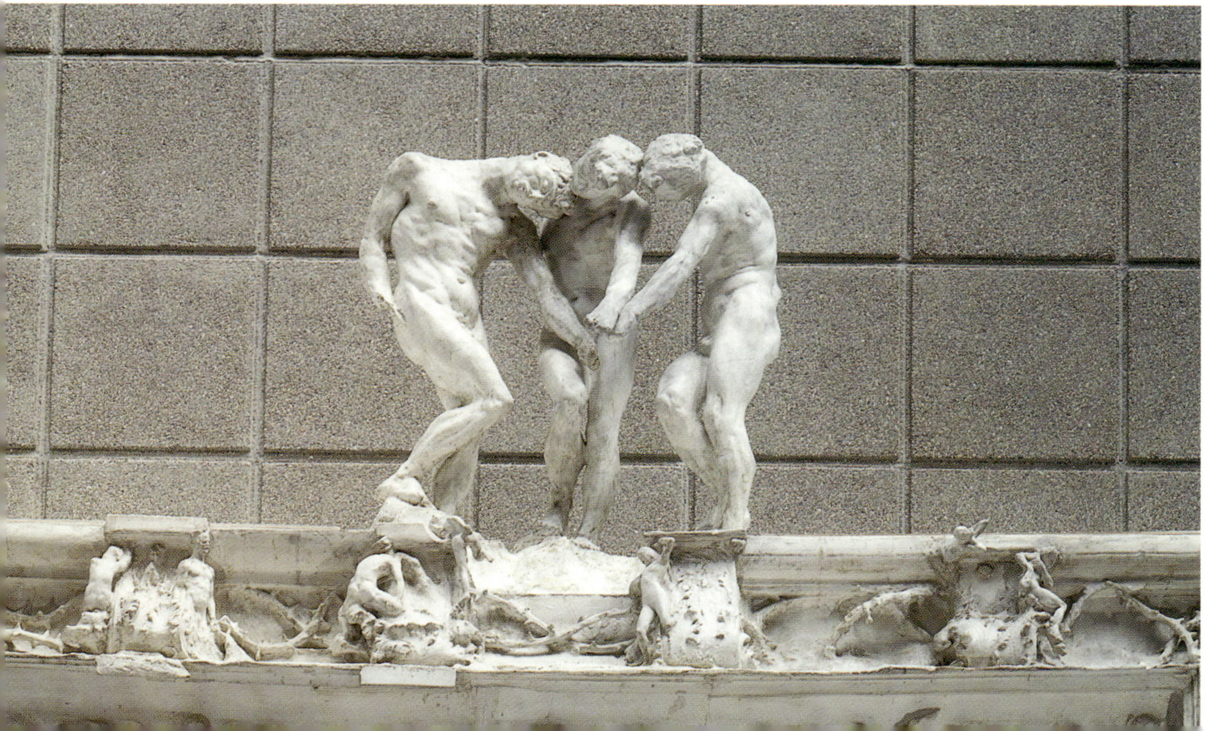

Antoine Coysevox
Shepherd Playing the Flute, 1709
Marble. 178 x 84 x 101 cm - ML

Auguste Rodin
The Gates of Hell, 1880-1889/1917, detail of *The Shades*
Plaster. 105 x 90 x 50 cm - MO

Toni Grand
*Green, squared, squared off then a partial notch,
squared off then two partial notches*, 1973
Wood. 160 x 180 cm - CP

Triads

In his flute-playing shepherd flanked by two listeners, Antoine Coysevox presents one of the most seductive examples of great sculpture 'for overall effect' of the century of Louis XIV. Each statue in the trio adopts its own attitude: the shepherd plies his charms, the hamadryad looks captivated, while Flora seems to pay scant heed to the melody.

On the other hand, the group of the *The Shades* that surmounts the *Gates of Hell* by Auguste Rodin repeats one and the same body of a man. As the artist declared: 'It is the succession of profile studies that endow a figure with a genuine quality of life.' Rodin completely reinvents the 'profile method' by means of which sculptors arranged the back, face and side-view of figures to present an all-round vision, as for example did Canova or Maillol when treating the theme of the Three Graces. By showing here three sides of an identical figure, Rodin seems instead to be reconstituting the effort of observation and analysis that takes place in the studio, so allowing the beholder to share in the creative process. The resultant rhythmical scansion can be compared to that produced by the repetition of the same chord in a piece of music by Beethoven or Stravinsky.

Toni Grand describes his sculpture: 'Too small in a space too large or too large in a space too small.' In this three-branched wood piece Grand, eschewing monumentality as much as decorativeness, instills a multiplicatory movement through two of its elements (thereby rotating the viewpoint), combined with a division that fragments then opens up the volume. It is as if the artist incorporates his own procedures into the living processes of natural growth. But the 'genesis narrative' constituted by the title shows the depth of thought behind the gesture.

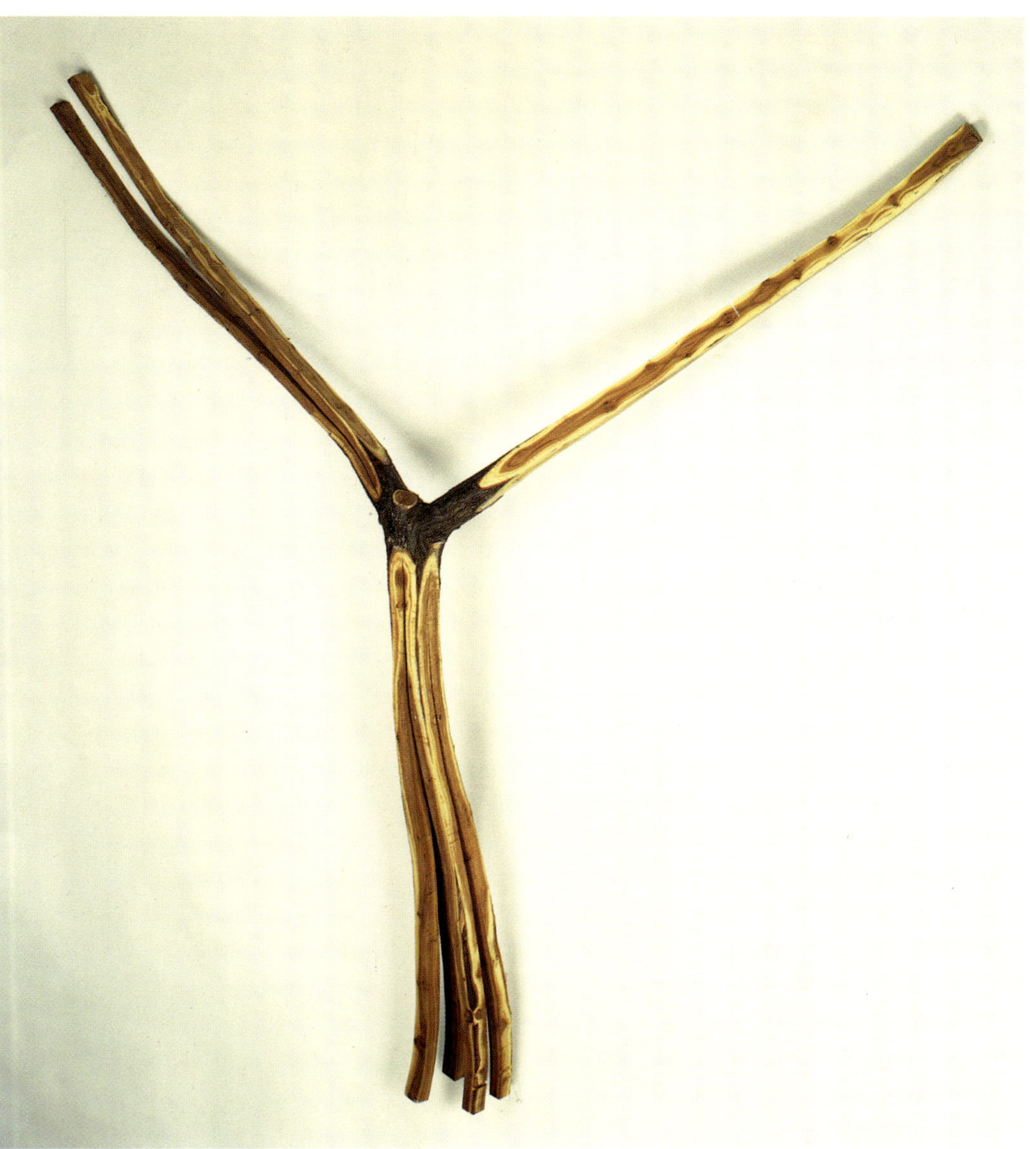

From every angle

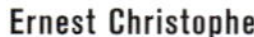

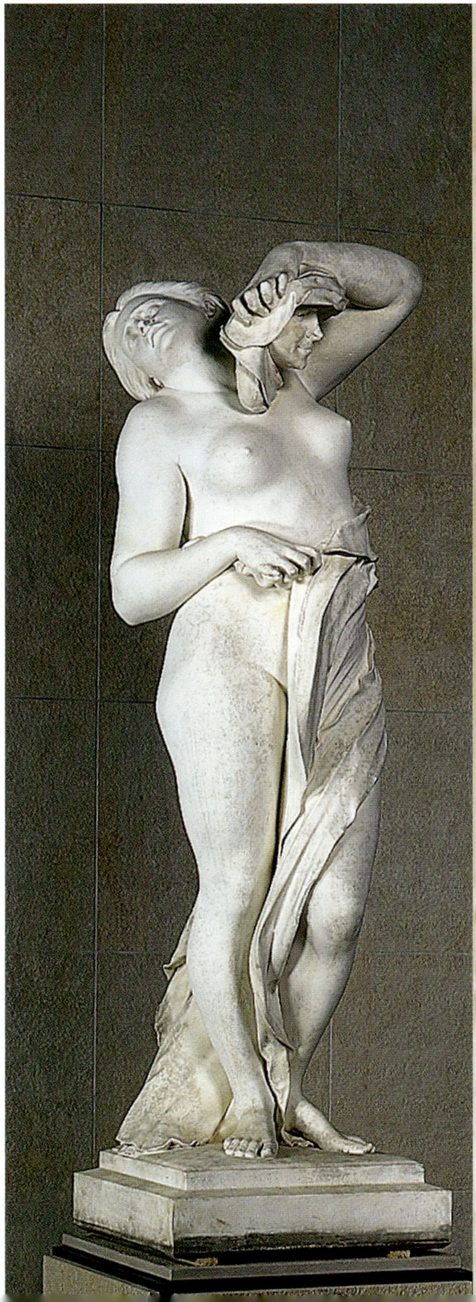

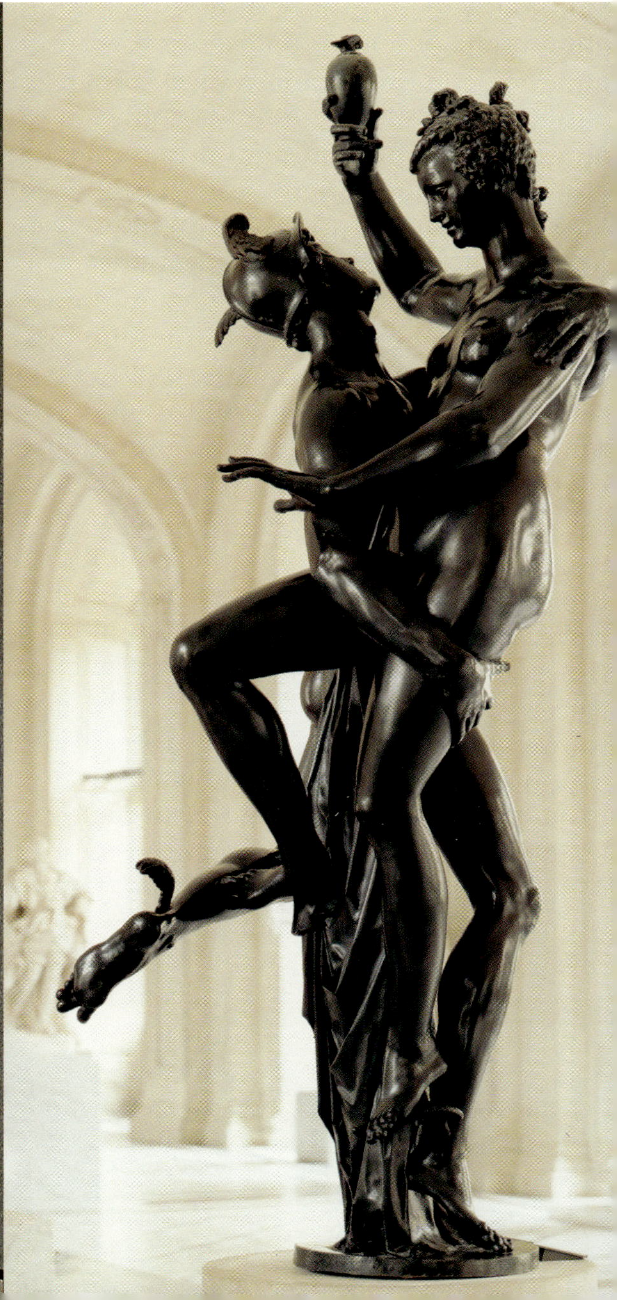

Ernest Christophe

The Human Comedy or *The Mask*, **1857/1876**

Marble. 245 x 85 x 72 cm - MO

Adriaen de Vries

Mercury Abducting Psyche, **1593**

Bronze. 215 x 92 x 72 cm - ML

Tony Cragg

Opening Spiral, **1982**

Mixed media. 152 x 260 x 366 cm - CP

'Multi-faciality' was one of the arguments most often advanced in favour of sculpture and its primacy over painting when the two arts were compared in the famous *paragone*. In his treatise *Of Sculpture* published in 1568 Benvenuto Cellini writes: 'Painting fixes but one of the eight principal points of view sculpture demands.' He is here contradicting Leonardo da Vinci who maintained that 'when a sculptor makes a figure in the round, he treats of only two forms [...]; of two figures, one is viewed from the front and the other from the rear.' Leonardo is wrong to belittle sculpture in this way, since the ancient *kouros* already offered beholders four different viewpoints. The new ideal of sculpture with multiple viewpoints that Cellini praises is perfectly illustrated by the group *Mercury Abducting Psyche* by Adriaen de Vries made in 1593 for Emperor Rudolf II. The viewer is no longer static but kinetic, the sculpture itself encouraging us to view it from every possible angle. Psyche is carried off to the heavens by a Mercury who touches the earth with just a single foot. In observance of an elegant Mannerist pre-

cept according to which a heavier object is borne up by a lighter, the goddess and her abductor are supported only by the drapery falling between them. The piece is designed according to the principle of serpentine lines first deployed in *The Rape of a Sabine* (1579-83) by De Vries' master Giambologna, a sculpture visible today in the Loggia dei Lanzi at Florence. The erotic charge of the body of the abducted Psyche, seen from every conceivable aspect, is evident, even though a symbolic reading invites us to see Psyche as the spirit of invention (*ingenium*) borne aloft by skill (*ars*).

'Let us contemplate this treasure of Florentine graces,' Baudelaire urges us in his poem 'Le Masque' published in *Les Fleurs du Mal*. Contrary to expectation, this was not applied to the work of De Vries but to *The Human Comedy* carved by Ernest Christophe in 1876. 'Let us turn around its beauty,' the poet continued. It is indeed only by moving that we can take in the sculpture: the mask of joy is but a facade (a *persona*) and the true face is one of pain. The aesthetics of 'surprise' (this is Baudelaire's word) that stems

from the multiple viewpoint is also to be found in certain sculptures by Picasso where, for instance, the alluring face of a young woman is replaced by a death's head as the beholder moves.

Perpetuum mobile: an 'endless motion' is evoked by *Opening Spiral* by British artist Tony Cragg. This sorcerer's apprentice of sculpture makes everyday objects dance, transforming an accelerating whirl of fragments and colours into a single, dynamic figure. The spiral recalls that of De Vries' Mannerist piece, but Cragg accentuates its 'multi-faciality' because each element is of a different size and orientation. Each time the sculpture is set up presents fresh opportunities for arrangements and different viewing angles.

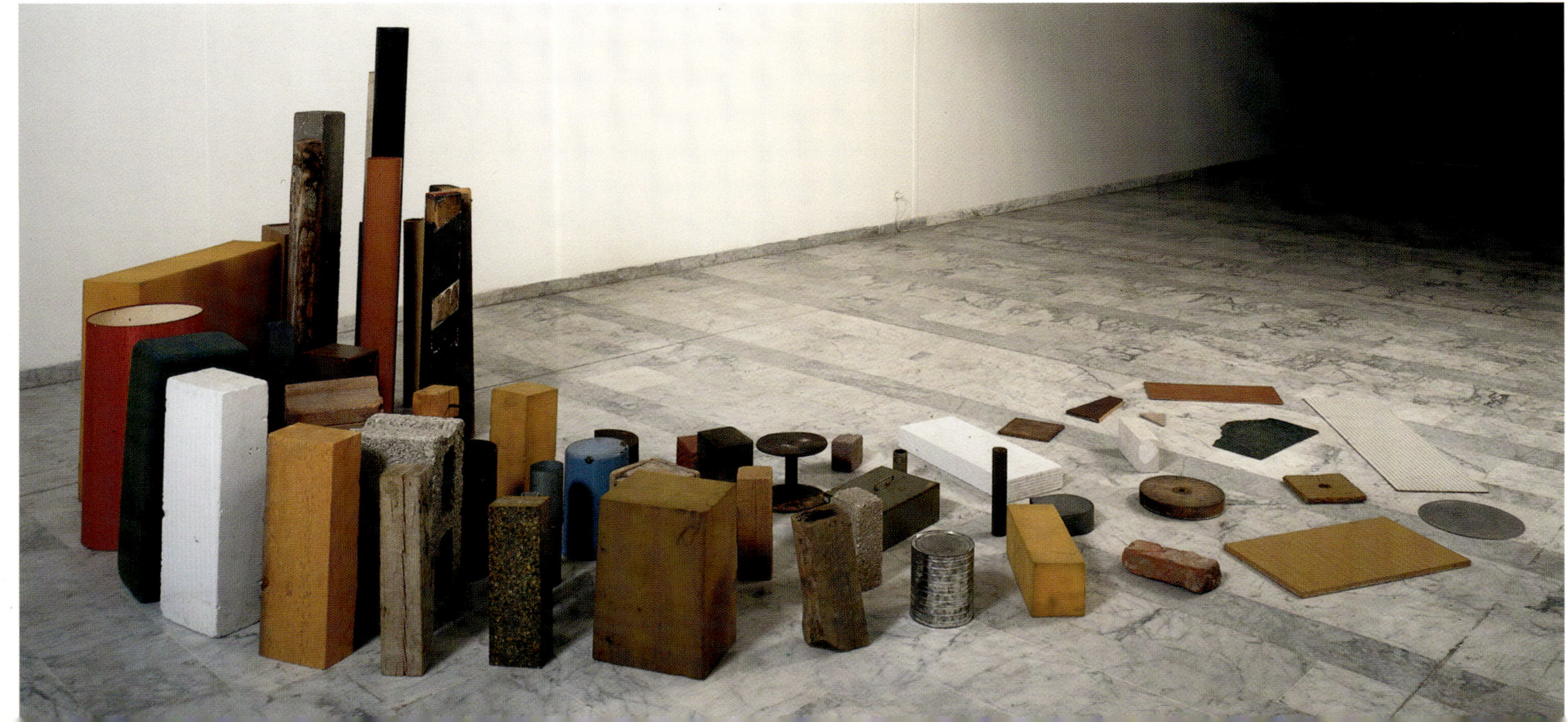

Drawing in space

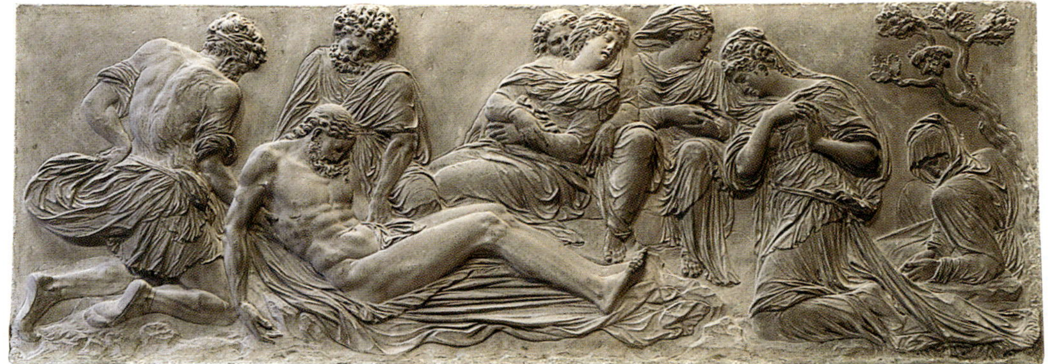

Jean Goujon
The Deploration of Christ
mid-16th century
Stone. 67 x 182 x 7 cm - ML

Antoine Pevsner
Model for the Construction of World, 1946
Brazed, varnished brass struts. 42 x 36 x 31 cm - CP

Honoré Daumier
Ratapoil, 1851-91
Bronze. 43 x 15 x 18 cm - MO

Julio González
Daphne, c. 1937
Bronze. 142 x 71 x 52 cm - CP

In the artistic milieu of the French Renaissance, greatly influenced by Italy and by Neo-Platonic theory, drawing was considered the foundation of sculptural expression. Around the body of the Redeemer, in the *Deploration of Christ* by Jean Goujon, an eloquent dramaturgy is set up based on the sinuous lines of the folded cloth and the epic rhetoric of the assistants, that outdoes even the tautly powerful musculature.

Honoré Daumier applied a caricaturist's vigorous line to sculpture. In 1831, Charles Philippon, publisher of the periodicals *Le Charivari* and *La Caricature*, ordered from him thirty-six busts in coloured unfired clay of the members of the Corps Législatif. This ensemble was to be used as a basis for the lithographic spoofs that go by the title *Le Ventre législatif* (The Legislative Belly). Daumier's drawing is characterised by a multitude of lines that endow his silhouettes with astonishing spatial plentitude and innate movement. Around 1850 in *Ratapoil*, Daumier lampooned the Bonapartist agitator and wheeler-dealer, one-time soldier and ragged-trousered blusterer, wearing his boots out stamping the path clear for the future Napoleon III's putsch.

Antoine Pevsner and Julio González knew to combine modern metalworking, welding in particular, with exceptional acuity of line, to the point that the Spanish artist's *Daphne* can well be termed a 'drawing in space'. As for Pevsner, in soldering together metal struts to form what he called 'developable surfaces', as here in *Maquette for the Construction of World*, he proclaims once more the intuitions, the techniques of a sculptor-craftsman, even though it has been demonstrated that both he and his brother Naum Gabo were adepts of mathematical modelling.

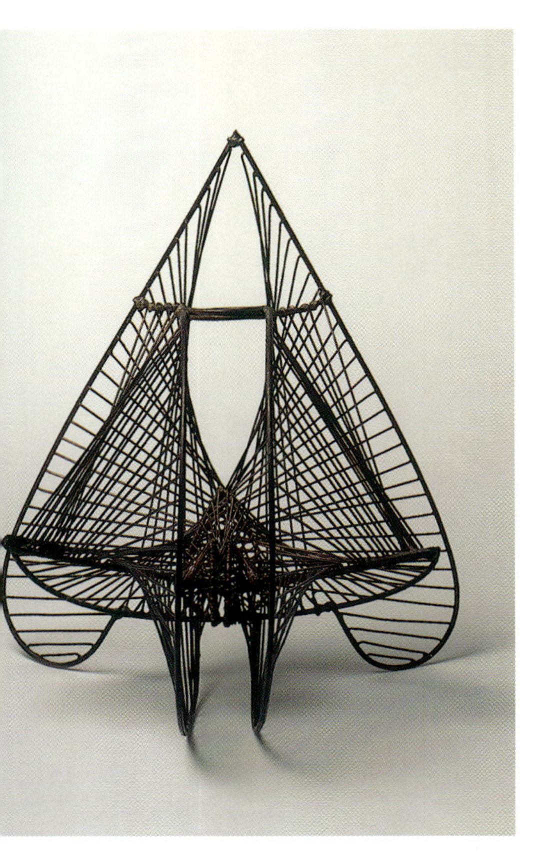 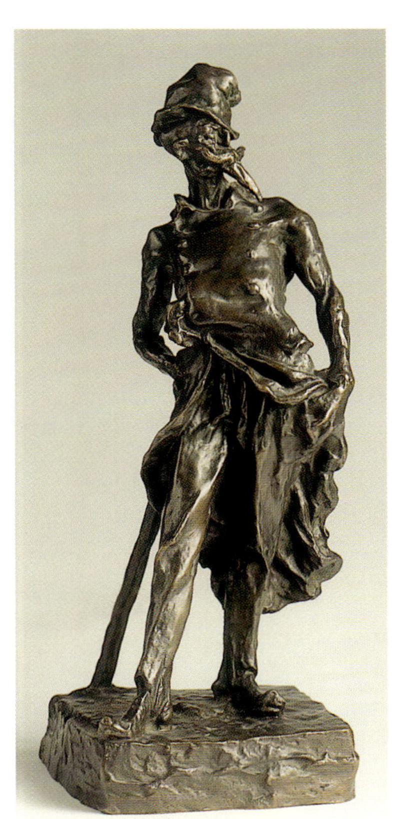 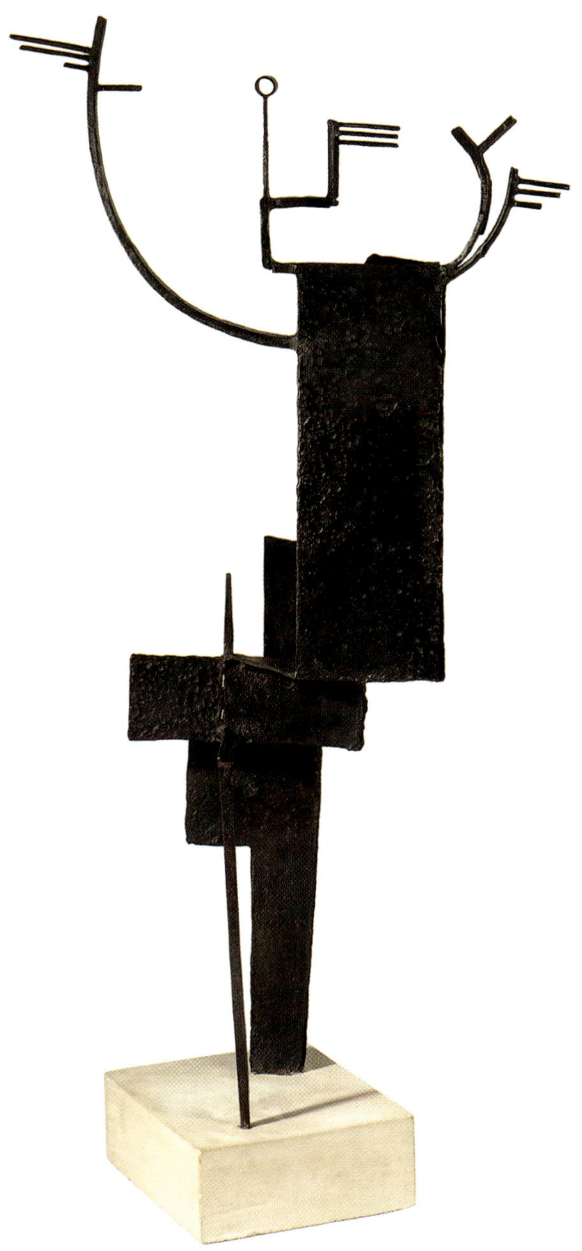

The powerful fascination of Germain Pilon's risen Christ owes much to the contrast created between the elevation — almost a levitation — of Jesus and the dead weight of the slumbering soldiers, as if bolted to the earth by some magnetic force. Christ, raising his right hand in blessing, surges forth in an expressive *contrapposto* from the grip of Death evoked by the prone bodies.

Rodin's *Ugolino*, on the other hand, gropes among the corpses of his children on all fours, prey to a kind of annihilation, in a vision that severs the sons from the father. Whereas Carpeaux had linked the group in a pyramid, Rodin deliberately destructures the tragic group, placing much emphasis on the drapery whose elegiac outpouring has in the end to reveal that which it cannot completely conceal.

Elevation and descent, the vertical and the horizontal, cohesion and dispersion, extension and concentration: all the forces that can affect a sculpture group are at work in the tangible choreography of Eva Hesse's *Seven Poles*. This piece, which the artist died too young to see completed, recalls the picture *Blue Poles*, where Barnett Newman drew straight vertical lines over a colourful interlace painted by his friend Jackson Pollock. According to Hesse, Pollock understood that chaos needs to be structured as if it were not chaos at all. In *Seven Poles*, the artist wrapped a wire armature suspended from the ceiling and whose vertical elements form an angle with the ground, in fibreglass, to fashion a six-fold suspension piece evocative of a cocoon — an image of a chrysalis. In this way the artist seeks to exorcise the melancholy of a descent into the inner world of the unconscious and a reemergence into life by means of the transparent, logical structure of artistic form.

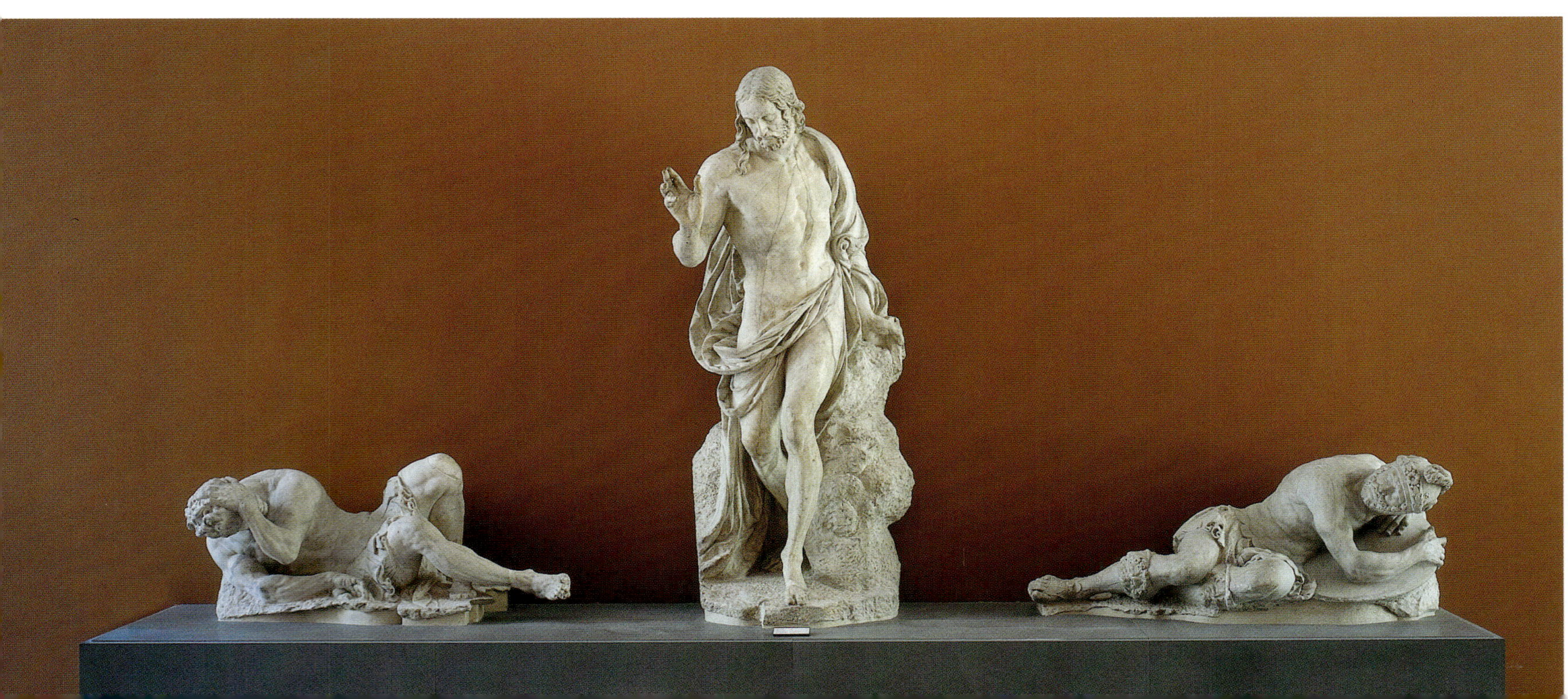

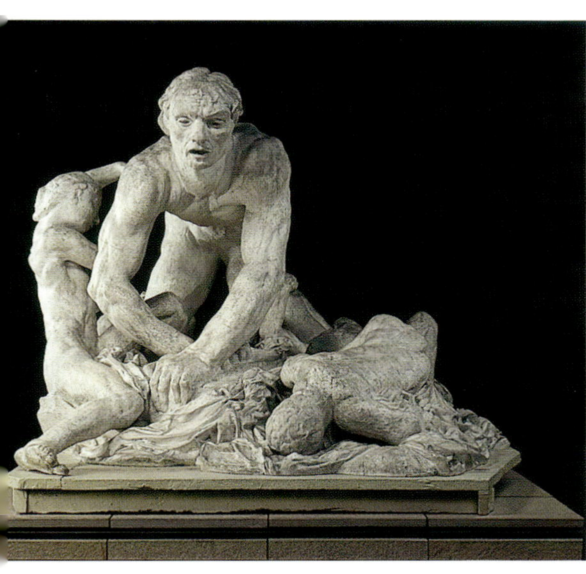

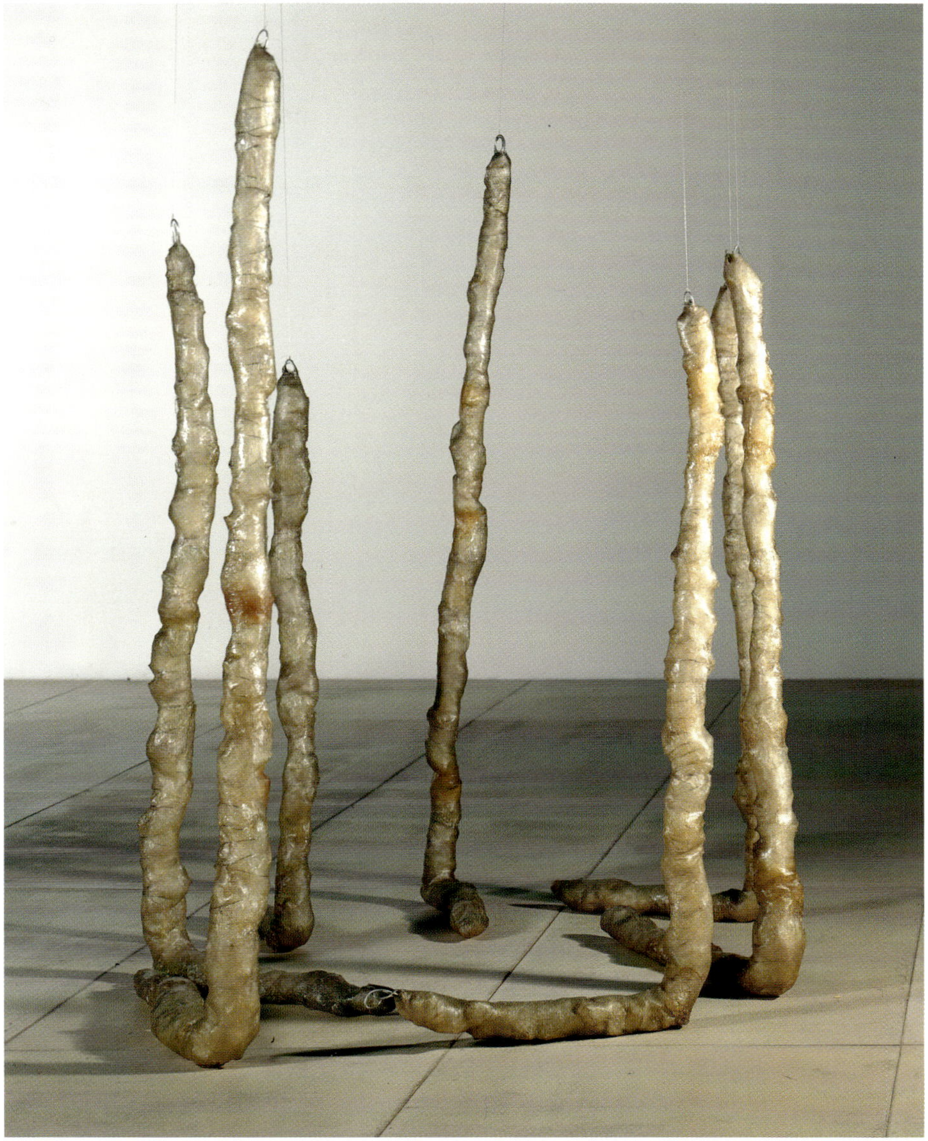

Germain Pilon
The Resurrection, second half of the 16th century
Marble. 215 x 188 x 74 cm - ML

Auguste Rodin
Ugolino, 1882/1906
Plaster. 139 x 173 x 278 cm - MO

Eva Hesse
Untitled (Seven Poles), 1970
Aluminium wire, polyethylene, resin, fibreglass. H: 188 to 282 cm - CP

Geometry

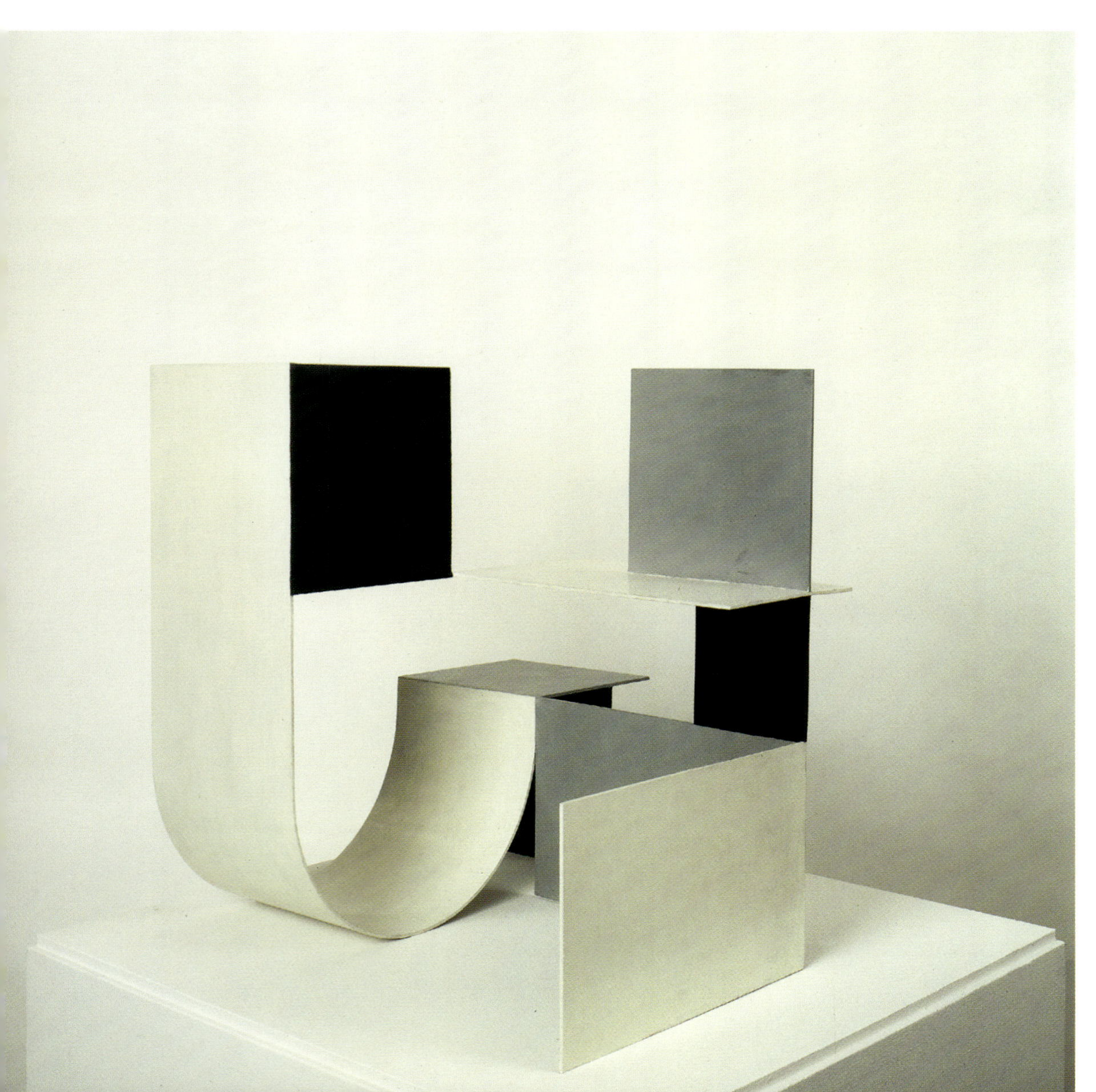

Katarzyna Kobro
Spatial Sculpture, c. 1928
Painted sheet-steel. 44.8 x 44.8 x 46.7 cm - CP

Aristide Maillol
Mediterranean, 1902-05
Marble. 118 x 142 x 71 cm - MO

Pierre Julien
Dying Gladiator, 1778
Marble. 60 x 48 x 42 cm - ML

A veritable manifesto for Neoclassicism, the *Dying Gladiator*, Pierre Julien's reception piece to the French Academy in 1779, goes well beyond its ancient model. If the attitude is verisimilar and the musculature rendered in all its details, the power of the piece lies in its geometrical superstructure: the spherical volume evinced by the drooping head, the circular surface of the vertically held shield, the complex triangulation of the crossed legs, the 'cubist' structure of the parallel limbs: all this is in the spirit of classical sculpture.
In his luminous *Mediterranean*, also called, and with some reason, *Thought*, Aristide Maillol attains the same complex equilibrium, with the same intercrossing lines with the legs. The sculptor's achievement — working in planes, laying in triangular forms — should not obscure his mastery of the relationship between the vig-

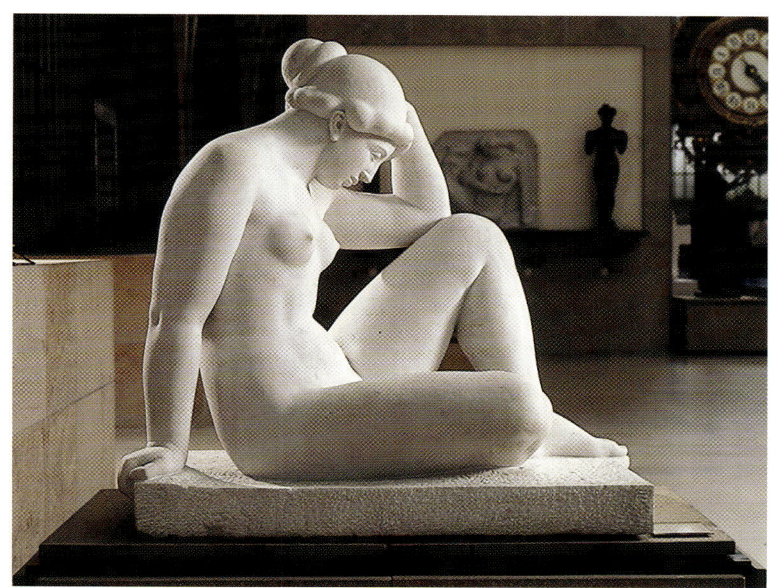

orous, full areas and the voids, which provides the modelled form with its buoyancy.

But the heritage of Greece is not the only place where classicism set down roots. The tendency to the abstraction of form, evident in the preceding sculptures, attains its apogee in *Spatial Sculpture* by the Polish artist Katarzina Kobro, a member of the Constructivist movement. Serge Lemoine wrote that it 'generates virtual volumes by an interplay of planes, it establishes a limit, allowing the free circulation of air and eye: its structure, completely imbricated in the space around, is an affirmation of the negation of mass.' Perhaps Constructionist art is the fruit of a classical sensibility and of a classical theory of art.

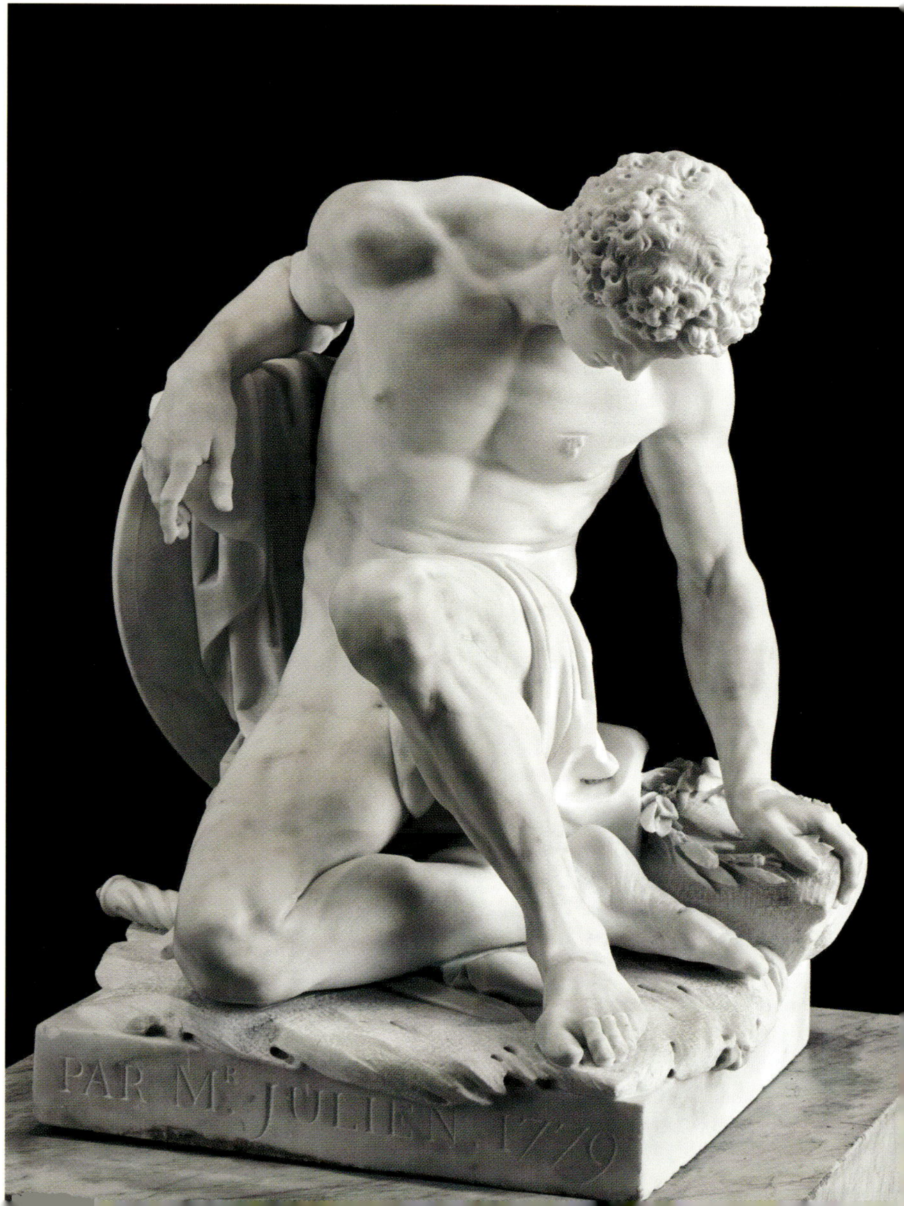

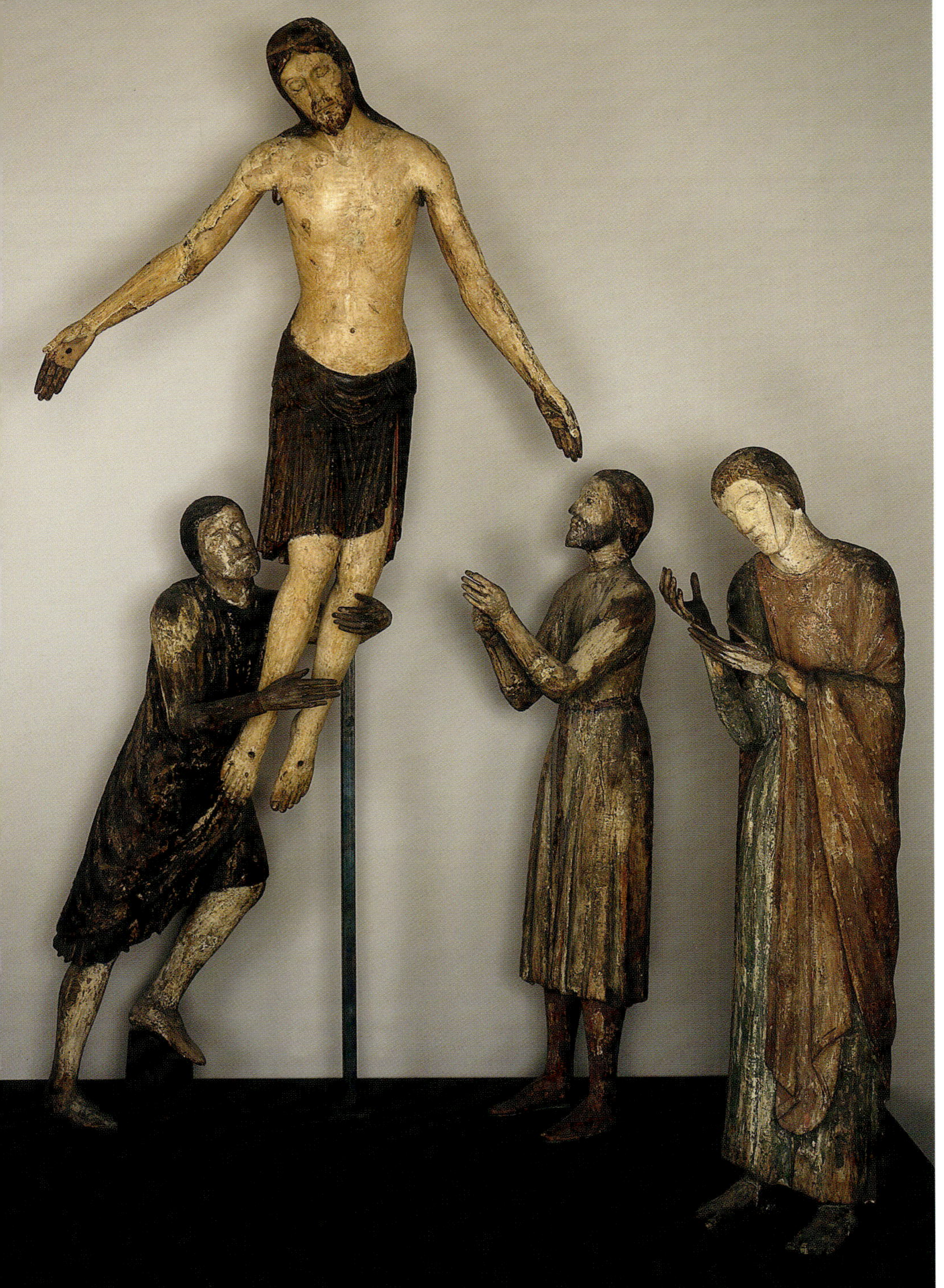

Cross

The theme of the cross in sculpture derives from the jointed crucifixes made of painted wood that were carried at one time in processions around churches. This polychrome wood *Descent from the Cross* from the 13th century takes on a deeper meaning if one recalls the importance of representing the dead Christ in combating the various dualistic heresies that denied his human nature — doctrines particularly prevalent in central Italy at this period. If the raised arms of the companions of Christ supporting his body at the foot of the Cross allude to the rite of the Mass, then the outstretched arms of Emmanuel Fremiet's knight, who holds a phylactery bearing the inscription 'Credo', following the example of saints in the Neo-Gothic churches being built at the time, mimic the Cross itself. Fremiet here establishes a perfect correspondence between the meaning of the word ('I believe'), the attitude of the knight opening his arms as if he were a living cross, and the structure of the statuette.

Therein lies the radical essence of the cross, where the horizontal meets the vertical, that so fascinated abstract artists such as the American Sol LeWitt. Hollowing out cubes so that only the risers remain, he effects a shift from sculptural object to drawing in space: the cross lies on the ground like a geometrical hopscotch.

The white modules — as 'ideal' as any marble — are tall enough to be on a level with the gallery goer as they make their way about them. They thus become aware of the irreducible difference between the ideal schema of the cross, that can be apprehended here only in the mind's eye (as it cannot be looked at from above), and the partial views of it experienced walking around the piece and seeing through it the space of the room.

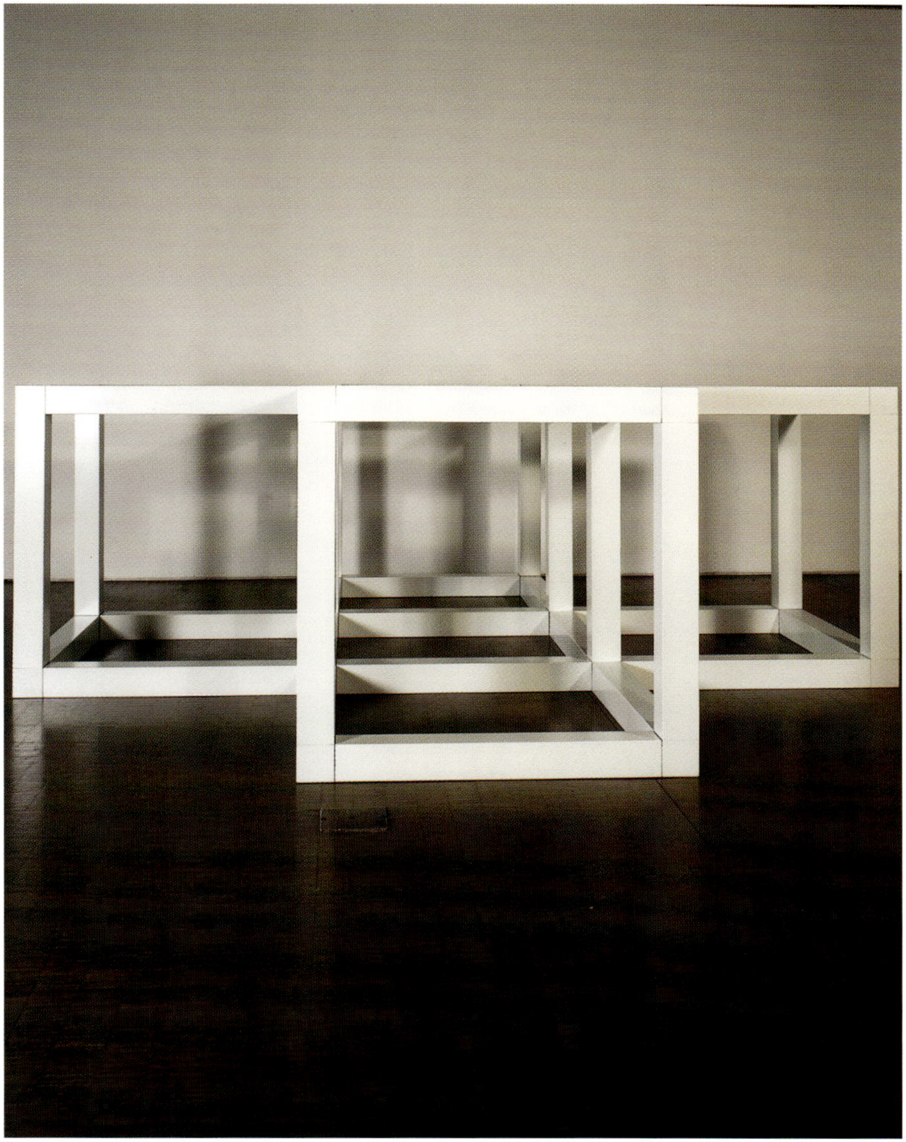

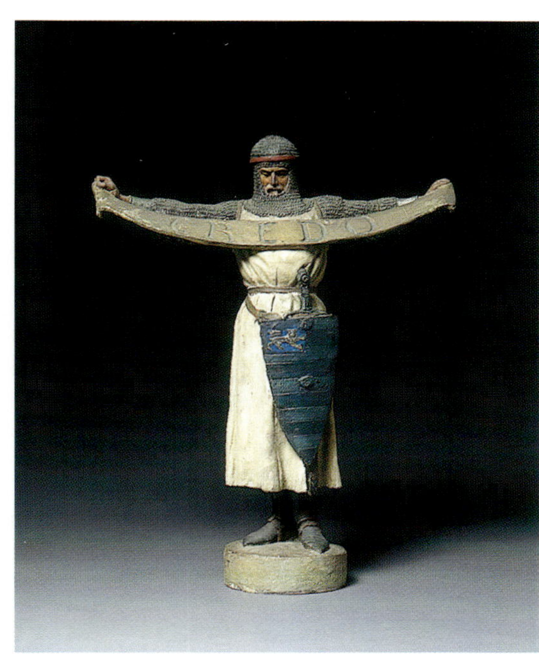

Descent from the Cross, Umbria,
second quarter of the 13th century.
Polychrome wood, marble. 183 cm x 123 cm - ML

Emmanuel Fremiet
Credo, 1885
Plaster covered in painted glued flock. 40 x 32 x 10 cm - MO

Sol LeWitt
5 Part Piece (Open Cubes) in Form of a Cross, 1966-69
Painted steel. 160 x 450 x 450 cm - CP

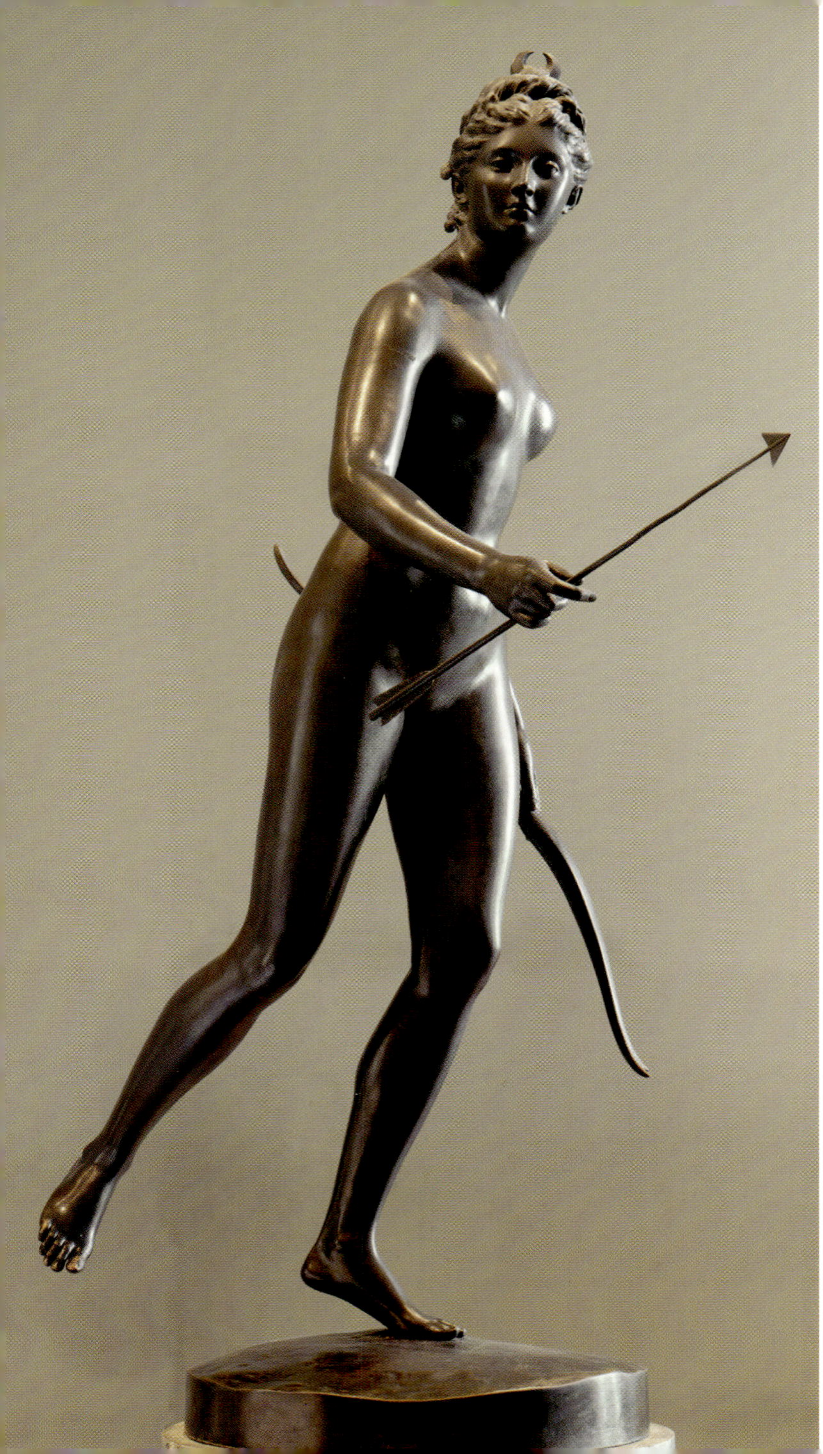

Balance

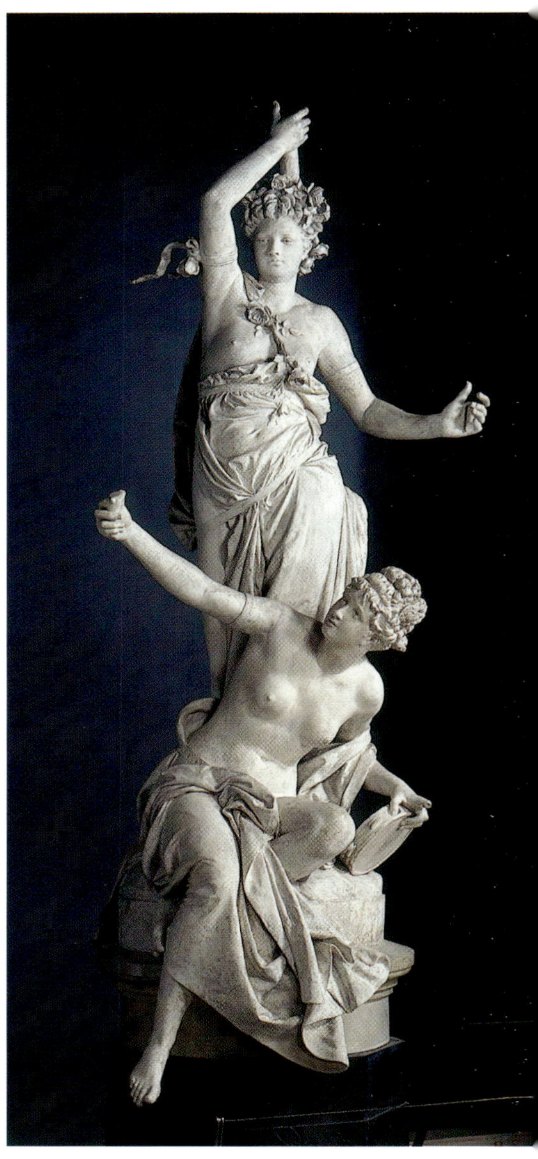

Diana the Huntress, represented entirely naked by Jean-Antoine Houdon (an unusual state for the unsullied, tunic-clad goddess!), has hardly posed a lightsome foot on the circular terrace that stands for the earth, like an airborne sister to Giambologna's *Mercury*. The figures in the *Torchère with Tambourine*, made for the interior of the Paris Opera by Carrier-Belleuse, can hardly maintain their balance in the air and stretch out their arms like a pair of scales. How can a sculptor capture 'the lightness of the divinities' of which Winckelmann spoke? By defying gravity.

It is to gravity, however, that Richard Serra paradoxically entrusts the responsibility of keeping up the metal partitions of the *Prop* pieces he has been erecting since the late 1960s. For these works, which resemble card houses made of metal, Serra chooses materials that are hard to maintain in positions of instability, such as lead. Balance in *5:30* results from the carefully calculated specifications of the intrinsic qualities of the materials, first and foremost, their weight. Alfred Pacquement observes that 'the sculpture exists only through its process of construction' adding that 'the various components are only physically connected by the force of gravity.'

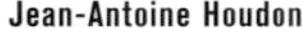

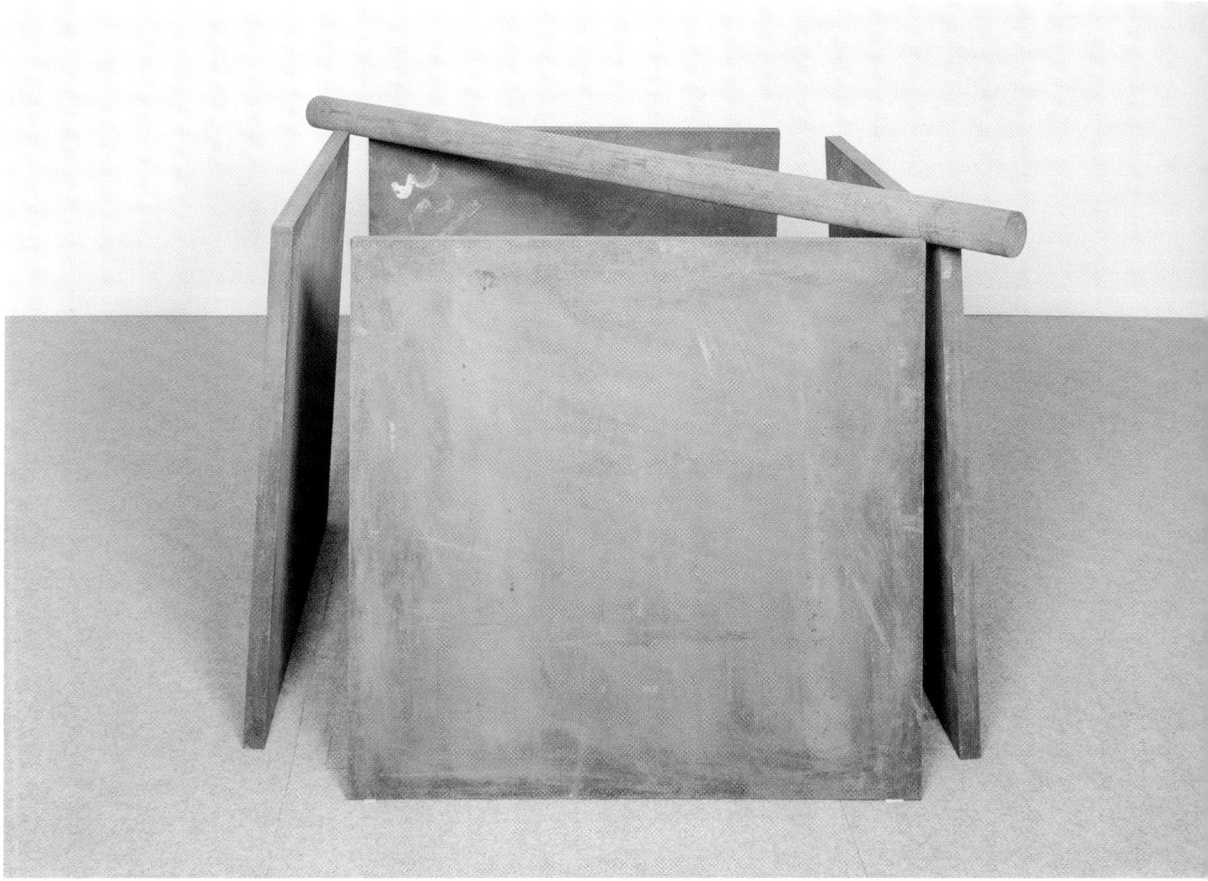

Jean-Antoine Houdon
Diana the Huntress, **1790**
Bronze. 192 x 90 x 114 cm - ML

Carrier-Belleuse
Torchère with Tambourine, **1873**
Plaster model. H: 260 cm; diam. (base): 90 cm - MO

Richard Serra
5:30, **1969**
Assemblage of four plates and one roll of Corten steel
124 x 124 x 5 cm (each plate) and 230 x 15 cm (roll) - CP

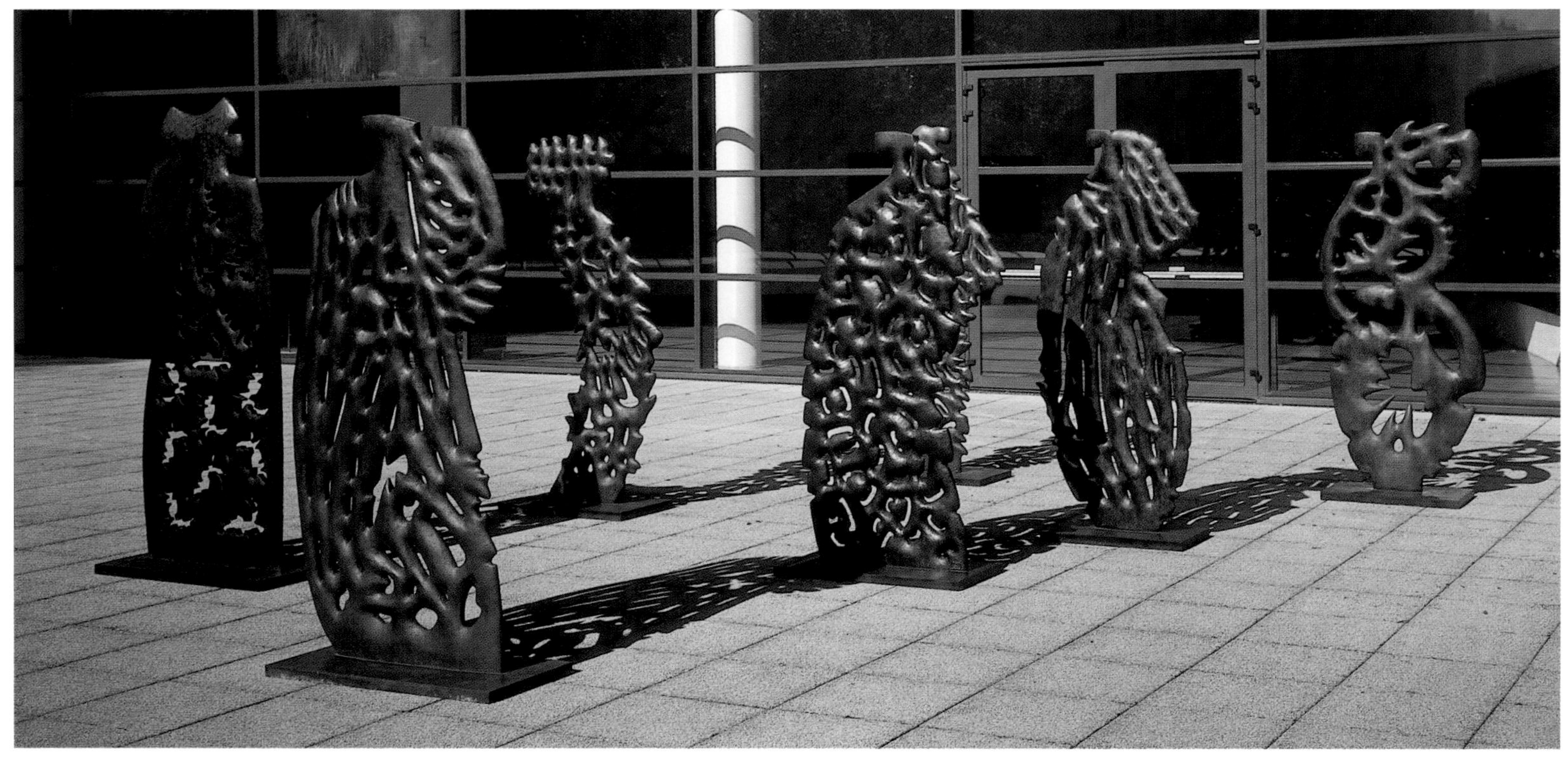

For *Perseus and Andromeda,* a group designed to stand out against a backdrop of green plants, Pierre Puget chose the moment when the figure of Perseus is at its maximum extension. The Greek hero literally leaps off ground to untie the captive who would fall forwards were she not held back by the hero: a 'contrast between force and liberated grace, between movement and languor,' as Geneviève Bresc-Bautier neatly put it.

Rodin's masterly intuition can be amply appreciated in this portrait of Camille Claudel entitled *Thought*. When the carver who cut the marble on the basis of the preparatory clay model of 1886 arrived at the stage where Camille's chin was visible yet remained in the 'stuff' of the block, Rodin ordered to him to down tools. The contrast between the compact block and the slightly inclined head detaching from it instates the dialectic of an ideal nexus that mirrors the formation of clear concepts from the still amorphous realm of intuitive thought.

The tireless observer of the world that is Etienne Hajdu takes up this idea to make a sculpture which, rare in this art of matter, is held together by light. Hajdu opens up the simple volumes of Brancusi's sculpture and manages to incorporate into his transparent, airy structures, the world of fluids, lightwaves and the gravitation of the elements. His two-dimensional *Grandes Demoiselles* are less an object than a surface for projecting light, a filter for the changing values of an environment. The artist had a passion for the scientific observation of nature. Following his death, some astrophysicist friends gave his name to a celestial body. It was Hajdu's contention that, if the world is above all energy, then sculpture should be so too.

Light defies gravity

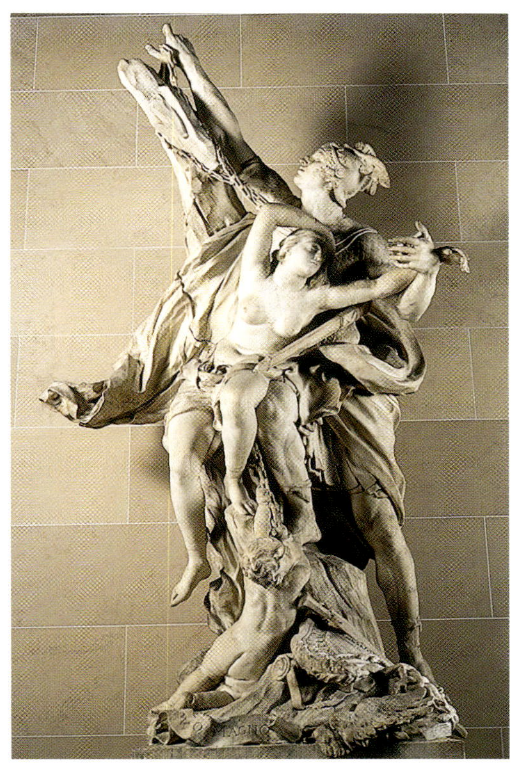

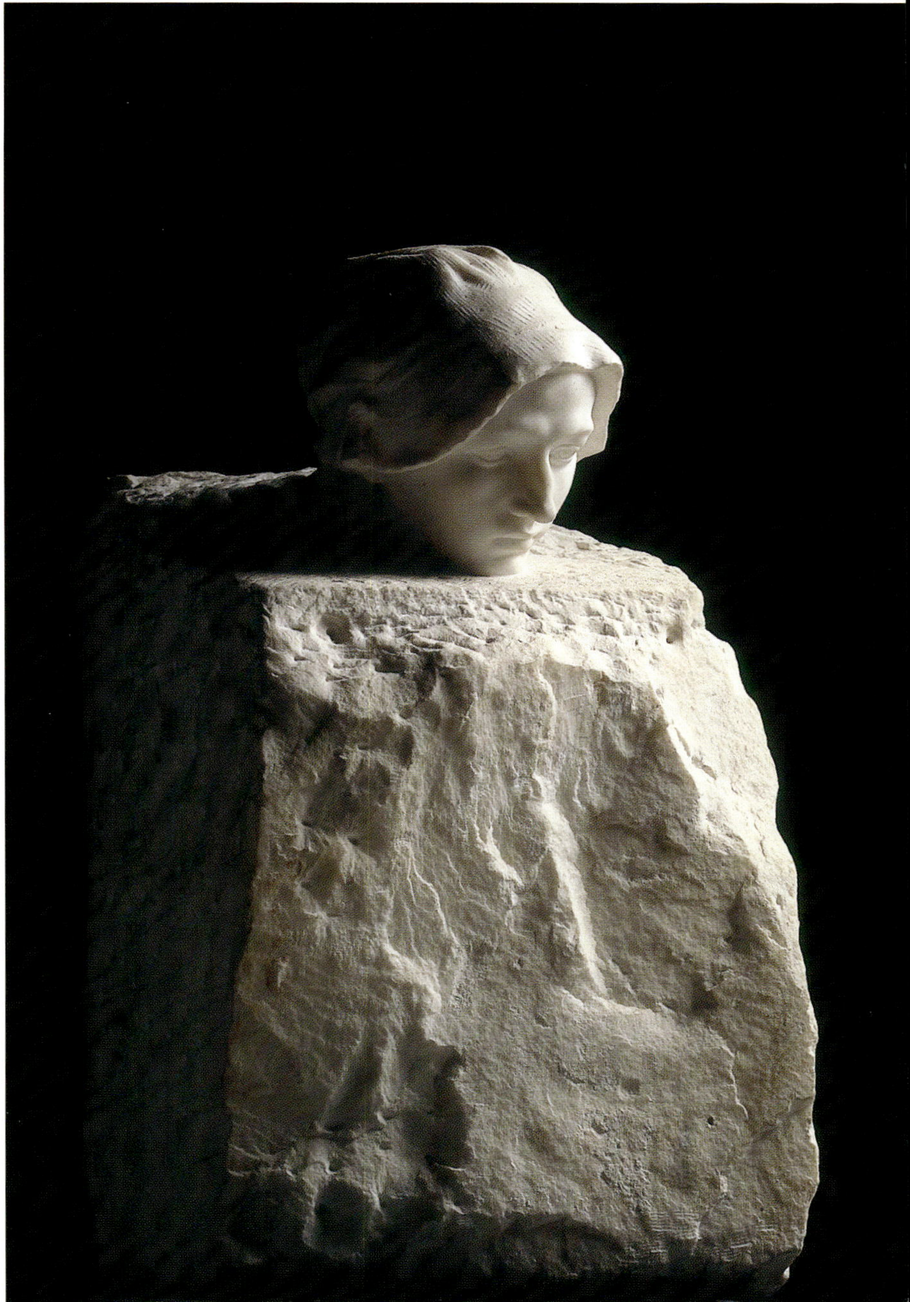

Etienne Hajdu
Grandes Demoiselles, 1979-82
Bronze. 189 to 206 x 72 to 94 cm - CP

Pierre Puget
Perseus and Andromeda, 1678-84
Carrara marble. 320 x 106 x 114 cm - ML

Auguste Rodin
Thought (Portrait of Camille Claudel), c. 1895
Marble. 74 x 43 x 46 cm - MO

Construction

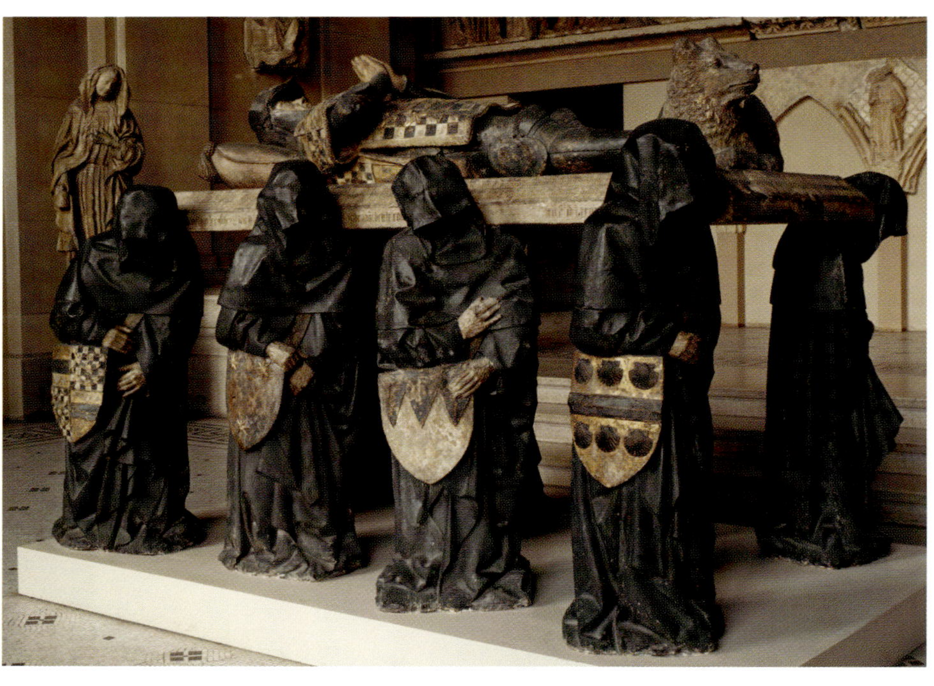

Tomb of Philippe Pot, Grand Sénéchal of Burgundy
last quarter of the 15th century
Polychrome stone. 181 x 260 x 167 cm - ML

Carl Andre
Hearth, 1980
44 cedarwood elements. 120.5 x 469 x 90 cm - CP

Albert Bartholomé
Monument of the Dead in the Père-Lachaise
central section, 1899
Bronze, reduction. 57 x 45 x 27 cm - MO

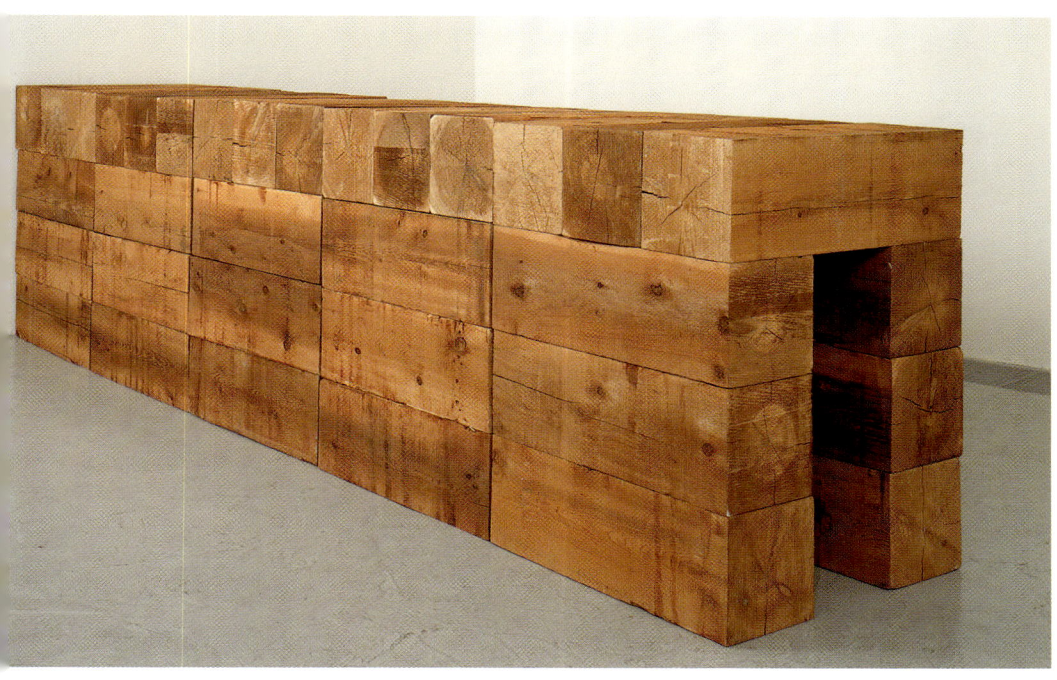

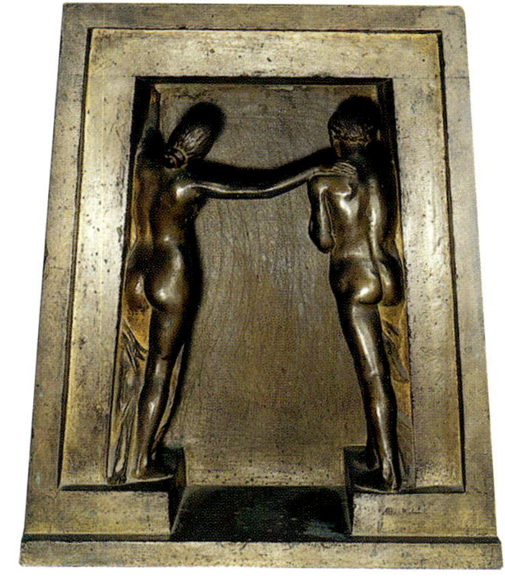

Ancient French chronicles often refer to the ceremony of bearing the body of the deceased. On the tomb of Philippe Pot, the *pleurants* ('mourners') wearing cowls followed the '*fierte*' borne shoulder-high on which the departed was laid. Their faces, hidden, convey their pain, but also the unknowability of death. Eight in number, they bear coats of arms corresponding to the quarters of nobility of the deceased. One of them is wholly imaginary: it belongs to Palamède, a hero of the Round Table to which Philippe Pot is thus fictitiously related. The *pleurants* here recall the '*deuillants*' ('wailers') on the tomb of Philippe the Bold and the sculptures at the *Well of the Prophets* at Champmol, near Dijon, by Claus Sluter.

Formally close to the tomb of Philippe Pot, Carl Andre's *Hearth* is a sculpture weighing more than a ton. Its red cedarwood beams — thirty longitudinal units bearing fifteen transverse ones — form a long tunnel, which, in addition to evoking the intimacy of a dwelling centred about a hearth, is reminiscent of megalithic tables, in particular those at Stonehenge.

Refining the composition of Canova's sculptural tombs, paring them down to their essence, Albert Bartholomé shows us only the backs of those who pass the threshold: modelled so as to provide a smooth surface over which flits a final glimmer of light, this is a wall of nothingness that absorbs the front half of the bodies, the face already lying hidden. The one lightly lays his hand on the shoulder of the other in a fraternal gesture, while the oppressive, trapezoid shape of the door suggests an entrance to a pyramid whence some infinite perspective will open out.

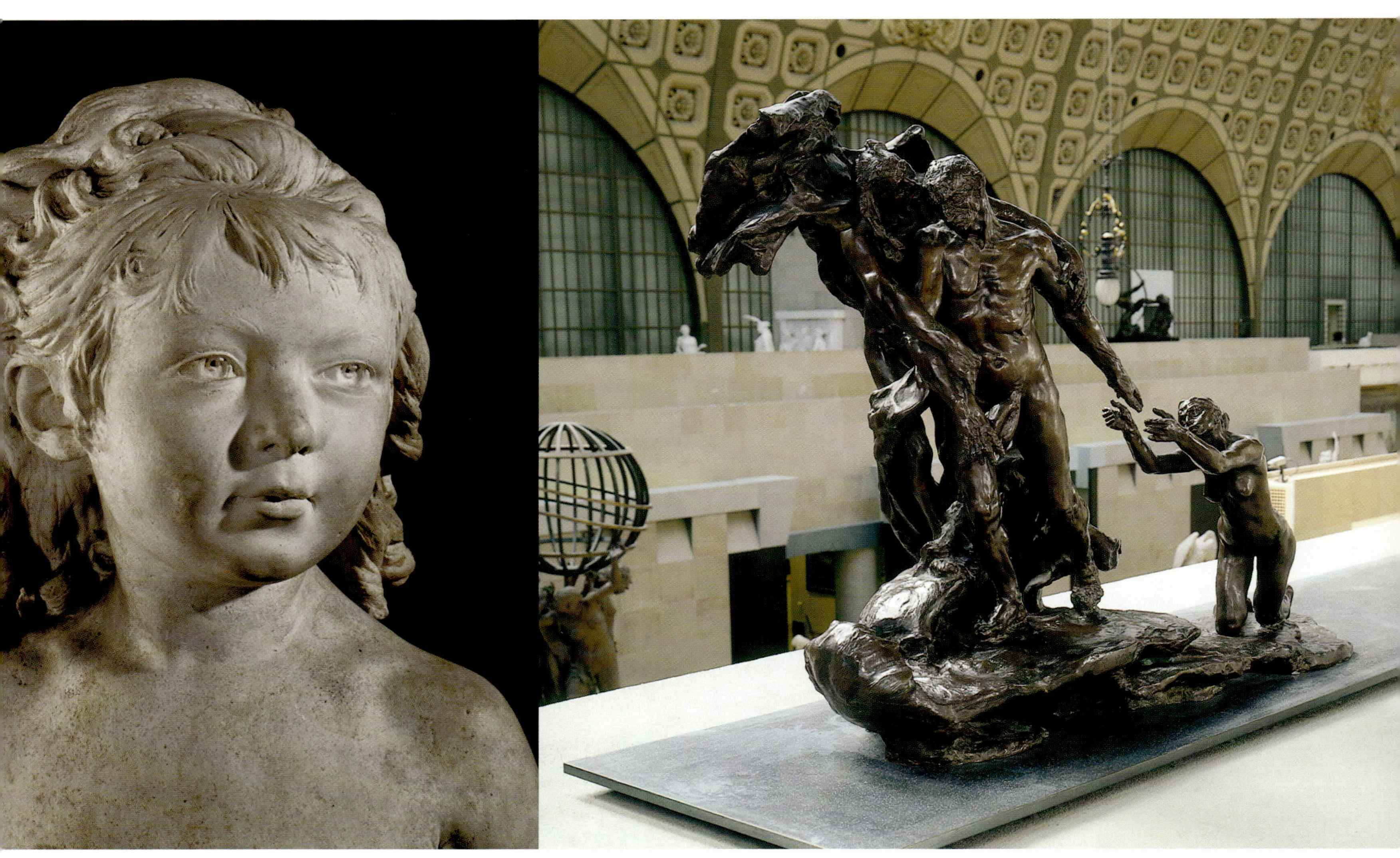

The ages of man

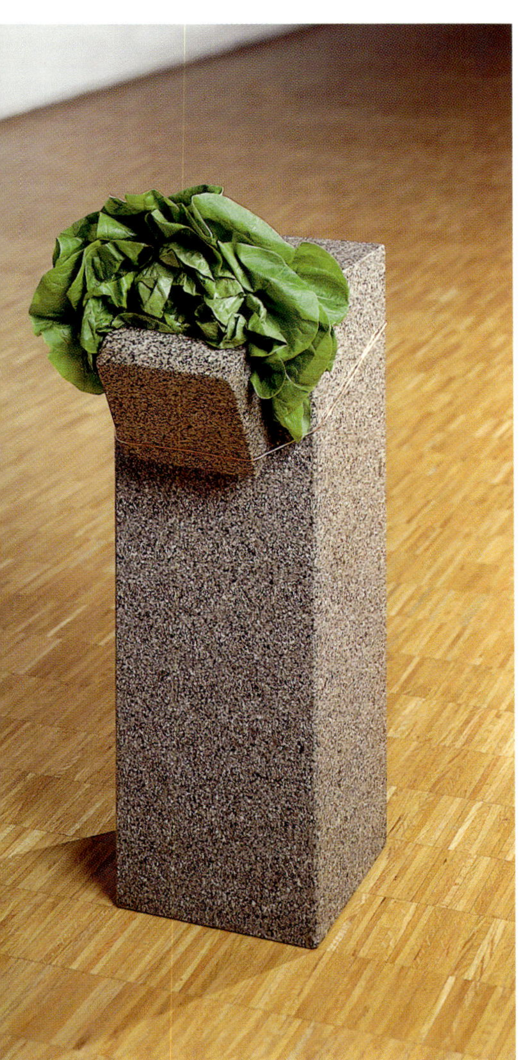

One might think that only painting is capable of the delicate task of portraying the various stages of life in people close to one — in one's child, one's lover, there where life passes closest. Yet sculpture excels here too. The portrait by Jean-Antoine Houdon of his daughter Sabine aged four proves as much. He had already made a bust of her before, when she was only ten months old. By carving the bust *all'antica*, the sculptor combined a finesse of psychological penetration with an artistic meditation on the Antique, regarded as the 'youth of art', which perfectly catches the child's wide-eyed gravity. Her look is especially finely rendered. As Guilhem Scherf noted, Houdon had a tendency to dig out the eye-socket relatively deeply, 'which permits an astonishing play of light and shade.' Beside the portraits he carried out of the foremost men of his time, including Diderot, Voltaire and Rousseau, Houdon is also plainly one of the great sculptors of the more intimate aspects of life and of childhood.

In this version of the theme of the three ages of life, executed in the middle of her traumatic break-up with Rodin, Camille Claudel attains the sublime. The roles are handed out and confrontation becomes inevitable: there is no place here for Giorgione's serene mediation in *The Three Philosophers*. Maturity is Rodin, a man turning his back on the youth of the kneeling Camille — as her brother Paul, the writer, immediately recognised — to turn away to old age, that of Rose Beuret, the sculptor's mistress, already clad in the shroud with which she is about to enwrap him. Arranged lengthwise, as if in motion, this scene shows time as a passage from light to growing shade. Kneeling symbolises the sacredness of distress, the way of the Cross of disappointed love.

Giovanni Anselmo's stele of temporality stands as a powerful *vanitas*: the lettuce is the incarnation of life caught between two poles, but it is the lettuce that makes the work possible. Following the example of other artists of Arte Povera like Mario Merz, Anselmo uses organic matter to renew traditional still life. If the museum curator — here the French word *conservateur* is particularly apt — doesn't change the salad occasionally, the structure collapses. The dying Buddha said: 'Every formation is perishable.' Thus does the Italian artist pose the question of the death of Art.

The flight of love

Diderot recalled that Madame de Pompadour, who adored sculpture, would hear no ill of Pigalle. When she'd ceased being Louis XV's favourite, she had herself carved, in a time-honoured mythological personification, as Friendship for her park at Bellevue. Pointing to her heart, she pleads with the king, a statue of whom stands opposite her own, not to let his friendship for her wither and die. The device Auguste Rodin sets up in *Fugit Amor* is entirely different. The artist here reworks the *Prodigal Son*, one of the figures on *The Gates of Hell*. Dishevelled, brilliant, he is strangely coupled to his lover in a vertiginous waltz redolent of a Möbius strip. Yet time comes between the lovers: the Prodigal Son sees his love escaping, on towards the void that existed before their encounter: the unrest of the soul, now deprived of that fervour for the future that love gives, is translated by the backward vault of the body.

In *The Bride*, by John Chamberlain, one of the foremost exponents of junk art, a form that appropriated industrial waste, the death of love is symbolised by an accident. The white car the mangled chassis once was evokes a wedding-dress. The wreck is reminiscent of *Car Crashes*, silkscreen prints on which Andy Warhol reproduced newspaper photos of automobile accidents.

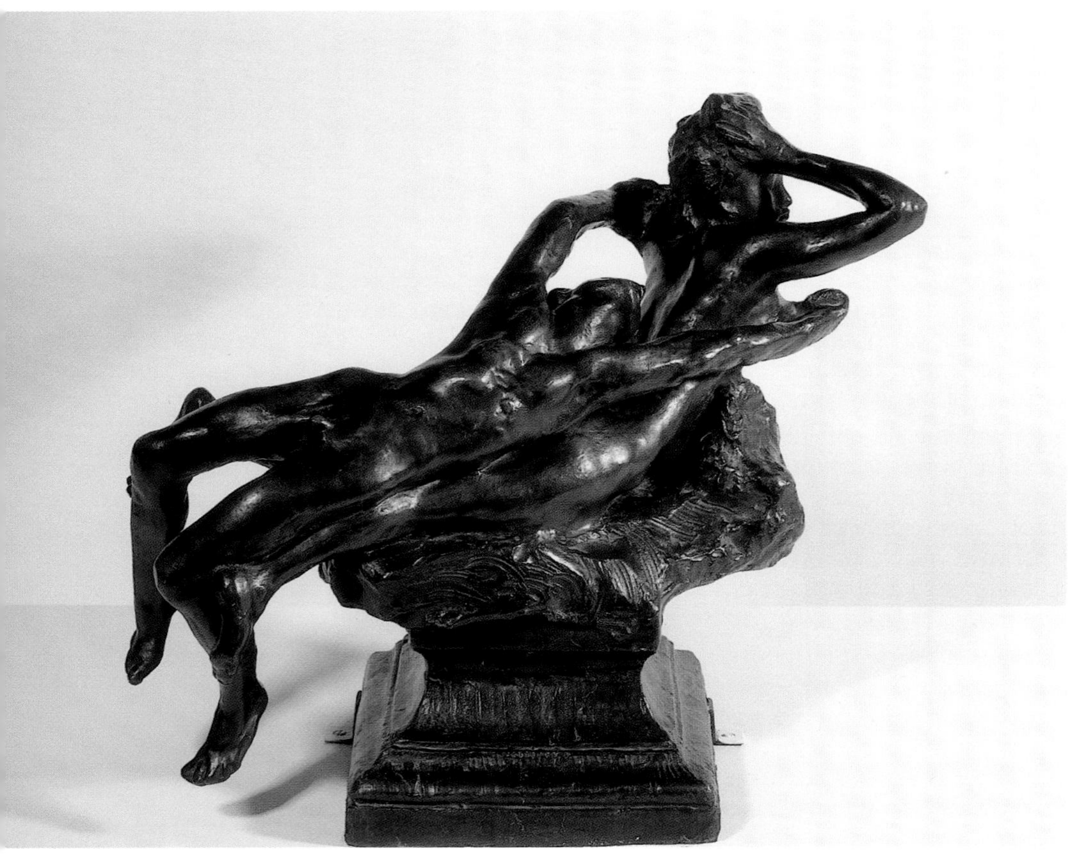

Auguste Rodin
Fugit Amor, 1886
Bronze. 38 x 46 x 33 cm - MO

John Chamberlain
The Bride, 1988
Chrome-plated and enamelled sheet metal. 216 x 120 x 114 cm - CP

Jean-Baptiste Pigalle
Friendship, 1750-53
Marble. 142 x 80 x 77 cm - ML

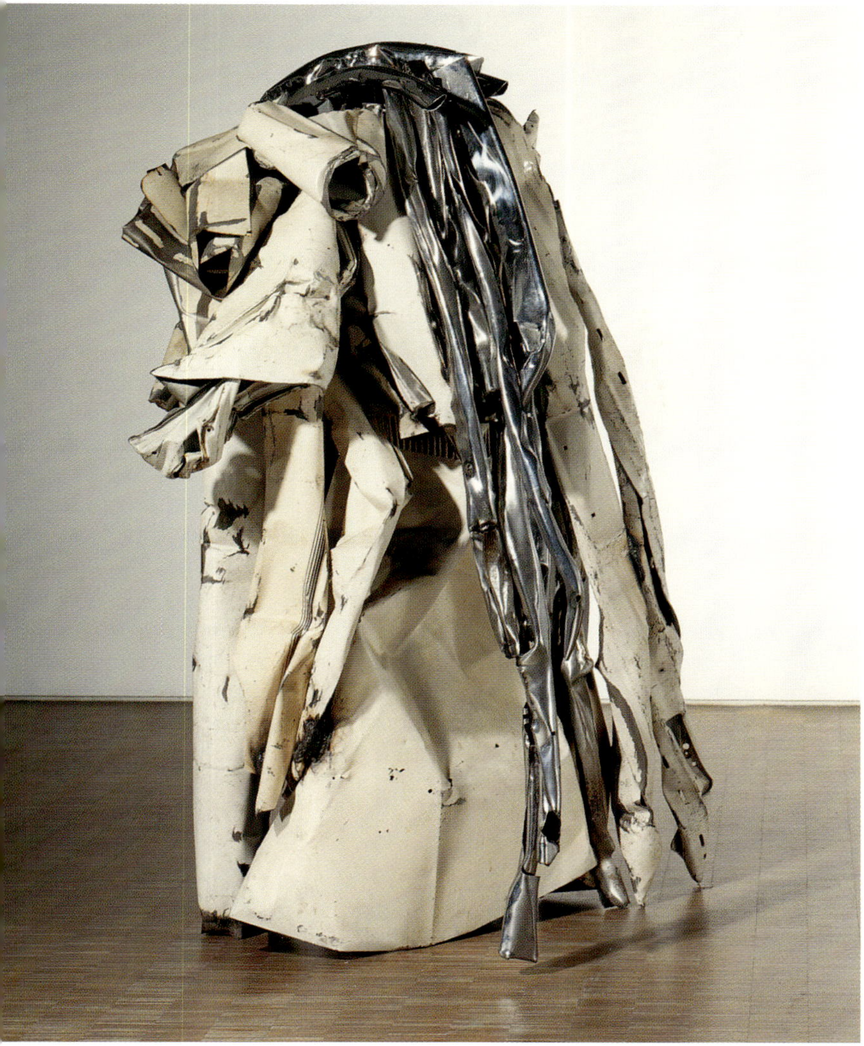

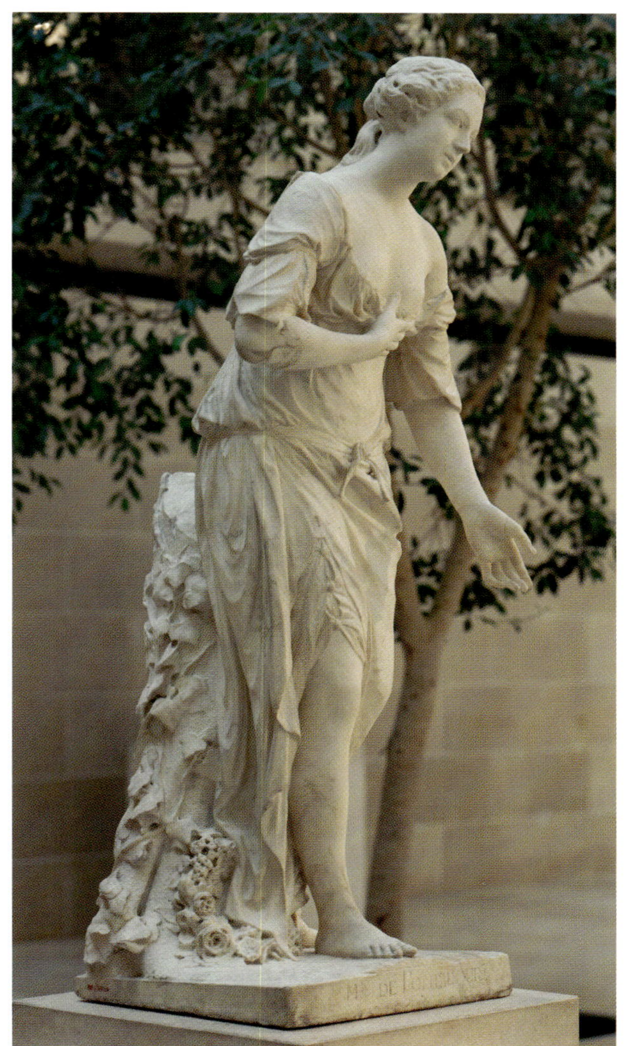

Vanitas

The funerary relief of Jeanne de Bourbon, Comtesse d'Auvergne (died 1511), is a forthright expression of metaphysical truth in the tradition of the late Middle Ages: as the image of a corpse eaten away by worms amply demonstrates, the body is mortal.

Jules Desbois also testifies to physical reality with his portrait of an *Old Woman*, even if he chose to append an allegorical subtitle — *Poverty* — as Rodin and Camille Claudel had done respectively in *Winter* and *Clotho*. Both moreover used the same elderly model as Desbois, by the name of Caira, who also lent her features to Death in *Maturity* (p. 160).

One might compare *Poverty* with *Celle qui fut la Belle Heaulmière* which Rodin carved shortly later harking back to these lines by the late medieval poet, François Villon, in which the old woman complains: 'And I live on, old and hoary. /When I think back, alas! to the good old days,/When I look at myself stark naked,/What am I? What have I become?/And I see myself so changed,/Poor, dried out, gaunt, shrivelled,/Why, I'm almost driven to distraction!'

Our body is a garment that hardens in the grip of *rigor mortis,* just as meat turns to leather. Born in Prague, the Canadian Jana Sterbak seemed to hark back to the *danses macabres* and to Baroque stagings of Death when, in 1968, she fled the repression of the Prague Spring and made her way to Canada, an essentially Protestant country. If the image of Rembrandt's *Flayed Ox* and the world of the painter Francis Bacon come to mind, the artist's actual intention was to reactivate the myth of Medea boiling Jason's uncle, Pelias, under the pretence making him young again. Sterbak is also addressing the idea of the female body as chattel, a topic she will return to in *Electric Dress.*

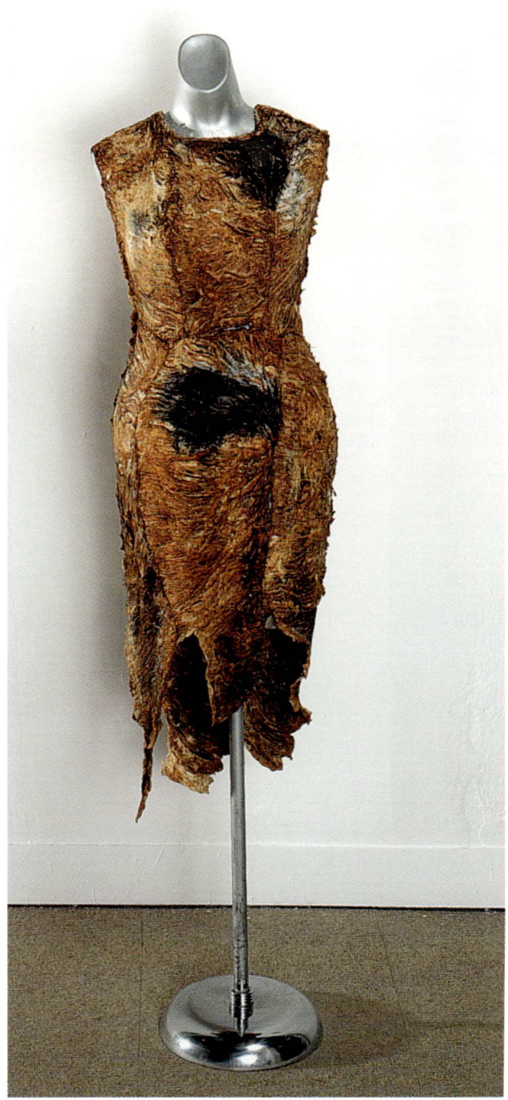

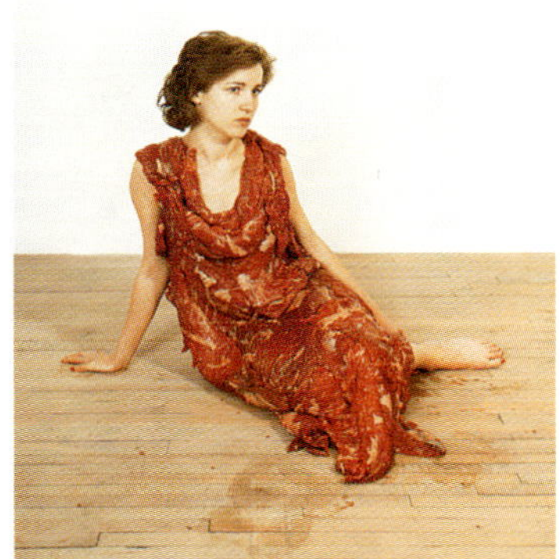

Jana Sterbak
Vanitas: Flesh Dress for an Albino Anorexic, 1987
Sewn raw beef. Photograph on live model and presentation on shop dummy. H: 113 cm (dummy) - CP

Jules Desbois
Old Woman (Poverty), 1884-94
Terracotta. 38 (42 with plinth) x 18 x 25 cm - MO

Jeanne de Bourbon, Countess of Auvergne,
Auvergne, first quarter of the 16th century
Stone. 178 x 78 x 29 cm - ML

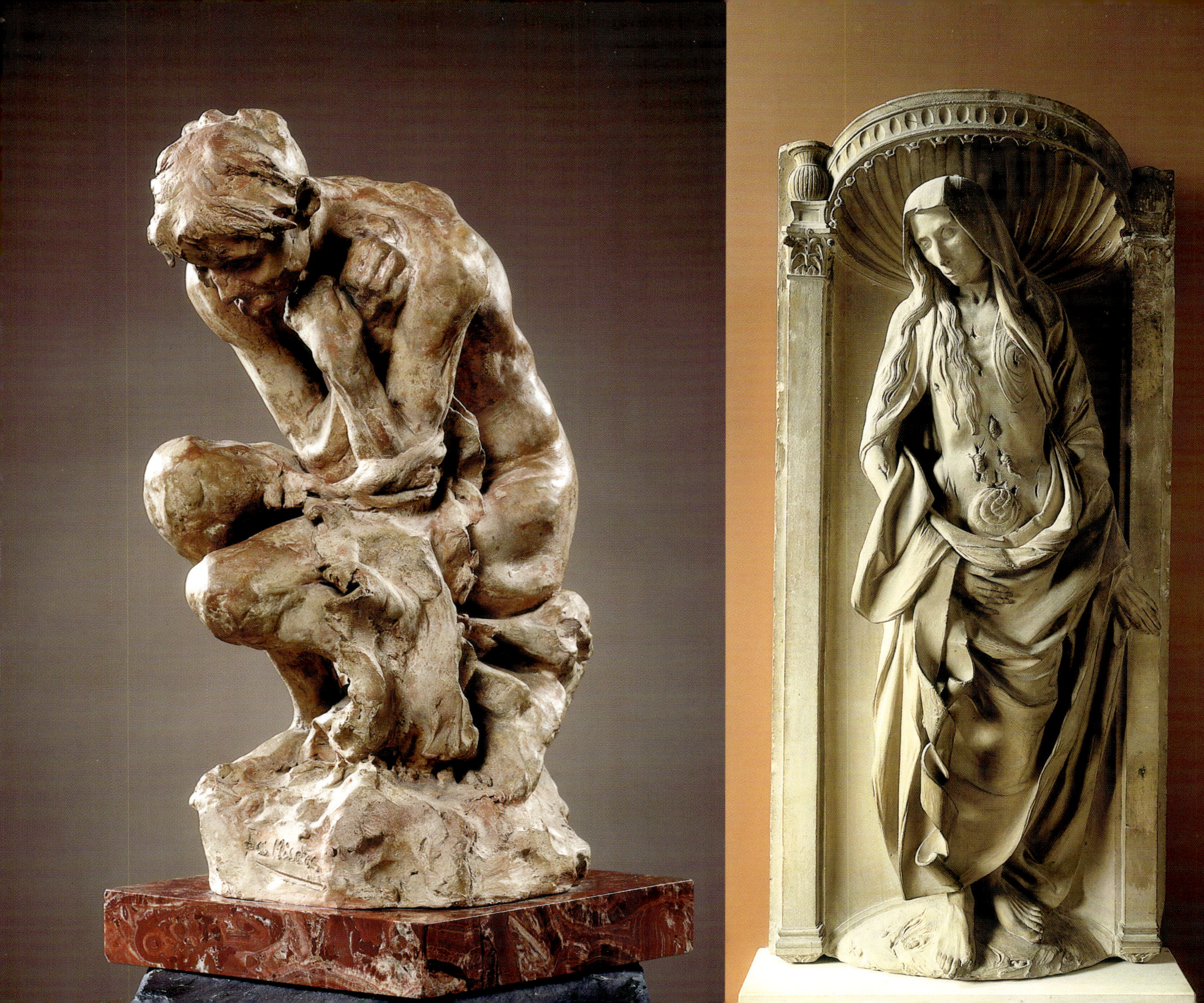

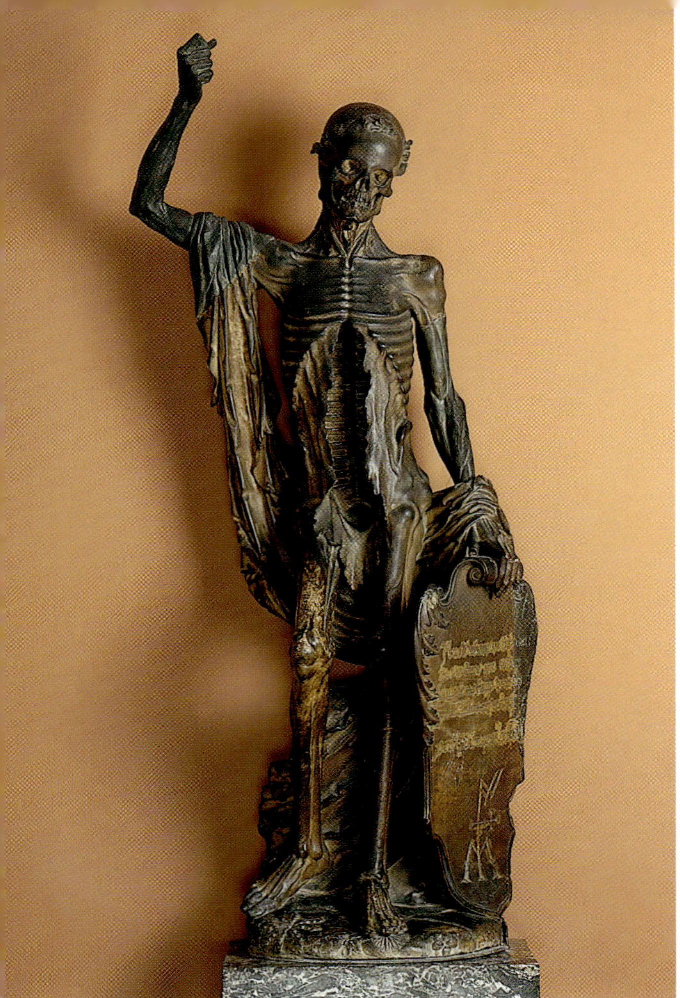

Ghosts

The Dead Saint Innocent, Ile-de-France, c. 1530
Alabaster. 120 x 55 x 27 cm - ML

Boleslas Biegas
The Sphinx, 1902
Plaster. 46 x 39 x 11 cm - MO

Jean Tinguely
Hell – a Small Beginning, 1984
Recycled junk, engines, miscellaneous objects
370 x 920 x 700 cm - CP

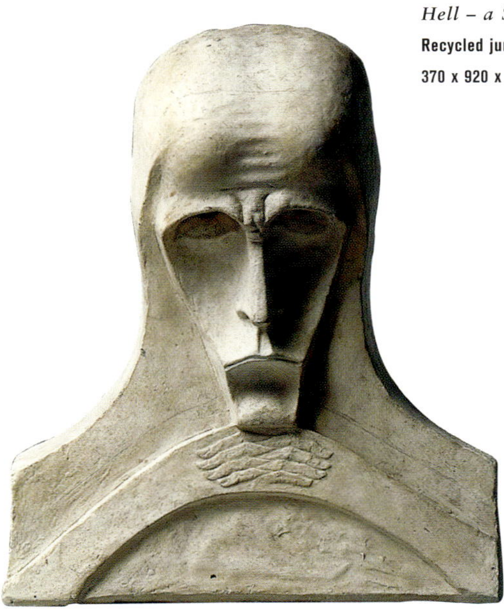

The skeleton in *The Dead Saint Innocent* would have looked like a sword of Damocles to visitors to the graveyard of the Innocents in the centre of Paris, which closed its doors in 1786. Placed in a box hanging from the tower of Notre-Dame-du-Bois right in the middle of the cemetery, like a memento mori this alabaster statue played the same admonishing role as the skeletons with which the Egyptians reputedly adorned their banqueting rooms.

With its mute expression and sinister glower, Boleslas Biegas'

Sphinx presents beholders with the enigma of pain. Why do we suffer? The sunken cheeks and the haggard features evoke the agony of Christ. The 'Egyptian' style, confined practically to two dimensions, accentuates the impression of ghostly evanescence.

Jean Tinguely, on the other hand, offers us a hurly-burly of forms shaking about in every direction that lifts a tiny corner of Hell. This large-scale piece is emblematic of the artist's late manner, with animal carcasses and skulls set into black-painted mechanisms

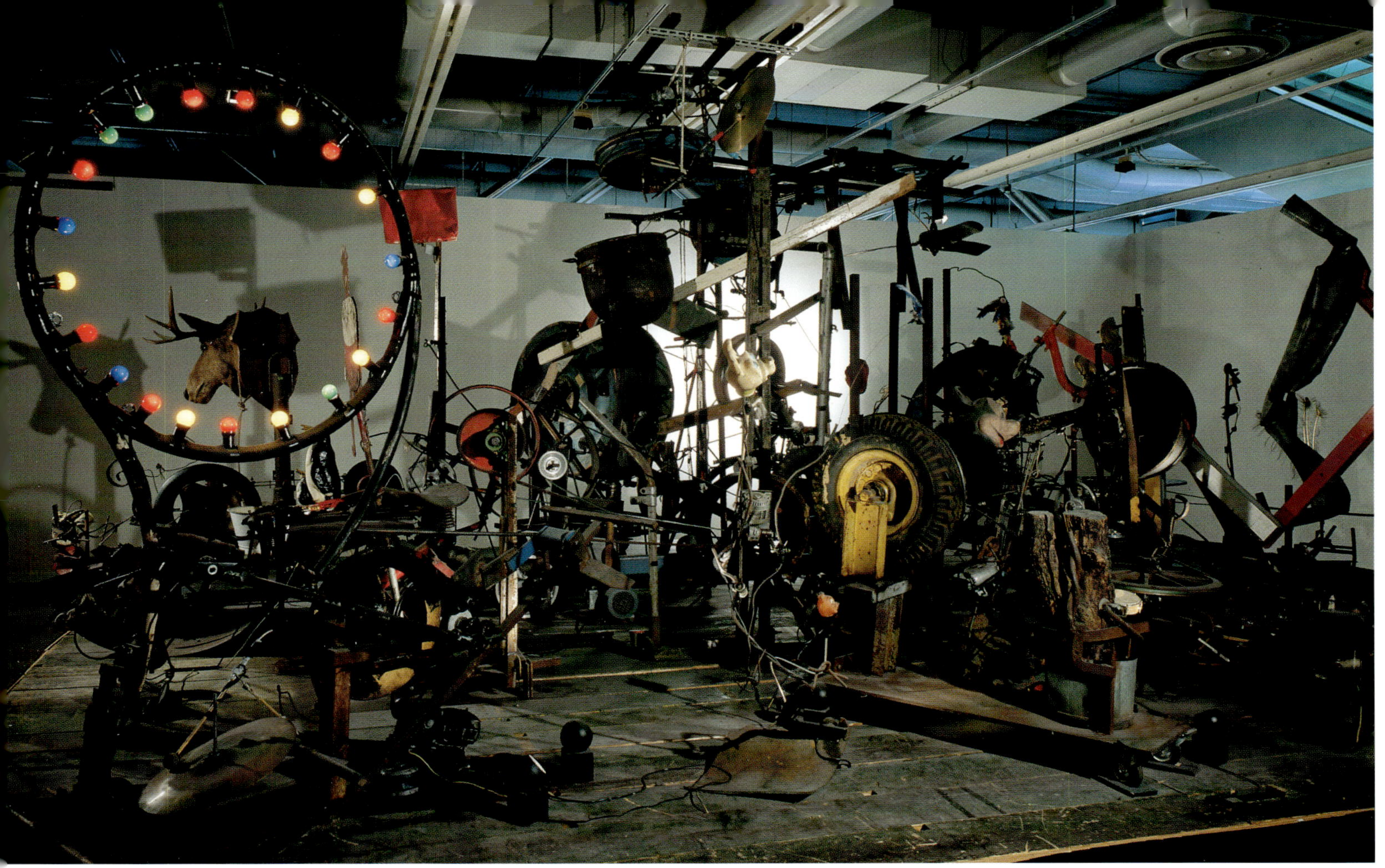

that let out an ear-splitting screech. A Formula 1 enthusiast, Tinguely almost lost his life in an accident. He had also been present at the death of friends and witnessed a serious fire in a farm near his workshop in Neyruz in Switzerland. By this point gravely ill himself, Tinguely here chose to face death with all the weapons at an artist's disposal: imagination and ingenuity.

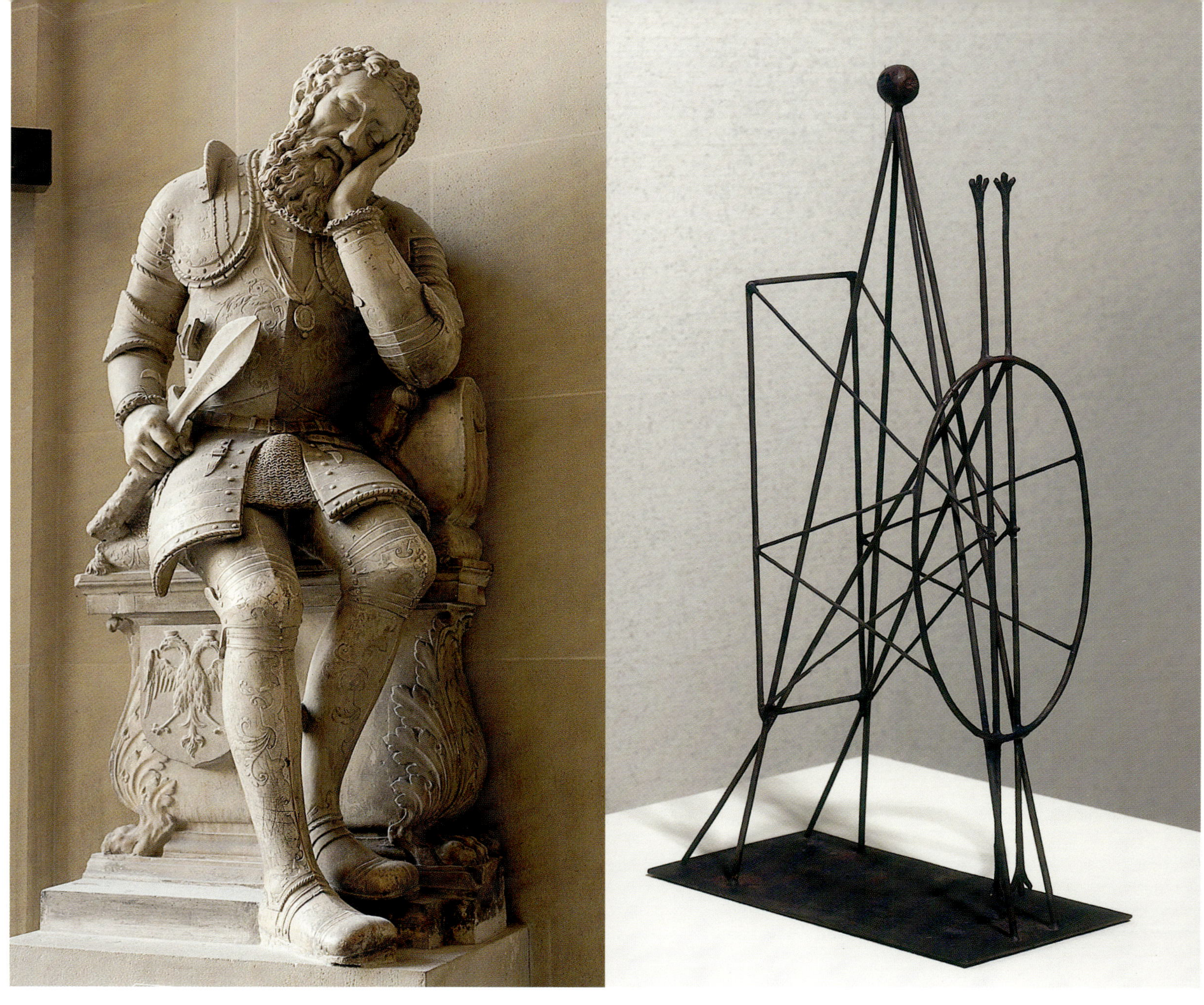

Memory

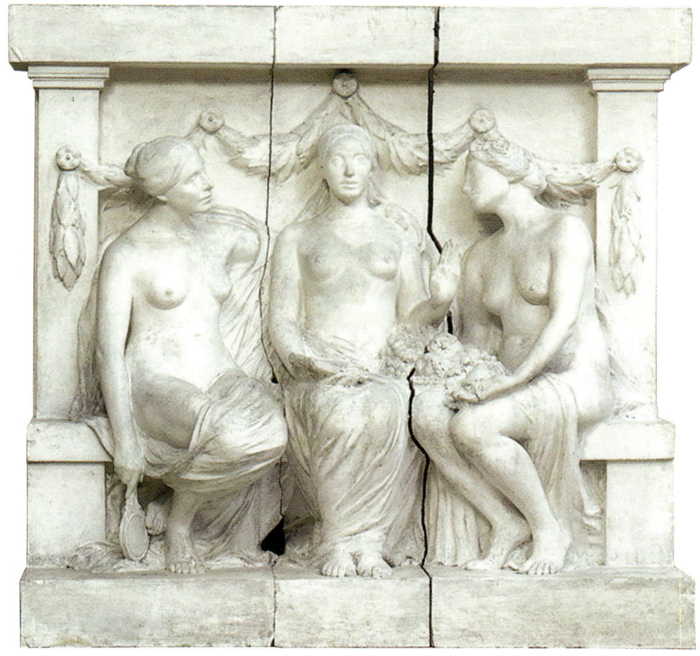

Sculpture opens three paths to remembrance. Each is associated with a register suited to its elected sign. Indeed, the Latin *moneo*, from which comes *monumentum* (monument), means 'to recall', 'to point out': the *icon* (the image of the departed), the *symbol* (the funeral oration), and the *index* (the direct evocation of the deceased's exploits).

Icon: the prone figure resting on its elbows, the *gisant accoudé* of the French Renaissance, such that of the Sieur de Maigny by Pierre Bontemps, is a euphemism turned into an image: the departed is only slumbering and remains 'at his post'. Since Antiquity — think of the Etruscan *Sarcophagus of the Couple,* for instance — Death likes to stretch out at funeral banquets.

Symbol: as in an oration by Bossuet or Malraux, the dead are evoked through the rhetorical mode of allegory: thus, the three figures of the plaster model of the central section of the *Monument to Jean-Jacques Rousseau*, commissioned in 1907 from Albert Bartholomé, the creator of the war memorial at Père-Lachaise cemetery (p. 158), and unveiled in the Panthéon in 1912. At the centre, *Philosophy* holds a book; to the right Truth puts an arm around her neck, while to the left Nature proffers her fruits and flowers. Philosophy's raised hand is a gesture of restraint to Nature: true wisdom is superior to the 'good savage'.

The *index*? Picasso made this *Figure* in autumn 1928 with the assistance of Julio González from sketchbooks brought back from one of his vacations in Dinard, and thought of using it in a monument to be dedicated to his friend the poet Guillaume Apollinaire, who died in 1918. The piece alludes to a passage in Apollinaire's novel *The Assassinated Poet*, where he refers to a 'monument in nothing'. Hence, it is an openwork structure, transparent, a 'drawing in space' in the apt expression of the art dealer Kahnweiler. Unfortunately this project for a monument, one that might be termed an 'index' because it bears the traces of Apollinaire's work, was never carried out.

Resonance: sounds emitted by matter

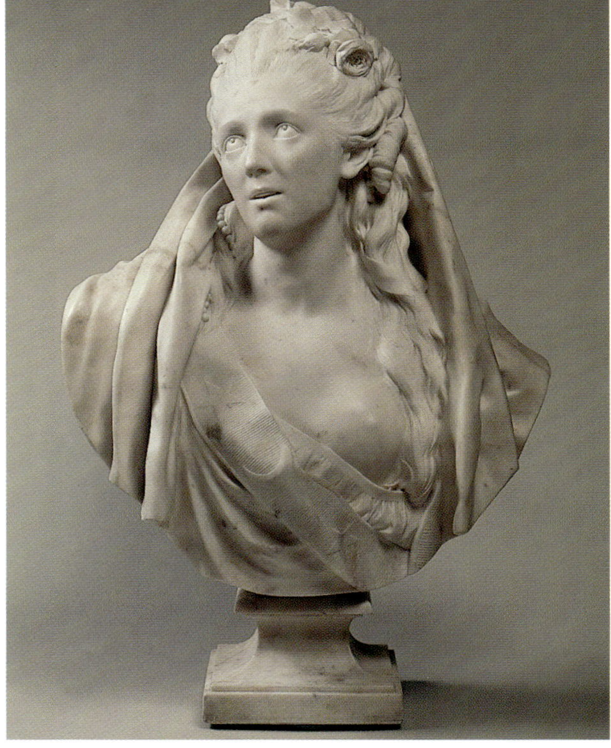

Jean-Antoine Houdon

Sophie Arnould Shown in the Role of Iphigenia, 1775

Marble. 81 x 51 x 29.5 cm - ML

Paul Dubois

Fifteenth-Century Florentine Singer, 1865

Silver-gilt bronze. 155 x 58 x 50 cm - MO

Berto Lardera

Two-Dimensional Sculpture, 1947

Copper, aluminium, iron. 130 x 90 x 25 cm - CP

Compare the face of one of the great solo singers of the 18th century, Sophie Arnould, captured by the sculptor Jean-Antoine Houdon, seemingly possessed by music in the disarray of her stage costume, to the absorbed, sublime visage of the *Fifteenth-Century Florentine Singer* by Paul Dubois, a member of the Florentine group of sculptors, who, after 1860, took their cue from the Italian Renaissance. If the Houdon vibrates with the sumptuous sensuality from which opera springs and which turned Diderot's head — he was a particular fan of Sophie — a more ethereal music seems to exhale from the slender form of the adolescent who appears to have stepped straight out of a fresco by Masaccio, Gozzoli or Pinturicchio. It should be said that Dubois was an impassioned observer of their art. This adolescent type met with enduring success if one thinks of Falguière's *Tarcisius* (p. 108) or of Minne's kneeling figures (p. 22). Carrying off its picturesque effect particularly well, this silver-plated bronze also represents a considerable technical *tour de force*.

Berto Lardera's *Sculpture in Two Dimensions* (1947) also presents the time-honoured theme of music transposed into the clang of metal: here, the visual sonority of the musical third, in copper-aluminium-iron, derives from the artist's memory of his mother playing the harp. Lardera who, like Antoine Pevsner, employed metal struts in his work, explained that he had 'wanted to replace volume, weight and mass by optical suggestions.' 'The forms opened, and could become havens of expressive light [...] the sculpture in two dimensions presented to the beholder two and only two side views on which its profound *raison d'être* was expressed in the rhythm between its empty and full spaces.'

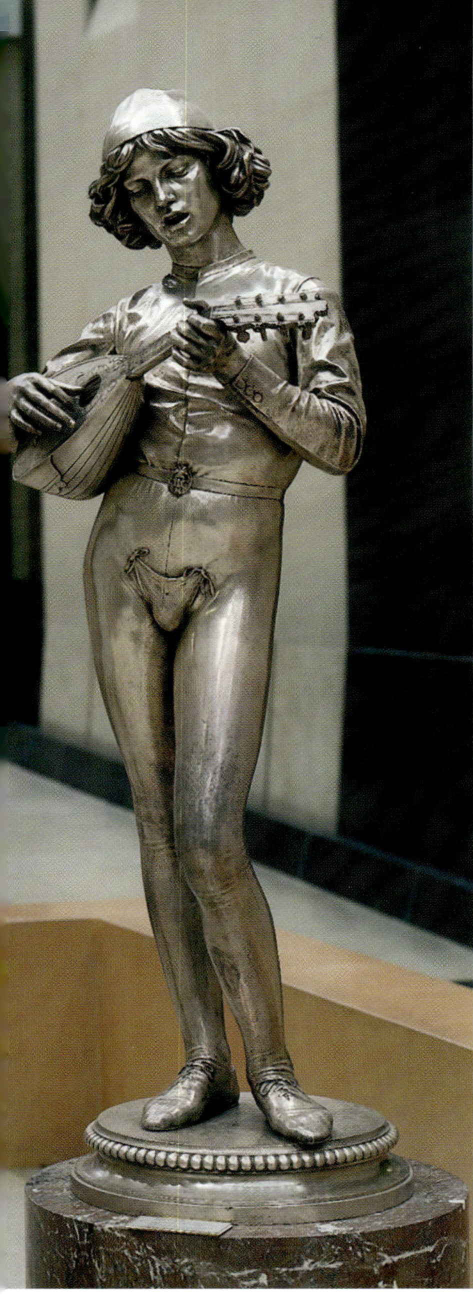

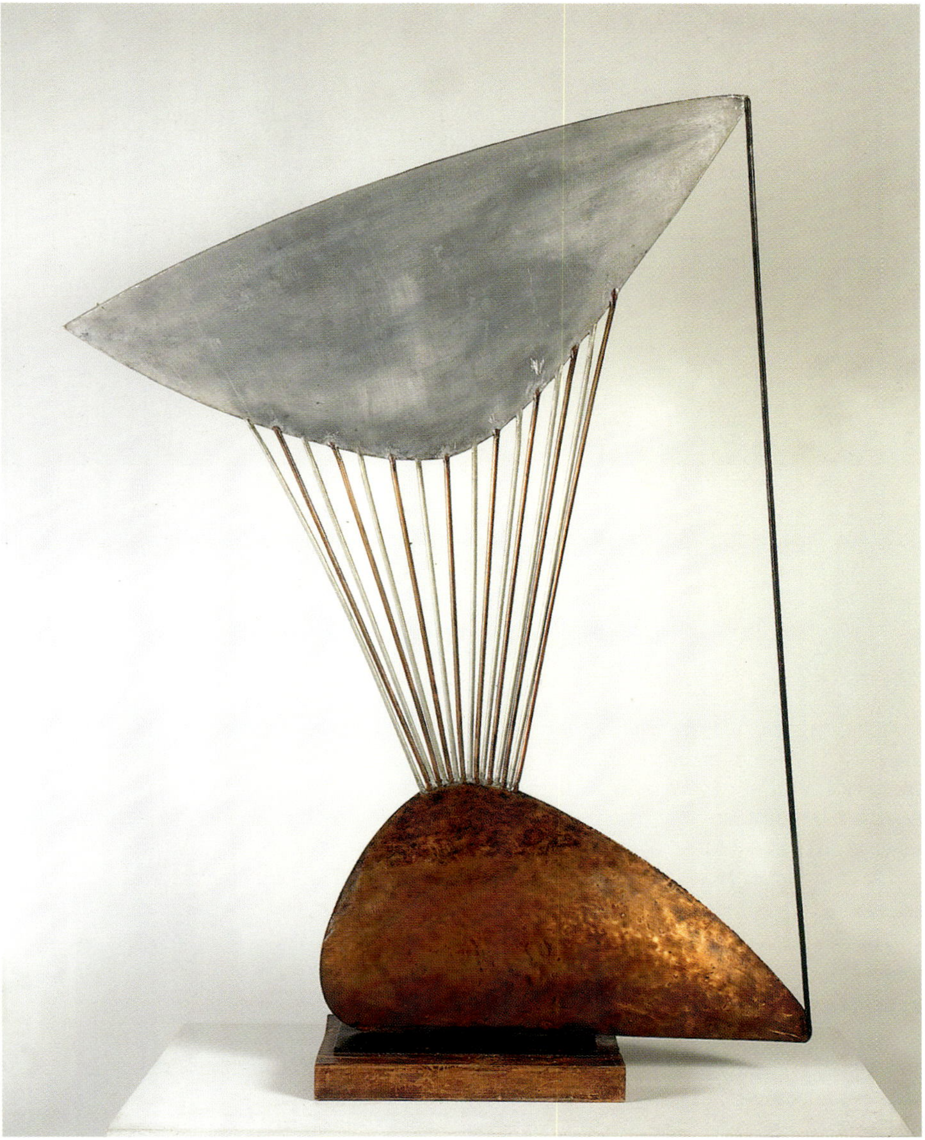

The circles of existence

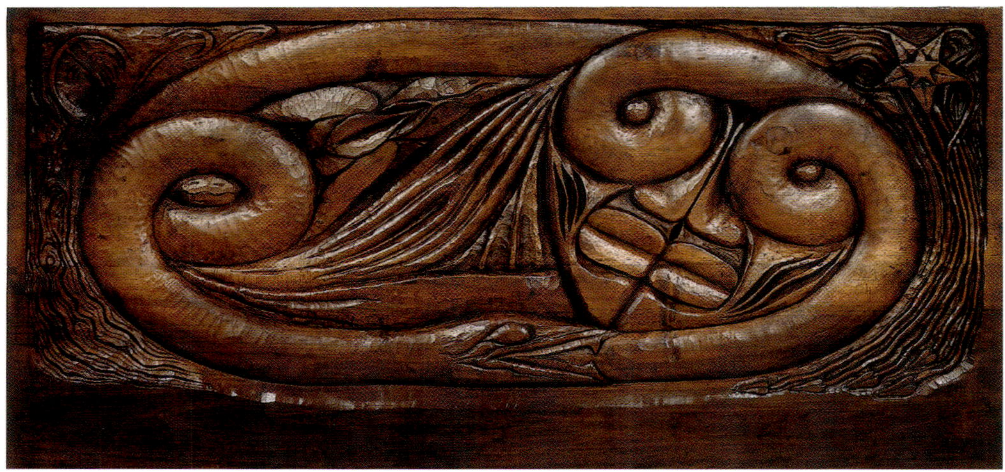

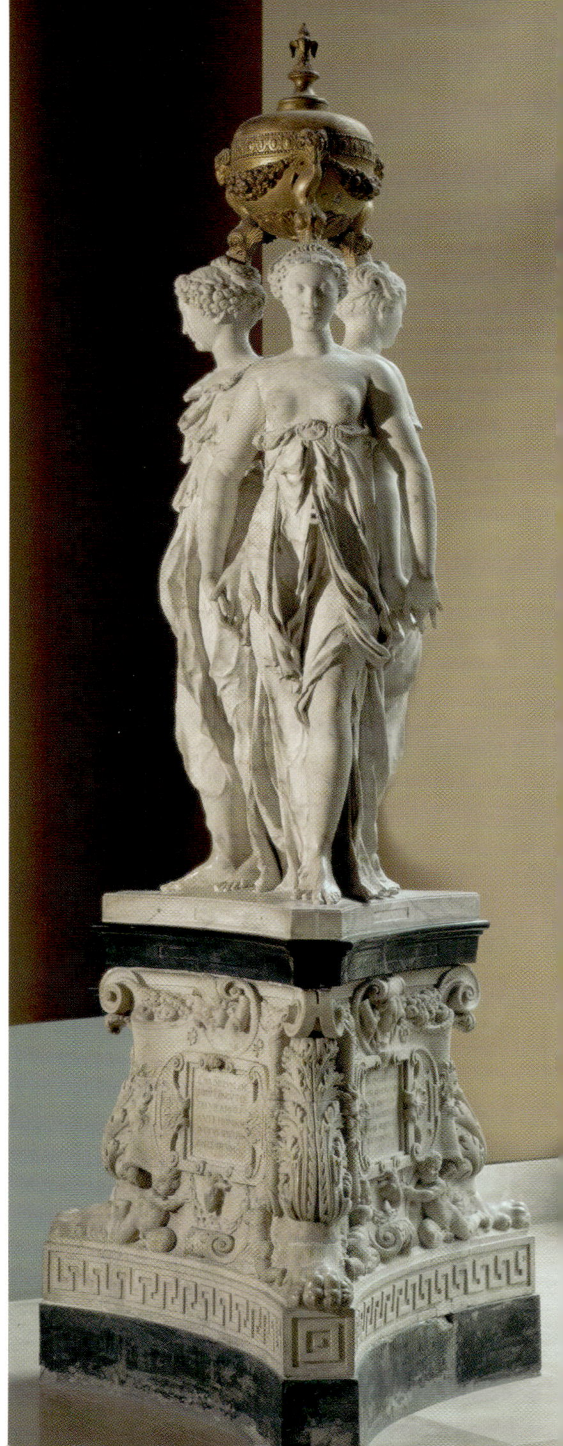

Georges Lacombe
Existence or *Bed*, 1894-96
Walnut. 68 x 142 x 6 cm - MO

Germain Pilon
Monument for the Heart of Henri II: The Three Graces,
1560-66
Marble. 150 x 75 x 75 cm - ML

Bruce Nauman
Smoke Rings (Model for Underground Tunnels), 1979
Eight plaster elements on wooden side pieces. Diam: 340 cm - CP

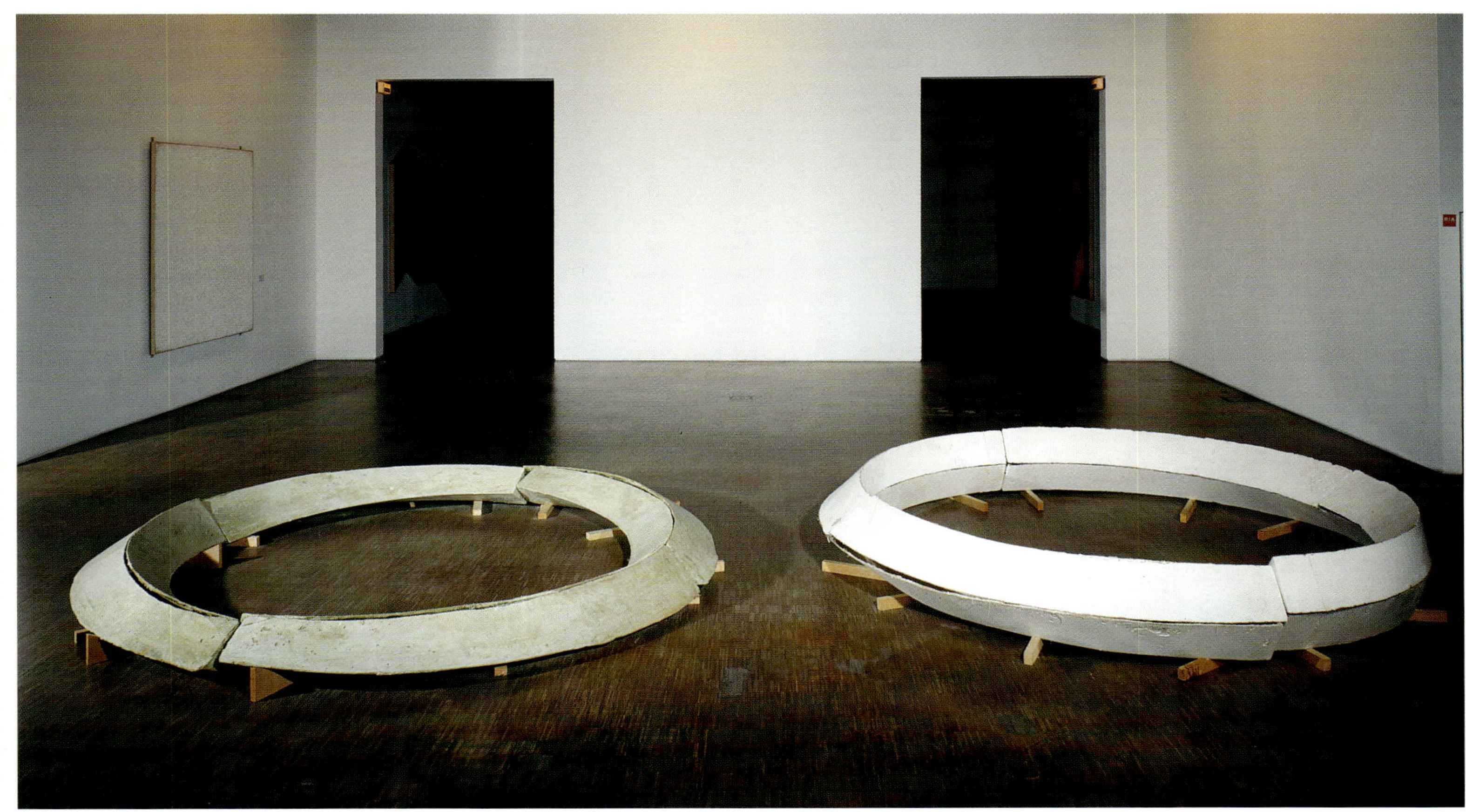

To surround the urn carrying the heart of King Henri II by the roundelay of the Three Graces is an act of a born courtier. Germain Pilon carried out this project begun by Primaticcio at the request of Catherine de' Medici in 1560. The Latin inscriptions along the base, completed by Dominique Florentin and treated in the orotund, elegant style typical of the School of Fontainebleau, enlightens us as to their meaning: unable, much against her wish, to keep it in her breast, the queen decides to give back what the text calls 'the former dwelling-place of the Graces', that is, the heart of her departed husband.

The snake biting its own tail, whose coil is fashioned into the eyes of this entwined primitivist couple, also lends its form to *Existence*, carved by the Nabi, Georges Lacombe. The artist cut seven shapes in wood featuring spermatozoids, which make their way towards the large lanceolate leaf in the centre that symbolises female genitals. In the upper right-hand corner appears a magic sign, the double pentagram. Nature gives birth to spring plants in an extended metaphor for fruitfulness.

Bruce Nauman sees *Smoke Rings* as a model for a utopian construction, underground tunnels perhaps. The fragility of the moulding and their temporary-looking arrangement suggest that the American artist, who has the habit of embedding his structures in the ready-made phraseology of language (such as in *From Hand to Mouth*), is thinking here of the quickly dissipated 'smoke rings' or 'pipe dreams' of inspiration and the precarity of human endeavour.

The fertile moment

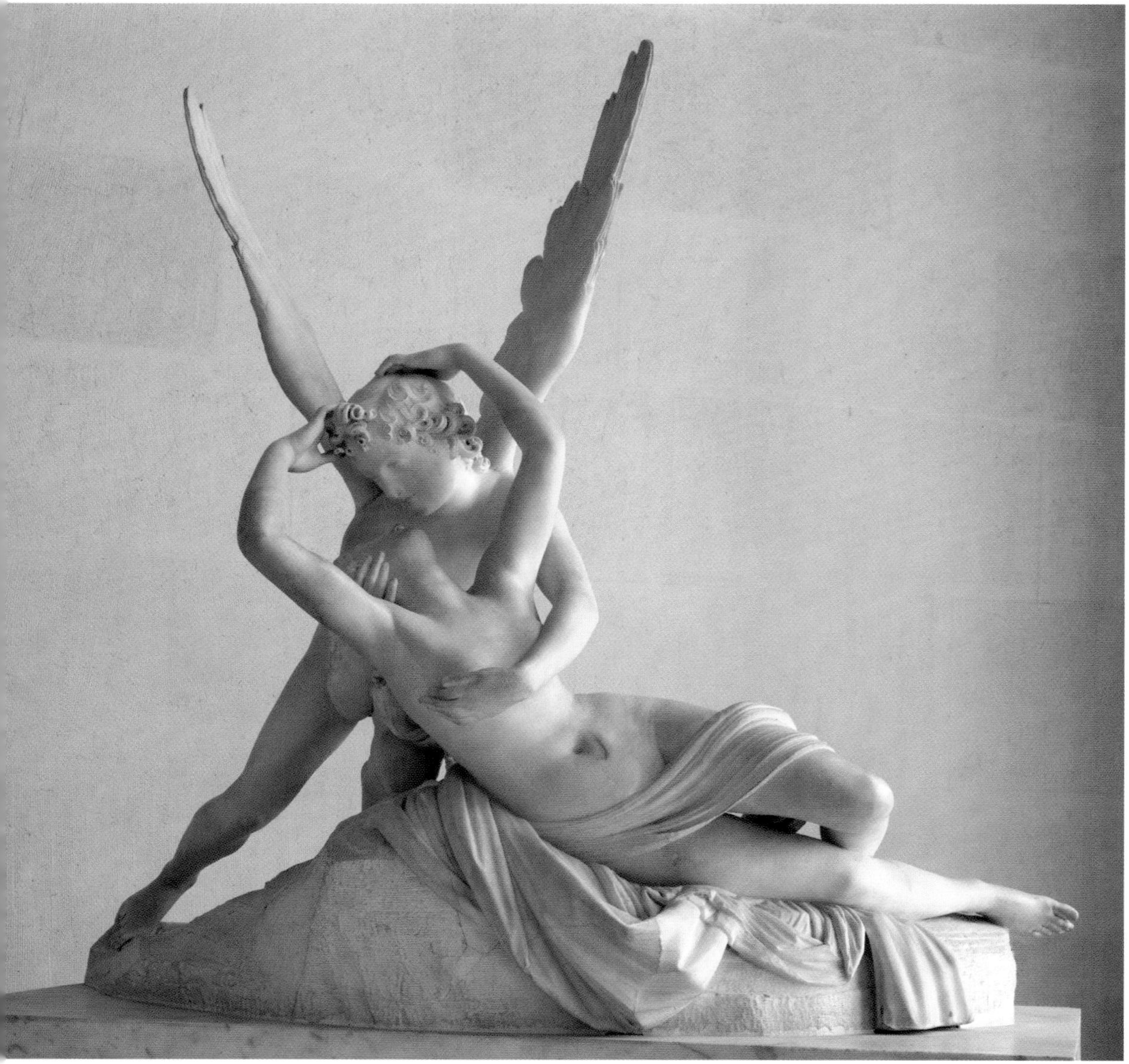

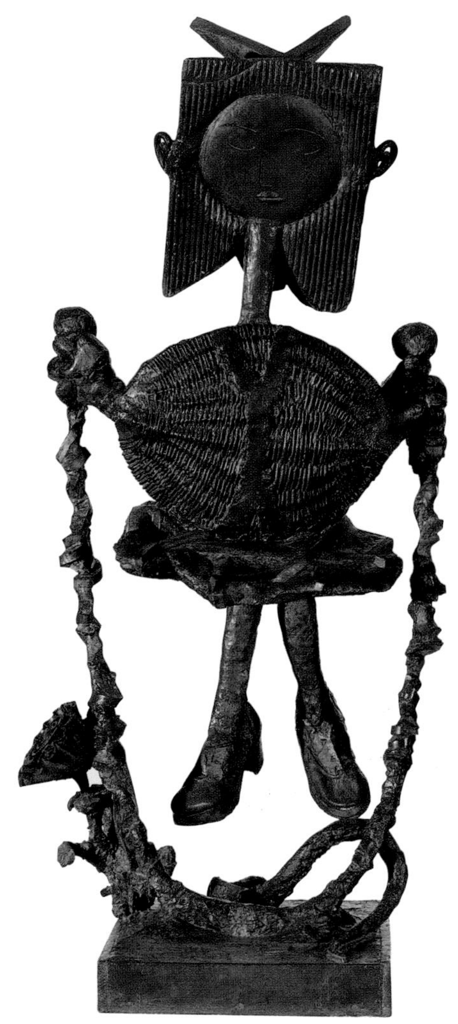

Antonio Canova
Psyche Revived by the Kiss of Love, 1787-1801
Marbre. 155 x 168 x 101 cm - ML

Pablo Picasso
Little Girl Skipping, 1950
Bronze. 153 x 62 x 65 cm - CP

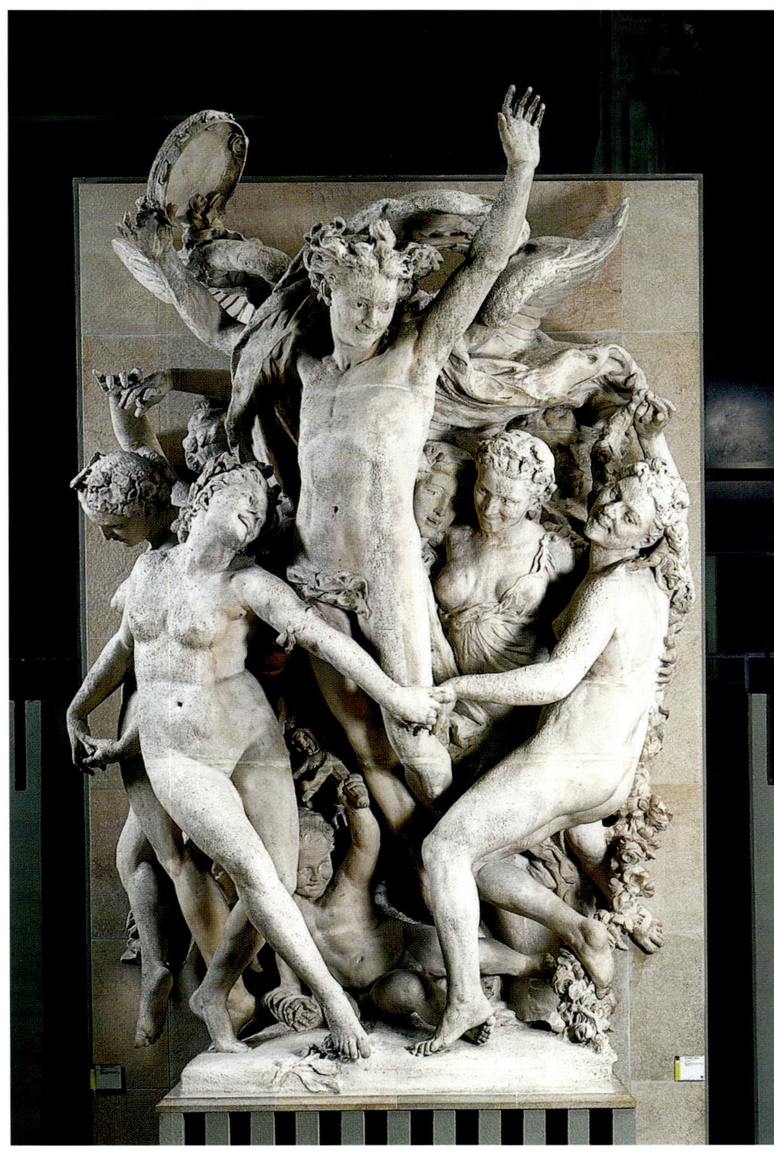

Jean-Baptiste Carpeaux
The Dance, 1868
Plaster model. 232 x 148 x 115 cm - MO

The question of which moment to depict, or which slice of action to propose to the viewer is a crucial one: Bernini called it the '*concetto*' and Lessing the 'fertile moment'. With this in mind, Antonio Canova constructed his *Psyche Revived by the Kiss of Love* (also known as *Psyche Revived by Cupid's Kiss*) around the slowly approaching mouths, just at the moment when a kiss is only the lightest touch. Psyche, exhausted, lies on the ground almost lifeless, while Love has barely come to rest next to her. Their double, enveloping gesture, the parallelism of the wings of one mimicking the arms of the other forms a kind of box that literally frames what the photographer Henri Cartier-Bresson used to call the '*instant décisif*'.

In Jean-Baptiste Carpeaux's *The Dance*, adorning the facade the Paris Opera, one 'of the most anti-tectonic dreams' of the sculptor (Catherine Chevillot), the youthful, gushing genius, like a faun, takes the breath away; the round of the nymphs' dance is broken as if by enchantment. Hidden away until this point amid the exultant troop, the dancer is shown leaping forward to the crash of the tambourine. His Dionysiac smile and the sheer sensual power of the movement, in conjunction with the nudity of the female figures, is so compelling that a passer-by, scandalised by what he regarded as intolerable license, threw a bottle of ink over the group in an iconoclastic gesture. The piece raised a howl of protest and only the outbreak of war in 1870 prevented its removal.

It took the sheer audacity of a Picasso and his vivid imagination to breathe new life into the theme of the 'woman with a snake' and turn the scene into something original. There too, the artist chooses, not without humour it must be said, the 'fertile moment'. The girl, produced prior to being cast in iron by way of a composite technique, half assemblage, half moulding — note for example the use of a cake-tin for the head and two wicker baskets for the body — is an incarnation of a thoroughly modern Eve suspended in the air as she jumps over a rope. She thus stays out of range for the snake writhing at her feet… but for how long?

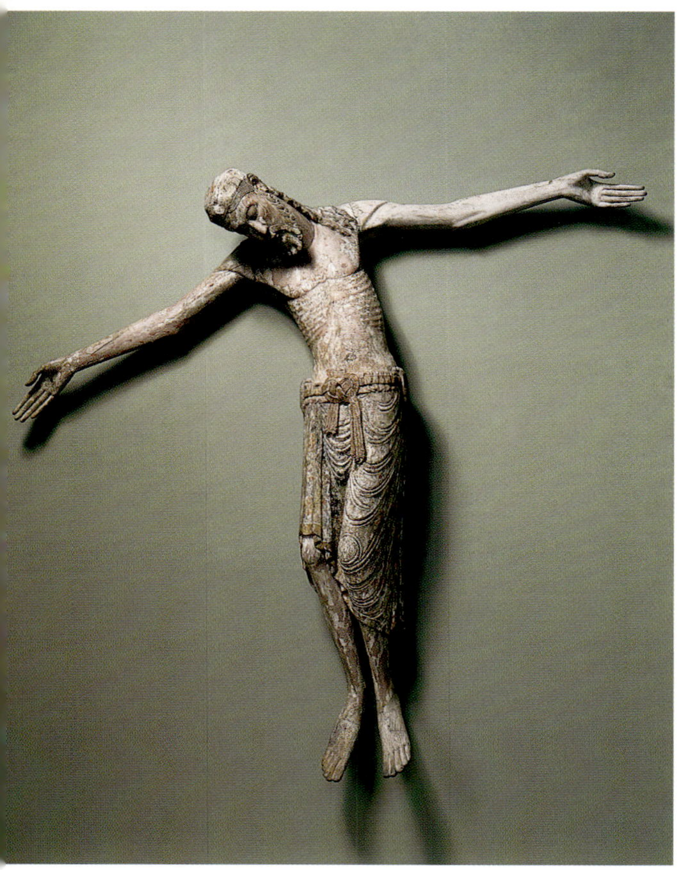

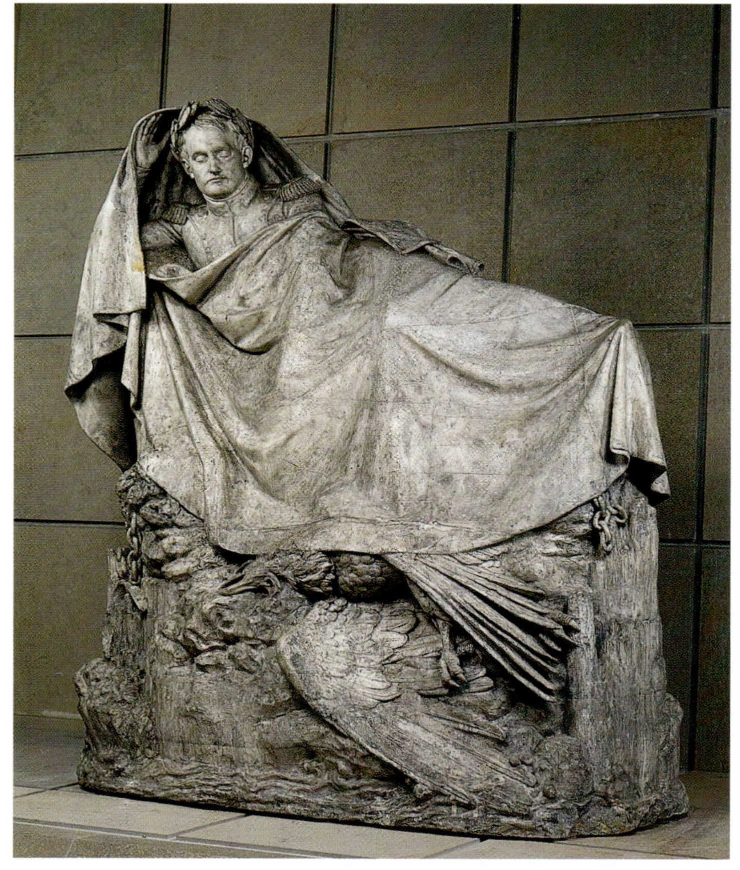

Just as sculpture was looking to be fixed for all eternity, it was revived by the visual empathy of the public. At a time when Gothic art was held in contempt, Louis Courajod, then director of the department of sculpture at the Louvre, experienced a pang of emotion gazing on the frozen movement of an admirable Burgundian Christ, today known as *The Courajod Christ*. Lent by its discoverer to the Paris World Fair of 1878, the sculpture, however, encountered an extremely hostile response. Piot spoke of this 'horrible piece', something like the 'fetishes of the wild tribes of Oceania'. The anti-Germanism of the immediate aftermath of the war of 1870 was one more reason to oppose the clarity of the Latin genius to the 'Gothic' pastime of 'Black Forest peasants spending long evenings carving knick-knacks'! Initially rejected by the museum board, this 'elite work', as Courajod was to call it in an article in the *Gazette des Beaux-Arts* in 1884, has today undergone what André Malraux would have termed its 'metamorphosis'. Nowadays, it is considered immortal, as much by its quality as a work of art, by *how* its conveys, that is, for its style (pure Romanesque), as by its content, by *what* it conveys, namely Christ in the Descent from the Cross.

Beside him, another 'immortal': Napoleon. François Rude executed this plaster of *Napoleon Awakening to Immortality* for a monument a captain in the Napoleonic army had erected in a park in his property at Fixin in Burgundy. The stroke of genius resides in how the sculptor purloins the apotheosis of the statesman from that of a

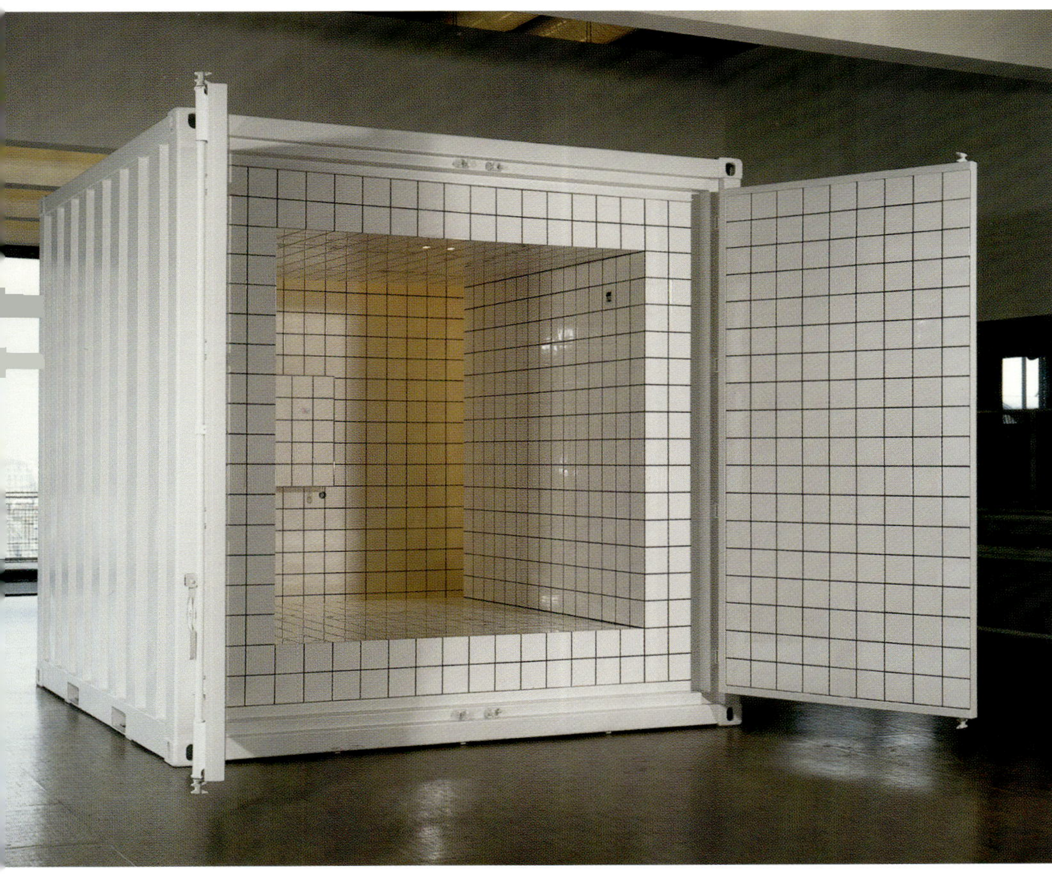

The Courajod Christ, Burgundy, second quarter of the 12th century.
Painted and gilded maple wood. 155 x 168 x 30 cm - ML

François Rude
Napoleon Awaking to Immortality, 1846
Plaster model. 215 x 195 x 96 cm - MO

Jean-Pierre Raynaud
Container Zéro, 1988
Steel, tiles, lighting. 330 x 330 x 330 cm - CP

saint: the eagle on Patmos is replaced by the imperial eagle. After religion, then, comes history. A veil is thrown over the captivity of the eagle, whose chain is hardly visible, and yet this visibility serves as a pointer to the truth to be unveiled by posterity — it is the latter that will do the emperor justice and render him glory, as testified by his forehead girded in laurel.

Immortality of faith, of history, and, finally, the immortality of the museum. Jean-Pierre Raynaud considers himself — thanks to the good offices of the directors of the Centre Pompidou — as but the 'conservator' of *Container Zero*. Inside this singular space, entirely lined in the artist's trademark white ceramic tiles, Raynaud places whatever he thinks fit: a rose, more recently and by way of homage on his death, a photograph of Pierre Restany, the founder of *Nouveau Réalisme*, or else, more frequently, a work chosen from the collection, and not always a sculpture at that!

Why sculpture survives

The death of sculpture has been foretold countless times. In 1828 Stendhal was of the opinion that the carved nude was no longer in step with modern taste, while Baudelaire, in his 1846 *Salon,* considered sculpture 'tedious', though he revised this judgement in that of 1859. At the beginning of the 20th century, Marinetti declared in his *Futurist Manifesto* (1909) that he preferred the beauty of an automobile to that of *The Winged Victory of Samothrace,* whereas Marcel Duchamp challenged his friend Brancusi to do better than an aeroplane propeller. Brancusi was to take up the gauntlet and in 1928 found himself having to defend the 'artistic' nature of his sculpture in an American courthouse for his pains!

If Boccioni judged that sculpture had to undergo a radical transformation, other artists were of the belief that even the word 'sculpture' was no longer suited to what they were doing: the Cubists spoke of 'construction' and their Russian epigones called themselves simply Constructivists. The idea of imitation ceased being the only legitimate path with the development of abstract art when the buzzword was 'forms'. Duchamp with his 'ready-mades', Picasso and Kurt Schwitters with their assemblages — even if some still call them 'assemblage sculptures' — and the Surrealists with their 'symbolically functioning objects' endowed the *objet trouvé* and the manufactured product alike 'with the dignity of a work of art' and broke with the 'trade' of the sculptor, understood as 'making' things, as a technique.

In the 1960s and 70s, artists such as the American Minimalists, who delegated the task of realising the works they designed (by drawing or some other means) to industry, began to employ terms like 'piece', 'specific object', 'work', 'project' or 'action'. Similarly, it was often the physical nature of the artistic act that provided the appellation for the finished work: 'accumulation' (Arman), 'compression' (César) and so on.

Has sculpture come to an end?

If one adheres solely to the dictionary definition (this one from the French *Petit Robert*): 'suggestion of an object in space by means of a material on which one imposes a predetermined form with an aesthetic aim', then the only answer can be 'yes'. An environment by Dubuffet or Beuys, an installation by Nam June Paik or Neto, or a Duchamp ready-made is far from being a 'suggestion of an object in space'. In addition, if one wants to preserve the idea of a sculpture as a lasting object, can Anselmo's *Structure that Eats* or Jana Sterbak's *Dress of Flesh* be dubbed sculpture? So let's put the dictionary away. For it is 'the idea of sculpture' — as Pontus Hulten commented on the art of Constantin Brancusi — that has changed.

In one of the rooms of this 'imaginary museum' of sculpture, a *Couple* by a American Hyperrealist stands next to the group of *Pygmalion and Galatea* that Falconet showed at the Salon of 1763, and Rodin's *Age of Bronze* of such verisimiltude that the work seemed — scandalously in the eyes of early viewers — to have been cast from the life. Yet these three sculptors possess very different conceptions of reality and *a posteriori* of the relationship that sculpture is supposed to maintain with it: the quest for anatomical and psychological truth for Falconet, symbolic power for Rodin, photographic likeness for De Andrea.

John De Andrea

Couple, **1971**

Acrylic on polyester, hair. H 173 cm - CP

Étienne-Maurice Falconet

Pygmalion et Galatée

[Pygmalion and Galatea], **1763 Salon**

Marble. 83 x 48 x 38 cm - ML

Auguste Rodin

Âge d'airain [Age of Bronze], **1877-80**

Bronze. 178 x 59 x 61 cm - MO

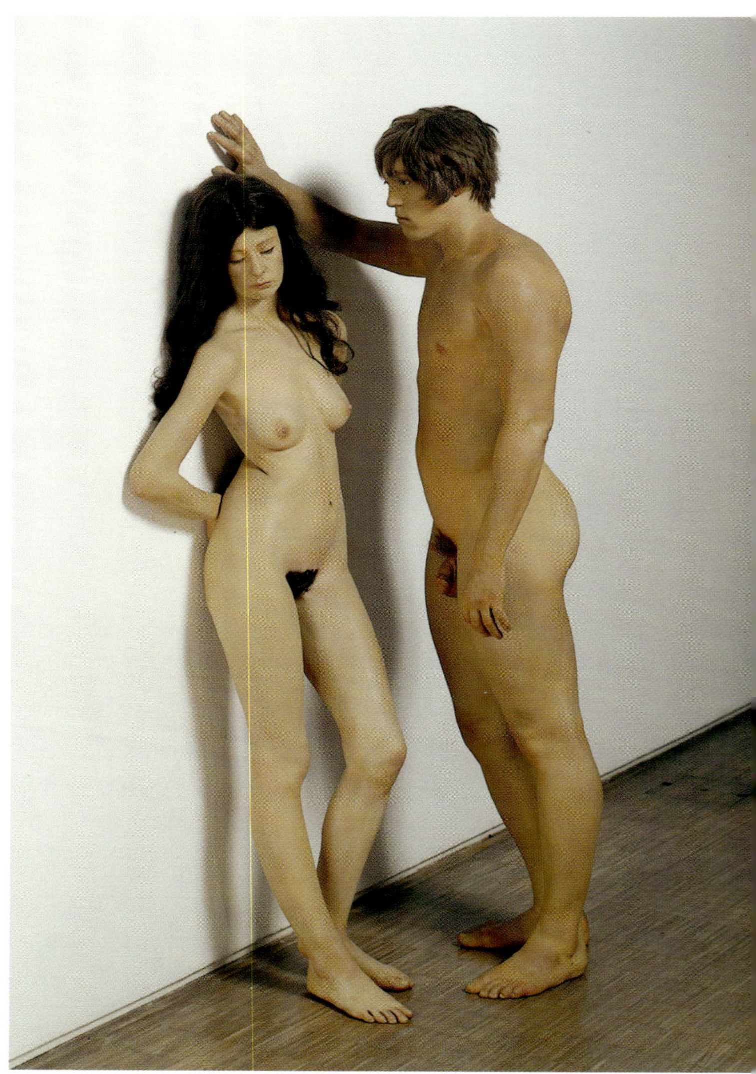

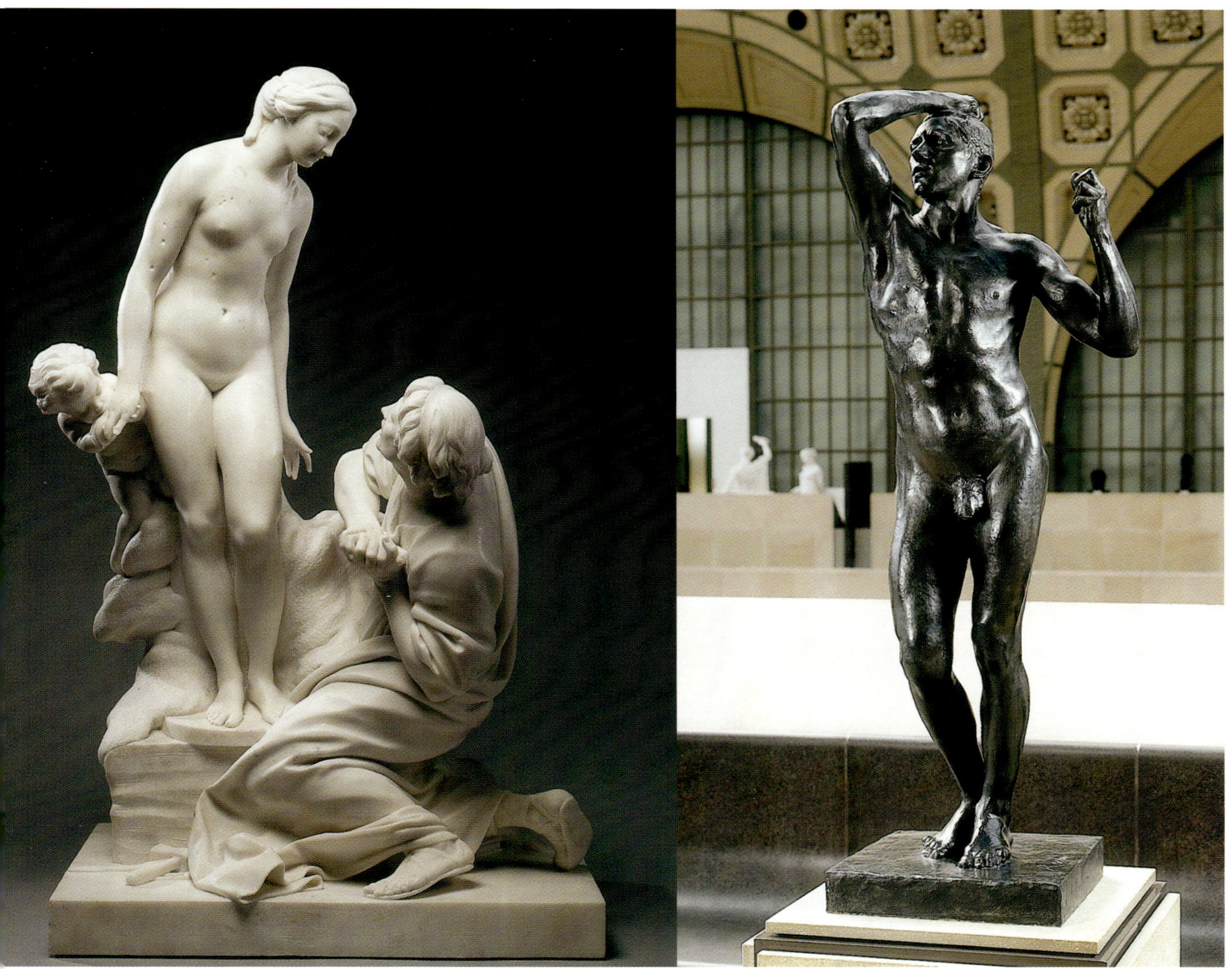

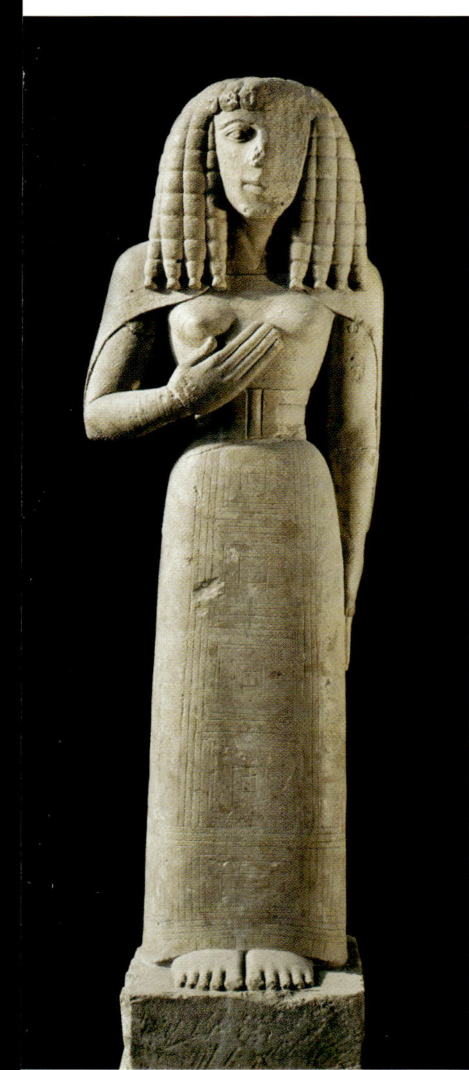

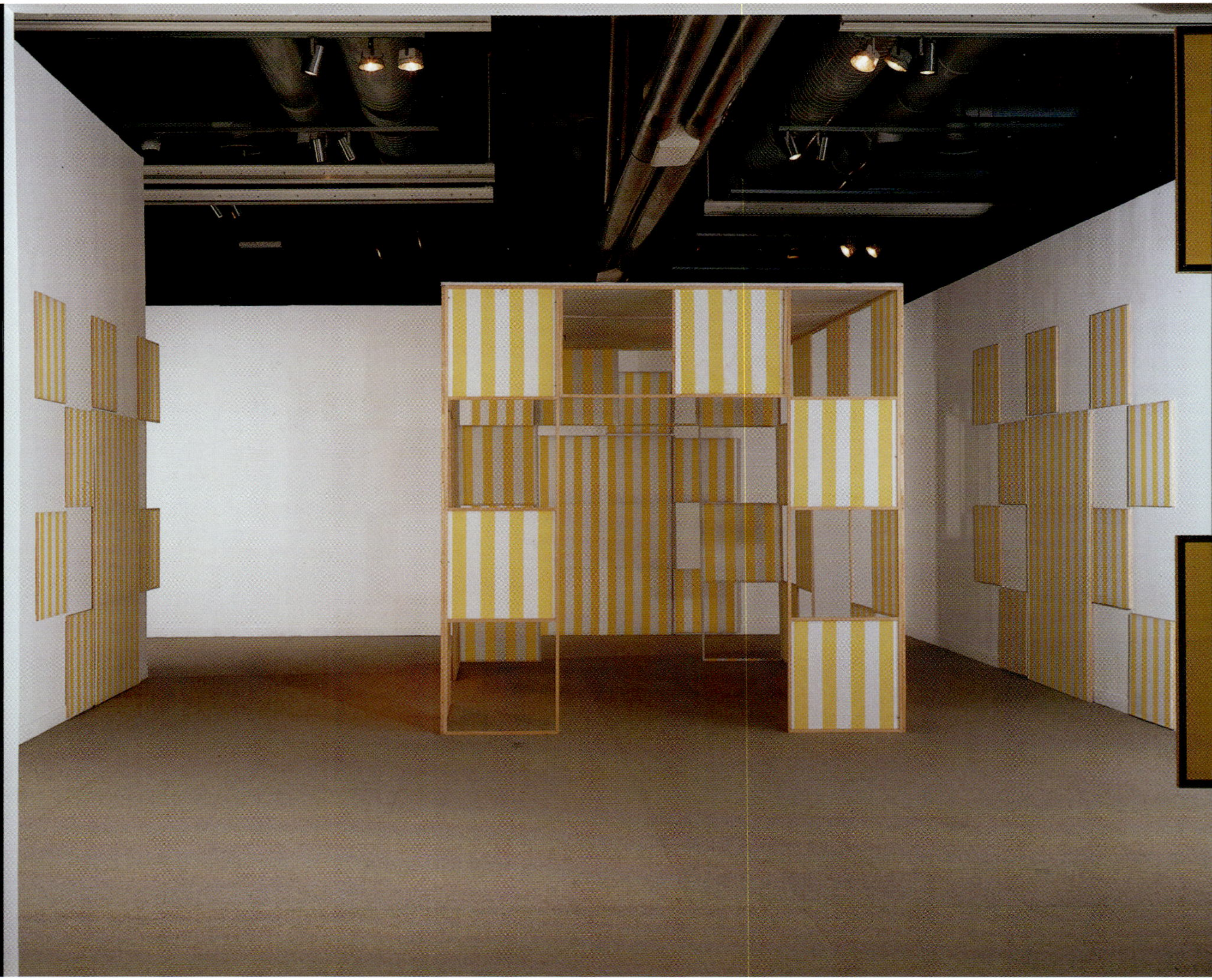

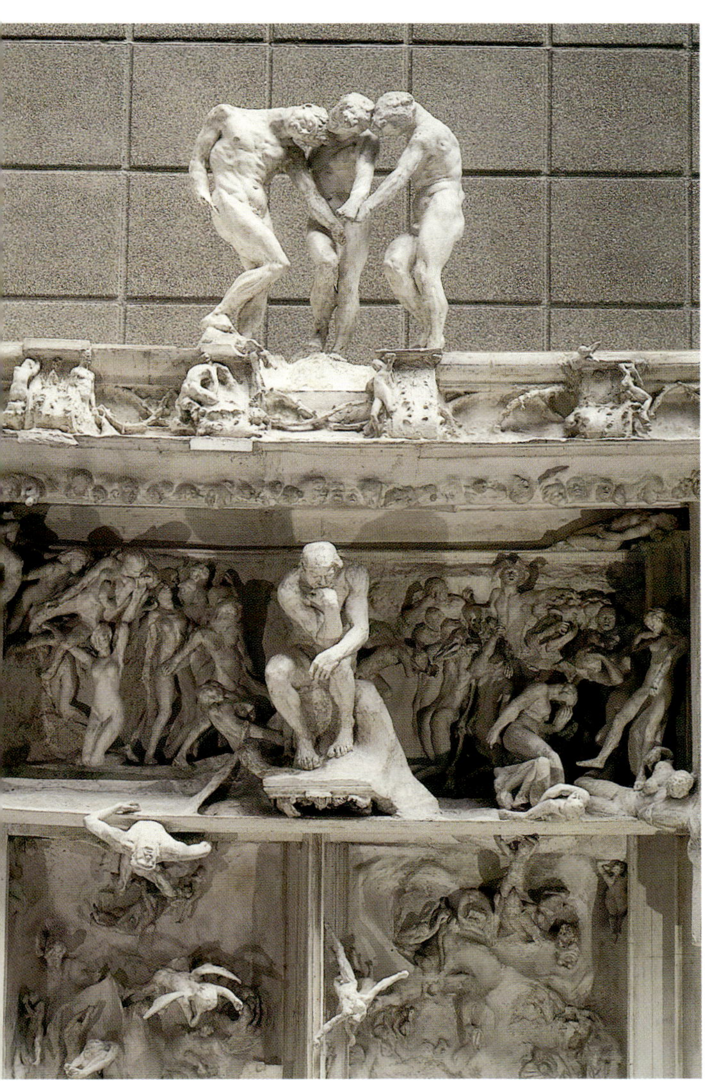

Another room is placed under the sign of the labyrinth, the maze. The garment worn by the *Dame d'Auxerre* (640-630 BC), in a style known as Dedalic because of the sense of movement it embodies, which differentiates it from the earlier Geometrical style, still shows signs of the squaring-up that guided the painter. A statue is still an object and the painted labyrinth remains imprisoned within the form. Opposite, stands Daniel Buren's *Cabane,* an installation in which both painting and sculpture achieve a balance with the museum's architecture that once again pushes back the frontiers of the art, the visitor being inviting to enter what is a 'large drawing exploded in space.'

There is no better work than the *Cabane* nor any better guide then Buren to draw attention to one final, all-important point: sculpture is experienced in space. Some works demand a wall, others, such as Carpeaux's *Ugolino* at the Musée d'Orsay, privilege a frontal view — the question is to know in what way exactly, the majority require a circumambulatory space so one can walk round them and take in the various views. They need space, and lots of it.

Marly courtyard - ML
The great nave of the Musée d'Orsay - MO
The Brancusi studio, Musée national d'art moderne - CP

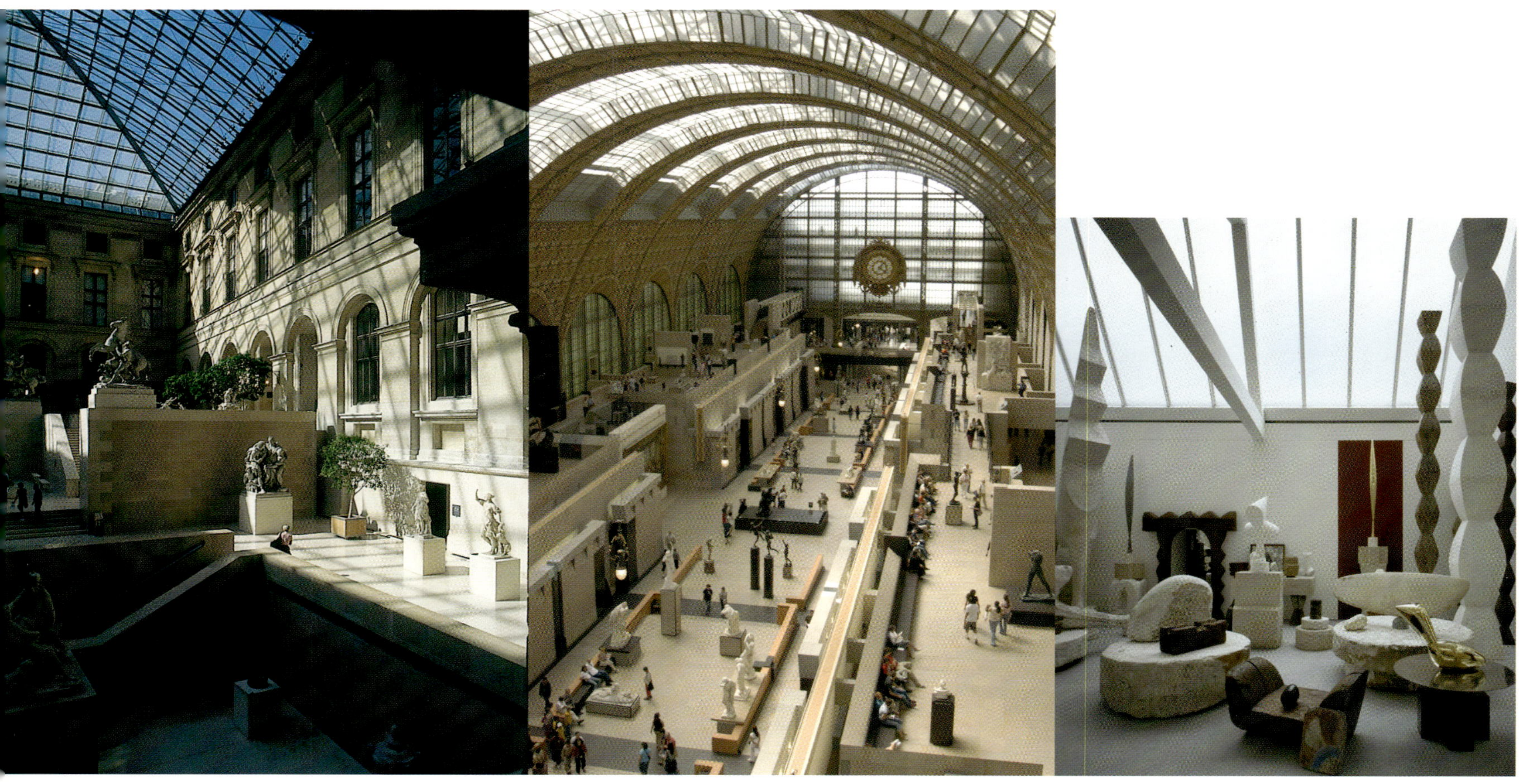

184

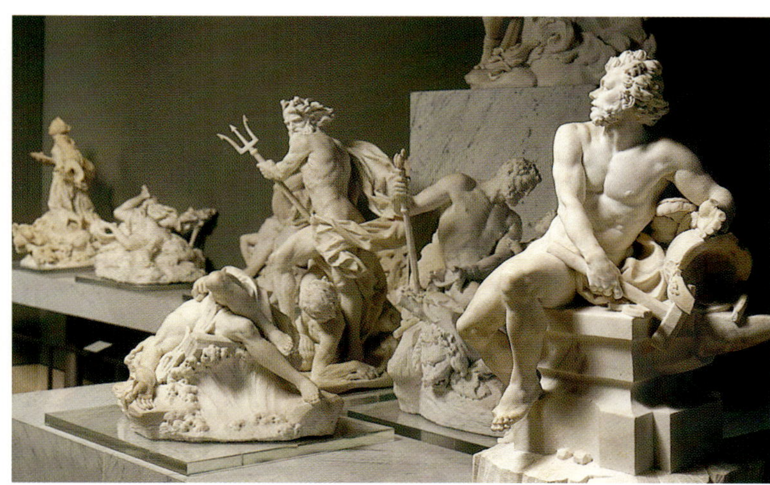

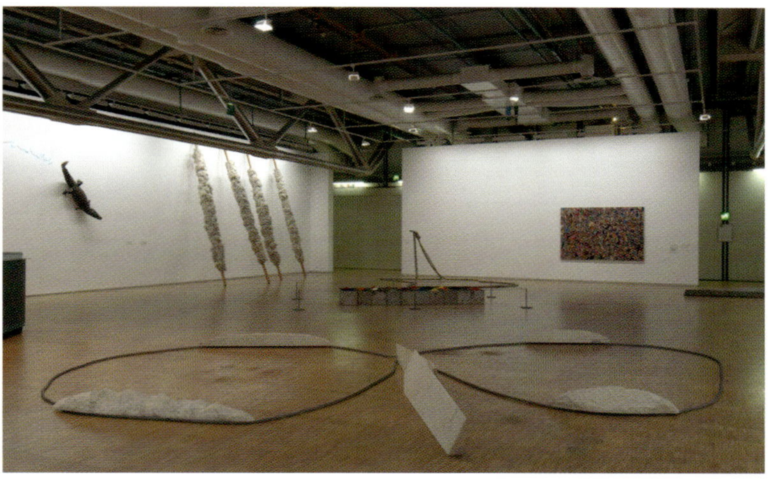

In the Puget and Marly courtyards in the Louvre, the external space of the royal parks is suggested beneath the glass canopy: the broad space, the depth of perspective, the many angles of sight allowed by the terracing provide for the eye, indeed for the whole body, a bracing dose of the open air. Still in the Louvre, the juxtaposition of Academy reception pieces with classical sculpture shows in a single glance their deep-rooted visual understanding of the Antique and their acute sense of how to vary their forms.

Better than any other place, the great nave of the Musée d'Orsay, where visitors move among sculptures vivified by the ever-changing light pouring in through the glass roof, recreates just how it must have been to go to one of those yearly art showcases, the Salons. Quips, animated discussion, excla-mations and laughter still resound around these walls and the audio guides have not quite drowned them out. People make comments and eavesdrop, they approve or condemn.

At the Centre Pompidou, landmark works by Duchamp, by Brancusi, whose studio reconstructed outside the Centre Pompidou is used for temporary exhibitions of contemporary art, by Matisse and Picasso present the major phases of 20th-century sculpture. The terraces provide an arena for samples of monumental sculpture; meanwhile, the room containing Arte Povera and post-Minimalist pieces, placed under the aegis of Mario Merz's neon Fibonacci sequence that runs across the wall, opens sculpture to the realm of space-time.

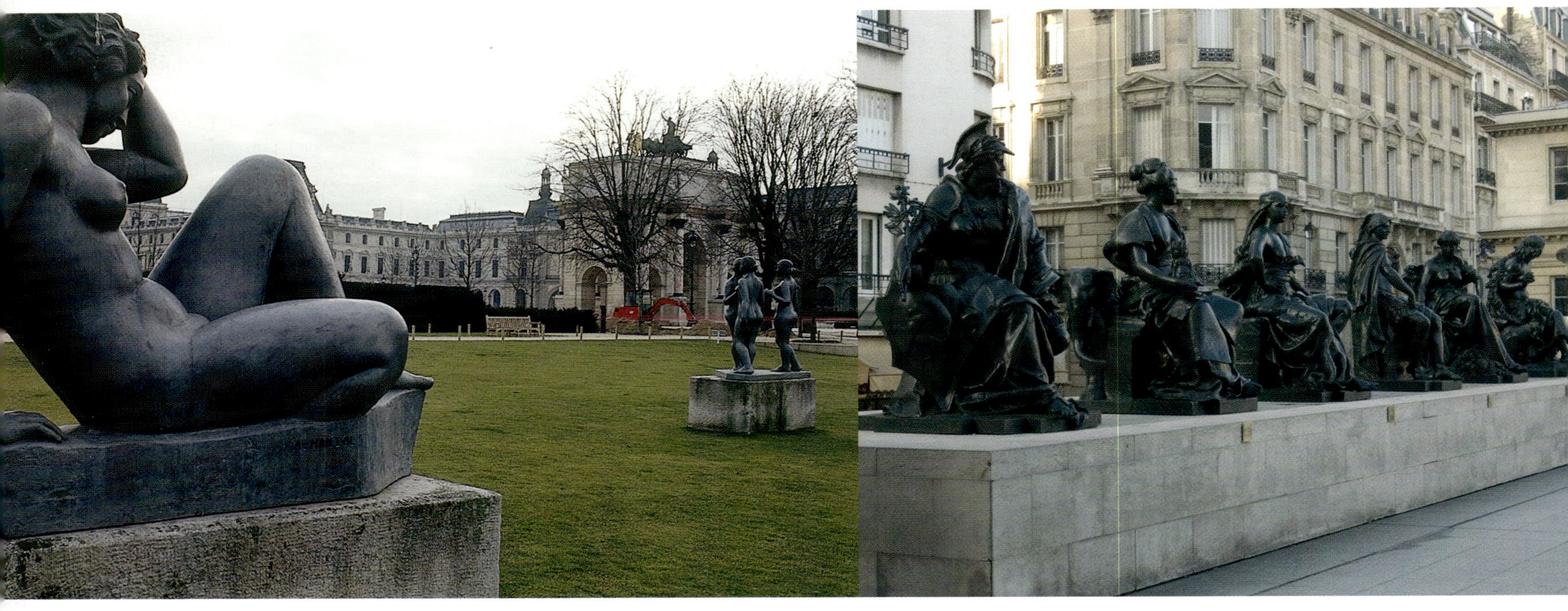

Soon, the mind is enriched with overlapping memories of all three museums. Indeed their immediate vicinity is generously adorned with sculpture: the equestrian sculpture of Louis XIV by Bernini in the courtyard of the Louvre, works by Maillol foreshadowing contemporary sculpture in the Tuileries gardens, and works for the World Fair of 1878, including The Six Continents, that greet tourists from the world over on the esplanade at the Musée d'Orsay, while on the terraces of the Centre Pompidou, monumental sculpture stands out against the Parisian sky.

It is then that Stendhal's phrase comes to mind:

'At the outset, it may be hard to take in a statue's expression; but, once one has, one dwells on it, often returning to it with a feeling of profound delight that borders on happiness.'

186

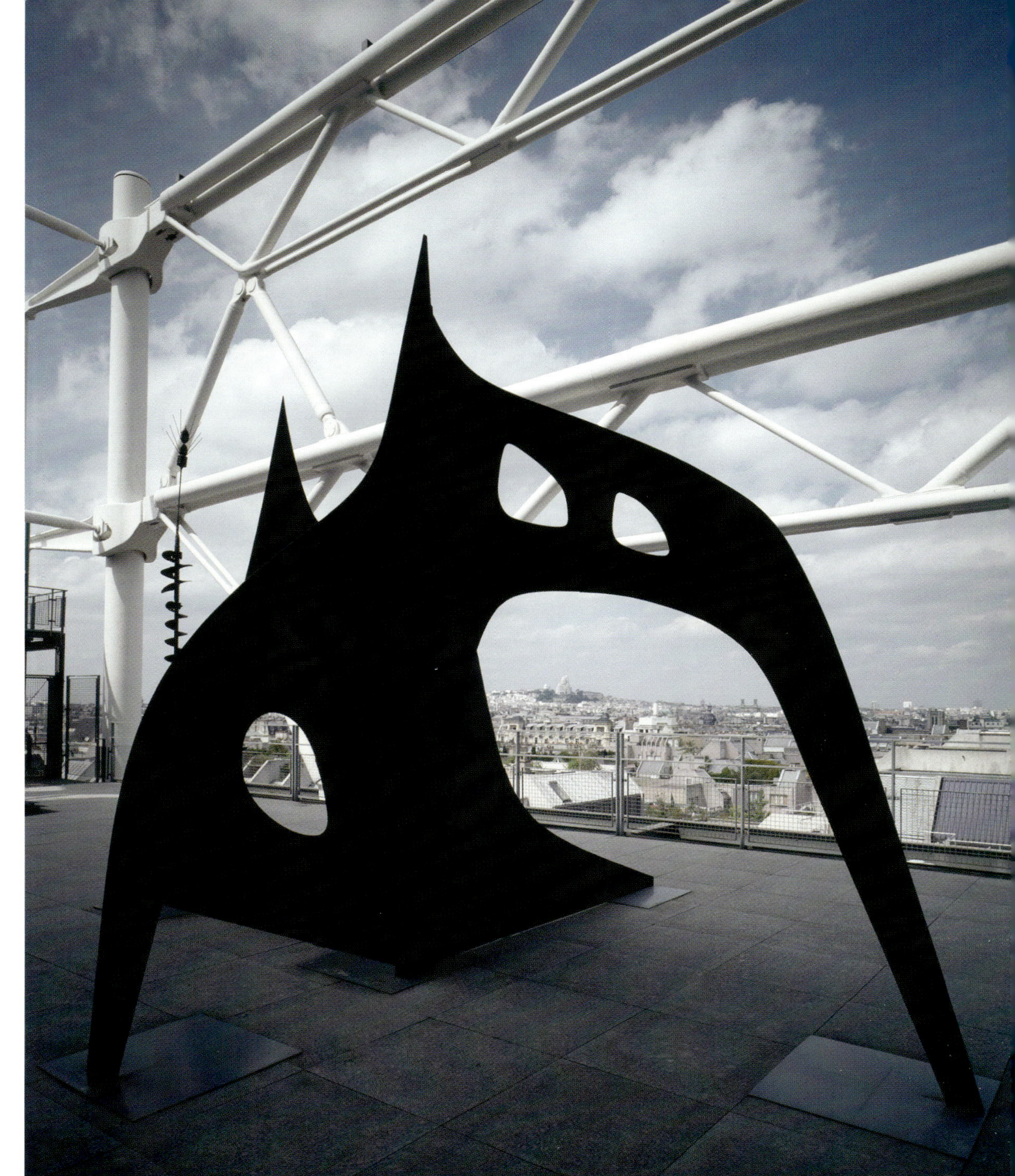

Calder of the terrace of the Musée national d'art moderne

Biographical Notes

Anonymous works

Oriental Antiquities

ML - *Statue in Human Form,* 7th millennium BC
Gypsum plaster, bitumen (eyelids and pupils). 105 x 33 x 13 cm / Excavation
at Ain Ghazal, Jordan, 1985. Loaned by the Direction of Antiquities, Jordan /
Department of Oriental Antiquities / DAO 96
This cult statue is one of the oldest human figures in the collections
of the Louvre. Modelled over a woven armature, the features of this
hieratic form were at one time highlighted in bitumen; it also
sported a hairpiece, hence the less-finished appearance of the top of
the skull.

Egyptian Art

ML - *The Seated Scribe,* 4th or 5th Dynasty, 2600-2350 BC
Painted limestone; eyes incrusted with rock crystal in copper. 53.70 x 44 x 35 cm /
Found at Saqqara / Department of Egyptian Antiquities / E 3023
Egyptian art reflects an intricately hierarchical society according to
which each man enters the world of the dead in the attitude of his
erstwhile function on earth. The pride of this scholar, who has
become a steward, betrays itself in the majestic pose of his head. An
X-ray study of the rock-crystal inlay marking the eyes, undertaken
by the laboratories of the French national museums, has greatly
broadened our appreciation of the piece: what might have appeared
as a fudge designed to cover up the artist's inability to render an eye
accurately turns out to be the result of a subtle analysis whose
purpose is to represent the known form of the organ as accurately
as possible.

ML - *Possession Figurine with Needles,* Roman Egypt, 3rd-4th centuries AD
Terracotta. 9.6 x 4.2 x 7.2 cm / Department of Egyptian Antiquities / E 27145 A
Showing a woman pierced with eleven needles, this statuette was
buried with a lead tablet bearing an inscription concerning a love
spell: Sarapammon calls upon the spirits of the dead to prevent
Ptolemais from experiencing pleasure and desire until she succumbs
to his love. Other papyri of a similar type attest to the practice of
this kind of magic.

Greek Art

ML - *Female Head,* Early Cycladic II (2700-2300 BC)
Marble. H: 27 cm / Rayet gift, 1873 / Department of Greek, Etruscan and Roman
Antiquities / Ma 2709
This head of an idol that once belonged to a large cult statue,
probably of the crossed-arms type, testifies to the high degree of
geometric abstraction attained by Cycladic carvers. It is an art
that inspired numerous 20th-century artists, in particular
Brancusi and Giacometti in the head-plaques of the late 1920s.
Its erudite sense of space is satisfying to contemporary eyes, just
as we now admire Romanesque buildings for their sobriety.
However, just as the walls of Romanesque constructions were in
fact painted, Cycladic heads too were stippled with red, black or
blue motifs.

ML - *Bell-Idol,* Thebes, Archaic period, c. 700 BC
Terracotta. H: 39.50 cm / Acquisition, 1893 / Department of Greek, Etruscan and
Roman Antiquities/ CA 573
The group of thirteen geometrically decorated Boeotian 'bell-
idols' discovered from the end of the 19th century on remains an
enigma. The Louvre possesses two of them. Are they articulated
dolls, as the jointed legs suggest? The size of the largest ones
makes this idea seem unlikely. Were they hung from trees as tributes to agrarian divinities? Do they commemorate the Boeotian
custom of the *Daedala,* a ritual procession of dolls representing
their main cities as recounted by the traveller Pausanias in the
2nd century? Their symbolic decoration militates in favour of a
funerary purpose. Or are they effigies representing some archaic
animal goddess? Most probably, they are idols intended to guide
the deceased to the next world. Carried aloft during the *ekphora,*
or funerary procession, their legs would have moved. These terracotta figures were then laid in the tomb.

ML - *Female Statuette,* known as *La Dame d'Auxerre,* Crete (?), c. 640-630 BC
Limestone with an incised pattern, originally painted. H: 75 cm / Exchange with the
Musée Municipal, Auxerre, 1909 / Department of Greek, Etruscan and Roman
Antiquities / Ma 3098
As of the end of the 9th century BC, the arrival in Crete of artists
from the East prepared the ground for a renaissance of Cretan art
in the 7th century. Characteristic of the advanced phase of the
Dedalic style, this cult statue can be considered to some extent an
ancestor of the korai (female figures) of the 6th century. The
cylindrical sleeve of the garment archaically recalls an archaic
stone block or squared-up beam, while the U-shaped face and
trapezoid stepped wig are conventional. The incised marking-up
visible on the dress served as a guide for painting a polychrome
decoration that some authorities believe was gaudily coloured.

ML - *Kore,* sanctuary of Hera at Samos, c. 570-560 BC
Marble. H: 192 cm / Acquisition, 1881 / Department of Greek, Etruscan and Roman
Antiquities / Ma 686
The inscription 'Chéramyes dedicated me to Hera as an offering',
engraved along the vertical edge of the veil draped over her back,
identifies this headless female figure as part of an ex-voto presented in the sanctuary of Hera at Samos. The circular sleeve sheathing the legs links this sculpture with primitive forms of Greek
religious art that originated in part in the worship of sacred trees.
The ***himation*** (a wool overmantle) and the ***chiton*** (a long pleated
tunic), however, conceal an effective rendering of the body.

ML - *Male Torso,* known as *The Torso of Miletos,* Miletos, c. 480-470 BC
Marble. H: 132 cm / Rayet and Thomas excavations. Rothschild gift, 1873 /
Department of Greek, Etruscan and Roman Antiquities / Ma 2792
This male torso comes from a *kouros* in the Severe style. He
stands naked in a frontal position, though without rigidity; the
left leg and probably the right arm project forward. Even if the
chest is presented conventionally and the pubic hair and back
sweep are still archaic in type, the patent drive to realism is characteristic of the transition towards Classicism.

ML - *Winged Victory of Samothrace,* Samothraki (Aegean Sea), c. 190 BC
Grey Lartos marble (boat), Paros marble (statue). H: 328 cm / C Champoiseau
missions, 1863, 1879 / Department of Greek, Etruscan and Roman Antiquities /
Ma 2369
Found by Champoiseau in 1863 and placed in the Hall of the
Caryatids in the Louvre in 1866, this Paros marble Nike (winged
goddess of Victory) today stands on a grey marble base in the
shape of the prow of a galley at the top of a staircase. This spectacular setting captures something of its original site on the
island of Samothrace in a niche towering above the sanctuary of
the Great Gods. Her right hand was probably raised in the air:
the statue gave thanks for a victory by the Rhodes fleet at the
beginning of the 2nd century BC.

ML - *Aphrodite,* known as the *Venus de Milo,* island of Melos (Cyclades, Greece),
c. 100 BC
Marble. H: 202 x 63 x 64 cm / Gift from the Marquis de Rivière to Louis XVIII,
1821 / Department of Greek, Etruscan and Roman Antiquities / Ma 399
'Our Lady of Beauty', as she was dubbed by the German writer
Henrich Heine, was found in 1820 on the island of Milo (Melos)
and is identified with the almost naked Aphrodite emerging from
the sea, or sometimes with Amphitrite, a marine goddess venera-
ted on the island. Created at the end of the Hellenistic period on
the type of *Aphrodite of Capua,* she attests to the return to the
past that marked the turn of the 1st century BC. The sculptor has
shown himself to be innovative, however, in the use of two
blocks of marble and in concealing the junction between them
beneath the drapery round the hips. The way the cloth seems to
slide down makes the pose look unusually natural and sponta-
neous. The left foot and arm were carved separately. The goddess
possibly belonged in a group with the *Ares Borghese.*

ML - *Fighting Warrior* (or *Fighting Gladiator*),
known as *The Borghese Gladiator,* Anzio (Antium), Italy, c. 100 BC
Marble. H: 199 cm / Formerly Borghese collection. Purchase, 1807 / Department of Greek, Etruscan and Roman Antiquities / Ma 527
Signed by Agasias of Ephesus, son of Dositheos, this nude warrior was discovered in pieces to the south of Rome (1609-11) and was reconstituted by Nicolas Cordier, Il Franciosino. It was initially identified with a gladiator, then with Achilles or Alexander. As the figure fought on foot against a horseman, some have even conjectured an Amazon. This 'anatomical wonder', as Théophile Gautier put it (1867), was carved according to the long-limbed canon of Lysippus of Sicyon, the great bronze sculptor of the 4th century BC. If the athletic stature does recall Lysippus, the emphatic gestures and musculature are more in the Hellenistic spirit. Commented on in the lectures at the Academy and a much-used model in anatomy courses, at the beginning of the 19th century it was even the subject of an écorché study by Jean-Galbert Salvage.

Etruscan and Roman art

ML - *Etruscan Canopic Jar,* Chiusi workshop, second half of the 6th century BC
Terracotta. H: 50 cm / Purchase, 1851 / Department of Greek, Etruscan and Roman Antiquities / D 162
Etruscan art was essentially funerary. The prosperous Etruscan city-states traded throughout the Mediterranean basin, notably Greece and Egypt. The lid of the cinerary urn, known as a *canope* by analogy to the Egyptian vases containing human organs, is modelled in the shape of a head, and arms are fixed to the handles. As with figures on the lids of Etruscan sarcophagi, the head is sculpted in the image of the deceased. These stylised effigies were then deposited inside tombs.

ML - *Nemi Aphrodite,* 4th century BC
Bronze. H: 50.5 cm / Department of Greek, Etruscan and Roman Antiquities / Br 321
The work of the Etruscan bronze-founders was famous throughout the Mediterranean basin. The collections of the Villa Giulia in Rome and many museums in the area of Tarquinia display typical elongated figures, which are in all probability ex-votos. From the 4th century BC on, this type of statuette was produced throughout central Italy. If the influence of Greek art is manifest in the idealised treatment of the face, the overall shape on the other hand shows links with the stylisation of archaic funerary art.

ML - *Captive Barbarian,* Rome, 2nd century
Red porphyry and white marble. H: 240 cm / Formerly Borghese collection. Purchase, 1807 / Department of Greek, Etruscan and Roman Antiquities / Ma 1385
Possessing a pendant in the Louvre also from the Borghese collection, this captive Dacian illustrates the tendency of the Roman Empire to depict the peoples it subdued during its military campaigns. He is represented in native costume, rendered in porphyry, in the attitude of a prisoner in a victory procession. The head, arms and hands are modern additions: it was their love for the Antique that prompted artists right up into the 19th century to restore the missing elements. The head is the work of Pietro Bernini, father of the great Gian Lorenzo.

ML – *Imperial Group as Mars and Venus,* c. 120-140; reworked c. 170-175
Marble. H: 173 cm / Formerly Borghese collection. Purchase, 1807 / Department of Greek, Etruscan and Roman Antiquities / Ma 1009
If the heads in this group are portraits, the bodies are simply types. The man is inspired by Alcamenes' *Borghese Ares* and the woman by the *Aphrodite of Capua* (4th century BC), from which the Venus de Milo also derives. A recurrent trend in the courtly world from the Renaissance to the 18th century, such mythological masquerades allowed the great and the good to share in the life of the gods. One might say the tradition continues today in the 'sword and sandals' epic.

ML – *Old Man Skinning an Animal* or *The Rustic Flayer,* Roman, Imperial period (1st-2nd century)
Marble. H: 107 cm / Department of Greek, Etruscan and Roman Antiquities / Ma 517
The *Rustic Flayer* belonged to the Albani collection. Seized under the Napoleonic regime, the piece was repurchased by Louis XVIII in 1815. An agrarian rite is here shown from a grotesque perspective.

Medieval art

ML – *The Courajod Christ,* Burgundy, second quarter of the 12th century
Painted and gilded maple wood. 155 x 168 x 30 cm / L Courajod gift, 1895 /
Department of Sculpture RF 1082
Originally, this statue belonged to a group of the *Deposition,* many
examples of which are found in central Italy and northern Spain.
Its provenance is unrecorded, but the style, close to the great *Christ
of Vézelay,* and the drapery — where the folds are represented by
pairs of lines reminiscent of Autun statuary — betray links with
Burgundian Romanesque art. It was presented by its discoverer
Louis Courajod at the 1878 World Fair, where it was disparaged as
akin to 'fetishes from the wild tribes of Oceania'. Courajod defended the work in *La Gazette des beaux-arts* and *La Gazette archéo-
logique,* before donating it to the Louvre, where he had become
conservator-in-chief of the Department of Sculpture.

ML - *Descent from the Cross,* Umbria (?), second quarter of the 13th century
Polychrome wood (poplar, willow, walnut), marble. 183 x 123 cm / Formerly
Van Stolk and Brimo de Laroussilhe collections. Acquisition, 1968 / Department
of Sculpture / RF 2966 to 2669
The appearance of carved groups in churches in Italy and France,
as well as in the Germanic countries and Spain, is a symptom of
statuary overcoming its role as decoration and attaining independence with respect to architecture. The scene of Christ taken
down from the Cross by Joseph of Arimathia and Nicodemus in
the presence of St John and the Virgin (here missing) echoes the
Mystery Plays, theatrical dramas on religious subjects. Appearing
tardily in Italy, Gothic here surfaces in the humanisation of the
figures, whereas the essentially static composition remains
Romanesque in spirit.

ML - *Virgin and Child,* Normandy, first third of the 14th century
Stone. 175 x 57 x 34 cm / Acquisition, 1850 / Department of Sculpture / ML 24
Originally from the abbey of the Premonstratensian Canons of
Blanchelande in Normandy, this piece was the first medieval
work bought for the Louvre, following the advice of Léon de
Laborde in 1850. The proliferation of depictions of the Virgin
and Child in the 14th century is linked to the development of
pietà moderna, which stressed the feelings of sacred figures, here
maternal affection and the spontaneity of the infant, who in fact
resembles a scaled-down man more than a child. Christ's real
humanity is here affirmed against the various heresies that denied
it. In the Virgin of Blanchelande naturalism extends to the teeth
exposed between the lips.

ML - *Virgin of the Annunciation,* Ile-de-France, second third of the 14th century
Alabaster, flecks of gilding. 69 x 20 x 12 cm / Félix Doistau gift, 1919 /
Department of Sculpture / RF 1661
In the 19th century, this group, which used to include an angel
now in the museum at Cleveland, stood in the church at
Javernant in Champagne. It is typical of 14th-century French
sculpture: the Virgin is portrayed standing, without a crown, the
hip projecting slightly, holding a book, and making a gesture of
reply to the angel. Thought to come from a Parisian workshop,
the workshop formulae employed here (round face, eyes flush
with the head, scornful mouth, artificial-looking tubular folds)
reappear in many Virgins from Champagne.

ML - *Tomb of Philippe Pot (1428-93), Grand Sénéchal of
Burgundy,* last quarter of the 15th century
Polychrome stone. 181 x 260 x 167 cm / From the chapel of St John the Baptist
at the abbey at Cîteaux in Burgundy / Acquisition, 1889 / Department of Sculpture /
RF 795
Long attributed to Antoine Le Moiturier (1425-c.1497), the tomb
of Philippe Pot is typical of Burgundian sculpture as marked by the
lesson of Claus Sluter. It represents the funerary procession. The
pleurants (mourners), bearing the tombstone on which the effigy of
the knight rests, carry blazons illustrating the eight quarters of the
deceased's coat of arms. The architectural power of the group goes
beyond ritual to also express a sense of grief.

Renaissance & Modern era

ML - *Jeanne de Bourbon, Countess of Auvergne (died 1511),*
Auvergne, first quarter of the 16th century
Stone. 178 x 78 x 29 cm / Purchase, 1899 / Department of Sculpture / RF 1212
At one time this flagstone was erected vertically in the recess
containing the gisant of Jeanne de Bourbon in the church of the
Franciscan Recollects at Vic-le-Vicomte (Puy-de-Dôme). This
funerary relief marks the juncture between the Middle Ages and
the Renaissance. Somewhat unrealistic anatomically, the macabre
figure of Jeanne de Bourbon is shown half putrefied and eaten by
worms. The *transi* is, however, presented upright, in an attitude
that refers to the Resurrection of the Flesh. This striking
ensemble is ensconced in a niche with pilasters surmounted by a
Renaissance-style shell.

ML - *La Mort Saint Innocent [The Dead Saint Innocent]*, Ile-de-France, c. 1530

Alabaster. 120 x 55 x 27 cm / Accession to the Louvre, 1866 / Department
of Sculpture / RF 2625

Originally from the cemetery of the Innocents in Paris, this herald
of mortality beat the death knell in a box suspended from the
tower of Notre-Dame-du-Bois in the centre of the graveyard. In
those days, cemeteries were not the remote and rather dubious
places of today: people would walk through them, even live in
them. With rags standing for wings, the death-dealing angel's right
hand strikes illiterate and erudite alike; the latter could read an inscription on the shield making it clear that the message concerned
him as much as anyone else.

ML – *Fountain of Diana*, mid-16th century

Marble. 211 x 258 x 134 cm / From the Musée des Monuments Français, 1823 /
Department of Sculpture / MR 1581, MR sup 123

This upper section of a fountain from the courtyard in the Château
at Anet (Eure-et-Loir), the residence of Diane de Poitiers, favourite
of Henri II, is the oldest extant garden sculpture in France. The
spirit of the School of Fontainebleau transpires in the beautiful
sinuous lines of the nude goddess and in the naturalistic treatment
of the animals. The sculpture has been successively ascribed to
Benvenuto Cellini (thinking perhaps of his bronze *Nymph*), Jean
Goujon, Germain Pilon and Ponce Jacquiot. But the piece is difficult to judge as, in 1799-1800, the sculptor Pierre-Nicolas
Beauvallet added at least the upper part of the torso and the head
— which contrary to what has previously been advanced is there-
fore not a portrait of the royal favourite.

ML - *Dead St Francis*, Spain, mid-17th century

Walnut, glass (eyes), bone (teeth), hemp (cord), original polychromy.
87 x 26 x 24 cm / Acquisition, 1988 / Department of Sculpture / RF 4211

Discovered in 1875 at the Rastro (flea market) in Madrid, this
Dead St Francis dates from the Spanish 'Siglo de Oro,' a time when
the mysticism of the Counter-Reformation was conveyed by a
realism bordering on the most theatrical illusionism. 'The world is a
dream', Calderón had written. The *realia* (real elements from daily
life) one finds in Zurbarán's *bodegones* (still lifes) are seamlessly
introduced into the sacred space, as in Velázquez's painting. This
Francis in ecstasy is a hallucinatory vision: according to Franciscan
legend, it was exactly in this manner that the body of the saint was
found in Assisi in the 15th century, standing upright, uncorrupted,
his eyes raised to heaven, the stigmatised foot still oozing blood.
This sacred vision is treated realistically, with glass and bone inlay
for the eyes and teeth, and a polychrome habit.

CP - *Fang Mask*, Gabon, late 19th century (?)

Dried gourd with pokerwork design. 42 x 28.5 x 14.7 cm / Alice Derain bequest,
1982 / AM 1982-248

In 1944, Vlaminck wrote: 'It is this mask that sparked off *art
nègre* [...] Derain offered to buy this mask off me and I let him
have it for twenty francs [...] Derain took the mask with him to
his studio on rue de Tourlaque, where [it] succeeded in per-
plexing and disturbing Picasso and Matisse, etc.' The mask
Vlaminck sold to Derain, and which the latter kept until his
death, thus had a palpable impact on the genesis of modern art,
Western art having ceased to be the only viable reference. Derain
indeed compiled a veritable 'imaginary museum' containing 210
pieces from every period and every continent, and was particularly fond of this mask.

Artists' biographies

Acconci, Vito

New York, 1940

CP - *Convertible Clam Shelter*, 1990

Sound installation: fibreglass, steel, rope, shells, lighting, sound environment.
Each shell: 150 x 240 x 280 cm / Gift by the Société des Amis du Musée National
d'Art Moderne, 1994 / AM 1994-262

Poet and visual artist, Acconci can think of words only in
conjunction with the voice that utters them, of creativity in
conjunction with the body that makes it real. He became known
for body art actions (1969-73), which both fascinated and distur-
bed his audience. Those works dealt with the involvement
between exhibitionist artist and voyeuristic spectator, and in
posing questions about intimacy, the relation between the body
and sexuality, and the transgression of the border between public
and private space. Gradually, the artist vanished physically from
his pieces: at first he started hiding from the public, leaving only
a voice that proffered the most disturbing messages (*Cultural
Space Pieces*, 1974-78), but, from the 1980s on, he went on to
disappear completely and produce objective sculptures. His giant
bras condense within a metaphorically charged envelope the psy-
choanalytical relationship to the mother and sexual fetishism, as
well as a personal preoccupation with the theme of the living
space in its dependence on the organic, the home and the phan-
tasmic. The piece in the Centre Pompidou belongs to a type of
production that has seldom led to works in outside venues and is
akin in spirit to Salvador Dalí's or Claes Oldenburg's appropria-
tions of architecture or furniture.

Achour, Boris

Marseille, 1966

CP - *Cosmos*, 2001

Coloured resin, engine, master recording on CD. 191 x 218 cm / Gift of the Société
Ricard, 2004, in the aegis of the Ricard Prize, 2002 / AM 2004-25

Like many artists of his generation, Achour has tackled a great
number of expressive techniques, including sculpture, video, installation and, more recently, digital graphics. This protean
approach to visual art followed a period of asceticism constituted
by his 'actions peu' of 1993-97, in which minute, absurd acts
were played out in urban spaces with whatever materials came to
hand, like a kind of asphalt-based land art. These interventions,
which Achour describes as 'soft' guerrilla actions, derive in part
from urban Situationism and Raymond Hains' 'pavement sculptures'. *Cosmos* belongs to a series dealing with the literary work
of Witold Gombrowicz: the title also covers an installation of
video cassettes classified by genre. It is within the 'weak' sign
constituted by a rolling videotape, a film camera, a looped record
that the artist finds, in accordance with Gombrowicz's postulate,
a 'strong' sign: the rotation of the earth, passing time and the
order (in Greek, *cosmos*) that is born out of chaos.

Adam, Lambert-Sigisbert

Nancy, 1700 - Paris, 1759

ML - *Neptune calmant les flots flots [Neptune Calming the Waters]*,
1733

Marble. 85 x 59 x 48 cm / Enrolled in the Académie Royale 1733. Academy reception
piece, 1737. Revolutionary seizure of the Academy collections / Department of
Sculpture / MR 1743

Born to a dynasty of sculptors from Nancy, Adam was one of the
finest French exponents of the *rocaille* style. Awarded the Prix de
Rome in 1723, he was an admirer of Bernini and the great
Baroque interiors. After his return to France in 1733, he devoted
himself to open-air statuary: the cascade in the park of St-Cloud,
The Triumph of Neptune and Amphitrite in the Bassin de
Neptune at Versailles, where he reused the theme of *Neptune
Calming the Waters,* as well as works for the palace of Sans-
Souci at Potsdam. His feeling for nature is allied to a genuine
talent for scene-setting and a taste for the gigantic.

Andre, Carl

Quincy (USA), 1935

CP - *144 Tin Square*, 1975

Assemblage on the ground of 144 tin squares in rows of 12. 367 x 367 cm /
Purchase, 1987 / AM 1987-1137

CP - *Hearth*, 1980

44 cedarwood elements. 120.5 x 469 x 90 cm / Purchase, 1988 / AM 1988-1177

Friend of the painter Frank Stella, who encouraged him to make
wooden sculptures, Andre discovered Brancusi's work while on a
trip to Paris in 1954. He also visited Stonehenge, going on to
combine the constructive monumentality of a megalithic site with
the serial production of industrial materials in simple forms (flag-
stones, beams, bricks, rails, etc). In 1966, the artist took part in
the very first exhibition of Minimalist art, 'Primary Structures'.
Defining sculpture as a location, from 1966 on, the artist produced *Floor Pieces* comprised of metal plates laid out on the
ground. In works dealing with horizontality, Andre allows
viewers to experience sculpture by walking over it. Another type
of piece composed of wooden modular elements arranged into
geometrical structures instigates a dialogue with architecture.

Anguier, François

Eu (Normandy), 1612 – Paris, 1686

ML - *Funerary Monument of Jacques-Auguste de Thou,*
detail of the sarcophagus with atlantes, 1647

Marble, stone, bronze. 146 x 126 x 63 cm / Executed for the Eglise St-André-des-Arts,
Paris. Transferred by the Musée de Versailles in 1851 and Ecole des Beaux-Arts in
1894 / Department of Sculpture / RF 972

A pupil of Simon Guillain — as was his brother Michel, who
carried out the *Nativity* for the Eglise du Val-de-Grâce in 1665
(now in Eglise St-Roch, Paris) — François Anguier stayed in
Rome for some ten years, working for Bernini's archrival,
Algardi. His knowledge of humanism and his balanced art with
its serene allegorical figures find expression chiefly in the monuments he executed for the great and the good of the kingdom,
such as the heart of the Duc de Longueville (1661, Louvre),
where four female figures symbolising the cardinal virtues are
arranged around the foot of an obelisk bearing the emblems of
power and of the arts.

Anselmo, Giovanni

Borgofranco d'Ivrea (Italy), 1934
CP - *Untitled,* 1968

Granite, lettuce, copper wire. 70 x 23 x 37 cm / Purchase, 1985 / AM 1985-177

Anselmo occupies a special place within the Arte Povera group, which came together under the aegis of Germano Celant at the Sperone Gallery in Turin in 1966. From slide projectors placed on the ground and beaming the word *particolare* (detail) on everything in their field, including the beholder's body, to gravity-defying blocks of granite fixed to the wall, the artist confronts viewers with their situation in the world and their relationship to the passage of time. A second major group of works employs perishable materials, such as sponge or lettuce, and functions as a 'real allegory' or *vanitas* designed to increase our awareness of transience. Anselmo represented Italy at the 1990 Venice Biennial.

Arman (Armand Pierre Fernandez)

Nice, 1928
CP - *Home, Sweet Home,* 1960

Gas masks in a box under Plexiglas. 160 x 140.5 x 20.3 cm / Purchase, 1986 / AM 1986-52

A member of the School of Nice formed in the late 1950s along with Ben and Yves Klein, Arman began as painter before, from 1959 on, constructing 'accumulations' of objects in series, one example being *Home, Sweet Home.* For this reason, critic Pierre Restany enrolled him in his Nouveau Réaliste group founded in 1960. Arman responded to the showing of Klein's empty *Vide* by transforming the Iris Clert gallery into a full-to-bursting *Plein,* saturating the space with everyday articles and rubbish. Whereas the appropriated objects under Plexiglas settle old scores with the cult of artistic display, his *Colères* (angers or rages, during which this martial arts expert would ritualistically smash objects — generally musical instruments — into smithereens) amount to grandiose iconoclastic gestures. In 1998, the artist, who now lives in the USA, expressed his rare sense of visual and tactile combination in the astonishing altars to post-industrial civilisation exhibited at the Jeu de Paume in Paris.

Arp, Jean (Hans Arp)

Strasbourg, 1886 – Basel (Switzerland), 1966
CP - *Pépin géant [Giant Pip],* 1937

Stone. 162 x 125 x 77 cm / Purchase, 1949 / AM 897 S

His acquaintance with the Expressionists of the Blaue Reiter, as well as with Apollinaire and Picasso, induced Arp to produce abstract collages in 1915, a path seconded by the artist Sophie Taeuber whom he was to marry in 1922. Arp then turned to painting wooden reliefs. In 1916, he was involved in founding the Dada group in Zurich, before bringing its revolutionary aesthetic to Cologne (1919-20). In 1926, he settled at Clamart, near Paris, participating simultaneously in Surrealism and in the development of Constructivist art, in addition contributing to the review *De Stijl,* and working with Van Doesburg on the decoration of the Aubette (Strasbourg, 1926-28). The use of the 'laws of hazard' and the spontaneity of gesture, patent in his 'torn papers' (1930 on), combined with a respect for the natural form of the material, culminated in an art in which abstraction competes with organic references that might be described as 'biomorphic'. From 1933, he produced 'concretions', plaster sculptures in the round, sometimes transposed into stone. The Arp Foundation at Clamart houses some admirable plaster pieces from this series.

Barre, Jean Auguste

Paris, 1811 – *ibid,* 1896
ML - *Rachel (1821-1858),* 1848

Ivory on a gilded bronze plinth. 46 x 13 x 13 cm / Dinah Félix bequest, 1910 / Department of Sculpture / RF 1508

Training under his father, an engraver and medallist, Barre was instrumental in promoting the statuette as the Romantic genre par excellence. His full-length standing figurines often depict actresses or dancers (Rachel, Fanny Elssler, Marie Taglioni), as well as official personages, such as Queen Victoria, of whom he also made a life-size statue (1860). Copies of his small-scale sculptures, where attitude is more telling than the schematic psychological portrait, were produced in both bronze and biscuit porcelain. Popular in aristocratic and bourgeois circles alike, they would have stood on a mantelpiece next to a caricature portrait by Dantan or an animal fight by Barye.

Barrias, Louis-Ernest

Paris, 1841 - *ibid,* 1905

MO - *Les Nubiens* or *Chasseurs d'alligators [The Nubians* or *The Alligator Hunters]*, **1894**

Plaster. 520 x 280 x 100 cm / Bronze commissioned by the anthropology gallery of the Natural History Museum under the title The Human Races in 1893 / RF 3743

MO - *La Nature se dévoilant à la Science [Nature Revealing Herself to Science* or *The Scarab]*, **1899**

Marble and polychrome Algerian onyx, grey granite (terrace), malachite (scarab), lapis-lazuli (ribbon). 200 x 85 x 55 cm / Commissioned for the staircase of the Conservatoire des Arts et Métiers in 1895 / RF 1409

Prix de Rome in 1861, Barrias was one of the main purveyors of monumental art for the Second Empire and, even more so, for the Third Republic. His two most famous monuments are the *Defense of Paris* (1883), a piece whose many-sidedness infringed the competition's criteria, and the *Monument to Victor Hugo* (1902), sadly destroyed during the Occupation, in which the poet was perched on a relief representing the rock of Guernsey, while winged allegories symbolising the various literary genres hover around the poet like seagulls. His *Fileuse de Mégare* (1870, Musée d'Orsay) and *Nature Revealing Herself to Science* testify to the eclectic taste of this academician accustomed to success at the Salon.

Bartholomé, Albert

Thiverval, 1848 - Paris, 1928

MO - *Monument of the Dead in the Père-Lachaise*, **central section, 1899**

Bronze, reduction. 57 x 45 x 27 cm / inaugurated 1 November 1899 at Père-Lachaise cemetery, Paris / RF 3881

MO - *Monument to Jean-Jacques Rousseau*, **1907-10;**
central high-relief: *Philosophy, Truth and Nature*

Plaster model. 215 x 230 x 95 cm / Commissioned 1907 / RF 3738, 3739, 3740

The artist to whom, in 1887, the state and the city of Paris entrusted the significant commission of a war memorial for Père-Lachaise cemetery was a painter who had only turned his hand to sculpting to build a tomb for his wife. Exhibited in 1895, the plaster model aroused great admiration and occasioned many subsequent orders, such as the *Monument to Jean-Jacques Rousseau*, inaugurated at the Panthéon in Paris in 1912. A remarkable portraitist and friend of Degas, whose wax figures he would restore, Bartholomé never deviated from a sense of well-modelled and well-balanced form that transcends realism and fits in skilfully with the architectural setting concerned.

Barye, Antoine-Louis

Paris, 1795 - *ibid,* 1875

ML - *Lion au serpent [Lion with Snake]*, **1835 Salon**

Lost-wax process bronze by Honoré Gonon in 1835. 135 x 178 x 96 cm / The plaster model dated 1832 was presented at the 1833 Salon / Commissioned for the Jardin des Tuileries where it stood 1836-1911. Acquisition, Louis-Philippe, 1836 / Department of Sculpture / LP 1184

MO - *La Paix [Peace]*, **1855**

Model third life-size, stained plaster. 105 x 91 x 70 cm / Gift of J Zoubaloff, 1912 / RF 1557

An avid reader of the naturalists Lacépède and Geoffroy St-Hilaire, who founded the menagerie in the Jardin des Plantes in Paris, it was Barye who raised animal sculpture to the status of a major genre. Impregnated with a romantic view of life in the wild, his own menagerie impressed not only the public but King Louis-Philippe, who saw the bronze lions he ordered from the artist as a paean to monarchy. Barye oversaw the casting of the bronzes himself, earning his living by marketing the many copies. His founder Gonon was so adroit he could execute a cast in a single pouring. The Second Empire allowed Barye to display his genius as a sculptor beyond his chosen field: the groups for the Louvre (*War, Order, Force, Peace*) 1854-55, and *Napoleon as a Roman Emperor* in Ajaccio (1865) are traditional in spirit and facture.

Bellmer, Hans

Katowice (Poland), 1902 - Paris, 1975

CP - *Die Puppe [The Doll]*, **1932/45**

Painted wood, hair, shoes, socks. 61 x 170 x 51 cm / Gift of the artist to the state, 1972; Transferred, 1976 / AM 1976-927

Bellmer was a visionary artist thrown into the cauldron of the 20th century on the Nazis' ascension to power, which led him to move to Paris in 1938. His singular body of work is shot through by a determination to counter the instrumentalisation of art by ideology. To this end, he chose a theme borrowed from childhood and playground and from popular art, but also from the German Romanticism of Novalis and E T A Hoffmann: the doll. A friend of Rilke and the author with Nora Mitrani of anagrams, the artist proceeded to disjoint and recombine the anatomy of the doll as one might a line of verse. The first doll dates to 1932-34 and the second to 1937. In 1949 Paul Eluard brought out a collection of poems entitled *Les Jeux de la poupée* illustrated with photographs by Bellmer. A dazzling draughtsman and a consummate photographer who set up his compositions meticulously, Bellmer has exerted a considerable influence on the contemporary art scene, in particular on body art and on the representation of the body in general, but also on the relationship between sculpture and photography.

Bernard, Joseph

Vienne (Isère), 1866 - Boulogne-Billancourt (Ile-de-France), 1931

MO - *Effort vers la nature [Effort Towards Nature]*, 1905-06

Lens stone. 32 x 29 x 31 cm / Gift of the artist's son, Jean Bernard, 1980 / RF 3513

MO - *Porteuse d'eau [The Water-Carrier]*, 1912

Bronze. 175 x 40 x 52 cm / Acquisition, 1917 / RF 3161

At the beginning of the 20th century, Bernard, son of a stonemason, was to revive the art of direct carving in the manner of Michelangelo, with the intention of creating a purified art nourished by archaic Greek and Asian sources. Bernard steered a course between the pioneering idea of form revealing material (*Effort Towards Nature*) and a stylised, harmonious figuration founded on simplified volumes and a sense of rhythm. These qualities reappear in his large-scale pieces, notably his *Monument to Michel Servet* (1911), executed in the city of his birth, and the frieze of the *Dance*, an enlarged version of which was commissioned by the state for the Pavillon du Collectionneur designed by Ruhlmann for the 1925 International Exhibition of Decorative Arts.

Beuys, Joseph

Clèves (Germany), 1921 – Düsseldorf, 1986

CP - *Plight*, 1985

Installation: 43 elements with 5 felt rolls each, grand piano, blackboard, thermometer. 310 x 890 x 1813 cm / Purchased with the aid of Anthony d'Offay and David Sylvester in memory of the artist, 1989 / AM 1989-545

Beuys's largely autobiographical oeuvre excels in transforming episodes from his life in the context of a strictly artistic logic, the consequence of which is to mythologise (and mystify) real life. From the memory of a tram-stop at Trier to the rather improbable episode of the Tartars who saved his life after he crash-landed his bomber in the Crimea in 1943, it is Beuys's lived experience, be it legendary or authentic, that lies at the origin of actions such as 'I Like America and America Likes Me', during which he spent a week shut up in the René Block gallery with a coyote (New York, 1974). Becoming professor at the Academy of Fine Art in Düsseldorf in 1959, the artist made performance (from actions proper to public debate) into such an integral mode of his expression — to the point of developing for himself a character who always wore an easily recognisable costume — that the ability of his productions to survive to him was sometimes brought into question. The installations or spatial arrangements of his fetish materials (fat, felt, musical instruments, shaman's stick) nevertheless still possess a strong participatory dimension: 'social sculpture', as this cofounder of the Green movement in Germany put it.

Biegas, Boleslas

Kozicyn (Poland), 1877 - Paris, 1954

MO - *The Sphinx*, 1902

Plaster. 46 x 39 x 11 cm / Acquisition, 1987 / RF 4187

This 'new Giotto', who (like Brancusi) worked as a shepherd until an adolescent, was discovered by his village priest and soon outstripped his masters. In 1901, he joined the Vienna Secession before making his way to Paris where he was to work for the rest of his life. He gravitated towards Symbolism, whose review, *La Plume*, acclaimed his work in 1902. If with its dense metaphysical and philosophical content his oeuvre readily takes inspiration from literary themes, it is equally impregnated by Polish folk art. In his reliefs Biégas manages to liberate forms that eschew all naturalism and in which spirit and geometry triumph in a kind of prefiguration of Cubism.

Bontemps, Pierre

Recorded 1536-68

ML - *Tomb of Charles de Maigny*, third quarter of 16th century

Verdun stone. 145 x 70 x 42 cm / From the Musée des Monuments Français, 1818 / Department of Sculpture / MR 1729

It was under Henri II that Pierre Bontemps, who had worked on the Château de Fontainebleau (1536), carried out the commission that was to make his name — the majority of the figures for the tomb of François 1er for the basilica of St-Denis (1548-52) — and the urn for the king's heart, commissioned by Primaticcio. There, the sculptor attained his true style, marked by a realism that is palpable in the gisants of the king and queen. His vocation proved to be the funerary effigy. The statue of Charles de Maigny (died 1556) is a prime example of the defunct sleeping, leaning on his elbows, seemingly drifting off from slumber into death, from life into nothingness. Converting to Protestantism just as the religious climate of the kingdom was becoming fraught, Bontemps left Paris in 1566.

Bosio, François-Joseph

Monaco, 1768 - Paris, 1845

ML - *Hercule combattant Achéloüs métamorphosé en serpent
[Hercules Fighting with Achelous Transformed into a Snake]*, 1824

Bronze cast by Carbonneaux. Plaster model exhibited at the 1814 Salon.

260 x 210 x 95 cm / Commission by Charles X, 1822 / Department of Sculpture /
LL 325

An adventurer in the Revolutionary army, rebuffed by his master
Pajou, taken up by Napoleon, and made a baron at the Restoration,
the sculptor Bosio was an artist at the crossroads. Between
Revolution and Empire on one hand and the Restoration on the
other, he oscillated between Neoclassicism and a Romanticism
verging on historicism. His works reflect an era that sought to
reconcile the present through the glories of the past: the *quadriga*
on the Arc du Carrousel, the *Louis XIV* in place des Victories and
the graceful *Salmacis Leaving the Bath* (1819-37), a counterpart to
the brutal *Hercules Fighting Achelous* (1814-24), which took the
essence of heroic Neoclassicism from Canova. He was also the
author of *Henri IV as a Child,* perhaps the first of the genre of
'famous children', many of which were to follow in the 19th
century, by Rude and Carpeaux, in particular.

Bouchardon, Edme

Chaumont-en-Bassigny (Champagne), 1698 - Paris, 1762

ML - *Sleeping Faun,* 1726-30

Marble. 184 x 142 x 119 cm / Entered the Louvre in 1892 /
Department of Sculpture / MR 1921

ML - *L'Amour se faisant un arc de la massue d'Hercule
[Love Cutting his Bow from the Club of Hercules]*, 1750

Marble. 173 x 75 x 75 cm / Entered the Louvre in 1824 / Department of Sculpture /
MR 1761

Pupil of Guillaume I Coustou and eternal rival of his comrade
Lambert-Sigisbert Adam, Bouchardon, as classical as Adam was
Baroque, was resident in Rome from 1722 to 1730. There he
executed much admired copies of the Antique (*Sleeping Faun*).
His portraits of Roman society, such as that of Von Stosch
(1727), marked the break with the taste for *rocaille*. If his projects for urban sculpture in Rome came to nothing, he did
manage to carry out the fountain on rue de Grenelle to the glory
of the city of Paris. With rigorous simplicity in line and composition, the sculpture more than holds its own against the architecture. In Bouchardon, an idea always lurks behind even the most
naturalistic form, with the result that his *Love Cutting his Bow*
met with total public incomprehension.

Bourdelle, Emile-Antoine

Montauban, 1861 - Le Vésinet (Ile-de-France), 1929

MO - *Héraklès tue les oiseaux du lac Stymphale,* or *Héraklès archer
[Hercules Killing the Stymphalian Birds,* also known as *Herakles
Archer]* (second version), 1909

Gilt bronze. 248 x 247 x 123 cm / Acquisition, 1924 / RF 3174

The 'faithful' Bourdelle, studio assistant and friend of Rodin, was
anything but a slavish follower. He possessed the temperament of
a lyric sculptor, at ease with powerful personalities, a Beethoven
or a Mickiewicz for instance, a visionary who composed epics in
bronze but who found sustenance in both the Roman tradition
and archaic Greece. And he was an innovator too. The War
Memorial at Montauban (1893-1902) marries the strength of
Puget to the dynamic sensitivity of Carpeaux or Rodin. As Rodin
was to remark, Bourdelle's *Head of Apollo* (1900) shows him
leaving the master and moving on to a synthetic manner that
overlays Rodin's analysis of form with a sense of structure
through planes and facets that is redolent of the early investiga-
tions of Cubism. *Herakles Archer* prizes open the carved block,
endowing it once again with depth and an orientation in space.
Bourdelle's sense of architecture transpires as much in his bas-
reliefs for the Théâtre des Champs-Elysées (1913) as in the
monuments to General Carlos María de Alvear (Buenos Aires,
1925) and to Mickiewicz (Paris, 1929). In that hive of international activity that was the Académie de la Grande-Chaumière, the
artist trained several generations of artists, including Alberto
Giacometti and Germaine Richier. In 1949, his daughter founded
a museum devoted to his work in his Montparnasse studio (the
Musée Bourdelle), which is a rewarding visit; the pungent prose
of this poet-sculptor is also enlightening.

Bourgeois, Louise

Paris, 1911

CP - *Precious Liquids*, 1992

Environment: water tank in cedarwood ringed in metal, glass, alabaster, fabric, embroidery, water, rubber balls. 427 x 442 cm / Purchase, 1993 / AM 1993-28

A student of Fernand Léger and a friend of Bonnard and André Breton, this American by adoption, who married the sculpture historian, Robert Goldwater, draws her inspiration from the boundless imagination of the dream. Taking up sculpture in 1949, she produced environments and performances in the 1970s before reverting to a more figurative vein in the 1980s. Constituents for the subjects of her sculpture appear in her 'drawings of insomnia' and her poetic writings, about childhood trauma, the relationship to the adult world and to female sexuality, and visions of a body transmogrified by phantasms. These preoccupations spawn a world of Richier-like insects (including a giant spider named *Maman*), but also eyes and sexually charged protuberances treated in various materials, from the most traditional, such as stone, to the most synthetic. In giving form to the artist's most intimate thoughts, her installations, like the *Magic Rooms (Cells)*, give viewers a sense of the unworldly.

Brancusi, Constantin

Pestisani (Romania), 1876 – Paris, 1957

CP - *The Newborn II*, 1915

Polished bronze, plinth in four parts: polished bronze (disc), marble (cross), oak, limestone (round). 17 x 25.5 x 17 cm / Constantin Brancusi bequest, 1957 / AM 4002-33

CP - *Mlle Pogany III*, 1933

Bronze. 44.5 x 19 x 27 cm / Constantin Brancusi bequest, 1957 / AM 4002-54

CP - *Le Coq [The Cockerel]*, 1935

Polished bronze, plinth in four parts: limestone, oak. 103.4 x 12.1 x 29.5 cm / Purchase, 1947 / AM 817 S

The exceptional gifts of the youthful shepherd from the Carpathians brought him to the art school in Bucharest (1898) and in 1904 to the Parisian studio of Antoine Mercié. Though influenced by Rodin's modelling and mixing in the cosmopolitan avant-garde, Brancusi was very much his own man. Like the Cubists, he abandoned the nude and from *Sleeping Muse* (1906) on created simple volumes stamped with a strong cosmic symbolism: the oval evokes an egg, the expanding form of the universe. Brancusi began by preferring to carve directly in stone, before working in wood from 1913. This artist-artisan was fond of combining materials and polished his gilded bronzes himself. Whenever he departed from the observed motif, in particular in portraits, such as *Mlle Pogany*, it was to pare it down to its abstract structure and dynamic power. Each new theme (*The Newborn, The Cockerel*) was produced in series in divers materials and treatments. For Brancusi, sculpture represented the essence of architecture: in India, he worked on a project for a Temple of Deliverance (1933), while in 1937-38 at Tirgu Jiu (Romania), he completed a memorial to the war dead comprising the *Gate of the Kiss*, the *Table of Silence* and the *Endless Column*. Through his renewal of the plinth, his serial and modular procedures, his geometric abstraction and his practice of photography (no less than 506 pictures of the studio and his works are preserved at the Centre Pompidou), Brancusi exerted a considerable influence over 20th-century art. The bequest of his workshop to the French state represents an exceptional memorial to the creativity of contemporary art. The studio has since been reconstituted in a building on the piazza in front of the Centre Pompidou.

Buren, Daniel

Boulogne-Billancourt (Ile-de-France), 1938

CP - *Cabane éclatée n° 6: les damiers,* 1985. Photo-souvenir: Philippe Migeat

Wooden structure and fabric with vertical stripes alternately white and golden yellow measuring 8.7 cm each; the joins between each bolt of cloth are painted white on the front. 283 x 424.5 x 283 cm / Purchase, 1990 / AM 1990-87

Initially a painter, in 1965 Buren unveiled his first canvas featuring vertical bands 8.7 cm wide at ground level and partly leaning against the wall. He then gained further exposure as a member of the BMPT group formed in 1967. His debut *Painting-Sculpture* dates to 1971 and was realised for a group show at the Guggenheim Museum, New York. A long, striped banner was to be hung from the glass canopy over the centre of the circular interior space, while a similar one was to be placed outside. The idea was to prevent the institution exerting control over the piece. Its rejection by the other artists in the exhibition, however, precluded its being installed. In the years 1970-80, these stripes appeared in various site-specific interventions, operating as a 'visual tool' for the analysis of space. Commonly known as 'Buren's columns', *Les Deux plateaux* in the Palais Royal (1986) in Paris caused a furore before being followed by a replica on place des Terreaux in Lyon. In 1982, Buren, who possesses no studio and who lives on the sites of the various projects he undertakes across the world, embarked on a series of *Cabanes* (Huts). These constituted the main theme of the retrospective devoted to the artist at the Centre Pompidou in 2002, entitled 'The Museum Which Does Not Exist'.

Caffieri, Jean-Jacques

Paris, 1725 - *ibid,* 1792

ML - *Canon Alexandre-Gui Pingré (1711-1796),* 1788

Terracotta. 51 x 51 x 34 cm / Accession to the Louvre 1909 / Department of Sculpture / RF 1496

Awarded the sculpture prize in 1748, Caffieri was the great rival of Houdon. Like the latter, he was a remarkable portraitist, known especially for busts of his contemporaries, such as this one of Canon Pingré, the reworked terracotta bozzetto for which was presented at the 1789 Salon. Through a physiognomic approach, Caffieri developed a penetrating psychological analysis of the sitter. He also produced posthumous portraits, so it was to this brilliant academician that D'Angiviller entrusted the statues of Molière and Corneille for his Galerie des Illustres.

Calder, Alexander

Philadelphia, 1898 – New York, 1976

CP - *Josephine Baker I,* also called *Dance,* 1926

Wire. 100.5 x 84 x 21 cm / Gift of the artist 1966 / AM 1518 S

CP - *Four Leaves and Three Petals,* 1939

Mobile on foot: sheet-steel, painted metal struts, wire. 205 x 174 x 135 cm / Gift in lieu, 1983 / AM 1983-56

Son and grandson of sculptors, Calder initially studied as an engineer before training at the Art Student League in New York. Sketches of the Barnum Circus for a newspaper (1923) culminated in *The Circus* (1926), a group of figurines made out of wire and wood, which he manipulated himself or had fitted with a motor. Following this wire sculpture phase and the introduction of motion in his work, in 1931 Calder joined the association Abstraction-Création. A visit to Mondrian's studio induced him to build coloured geometrical forms in metal, first 'stabiles' (1931), then 'mobiles' (1932), which he allowed to move freely in the air, rather than by motor. His cutout aerial structures, such as his last large-scale mobile realised for the National Gallery of Washington, were extremely complex. Calder, who spent the last years of his life at Saché in the Touraine, produced an impressive number of monumental *stabiles* all over the world, which have become landmarks in their cities.

Canova, Antonio

Possagno, 1757 - Venice, 1822

ML - *Psyche Revived by the Kiss of Love,* 1787-1801

Marbre. 155 x 168 x 101 cm / Commissioned by Colonel John Campbell in 1787 / Acquisition, 1801 by Joachim Murat / Department of Sculpture / MR 1777

The foremost Neoclassicist — and Stendhal's favourite sculptor — trained in Venice before settling in Rome in 1780. There his *Theseus and the Dead Minotaur* (1781-83), created in the spirit of Winckelmann's ideal beauty, earned him the support and friendship of the art and architectural theorist Quatremère de Quincy. Canova's rigour found perfect expression in monuments carved for popes and other great figures, including Maria Cristina of Austria, while his mythological compositions, such as the *Cupids* and his *Psyche* in the Louvre, kindled a vogue for a refined style in which graceful figures of androgynous adolescents fuse sensuality, eroticism and formal purity. A notable portraitist — think of his effigy of the nude Pauline Borghese — he could master the heroic, when inspired by the ancient poets, as well as a more pathetic vein, in the religious subjects of the end of his life. Painter, director of the pontifical museums and responsible for the restitution of artworks taken to France by Napoleon during his Italian campaign, Canova erected a Pantheon in his birthplace at Possagno. His plaster models were reunited in his house-studio after his death.

Carpeaux, Jean-Baptiste
Valenciennes, 1827 – Courbevoie (Ile-de-France), 1875

ML - *Pêcheur à la coquille*
[Young Fisherman with a Shell or *The Fisherboy]*, 1858
Original plaster model. 91 x 47 x 54 cm / Acquisition, 1900 / Department
of Sculpture, deposit by Musée d'Orsay / RF 1317

MO - *Anna Foucart*, 1860
Patinated plaster mask. 19 x 13 x 7 cm / Gift of the heirs of Mme Schommer, 1979 /
RF 3415

MO - *Ugolin [Ugolino]*, 1860
Bronze. 194 x 148 x 119 cm / Commissioned 1862 / RF 2994

MO - *La France impériale portant la lumière dans le monde
et protégeant l'Agriculture et la Science [Imperial France Bringing
Light to the World and Protecting Agriculture and Science]*, 1866
Half-size original plaster model. 268 x 427 x 162 cm / Stone sculpture commissioned
1863. Acquired from the sculptor's widow in 1892 / RF 1948-50

MO - *La Danse [The Dance]*, 1868
Half-size original plaster model. 232 x 148 x 115 cm / Stone sculpture commissioned
by Charles Garnier for the facade of the Palais Garnier in 1863. Acquisition, 1889 /
RF 818

MO - *Les Quatre Parties du monde soutenant la sphère céleste
[The Four Quarters of the World Bearing the Celestial Sphere]*, 1873
Plaster model with bronze patina. 280 x 177 x 145 cm / Bronze commissioned
by the city of Paris in 1867 / Acquisition, 1889 / RF 817

A sign of changing times: Carpeaux was one of the last major sculptors to strive to win the Prix de Rome, obtaining it after a ten-year struggle in 1854. His bold originality, however, steered him increasingly into the orbit of Rude, whom he admired, rather than towards the Academy. The striking *Ugolino* group (1860) shows that the artist who came to exemplify the reign of Napoleon III possessed ambitions that exceeded those of a mere decorator. Besides sculptures made for the Louvre and his portrait of the imperial prince (1865), Carpeaux, who was also a painter, executed sculpture groups, such as *The Dance* for the Paris opera house and *The Four Quarters of the World* for the fountain in the Jardins de l'Observatoire, which testify to a seldom equalled control of intricacy and movement. The liveliness of his figures, initially expressed in brilliantly executed sketches, is transferred intact to the jubilant smiles in the final versions. Carpeaux was also the author of remarkably lifelike portraits in the vein of Houdon, such as that of his friend and protector, the architect Charles Garnier. It is impossible to understand Rodin without reference to Carpeaux.

Carrier-Belleuse (Albert-Ernest Carrier de Belleuse)
Anisy-le-Château (Picardy), 1824 – Sèvres (Ile-de-France), 1887

MO - *Hébé endormie [Sleeping Hebe]*, 1869
Marble. 207 x 146 x 85 cm / Commissioned 1868 / RF 163

MO - *Torchère au tambourin [Torchère with Tambourine]*, 1873
Plaster model. H: 260 cm; diam (base): 90 cm / Gift of Mme Carrier-Belleuse to the
Union Centrale des Arts Décoratifs, 1891 / DO 1979-88

Nephew of the astronomer François Arago, pupil at the Petite Ecole that catered for all those who, like Rodin, failed the entrance exam to the Ecole des Beaux-Arts, friend of Carpeaux and Charles Garnier, Carrier-Belleuse is often regarded as an artist of second-rank whose finest pieces are only 'overmantels'. He is, admittedly, a decorative sculptor, who modelled figures for porcelain pieces before becoming director of artistic works at the Manufacture at Sèvres in 1876, where he employed a young Rodin. Nonetheless, when tackling life-size and even monumental pieces, he brought the freshness and vivacity of the School of Fontainebleau he so admired to the eclectic art of his day. His airy, often dizzying manner culminates in *Sleeping Hebe* and in the *Torchères* he made for the Paris Opéra. Author of many pattern books, Carrier-Belleuse was also instrumental in promoting the industrial arts. He was one of the founder members of the Union Centrale des Arts Décoratifs, which in 1864 replaced the Société du Progrès de l'Art Industriel founded in 1845.

Carriès, Jean-Joseph-Marie
Lyon, 1855 - Paris, 1894

MO - *Masque d'horreur [Masque of Horror]*, 1891
Enamelled stoneware. 28 x 22 cm / Acquisition, 1993 / OAO 1269

MO - *Faun*, 1893
Bronze. 35.3 x 34 x 23 cm / Formerly Leys collection. Acquisition, 1984 / RF 3679

This artist from Lyon, who settled in Paris in 1874 as a student of Jacques-Edme Dumont, started out with masks depicting wretched-looking or impoverished figures. His work was remarked on at the 1881 and 1883 Salons, where he exhibited a plaster piece, *Charles I* (Musée d'Orsay), inspired by a funeral mask, and the bust of a bishop. Excellent portraitist, he also mastered the elevated style in portraits of types: nun, warrior, miner, baby, etc. Fascinated by the bizarre, he depicted himself in the guise of a faun. In tandem with master-founder Pierre Bingen, he gave a new lease of life to the lost-wax process, in the process obtaining some astonishing patinas. His encounter with Japanese ceramics led him to pottery. His great work is a project for the *Gate of Parsifal* in enamelled stoneware commissioned in 1889 by Princess Scey-Montbéliard to house Wagner's manuscript. Of symbolist and fantastic inspiration, certain elements of the Gate were exhibited to acclaim at the Salon de la Société Nationale des Beaux-Arts in 1892. The painted plaster model is now in the Musée du Petit Palais in Paris.

César (César Baldiccini)

Marseille, 1921 – Paris, 1908

CP - *Expansion No. 14,* 1970

Expanded polyurethane, laminated and varnished. 100 x 270 x 220 cm / Purchased
by the State, 1971; attribution: 1976 / AM 1976-938

The first successful work by this Marseille-born artist of Italian extraction, who travelled up to Paris in 1943, was a scrap-iron bestiary (1954), which combined the influences of the masters of metal sculpture (González, Picasso) with those of Giacometti and Germaine Richier. After producing sculptures in the round and *Plaques,* he created a scandal at the 1960 Salon de Mai with a display of three crushed car *Compressions.* Pierre Restany enrolled him in the group of Nouveaux Réalistes. The enormous orange *Expansion* at the 1967 Salon de Mai was the first of his expanded polyurethane foam 'castings', a spectacular conjunction of technology and random processes. Experimenting with the most diverse materials, the sculptor then created enlarged imprints of body parts, starting with *Thumb* in 1965. Gaining in celebrity, he garnered commissions for monumental pieces, such as *The Centaur* (Carrefour de la Croix-Rouge, Paris, 1983) and the *Plaque Eiffel* at the Cartier Foundation at Jouy-en-Josas (1984-89). From then until his death, he continued in a more introspective vein that ranged from squared-up self-portraits to *Vanitas* with more than a hint of Surrealist assemblage.

Chamberlain, John

Rochester (Indiana), 1927

CP - *The Bride,* 1988

Chrome-plated and enamelled sheet metal. 216 x 120 x 114 cm / Purchase, 1990 /
AM 1990-226

A graduate of the artistic hotbed that was Black Mountain College (North Carolina), Chamberlain is, with Richard Stankiewicz, one of the foremost exponents of junk art, which specialises in recycling rubbish. As early as 1956 in an installation in New York, he incorporated car bodies in soldered metal sculptures with the twofold effect of bringing art closer to social reality and introducing colour. By analogy with Pollock's Action painting, one might describe his work as 'action sculpture'. In effect, the artist acts on his materials, twisting, warping, and soldering the sheet metal in interventions that remain visible in the end product. Like the Frenchman César, Chamberlain explores the expressive possibilities of modern materials, while participating in the great creative recycling of industrial civilisation undertaken simultaneously on either side of the Atlantic by Rauschenberg and the neo-Dadaists on one hand and French *affichistes* and Nouveaux Réalistes on the other.

Chapu, Henri

Le Mée-sur-Seine (Ile-de-France), 1833 – Paris, 1891

MO - *Jeanne d'Arc à Domrémy [Joan of Arc at Domrémy],* 1870/1871

Marble exhibited at the 1870 Salon. 117 x 92 x 83 cm / Acquisition, 1872.
Deposited at Amboise, 1967 / Transferred to Musée d'Orsay, 1999 / RF 166

Of modest origins, Chapu first trained in a free drawing school, and then at the Ecole des Beaux-Arts in Paris where he was a pupil of James Pradier. Awarded the Prix de Rome in 1855, he spent six years at the Académie de France, copying ancient statues such as the *Spinario* (marble, 1858, Ecole des Beaux-Arts, Paris) and *Mercury Inventing the Caduceus* (marble, 1862, Musée d'Orsay). In pieces of his own authorship, like *Christ with the Angels* (1857, Musée Chapu, Le Mée), a striving for an original expressive intensity distinguishes his art from the academic. He encountered great success with *Joan of Arc* (1872), long displayed at Amboise. As testified in *Youth* (1875, Ecole des Beaux-Arts, Paris) and the recumbent statue of the Duchesse d'Orléans (1885, chapel royal at Dreux), Chapu knew better than most how to render drapery discreetly yet effectively so as to emphasise attitudes of conviction. There is a museum devoted to his work in his native town.

Chaudet, Antoine-Denis

Paris, 1763 - *ibid,* 1810

ML - *Peace,* 1806

Silver, silver gilt, bronze and gilded bronze. 167 x 108 x 84 cm / Commissioned
on the occasion of the Peace of Amiens and cast by Jean-Baptiste Chéret (1760-1832),
under the direction of Dominique Vivant Denon, director of the Musée Napoléon /
Department of Sculpture / MR 3554

With his relief *Joseph Sold by His Brothers* (1784), Chaudet emerged as the most remarkable French Neoclassical sculptor of the Napoleonic era. After a stay in Rome (1784-88), he executed the statue of Napoleon that adorned — until its demolition under the Commune — the top of the column in place Vendôme in Paris. If Canova's influence remains perceptible in his work, especially in its elegant handling and use of allegory, the Frenchman is deliberately more severe than the Italian, preferring compact forms and revelling in combinations of rare metals, as in *Peace.* Even more than his *Oedipus and Phorbas* (1799), Chaudet's fame was assured by his posthumous marble *Love,* finished by Cartellier (1817, Louvre), in which a gracefully kneeling Eros holds out a rose to a butterfly, the incarnation of the soul (Psyche), which has a finesse of allusion and subtlety of meaning untainted by the affectation that afflicted so many of Canova's epigones.

Chillida, Eduardo

1924, San Sebastián (Espagne) – *ibid,* 2002

CP - *Gravitation,* **1989**

Cut-outs and Indian ink on handmade amate paper glue-mounted on paper.

122 x 80.5 cm / Purchase, 1992 / AM 1992-90

Returning to San Sebastián, the capital of the Spanish Basque country, after starting a course of architecture in Madrid, Chillida developed an abstract art founded on the painstaking and sensitive implementation of materials, such as iron, alabaster, steel and cement. He became particularly interested in Basque carved funerary steles and traditional metalworking. His great love of Greek civilisation led him to create an art that could mediate between man and the world, in the sense that sculpture would both 'eulogise' and be the stage for an 'encounter' (words that recur in his titles) between the elements of air (space), earth (matter), fire (light) and water (sea). He thus produced monumental sculptures such as *Zuhaitz* (Grenoble) and the *Wind Combs* that are built into the rocky shoreline near San Sebastián. Drawing also constituted an essential activity, all the more so since his sculpture can be considered from the perspective of engraving and the symbolism of signs. The *Gravitations* made of cut out, suspended sheets are a fascinating demonstration of this relationship. The Chillida Foundation near San Sebastián provides an opportunity to take the measure of his oeuvre.

Christo (Christo Javacheff)

Gabrovo (Bulgaria), 1935

CP - *Package on a Table,* **1961**

Wood, various objects, velvet, canvas, string. 134.5 x 43.5 x 44.5 cm / Purchase, 1982 / AM 1982-323

Christo was still a student at the Academy of Fine Arts at Sofia (1952-56) when he participated on a landscaping project for the Orient Express line. He moved to the West in 1956, settling in Paris in 1958 where he mixed with the Nouveau Réaliste group and produced object 'wrappings'. Perhaps his taste for engaging in long and complicated projects that require all kinds of authorisations and preliminary discussions derives from past confrontations with state bureaucracy or from an enthusiasm for his newfound freedom — or perhaps both at once. Assisted by his wife, Jeanne-Claude, after having wrapped the Kunsthalle in Bern in 1968, he constructed *The Running Fence,* a 'fleeing enclosure' visible from the moon (1976), surrounded Florida islands with pink corollas floating on the sea (*Surrounded Islands,* 1983, off Miami), wrapped the Pont-Neuf in Paris (1985), and opened simultaneously hundreds of parasols on both sides of the Atlantic (1991). Their pieces are all financed by sales of byproducts from earlier operations (drawings, photographs, collages). Their most recent project, entitled *The Gates,* placed 7,500 arches draped in saffron-coloured cloth banners along paths in New York's Central Park (February 2005).

Christophe, Ernest

Loches (Indre-et-Loire), 1827 - Paris, 1892

MO - *La Comédie Humaine* or *Le Masque [The Human Comedy* or *The Mask],* **1857/76**

Marble. 245 x 85 x 72 cm / Acquisition, 1876 / RF 285

A pupil of François Rude — who moreover signed the tomb of Godefroy Cavaignac with the words 'Rude and Christophe, his young pupil' — Christophe, like all the Romantic sculptor's disciples, encountered considerable difficulties with the officials of the Salon. Inclined to envisage existence from a tragic perspective that only the love of art could allay, he exacerbated his situation by joining the ranks of the Symbolists. The Third Republic nonetheless purchased this work, the inspiration behind Baudelaire's poem of same name, dedicated to the artist that appeared in *The Flowers of Evil:* the factitious mask of joy removed, there remains only a face in pain. The Musée d'Orsay also possesses two of Christophe's groups: *Fatality* and *The Supreme Kiss. Douleur (Suffering)* by his own hand appears on the artist's tomb in Batignolles cemetery in Paris.

Claudel, Camille

Fère-en-Tardenois (Picardy), 1864 - Villeneuve-lès-Avignon, 1943

MO - *L'Âge mûr [The Age of Maturity],* **1899-1903**

Bronze group in three parts. 114 x 163 x 72 cm / Acquisition, 1982 / RF 3606

Sister of the writer Paul Claudel, Camille Claudel was both a model for (as in *Thought,* 1886) and a pupil of Rodin, with whom she engaged in a passionate affair. Her strength lies in a capacity to elevate to a level seldom attained the fusion between plastic themes inherited from tradition or from Rodin and dramatic autobiographical accents. Corresponding to the period of her breakup with Rodin (1898), works, such as *Clotho* (1893-99) and *The Age of Maturity* (1895-99), are deeply rooted in her personal life. *Sakountala* (1886-1905) and *The Waltz* (1889-1905), the return to direct carving in *Perseus and the Gorgon* (1898-1902), the taste for polychromy using unusual materials and Art Nouveau spirit of *The Wave,* and her delicate interpretation of informal and feminine themes show her ability to innovate, even if Rodinian themes are noticeably recurrent. Sectioned in 1913, Camille Claudel's correspondence (later published) is poignant. As Rodin himself stipulated, the Musée Rodin in Paris has a room set aside for her work.

Clésinger, Auguste (Jean-Baptiste Clésinger)
Besançon, 1814 - Paris, 1883
MO - *Femme piquée par un serpent [Woman Bitten by a Snake]*, 1847
Marble. 56 x 180 x 70 cm / Acquisition, 1931 / RF 2053
Son of a sculptor, briefly pupil of Thorvaldsen and of David
d'Angers, Clésinger is a man of one work: the artist behind the
scandal of *The Woman Bitten by a Snake*, presented at the 1847
Salon. But let there be no mistake: the artist did not thereby
become the Courbet of sculpture; the realistic moulding sought in
fact to flatter the eye and did not lead him to naturalism. From
1859 to 1863, he lived in Italy. On his return in 1864, the Second
Empire made him one of its official sculptors. For the Palace of
Industry he realised equestrian statues of Napoleon and
Charlemagne, as well as a Napoleon III, together with portraits
of George Sand for the Théâtre Français, and the actress Rachel,
who also posed for him as Tragedy. After the fall of the Second
Empire in 1871, Clésinger's popularity waned, though he did
obtain an order for four equestrian statues, originally intended
for the facade of the Ecole Militaire, of which only three (Hoche,
Kléber and Marceau) were ever carried out.

Clodion (Claude Michel)
Nancy, 1738 - Paris, 1814
ML - *Pan poursuivant Syrinx sous le regard de l'Amour*
[Pan and Syrinx or *Pan Pursuing Syrinx as Love Looks On]*, 1782
Tonnerre stone. 104 x 323 x 23 cm / From the bathroom at the Hôtel de Besenval,
Paris / Gift in lieu, 198 / Department of Sculpture / RF 4200
A nephew of the Adam brothers, the young Clodion trained with
Lambert-Sigisbert Adam and Jean-Baptiste Pigalle before staying in
Italy from 1762 to 1771. He is at his best in modest formats, his
favourite material being terracotta. He produced reliefs and vases for
a discerning clientele who particularly prized his at once graceful
and lively treatment of mythological subjects. He was inseparable
from the architect Alexandre Théodore Brongniart and together
they were responsible for building and decorating any number of
private mansions in Paris, in particular Baron de Besenval's *hôtel
particulier* in the Faubourg-St-Germain. As a statue of Montesquieu
betrays (Louvre, 1783), he proved less at ease in marble statuary
than in the countless highly imaginative little groups turned out by
his studio in which his three brothers also practiced. In a neo-
Alexandrine taste, putti compete with the fluid folds engulfing
young women, whose sensuality is further enhanced by the warm
tones of terracotta. The Revolution was like the arrival of
Savonarola for this Botticelli of modelling: under the prevalent
Neo-Greek taste, Clodion's 18th-century *galanterie* was outmoded.
Although never really at home with the heroic nude or with colossal

formats, during the Empire, he nonetheless worked on the relief
on the Arc du Carrousel and for the Senate (*Cato of Utica*)
before dying forgotten; his reputation, however, has long since
been reestablished.

Colombe, Michel
c. 1430 - Tours, c. 1512-15
ML - *Saint Georges combattant le dragon*
[St George Slaying the Dragon], 1509-1510
Marbre. 128 x 182 x 17 cm / Executed in 1509-10 in Tours for the attarpiece
of the upper chapel at the Château de Gaillon (Eure) / Entry in 1816 / Department
of Sculpture / MR 1645
Unfortunately little evidence remains of the career of this sculptor from the Berry. Settling in Tours around 1495, he nevertheless
enjoyed many commissions from major figures in the royal
entourage at a time when the Loire Valley was the beating heart
of the kingdom, as well as from religious communities. The
quality of his art, which introduced Italian idioms into the
Gothic tradition, can be gauged from his masterpiece, the tomb
of François II of Brittany and Marguerite de Foix (1502-07) in
Nantes cathedral, commissioned by Anne de Bretagne. As for the
relief of *St George Slaying the Dragon*, it is a very late piece made
for the altarpiece in the upper chapel in the Château de Gaillon
(Eure), dedicated to St George, patron saint of the Cardinal
d'Amboise.

Cordier, Charles

Cambrai, 1827 - Algiers, 1905

MO - *Nègre du Soudan*, ou *Nègre en costume algérien [Negro of the Sudan or Negro in Algerian Costume]*, 1856

Bronze and marble-onyx (bust), Vosges porphyry (stand).

96 (of which stand: 20) x 66 x 36 cm / Acquisition, 1857 / RF 2997

A pupil of François Rude, who settled in Paris from 1846, the artist who might be characterised as an 'ethnographic sculptor' managed, through fieldwork undertaken in Algeria (1856), Greece (1858) and Egypt (1865), to transcend the superficial fashion for Orientalism. His busts depicting a typology of different races (1860) earned him orders from the Museum of Natural History in Paris. With an eye for new techniques, such as galvanoplasty, as well as for seductive combinations of diverse materials, he specialised in polychrome sculpture, notably the sumptuous caryatids for the Palais Garnier. He also obtained many commissions for decorative and large-scale work in Paris as well as abroad. The Musée d'Orsay recently held an exhibition of his work.

Corradini, Antonio

Este (near Venice), 1668 - Naples, 1752

ML - *Veiled Woman* or *Faith*, first half of the 18th century

Marble. 138 x 48 x 36 cm / Acquisition, 1976 / Department of Sculpture/ RF 3088

Some sculptors enjoy a reputation during their lifetime that is not sustained by posterity: this is the case with the Italian Baroque sculptor Corradini. Impregnated with a typically Neapolitan refinement and a theatrical faith, his is an art of Rococo suavity. However, his greatest creation, the *Modesty* in the chapel of Sansevero di Sangro in Naples, of which the work in the Louvre is a reinterpretation on reduced scale, is wonderfully alluring in the sensual suggestiveness of its rose-strewn veil. The body-hugging folds recall the transparent cloth in Sanmartino's *Christ with the Shroud* in the same chapel.

Coustou, Guillaume the Elder

Lyon, 1677 - Paris, 1746

ML - *Daphné poursuivie par Apollon [Daphne Pursued by Apollo]*, 1710

Marble. 132 x 135 x 65 cm / Commission for the Bassin des Carpes in the Parc de Marly. Installed in the Jardin des Tuileries 1798-1940 / Department of Sculpture / MR 1807

ML - *Cheval retenu par un palefrenier* or *Cheval de Marly [Horse Restrained by a Groom* also known as *Cheval de Marly]*, 1739-45

Carrara marble. 340 x 284 x 127 cm / Previously in the Parc de Marly and place de la Concorde, until 1984 / Department of Sculpture / MR 1802

Brother of Nicolas, with whom he executed a number of works as pairs, such as the *Daphne* of 1710, Guillaume Coustou the Elder trained like his brother in the studio of their uncle, Antoine Coysevox, and then in Rome (1697-before 1703) with Pierre Legros the Younger. He espoused the classical heritage of the age of Louis XIV, which he tried to square with the international vogue for the Baroque. A vigorous chiseller, he shows great skill in the portraits of his brother and of Marie Leszczynska, but excelled in the famous *Horses*, set up at the Parc de Marly in 1745. These latter, a counterpart to Coysevox's pair, testify not only to exceptional virtuosity — the marble was carved in just two years — but still more to Coustou's ability to renew the equestrian theme by breaking with allegory and focusing instead on the elementary forces at work in what is a pre-Romantic vision. His son, Guillaume Coustou the Younger, also followed a career as an academic sculptor.

Coustou, Nicolas

Lyon, 1658 - Paris, 1733

ML - *Apollon poursuivant Daphné [Apollo Pursuing Daphne]*, 1713

Marbre. 135 x 106 x 113 cm / Commission for the Bassin des Carpes in the Parc de Marly. Installed in the Jardin des Tuileries 1798-1940 / Department of Sculpture / MR 1805

Brother of Guillaume Coustou the Elder, he followed a similar course. Awarded the sculpture prize at the Académie Royale in 1682, he left for the French Academy in Rome in 1683. On his return he put his knowledge of the Antique to work in the great royal projects. It was in the Parc de Marly that he truly asserted his style, seen in balanced yet lively sculptures such as *Meleager Killing a Deer* (marble, 1703-06, Marly), noble figures such as his *Nymph with a Quiver* (1710, Louvre) and the dynamic *Apollo Pursuing Daphne*, in which one can easily read the influence of Bernini. In 1725, his *Virgin of the Pity*, with more disciplined handling, was erected in the choir of Notre-Dame cathedral in Paris.

Coysevox, Antoine

Lyon, 1640 - Paris, 1720

ML - *Louis II de Bourbon called le Grand Condé (1621-1686),* 1688

Bronze. 60 x 68 x 34 cm / Seized at the Revolution / Department of Sculpture / MR 3343

ML - *La Renommée montée sur Pégase [Fame Mounted on Pegasus],* 1699-1702

Carrara marble. 315 x 291 x 128 cm / Commissioned for the Parc de Marly. Placed in 1719 at the western entrance to the Jardin des Tuileries and replaced by a moulding in 1986 / Department of Sculpture / MR 1824

ML - *Berger jouant de la flûte [Shepherd Playing the Flute],* 1709

Marble. 178 x 84 x 101 cm / Originally in the Jardin des Tuileries, 1870 / Department of Sculpture / MR 1820

Hailing from Lyon, Coysevox who unusually did not go to Rome, became sculptor to the king in 1666 and embarked on an academic career in Paris in 1678. Perfectly at ease in the Antique manner, as his copy of *Venus with the Shell* testifies, he joined Le Brun's team at Versailles, with sculptures for the château's facades and the water parterre, and worked on the *Triumph of Louis XIV* in the Salon de la Guerre. We then meet him in the dome of Les Invalides and at the Château de Marly, for which he carved his celebrated horses. In parallel with his royal commissions, he executed more than fifty busts, including *Le Grand Condé,* evidence of his staggering talent as a portraitist. In addition to prestigious tombs, such as those of Colbert in the Eglise St-Eustache and Mazarin at the Institut de France, he produced an equestrian statue of Louis XIV for the city of Rennes, unfortunately destroyed during the Revolution. One of his last works, and the quintessential expression of his at once realist and noble genius, is the marble characterisation of Louis XIV in *Le Voeu de Louis XIII* in Notre-Dame cathedral in Paris.

Cragg, Tony (Anthony Cragg)

Liverpool, 1949

CP - *Opening Spiral,* 1982

Installation: mixed media. 152 x 260 x 366 cm / Purchase, 1988 / AM 1988-1061

Tony Cragg is one of the most inventive representatives of a generation that also includes Richard Long and Richard Deacon, which breathed new life into British sculpture in the 1970s and 80s. In his vast puzzles of coloured plastic debris placed initially on the ground, and later on the wall, the object dissolves, to be reconstituted anew — very like in a Schwitters collage. Diverse materials including wood and metal take their place in this dance of dynamic forms, as exemplified in *Opening Spiral.* Tony Cragg scaled-up this technique in stacks of metal shapes and enormous cast-iron sculptures. More recently, the artist has made use of glass, embarking on an investigation of biological form and the geometry of the living.

Dalou, Aimé-Jules

Paris, 1838 - *ibid,* 1902

MO - *Bacchanale,* 1879/1899

Bronze (unique example cast 1899). 59 x 19 cm / Gift of Zoubaloff in 1920 / RF 1692

MO - *Grand Paysan [Large Peasant],* 1899-1902

Bronze. 197 x 70 x 68 cm / Acquisition, 1905 / RF 2999

Noticed by Carpeaux, Dalou earned initial success in 1870 with the *Brodeuse* (*Woman Embroidering*). His commitment to the Paris Commune forced him into exile to London from 1871 to 1880, where he gained a good reputation. From London, he dispatched a model for what was to prove his masterpiece, the *Triumph of the Republic* (1880-99), commissioned by the Paris city council for the place de la Nation. Back in Paris, this committed humanist and left-wing sculptor — as we might call him today — conveyed his enthusiasm for the Republic in a classical style, which owes much to the simplicity of decorative sculpture of the reign of Louis XIV. His allegories are often couched in the features of his immediate circle, in particular his wife. As with Constantin Meunier and Rodin, cherished plans for a Monument to Labour never came to fruition.

Dampt, Jean

Venarey (Burgundy), 1854 – *ibid,* 1946

MO - *Fireplace for the Salle du Chevalier,* 1900-06

Bas-relief in Comblanchien marble. 196 x 224 x 14 cm / Made for the reception room at the residence of the Comtesse de Béarn / Gift of the patron to the Musée des Arts Décoratifs, 1927. Deposit at Musée d'Orsay, 1984 / DO 1980-16

With Jean Dampt, Symbolism takes on a *fin-de-siècle* accent. Far from the literary gravitas of Christophe or Préault, Dampt's art is one of refinement, whose mystery derives more from the manner in which it combines materials than from its subject-matter. He was one of the founders of the group Art dans Tout (Art in Everything), whose intention, modelled on the late 19th-century English Arts and Crafts movement championed by William Morris, was to attain nobility for the industrial crafts by means of a thorough-going renewal of decorative arts. The decoration of the residence of the Comtesse de Béarn, carried out in collaboration with a number of others, falls totally within this sphere.

Daumier, Honoré

Marseille, 1808 - Valmondois (Ile-de-France), 1879

MO - *Ratapoil,* **1851-1891**

Bronze. 43 x 15 x 18 cm / Acquisition, 1891/ RF 927

If he is known as a fine painter and if his lithographs made him famous, Daumier was incontrovertibly a sculptor way ahead of his time. Whereas official sculpture tended to prettify and idealise, he was direct and satirical. His independence of spirit was equalled only by a freedom in modelling that highlighted features from the real with exceptional clarity, thereby turning sculpture into a tool of political and public debate. His painted terracotta busts of members of parliament (1832-35) derive their small format from the Romantic statuette and their expressivity from a searing realism. Like the reliefs for *The Fugitives, Ratapoil* is an example of sculpture impregnated with a powerful social message.

David d'Angers (Pierre-Jean David)

Angers, 1788 - Paris, 1856

MO - *Johann Wolfgang von Goethe (1749-1832),* **1829**

Plaster. 83 x 58 x 51 cm / David d'Angers bequest to the town of Saumur, 1857.

Deposit at Musée d'Orsay, 1986 / DO 1986-5

Although Grand Prix de Rome in 1811, and famous soon after his return in Paris in 1816, David d'Angers has been largely forgotten today. He is only occasionally remembered for an extraordinary series of medallions of the celebrities of his time struck between 1825 and 1850. Romantic and Republican, a friend of Victor Hugo, he nurtured an elevated sense of his profession and remained committed to the ethical value of sculpture. In his eyes, only sculpture could transcend the commonplace reality of the visible and reveal the moral beauty and energy of exceptional beings. His art was thus entirely dedicated to commemorative statuary. From the expressive *Tomb of General Bonchamp* (1824) at St-Florent-le-Vieil to the pediment of the Panthéon in Paris, he knew better than anyone how to bring clarity to complex reliefs and focus on the essential actions of his figures. He was master of the 'expressive' or 'character' head, a genre much in vogue in the 19th century. There is a museum devoted to his work in Angers.

Deacon, Richard

Bangor (Wales), 1949

CP - *Breed,* **1989**

Wood, hardboard, laminate, aluminium, epoxy, pigments. 138 x 285 x 150 cm and 142 x 287 x 150 cm / Purchase, 1989 / AM 1989-548

A student at the renowned St Martin's School of Art in London in the 1980s, a forcing-ground for the young tyros of British sculpture, Deacon is, like Cragg, an assembler of recycled materials. Privileging organic forms with curved lines in the spirit of Moore, but transposed into manufactured products, Deacon regards drawing as the core language of sculpture: 'All drawings have an enclosure, a line of closure, that, in some ways, creates an opening.' With daubs of paint, splurges of glue and exposed rivets, *Breed* illustrates the emphasis Deacon lays on the gesture of the sculptor, as well as on the meticulous positioning of a piece with respect to the ground. His biomorphic and transparent work is structured like an interwoven narrative that highlights links between the manufacture of utilitarian articles and the myths of primitive art. It evokes the universally recognisable lines of the fishing net, the boat, the agricultural tool, within the framework of a sophisticated art with many complex levels of interpretation.

De Andrea, John

Denver, 1941

CP - *Couple,* **1971**

Acrylic on polyester, hair. H 173 cm / Gift of Odette Plouvier, 1978 / AM 1977-65

Together with sculptor Duane Hanson and painters Richard Estes and Chuck Close, De Andrea is one of the most prominent figures in American hyperrealism. De Andrea made his mark with nude figures of a frozen and almost timeless eroticism. Moulded on the model, like those of George Segal, his works in polyester and fibreglass are of impeccable photographic veracity, whereas Segal's plaster casts introduce a sense of distance. Such perfect illusion is obtained by the use of a spray gun and the addition of natural head and body hair. The artist thus exploits the ambiguity arising from the clinical restitution of the most banal facets of Western aesthetic models.

Degas, Edgar

Paris, 1834 - *ibid*, 1917

ML - *Quatre Etudes d'une danseuse danseuse [Four Studies of a Dancer]*, 1878-79

Charcoal, white highlights on vellum. 49 x 32.1 cm / RF 4646

MO - *Petite Danseuse de 14 ans,* or *Grande Danseuse habillée [Little Fourteen-Year-Old Dancer* or *Large Dressed Dancer]*

(Marie Van Goethem, born 1865, pupil at the ballet school at the Opéra), 1881

Bronze patinated in various tints (black for the hair, blonde for the bodice, pink for the slippers), tulle (tutu), satin ribbon (in hair), wood (plinth). 98 x 35 x 24 cm (with plinth: 103 x 48 x 50 cm) / P series, acquired in 1930 through the generosity of the artist and of the Hébrards / RF 2137

MO - *Le Tub [The Bathtub]*, 1889

Bronze. 22 x 43 x 45 cm / P series, acquired in 1930 through the generosity of the artist and of the Hébrards / RF 2120

MO - *Danseuse regardant la plante de son pied droit [Dancer Looking at the Sole of her Right Foot],*

first preliminary study, 1895-1910

Wax statuette on wooden plinth. 45 x 21 x 18 cm; 51 x 24 x 27 cm with plinth

Paul Mellon Gift to the Musée du Louvre, 1956. Transfer to Musée d'Orsay, 1986 / RF 2771

Like Renoir, the painter Degas worked on sculpture mainly at the end of his life, at a time when he had nearly lost his sight. Of the some hundred and fifty or so works in clay or wax, only half survive, chiefly thanks to the efforts of sculptor Albert Bartholomé who restored them. The artist tended to work in series: studies of ballerinas that render the very essence of movement such as it is developed in his paintings by way of colour schemes of astonishing richness; studies of horses elaborated from Muybridge's time-lapse photographs. *The Little Fourteen-Year-Old Dancer,* in which Degas pushes realism to the point of dressing the figure in a real tutu, was the only work to be presented publicly, at the Impressionist exhibition of 1881. For many contemporary artists, these 'painter's sculptures' by Degas provide a benchmark in two senses: for the art of assemblage and for their distilled abstraction of line.

Derain, André

Chatou (Ile-de-France), 1880 – Garches (Ile-de-France), 1954

CP - *Nu debout [Standing Nude]*, 1907

Stone. 95 x 33 x 17 cm / Gift in lieu, 1994 / AM 1994-76

Derain's sculpture is a painter's sculpture. Like him, his painter friends Matisse and Picasso were also significant sculptors, but Derain's practice is less well known and rarely left the inner sanctum of the studio. Moreover, it corresponds to a brief, well-defined period around 1907, when, wearying of the chromatic excesses of Fauvism, Derain returned to a study of Cézanne and his explorations of the art of the past. His enthusiasm for African art, to which he introduced his friends and of which he possessed a rich collection, including the Fang mask reproduced page 21, guided his choice of compact forms comparable in their three-dimensional density to African examples. His *Squatting Man and Standing Nude* (where the treatment of volume can be compared with that in the *Bathers,* also painted in 1907, as if as in response to Picasso's *Demoiselles d'Avignon*) evidence an almost coarse directness in carving redolent of Gauguin.

Desbois, Jules

Parçay-les-Pins (Maine-et-Loire), 1851 - Paris, 1935

MO - *Vieille Femme (La Misère) [Old Woman (Poverty)]*, 1884-94

Terracotta. 38 (42 with plinth) x 18 x 25 cm / Formerly Maurice Kahn-Sriber Collection. Acquisition, 2003/ RF 4698

Entering the workshop of Rodin, whose friend, carver and collaborator he became, Desbois was sometimes the innovative one: his *Poverty,* in which this anarchist at heart leaps to the defense of the downtrodden, precedes Rodin's *Celle qui fut la Belle Heaulmière,* as well as Rodin's *Winter* that also derives from it and for which the master used the same old woman as his model. Like that of Camille Claudel, the art of Desbois, illustrated by *Winter* (1907) and the pacifist *Mort casquée (Death in a Helmet)* (1887-1920), well demonstrates the fecundity of Rodin's studio.

De Vries, Adriaen

The Hague, 1556 - Prague, 1626

ML - *Mercure enlevant Psyché [Mercury Abducting Psyche]*, 1593

Bronze. 215 x 92 x 72 cm / Made in Prague, Swedish war booty in 1648. Brought to France by Christina of Sweden in 1654. Transferred from the Jardin des Tuileries / Department of Sculpture / MR 3270

A pupil of Giambologna between 1581 and 1588, De Vries' two groups taking the subject of Psyche, now in the Louvre and in Stockholm, represent the artistic culmination of Giambologna's principle by which sculpture can be viewed from every angle — as borne out in Jan Muller's engravings after his works. From 1596 to 1602, the artist worked on the monumental decoration of the town of Augsburg. Between 1601 and 1612, he was sculptor at the court of Rudolf II in Prague where the finest current of European Mannerism held sway. De Vries mastered practically all genres, from small bronzes in an Antique vein, to portraits (such as one of Rudolf II executed in 1603) and reliefs, to large-scale bronzes.

Dodeigne, Eugène

Rouvreux (Belgium), 1923

CP - *Grand Torse [Large Torso]*, 1960-61

Black granite. 120 x 56 x 45 cm / State purchase, 1961; transfer 1963 / AM 1366 S

This son of a stonemason, a friend of Etienne Hajdu and Germaine Richier, has lived at Bondues, near Lille, since 1950. Ever respectful of his material, and receptive to its lessons, he worked initially in wood, before moving on to stone, in particular to the beautiful blue stone from Soignies that he carves into powerful forms reminiscent of monumental megalithic art. His art is frequently fantastical in shape, though never less than rigorous its quasi-abstract planes. The vigour of his carving is best appreciated from close up, while viewing it from further away brings the figures into focus. Dodeigne has also always drawn and modelled (his Torses are derived from terracottas).

Dubois, Paul

Nogent-sur-Seine (Champagne), 1829 - Paris, 1905

MO - *Chanteur florentin du XVe siècle [Florentine Singer of the 15th Century]*, 1865

Silvered bronze. 155 x 58 x 50 cm / Commissioned in 1865 / RF 2998

After studying briefly at the Ecole des Beaux-Arts in Paris, this great-nephew of Pigalle financed himself four crucial years in Italy from 1859, studying Renaissance sculpture, especially that of Florence. At the Salon he made his name with *St John the Baptist as a Child* (1861) and, still more, with this *Florentine Singer* (1865). Dubois carved the monument to Lamoricière (1879) in Nantes cathedral, while his statue of Joan of Arc (1896), intended for the parvis of Reims cathedral, testifies to a sophisticated, historicising art. A member of the group of 'Florentines' with Delaplanche and Falguière, in 1873 Dubois was appointed curator at the Musée du Luxembourg in Paris and director of the Ecole des Beaux-Arts from 1878 to 1905.

Dubuffet, Jean

Le Havre, 1901 – Paris, 1985

CP - *Le Jardin d'hiver [The Winter-Garden]*, 1968-70

Polyurethane paint on epoxy. 480 x 960 x 550 cm / State purchase 1973; transfer 1977 / AM 1977-251

Dubuffet made his first forays into sculpture in 1954 with 'statues of precarious life', in which strange debris — roots, sponges, furnace slag, etc — were revitalised by the imagination. After trying his hand at ceramics, and, in 1966, expanded polystyrene, the following year he turned to a more resistant epoxy resin to which his paintings could be transferred and enlarged. In conjunction with a team of assistants, he began working on the *Cabinet Logologique* (1967), installed in 1976 at the Villa Falbala at Périgny-sur-Yerres, and on the *Tower with Figures* (1968), set up after his death on the Ile St-Germain near Paris. Like the *Jardin d'émail* at Otterlo (1974) and *Le Jardin d'hiver*, these are *sculptures-habitacles* — 'cockpit-' or 'dwelling-sculptures'. Like Calder, Dubuffet created large-scale works that have become landmarks in the cities in which they were erected, as with the *Group of Four Trees* (1972) in New York and the *Monument with Standing Beast* (1984) in Chicago. The Dubuffet Foundation in Paris is a source of further information on this non-conformist artist.

Duchamp, Marcel

Blainville-Crevon (Normandy), 1887 – Paris, 1968

CP - *Roue de bicyclette [Bicycle Wheel],* 1913/1964
Ready-made: metal, painted wood. 126.5 x 31.5 x 63.5 cm / Purchase, 1986 / AM 1986-286

CP - *Feuille de vigne femelle [Female Fig-Leaf],* 1950/1951
Green-painted plaster. 8.5 x 13 x 11 cm / Purchase, 1990 / AM 1990-104(1)

CP - *With my Tongue in my Cheek,* 1959
Plaster, pencil on paper mounted on wood. 25 x 15 x 5.1 cm / Gift in lieu, 1993 / AM 1993-123

Did he who invented the ready-made (1913-15) turn to the manufactured object as an escape from painting? Born to a middle-class Normandy family, all of whose children became artists, Marcel proved the most original. With the 'assisted' ready-made, the pre-Dada found object (*Bicycle Wheel,* 1913, *Fountain,* 1917) evolved into the Surrealist assemblage. André Breton appointed Duchamp technical curator for various exhibitions by the Surrealist group. A precursor of kinetic and Op art, notably in his *Roto-reliefs* (1935), Duchamp was in part inspired by scientific and technical advances. Rehabilitating moulding as a process, he left a strange last testament in the shape of an environment entitled *Etant donnés: 1° La chute d'eau 2° Le gaz d'éclairage,* executed in the strictest secrecy between 1946 and 1966. Travelling to-and-fro between France and the USA, Duchamp paved the way for Nouveau Réalisme on one side of the Atlantic and for Neo-Dadaism, and even Pop art, on the other. Every facet of 20th-century art can be seen as stemming from this artist's intuitions: performance, transitory art, Anti-Form, Conceptual art... His work, reductions of which were contained in the *Boîte en valise* (1936), is well represented at the Philadelphia Museum of Art and the Centre Pompidou in Paris.

Duchamp-Villon, Raymond

Damville (Normandy), 1876 – Cannes, 1918

CP - *Le Cheval majeur,* 1914/1976
Bronze with black patina. 150 x 97 x 153 cm / Purchase, 1976 / AM 1977-206

Of the three Duchamp brothers, Raymond was the most authentically a sculptor; he came away from the Sunday meetings of the Puteaux group with the conviction that Cézanne, on the one hand, and archaic models, on the other, could constitute the bases for a new type of sculpture. Shaking off Rodin's manner of modelling, *Baudelaire* (1911) and *Maggy* (1912) show how Duchamp-Villon intuitively devised a forward-looking language, comprised of near-abstract forms whose geometry recalls black African art. He also made sculptures for the *Cubist House* unveiled at the 1911 Salon. Examples of a stylisation at once machinist and Cubo-Futurist in spirit, *Le Petit Cheval* (plaster in the Musée de Grenoble) and the bronze *Le Cheval Majeur* derived from it should be compared less to his brother's *Bicycle Wheel* than to the aerodynamism of the Italian Futurist Umberto Boccioni. Like the latter, Duchamp-Villon died in World War I.

Duseigneur, Jehan (Jean Bernard Duseigneur)

Paris, 1808 – *ibid,* 1866

ML - *Roland furieux [Orlando Furioso],* 1867
Bronze cast by Charnod. 130 x 140 x 90 cm / Acquired by Napoleon III, 1868 / Department of Sculpture / RF 2993

Discovered at only twenty-three when *Orlando Furioso* was unveiled at the 1831 Salon, Duseigneur was considered the Victor Hugo of Romantic sculpture. However, despite the plaudits lavished on him by Théophile Gautier, he did not continue in the same vein. Under the July Monarchy (1830-48), his multi-talented activity turned to the medallion and the bust, as well as to religious sculpture. During the Second Empire, his taste for archaeology and history led him to contribute to the *Revue universelle des arts* and to compile a history of early Renaissance sculpture.

Erhart, Gregor

Ulm, c. 1470 - Augsburg, 1540

ML - *Mary Magdalene*, c. 1515-20

Limewood, original polychromy. 177 x 44 x 43 cm / Originally from the Dominican
church at Augsburg (?) / Base replaced in the 19th century / Formerly collection
Siegfried Lämmle. Acquisition, 1902 /Department of Sculpture / RF 1338

Except for a period of activity in Augsburg (between 1494 and
1508), the life and work of this son of a sculptor, born in Ulm,
remain sketchy. Apart from an equestrian statue of Emperor
Maximilian, his religious output is by far the most important.
Erhart collaborated with Hans Holbein the Elder on the high
altar of the abbey church at Kaisheim (1502), also executing a
Virgin of Mercy (destroyed during World War II) for the same
church. The *Mary Magdalene* in the Louvre, attributed to the
master due to its similarity in terms of facture with the preceding
example, attests to the fusion of Italianate models with the tradition of Swabian statuary. The sensuality of the Renaissance nude
is here wedded to the formal elegance of Late Gothic.

Etienne-Martin (Etienne Martin)

Loriol-sur-Drôme, 1913 – Paris, 1995

CP - *Le Manteau (Demeure 5) [Coat (Dwelling 5)]*, 1962

Fabric, trimmings, rope, leather, metal, tarpaulin. 250 x 230 x 75 cm /
State purchase, 1973; transfer: 1976 / AM 1976-965

The artist never forget the house in Loriol where he was born; it
became the inescapable reference for his future relationships to
the intimacy of space — an inhabited space that resurfaces in his
aptly entitled *Demeures* (residences or dwelling places). Trained
at the Ecole des Beaux-Arts in Lyon, Etienne-Martin joined the
Témoignage group founded by the poet and art dealer, Marcel
Michaud. His *Virgin with Child*, created in 1943 in a quarry at
Dieulefit, is a testimony to a heartfelt faith as well as foreshadowing
land art. His innovative streak is also apparent in his use, as early
as 1948, of textile in making his *passementeries* (trimmings or
haberdashery) and 'coats' and, from 1969, in his *Demeures*
(about twenty in total), made out of painted wood, mixed materials, or cast in bronze, and preceded by wire models. This personal mythology fascinated Harald Szeemann, who invited him to
Documenta 5 in Kassel in 1972. In addition to the exhibition of
the *Demeures* at the Centre Pompidou (1984), several public
commissions and a piece in the Jardin des Tuileries have given
additional exposure to this strange body of work.

Fabro, Luciano

Turin, 1936

CP - *Piede [Foot]*, 1968-72

Murano glass, silk shantung. 333.5 x 108 x 79 cm / Purchase, 1989 / AM 1989-134

One of the six founder members of Arte Povera, Fabro views the
artist as a storyteller delving into the memory of the world; for
him, the use of blocks of marble inescapably refers to the history
of sculpture, though he is not immune to the allure of colour. If
the entire history of art is convened — notably in *Lo Spirato*
(1968-73), a recumbent marble statue, and in *Io* (1978, Rome),
an ovoid Neo-Baroque fountain — Fabro also undertakes almost
imperceptible interventions in the natural environment, which
link him to the recent generation of land artists, such as Nils Udo
or Andy Goldsworthy. Fabro constantly returns to the same
themes on which he confers new meaning. The *Piede* — of which
he made fifteen versions between 1968 and 1972 — present a
bipartite structure reminiscent sometimes of antique statuary,
sometimes of great trees. In addition Piede alludes to the 'boot' of
Italy, an image Fabro has drawn on in fifteen or so hanging
'sculpture-maps' entitled *Italia*.

Falconet, Etienne-Maurice

Paris, 1716 - *ibid*, 1791

ML - *Baigneuse [Bather]*, 1757

Marble. 80 x 25 x 29 cm / Falconet exhibited a *Nymph Leaving the Bath* at the 1757
Salon, that in the Louvre is a replica executed for Madame Du Barry that was part
of the collection seized at Louveciennes in 1793 during the Revolution / Accession,
before 1855 / Department of Sculpture / MR 1846

ML - *Pygmalion et Galatée [Pygmalion and Galatea]*, 1763 Salon

Marble. 83 x 48 x 38 cm / Félix Guyon bequest, 1920. Accession to the Louvre
in 1930 / Department of Sculpture/ RF 2001

Of modest origin, Falconet was, with Pigalle, a protégé of
Madame de Pompadour. His master, Jean-Baptiste Lemoyne the
Younger, encouraged him to engage with the sculpture of Puget, a
figure Falconet greatly admired: his Academy reception piece was
a singularly personal interpretation of the Milon of Crotona. An
Enlightenment figure, admired by Goethe, Falconet correspon-
ded with Diderot, who published one of his texts by the
Encyclopaedia. Convinced of the moral value of his art, for the
equestrian statue commissioned by Catherine the Great of Russia
(St Petersburg, 1767-82), Falconet opted to depict Peter the
Great as a legislator. Yet he believed even more strongly in the
authenticity of the emotions aroused by the sensitive rendering of
anatomy, as in this 1757 *Bather* and he always preferred this to
the 'Antique taste'. His writings on sculpture, *Le Cavalier
d'Airain* in particular, are enthralling.

Falguière, Alexandre

Toulouse, 1831 - Paris, 1900

MO - *Tarcisius, martyr chrétien [Tarcisius, Christian Martyr]*, 1868

Marble. 64 x 140 x 59 cm / Acquisition, 1867 / RF 174

Prix de Rome in 1859, in Italy Falguière discovered Florentine Renaissance sculpture and became part of the Florentine group. An excellent portraitist in his busts, he was an untiring provider of monuments to the great and the good, catering for the lion's share of the Third Republic's statuomania. His skill at combining idealisation with photographic realism won him considerable success. *Tarcisius* was based on the documentary use of photographs of *tableaux vivants*. His *Pasteur* (place de Breteuil, Paris) also depicts edifying scenes around its lofty pedestal. The striking discrepancy between the freshness of his preparatory studies and the final realisation can best be explained by the contemporary conventions surrounding public commissions.

Fix-Masseau (Pierre-Félix Masseau)

Lyon, 1869 - Paris, 1937

MO - *Secret*, 1894

Mahogany, ivory casket, polychrome traces; reverse of the fold of the veil green; gilt tassels and band. 76 x 17 x 18 cm / Acquisition, 1894 / RF 3638

Fix-Masseau played a noteworthy role in Art Nouveau, which can be regarded as the last major style to affect every artistic field, from architecture to furniture. His subject of predilection was the female figure, surrounded, as befitted his talent as a painter, by floral patterns, and treated in the Symbolist manner, as in *Secret*. He was active in the applied arts and in 1935 became director of the Ecole Nationale des Arts Décoratifs at Limoges. The mix of materials and colours, the exploitation of changes in scale render his statuettes and domestic articles particularly appealing.

Flavin, Dan

New York, 1933 – *ibid*, 1996

CP - *Untitled (Monument for Vladimir Tatlin)*, 1975

Fluorescent light tubes, metal. 304.5 x 62.5 x 12.5 cm / Gift of Leo Castelli and the Georges Pompidou Art and Culture Foundation, 1992 / AM 1992-16

An art history graduate, Flavin is, with Morris and Judd, emblematic of a generation of artists who approached the creative arts with a solid intellectual background. At the outset a painter, Flavin's early religious vocation grew into a meditation that centred on the image of light. From 1961, he began using electric light to confer spatial radiation to monochrome pictures, using the term 'icons'. From 1963 on, he worked exclusively with fluorescent light tubes. Standard in format, they are arranged on the wall or around openings in geometrical, formal progressions and structures reminiscent of Russian Constructivism. Transcending the opposition between painting and sculpture, his light installations constitute some of the most evocative forms in all American Minimalist art.

Fremiet, Emmanuel

Paris, 1824 - *ibid*, 1910

MO - *Credo*, 1885

Plaster statuette covered in glued flock. White robe, flesh colours, blue and gilt highlights. 40 x 32 x 10 cm / Gift of Mme Fauré-Fremiet in 1979 / RF 3434

MO - *St Michel terrassant le dragon [St Michael Slaying the Dragon]*, 1897

Hammered copper. 617 x 260 x 120 cm / Replica of the finial on Mont-St-Michel / Gift of Madame G Pasquier to the Monuments Historiques / Deposit Musée d'Orsay, 1983 / DO 1983-80

Watch out for the gorilla! Exhibited beneath a wall-hanging in 1859, the plaster *Female Gorilla Making off with a Negress* testified to an in-depth knowledge of animal and human anatomy. A distant precursor of Senegalese sculptor Ousmane Sow, this nephew of Rude rarely resisted an opportunity to present the public with some horrendous scene: orang-utan strangling a savage in Borneo, she-bear killing someone poaching her cubs... His commissions for the Museum of Natural History marry a taste for depicting the animal world and the then-growing interest in prehistory. His sculpture thus became increasingly marked by historical realism. Fremiet is also responsible for the Joan of Arc in place des Pyramides, Paris, and for the *Napoleon I* at Laffrey, a village on the Route Napoléon.

Gauguin, Paul

Paris, 1848 - Atuana (Marquesas Islands), 1903

MO - *Soyez mystérieuses [Be Mysterious]*, 1890

Painted limewood. 73 x 95 x 5 cm / Formerly Gustave Fayet collection,
Mme d'Andoque. Acquisition, 1979 / RF 3405

MO - *Idole à la coquille [Idol with Shell]*, 1892

Ironwood (tua), mother-of-pearl, pharyngeal tooth from a parrot-fish.
34 x 12 x 11 cm / Formerly Daniel de Monfreid collection. Acquisition, 1951 /
OA 9540

MO - *Oviri*, 1894

Partially enamelled vitrified stoneware. 75 x 19 x 27 cm / Formerly Gustave Fayet
collection, 1925. Acquisition, 1987 / OAO 114

MO - *Femme nue et arbre aux fruits rouges [Nude Woman
and Tree with Red Fruit]*, 1901

Right door jamb from the Maison du Jouir: polychrome giant sequoia wood.
159 x 40 x 2 cm / Formerly Victor Segalen collection. Acquisition, 1952 / RF 2722

MO - *Soyez amoureuses, vous serez heureuses*, 1901

Right-hand plinth from the Maison du Jouir: polychrome giant sequoia wood.
45 x 204 x 2 cm / Formerly Victor Segalen collection. Acquisition, 1952 / RF 2720

Numbering some 165 recorded pieces, Gauguin's sculptural
oeuvre is far from negligible and he was instrumental in the
rebirth of wood carving, as well as a revival in ceramics. From
his first voyage to Tahiti (1891-93), primitive art became a
constant source of inspiration for his reliefs and 'idols'. It was in
this way that he went beyond the Symbolist aesthetic of his for-
mative period. After a brief return to France, in 1895 he settled
definitively the tropics, carving for his house on the Marquesas
Islands wood panels that encapsulate his philosophy of life. His
work as a sculptor and potter, which holds such a decisive place
in the evolution of modern sculpture, also constitutes a recurrent
motif in his painting.

Gérôme, Jean-Léon

Vesoul, 1824 - Paris, 1904

MO - *Tanagra*, 1890

Marble (at one time polychrome), holding in her hand the (polychrome marble)
Danseuse au cerceau [Dancer with a Hoop] 154 x 56 x 57 cm / Acquisition, 1890 /
RF 2514

MO - *Sarah Bernhardt*, 1895

Stained marble. 69 x 41 x 29 cm./ Artist bequest, 1904 / RF 1393

MO - *Les Gladiateurs, 1878. Monument à Gérôme
[The Gladiators, 1878. Monument to Gérôme]*, 1909

Bronze. 360 x 182 x 170 cm / Statue of Gérôme by Aimé Morot /
Commissioned 1905 / RF 3517

Gérôme only took up sculpture after having gained fame as a
painter and acquiring eminently official status as a professor and
member of the Institut. Moreover, he continued to paint his statues
or coat them in wax. The vogue for Orientalism and archaeology,
which in part motivates this *Tanagra*, often joins forces with a
realism bordering on the photographic. In fact, the study of live
models was backed up by the use of photography. Gérôme also cul-
tivated effects created combining materials, and, in executing multiple versions of his pieces, seems to have been willing to open up
sculpture to industrial methods.

Giacometti, Alberto

Stampa (Suisse), 1901– Coire (Suisse), 1966

CP - *Boule suspendue [Suspended Ball],* 1930-31

Wood, iron, string. 60.4 x 36.5 x 34 cm / Purchase, 1996 / AM 1996-205

CP - *Figurine dans une boîte entre deux maisons [Figurine in a Box between Two Houses],* 1950

Painted bronze. 29.5 x 53.5 x 9.4 cm / Gift in lieu, 1982 / AM 1982-100

CP - *Bust of Diego,* 1954

Bronze. 40 x 33.7 x 19 cm / State purchase, 1961. Transfer, 1964 / AM 1424 S

CP - *Femme de Venise V [Woman of Venice V],* 1956

Bronze. 110.5 x 31.3 x 14 cm / Gift in lieu, 1991 / AM 1991-301

CP - *Annette X,* 1965

Bronze. 44 x 18.5 x 13.5 cm / Louise and Michel Leiris donation, 1984 / AM 1984-517

From a family of artists from Italian-speaking Switzerland, Giacometti trained with Bourdelle in Paris. From the end of the 1920s, his planar sculptures, and especially his 'cages', earned the approval of the Surrealist group. Under the stewardship of Breton and Dalí, there then followed a period of dream-like objects that came to a stop in 1934-35, when the sculptor decided to return to the figure. Giacometti pursued his experiments for fully ten years: he discovered that nothing was as he thought, that reality was always one step ahead. From 1947 to the end of the 1950s, he created his unforgettable *Femmes debout* (*Standing Women*) and *Hommes qui marchent* (*Walking Men*). If the genres (bust, full-length statue, head) and elements (bases, steles) involved remain traditional, the approach adopted was certainly not: Giacometti eliminates anything (volume, normal size, contours) liable to reconcile the spirit with the unknown. Like his painted figures, his sculpture possesses the obsessive power of a pure phenomenon, almost without a material core.

Girardon, François

Troyes, 1628 - Paris, 1715

ML - *Vierge de douleur [Virgin of Sorrows],* 1657

Marble. 85 x 65 x 10 cm / Reception piece to the Académie Royale de Peinture et de Sculpture, presented 7 July 1657 / Department of Sculpture / RF 3148

Through the good offices of his friend, the painter Charles Le Brun, Girardon obtained complete control over the sculpture for the building works of Louis XIV. A first-rate decorator, he worked on the Galerie d'Apollon (recently restored) in the Louvre. For the Grotto of Thetis at Versailles, he provided his masterpiece, *Apollo Served by Nymphs* (1666), marked by its uncluttered composition, the delicate gestures and the elegant draperies. The piece earned him a wealth of orders for the park at Versailles in 1674 that were met by other, equally fine sculptures: *The Rape of Persephone and Winter*. He also executed sumptuous tombs, such as in that of Cardinal de Richelieu for the chapel in the Sorbonne (1675-94), while his busts of the royal couple or the theologian Antoine Arnauld attest to his talent as a portraitist. He carved an equestrian statue of *Louis XIV* for place Vendôme, which was not to survive the Revolution, and retouched Bernini's *Louis XIV*. A collector of antiques, Girardon also restored a great number for the king.

González, Julio

Barcelone, 1876 – Arcueil, 1942

CP - *Daphne,* vers 1937

Bronze. 142 x 71 x 52 cm / Gift of Roberta González, 1966 / AM 1491 S

CP - *Masque de Montserrat criant [Mask of Montserrat, Shouting],* c. 1938-39

Welded wrought iron, patina. 22 x 15.5 x 12 cm / Gift of Roberta González, 1964 / AM 1403 S

The son of an ironworker and goldsmith, González settled in Paris in 1900, producing wrought-iron masks and cut-out figures at the end of the 1920s. Along with Picasso, to whom he taught iron welding, he was one of the inventors of Cubist sculpture. His temperament speaks loud and clear in the *Mask of Montserrat, Shouting* and his *Montserrat* — with *Guernica,* the lynchpin at the pavilion of the Spanish Republic at the 1937 World Fair. The expressionism of both these pieces, executed in response to the Spanish Civil War and the worsening crisis in Europe, is wholly at one with the absolute rigour of their formal procedures. Juggling abstraction and figuration, his art opens up a dialogue between line and volume and the space they enclose: a 'drawing in space'.

Goujon, Jean

Recorded 1540-63

ML - *Déploration du Christ, ou Notre-Dame de Pitié*
[The Deploration of Christ or Our Lady of Sorrows], mid-16th century
Stone. 67 x 182 x 7 cm / Relief from the rood screen of St-Germain-l'Auxerrois, Paris.
Provenance: Musée des Monuments Français, 1818 / Department of Sculpture /
MR 1731
ML - *Nymphe et triton [Nymph and Triton]*, mid-16th century
Stone. 73 x 195 x 12 cm / The composition is inspired by an Antique sarcophagus
now conserved at Grottaferrata, which often appears in 16th-century drawings /
Transferred to the Louvre in 1818 / Department of Sculpture/ MR 1737

Although no document attests to the fact with certainty, it is
more than likely that Goujon gained familiarity with Antique art
during an early stay in Italy. Additionally an architect, he was
one of those artists who were to translate the models of Italian
Renaissance painting into sculpture. It can be demonstrated, for
example, that the composition of his *Deploration of Christ* was
inspired by Parmigianino or Rosso. From 1547 to 1562, he lived
in Italy where he worked in the service of the king of France.
Drawing played a key role in the idealisation of the figures by
this great Mannerist, who excelled in monumental sculpture. The
relationship between sculpture and architecture is always harmonious. His reliefs and caryatids display wonderfully undulating
lines, while the flat transitions are sensuous and soft. The elongated, Primaticcio-style canon of his mythological figures, such as
Nymph and Triton for the Fontaine des Innocents (1549), is characteristic of the School of Fontainebleau. Goujon introduced
into sculpture a striving for balletic rhythms and dynamic equilibrium that foreshadows Classicism.

Grand, Toni

Gallargues-le-Montueux (Gard), 1935

CP - *Vert, équarri, équarri plus une refente partielle, équarri plus
deux refentes partielles [Green, squared, squared off then a partial
notch, squared off then two partial notches]*, 1973
Forked and squared-off branch of wood. 160 x 180 cm / Purchase, 1983 /
AM 1983-368

Toni Grand only spent one year at the Ecole des Beaux-Arts in
Montpellier. In 1967, he exhibited *Prélèvements*, abstract forms
truncated in metal structures, at the Venice Biennale. Believing
that the possibilities of modern sculpture had been exhausted, he
found a way to renew the art through an analysis of the transformation of materials in the deconstructive practices of the artists
of Supports-Surfaces, who he encountered in 1969 when he
moved to Nice. Thus, for *Vert, équarri*, the complete title records
the genesis of the creative process. Since the late 1970s, he has
used laminated polyester in conjunction with wood, stones or
bone. Fish and animal remains (as in *Untitled, Le Cheval majeur*,
1985, also owned by the Centre Pompidou) dipped in polyester
produced surprising fossilised forms, in which nature and abstraction meet. In 1988, the artist was awarded the Grand Prix
National de Sculpture.

Guillaume, Eugène

Montbard (Burgundy), 1822 - Rome, 1905

MO - *The Gracchi*, 1847/53
Bronze. 85 x 90 x 60 cm / Acquisition, 1853 / RF 1

A pupil of James Pradier, awarded the Prix de Rome in 1845,
Guillaume turned back to subjects from Roman history. *The
Gracchi* constitutes the finest example of this revival in
Neoclassical style. A scholarly sculptor with an austere manner,
he climbed the slippery pole of academia under successive political regimes. Guillaume produced numerous statues of great men,
portraits, and even six busts of Bonaparte represented at various
ages. He also worked on the carved decoration of the churches of
St-Eustache, Ste-Clotilde and the Trinité in Paris, as well as the
sculptures on the Bourse and law courts in Marseille.

Hajdu, Etienne

Turda (Romania), 1907 – Bagneux (Ile-de-France), 1996

CP - *Grandes Demoiselles*, 1979-82
Bronze. 189 to 206 x 72 to 94 cm / Gift in lieu, 1999 / AM 1999-107

Arriving in Paris from Romania in 1927, Hajdu belonged to the
Second School of Paris, which arose in the interwar period under
the influence of Rodin, Laurens, Cubism and Brancusi. The work of
Fernand Léger, which he discovered in 1929, led him to express
modern themes and to combine geometric and biological elements.
From 1945 to the end of the 1950s, Hajdu produced bas-reliefs in
hammered metal or in stone, whose forms lie at the limit of sign and
object. Gradually, his works gained in volume to the point that one
may regard them as sculptures in the round, although they remain
primarily double-sided or openwork. He also executed carved
groups such as the *Seven Columns for Stéphane Mallarmé* (1969-
71) and the *Grandes Demoiselles*.

Hausmann, Raoul

Vienna, 1886 – Limoges, 1971

CP - *The Spirit of Our Time* or *Mechanical Head*, 1919

Wooden dummy head with various materials. 32.5 x 21 x 20 cm / Purchase, 1974 /
AM 1974-6

Founder of the Dada Club in Berlin in 1918 and of the review
Der Dada, Hausmann began developing his photomontage technique in 1919, and, together with John Heartfield, made it into
an effective satirical and political tool for Berlin Dadaism. A
brilliant Jack of all trades — poet, photographer, abstract artist
and creator of collages and assemblages, such as this *Mechanical
Head* — he was also interested in optics, and in 1927 created the
Optophone, a machine that conveyed colour through music.
When Hitler came to power, the artist, considered 'degenerate',
was driven from Germany in 1933. After stays in Paris and
several other European cities, Hausmann settled in Limoges in
1944, where he continued his work and wrote his memoirs.

Hesse, Eva

Hamburg, 1936 – New York, 1970

CP - *Untitled (Seven Poles)*, 1970

Seven elements hanging from the ceiling: aluminium wire, polyethylene, resin,
fibreglass. H: 188 to 282 cm (floor area varies) / Purchase, 1986 / AM 1986-248

Hesse's family left Germany in 1939 to settle in the USA in 1945.
A meteoric talent, Hesse soon reacted against the Minimalist art
that was to dominate the artistic arena. Her flexible sculptures in
resin, latex, rubber and felt are characteristic of the 'Anti-Form'
tendency, also expressed by Robert Morris and Bruce Nauman.
Of exceptional tactile sensitivity, her installations, hanging from
the ceiling, laid out on the ground, or even tumbling down walls,
remind one of Pollock's drip paintings or of the dreamworld of
the Surrealists and Arshile Gorky. Hesse working in series, tackling the inner experience of the body and psyche in various regis-
ters, ranging from reverie to sarcasm, from humour to fantasy. In
this manner, she opened the way for the artistic expression of the
body, in which other women artists, such as Lygia Clark and
Yahoi Kusama, have also excelled.

Hoetger, Bernhard

Hörde (Germany), 1874 - Beatenburg (Switzerland), 1949

MO - *The Human Machine*, 1902

Bronze. 44 x 37 x 18 cm / Gift of Mme Marcel Duchamp to the MNAM in 1977,
deposited with Musée d'Orsay in 1983 / DO 1983-75

Originally a stonemason, Hoetger came into contact with the
avant-garde during a sojourn in Paris from 1900 to 1907, when
he also met Rodin and Maillol. It was at this time he carved his
Art Nouveau female figures, such as *Loïe Fuller* (1900), and his
Workers, accursed beings (*The Human Machine*, 1902) in which
a drive for the monumental is enriched by lessons from Rodin.
Back in Germany, Hoetger joined the artistic colonies at
Darmstadt and then at Worpswede. As an architect, after World
War I he built the Paula Moderson Haus in Bremen. Fleeing Nazi
Germany, his style evolved from Expressionism to perfect geome-
trical rigour and he spent the end of his life in Switzerland.

Houdon, Jean-Antoine

Versailles, 1741 - Paris, 1828

ML - *Sophie Arnould (1740-1802), cantatrice, représentée
dans son rôle d'Iphigénie [Sophie Arnould (1740-1802) Shown
in the Role of Iphigenia]*, 1775

Marble. 81 x 51 x 29.5 cm / Gift of Mme Edgard Stern and her children, 1947 /
Department of Sculpture / RF 2596

ML - *Diane chasseresse [Diana the Huntress]*, 1790

Bronze. 192 x 90 x 114 cm / Acquired from the artist's heirs, 1829 / Department
of Sculpture / CC 204

ML - *Sabine Houdon (1787-1836) âgée de quatre ans
[Sabine Houdon (1787-1836) aged four]*, 1791 Salon (?)

Original plaster. 40 x 30 x 24 cm / Acquisition, 1905 / Department of Sculpture /
RF 1392

A student of Michel-Angel Slodtz, Houdon carried off the first prize
at the Académie Royale in 1761, gaining a thorough knowledge of
the Antique during his stay in Italy (1764-68). His commitment to
verity led him to produce an *écorché* in 1766-67, which marked a
turning-point in anatomical realism. Houdon's driving ambition was
to reconcile the simplicity of Antique classicism with a respect for
nature. His religious subjects, such as the St Bruno in Santa Maria
degli Angeli (Rome), and his mythological subjects, such as *Diana the
Huntress,* share a manifest purity of line with a penetrating sense of
formal integrity. Houdon was also a hugely talented portraitist, for
whom many leading figures of the day posed (from Diderot to
Benjamin Franklin), not forgetting many admirable likenesses of his
intimate circle. His works were widely disseminated, often by way of
editions executed by the artist himself.

Jean de Liège

Known from 1361 - died 1381

ML - *Tombeau des entrailles de Charles IV le Bel et Jeanne d'Evreux [Tomb for the Entrails of Charles the Fair and Jeanne d'Evreux],* second half of the 14th century

Charles IV the Fair (died 1328) and Jeanne d'Evreux (died 1371)

Marble. 135 x 36 x 160 cm / From the Abbaye de Maubuisson. Gift of the Société des Amis du Louvre, 1907 / Department of Sculpture / RF 1436, RF 1437

Originally from northern Flanders, Jean de Liège made his way to Paris in 1361 when, under the protection of Charles V, he worked in the Louvre, carving statues of the royal couple, today lost. He also executed the tomb of Philippa de Hainaut, wife of King Edward III, destined for Westminster Abbey. After making the tomb for the heart of Charles V in Rouen cathedral, he carved recumbent statues containing the entrails of Charles IV and Jeanne d'Evreux for the abbey at Maubuisson (1370-72). His style, which has occasionally been described as 'cold', is of a courtly elegance that transpires especially in the smiles and in the modelling of the features. The drapery is balanced to perfection. A marble bust of Marie de France for the abbey at St-Denis (Metropolitan Museum of Art, New York) testifies to his qualities as a portraitist.

Judd, Donald

Excelsior Springs (USA), 1928 – New York, 1994

CP - *Stack,* 1972

Stainless steel, red Plexiglas. 470 x 102.5 x 79.2 cm / State purchase, 1973; Transfer 1980 / AM 1980-412

A graduate in philosophy and history of art, Judd was active as an art critic and teacher, in parallel with his artistic work. At first a painter, he moved on to reliefs (1960) and then to three-dimensional objects (1962), without abandoning his qualities as a colourist. His *Specific Objects* (1965), a manifesto of Minimalist art, gathered together under this generic term works which, in the wake of Carl Andre or Robert Morris, situate their action in the immediate space of the viewer and cannot be pigeonholed into traditional categories of painting or sculpture. The rapport between Judd's work and industrial production recalls that between Pop art and mass-media imagery. The rejection of expressionist gesture and subjectivity fed into a classicism of a novel type, the impact of which can be gauged at the Chinati Foundation, Mafra (Texas), where the artist himself displayed his works.

Julien, Pierre

Saint-Paulien (Auvergne), 1731 - Paris, 1804

ML - *Gladiateur mourant [Dying Gladiator],* 1778

Marble. 60 x 48 x 42 cm / Elected to the Académie Royale in 1778. Academy reception piece, 1779 / Seized at the Revolution / Department of Sculpture / RF 4623

ML - *Jean de La Fontaine (1621-1695),* 1785 Salon

Marble. 173 x 110 x 129 cm / Accession to Louvre, 1960 / Department of Sculpture / RF 2983

A pupil of Guillaume Coustou the Younger, Prix de Rome (1765), Julien stayed in Italy from 1768 to 1773. In 1779, he was accepted into the Académie Royale with his *Dying Gladiator,* which exemplifies a style thoroughly imbued with the lessons of the Antique. The sculptor demonstrated the range of his talents in an almost anecdotal statue of La Fontaine in period dress and in another of Poussin sporting a perfectly Neoclassical drapery for the series of 'great men' destined for the Louvre's Grande Galerie. For Marie-Antoinette's dairy in the Parc de Rambouillet, he adopted Jean-Jacques Rousseau's bucolic utopianism and carved *Girl with a Goat,* wedding sensual physicality to an idealised line. The Musée Crozatier at Puy-in-Velay has a collection of terracottas by this native of the region.

Kienholz, Edward

Fairfield (USA), 1927 – Hope (USA), 1994

CP - *While Visions of Sugar Plums Danced in their Heads,* 1964

Sound installation: furniture, bedding, radio, framed prints, fibreglass dummies. 180 x 360 x 270 cm / State purchase, 1971; transfer, 1976 / AM 1976-984

In his painted wood reliefs (from 1954) and later 'environments' (1960s), self-taught artist Kienholz transcribed the world of America as he experienced it when he held down a series of dead-end jobs. This Kerouac of sculpture reconstituted bars, brothels, automobiles and domestic interiors, without illusion perhaps, but not without a certain retrospective tenderness. Deflating the American dream as promoted by cinema, advertising, official propaganda and the media, his political art denounced the Vietnam War (*The Portable War Memorial,* 1968), repressive psychiatry, sexual frustration (*While Visions of Sugar Plums Danced in their Heads,* 1964) or ridiculed the art world (*The Art Show,* 1963-77). His wife, Nancy Redding, was co-author with Kienholz of his complex assemblages.

Klein, Yves

Nice, 1928 - Paris, 1962

CP - *Portrait-relief Arman*, 1962

Bronze, plywood, gold-leaf. 175 x 95 x 26 cm / State purchase, 1968; Transfer, 1970 / AM 1708 S

When Yves Klein made the ultramarine-impregnated sculptures in various materials, which became his hallmark, such as the sponge reliefs for the opera house at Gelsenkirchen (1957-59), or when he used the bodies of his models as living brushes, as in *Anthropométries* (1960), was he a painter or sculptor? The artist always preferred emptiness to volume, as in the exhibition 'Le Vide' at the Galerie Iris Clert in 1958. His collaboration with Jean Tinguely in the same gallery led to a joint display of rotary discs, six of them blue, 'Pure Speed and Monochromic Stability' in November 1958. The artist, a fine judoka, excelled in performance: *Saut dans le Vide* (1960), captured in a photo-montage, remains famous. He dreamed of illuminating the obelisk on the place de la Concorde in blue light, but the Préfecture forbade the action at the last moment. If the lion's share of his activity was conceptual, questioning space in its elementary dimension (pieces made with the elements of air, water and fire, for instance), or else metaphysical (as in the *spaces of pictorial sensitivity*), Klein ended up reverting to the imprint and the relief, in particular in this 'portrait-relief' of Arman.

Klinger, Max

Leipzig, 1857 – Grossjena (Germany), 1920

MO - *Cassandra*, 1886-95/1903 (?)

Bronze (bust), orange/red cornelian incrustations (eyes), traces of gold (hair ribbon). 59 x 32 x 35 cm / Acquisition, 1990 / RF 4302

A painter and engraver highly respected in Symbolist circles, Klinger came late to sculpture, with a bust of Friedrich von Schiller in 1883. During sojourns in Paris, when he began practicing statuary and more particularly developing aesthetic conceptions which he expounded in the 1891 treatise *Malerei und Zeichnung* (*Painting and Drawing*), he started advocating a total art that would be open to space (*Raumkunst*). It was in this perspective that Klinger turned to polychrome sculpture, a sort of spatialised painting, realising, in addition to busts of Symbolist figures, such as Salome and Cassandra, a heroic bust of Beethoven that formed, together with the frieze Gustav Klimt devoted to the musician, the focal point of the Vienna Secession building in 1902.

Kobro, Katarzyna

Moscow, 1898 – Lodz (Poland), 1951

CP - *Spatial Sculpture*, c. 1928

Painted sheet-steel. 44.8 x 44.8 x 46.7 cm / Purchase, 1985 / AM 1985-18

Of Polish origin, Kobro studied sculpture in Moscow (1917-20), joining the Unovis group headed by Malevich. In 1920, she married the Unist painter Wladyslaw Strzeminski. In 1924, the couple settled in Poland, in 1929 founding 'a-r' ('revolutionary artists'), which forged links with the Parisian group, Abstraction-Création. Her open and often suspended constructions (1921-24) herald Calder and Kinetic art. Beginning in 1925, her 'compositions in space' structure space by means of secant planes of metal assembled in accordance with mathematical modules that define the relations between form and surface. The use of colour and the sense of spatial continuity characteristic of Unism endow Kobro's 'spatial sculpture', in particular the one reproduced here, with a distinct originality amply borne out in a recent exhibition at the Centre Pompidou. The artist published theoretical writings, alone ('Sculpture and the Solid', 1929) or with Strzeminski ('The Composition of Space'), which call for a functional, clear art adapted to urban life. In 1931, together they founded the museum at Lodz (which with Société Anonyme, created in 1920 by Marcel Duchamp and Man Ray, was one of the very first museums devoted to modern art), which became an international arena for creation and teaching. The Nazis destroyed most of its contents, known today primarily through reconstructions.

Kounellis, Jannis

Piraeus (Greece), 1936

CP - *Untitled*, 1969

Metal, hair. 100.5 x 70.5 x 5 cm / Purchase, 1981 / AM 1981-1

Kounellis's elective homeland is the Italy of Alberto Burri and Lucio Fontana. It is from their works, as from those of Yves Klein and Piero Manzoni, that the artist draws his conceptual approach to organic materials using wool, hair, string, coal and cloth bags. In 1969, he even exhibited live horses in the L'Attico gallery in Rome, thus providing a new take on the tradition of sculpture 'from the life'. Kounellis also incorporated smells and sounds into sculpture, as well as an exceptional expressionist power vehicled by the use of dangerous materials, such as gas and fire, by claustrophobic space (blocked off exits, suffocating mazes), and by the monumental vigour of sheet steel.

Lacombe, Georges (Paul Lacombe)
Versailles, 1868 - Saint-Nicolas-des-Bois (Normandy), 1916
MO - *L'Existence [Existence]*, 1894-96
Walnut. 68 x 142 x 6 cm / Acquired from Mme Mora Lacombe,
the artist's daughter, 1956 / R.F. 3221
MO - *Isis*, 1895
Partially polychrome mahogany. 111 x 62 x 17 cm / Acquisition, 1982 / RF 3627
Introduced to the Nabis by Paul Sérusier in 1892, Lacombe was
to become the group's most important sculptor. Under the
influence of Gauguin's wood carving and of Breton folk art, the
four panels of his *Bed* were dedicated to the theme of the human
condition. Symbolist in spirit, laden with references, his art is
nonetheless very straightforward, as much in the choice of its
subjects as in its realist handling. If the polychrome two-level
relief is Lacombe's privileged mode of expression, he also carved
a number of sculptures in the round, in particular a *Mary
Magdalene*, a *Christ on the Cross* and a self-portrait, as well as
portraits, including one of Bonnard.

Laib, Wolfgang
Metzingen (Germany), 1950
CP - *Milk-Stone*, 1977
Marble and milk. 143.5 x 139.5 x 2 cm / Purchase, 1991 / AM 1991-314
Laib came away from his medical studies with the sensation that,
in the West, knowledge of the body and of nature is grounded
more in the prohibitions of hygiene and the idea of control than in
a principle of communion. To make his visions reality, he thus
turned to art, producing his first *Milk-Stones*. Two years later, he
gathered pollen (pine, dandelion) collected during the summer
months and spread it over the ground, thereby obtaining simple
forms whose intense colours bewitch the beholder. Such actions
chime in perfectly with a carefully contrived, deliberately artistic
lifestyle: life in a remote village, knowledge of the botanical environment and of flowering periods, patient gathering, ritual installation in the exhibition space. The artist pours out the contents of
the pollen flasks in a kneeling position; a relationship to the earth
symptomatic of his whole approach. Each of his works seems to
offer a concentrate of life. In more recent pieces, he piles up heaps
of rice or builds houses out of various materials, including wax: in
Laib, homeopathic doses of Far Eastern sensitivity seem to perco-
late through to Western culture.

Lardera, Berto
La Spezia (Italy), 1911 – Paris, 1989
CP - *Two-Dimensional Sculpture*, 1947
Copper, aluminium, iron. 130 x 90 x 25 cm / Gift of the artist to the state, 1970;
transfer, 1976 / AM 1976-992
The early works of Lardera glorify the Italian Resistance in
which he himself took part. In 1947, he settled in Paris. The
result of an intricate process of cutting and welding iron or stainless steel plates, his sculpture, initially in two, and subsequently
in three dimensions, marries cold and lyrical abstraction. Paris
gallerist Denise René acclaimed his work at an early stage and in
1948 dedicated an exhibition to him. Moving between Paris and
Hamburg, Lardera followed a dual career as a sculptor and a
teacher, and created about thirty large-scale works now dispersed
across the world.

Laurana, Francesco
Vrana (near Zara), c. 1430 - Avignon, 1502
ML - *Unknown Princess*, second half of the 15th century
Marble. 44 x 44 x 24 cm / Seized in 1793 with the collections of the Condé family
at the Château d'Ecouen. Accession to the Louvre, 1818 / Department of Sculpture /
MR 2597
Brother of the architect Luciano Laurana, Francesco entered the
service of Alfonso of Aragon in Naples. From 1453 to 1458, he
worked on the carved decoration of the triumphal arch of the
Castel Nuovo. He then moved to Provence (1461-66) in the
entourage of King René and subsequently to Sicily (1467-72),
where he was responsible for several Madonnas, and Naples
(1474). His activity as a sculptor was thereafter to be divided
between the south of France and Naples. His marble busts of
women are imbued with an aristocratic elegance. Idealised and
rendered through pure geometrical forms, they are nonetheless
always based on acute observation of the sitter.

Laurens, Henri

Paris, 1885 – *ibid,* **1954**

CP - *Construction, Small Head,* **1915**

Wood, polychrome iron sheeting. 30 x 13 x 10 cm / Claude Laurens donation, 1967 / AM 1537 S

CP - *Autumn,* **1948**

Bronze. 80 x 170 x 57 cm / Claude Laurens donation, 1967 / AM 1632 S

Laurens discovered Cubism in 1908 in the studios at La Ruche in Paris while still a humble stone-carver. Working in solitude and studying Romanesque and Gothic sculpture, in 1911 he became friends with Georges Braque. After assimilating Analytical Cubism, in 1915 he carried out his first *Constructions,* which focused on the theme of the bottle and the glass. The colour he applied to his wood and plaster pieces sought to open up volume, conveying a comprehension of the object that associates intellectual analysis with a tactile rendering. After World War I, he married his treatment of forms with the newfound freedom of Surrealism, though he avoided imagery, committed as he was to the plastic depiction of the female body and to the harmony between line and volume.

LeWitt, Sol

Hartford (USA), 1928

CP - *5 Part Piece (Open Cubes) in Form of a Cross,* **1966-1969**

Painted steel. 160 x 450 x 450 cm / State purchase 1976; transfer, 1977 / AM 1977-108

After studies at Syracuse University (New York), Sol LeWitt worked as a graphic designer in the practice of the architect I M Pei. Through a stay in the Far East, he became familiar with Oriental art and the concept of the void. It is the influence of Constructivism and of the Bauhaus, however, which seems paramount in his earliest paintings with lines and squares (1961-64), and from 1966 in his sculptures, variations on the cube disposed in space based on a machined module in varnished iron, wood or white-painted steel. In 1967 and 1969, he brought out two manifestoes on Conceptual art (*Paragraphs on Conceptual Art* and *Sentences on Conceptual Art*) and embarked on his temporary *Wall Drawings.* The concept of the work, as illustrated in the drawing in a sketchbook, may or may not be realised: the colour or monochrome material manifestation serves solely to visualise the ideas.

Lipchitz, Jacques

Druskininkai (Russia), 1891 – Capri (Italy), 1973

CP - *Figure,* **1926-30**

Painted plaster. 220 x 95 x 75 cm / Donation by the Jacques and Yulla Lipchitz Foundation, 1976 / AM 1976-822

Coming to Paris to learn sculpture, Lipchitz was diverted from academic study by an encounter with Mexican painter Diego Rivera. Lipchitz created a massless abstraction, his early sculpture possessing a Cubist character close to the constructions of Picasso or Laurens, before turning post-Cubist, even Surrealist in the 1920s. Often openwork, these pieces constitute a transparent sculpture whose invention the artist claimed jealously. From the 1930s, the reintroduction of mythological or Biblical subjects was accompanied by compositions in curved bands that appear somewhat baroque in spirit. Still restrained in Figure (1926-30), a sense of energy explodes in powerful monumental works, such as *Le Chant des voyelles* (1931-32) and *Prometheus* (1936).

Maillol, Aristide

Banyuls-sur-Mer, 1861 – *ibid,* **1944**

MO - *Baigneuse debout [Standing Bather],* **1898-1900**

Bronze. 78 x 25 x 15 cm / Transferred by order of the Commission de Récupération Artistique in 1949 / RFR 3

MO - *Méditerranée [Mediterranean],* **1902-05**

Bronze, artist's proof. 118 x 142 x 71 cm / Gift of Mme Dina Vierny, 1986 / RF 4096

MO - *Désir [Desire],* **1905-07**

Lead. 120 x 115 x 25 cm / Transferred by order of the Commission de Récupération Artistique in 1949 / RFR 14

MO - *Jeunesse [Youth],* **1910**

Marble. 106 x 44 x 34 cm / Gift of J Zoubaloff in 1927 / RF 3240

Initially a painter and creator of tapestries, Maillol began sculpting late and self-taught. He modelled clay and carved wood intuitively, with a love for rounded forms that owe as much to his temperament as to a taste for Classical art, which he was to explore further during a journey to Greece. Of a literally tactile geometry, his female figures, such as *Mediterranean,* appeal as much to the hand as to the mind. Energy in the service of an idea, this is also the mainspring of *L'Action Enchaînée,* carved for the monument dedicated to Auguste Blanqui in Puget-Théniers (1906). Like Brancusi, with whom he shares a marked simplicity, each given formal type is tackled in numerous variants. The natural light in the garden at the Tuileries much enhances the opulence of Maillol's serene and sober art. The Musée Maillol in Paris is devoted to his work.

Man Ray (Emanuel Rudnitsky)

Philadelphia, 1890 – Paris, 1976

CP - *Lampshade,* **1919 /1954**

Painted aluminium. 152.5 x 63.5 cm / Gift in lieu, 1994 / AM 1994-300

Friend of Marcel Duchamp, Man Ray began producing Dadaist pieces, such as the *Objet à détruire* (1923), comprising a metronome whose needle has a photograph of an eye attached to it. Accompanying instructions stipulated that it should be smashed to pieces with a hammer, but it was actually destroyed in an act of vandalism after World War II. Its replacement was entitled the *Indestructible Object* — though this only after a lawsuit forced the insurance company concerned to accept the ready-made's increase in artistic value! Man Ray also made constructions, which he destroyed after taking mysterious-looking photographs of them, for instance *The Enigma of Isidore Ducasse* (1935), featuring a sewing-machine and an umbrella concealed beneath a cover carefully bound up with string in a kind of Christo before the event. *Lampshade* was also one of the sculptures that he photographed.

Matisse, Henri

Cateau-Cambrésis, 1869 – Nice, 1954

CP - *Nu de dos, premier état* or *Dos I [Nude from the Back - First State],* **1950**

Lost-wax process bronze. 190 x 116 x 17 cm / State purchase, 1964; transfer, 1970 / AM 1710 S

CP - *Nu de dos, quatrième état* or *Dos IV [Nude from the Back - Fourth State],* **1960-63**

Bronze, dark patina. 190 x 114 x 16 cm / State purchase, 1964; transfer, 1970 / AM 1711 S

An illustrious promoter of 'painter's sculpture' who transformed the history of the art at the beginning of the 20th century, Matisse modestly averred that he sculpted only as a rest from painting. The change of medium was not without impact on sculpture, nor on his own painting, in which his sculptures often appear. However, while he would paint constantly, Matisse might remain years without sculpting. His oeuvre numbers 59 works, produced in bursts of activity, but only a single relief, for Matisse was a modeller, like Carpeaux and Rodin, whom he admired. In his studies of movement, he pursued Rodin's explorations, liberating line from volume, as in the *Serpentine.* Matisse also revelled in dense forms deriving from Gauguin and black African art. Two constants are noticeable in his work: the use of series (from the *Madeleines* through the *Jeannettes* to the *Backs*) and the tendency to abstract from the model.

Meissonier, Ernest

Lyon, 1815 - Paris, 1891

MO - *Voyageur dans le vent [Traveller in the Wind,* also known as *Napoleon during the Russian Campaign. Maréchal Ney. Officer of the Empire in Torment],* **1878**

Grey (plinth) and red (horse and rider) wax, cloth (cloak, saddle rug), leather (reins) on wooden plinth. 47 x 60 x 39 cm / Gift of M. du Pasquier en 1984 / RF 3672

A major painter of genre and military subjects, in which not a single gaiter button is ever out of place, a foremost contributor to the Napoleonic epic in painting, an observer hailed by the official art world, Meissonier was also an artist with doubts who left nothing to chance and who turned his hand to sculpture in an effort to improve his painting. Thus the wax models he made from 1860 on were intended as studies for figures in his pictures. In his quest for verisimilitude, he built meticulous models out of miscellaneous materials in an approach that might be contrasted with Degas' horses, constructed with singular formal economy. Dalí admired Meissonier's verism, seeing him as sharing in his own 'paranoiac' concern to convince viewers of the truth of the simulacra before him. Of the score or so models by Meissonier, eight were cast and he was widely collected.

Mercié, Antonin

Toulouse, 1845 - Paris, 1916

MO - *David,* **1869-70/1873**

Bronze. 184 x 76 x 83 cm / Commissioned 1872 / RF 186

A pupil of Falguière and Prix de Rome (1868), Mercié enjoyed success at the Salon with his David, conceived in Rome (1869-73) in the spirit of Florentine models. His *Gloria Victis* bought by city of Paris is for its part a patriotic piece. Among the many monuments for which he was responsible, special mention should be made of the *Genius of the Arts* for the entryway to the Carrousel du Louvre (Louvre), which bears his hallmark: a supple, elegant lightness. His swelling order book included tombs for Père-Lachaise cemetery, funerary statues for the Orléans family at Dreux, *Faidherbe* in Lille and a *Fame* (since destroyed) for the Trocadéro in Paris.

Merz, Mario
Milan, 1925 – Turin, 2003
CP - *Igloo di Giap*, 1968
Iron armature, plastic bags filled with earth, neon tubes, batteries. 120 x 200 cm /
Purchase, 1982 / AM 1982-334
Although this politically engaged artist began as a painter, as
early as 1965 he was making assemblages of objects and various
media given an ethereal touch by the use of neon lighting. The
first igloos appeared in 1968. Fusing sculpture and primitive
architecture, these primaeval heaps emerging from the earth each
represent a revolt against the domination of the industrial
powers. The clash between natural materials, such as straw, wax
and faggots of wood, and industrial products, such as neon and
metal struts, serves to telescope our sense of time — a predomi-
nant subject in Merz from the 1970s. The use of the Fibonacci
mathematical series, the spiral-shaped tables covered in food,
and the piles of unsold newspapers always strive to materialise
the infinite. The juxtaposition of prehistoric animals, crocodiles,
motorcycles, tent-like shelters and strip lights endow his installations with the disturbing feel of a time machine.

Michelangelo (Michelangelo Buonarroti)
Caprese, 1475 - Rome, 1564
ML - *The Captive* or *The Rebel Slave*, 1513-15
Marble. 209 x 49 x 75.5 cm / Executed for the tomb of Pope Julius II /
Accession to the Louvre, 1794 / Department of Sculpture / MR 1589
The young Michelangelo first encountered Antique statuary in the
residence of Lorenzo the Magnificent in Florence, where he moved
in Neo-Platonic Humanist circles. In 1496, he settled in Rome,
carving his first masterpieces, such as the *Pietà* in St Peter's (1499)
and *The Virgin with Child with the Infant St John the Baptist*
(1504-05). He carved his *David* (1501-04) on his return to
Florence, where he was much affected by the preaching of
Savonarola. He was then recalled to Rome by Pope Julius II, who
entrusted him with the execution of his tomb. The *Slaves* in the
Louvre and *Moses* were started in 1513 for the second version of
this tomb, which was to be reworked several more times before its
eventual completion in 1545. Betweentimes, Michelangelo was to
work on the Medici tombs in the church of San Lorenzo in
Florence. For the sculptor, who was also a remarkable poet, the
idea always precedes form and always exceeds it: hence, the opposition between the polished sculpture, in which the concept asserts
itself, and the *non finitò*, where it remains imprisoned in matter.

Minne, Georges
Ghent, 1866 - Laethem-Saint-Martin (Belgium), 1941
MO - *Kneeling Youth at the Fountain*, 1898
Bronze. 78 x 19 x 43 cm / Gift of Enrique Mistler, c. 1933 / RF 3256
This Belgian artist, who worked in Paris and was a friend of the
Symbolist poets Maurice Maeterlinck and Emile Verhaeren,
aimed directly at the human soul, without the detour via the phy-
sical body advocated by Rodin. The anorexic figures of his
Kneeling Youths seem blissfully unaware of the hustle and bustle
of the world, intent as they are solely on their meditation.
Minne's secret, one that only Wilhelm Lehmbruck succeeded in
recapturing, is to exalt line and invest it with heartfelt emotion.
In 1898, Minne joined the colony of artists at Laethem-St-
Martin, where he pursued his work as a sculptor and engraver.

Mino da Fiesole (Mino di Giovanni)
Poppi, 1431 – Florence, 1484
ML - *Dietisalvi Neroni (1406-1482)*, 1464
Marble. 57 x 50 cm / Formerly Eugène Piot and Charles Timbal collections.
Gift of Mme Dreyfus, née Henriette Obermayer, and her children in remembrance
of the collector Gustave Dreyfus (1837-1914) / Department of Sculpture / RF 1669
From his master Desiderio da Settignano, Mino learnt a sense of
elegance borne out in his marble relief *Charity* for the tomb of
Ugo, duke of Tuscany (1469-81), in the church of La Badia in
Florence. In his marble busts depicting the Florentine aristocracy
of the Medici and Strozzi families, Mino da Fiesole reverts to the
tradition of Antique portraiture, while at the same time capturing, as in the bust of Dietisalvi Neroni, the individual expression
of the sitter with an amplitude and a humanist grace quite unlike
Donatello's incisive line.

Miró, Juan
Barcelona, 1893 – Palma de Majorca, 1983
CP - *L'Objet du couchant*, 1935-36
Assemblage: painted carob-tree trunk, bedspring, gas jet, gas burner, chain, shackle,
string. 68 x 44 x 26 cm / Made at Montroig and Barcelona / Purchase, 1975 /
AM 1975-56
Would Miró ever have made sculpture without Montroig, the
Catalan village where he would collect the stones, branches and
other objects that filled his workshop before one day finding
their place in an assemblage? His 'poetic objects' (1930s), close
in spirit to the concerns of the Surrealists, stem from these kinds
of found objects. In 1944, he discovered with Artigas the technique of *grand feu* firing that gives incomparable strength of
colour to ceramics. At the same time, Miró also worked on
bronzes, which started from strange assemblages reminiscent of
those of Picasso. In the 1960s, in his own inimitable fashion he
started incorporating manufactured or mass-produced objects
into his pieces. His large-scale pieces in painted resin, such as the
one on the esplanade at La Défense in Paris (1978), have something of the primitive sign or child's model about them, and bring
to public sculpture an imaginative power and malleability that is
unparalleled.

Morris, Robert
Kansas City, 1931
CP - *Wall Hanging*, 1971-1973
Cut felt. 247 x 355 x 120 cm / Daniel Cordier donation, 1989 / AM 1989-459
Following engineering studies undertaken in parallel with a training
in art, Morris' creativity engaged on all fronts: painting, theatre,
dance, cinema, happenings... Settling in New York in 1961, he
only opted for sculpture in 1964-65, taking part in the exhibition
that sparked off Minimalist art, 'Primary Structures' at the
Jewish Museum, New York, in 1966. Published in *Artforum,* his
'Notes on Sculpture' propose a theoretical approach that shakes
off Judd's Gestaltist sculpture and focuses instead on the life of
materials: his 'Felt Works', for example, fold and droop under
their own weight. Morris undertook a vast number of experiments in the field: earthworks, videos, time-variable installations,
imprints, performances, etc. In a new direction that again
demonstrates the unclassifiable character of his oeuvre, the
frames of Morris' most recent pieces possess a relief of neo-
Baroque inspiration.

Nauman, Bruce
Fort Wayne (USA), 1941
CP - *Smoke Rings (Model for Underground Tunnels)*, 1979
Eight plaster elements on wooden side pieces. Diam: 340 cm / Purchase, 1985 /
AM 1985-140
Eight plaster elements on wooden side pieces. Diam: 340 cm /
Purchase, 1985 / AM 1985-140
From 1968 to 1971, Nauman worked on taking his own image,
using the dual frame of the space in which he moved and a video-
camera. During the same period, he also used wax, rubber and,
later, neon tubes to mould parts of his body. His creative career
has developed through a constant process of interchange between
different disciplines: moulding human or animal bodies (as in the
'carrousels' of 1988), geometric structures designed to posit body
and space simultaneously (perceptual *Corridors*, 'suspensions'),
pre-programmed neon installations in which everyday words
clash... *Corridors* and videos combine: human relationships
(power, sex, food) are conveyed through schematic neon figures
or by videos in which a series of words (*Good Boy, Bad Boy,*
1985) is mindlessly repeated. Nauman is symptomatic of the
desire to recover a lost unity by bridging the gap between image
and sensation, between interior and exterior, the individual and
the social, the mind and the body, for which his circular *Tunnels*
constitute an active metaphor.

Neto, Ernesto
Rio de Janeiro, 1964
CP - *We Stopped Just Here at the Time*, 2002
Cloth, love, turmeric, cumin, pepper. 400 x 506 x 506 cm / Gift of the Société
des Amis du Musée National d'Art Moderne, 2003 / AM 2003-242
Neto is regarded as heir apparent to a Brazilian school that has
numbered names of the calibre of Hélio Oiticica and the two
Lygias, Clark and Pape. In the 1960s, in the era of Neoconcretism,
a geometrical abstractionism originating in Europe (notably by
Max Bill and Zurich Concrete art) melded with a more biomorphic
expressiveness receptive to sensory experience. A new, more participatory relationship was sought between work and spectator. In a
similar spirit, Neto worked on a number of series, the *Ovaloids,*
polystyrene-filled Lycra sheaths that can be slipped over the arm,
then the *Humanoids* and *Naves,* which can be physically entered.
Set up according to a precise protocol, *We Stopped Just Here at the
Time* alludes to skin and vessels, to capillarity and networks, to
which the incorporation of aromatic spices adds the sense of smell.
The artist represented Brazil at the 2001 Venice Biennale.

Oldenburg, Claes

Stockholm, 1929

CP - *Ghost Drum Set,* 1972

Installation: ten elements in sewn and painted cloth containing polystyrene balls.
80 (with plinth) x 183 x 183 cm / Gift of the Menil Foundation in memory
of Jean de Menil, 1975 / AM 1975-64

After moving to New York in 1956, Oldenburg became one of the
earliest exponents of the 'happening'. In *The Street* (1959) and *The
Store* (1960-62), objects made of cardboard, cloth and papier-
mâché, painted in the manner of Abstract Expressionism, were sold
to visitors. He subsequently used plastic in outsized, floppy versions
of modern furnishings that he called *Soft Sculptures,* phantoms of
the everyday in the era of Pop art. In 1965, he began filling sketchbooks with designs for monumental projects that drift hauntingly
through the urban landscape, some of which were later to be realised: *Lipstick,* Yale, 1969; *Clothespin,* Philadelphia, 1976; *Bat
Column,* Chicago, 1977. Since then, Oldenburg, who lives part of
the year in France, has, in collaboration with Coosje Van Bruggen,
become a significant producer of public art. His success is due to a
thorough examination of the site prior to each design and to his
unrestrained attitude with respect to architecture, as visible in the
Buried Bicycle at La Villette (Paris, 1990).

Pagès, Bernard

Cahors, 1940

CP - *Dix Assemblages bout à bout [Ten Assemblages
End to End],* 1974

Wood, annexed devices. 40 x 110 cm / Purchase, 1984 / AM 1984-367

'Born at Cahors in the Lot early on September 21, 1940. Childhood
on the farm. Strong presence of the cliffs and rocks, but also of water
and sand. 1950: First drawings, then watercolours and gouaches.
1959: Paris. Greatly impressed by Brancusi's studio at the Musée
d'Art Moderne. 1965-6. Coaraze: village in the Nice hinterland.
More space. Meet Jacques Lepage who introduced me to C Viallat,
B - Venet, E - Dietman, then later P - Saytour, D Biga, D Dezeuze.
Nouveaux Réalistes show at Nice. 1968-9. Exhibition in the village,
1970. Break-up with the people from Supports/Surfaces.' This is
how Pagès summarised his artistic biography up to 1970 when exhi-
biting his famous *Abri de Jardin Manufrance,* a work that distanced
him from Supports/Surfaces. Subsequently his 'nomenclatures' and
assemblages mixed natural objects and instruments in combinatory
processes. From 1980 on, his *Composite Columns* opened up his
sculpture to architecture. Since then the intensity of colour, the
variety of texture, and the energy of the spatial devices in his production display a new mastery of space that goes beyond structural
constructability and engages with the eye and body of the viewer.

Paik, Nam June

Seoul (South Korea), 1932

CP - *Moon is the Oldest TV,* 1965

Installation: 12 to 17 black and white TV sets, 12 to 17 magnets.
Darkroom from 10 x 7 m / Purchase, 1985 / AM 1985-142

After studying musicology in Tokyo, Nam June Paik settled in
Germany in 1956-57. Meeting Stockhausen, who introduced him
to electro-acoustic music, and John Cage, who drew him into the
Fluxus movement, he developed the idea of a total art founded on
the Event. Not afraid of iconoclastic gestures (*Klavier integral,*
1958-63), one of his actions at Fluxus festivals centred on the destruction of musical instruments. On moving to the USA (1964),
Paik turned to video-sculpture and work on the audiovisual signals
emitted by television. Making use of magnets and satellite, he
creates images that subvert the small screen. The impact of his television installations — robot families and strange hybrids, such as a
Buddha and a TV monitor, or goldfish in front of a television
set/aquarium — derives from their humour and critical insight, as
well as from the Eastern perspective they offer on Western culture.

Pajou, Augustin

Paris, 1730 - *ibid,* 1809

ML - *Psyché abandonnée [Psyche Abandoned],* 1785/90

Marble. 177 x 86 x 86 cm / Accession to the Louvre in 1829 /
Department of Sculpture / MR SUP 62

Professor at the Académie Royale by 1760, remarkable draughtsman, Pajou was also the talented decorator of the Opera at
Versailles (1768-70), the Palais Royal (1769), and the Hôtel
d'Argenson, as well as the creator of the *St Augustine* for Les
Invalides (1761 Salon). Hardly the CV of a troublemaker. And yet,
if he remains known to the general public, it is largely thanks to this
Psyche Abandoned. With its daring show of flesh, it stirred up such
a scandal at the 1785 Salon that eventually the plaster model could
be shown only in the artist's studio. A virtuoso marble carver, Pajou
was able to simultaneously capture and idealise his figures, as in his
Du Barry (1773), and *Buffon* in the Museum of Natural History
(1776), who is posed in the Antique style, with the beautiful abstract form of a crystal at his feet.

Pane, Gina

Biarritz, 1939 – Paris, 1990

CP - *Francis of Assisi Three Times with the Stigmata*, 1985-87

Zinc-plated iron, iron, rust, frosted glass. 169.6 x 198 x 2.2 cm / Purchase, 1989 / AM 1989-3

A major figure in French body art, Gina Pane was much affected by Italy, where she lived until 1961, prior to coming to study at the Ecole des Beaux-Arts in Paris. There, she worked at the Atelier d'Art Sacré founded by Maurice Denis. From 1968 to 1971, she developed 'actions' in the natural world, without an audience. It was only at the beginning of the 1970s that she began executing actions in the studio and finally in public. In her explorations of risk-taking and of the dialectic between pleasure and pain, Gina Pane eschewed all theatricality: 'To live one's body', the artist writes, 'is to also uncover one's weaknesses, the tragic and pitiless servitude of one's shortcomings, one's debilitation and precariousness.' Beyond limits, this oeuvre engaged with the collective as much as with the individual, however: social therapy and political protest revolve around the manifestation of the body. These experiments were accompanied by many preparatory drawings, texts and photographs. In 1981, Pane drew her cycle of actions to a close and began creating plastic works, such as *Partitions,* which tackle matter rather than the body. The question of the sacred and its mediation resurfaced in her late pieces on the saints, as in this *St Francis.* The Centre Pompidou staged a retrospective of her work in February-May 2005.

Pascali, Pino

Bari, 1935 - Rome, 1968

CP - *Le Penne di Esopo [Aesop's Feathers],* 1968

Bird feathers, braided steel wool mounted on a wooden plank.

Diam: 150 cm; depth: 35 cm / Purchase 1991/ AM 1991-98

The untimely death of Pascali at the age of 33 deprived the contemporary art world of one of its most promising talents. A graduate of the art school in Rome in 1959, he initially made a name as a set designer. His one-man show at the Tartaruga gallery (Rome, 1965), another in the Iolas gallery in Paris (1968), together with his participation at the 34th Venice Biennale, where he was awarded the international sculpture prize, crowned three years of intense activity that brought him worldwide acclaim. With its deep roots in the myths of the Mediterranean basin, his culture overlaps with that of Pasolini. One can sometimes sense a glimmer of nostalgia, as for instance in his feather tribute to Aesop. His work often employs fragile, ephemeral materials in brutal contrast to mechanical weapons, as in the series of guns (*Armi*), a silent protest against war.

Penone, Giuseppe

Garessio (Italy), 1947

CP - *Albero [Tree]*, 1973

Wood. 550 x 19.5 x 7.5 cm / Purchase, 1982 / AM 1982-133

CP - *Soffio 6 [Breath 6]*, 1978

Terracotta. 158 x 75 x 79 cm / Purchase, 1980 / AM 1980-42

For Penone, Arte Povera was a way of asserting his empathy with the earth and its forests. In 1969, he started the series of *Alberi* (*Trees*) with the *Four-Meter Tree,* unveiling the whole collection in *Ripetere il Bosco.* His art is based on metonymies in which parts of the body leave imprints — as in the drawing *Eyelid* (1977), measuring more than 10 m — or casts. In the late 1970s, Penone grew potatoes and marrows in moulds in the shape of parts of his body. The *Soffii (Breaths,* 1978) meanwhile are clay vases on a human scale. Yet Penone's sculpture is also analogical: in *Being a River* (1981), he identifies himself with nature's work in reproducing the effect of water eroding a stone. After pieces in thermoformed glass, such as the fingernails of *Nails* (1987-94) and *Anatomies* (1994-97), blocks of marble whose exposed veins are made to appear alive, like human skin, the artist returned to the thematic of the tree. His *Crystal Trees* were an investigation of light, *Respirare l'ombra (Breathing Shadow),* a room papered with bay leaves (2000), an exploration of shadow and the sense of smell. In 1999, *The Tree of Vowels,* a huge bronze tree from which suckers emerge, was set up in the Jardin des Tuileries in Paris. The Centre Pompidou devoted a retrospective to his oeuvre in 2004, an occasion on which *The Cedar of Versailles* was unveiled in the forum.

Pevsner, Antoine

Klimovitchi (Russia), 1884 – Paris, 1962

CP - *Mask*, 1923

Celluloid, zinc. 33 x 20 x 20 cm / Purchase, 1974 / AM 1974-24

CP - *Model for the Construction of 'A World'*, 1946

Brazed, varnished brass struts. 42 x 36 x 31 cm / Gift of Virginie Pevsner, 1962 / AM 1347 S

Drawn to Paris at an early age, and living there from 1911 to 1915, Pevsner, then a painter, decided, in the company of his brother, Naum Gabo, to return to Russia in 1917, just as the Revolution was breaking out. While there the two brothers signed the *Realist Manifesto* in 1920. In 1922, however, they opted to leave Soviet Russia. Antoine settled in Paris and Gabo in New York. If the latter increasingly used materials such as plastic, nylon and glass, Antoine Pevsner employed metal, welding together individual brass or copper wires. These pieces, which, like his *Developable Columns,* can be designed on a monumental scale, express the essence of movement, and incorporate a fourth dimension, that of time, into sculpture. The Centre Pompidou holds the most comprehensive collection of works by this artist who acquired French nationality.

Picasso, Pablo

Málaga (Spain), 1881 – Mougins (France), 1973

CP - *Le Verre d'absinthe [The Absinthe Glass]*, 1914

Painted and sand-coated bronze, absinthe spoon. 21.5 x 16.5 x 6.5 cm /
Louise and Michel Leiris donation, 1984 / AM 1984-629

CP - *Figure*, 1928

Wire (iron) sheet-metal. 37.5 x 10 x 19.6 cm / Gift in lieu, 1979. Musée Picasso /
On deposit at the Musée National d'Art Moderne, Centre Pompidou /
AM 1984-DEP 20

CP - *Petite Fille sautant à la corde [Little Girl Skipping]*, 1950

Bronze. 153 x 62 x 65 cm / Louise and Michel Leiris donation, 1984 /
AM 1984-642

Although one might well like the *Fou [Fool]* of 1905 or the *Head of a Woman* (*Fernande*) of 1909, a not especially convincing exploration of sculpture in facets, Picasso's first genuine contribution to modern sculpture appears in Cubists constructions, such as *The Absinthe Glass*. In 1928-29, helped by Julio González he made soldered iron *Constructions,* including the *Project for a Monument to Apollinaire*. In the 1930s Boisgeloup was the stage for various experiments: reclining figures in wood, imposing sculptures in ronde-bosse, Surrealist assemblages. Concerned as it is with a newfound harmony, the *Bull's Head* (1943) is as unconstrained as *Man with Sheep* (1944). In the 1950s, Picasso created hybrid pieces in which the figure takes shape around some accompanying object, as in *Little Girl Skipping* and *She-Ape with Young* (1952-55). From the early cut-outs in sheet bronze (1960s) to large-scale works in metal or cement made from his models, Picasso's sculptural output numbers some 350 pieces, not including his ceramics.

Pigalle, Jean-Baptiste

Paris, 1714 - *ibid*, 1785

ML - *Amitié [Friendship]*, 1750-53

Marble. 142 x 80 x 77 cm / Accession to the Louvre in 1879 / Department
of Sculpture / RF 297

ML - *Mercure attachant ses talonnières [Mercury Tying his Talaria]*, 1753

Lead. 187 x 108 x 106 cm / Restored with help from the RATP / From the Château
d'Anet, then Jardin du Luxembourg. Accession to the Louvre,1872 /
Department of Sculpture / RF 3023

ML - *Voltaire nu [Voltaire Nude]*, 1770-76

Marble. 150 x 89 x 77 cm / Commissioned by subscription in 1770.
Left by Voltaire to his great-nepthew. Given to the Institut de France, 1807.
On deposit, 1962 / Department of Sculpture / Ent 1962. 1

ML - *Autoportrait [Self-Portrait]*, c. 1777

Terracotta. 44 x 27 x 25 cm / Acquisition, 1949 / Department of Sculpture /
RF 2670

Dubbed the 'donkey of sculpture' due to his tireless labour, Pigalle paid for his training in Rome out of his own pocket. At the 1742 Salon, he exhibited a plaster *Mercury Tying his Talaria* inspired by the Flemish painter Jordaens, with a pendant, a *Venus*, marble versions of which, today in Berlin, were presented by Louis XV to Frederick II of Prussia. Acceding to the Academie Royale in 1744, Pigalle's career flourished under the patronage of Madame de Pompadour, a portrait of whom appears in *Friendship*. His *Child with a Cage* (1750), the pieces for the marquise's château at Bellevue, his *Virgin and Child* (Eglise St-Sulpice, Paris, 1754) and *Voltaire Nude* all show an intense concern with realism, marked by an extreme individualisation of the features, of which the *Self-Portrait* constitutes another masterly example. If his rejection of idealisation, most notable in *Voltaire Nude,* left contemporaries bewildered, it enabled him to create two monuments whose immediacy of expression is of unusual power. Referring to the mausoleum for the Maréchal de Saxe (1776, St-Thomas Protestant church, Strasbourg), Alberto Giacometti wrote: 'With Pigalle, death is as relentless as his realism.' The sculptor himself (letter to Voltaire, 1763) described his monument to Louis XV for Reims, which presented the king on foot and stretching out a hand protectively over his people, as being that of a 'happy citizen'. Only the figures from the pedestal survive.

Pilon, Germain

Paris, known from 1540 - *ibid*, 1590

ML - *Mask of Henri II*, second half of the 16th century

Terracotta. 21 x 16 x 11 cm / Removed from St-Denis, 1881 / Department of
Sculpture / RF 446

ML - *Monument for the Heart of Henri II: The Three Graces*, 1560-66

Marble. 150 x 75 x 75 cm / Previously in the Couvent des Célestins, then the Musée
des Monuments Français, 1817 / Department of Sculpture / MR 1591 A

ML - *The Resurrection*, second half of the 16th century

Marble. 215 x 188 x 74 cm / Originally in the Salle des Antiquités at the Louvre,
before dispersion: Christ in the Eglise St-Paul-St-Louis, Paris, 1933; soldiers
in the Musée des Monuments Français, 1821 / Department of Sculpture /
RF 2292, MR 1592, MR 1593

ML - *Virgin of Sorrows*, 1590

Polychrome terracotta and gypsum. 159 x 119 x 81 cm / Previously in the Sainte-
Chapelle, then Musée des Monuments Français, then the chapel in the Ecole Militaire,
St-Cyr / Department of Sculpture / RF 3147

Trained under his father, it is conceivable that Germain Pilon travelled to Italy, though this has not been proved. From 1561 to
1563, he carved the *Three Graces* carrying the urn containing the
heart of Henri II for the Couvent des Célestins in Paris.
Following designs by Primaticcio, he then carried out the recumbent statues of the royal couple, the praying figures in bronze,
two of the Virtues and reliefs on the base (1562-73) for the tomb
of the same monarch for the Rotonde des Valois in the abbey at
St-Denis. His *Resurrection,* also originally conceived for the
Rotonde, and *Virgin of Sorrows* testify to his sense of grandeur
in composition and to an astute penetration of mental states.
Such qualities of intensity and nobility characterise the fifteen or
so tombs by his hand, most of them severely damaged today.

Pompon, François

Saulieu (Burgundy), 1855 - Paris, 1933

MO - *Ours blanc [Polar Bear]*, 1922/1929

Lens stone. Plaster presented at the 1922 Salon d'Automne. 163 x 251 x 90 cm /
Accession to the Musée du Luxembourg in 1929 / RF 3269

Son of a cabinetmaker, Pompon was the greatest early 20th-century
animal sculptor. From 1890, he acted as master carver to Rodin,
who encouraged him to develop his taste for the animal figure. His
synthetic manner, which, above and beyond its Art Deco accents,
bears the hallmarks of the Egyptian art he so admired, culminated
in the *Polar Bear,* which met with great success at the 1922 Salon
d'Automne. The sculptor also carved a *Bull* (1931) that was erected
after his death on the main square in his native town of Saulieu.
Pompom bequeathed more than 300 works to the French state.

Ponce, Jacquiot, also known as Master Ponce (attributed to)

Rethel, flourished from 1527 - Paris, 1572

ML - *André Blondel de Rocquencourt* (died 1558), third quarter
of the 16th century

Bronze. 59 x 173 x 6 cm / Previously in the Musée des Monuments Français, 1823 /
Department of Sculpture / MR 1710

Ponce Jacquiot's early works in France and Italy earned him a
mention in the pages of Vasari and a summons to the abbey at St-
Denis. Together with Germain Pilon, he there executed bronzes of
Strength and *Temperance* for the tomb of Henri II (1563-70). Ponce
translates into sculpture the elegance of line typical of Primaticcio,
then superintendent of the king's works. He was also responsible
for a terracotta *Tireuse d'épine* (Louvre) and the splendid bas-relief
on the tomb of the Sieur de Rocquencourt, controller general of
finances. The *Diana* at Anet is also sometimes ascribed to him.

Pradier, James (Jean-Jacques Pradier)

Geneva, 1790 – Bougival (Ile-de-France), 1852

ML - *Satyre et Bacchante [Satyr and Bacchante]*, 1834

Marble. 125 x 112 x 78 cm / Acquired with the participation of the Société des Amis
du Louvre, 1980 / Department of Sculpture / RF 3475

Prix de Rome in 1813, Pradier returned from Italy with a
Bacchante of unbridled sensuality and a *Wounded Niobid* that
carried all before them at the 1822 Salon. These sculptures exem-
plifying the duality of an oeuvre which, on the one hand, leads
towards a pristine Neo-Greek style, and, on the other, as in *Satyr
and Bacchante,* tends towards an eroticism that shocked the
morals of the day. He might be dubbed the 'Ingres of sculpture',
for he, too, produced *Odalisques,* while his *Sappho* is grandly
noble in inspiration, were it not for his fondness for sculpture of
a more libertine spirit, which he tested first on the public with
statuettes before launching into marble. Curiously, once successful he was awarded many official commissions, such as the
Fames on the Arc de Triomphe, the statues of *Lille* and
Strasbourg in place de la Concorde, the *Victories* on the tomb of
Napoleon at Les Invalides, and a monumental fountain in Nîmes.

Préault, Auguste

Paris, 1809 - *ibid*, 1879

MO - *Ophelia*, 1843/1876

Bronze. 75 x 200 x 20 cm / State commission, 1876, transferred to the Musées
Nationaux, 1982 / RF 3641

MO - *Virgil*, 1853

Colossal oval medallion, bronze. 95 x 85 x 23 cm / Acquired by Napoleon III
in 1853 / RF 3

A pupil of David d'Angers, Préault was a Romantic in his choice
of subject (*Ophelia, Dante and Virgil in Hell*) and lyric style,
with its splitting line and tumultuous sense of movement. His
Clémence Isaure for the Luxembourg gardens is an apt transla-
tion of the historicism of the time, while, with *Ophelia* and the
noble profile of his *Virgil*, the medallion of *Silence* erected over
the tomb of Jacob Robles in Père-Lachaise cemetery, is his most
mysterious work. It was only after the Revolution of 1848 that
he was accepted at the Salon and received official orders from the
Second Empire for the Louvre, Versailles and several Paris
churches.

Puget, François

Toulon, 1651 - Marseille, 1707

ML - *Milon de Crotone aux mains emprisonnées dans un tronc
de chêne [Milon of Crotona, his Hands Trapped in the Trunk
of an Oak Tree]*, second half of the 17th century

Pen and brown ink, lead pencil, grey wash. 45 x 31 cm / Bequest, 1881 /
Graphic Arts Department, drawings and miniatures collection / RF 1177, recto

After training with his father, the sculptor Pierre Puget, François
turned to painting. In 1682, he presented to the king his father's
Milon of Crotona from which he made this drawing, followed by
the *Perseus and Andromeda* in 1685. Repairing to Toulon and
Marseille, he there devoted himself to religious painting and portraiture. His most famous picture is the *Réunion d'amateurs* (1684,
Louvre), which some experts believe contains a portrait of the com-
poser Lully.

Puget, Pierre

Marseille, 1620 - *ibid*, 1694

ML - *Milon de Crotona*, 1670-82

Carrara marble. 270 x 140 x 80 cm / Commissioned by the Bâtiments du Roi
in 1670. Placed in the park at Versailles, 1683. Accession to the Louvre, 1829 /
Department of Sculpture / MR 2075

ML - *Alexander and Diogenes*, 1670-89

Carrara marble. 332 x 296 x 44 cm / Commissioned by the Bâtiments du Roi.
Transferred by the Musée de Versailles, 1833 / Department of Sculpture /
MR 2776

ML - *Perseus and Andromeda*, 1678-84

Marble. 320 x 106 x 114 cm / Illustration of an episode in Ovid's Metamorphoses /
Executed for Louis XIV, probably in collaboration with Christophe Veyrier. Erected
at Versailles at the Tapis Vert in 1685 / Transferred from the park at Versailles,
1850 / Department of Sculpture / MR 2076

Son of a Marseille stonemason, longtime carver to the royal ships
in the arsenal at Toulon, who shuttled between Genoa, the cities
of southern France and Paris, Puget was a Baroque genius maroo-
ned in Classical France. He was nonetheless feted by his peers as
well as by Louis XIV's minister Colbert, who, in 1670, made over
to him the blocks of marble from which he was to carve three
indisputable masterpieces. The first, *Milon of Crotona*, widely
admired was installed in the park at Versailles, followed by
Perseus and Andromeda. Puget's pugnacious temperament led
him to heroic figures, such as Hercules, and towards dramas of
violence and faith. A painter and architect as well as sculptor, he
also designed the magnificent chapel topped by an ovoid dome at
the former charity hospital of the Vieille Charité in Marseille.

Raynaud, Jean-Pierre
Courbevoie (Ile-de-France), 1939
CP - *Container Zéro*, 1988
Site-specific; steel, tiles, lighting. 330 x 330 x 330 cm / Purchased with aid
from the Centre National des Arts Plastiques, 1988 / AM 1988-2
In the 1960, this gardener, who so hated seeing his plants die that
he set them in concrete, this city-dweller, distraught by what he
saw as the horrendous, dehumanising invasion of mass-media
messages, began to work on red and white *Psycho-objects*
(gauges, ladders, first-aid equipment, traffic signs, flower pots).
Focusing less than on the objects themselves than on the sense of
alienation individuals feel when confronted by the signs produced
by the collectivity, he went on to completely surrender his private
life, opening up his house, lined entirely in white tiling (1974),
and publishing its contents (1988), before destroying it and dis-
playing the remains in pots at the CAPC contemporary art
museum in Bordeaux. The same uneasy asceticism transpires in
the stained-glass for the Cistercian abbey at Noirlac (1977) and in
the 'zero spaces', from which the 1988 piece derives. One of
Raynaud's great regrets was the failure of the *Tour Blanche* at
Vénissieux, a plan to 'immolate' an abandoned high-rise by covering
it entirely in white tiles.

Renoir, Pierre-Auguste and Guino, Richard
Limoges, 1841 - Cagnes-sur-mer, 1919
Girone (Spain), 1890 - Anthony (France), 1973
MO - *Madame Renoir (1859-1915) [Renoir's Wife (1859-1915)]*, 1916
Bust, polychrome mortar. 82 x 53 x 34 cm / Acquisition, 1955 / RF 2764
Renoir came to sculpture only after 1913, by which time he was
almost paralysed. His few works (a score or so pieces) were carried
out according to his specifications by Guino (as in the case with
this portrait of his wife), to the extent that, in 1973, the latter was
legally pronounced joint author of Renoir's sculptures. *Venus
Victrix* (1915-16) and the *Grande Baigneuse* (1917) are both tributes to womanhood and fertility. The sculptor here allows the
generous proportions of the female figures he liked to paint to take
possession of the space, in a fusion of form and surroundings
that paves the way for another Renoir — his son, the future film
director, Jean.

Richier, Germaine
Granz (France), 1904 – Montpellier, 1959
CP - *L'Orage [The Storm]*, 1947-48
Bronze. 200 x 80 x 52 cm / Purchase, 1949 / AM 887 S
A pupil of Antoine Bourdelle at the Grande Chaumière in
Montparnasse, and wife of the writer René de Solier, Richier
extrapolates in a fantastic idiom the hybrid forms that Bourdelle
introduced in his *Centaurs*. The outbreak of World War II
brought forth an insect- and bat-infested world reminiscent of
Goya's *Sleep of Reason,* while spiders and other surreal creatures
entrap space in a wire net. The human figure returns dramati-
cally in the guise of fearsome beings like *The Storm* and *The
Hurricane.* Inventive in approach, Richier puts man back in his
place in the bosom of nature by using natural materials — though
she could also humanise bizarre creations somewhat reminiscent
of paintings by her friends Hans Hartung, Vieira da Silva and
Zao Wou-Ki.

Riemenschneider, Tilman
Heiligenstadt-im-Eichesfeld, c. 1460 - Würzburg, 1531
ML - *Virgin of the Annunciation*, c. 1495
Alabaster, polychrome highlights. 53 x 40 x 19 cm / From St Peter's, Erfurt,
Germany / Wurschmidt collection; Léopold Goldschmidt collection.
Acquisition, 1904 / Department of Sculpture / RF 1384
Tilman Riemenschneider was one of the foremost exponents of
late Gothic German sculpture. He worked in Würzburg, where he
became a master in 1485. He excelled in carving all materials
(limewood, stone, marble, alabaster), with a particular refinement
in the details and surfaces. His delicate, lyrical style is recognisable
in his treatment of the broken draperies, his graceful features and
the gentle expressions of his male and female figures. The master
and his studio were responsible for large limewood altarpieces and
marble and stone statues, as well as tombs, in Würzburg and
Bamberg. A telling example of the social ascendancy of the artist,
in 1520-21, Riemenschneider became burgomaster, only to be mis-
treated during the Peasants War in 1525 for his pains.

Rodin, Auguste

Paris, 1840 - Meudon, 1917

MO - *L'Homme au nez cassé [Man with a Broken Nose]*, **1864/1878**

Bronze mask on white marble stand. 39 (of which stand: 13) x 21 x 23 cm /
Acquisition, 1906 / RF 2238

MO - *Âge d'airain [Age of Bronze]*, **1877-80**

Bronze. 178 x 59 x 61 cm / Acquisition, 1880/ RF 676

MO - *St John the Baptist*, **1879-81**

Bronze. 204 x 63 x 113 cm./ Acquisition, 1881/ RF 670

MO - *Porte de l'Enfer [The Gates of Hell]*, **1880-89/1917**

Plaster. 635 x 400 x 85 cm, surmounted by the group *The Shades* /
Rodin donation, 1916. Deposit at Musée d'Orsay, 1986 / DO 1986-4

MO - *Ugolino*, **1882, enlargement with drapery 1906**

Plaster. 139 x 173 x 278 cm / Rodin donation, 1916 / DO 1986-1

MO - *Fugit amor*, *Le Rêve* or *Amour qui passe [Fugit amor,
The Dream* or *Love that Passes]*, **1886**

Bronze. 38 x 46 x 33 cm / Formerly Sée collection. Cosson bequest, 1926 / RF 2241

MO - *La Pensée [Thought (Portrait of Camille Claudel]*, **c. 1895**

Marble. 74 x 43 x 46 cm / Gift of Mme Durand en 1902 / RF 4065

MO - *Honoré de Balzac (Tours, 1799 - Paris, 1850), Writer*, **1898**

Plaster. 275 x 121 x 132 cm / Rodin donation, 1916 / DO 1986-2

MO - *Homme qui marche [Walking Man]*, **1905**

Bronze. 213 x 161 x 72 cm / Gift to the French state, 1911 / RF 409

A towering figure of sculpture, we still much have to learn about
Rodin. He was once seen as an insatiable modeller, at ease with
every subject, capable of untold expressiveness, and whose intuitions were so far ahead of their time that his *Gates of Hell*, commissioned in 1880, like his *Balzac* (1898), were bound to be
misunderstood by the contemporary public. He was seen too as
the creator of groups unified by action or by the dream, such as
The Burghers of Calais (1884-95) or *The Kiss* (1886). A friend of
Claude Monet, he was also the sculptor of light, a counterpart to
the Impressionists in sculpture. Since the 1960s, it has become
clear that many of his processes and ideas anticipate the changing
face of contemporary sculpture: subjects treated in series developed over a number of years, the reworking of earlier elements
into new sculptures, the use of typological body parts (arms, legs)
as if they were prefabricated units (the famous *abbatis*), the
inventive use of imprints, etc. The Rodin donation to the state in
1916 paved the way for the setting up of a museum devoted to
his work in Paris.

Rosso, Medardo

Turin, 1858 - Milan, 1928

MO - *Aetas aurea* or *L'Âge d'or [The Golden Age]* **(Portrait of Rosso's wife and
son, Francesco, born 1885), 1886**

Bronze. 50 x 37 x 26 cm./ Formerly collection Eugène Carrière. Acquisition, 1989 /
RF 4231

MO - *Ecce Puer* or *Impression d'enfant* **(Portrait of Alfred Mond, aged six), 1906**

Bronze. 44 x 37 x 27 cm / Gift of Francesco Rosso, the artist's son, in 1928, in
exchange for the plaster acquired in 1907 / RF 3285

If Rodin needed a rival, it would have to be Rosso. Rosso, who lived
primarily in Paris, went even further in creating sculptures verging
on pure visions, exempt from the strictures of objective volume. The
subject seems to dissolve, leaving light playing over a continuous
surface open to the world outside. In this perspective, Rosso also
foreshadowed Futurist concerns. He treated humdrum subjects
(hooligan, janitor), or his close relations (mother and child), going
beyond the taste for the anecdotal common among the
Impressionists. If his work in wax recalls Degas, it in fact conveys the
sculptor's new relationship to matter, in which the immediate environment is imprinted, modulated and absorbed.

Rouillard, Pierre-Louis

Paris, 1820 - *ibid*, 1881

MO - *Cheval à la herse [Horse with a Harrow]*, **1878**

Cast iron. 350 x 223 x 220 cm / Commissioned for the Palais du Trocadéro for the
1878 World Fair / RF 3754

Rouillard experienced his hour of glory as a sculptor of animal
figures for palatial interiors. In the Louvre, he oversaw teams including powerful personalities, such as Fremiet and Jacquemart. His
services were in addition called upon at the Opera and the Tribunal
de Commerce in Paris. Professor of sculpture at the Ecole de Dessin
(the future Ecole des Arts Décoratifs) from 1840 to 1881, he was
also Pompon's master. The equestrian theme was his favourite
subject, and in the Louvre horses can be seen leaping through palm
fronds or straining at the harrow. His *Elk* met with a certain
success, and Rouillard was also summoned to Constantinople to
execute twenty-four groups of animals as well as bas-reliefs on the
Belerbeyi palace. Whereas animal movement in Barye's work is
wholly uncompromising, Rouillard's beasts are imbued with an
effortless grace; the attitude is somewhat condescending and man
remains the dominant observer.

Rude, François

Dijon, 1784 - Paris, 1855

ML - *Pêcheur napolitain jouant avec une tortue [Neapolitan Fisherman Playing with a Tortoise],* **1833 Salon**

Marble. (Plaster model presented at the 1831 Salon) 82 x 88 x 48 cm / Acquired by Louis-Philippe, 1833 / Department of Sculpture / LP 63

MO - *Génie de la Patrie,* **1836/1898**

Plaster. 224 x 196 x 90 cm / Cast of the relief on the Arc de Triomphe in Paris, *The Departure of the Volunteers* of 1792 (1836). Commissioned by the city of Dijon in 1887. Executed by Pouzadoux in 1898 / DO 1985-2

ML - *Louis David, Painter (1748-1825),* **1838**

Marble. 86 x 75 x 50 cm / Executed in 1838 for the painting galleries in the Louvre / Acquired by Louis-Philippe / Department of Sculpture / LP 1780

MO - *Napoléon s'éveillant à l'immortalité [Napoleon Awaking to Immortality],* **1846**

Plaster model. 215 x 195 x 96 cm / Acquisition, 1892 / RF 904

Following the fall of the First Empire in 1815, Rude (Prix de Rome, 1812) followed David to Brussels. Back in Paris in 1828, he was soon at loggerheads with the Academy, which refused him honours and excluded his pupils. His *Neapolitan Fisherman* treated a contemporary subject with a daring freshness of vision. Nonetheless, Rude had his enthusiasts, such as Adolphe Thiers, who commissioned the *Departure of the Volunteers of 1792* (*The Marseillaise*) for the Arc de Triomphe (1836). In fact, Rude was often to celebrate the Napoleonic epic: Napoleon (1846) and Ney (1852-53) were both innovative treatments of the theme of the great man. In *Cavaignac* (1847, Montmartre cemetery), the artist shows how to draw useful lessons from the art of the past in an authentic expression of the present. His eclecticism did much to foster the art of his pupils, Carpeaux in particular. There is a museum dedicated to his work in his birthplace, Dijon, where the Musée des Beaux-Arts also possesses significant holdings.

Saint-Marceaux, Charles-René de Paul de

Reims, 1845 - Paris, 1915

MO - *Génie gardant le secret de la tombe [Genius Keeping the Secret of the Tomb],* **1879**

Marble. 168 x 95 x 119 cm / Acquisition, 1879 / RF 300

Attention was first drawn to the work of this son of a champagne merchant by the recumbent figure of Abbé Miroy (1870), at the cemetery in north Reims. Saint-Marceaux admired Florentine art, above all the tutelary genius of Michelangelo, and leaned heavily on these sources for *Genius Keeping the Secret of the Tomb* and *Harlequin* (Musée des Beaux-Arts, Reims). His evolution is symptomatic of the Symbolist inclinations of his generation. The suggestion of the idea is more in evidence in his public monuments and masks than in the expressive treatment that characterised his earlier busts. He is also author of the monument to Alexandre Dumas fils in place Malesherbes in Paris, as well as the monument at the Postal Union in Bern (1909).

Saint Phalle, Niki de (Marie-Agnès Fal de Saint Phalle)

Neuilly-sur-Seine, 1930 – San Diego (USA), 2002

CP - *Le Monstre de Soisy [The Monster of Soisy],* **c. 1962-63**

Painting and various objects on a metal structure. 253 x 161 x 63.3 cm / Gift of Pontus Hulten, 2004 / EC-2004-4-AP

Niki de Saint Phalle's life and creative work were governed by several passions: Jean Tinguely, with whom she formed a mythical artistic couple, the curator and director of the Musée National d'Art Moderne, Pontus Hulten, who supported her work from the very start, the United States, where she spent both her childhood and her final years, France, naturally, and Italy, where she carried out her major work, the *Garden of the Tarots,* started in 1979 (Garavicchio, Tuscany). An unconventional figure, she first became known in the 1960s through her free-spirited *Shootings,* her *Nanas* (sideways tributes to womanhood), and her tame, carnival-like *Monsters.* Luxuriant in form and colour, and generally executed in tandem with Tinguely, she has sculptures in a number of cities, including the famous *Stravinsky Fountain* outside the Centre Pompidou. Conversely, she could also lend a hand with Tinguely's work, providing for example the mirror-glass face for the gigantic figure of the Cyclops at Milly-la-Forêt.

Sarazin, Jacques
Noyon, 1592 - Paris, 1660
ML - *Monument du cœur du cardinal Pierre de Bérulle (1575-1629)*
[Monument for the heart of Cardinal Pierre de Bérulle (1575-1629)], 1653-57
Marble. 216.5 (including plinth) x 80 x 135 cm / Previously in the Eglise des Carmelites, Paris. Accession 1906 / Department of Sculpture / RF 1430
From the time of his stay in Rome (1610-27), during which he rubbed shoulders with Domenichino, Poussin and Simon Vouet, Sarazin fused the classical spirit with an impetuous vitality that hints at the Baroque. Back in France, he was appointed *Sculpteur du Roi,* Vouet being *Premier Peintre.* He exercised his art in the Louvre (1639-41), in the monument for the heart of Louis XIII, in devotional works and funerary pieces, such as the tomb of Cardinal de Bérulle, and the vault for the heart of the Prince de Condé at Chantilly. The success of *Children with a Goat* in the Louvre (1640) attracted wealthy private clients. His formal exactitude and the naturalness of his poses — the direct expression of interior feeling — make him one of the initiators of French Classicism for the first generation of pupils at the Académie de Peinture et de Sculpture, a institution he helped to set up in 1648.

Schoenewerk, Pierre-Alexandre
Paris, 1820 - *ibid,* 1885
MO - *Jeune Tarentine [Young Tarentine]*, 1871
Marble. 74 x 171 x 68 cm / Acquisition, 1872 / RF 215
Schoenewerk was one of the most active representatives of 19th-century eclecticism, a current which catered for the Second Empire and Third Republic middle-classes with illustrations of its culture that flattered its sense of superiority. He was the creator of *Psyches,* droopingly beautiful allegorical girls, subjects drawn from literature and Antiquity in accordance with the diktats of the Academy. His *Young Tarentine* obtained notable success. Inspired by a poem by André Chénier, it is the story of a girl engaged to be married who dies on the sea voyage to her intended husband, who can only embrace her corpse. In his sarcastic review in the *Salon de 1872,* Zola was in a distinct minority, though it should be said that the writer was an advocate of Realism, which took a view diametrically opposed to eclecticism: Courbet or Manet, then, against Cabanel's *Venus* and Clésinger's *Woman Bitten by a Snake.*

Séchas, Alain
Colombes, 1955
CP - *Le Mannequin [The Dummy]*, 1985
Foam rubber, textile, plastic, plaster. 185 x 130 x 76 cm / Purchase, 1985 / AM 1985-145
Foam rubber, textile, plastic, plaster. 185 x 130 x 76 cm / Purchase, 1985 / AM 1985-145
The jokey, cartoon-like figures drawn or sculpted by this Parisian artist generally seem to be based on puns (including the *chat* — cat — in Séchas). His cats are patently disguised self-portraits in which the artist allows free rein to his manias and crazes. As in the world of Buster Keaton, the humour is deadpan. In *Mannequin,* for example, it 'rains men' into the plaster in a world turned upside down. His *Professor Suicide* (1995) is even more corrosive. These burlesque sketches remind one of another icily satirical voice in contemporary art: Maurizio Cattelan. Séchas can also be compared to a whole school of the unhinged characteristic of the work of other contemporary French artists, such as Gilles Barbier.

Segal, George
New York, 1924 – *ibid,* 2000
CP - *Movie House,* 1966-67
Light installation: plaster, wood, Plexiglas, electric lamps. 259 x 376 x 370 cm / State purchase, 1969; transfer, 1976 / AM 1976-1018
George Segal began as a painter of almost abstract landscapes tributary of an expressionist aesthetic. In 1958, in an effort to 'concretise' one of his pictures, he placed in front of it three life-size plaster figures. He subsequently gave up painting and started wrapping living models in strips of cloth dipped in plaster and arranging the casts in routine, almost banal poses against a backdrop of real objects. The strangeness of the figures contradicts the prosaic nature of the scenes. Anonymous, yet undoubtedly human, they have been caught on the hop and seem less real than the objects. The scene tells no story; the artist is simply questioning the human condition as it is instrumentalised by functional and material contingencies.

Sergel, Johan Tobias

Stockholm, 1740 - *ibid,* **1814**

ML - *Nymph in her Bath,* **c. 1775-1812**

Marble. 78.8 x 63.3 x 13 cm / Acquisition, 1994 / Department of Sculpture /
RF 4463

Trained in Sweden and based in Rome between 1767 and 1778, Sergel is symptomatic of the junction between the last gasp of the Baroque and the lessons of the Antique that led to Neoclassicism. His mythological subjects are treated with great freedom, as witness his *Drunken Faun,* carved when he was thirty years old and which made him known, and his *Nymph in the Bath,* a bas-relief inspired by an Antique sarcophagus. Recalled to Sweden by Gustav III in 1778, he was received into the Académie Royale during a stay in Paris. Although later appointed official sculptor to the Swedish court, his sculpture never became constrained or cold, as Thorvaldsen's sometimes did. His pen and pen-and-wash drawings demonstrate singular qualities of observation and vivacity, and his sketches often evince an energy reminiscent of Carpeaux.

Serra, Richard

San Francisco, 1939

CP - *Hand Catching Lead,* **1968**

16 mm. black and white silent film stock. Length: 3 min. / AM 1974-F0282

CP - *5:30,* **1969**

Assemblage of four plates and one roll of Corten steel. 124 x 124 x 5 cm (each plate)
and 230 x 15 cm (roll) / Purchase, 1983 / AM 1983-454

CP - *Père Lachaise,* **1990**

Lithograph on vellum with paintstick highlights. 119 x 190 cm / AM 1991-85

After university studies (1957-64) and meeting Josef Albers (1963), Richard Serra came to Paris in 1964, where he studied the work of Brancusi in his studio reconstituted at the Musée d'Art Moderne, then housed in the Palais de Tokyo. On his return to New York in 1966, he made pieces in rubber (the *Belts*) and neon. His molten lead *Splashings* (1968), his *Prop Parts* (precariously balanced lead sheets, 1968-69), and his dispersion pieces are emblematic of process art, which lay special emphasis on the creative gesture and the physical existence of materials. It was inevitable then that his work should feature in the exhibition, 'When Attitudes Become Form' (Bern, 1969). Thereafter, his pieces increased in size to exploit the emotional reaction of viewers faced with metal plates that encroach upon their space and seem to threaten them. Serra went on to create large-scale site-specific pieces that seek to identify sculpture with a critique of the architectural and social context. The sculptor's deliberately disturbing interventions into the urban fabric have sometimes been dismantled, as it was the case in 1989 for *Tilted Arc,* a long curvilinear steel plate span-

ning Federal Plaza in New York. The artist inevitably condemns such removals carried out on the initiative of the commissioning authorities as being akin to destroying his work.

Sterbak, Jana

Prague, 1955

CP - *Vanitas: Flesh Dress for an Albino Anorexic,* **1987**

Raw beef sewn onto a dummy figure (H: 113 cm), photograph / Purchase, 1996 /
AM 1996-524

Born in Czechoslovakia where she lived until 1968 when her family emigrated to Canada, Sterbak lived an itinerant existence between Toronto, New York, Paris and Barcelona, before settling in Montreal. In 2003 she represented Canada at the Venice Biennale. She has gradually built up a complex body of work using unconventional materials and appropriating everyday articles so as to uncover the varieties of conditioning to which modern man is subjected. Her *Seduction Couch* (1986-87) gives electrostatic shocks, while *Declaration* (7 min. video, 1993) the text of Thomas Paine's *Rights of Man* is read out by someone with a stammer. Ageing and death are also recurring themes that appear in *Flesh Dress.* Sterbak has also explored other means of expression, such as installation, performance, video and film.

Taeuber-Arp, Sophie

Davos (Switzerland), 1889 – Zurich, 1943

CP - *Dada Head,* **1920**

Painted lathed wood. H: 29.4 cm / Purchase, 2003 / AM 2003-332

After studying applied art in Switzerland and Germany, Sophie Taeuber taught textile design in Zurich from 1915 to 1925. There, she mixed with the Dada group and met Hans Arp, who she married in 1921. From this period date the *Duos-Collages* with abstract colour patterns woven for her husband as well as the lathe-turned and painted wooden *Heads,* which had been preceded by the puppets the artist made for a stage production in 1918. These object-heads, where caricature is less germane than decorative effect, are contemporary with Raoul Hausmann's *Mechanical Head* (1919). In the 1930s, the artist painted pictures featuring elementary geometric motifs arranged according to visual rhythms which show links to the researches of the Cercle et Carré and Abstraction-Création groups. Settling in Meudon with Arp, she edited the review *Plastique* (together with the painter César Domela) and painted wood reliefs.

Takis (Panayotis Vassilakis)

Athens, 1925

CP - *Le Grand Signal,* 1964

Metal and light signal. 499 x 50 x 34 cm / Purchase, 1982 / AM 1982-137

Before his arrival in Paris in 1954, Takis had already produced sculptures evocative of Giacometti's spindly and elongated works. However, a fascination with the signs of the modern world — his earliest *Signals* date back to 1955 — explains the advent of electro-magnetic works in the 1960s. With his *Télélumières* and *Télésculptures,* in which magnetism turns the convention of gravity on its head, Takis endeavours to prove that James Clerk Maxwell, inventor of magnetic field theory, was perhaps as signifi-cant a figure as Albert Einstein. At about the same time, Takis and Yves Klein, in a kind of parody of the conquest of space, both made reference to a man being suspended in space by means of electromagnetic attraction. Takis's work continues to evolve, inte-grating sound effects and increasing significantly in scale, as in the luminous aerials at La Défense (1987).

Tatlin, Vladimir

Kharkov (Russia), 1885 - Novodevechi (USSR), 1953

CP - *Model for the Monument to the Third International,* 1919

Reconstitution, 1979: wood, metal. H: 500 cm; diam (base): 300 cm /
Purchase, 1979 / AM 1979-413

As a young painter, Tatlin belonged to the West-orientated wing of the early 20th-century Russian avant-garde. Some time during a mysterious voyage to Paris (1913), he probably met Archipenko and succeeded in sneaking into Picasso's studio pretending to be a balalaika player! Before being shooed away by the master, ever jealous of his creations, he would have had time to catch a glimpse of his new Cubist constructions… Returning to Moscow, Tatlin produced painted 'counter-reliefs' before creating 'corner counter-reliefs', abstract forms suspended in space, in 1915; a major contri-bution to the history of sculpture that was unveiled at the famous '0.10' exhibition. After 1917, Tatlin's artistic materialism seems to have destined him to become the model Revolutionary artist: he was appointed to a teaching post at the Moscow Vhutemas and was entrusted with the project for the Monument to the Third International (1919). Nothing came of all these plans, however, in spite of a late experimental flying machine, exhibited in 1932, christened the *Letatlin.* Marginalised, in common with practically all the artists of the early avant-garde, by the advent of Socialist Realism, Tatlin died forgotten in a home for artists. His work, for the most part no longer extant, has been the subject of reconstitu-tions, particularly in the context of the great 'Paris-Moscow' exhi-bition held at the Centre Pompidou in 1979.

Tinguely, Jean

Fribourg (Switzerland), 1925 - Bern, 1991

CP - *Requiem pour une feuille morte [Requiem for Dead Leaf],* 1967

Painted steel and wood, leather. 305 x 1105 x 80 cm / Collection d'Art Moderne Renault / On deposit at the Centre Pompidou, 2002 / AM 2003-DEP 48

CP - *L'Enfer, un petit début [Hell – a Small Beginning],* 1984

Recycled junk, engines, miscellaneous objects. 370 x 920 x 700 cm /
Purchase, 1990 / AM 1990-27

Tinguely started out as a painter, but could never be satisfied with just one composition: he was more interested in putting forms into motion and in obtaining an infinite number of pictures. He used crankshafts in wire constructions called *Moulins à prière (Prayer wheels),* before, in 1953, powering them by engines concealed in the frame of geometrical forms that swung on pivots: it seemed as if a picture by Malevich, Kandinsky or Herbin had suddenly started to move. The invention of the 'painting machines' (*Meta-Matic*), unveiled at the first Paris Biennial (1959) in the presence of an André Malraux much amused by the resulting scandal, is not without links to the indirect painting using women as 'live brushes' by his friend Yves Klein, who he had met in 1956. This was more enough to awaken the interest of Pierre Restany and the Nouveaux Réalistes, but in this respect Tinguely remained a fellow traveller. With Tinguely, the machine becomes surprisingly human, a mirror to our emotions and to the history of humankind. The machine lives and dies (like the self-destroying machine in *Homage to New York,* 1960), it vocalises, consumes, is consumed. On a large scale it takes over public space, with Niki de Saint Phalle's *Nanas* often providing a fitting coupling. Together with his friend Luginbühl, Tinguely also oversaw the making of some colossal sculptures, his political and artistic legacy being the *Cyclops* (1969-87) erected in the Forêt de Fontainebleau at Milly-la-Forêt.

Veilhan, Xavier

Lyon, 1963

CP - *The Rhinoceros,* 1999-2000

Resin, polyester paint, varnish. 110 x 415 x 140 cm / Made for the Yves Saint-Laurent
Rive Gauche Homme store in New York and unveiled February to May 2000
at the Centre Pompidou. Purchase, 2001 / AM 2001-26

Veilhan is one of the chief exponents of hyper Pop which, in the
1990s, once again derived artistic mileage from the worlds of
consumerism, the everyday and industrial design. It is as advertising
material that his 'animals' begin to exist, in an offbeat yet stereoty-
pical world — as in *Penguin at the Supermarket,* one of a series of
photographic tableaux (1997-98) and *Rhinoceros.* The subjects of
his photographs, sculptures and installations, all derived from
nature, history, or culture form an encyclopedia of images which,
using modern technical means, recall updated versions of those
illustrations in 19th-century scientific adventure novels in the Jules
Verne vein or the visual universe of H P Lovecraft's science fiction.
No surprise then that narrative plays such a prominent role in his
work, as much as in his short films as in his generally mysterious
environments, like his 'forest of felt' (*La Forêt,* Magasin, Grenoble,
2000) or his *Light Machines,* whose luminous screen of thousands
of light bulbs emits an image that can be modified by changes in
light intensity. One of these machines was presented at the Centre
Pompidou in autumn 2004.

Zorio, Gilberto

Andorno Micca (Italy), 1944

CP - *Pugno fosforescente [Phosphorescent Fist],* 1971

Phosphorescent wax, two wood lamps. 170 x 180 x 50 cm / Purchase, 1984 /
AM 1984-386

One of the most authentic voices in Italian Arte Povera, Zorio's
principal theme was the expression of energy in all its forms. His
works include a whole range of devices that transmit and focus
visual and audio messages. His hanging 'javelins' reconfigure the
paradox of the Greek philosopher Zeno, according to whom
movement is comprised of successive phases of immobility.
Grouped into star shapes, they crisscross space and time like
beams of light. The works 'to purify the word' are made up of precariously balanced containers, conductors and tubes filled with
alcohol or other fragile substances. The works' contained violence
is released in the word Odio (Hatred) spelt out on the wall by
dents made with an axe, or in the phosphorescent wax of *Pugno
fosforecente.* Zorio is engaged on a quest back to the magical or
alchemical animation of form. Site-specific works by the artist can
be seen in the Castello di Rivoli, near Turin.

Index of illustrations

Bibliography

This bibliography is confined to just a few basic publications, and titles consulted by the author, so it is obviously not exhaustive. Readers may also refer to the collection catalogues published by the three partner institutions, as well as the *catalogues raisonnés* of the sculptors in question. Among exhibition catalogues focusing on general subjects, let us mention *La Sculpture française au XIXᵉ siècle*, Paris, Galerie nationale du Grand Palais, 10 April-28 July 1986, Réunion des Musées Nationaux, 1986; *Qu'est-ce que la sculpture moderne?*, Paris, Musée national d'art moderne, Centre Pompidou publications, 1986, and *D'après l'Antique*, Paris, Louvre, October 2000-January 2001, Paris, Réunion des Musées Nationaux, 2000. Lastly, we should mention the well documented book *Mille Sculptures de France*, Paris, Gallimard, 1998, and the extremely accessible volume *La Sculpture sous tous les angles*, by Manon Potvin, edited by Geneviève Bresc-Gautier, Musée du Louvre, 1995.

Baudry, Marie-Thérèse et Bozo, Dominique, *La Sculpture : méthode et vocabulaire*, Paris, Inventaire général, Imprimerie nationale [1978], 1990

Benoist, Luc, *La Sculpture romantique*, Paris, Renaissance du Livre, 1927

Bresc-Bautier, Geneviève et Pingeot, Anne, *Sculptures des jardins du Louvre, du Carrousel et des Tuileries,* Paris, Réunion des musées nationaux, 1986

Charbonneaux, Jean et Pradel, Pierre, *Architecture et sculpture des origines à nos jours*, Paris, Nathan, 1970-1971, t. 4

Chevillot, Catherine, *La République et ses grands hommes*, Paris, Hachette/Réunion des musées nationaux, 1990

Elsen, Albert E., *Origins of Modern Sculpture: Pionners and Premises*, Londres, Phaidon, 1973 et New York, Georges Braziller, 1974

Focillon, Henri, *L'Art des sculpteurs romans* [1931], Paris, P.U.F., 1964

Francastel, Pierre (ed.), *Les Sculpteurs célèbres,* Paris, Mazenod, 1954

Freedberg, David, *Le Pouvoir des images* [1989], Paris, Gérard Monfort, 1998

Frontisi-Ducroux, Françoise, *Dédale, Mythologie de l'artisan en Grèce ancienne* [1975], Paris, La Découverte, 2000

Fuchs, Heinz R., *La Sculpture contemporaine*, Paris, Albin Michel, 1972

Gaborit, Jean-René, *Art gothique*, Paris, Hachette, 1978

Giedion-Welcker, Carola, *Contemporary Sculpture, an Evolution in Volume and Space*, [1956], New York, George Wittenborn, 1961

Hammacher, Abraham M., *La Sculpture*, Paris, Cercle d'art, 1988

Hulten, P., Dumitresco, N. et Istrati, A., *Brancusi*, Paris, Flammarion, 1986

Janson, H.W., *19th-Century Sculpture*, New York, Harry N. Abrams, 1985

Krauss, Rosalind, *Une histoire de la sculpture de Rodin à Smithson,* [1957], Paris, Macula, 1997

La Sculpture, histoire d'un art, Genève, Skira :
Bruneau, Philippe, Torelli, Mario et Barral I Altet, Xavier, *Le Prestige de l'Antiquité* (1991);
Bresc-Bautier, Geneviève, Ceysson, Bernard, Fagiolo Dell'Arco, Maurizio et Souchal, François, *La Grande Tradition de la sculpture du XVᵉ au XVIIIᵉ siècle* (1987);
Duby, Georges, Barral I Altet, Xavier et Guillot de Suduiraut, Sophie, *Le Grand Art du Moyen-Âge. Du Vᵉ au XVᵉ siècle* (1989);
Le Normand-Romain, Antoinette, Pingeot, Anne et Hohl, Reinhold, *L'Aventure de la sculpture moderne (XIXᵉ-XXᵉ siècle)* (1986)

Le Cadre et le socle dans l'art du XXᵉ siècle, Serge Lemoine ed, Dijon, Université de Bourgogne/Paris, Centre Pompidou, Centre national des arts plastiques, 1987

Le Normand-Romain, Antoinette, *La Tradition classique et l'esprit romantique*, Rome, Edizioni dell'Elefante, 1981

Lucie-Smith, Edward, *Sculpture since 1945*, Londres, Phaidon, 1987

Malraux, André, *Le Musée imaginaire de la sculpture mondiale*, Paris, Gallimard, 1954

Mc Evilley, Thomas, *Sculpture in the Age of Doubt*, New York, Allworth Press, 1999

Read, Herbert, *The Art of Sculpture*, Princeton, Princeton University Press, 1956

Rheims, Maurice, *La Sculpture au XIXᵉ siècle*, Paris, Arts et métiers graphiques, 1972
Rickey, George, *Constructivism. Origins and Evolution*, New York, Braziller, 1967

Rolley, Claude, *La Sculpture grecque*, 2 vol., Paris, Picard, 1994-1996

Sauerländer, Willibald, *La Sculpture gothique en France, 1140-1270*, Paris, Flammarion, 1972

Sculpter-Photographier. Photographie-Sculpture, Paris, Marval - Musée du Louvre, 1993

Seuphor, Michel, *La Sculpture de ce siècle. Dictionnaire de la sculpture moderne*, Neuchâtel, éd. du Griffon, 1959

Souchal, François, *French Sculptors of the Seventeenth and Eighteenth Centuries*, Oxford, Cassirer, 1977

Wittkower, Rudolf, *Qu'est-ce que la sculpture? Principes et procédures, de l'Antiquité au XXᵉ siècle,* [1977], Paris, Macula, 1995

Photos Credits

Photolithography:
APS-CHROMOSTYLE, Tours, France
Printing:
Printed in October 2005 by MAME, in Tours, France